PHILOSOPHY

A LITERARY AND CONCEPTUAL APPROACH

SECOND EDITION

PHILOSOPHY

A LITERARY AND CONCEPTUAL APPROACH

SECOND EDITION

BURTON F. PORTER

RUSSELL SAGE COLLEGE

HARCOURT BRACE JOVANOVICH, INC.

NEW YORK   SAN DIEGO   CHICAGO   SAN FRANCISCO   ATLANTA
LONDON   SYDNEY   TORONTO

For Anastasia

ISBN: 0-15-570553-9

Library of Congress Catalog Card Number: 79-92895

Printed in the United States of America

Cover drawing: Illustration by Pablo Picasso, from Nestor's Tales of the Trojan War from Ovid's
"Metamorphosis." Reproduced by permission of The Baltimore Museum of Art — The Cone
Collection, formed by Dr. Claribel Cone and Miss Etta Cone of Baltimore, Maryland.

Copyright and Acknowledgments appear on pages 495-96, which constitute a
continuation of the copyright page.

Preface

This book introduces the reader to philosophy by presenting major literary and philosophic works arranged under common conceptual headings. The assumption underlying this approach is that the combination of the two can be advantageous, shedding a double light on basic philosophic issues. Literature and philosophy are thereby taken to be compatible rather than antagonistic, and capable of being combined in mutually beneficial ways.

Historically, philosophers have sometimes been skeptical about this union, and have preferred to link philosophy with science rather than with any form of art. Thinkers as far apart in time as Aristotle (384–322 B.C.), Francis Bacon (1561–1626), and Bertrand Russell (1872–1970), for example, esteemed the rigor and precision of the scientific method and adapted it to their philosophic investigations. Science, it was argued, concentrated on the objective world divorced from those subjective emotions that distorted truth, providing a model of procedure and standards by which philosophic theories could be judged.

Some philosophers within this tradition not only endorsed science but distrusted art for its emotive power. Art persuaded people to accept beliefs by generating a passionate response within them, by engaging their senses but muddling their minds. It seduced them into assent by exploiting the feelings that surrounded ideas rather than promoting the cool consideration of intellectual matters in terms of logic. Whether through a line of verse, a cathedral, or a piano concerto, whether it used the language of color, melody, or poetic metaphor, art moved people to accept ideas because of their aesthetic appeal. Surely, it was argued, reality could be understood only through argumentation, investigation, and dispassionate evaluation of competing theories, by comprehension and reflection, by thinking deeply, not feeling strongly. Although truth could be aesthetically pleasing, the aesthetically pleasing is not *ipso facto* true. Through its emotive power, art blurred this distinction and induced people to believe nonsense that had been presented in an imaginative and emotionally enticing way.

These philosophers further believed that art generally deflected attention from political, social, and economic concerns and, to that extent, could be morally condemned as deficient in humanity. Instead of attempting to im-

v

prove the conditions of human existence, artists directed their energies toward achieving moments of heightened experience and influenced others to neglect their obligations to society and seek instead the momentary joy. Since aesthetic satisfaction would be achieved at the expense of human welfare, an orientation of this kind was perceived to be not only frivolous but selfish. How could Mozart have taken no notice of the French revolution happening around him?

Although the above indictment against art is severe, it also pays a left-handed compliment to the power of art in capturing the human spirit, and philosophers have, from time to time, defended this power as salutary, not harmful, to human progress and understanding. A viable case has been made for art as its own excuse (*ars gratia artis*), but, that theory aside, it can also be argued that art can contribute to the quality of life by offering people an intensification and enhancement of existence. Through the magic of Mozart or Homer or da Vinci the individual can experience that enrichment which the moralist strives to realize in his distant utopia. Rather than neglecting humanity, art imbues human life with vividness, depth, and charm. Through the artist's vision, the world can be made to yield its inner resonance and savor, and daily living can be raised from the banal. Surely the moralist cannot criticize this elevation of life that art provides, for it is integral to the moralist's own ideal for humanity.

In addition, art can provide new insights into reality, and function as a vehicle rather than an impediment to truth. Undoubtedly, we should be suspicious of a mode of appeal that defies verification, enchanting the critical faculties rather than engaging them, but perhaps art transmits truths that are otherwise inexpressible. Perhaps, through sensuous forms, people can come to realizations that transcend laboratory findings or the careful reasoning of the logician. Indeed, people have sometimes felt the superiority of artistic insights, and it would be mere prejudice to regard empirical and intellectual knowledge as more trustworthy than sensible and emotional understanding.

When philosophers are impressed with the truth value of art, they are struck by the intimate relation between art and some precious essence of reality. Art seems capable of touching the very "inscape" of life; philosophic theories begin to appear as poor abstractions by comparison, and philosophic criticisms become hollow and cheap. Viewed in these terms, art may be indispensable to the philosopher in the search for genuine understanding, transmitting insights that are otherwise inaccessible.

Art may also be compatible with philosophy in the coherence of its structure, which parallels the organization of reasoned argument. When the composer arranges formal elements of texture and timbre, harmony, melody, and rhythm into an aesthetically pleasing musical composition, and when the writer uses certain symbols and images and a particular plot and language style in constructing a literary work, the resulting structure strongly resembles a philosophic system of ideas.

Furthermore, the constructions of art present a world view, a vision of the meaning and place of human beings in the universe that the philosopher also tries to achieve through metaphysical theories. Each offers a microcosm of life, and each is committed to creating a model that truly diagrams reality; Leo Tolstoy's novel *War and Peace* is as much an interpretation of the human condition as is the philosophical *Meditations* of René Descartes.

The philosopher, then, may come to recognize the essential similarities between art and philosophy and to think of philosophy itself as a kind of art. The thinker can be viewed as an imaginative and perceptive artist who, through a blend of inspiration and reason, experience and logic, creates an intellectual work of art that expresses a conception of the universe. Even if we do not take the analogy this far, it is at least clear that the artist and the philosopher are not in opposition but are highly compatible. Thus, Plato can award the Muses a place in disciplining the character of the youth, Schopenhauer can find liberation from the unceasing desires of Will in aesthetic contemplation, and Whitehead can maintain that individuality and personal development may be deepened through habits of aesthetic apprehension.

It was in light of these considerations concerning philosophy and art that this book was conceived. Through the medium of literature, we may hope to gain unique insights and fresh perspectives on philosophic issues and to find those issues rendered vital and immediate by the aesthetic force of the art. We may expect that the philosophic issues will gain in meaning by being presented in literary as well as in philosophic form and that they will come alive to challenge and intrigue us.

BURTON F. PORTER

Contents

THREE FREE WILL AND DETERMINISM 201

PHILOSOPHY

A LITERARY AND CONCEPTUAL APPROACH

SECOND EDITION

*"Surely philosophy is no other than
sophisticated poetry."*
—MONTAIGNE

Introduction

THE NATURE OF PHILOSOPHY

Philosophy may be defined as the critical and systematic attempt to understand human existence at its most fundamental level. This means that philosophy deals with essential questions concerning the meaning of life, employing high standards of logical precision, coherence, and scope in both presenting and evaluating various theories. Rather than speculating in an undisciplined and haphazard way, the philosopher tries to think deliberately and rationally, stretching the human intellect in order to comprehend the general character of the world and man's place in the total scheme of things.

Traditionally, philosophy has been divided into five major branches, each of which is interrelated with the others—metaphysics, epistemology, logic, ethics, and aesthetics. Each branch consists of various theories, some of which are in direct opposition to each other.

Metaphysics, the most basic branch of philosophy, is concerned with the nature of reality, or, more specifically, with the essence of the universe—its basic constitution, structure, and process of development. *Idealism,* for example, is a metaphysical theory which maintains that the ultimate reality is spiritual or psychical rather than physical, and that the universe is the embodiment of spirit or mind. To understand the universe, the idealist claims, we must look within ourselves at such things as our personality, rational activity, ego, values, and ideals, for the universe possesses the same spiritual element at its core. *Naturalism,* the opposite metaphysical theory, maintains that the universe can be explained wholly in natural terms without any reference to spiritual essences. According to the naturalist, it is only a psychological weakness that induces us to believe in a spiritual universe resembling ourselves, and even our own spiritual values, personality, and reasoning are merely reflections of our organic needs, the result of a natural evolutionary process.

In addition to the idealist–naturalist controversy, metaphysics is concerned with collateral issues, such as whether the universe has a purpose or a goal toward which it is destined—an ultimate end such as an apocalypse or the maximum evolutionary development of all life.

1

This poses further questions concerning the existence and nature of God: Should we consider God an imaginative construct which man conceived out of insecurity, fear, and the need for immortality, or a real entity with qualities such as absolute wisdom and love, omnipresence, omnipotence, and eternality? If God is real, can we think of him as a personal being or an impersonal force that created and sustains the world? On a more technical level, the metaphysician inquires about the nature of "being," that is, the order of existing things, and about the relation between form and matter, thought and action, the reality of time and space, soul and self.

Epistemology, a second branch of philosophy, concentrates on the question of whether genuine knowledge is at all possible and if so, on what would be the most reliable means of knowing. It is the senses that are usually assumed to disclose reality, but sense perception can be grossly misleading. For example, there are numerous cases of optical illusions and hallucinations, and the telescope and microscope reveal a world far different from that which was formerly considered real. The earth does not stand still, despite appearances, and the sun does not rise or set. Furthermore, theoretical knowledge, such as that involved in mathematical systems or historical assumptions, is beyond the scope of sense perception, which indicates that sense perception is not sufficiently comprehensive to embrace the whole of reality.

For these reasons a reliance upon *reason* rather than upon sense perception has been urged by those who feel that the senses are too limited and fallible to be trusted. Here we trust the conclusions arrived at through rational deliberation and accept only logically consistent systems of ideas. But reason too has its weaknesses. Rational systems of thought can be pure inventions without any relation to reality. The scientist, for example, is often impatient with rational philosophic schemes for precisely this reason, for the parts may be consistent with each other but the whole may be entirely false. At the same time the religious person criticizes reason for failing to acknowledge truths that surpass rational confirmation, especially the truths about a transcendent God.

The latter criticism naturally leads to the affirmation of *intuition* as the essential means of knowing reality, and the religious believer and the artist will often champion intuition above all else. Intuition means an immediate apprehension or sudden awareness of reality which has not been filtered through reason or the senses as, for example, in the case of religious revelation and artistic inspiration. But the usual objection leveled against knowledge gained in this way is that it is so highly personal and private that no public verification can be offered for its authenticity. Therefore, we have no valid means of differentiating between delusions and authentic knowledge.

The epistemologist must adjudicate between these conflicting claims, assessing their strengths and weaknesses to fully arrive at a sound theory of knowledge. The epistemologist must also address questions such as: Does the world exist independent of any observer or does it depend upon an observer for its existence? Are qualities such as hardness, redness, and sweetness a part of objects that contain them or are they qualities we supply by our perception of objects? How much can we know of reality and how much is mere appearance?

Logic, or theory of proof, is a third major field of philosophy, and it takes the problem of valid reasoning as its central concern. Logic does not focus primarily on the truth of statements but on the correctness of the formal process of reasoning. For example, if someone were to argue that, "Feminists favor abortion; Alice favors abortion; therefore, Alice is a feminist," this would be judged unsound thinking. For, although all feminists may be in favor of abortion, not all those in favor of abortion are necessarily feminists. In other words, we do not know from the argument that *only* feminists favor abortion.

Logic is concerned with detecting fallacies of this sort (and errors of much greater subtlety) in all forms of argumentation, and more positively, with the construction of a sound base of reasoning for all philosophic conclusions. By extension, logic also involves the examination of scientific method, the analysis of the concepts of symbolism, analogy, and explanation, and the classification of the uses of language.

Ethics and *aesthetics* are the remaining two branches of philosophy, and they are often grouped together under the heading of axiology or value theory. Questions of ethical value and aesthetic value are alike in many respects, especially with regard to the problem of justifying value judgments.

Ethics deals with man's moral duties and obligations, with theories of right and wrong conduct, and with good and bad ways of living. It attempts to assess the moral worth of acts such as truth-telling and promise-keeping, mercy-killing and suicide, and self-assertion or self-denial. (A fuller discussion of ethics appears in Part IV, Ethical Ideals: The Good Life.)

The fifth and last division of philosophy, aesthetics, pivots round the question of what makes an art object aesthetically pleasing. One theory maintains that it is the representational or imitative quality of the work of art, as best exemplified by realistic painting and literature that shows a slice-of-life. Another theory holds that it is "significant form," which means a pleasing combination of formal elements as in abstract painting, while still another asserts that a good work of art expresses emotion in a moving way, as in Romantic novels and music. The aesthetician tries to evaluate each of these theories (plus others not mentioned) in an attempt to justify aesthetic judgments, for unless we can state why, for example, the classical symphony is better than military marches, or French Impressionism is superior to children's

Sunday school paintings, then everything could qualify as good art without discrimination.

Aesthetics also inquires into the distinction between art and nonart (for example, whether sunsets, traffic noises, and chimpanzee paintings could be classified as art); the relation between art and morality, politics, and religion; the process of artistic creation; the status of art with regard to truth; and so forth.

Such, in brief, are the main branches of philosophy, but there are other ways of dividing the subject. One can also refer to the philosophy of science, the philosophy of history, the philosophy of religion, the philosophy of art, the philosophy of politics, the philosophy of mathematics, and so on. The philosophic approach to these fields means the critical examination of their fundamental presuppositions. Ultimately, the same philosophic ground is covered, but from a different perspective.

In this book, philosophy has been presented from the perspective of several key philosophic issues: the concept of self, the problem of evil, free will and determinism, ethical ideals, and the nature of reality. These issues involve each of the major branches of philosophy as well as being intrinsically interesting in their own right, thus providing an engrossing introduction to the subject. Other philosophic issues might have been chosen, but none appear as readily in both literary and philosophic sources; the particular pedagogical approach of this book, therefore,. is best served by these topics.

In the following pages, then, the reader will find discussions of selfhood, evil, free will, ethical ideals, and reality, together with literary and philosophic selections appropriate to them. If these basic issues are confronted and grasped, then a substantial portion of fundamental philosophy will have been understood.

ONE

THE CONCEPT OF SELF

There are certain things we think we know until we are called upon to explain them. The idea of self falls into this category, for nothing seems more obvious than our very self, but when we attempt to define its nature we tend to become confused. Part of the problem is that we ourselves are analyzing our selves, which is rather like trying to point a flashlight at its own beam of light. The principal problem, however, stems from the complex nature of self which renders it extremely difficult to characterize.

On the one hand, we think of the self as a physical entity that exists in the same tangible form as a rock or a tree, and whose existence is verified by sense perception. We recognize our own self and other selves as corporeal beings, acting in a concrete world of objects and events. In short, self can be conceived of as *embodied,* and our body as that which we are, rather than something we have.

On the other hand, we sometimes regard this conception of self-hood as superficial and irrelevant, and feel that the self can be more adequately described as the spiritual entity lying beneath our physical appearance and behavior; it is the nonbodily source of our bodily actions. In this view, the essential self is thought to be known through an introspective process whereby we look inside our own being and discover its spiritual center. The body serves as a shell or housing within which the self resides, issuing orders, receiving impressions, storing memories, reflecting and deliberating; in short, the self is here identified with our psychical reality or spiritual mind.

However, this concept of self is difficult to defend in scientific terms and resembles certain extreme religious beliefs that also claim to be based on private knowledge. We cannot be sure, therefore, whether the self is a real spiritual entity, surpassing all scientific understanding, or whether belief in such a concept is merely a delusion.[1]

These two alternatives, of identifying the self with the body or with the mind, are thus fraught with problems, nevertheless, they are natural and persistent ways of thinking. They are also two of the principal philosophic theories as to the nature of self and, for these reasons, deserve further discussion. *Reductive materialism* is the technical name for the theory that the self is coextensive with the physical being; the view that the self is explicable in terms of the mind or spirit is called *panpsychism*.

The theory of reductive materialism rejects the notion of mind altogether and explains all activities in terms of mechanical sequences of a physiological kind. "Brain" is substituted for "mind" as the agency responsible for actions, and the self is treated as identical with the physical organism, which includes the brain as well as the nerves, muscles, organs, skin, and so on. According to this theory, we are nothing but our anatomical parts and physiological processes.

Not only is a physical explanation thought to be adequate to account for all activities of the self, but the concept of mind is vigorously challenged on the grounds that there can be no possible evidence for its existence. It is argued that mind, by its very nature, belongs to a permanently unknowable realm beyond the reach of either scientific verification or the evidence of the senses. It cannot be seen, touched, heard, smelled, or tasted; no conceivable test could detect its presence within the body. For example, if a person reaches for a fork, then a train of physiological events occurring in a cause and effect pattern can be described: His muscles contracted on certain nerve impulses that were triggered by certain neural events occurring in his brain. But no evidence can be offered to substantiate the assumption that a nonphysical entity called "mind" was responsible for the movement of his arm.

Sometimes the reductive materialist charges that the existence of mind can only be asserted using an *argumentum ad ignorantiam:* We do not know what lies behind the physiological processes (assuming that something must), consequently we claim that mind is this funda-

[1] See David Hume, *A Treatise of Human Nature,* Vol. 1, Book 1, Part IV.

mental source. Obviously this is logically invalid, for a lack of knowledge cannot be taken as grounds for any conclusion; a theory is neither proven by not having been disproven nor disproven by not having been proven. If we do not know the cause of action, we cannot conclude that the cause must be the mind.

On the basis of these points, the reductive materialist rejects the notion of mind and defines the self strictly in terms of its physical components; the "I" is thus reduced wholly to matter without any spiritual or mental part.

Panpsychism is the name of the opposite theory which maintains that the self is basically spiritual or psychical in nature; even our physical body is thought to be in some way mental. Rather than the mind being in the body, the body is contained in the mind. Panpsychism rejects the materialistic view of self and regards it as having arisen from a prejudice for scientific explanations—a prejudice that is inconsistent with our experiences of phenomena such as remembering, desiring, deliberating, reflecting, and acting in accordance with a conscious purpose. To reduce phenomena of this sort to physiological terms does violence to our deep feeling that something other than a physical process is occurring when, for example, we are experiencing aesthetic joy or the emotion of love. The materialistic explanation also arbitrarily narrows man by declaring that he cannot be anything other than that which is empirically verifiable, that is, known by sense experience. Such a reduction is not only repugnant but depends upon an unfounded criterion for genuine knowledge.

As an alternative, the panpsychist declares that the essential self consists of mind or spirit, and that the reality of any physical aspect of self can be doubted. Viewed from this context, a supposedly physical event such as drinking some wine is only the sense of mellowness and well-being, a morning swim is the feeling of invigoration, with both experiences perhaps being increased further by anticipation and recollection which also belong to the mental realm. According to the panpsychist, all "physical" occurrences ultimately come down to internal experiences and are nothing but these experiences. We are not aware of our body being injured, for example, but rather injury is that mental event of experiencing pain. There is no physical self that is wounded, but only a mental self that is suffering; the *consciousness* of suffering is what being injured or wounded means. The same is said to be true of any alleged bodily event.

The panpsychist also argues that everyone recognizes himself to be that spiritual being lying within the animal form rather than the form itself. We know this through first-hand experience which gives us immediate and direct assurance that our mind, and not our body, constitutes the core of our self.

Some panpsychists go so far as to claim that, by analogy with the human self, the entire range of objects in the world—from animals to plants to rocks—might possess an internal spirit and some degree of awareness. For just as we know our own self to lie behind that which is externally apparent, other entities too could possess centers of consciousness within. In the case of flowers and trees the level of awareness would be quite low; for fish and birds it would be somewhat higher. But a mode of consciousness might be asserted to reside within every object in the universe, with the sum total of these spiritual centers constituting reality. Such a position is a variety of what is called philosophical idealism.

Whether or not we feel persuaded to adopt this position, it does seem plausible to trust our primary awareness that our minds are real and, perhaps, central to our selves. We may not be willing to accept the theory that mind is the only reality, or attribute consciousness to inanimate objects, but we do tend to accept the assumption that our minds, as well as our bodies, are real. Once we assert the reality of mind and body, we are faced with the theoretical problem of how interaction can occur between such radically different entities, but at least we are in harmony with our reflective understanding that the self includes both. In panpsychism and reductive materialism, a certain consistency is gained at the expense of common sense, but neither our mental part nor our physical part seems reducible to the other.

If the self does embrace both mind and body, then a further set of questions becomes relevant: To what extent are we physical beings and to what extent mental? [2] The self cannot be identified wholly with the body since we are more than the sum of our physical parts; nevertheless, the body seems to be a definite part of the self. And although the self is closely identified with the mind, it is not just mind but omething more encompassing. (If self were only that series of mental phenomena making up mind then it would be impossible to account for the fact of self-awareness. To quote the nineteenth-century English philosopher John Stuart Mill, we would have to "accept the paradox that something which *ex hypothesi* is but a series of feelings, can be aware of itself as a series"; or, that "I feel" is the same as "I know that I feel." That is, consciousness cannot be the same as self-consciousness.)

What then are the boundaries of the self? How much or what part of our bodies would have to be lost before we felt a diminution of selfhood? When our bodies grow, decay, and otherwise change throughout our lives, how is the self affected? How can the self reflect upon itself, be both subject and object; how can "I" contemplate "me"?

Related to these questions are others concerning the relation of the

---

[2]It is one thing, incidentally, to distinguish between mind and body, and quite another to say that mind can exist after the body has decayed. Belief in the distinction between mind and body does not logically entail belief in disembodied existence; a separate argument is needed to prove the immortality of the spirit.

self to the nonself: What should necessarily be included as essential to the self and what should be excluded as extraneous to it? What lies outside as object and what within as subject? The self has sometimes been said to include the people one loves and personal property, especially objects such as tools worn from a lifetime of use, one's land and home, special books or paintings, a favorite chair, or clothing that has conformed to the body from repeated wearing. As Henry David Thoreau writes in Walden:

> Kings and queens who wear a suit but once, though made by some tailor or dressmaker to their majesties, cannot know the comfort of wearing a suit that fits. They are no better than wooden horses to hang the clean clothes on. Every day our garments become more assimilated to ourselves, receiving the impress of the wearer's character, until we hesitate to lay them aside, . . . even as our bodies.

Or one can enlarge the self to embrace the whole of mankind within one's consciousness, as John Donne declares in his *Meditation XVII:*

> No man is an island, entire of itself; every man is a piece of the continent, a part of the main; if a clod be washed away by the sea, Europe is the less, as well as if a promontory were; as well as if a manor of the friends or of thine own; any man's death diminishes me, because I am involved in mankind; and therefore never send to know for whom the bell tolls; it tolls for thee.

The question is that of deciding the *extent* of the self: How wide or narrow can we interpret it to be? Perhaps William James is correct when he states that an individual is "the sum total of all that he can call his."

Just as we may question the extent of the self in "space," we may also inquire about the persistence of the self through "time." Here we wish to determine what core or personal essence survives all the changes that take place during one's life. Seemingly every facet of our being changes without any thread of continuity existing throughout. Our thoughts, attitudes, aspirations, and values change between childhood and old age. Our memories may grow dim; our disposition can vary from extreme compassion to bitter cynicism and misanthropy; our bodies undergo a virtual metamorphosis as every cell is replaced; and growth and degeneration proceed continually between birth and death. What, then, remains constant? In temporal terms, the self is whatever entitles us to declare we are the same person throughout our lifetime, legitimately referred to by the same name. Whatever is seen as the persistent pattern, the constant ground of our being, that principle of personal unity underlying all change is our essential self.

As a final point it should be mentioned that some philosophic systems of a mystical nature have denied the reality of self altogether.

Indian philosophies, for example, will often make this claim, treating the self as an illusion (Maya) that we maintain through ignorance. They assert that the enlightened man understands that there are no separate selves and no genuine duality between people and the world they inhabit. Reality is one, without inner and outer parts, and the separation of the individual soul and the world soul is a distinction without a difference. The Indian philosophy further maintains that we can experience the unitary character of reality in privileged moments of heightened awareness, provided that we are receptive to Enlightenment and do not, among other things, retain a false belief in our individual existence. If our spirit is properly prepared, then the Oneness of the universe can be revealed to us in a mystical experience in which our sensations are melted and fused, our bones become liquefied, and we are absorbed into the cosmic All.

To conceive of the self in this way, as undifferentiated and consequently unreal, is extremely appealing when our lives are painful and we long for escape. But for good or ill, wishes do not necessarily correspond to actualities; the world exists independent of our heart's desires. However much our individual loneliness or the consciousness of pain may induce us to believe that our separate self is unreal, we are aware of our selves with a vividness, immediacy, and power that seems to guarantee authenticity and to render all denials absurd. Western philosophers generally argue that if the "I" is not real, then everything is an illusion, for few things strike us as more certain. Thus the Indian equation of the self and the universe as fundamentally one violates our "self-awareness." [8]

If we are prepared to assert the reality of self, we then face the more puzzling issue of defining its nature. That is, once we are satisfied *that* the self is, we must then ask *what* it is, and this question has occupied philosophy since the time of Plato.

In the literary and philosophic works that follow, various answers to this question are proposed for consideration. Since the concept of self is not an easy matter, we should not expect to find facile solutions, but we can expect to be engaged in an interesting inquiry. For the nature of the self is both an intriguing academic problem and a highly personal issue.

---

[8] The same point can be made against Sufism, Neoplatonism, Christian mysticism, and Walt Whitman's ecstatic spiritualism.

1
Personal Identity
as
Essentially Internal

THE NOTEBOOKS OF MALTE LAURIDS BRIGGE

RAINER MARIA RILKE

(trans. by M. D. Herter Norton)

Rainer Maria Rilke (1875–1926) was an Austrian poet and prose writer who is best known for his poetic works *The Duino Elegies* and *Sonnets to Orpheus* and two novels, *The Tale of Love and Death of Cornet Christopher Rilke* and *The Notebooks of Malte Laurids Brigge*. His ability to express abstract ideas in concrete images has influenced twentieth-century British and American poetry to a considerable extent.

In *The Notebooks of Malte Laurids Brigge,* Rilke refuses to identify the person with his body and appearance, distinguishing clothing, faces, and hands, in particular, as extraneous to self. Faces are masks, clothing is costume, and both are assumed by the individual in a continuous series of impersonations. They do not function as reflections of our nature, but are roles imposed upon us by society that we might be unable to stop playing when we try to be ourselves. Even hands are a part of the world, divorced from us to the point of having separate autonomy, and they bear a greater affinity to faces than to our volitional selves. To Rilke, the authentic self consists of internal forces, dynamic and spiritual, and *will* above all, which courses through men, nature, and objects.

In his other writings, Rilke develops his concept of the primacy of inner forces. He describes cathedrals that have heaped themselves up until the molten rock crystalizes in the air while the surrounding houses are shocked into silence by the volcanic eruption. Trees surge toward the sky, the sap collecting and rising, the branches thrusting through the bark, the leaves unfolding and spreading. Single flowers stand up and shout "Red" in frightened voices, and houses grouped round a square pile on top of one another wanting to see everything. Rilke believes that it is the internal aspect of all things (human beings especially) which defines their nature, and that people must resist the self-alienation that comes from defining themselves by looking in a mirror. The "I" is known through "interior apprehension," which discloses indwelling spiritual centers as the essence of the individual.

11

FACES

Have I said it before? I am learning to see. Yes, I am beginning. It still goes badly. But I intend to make the most of my time.

To think, for instance, that I have never been aware before how many faces there are. There are quantities of human beings, but there are many more faces, for each person has several. There are people who wear the same face for years; naturally it wears out, it gets dirty, it splits at the folds, it stretches, like gloves one has worn on a journey. These are thrifty, simple people; they do not change their face, they never even have it cleaned. It is good enough, they say, and who can prove to them the contrary? The question of course arises, since they have several faces, what do they do with the others? They store them up. Their children will wear them. But sometimes, too, it happens that their dogs go out with them on. And why not? A face is a face.

Other people put their faces on, one after the other, with uncanny rapidity and wear them out. At first it seems to them they are provided for always; but they scarcely reach forty—and they have come to the last. This naturally has something tragic. They are not accustomed to taking care of faces, their last is worn through in a week, has holes, and in many places is thin as paper; and then little by little the under layer, the no-face, comes through, and they go about with that.

But the woman, the woman; she had completely collapsed into herself, forward into her hands. It was at the corner of rue Notre-Dame-des-Champs. I began to walk softly as soon as I saw her. When poor people are reflecting they should not be disturbed. Perhaps their idea will yet occur to them.

The street was too empty; its emptiness was bored; it caught my step from under my feet and clattered about with it hither and yon, as with a wooden clog. The woman startled and pulled away too quickly out of herself, too violently, so that her face remained in her two hands. I could see it lying in them, its hollow form. It cost me indescribable effort to stay with those hands and not to look at what had torn itself out of them. I shuddered to see a face from the inside, but still I was much more afraid of the naked flayed head without a face. . . .

HANDS: A CHILDHOOD EXPERIENCE

. . . I was drawing a knight, a solitary, easily recognizable knight, on a strikingly caparisoned horse. He became so gaily-colored that I had to change crayons frequently, but the red was most in demand, and for it I reached again and again. Now I needed it once more, when it rolled (I can see it yet) right across the lighted sheet to the edge of the table and, before I could stop it, fell past me and disappeared. I needed it really urgently, and it was very annoying to clamber down after it. Awkward as I was, I had to make all sorts of preparations to get down; my legs seemed to me far too long, I could not pull them out from under me; the too-prolonged kneeling posture had numbed my limbs; I could not tell what belonged to me, and what to the chair. At last I did arrive down there, somewhat bewildered, and found myself on a fur rug that stretched from under the table as far as the wall. But here a fresh difficulty arose. My eyes, accustomed to the brightness above and all inspired with the colors on the white paper, were unable to distinguish anything at all beneath the table, where the blackness seemed to me so dense that I was afraid I should knock against it. I therefore relied on my sense of touch, and kneeling, supported on my left hand, I combed around with my other hand in the cool, long-haired rug, which felt quite friendly; only that no pencil was to be found. I imagined I must be losing a lot of time, and was about to call to Mademoiselle and ask her to hold the lamp for me, when I noticed that to my involuntarily strained eyes the darkness was gradually growing more penetrable. I could already distinguish the wall at the back, which ended in a light-colored molding; I oriented myself with regard to the legs of the table; above all I recognized my own out-spread hand moving down there all alone, a little like an aquatic animal, examining the ground. I watched it, as I remember still, almost with curiosity; it seemed as if it knew things I had never taught it, groping down there so independently, with movements I had never noticed in it before. I followed it up as it pressed forward, I was interested in it, ready for all sorts of things. But how should I have been prepared to see suddenly come to meet it out of the wall another hand, a larger, extraordinarily thin hand, such as I had never seen before. It came groping in similar fashion from the other side, and the two outspread hands moved blindly toward one another. My curiosity was not yet used up but suddenly it came to an end, and there was only terror. I felt that one of the hands belonged to me, and that it was committing itself to something irreparable. With all the authority I had over it, I checked it and drew it back flat and slowly, without taking my eyes off the other, which went on groping. I realized that it would not leave off; I cannot tell how I got up again. I sat deep in the armchair, my teeth chattered, and I had so little blood in my face that it seemed to me there could be no more blue in my eyes. . . .

COSTUMES: A CHILD'S GAME OF IMPERSONATION

It was then that I first learned to know the influence that can emanate directly from a particular costume itself. Hardly had I donned one of these suits, when I had to admit that it got me in its power; that it prescribed my movements, my facial expression, yes, even my ideas. My hand, over which the lace cuff fell and fell again, was anything but my usual hand; it moved like a person acting; I might even say that it was watching itself, exaggerated though that sounds. These disguises never, indeed, went so far as to make me feel a stranger to myself; on the contrary, the more varied my transformations, the more convinced did I become of myself. I grew bolder and bolder; I flung myself higher and higher; for my dexterity in recapture was beyond all doubt. I did not notice the temptation in this rapidly growing security. To my undoing, the last closet, which I had heretofore thought I could not open, yielded one day, to surrender to me, not specific costumes, but all kinds of random paraphernalia for masquerades, the fantastic peradventures of which drove the blood to my cheeks. It is impossible to recount all I found there. In addition to a baútta that I remember, there were dominos in various colors, there were women's dresses that tinkled brightly with the coins with which they were sewn; there were pierrot-costumes that looked silly to me, and braided Turkish trousers, all folds, and Persian fezzes from which little camphor sacks slipped out, and coronets with stupid, expressionless stones. All these I rather despised; they were of such a shabby unreality and hung there so peeled-off and miserable and collapsed so will-lessly when one dragged them out into the light. But what transported me into a sort of intoxication were the capacious mantles, the wraps, the shawls, the veils, all those yielding, wide, unused fabrics, that were so soft and caressing, or so slithery that one could scarcely take hold of them, or so light that they flew by one like a wind, or simply heavy with all their own weight. In them I first discerned really free and infinitely mobile possibilities: being a slave-girl about to be sold, or being Jeanne d'Arc or an old king or a wizard; all this lay to hand, especially as there were also masks, large, threatening or astonished faces with real beards and full or high-drawn eyebrows. I had never seen masks before, but I understood at once what masks ought to be. I had to laugh when it occurred to me that we had a dog who looked as if he wore one. I recalled his affectionate eyes, that always seemed to be looking as from behind into his hirsute visage. I was still laughing as I dressed up, and in the process I completely forgot what I had intended to represent. No matter; it was novel and exciting not to decide till afterward before the mirror. The face I fastened on had a singularly hollow smell; it lay tight over my own face, but I was able to see through it comfortably, and not till the mask sat firm did I select all sorts of materials, which I wound about my head like a turban, in such a way that the edge of the mask, which reached downward into an immense yellow cloak, was almost entirely hidden also on top and at the sides. At length, when I could do no more, I considered myself sufficiently disguised. I seized in addition a large staff, which I made walk along beside me at arm's length, and in this fashion, not without difficulty, but, as it seemed to me, full of dignity, I trailed into the guest-room toward the mirror.

It was really grandiose, beyond all expectation. And the mirror gave it back instantly, it was too convincing. It would not have been at all necessary to move much; this apparition was perfect, even though it did nothing. But I wanted to discover what I actually was, so I turned a little and finally raised both arms: large, almost conjuring gestures were, I saw immediately, the only fitting ones. But just at this solemn moment I heard quite near me, muffled by my disguise, a very complicated noise; much frightened, I lost sight of the presence in the mirror and was badly upset to perceive that I had overturned a small round table with heaven knows what, probably very fragile objects. I bent down as well as I could and found my worst fears confirmed: it looked as though everything were in pieces. The two useless green-violet porcelain parrots were of course shattered, each in a different malign fashion. A box, from which rolled bonbons that looked like insects in silken cocoons, had cast its cover far away; only half of it was to be seen, and the other had totally disappeared. But most annoying of all was a scent-bottle that had been shivered into a thousand tiny fragments, from which the remainder of some sort of old essence had spurted that now formed a spot of very repulsive profile on the clear parquet. I wiped it up quickly with something or other that was hanging down about me, but it only became blacker and more unpleasant. I was indeed desperate. I picked myself up and tried to find something with which to repair the damage. But nothing was to be found. Besides I was so hampered in my vision and in every movement, that wrath rose in me against my absurd situation, which I no longer understood. I pulled at all my garments, but they clung only the tighter. The cords of the mantle strangled me, and the stuff on my head pressed as though more and more were being added to it. Furthermore the atmosphere had become dim and as though misty with the oldish fume of the spilled liquid.

Hot and angry, I rushed to the mirror and with difficulty watched through the mask the working of my hands. But for this the mirror had just been waiting. Its moment of retaliation had come. While I strove in boundlessly increasing anguish to squeeze somehow out of my disguise, it forced me, by what means I do not know, to lift my eyes and imposed on me an image, no, a reality, a strange, unbelievable and monstrous reality, with which, against my will, I became permeated: for now the mirror was the stronger, and I was the mirror. I stared at this great, terrifying unknown before me, and it seemed to me appalling to be alone with him. But at the very moment I thought this, the worst befell: I lost all sense, I simply ceased to exist. For one second I had an indescribable, painful and futile longing for myself, then there was only he: there was nothing but he.

I ran away, but now it was he that ran. He knocked against everything, he did not know the house, he had no idea where to go; he managed to get down a stairway, and in his course stumbled over someone who shouted in struggling free. A door opened, several persons came out: Oh, oh, what a relief it was to know them! There were Sieversen, the good Sieversen, and the housemaid and the butler: now for a decision. But they did not spring forward to the rescue; their cruelty knew no bounds. They stood there and laughed; my God, they could stand there and laugh. I wept, but the mask did not let the tears escape; they ran down inside over my cheeks and dried at once and ran again and dried. And at last I knelt before them, as no human being ever knelt; I knelt, and lifted up my hands, and implored them: "Take me out, if you still can, and keep me," but they did not hear; I had no longer any voice.

AN INTRODUCTION TO METAPHYSICS

HENRI BERGSON

(trans. by T. E. Hulme)

Henri Bergson (1859–1941) was a French philosopher famous for his theory of "creative evolution" which exerted a considerable impact on the philosophy and literature of his day. To Bergson, evolution is the result of a thrust of life (*élan vital*) which counteracts the tendencies of matter toward repetition and dissipation of energy. In *Time and Free Will, Matter and Memory,* and *The Two Sources of Morality and Religion,* he develops his dynamic view of the material world and correlates it with a theory of knowledge.

In the following selection from his *Introduction to Metaphysics,* Bergson (like Rilke) affirms the view that the self resides within and is known by intuitive apprehension. On the surface of the sphere of self lie perceptions, memories, tendencies, and motor habits, while within there exists a continuous flux, both manifold and one, which is the essence of self continually developing in time.

There is one reality, at least, which we all seize from within, by intuition and not by simple analysis. It is our own personality in its flowing through time—our self which endures. We may sympathize intellectually with nothing else, but we certainly sympathize with our own selves.

When I direct my attention inward to contemplate my own self (supposed for the moment to be inactive), I perceive at first, as a crust solidified on the surface, all the perceptions which come to it from the material world. These perceptions are clear, distinct, juxtaposed or juxtaposable one with another; they tend to group themselves into objects. Next, I notice the memories which more or less adhere to these perceptions and which serve to interpret them. These memories have been detached, as it were, from the depth of my personality, drawn to the surface by the perceptions which resemble them; they rest on the surface of my mind without being absolutely myself. Lastly, I feel the stir of tendencies and motor habits—a crowd of virtual actions, more or less firmly bound to these perceptions and memories. All these clearly defined elements appear more distinct from me, the more distinct they are from each other. Radiating, as they do, from within outwards, they form, collectively, the surface of a sphere which tends to grow larger and lose itself in the exterior world. But if I draw myself in from the periphery towards the centre, if I search in the depth of my being that which is most uniformly, most constantly, and most enduring myself, I find an altogether different thing.

There is, beneath these sharply cut crystals and this frozen surface, a continuous flux which is not comparable to any flux I have ever seen. There is a succession of states, each of which announces that which follows and contains that which precedes it. They can, properly speaking, only be said to form multiple states when I have already passed them and turn back to observe their track. Whilst I was experiencing them they were so solidly organized, so profoundly animated with a common life, that I could not have said where any one of them finished or where another commenced. In reality no one of them begins or ends, but all extend into the other.

This inner life may be compared to the unrolling of a coil, for there is no living being who does not feel himself coming gradually to the end of his role; and to live is to grow old. But it may just as well be compared to a continual rolling up, like that of a thread on a ball, for our past follows us, it swells incessantly with the present that it picks up on its way; and consciousness means memory.

But actually it is neither an unrolling nor a rolling up, for these two similes evoke the idea of lines and surfaces whose parts are homogeneous and superposable on one another. Now, there are no two identical moments in the life of the same conscious being. Take the simplest sensation, suppose it constant, absorb in it the entire personality: the consciousness which will accompany this sensation cannot remain identical with itself for two consecutive moments, because the second moment always contains, over and above the first, the memory that the first has bequeathed to it. A consciousness which could experience two identical moments would be a consciousness without memory. It would die and be born again continually. In what other way could one represent unconsciousness?

It would be better, then, to use as a comparison the myriad-tinted spectrum, with its insensible gradations leading from one shade to another. A current of feeling which passed along the spectrum, assuming in turn the tint of each of its shades, would experience a series of gradual changes, each of which would announce the one to follow and would sum up those which preceded it. Yet even here the successive shades of the spectrum always remain external one to another. They are juxtaposed; they occupy space. But pure duration, on the contrary, excludes all idea of juxtaposition, reciprocal externality, and extension.

Let us, then, rather, imagine an infinitely small elastic body, contracted, if it were possible, to a mathematical point. Let this be drawn out gradually in such a manner that from the point comes a constantly lengthening line. Let us fix our attention not on the line as a line, but on the action by which it is traced. Let us bear in mind that this action, in spite of its duration, is indivisible if accomplished without stopping, that if a stopping-point is inserted, we have two actions instead of one, that each of these separate actions is then the indivisible operation of which we speak, and that it is not the moving action itself which is divisible, but, rather, the stationary line it leaves behind it as its track in space. Finally, let us free ourselves from the space which underlies the movement in order to consider only the movement itself, the act of tension or extension; in short, pure mobility. We shall have this time a more faithful image of the development of our self in duration. . . .

Let us try for an instant to consider our duration as a multiplicity. It will then be necessary to add that the terms of this multiplicity, instead of being distinct, as they are in any other multiplicity, encroach on one another; and that while we can no doubt, by an effort of imagination, solidify duration once it has elapsed, divide it into juxtaposed portions and count all these portions, yet this operation is accomplished on the frozen memory of the duration, on the stationary trace which the mobility of duration leaves behind it, and not on the duration itself. We must admit, therefore, that if there is a multiplicity here, it bears no resemblance to any other multiplicity we know. Shall we say, then, that duration has unity? Doubtless, a continuity of elements which prolong themselves into one another participates in unity as much as in multiplicity; but this moving, changing, colored, living unity has hardly anything in common with the abstract, motionless, and empty unity which the concept of pure unity circumscribes. Shall we conclude from this that duration must be defined as unity and multiplicity at the same time? But singularly enough, however much I manipulate the two concepts, portion them out, combine them differently, practise on them the most subtle operations of mental chemistry, I never obtain anything which resembles the simple intuition that I have of duration; while, on the contrary, when I replace myself in duration by an effort of intuition, I immediately perceive how it is unity, multiplicity, and many other things besides. These different concepts, then, were only so many standpoints from which we could consider duration. Neither separated nor reunited have they made us penetrate into it.

We do penetrate into it, however, and that can only be by an effort of intuition. In this sense, an inner, absolute knowledge of the duration of the self by the self is possible.

2
The Duality
of
Mind and Body

THE METAMORPHOSIS
(Part I)

FRANZ KAFKA
(trans. by Willa and Edwin Muir)

Franz Kafka (1883–1924) was an Austrian novelist and short story writer whose works depict the displacement and alienation between man, on the one hand, and society, God, and his own authentic self, on the other. *The Castle* and *The Trial* are Kafka's major novels; his outstanding short stories include *The Metamorphosis, The Penal Colony,* and *The Country Doctor.*

The fantastic transformation of a man into a beetle forms the theme of Kafka's story.*The Metamorphosis.* As a metaphysical parable it can be understood on numerous levels, and the ambiguity is intended to stimulate reflection on the state of man. A common interpretation treats Gregor Samsa as an insect from beginning to end, formerly in human form and ultimately inhabiting the appropriate beetle body. As a salesman living the unreflective, repetitive life of a food gatherer, Gregor had been a diligent provider but he had not developed beyond this function, which is exactly the point. Humanness and personal identity begin where activities directed at securing the necessities of life leave off. It is precisely with regard to human and individual qualities that Gregor is deficient, consequently his metamorphosis into a beetle is poetically just.

Another interpretation that can be made is of greater philosophic interest. In depicting Gregor, Kafka might well be symbolically representing *the disparity between mind and body.* Internally, Gregor remains fundamentally unchanged; the metamorphosis into an insect is wholly external. Yet the metamorphosis circumscribes the limits of his actions in the same way that we are all imprisoned within the shell of our bodies, subject to its demands for sleep, nourishment, and shelter, and obliged to keep it exercised, healthy, and in good repair. In short, we may not identify primarily with the body we inhabit, but it determines our behavior in significant ways. Furthermore, we are "chained to a dying animal," and Gregor's transformation could stand for the degeneration of our bodies in old age. In this sense, we all undergo a metamorphosis from birth to death, and toward the end of life our skin

20

too becomes crusty, our voices grow shrill and thin, our eyesight degenerates, and our mouths become toothless. We must be careful in our movements because our bodies become sluggish, and getting out of bed in the morning becomes difficult because we have grown stiff in the night and our thin legs hardly support us. Finally, unable to communicate with others (although making perfect sense to ourselves), surrounded by neglect and rejection, we die and disappear from sight—to everyone's relief.

As Gregor Samsa awoke one morning from uneasy dreams, he found himself transformed in his bed into a gigantic insect. He was lying on his hard—as it were, armor-plated—back, and when he lifted his head a little, he could see his dome-like brown belly divided into stiff arched segments, on top of which the bedquilt could hardly keep in position and was about to slide off completely. His numerous legs, which were pitifully thin compared to the rest of his bulk, waved helplessly before his eyes.

"What has happened to me?" he thought. It was no dream. His room, a regular human bedroom, only rather too small, lay quite inside the four familiar walls. Above the table, on which a collection of cloth samples was unpacked and spread out—Samsa was a commercial traveler—hung the picture that he had recently cut out of an illustrated magazine and put into a pretty gilt frame. It showed a lady, with a fur cap and a fur stole, sitting upright and holding out to the spectator a huge fur muff into which the whole of her forearm had vanished.

Gregor's eyes turned next to the window, and the overcast sky—one could hear raindrops beating on the window gutter—made him quite melancholy. "What about sleeping a little longer and forgetting all this nonsense?" he thought; but it could not be done, for he was accustomed to sleep on his right side, and in his present condition he could not turn himself over. However violently he forced himself toward his right side, he always rolled onto his back again. He tried it at least one hundred times, shutting his eyes to keep from seeing his struggling legs, and only desisted when he began to feel in his side a faint dull ache that he had never experienced before.

"Oh God," he thought, "what an exhausting job I've picked on! Traveling about, day in, day out. It's much more irritating work than doing the actual business in the office, and on top of that there's the trouble of constant traveling, of worrying about train connections, the bed and irregular meals, casual acquaintances who are always new and never become intimate friends. The devil take it all!" He felt a slight itching up on his belly; slowly pushed himself on his back nearer to the top of the bed so that he could lift his head more easily; identified the itching place, which was surrounded by many small white spots, the nature of which he could not understand, and made to touch it with a leg, but drew the leg back immediately, for the contact made a cold shiver run through him.

He slid down again into his former position. "This getting up early," he thought, "makes one quite stupid. A man needs his sleep. Other commercials live like harem women. For instance, when I come back to the hotel of a morning to write up the orders I've got, these others are only sitting down to breakfast. Let me just try that with my chief; I'd be sacked on the spot. Anyhow, that might be quite a good thing for me, who can tell? If I didn't have to hold my hand because of my parents, I'd have given notice long ago, I'd have gone to the chief and told him exactly what I think of him. That would knock him endways from his desk! It's a queer way of doing, too, this sitting on high at a desk and talking down to employees, especially when they have to come quite near because the chief is hard of hearing. Well, there's still hope; once I've saved enough money to pay back my parents' debts to him—that should take another five or six years—I'll do it without fail. I'll cut myself completely loose then. For the moment, though, I'd better get up, for my train goes at five."

He looked at the alarm clock ticking on the chest. "Heavenly Father!" he thought. It was half past six o'clock and the hands were quietly moving on. It was even past the half-hour; it was getting on toward a quarter to seven. Had the alarm clock not gone off? From the bed one could see that it had been properly set for four o'clock; of course it must have gone off. Yes, but was it possible to sleep quietly through that ear-splitting noise? Well, he had not slept quietly, yet apparently all the more soundly for that. But what was he to do now? The next train went at seven o'clock; to catch that he would need to hurry like mad, and his samples weren't even packed up, and he himself wasn't feeling particularly fresh and active. And even if he did catch the train he wouldn't avoid a row with the chief, for the firm's porter would have been waiting for the five-o'clock train and long since would have reported his failure to turn up. The porter was a creature of the chief's, spineless and stupid. Well, supposing he were to say he was sick? But that would be most unpleasant and would look suspicious, as during his five years' employment he had not been ill once. The chief himself would be sure to come with the sick-insurance doctor, would reproach his parents with their son's laziness, and would cut all excuses short by referring to the insurance doctor, who of course regarded all mankind as perfectly healthy malingerers. And would he be so far wrong on this occasion? Gregor really felt quite well, apart from a drowsiness that was utterly superfluous after such a long sleep, and he was even unusually hungry.

As all this was running through his mind at top speed without his being able to decide to leave his bed—the alarm clock had just struck a quarter to seven—there came a cautious tap at the door behind the head of his bed. "Gregor," said a voice—it was his mother's—"it's a quarter to seven. Hadn't you a train to catch?" That gentle voice! Gregor had a shock as he heard his own voice answering hers, unmistakably his own voice, it was true, but with a persistent horrible twittering squeak behind it like an undertone, leaving the words in their clear shape only for the first moment and then rising up reverberating around them to destroy their sense, so that one could not be sure one had heard them rightly. Gregor wanted to answer at length and explain everything, but in the circumstances he confined himself to saying: "Yes, yes, thank you, Mother, I'm getting up now." The wooden door between them must have kept the change in his voice from being noticeable outside, for his mother contented herself with this statement and shuffled away. Yet this brief exchange of words had made the other members of the family aware that Gregor was still in the house, as they had not expected, and at one of the side doors his father was already knocking, gently, yet with his fist.

"Gregor, Gregor," he called, "what's the matter with you?" And after a little while he called again in a deeper voice: "Gregor! Gregor!"

At the other side door his sister was saying in a low, plaintive tone: "Gregor? Aren't you well? Are you needing anything?"

He answered them both at once: "I'm just ready," and did his best to make his voice sound as normal as possible by enunciating the words very clearly and leaving long pauses between them. So his father went back to his breakfast, but his sister whispered: "Gregor, open the door, do." However, he was not thinking of opening the door, and felt thankful for the prudent habit he had acquired in traveling of locking all doors during the night, even at home.

His immediate intention was to get up quietly without being disturbed, to put on his clothes and above all eat his breakfast, and only then to consider what else was to be done, as in bed, he was well aware, his meditations would come to no sensible conclusion. He remembered that often enough in bed he had felt small aches and pains, probably caused by awkward postures, which had proved purely imaginary once he was up, and he looked forward eagerly to seeing this morning's delusions gradually fall away. That the change in his voice was nothing but the precursor of a severe chill, a standing ailment of commercial travelers, he had not the least possible doubt.

To get rid of the quilt was quite easy; he had only to inflate himself a little and it fell off by itself. But the next move was difficult, especially because he was so uncommonly broad. He would have needed arms and hands to hoist himself up; instead he had only the numerous little legs, which never stopped waving in all directions, and which he could not control in the least. When he tried to bend one of them, it was the first to stretch itself straight; and did he succeed at last in making it do what he wanted, all the other legs meanwhile waved the more wildly in a high degree of unpleasant agitation. "But what's the use of lying idle in bed?" said Gregor to himself.

He thought that he might get out of bed with the lower part of his body first, but this lower part, which he had not yet seen and of which he could form no clear conception, proved too difficult to move because it shifted so slowly; and when finally, almost wild with annoyance, he gathered his forces together and thrust out recklessly, he had miscalculated the direction and bumped heavily against the lower end of the bed, and the stinging pain he felt informed him that precisely this lower part of his body was at the moment probably the most sensitive.

So he tried to get the top part of himself out first, and cautiously moved his head toward the edge of the bed. That proved easy enough, and despite its breadth and mass the bulk of his body at last slowly followed the movement of his head. Still, when he finally got his head free over the edge of the bed he felt too scared to go on advancing, for after all if he let himself fall in this way it would take a miracle to keep his head from being injured. And at all costs he must not lose consciousness now, precisely now; he would rather stay in bed.

But when after a repetition of the same efforts he lay in his former position again, sighing, and watched his little legs struggling against one another more wildly than ever, if that were possible, and saw no way of bringing any order into this arbitrary confusion, he told himself again that it was impossible to stay in bed and that the most sensible course was to risk everything for the smallest hope of getting away from it. At the same time he did not forget meanwhile to remind himself that cool reflection, the coolest possible, was much better than desperate resolves. In such moments he focused his eyes as sharply as possible on the window, but, unfortunately, the prospect of the morning fog, which muffled even the other side of the narrow street, brought him little encouragement and comfort. "Seven o'clock already," he said to himself when the alarm clock chimed again, "seven o'clock already, and still such a thick fog." And for a little while he lay quiet, breathing lightly, as if perhaps expecting such complete repose to restore all things to their real and normal condition.

But then he said to himself: "Before it strikes a quarter past seven I must be quite out of this bed, without fail. Anyhow, by that time someone will have come from the office to ask for me, since it opens before seven." And he set himself to rocking his whole body at once in a regular rhythm, with the idea of swinging it out of the bed. If he tipped himself out in that way, he could keep his head from injury by lifting it at an acute angle when he fell. His back seemed to be hard and was not likely to suffer from a fall on the carpet. His biggest worry was the loud crash he would not be able to help making, which would probably cause anxiety, if not terror, behind all the doors. Still, he must take the risk.

When he was already half out of the bed—the new method was more a game than an effort, for he needed only to hitch himself across by rocking to and fro—it struck him how simple it would be if he could get help. Two strong people—he thought of his father and the servant girl—would be amply sufficient; they would only have to thrust their arms under his convex back, lever him out of the bed, bend down with their burden, and then be patient enough to let him turn himself right over onto the floor, where it was to be hoped his legs would then find their proper function. Well, ignoring the fact that the doors were all locked, ought he really to call for help? In spite of his misery, he could not suppress a smile at the very idea of it.

He had got so far that he could barely keep his equilibrium when he rocked himself strongly, and he would have to nerve himself very soon for the final decision, for in five minutes' time it would be a quarter past seven—when the front doorbell rang. "That's someone from the office," he said to himself, and grew almost rigid, while his little legs only jigged about all the faster. For a moment everything stayed quiet. "They're not going to open the door," said Gregor to himself, catching at some kind of irrational hope. But then of course the servant girl went as usual to the door with her heavy tread and opened it. Gregor needed only to hear the first good-morning of the visitor to know immediately who it was—the chief clerk himself. What a fate, to be condemned to work for a firm where the smallest omission at once gave rise to the gravest suspicion! Were all employees in a body nothing but scoundrels, was there not among them one single loyal, devoted man who, had he wasted only an hour or so of the firm's time in a morning, was so tormented by conscience as to be driven out of his mind and actually incapable of leaving his bed? Wouldn't it really have been sufficient to send an apprentice to inquire— if any inquiry were necessary at all? Did the chief clerk himself have to come, and thus indicate to the entire family, an innocent family, that this suspicious circumstance could be investigated by no one less versed in affairs than himself? And more through the agitation caused by these reflections than through any act of will Gregor swung himself out of bed with all his strength. There was a loud thump, but it was not really a crash. His fall was broken to some extent by the carpet; also, his back was less stiff than he had thought, and so there was merely a dull thud, not so very startling. Only he had not lifted his head carefully enough and had hit it; he turned it and rubbed it on the carpet in pain and irritation.

"That was something falling down in there," said the chief clerk in the next room to the left. Gregor tried to suppose to himself that something like what had happened to him today might some day happen to the chief clerk; one really could not deny that it was possible. But as if in brusque reply to this supposition the chief clerk took a couple of firm steps in the next room, and his patent-leather boots creaked. From the right-hand room his sister was whispering to inform him of the situation: "Gregor, the chief clerk's here."

"I know," muttered Gregor to himself: but he didn't dare to make his voice loud enough for his sister to hear it.

"Gregor," said his father now from the left-hand room, "the chief clerk has come and wants to know why you didn't catch the early train.

We don't know what to say to him. Besides, he wants to talk to you in person. So open the door, please. He will be good enough to excuse the untidiness of your room."

"Good morning, Mr. Samsa," the chief clerk was calling amiably meanwhile.

"He's not well," said his mother to the visitor, while his father was still speaking through the door, "he's not well, sir, believe me. What else would make him miss a train! The boy thinks about nothing but his work. It makes me almost cross the way he never goes out in the evenings. He's been here the last eight days and has stayed at home every single evening. He just sits there quietly at the table reading a newspaper or looking through railway timetables. The only amusement he gets is doing fretwork. For instance, he spent two or three evenings cutting out a little picture frame; you would be surprised to see how pretty it is; it's hanging in his room; you'll see it in a minute when Gregor opens the door. I must say I'm glad you've come, sir; we should never have got him to unlock the door by ourselves, he's so obstinate; and I'm sure he's unwell, though he wouldn't have it to be so this morning."

"I'm just coming," said Gregor slowly and carefully, not moving an inch for fear of losing one word of the conversation.

"I can't think of any other explanation, madam," said the chief clerk, "I hope it's nothing serious. Although on the other hand I must say that we men of business—fortunately or unfortunately—very often simply have to ignore any slight indisposition, since business must be attended to."

"Well, can the chief clerk come in now?" asked Gregor's father impatiently, again knocking on the door.

"No," said Gregor. In the left-hand room a painful silence followed this refusal; in the right-hand room his sister began to sob.

Why didn't his sister join the others? She was probably newly out of bed and hadn't even begun to put on her clothes yet. Well, why was she crying? Because he wouldn't get up and let the chief clerk in, because he was in danger of losing his job, and because the chief would begin dunning his parents again for the old debts? Surely these were things one didn't need to worry about for the present. Gregor was still at home, and not in the least thinking of deserting the family. At the moment, true, he was lying on the carpet and no one who knew the condition he was in could seriously expect him to admit the chief clerk. But for such a small discourtesy, which could plausibly be explained away somehow later on, Gregor could hardly be dismissed on the spot. And it seemed to Gregor that it would be much more sensible to leave him in peace for the present than to trouble him with tears and entreaties. Still, of course, their uncertainty bewildered them all and excused their behavior.

"Mr. Samsa," the chief clerk called now in a louder voice, "what's the matter with you? Here you are, barricading yourself in your room, giving only 'yes' and 'no' for answers, causing you parents a lot of unnecessary trouble, and neglecting—I mention this only in passing—neglecting your business duties in an incredible fashion. I am speaking here in the name of your parents and of your chief, and I beg you quite seriously to give me an immediate and precise explanation. You amaze me, you amaze me. I thought you were a quiet, dependable person, and now all at once you seem bent on making a disgraceful exhibition of yourself. The chief did hint to me early this morning a possible explanation for your disappearance—with reference to the cash payments that were entrusted to you recently—but I almost pledged my solemn word of honor that this could not be so. But now that I see how incredibly obstinate you are, I no longer have the slightest desire to take your part at all. And your position in the firm is not so unassailable. I came with the intention of telling you all this in private, but since you are wasting my time so needlessly, I don't see why your parents shouldn't hear it too. For some time past your work has been most unsatisfactory; this is not the season of the year for a business boom, of course, we admit that, but a season of the year for doing no business at all, that does not exist, Mr. Samsa, must not exist."

"But, sir," cried Gregor, beside himself and in his agitation forgetting everything else, "I'm just going to open the door this very minute. A slight illness, an attack of giddiness, has kept me from getting up. I'm still lying in bed. But I feel all right again. I'm getting out of bed now. Just give me a moment or two longer! I'm not quite so well as I thought. But I'm all right, really. How a thing like that can suddenly strike one down! Only last night I was quite well, my parents can tell you, or rather I did have a slight presentiment. I must have showed some sign of it. Why didn't I report it at the office! But one always thinks that an indisposition can be got over without staying in the house. Oh, sir, do spare my parents! All that you're reproaching me with now has no foundation; no one has ever said a word to me about it. Perhaps you haven't looked at the last orders I sent in. Anyhow, I can still catch the eight-o'clock train, I'm much the better for my few hours' rest. Don't let me detain you here, sir; I'll be attending to business very soon, and do be good enough to tell the chief so and to make my excuses to him!"

And while all this was tumbling out pell-mell and Gregor hardly knew what he was saying, he had reached the chest quite easily, perhaps because of the practice he had had in bed, and was now trying to lever himself upright by means of it. He meant actually to open the door, actually to show himself and speak to the chief clerk; he was eager to find out what the others, after all their insistence, would say at the sight of him. If they were horrified, then the responsibility was no longer his and he could stay quiet. But if they took it calmly, then he had no reason, either, to be upset, and could really get to the station for the eight-o'clock train if he hurried. At first he slipped down a few times from the polished surface of the chest, but at length with a last heave he stood upright; he paid no more attention to the pains in the lower part of his body, however they smarted. Then he let himself fall against the back of a near-by chair and clung with his little legs to the edges of it. That brought him into control of himself again, and he stopped speaking, for now he could listen to what the chief clerk was saying.

"Did you understand a word of it?" the chief clerk was asking. "Surely he can't be trying to make fools of us?"

"Oh dear," cried his mother, in tears, "perhaps he's terribly ill and we're tormenting him. Grete! Grete!" she called out then.

"Yes, Mother?" called his sister from the other side. They were calling to each other across Gregor's room.

"You must go this minute for the doctor. Gregor is ill. Go for the doctor, quick. Did you hear how he was speaking?"

"That was no human voice," said the chief clerk in a voice noticeably low beside the shrillness of the mother's.

"Anna! Anna!" his father was calling through the hall to the kitchen, clapping his hands, "get a locksmith at once!" And the two girls were already running through the hall with a swish of skirts—how could his sister have got dressed so quickly?—and were tearing the front door open. There was no sound of its closing again; they had evidently left it open, as one does in houses where some great misfortune has happened.

But Gregor was now much calmer. The words he uttered were no longer understandable, apparently, although they seemed clear enough to him, even clearer than before, perhaps because his ear had grown accustomed to the sound of them. Yet at any rate people now believed that something was wrong with him, and were ready to help him. The positive certainty with which these first measures had been taken comforted him. He felt himself drawn once more into the human circle and hoped for great and remarkable results from both the doctor and the locksmith, without really distinguishing precisely between them. To make his voice as clear as possible for the decisive conversation that was now imminent he coughed a little, as quietly as he could, of course, since this noise too might not sound like a human cough, for all he was able to judge. In the next room meanwhile there was complete silence. Perhaps his parents were sitting at the table with the chief clerk, whispering; perhaps they were all leaning against the door and listening.

Slowly Gregor pushed the chair toward the door, then let go of it, caught hold of the door for support—the soles at the end of his little legs were somewhat sticky—and rested against it for a moment after his efforts. Then he set himself to turning the key in the lock with his mouth. It seemed, unhappily, that he hadn't really any teeth—what could he grip the key with?—but on the other hand his jaws were certainly very strong; with their help he did manage to set the key in motion, heedless of the fact that he was undoubtedly damaging them somewhere, since a brown fluid issued from his mouth, flowed over the key, and dripped on the floor.

"Just listen to that," said the chief clerk next door; "he's turning the key." That was a great encouragement to Gregor; but they should all have shouted encouragement to him, his father and mother too: "Go on, Gregor," they should have called out, "keep going, hold on to that key!"

And in the belief that they were all following his efforts intently, he clenched his jaws recklessly on the key with all the force at his command. As the turning of the key progressed he circled round the lock, holding on now only with his mouth, pushing on the key, as required, or pulling it down again with all the weight of his body. The louder click of the finally yielding lock literally quickened Gregor. With a deep breath of relief he said to himself: "So I didn't need the locksmith," and laid his head on the handle to open the door wide.

Since he had to pull the door toward him, he was still invisible when it was really wide open. He had to edge himself slowly round the near half of the double door, and to do it very carefully if he was not to fall plump upon his back just on the threshold. He was still carrying out this difficult maneuver, with no time to observe anything else, when he heard the chief clerk utter a loud "Oh!"—it sounded like a gust of wind—and now he could see the man, standing, as he was, nearest to the door, clapping one hand before his open mouth and slowly backing away as if driven by some invisible steady pressure. His mother—in spite of the chief clerk's being there her hair was still undone and sticking up in all directions—first clasped her hands and looked at his father, then took two steps toward Gregor and fell on the floor among her outspread skirts, her face quite hidden on her breast. His father knotted his fist with a fierce expression on his face as if he meant to knock Gregor back into his room, then looked uncertainly around the living-room, covered his eyes with his hands, and wept till his great chest heaved.

Gregor did not go now into the living-room, but leaned against the inside of the firmly shut wing of the door, so that only half his body was visible and his head above it bending sideways to look at the others. The light had meanwhile strengthened; on the other side of the street one could see clearly a section of the endlessly long, dark-gray building opposite—it was a hospital—abruptly punctuated by its row of regular windows; the rain was still falling, but only in large singly discernible and literally singly splashing drops. The breakfast dishes were set out on the table lavishly, for breakfast was the most important meal of the day to Gregor's father, who lingered it out for hours over various newspapers. Right opposite Gregor on the wall hung a photograph of himself in military service, as a lieutenant, hand on sword, a carefree smile on his face, inviting one to respect his uniform and military bearing. The door leading to the hall was open, and one could see that the front door stood open too, showing the landing beyond and the beginning of the stairs going down.

"Well," said Gregor, knowing perfectly that he was the only one who had retained any composure. "I'll put my clothes on at once, pack up my samples, and start off. Will you only let me go? You see, sir, I'm not obstinate, and I'm willing to work; traveling is a hard life, but I couldn't live without it. Where are you going, sir? To the office? Yes? Will you give a true account of all this? One can be temporarily incapacitated, but that's just the moment for remembering former services and bearing in mind that later on, when the incapacity has been got over, one will certainly work with all the more industry and concentration. I'm loyally bound to serve the chief, you know that very well. Besides, I have to provide for my parents and my sister. I'm in great difficulties, but I'll get out of them again. Don't make things any worse for me than they are. Stand up for me in the firm. Travelers are not popular there, I know. People think they earn sacks of money and just have a good time. A prejudice there's no particular reason for revising. But you, sir, have a more comprehensive view of affairs than the rest of the staff, yes, let me tell you in confidence, a more comprehensive view than the chief himself, who, being the owner, lets his judgment easily be swayed against one of his employees. And you know very well that the traveler, who is never seen in the office almost the whole year round, can so easily fall a victim to gossip and ill luck and unfounded complaints, which he mostly knows nothing about, except when he comes back exhausted from his rounds, and only then suffers in person from their evil consequences, which he can no longer trace back to the original causes. Sir, sir, don't go away without a word to me to show that you think me in the right at least to some extent!"

But at Gregor's very first words the chief clerk had already backed away, merely staring at him with parted lips over one twitching shoulder. And while Gregor was speaking he did not stand still one moment, but stole away toward the door without taking his eyes off Gregor, yet only an inch at a time, as if obeying some secret injunction to leave the room. He was already at the hall, and the suddenness with which he took his last step out of the living-room would have made one believe he had burned the sole of his foot. Once in the hall, he stretched his right arm before him toward the staircase, as if some supernatural power were waiting there to deliver him.

Gregor perceived that the chief clerk must on no account be allowed to go away in this frame of mind if his position in the firm were not to be endangered to the utmost. His parents did not understand this so well; they had convinced themselves in the course of years that Gregor was settled for life in this firm, and besides they were so preoccupied with their immediate troubles that all foresight had forsaken them. Yet Gregor had this foresight. The chief clerk must be detained, soothed, persuaded, and finally won over; the whole future of Gregor and his family depended on it! If only his sister had been there! She was intelligent; she had begun to cry while Gregor was still lying quietly on his back. And no doubt the chief clerk, so partial to ladies, would have been guided by her; she would have shut the door of the flat and in the hall talked him out of his horror. But she was not there, and Gregor would have to handle the situation himself. And without remembering that he was still unaware what powers of movement he possessed, without even remembering that his words in all possibility, indeed in all likelihood, would again be unintelligible, he let go the wing of the door, pushed himself through the opening, started to walk toward the chief clerk, who was already ridiculously clinging with both hands to the railing on the landing; but immediately, as he was feeling for a support, he fell down with a little cry upon all his numerous legs. Hardly was he down when he experienced for the first time this morning a sense of physical comfort; his legs had firm ground under them; they were completely obedient, as he noted with joy; they even strove to carry him forward in whatever direction he chose; and he was inclined to believe that a final relief from all his sufferings was at hand. But at the moment when he found himself on the floor, rocking with suppressed eagerness to move, not far from his mother—indeed, just in front of her—she, who had seemed so completely crushed, sprang all at once to her feet, her arms and fingers outspread, cried: "Help, for God's sake, help!" bent her head down as if to see Gregor better, yet on the contrary kept backing senselessly away; had quite forgotten that the laden table stood behind her; sat upon it hastily, as if in absence of mind, when she bumped into it; and seemed altogether unaware that the big coffeepot beside her was upset and pouring coffee in a flood over the carpet.

"Mother, Mother," said Gregor in a low voice, and looked up at her. The chief clerk, for the moment, had quite slipped from his mind; instead, he could not resist snapping his paws together at the sight of the streaming coffee. That made his mother scream again. She fled from the table and fell into the arms of his father, who hastened to catch her. But Gregor had now no time to spare for his parents; the chief clerk was already on the stairs; with his chin on the banisters he was taking one last backward look. Gregor made a spring, to be as sure as possible of overtaking him. The chief clerk must have divined his intention, for he leaped down several steps and vanished; he was still yelling "Ugh!" and it echoed through the whole staircase.

Unfortunately, the flight of the chief clerk seemed completely to upset Gregor's father, who had remained relatively calm until now, for instead of running after the man himself, or at least not hindering Gregor in his pursuit, he seized in his right hand the walking-stick that the chief clerk had left behind on a chair. Together with a hat and greatcoat, snatched in his left hand a large newspaper from the table, and began stamping his feet and flourishing the stick and the newspaper to drive Gregor back into his room. No entreaty of Gregor's availed; indeed, no entreaty was even understood; however humbly he bent his head, his father only stamped on the floor the more loudly. Behind his father, his mother had torn open a window despite the cold weather and was leaning far out of it with her face in her hands. A strong draft set in from the street to the staircase, the window curtains blew in, the newspapers on the table fluttered, stray pages whisked over the floor. Pitilessly Gregor's father drove him back, hissing and crying "Shoo!" like a savage. But Gregor was quite unpracticed in walking backwards, it really was a slow business. If he only had a chance to turn around he could get back to his room at once, but he was afraid of exasperating his father by the slowness of such a rotation and at any moment the stick in his father's hand might hit him a fatal blow on the back or on the head.

In the end, however, nothing else was left for him to do since to his horror he observed that in moving backwards he could not even control the direction he took; and so, keeping an anxious eye on his father all the time over his shoulder, he began to turn round as quickly as he could, which was in reality very slowly. Perhaps his father noted his good intentions, for he did not interfere except every now and then to help him in the maneuver from a distance with the point of the stick. If only he would have stopped making that unbearable hissing noise! It made Gregor quite lose his head. He had turned almost completely round when the hissing noise so distracted him that he even turned a little the wrong way again. But when at last his head was fortunately right in front of the doorway, it appeared that his body was too broad simply to get through the opening. His father, of course, in his present mood was far from thinking of such a thing as opening the other half of the door, to let Gregor have enough space. He had merely the fixed idea of driving Gregor back into his room as quickly as possible. He would never have suffered Gregor to make the circumstantial preparations for standing up on end and perhaps slipping his way through the door. Maybe he was now making more noise than ever to urge Gregor forward, as if no obstacle impeded him; to Gregor, anyhow, the noise in his rear sounded no longer like the voice of one single father; this was really no joke, and Gregor thrust himself—come what might—into the doorway. One side of his body rose up, he was tilted at an angle in the doorway. His flank was quite bruised; horrid blotches stained the white door; soon he was stuck fast and, left to himself, could not have moved at all. His legs on one side fluttered trembling in the air; those on the other were crushed painfully to the floor—when, from behind, his father gave him a strong push, which was literally a deliverance, and he flew far into the room, bleeding freely. The door was slammed behind him with the stick, and then at last there was silence.

MEDITATIONS ON FIRST PHILOSOPHY

RENÉ DESCARTES

René Descartes (1596–1650) was a French philosopher often considered to be the father of modern philosophy because of his rigorous methodology and his emphasis upon the theory of knowledge as the starting point for all philosophic speculation. *The Discourse on Method* and *Meditations on First Philosophy* develop his system of thought in the style of a spiritual autobiography.

In his *Meditations,* Descartes affirmed only "clear and distinct" ideas as certain, and pressed his method of "systematic doubt" to the point of denying reality to everything but the thinking self. We may be deceived about empirical matters by God, an evil spirit, or dreams which are sometimes indistinguishable from waking life, but the proposition *cogito, ergo sum* (I think, therefore I am) cannot be doubted. It is, in fact, affirmed even in the act of doubting it, for we must exist in order to doubt. Descartes consequently defines the "I" as "a thing which thinks," that is, "a thing which doubts, understands, [conceives], affirms, denies, wills, refuses, which also imagines and feels." Since he subsequently affirms the reality of the body as well, he is considered to hold a dualistic concept of self.

MEDITATION I.

Of the things which may be brought within the sphere of the doubtful.

It is now some years since I detected how many were the false beliefs that I had from my earliest youth admitted as true, and how doubtful was everything I had since constructed on this basis; and from that time I was convinced that I must once for all seriously undertake to rid myself of all the opinions which I had formerly accepted, and commence to build anew from the foundation, if I wanted to establish any firm and permanent structure in the sciences. But as this enterprise appeared to be a very great one, I waited until I had attained an age so mature that I could not hope that at any later date I should be better fitted to execute my design. This reason caused me to delay so long that I should feel that I was doing wrong were I to occupy in deliberation the time that yet remains to me for action. To-day, then, since very opportunely for the plan I have in view I have delivered my mind from every care [and am happily agitated by no passions] and since I have procured for myself an assured leisure in a peaceable retirement, I shall at last seriously and freely address myself to the general upheaval of all my former opinions.

Now for this object it is not necessary that I should show that all of these are false—I shall perhaps never arrive at this end. But inasmuch as reason already persuades me that I ought no less carefully to withhold my assent from matters which are not entirely certain and indubitable than from those which appear to me manifestly to be false, if I am able to find in each one some reason to doubt, this will suffice to justify my rejecting the whole. And for that end it will not be requisite that I should examine each in particular, which would be an endless undertaking; for owing to the fact that the destruction of the foundations of necessity brings with it the downfall of the rest of the edifice, I shall only in the first place attack those principles upon which all my former opinions rested.

All that up to the present time I have accepted as most true and certain I have learned either from the senses or through the senses; but it is sometimes proved to me that these senses are deceptive, and it is wiser not to trust entirely to any thing by which we have once been deceived.

But it may be that although the senses sometimes deceive us concerning things which are hardly perceptible, or very far away, there are yet many others to be met with as to which we cannot reasonably have any doubt, although we recognise them by their means. For example, there is the fact that I am here, seated by the fire, attired in a dressing gown, having this paper in my hands and other similar matters. And how could I deny that these hands and this body are mine, were it not perhaps that I compare myself to certain persons, devoid of sense, whose cerebella are so troubled and clouded by the violent vapours of black bile, that they constantly assure us that they think they are kings when they are really quite poor, or that they are clothed in purple when they are really without covering, or who imagine that they have an earthenware head or are nothing but pumpkins or are made of glass. But they are mad, and I should not be any the less insane were I to follow examples so extravagant.

At the same time I must remember that I am a man, and that consequently I am in the habit of sleeping, and in my dreams representing to myself the same things or sometimes even less probable things, than do those who are insane in their waking moments. How often has it happened to me that in the night I dreamt that I found myself in this particular place, that I was dressed and seated near the fire, whilst in reality I was lying undressed in bed! At this moment it does indeed seem to me that it is with eyes awake that I am looking at this paper; that this head which I move is not asleep, that it is deliberately and of set purpose that I extend my hand and perceive it; what happens in sleep does not appear so clear nor so distinct as does all this. But in thinking over this I remind myself that on many occasions I have in sleep been deceived by similar illusions, and in dwelling carefully on this reflection I see so manifestly that there are no certain indications by which we may clearly distinguish wakefulness from sleep that I am lost in astonishment. And my astonishment is such that it is almost capable of persuading me that I now dream.

Now let us assume that we are asleep and that all these particulars, e.g. that we open our eyes, shake our head, extend our hands, and so on, are but false delusions; and let us reflect that possibly neither our hands nor our whole body are such as they appear to us to be. At the same time we must at least confess that the things which are represented to us in sleep are like painted representations which can only have been formed as the counterparts of something real and true, and that in this way those general things at least, i.e. eyes, a head, hands, and a whole body, are not imaginary things, but things really existent. For, as a matter of fact, painters, even when they study with the greatest skill to represent sirens and satyrs by forms the most strange and extraordinary, cannot give them natures which are entirely new, but merely make a certain medley of the members of different animals; or if their imagination is extravagant enough to invent something so novel that nothing similar has ever before been seen, and that then their work represents a thing purely fictitious and absolutely false, it is certain all the same that the colours of which this is composed are necessarily real. And for the same reason, although these general things, to wit, [a body], eyes, a head, hands, and such like, may be imaginary, we are bound at the same time to confess that there are at least some other objects yet more simple and more universal, which are real and true; and of these just in the same way as with certain real colours, all these images of things which dwell in our thoughts, whether true and real or false and fantastic, are formed.

To such a class of things pertains corporeal nature in general, and its extension, the figure of extended things, their quantity or magnitude and number, as also the place in which they are, the time which measures their duration, and so on.

That is possibly why our reasoning is not unjust when we conclude from this that Physics, Astronomy, Medicine and all other sciences which have as their end the consideration of composite things, are very dubious and uncertain; but that Arithmetic, Geometry and other sciences of that kind which only treat of things that are very simple and very general, without taking great trouble to ascertain whether they are actually existent or not, contain some measure of certainty and an element of the indubitable. For whether I am awake or asleep, two and three together always form five, and the square can never have more than four sides, and it does not seem possible that truths so clear and apparent can be suspected of any falsity [or uncertainty].

Nevertheless I have long had fixed in my mind the belief that an all-powerful God existed by whom I have been created such as I am. But how do I know that He has not brought it to pass that there is no earth, no heaven, no extended body, no magnitude, no place, and that nevertheless [I possess the perceptions of all these things and that] they seem to me to exist just exactly as I now see them? And, besides, as I sometimes imagine that others deceive themselves in the things which they think they know best, how do I know that I am not deceived every time that I add two and three, or count the sides of a square, or judge of things yet simpler, if anything simpler can be imagined? But possibly God has not desired that I should be thus deceived, for He is said to be supremely good. If, however, it is contrary to His goodness to have made me such that I constantly deceive myself, it would also appear to be contrary to His goodness to permit me to be sometimes deceived, and nevertheless I cannot doubt that He does permit this.

There may indeed be those who would prefer to deny the existence of a God so powerful, rather than believe that all other things are uncertain. But let us not oppose them for the present, and grant that all that is here said of a God is a fable; nevertheless in whatever way they suppose that I have arrived at the state of being that I have reached—whether they attribute it to fate or to accident, or make out that it is by a continual succession of antecedents, or by some other method—since to err and deceive oneself is a defect, it is clear that the greater will be the probability of my being so imperfect as to deceive myself ever, as is the Author to whom they assign my origin the less powerful. To these reasons I have certainly nothing to reply, but at the end I feel constrained to confess that there is nothing in all that I formerly believed to be true, of which I cannot in some measure doubt, and that not merely through want of thought or through levity, but for reasons which are very powerful and maturely considered; so that henceforth I ought not the less carefully to refrain from giving credence to these opinions than to that which is manifestly false, if I desire to arrive at any certainty [in the sciences].

But it is not sufficient to have made these remarks, we must also be careful to keep them in mind. For these ancient and commonly held opinions still revert frequently to my mind, long and familiar custom having given them the right to occupy my mind against my inclination and rendered them almost masters of my belief; nor will I ever lose the habit of deferring to them or of placing my confidence in them, so long as I consider them as they really are, i.e. opinions in some measure doubtful, as I have just shown, and at the same time highly probable, so that there is much more reason to believe in than to deny them. That is why I consider that I shall not be acting amiss, if, taking of set purpose a contrary belief, I allow myself to be deceived, and for a certain time pretend that all these opinions are entirely false and imaginary, until at last, having thus balanced by former prejudices with my latter [so that they cannot divert my opinions more to one side than to the other], my judgment will no longer be dominated by bad usage or turned away from the right knowledge of the truth. For I am assured that there can be neither peril nor error in this course, and that I cannot at present yield too much to distrust, since I am not considering the question of action, but only of knowledge.

I shall then suppose, not that God who is supremely good and the fountain of truth, but some evil genius not less powerful than deceitful, has employed whole energies in deceiving me; I shall consider that the heavens, the earth, colours, figures, sound, and all other external things are nought but the illusions and dreams of which this genius has availed himself in order to lay traps for my credulity; I shall consider myself as having no hands, no eyes, no flesh, no blood, nor any senses, yet falsely believing myself to possess all these things; I shall remain obstinately attached to this idea, and if by this means it is not in my power to arrive at the knowledge of any truth, I may at least do what is in my power [i.e. suspend my judgment], and with firm purpose avoid giving credence to any false thing, or being imposed upon by this arch deceiver, however powerful and deceptive he may be. But this task is a laborious one, and insensibly a certain lassitude leads me into the course of my ordinary life. And just as a captive who in sleep enjoys an imaginary liberty, when he begins to suspect that his liberty is but a dream, fears to awaken, and conspires with these agreeable illusions that the deception may be prolonged, so insensibly of my own accord I fall back into my former opinions, and I dread awakening from this slumber, lest the laborious wakefulness which would follow the tranquillity of this repose should have to be spent not in daylight, but in the excessive darkness of the difficulties which have just been discussed.

MEDITATION II.

Of the Nature of the Human Mind; and that it is more easily known than the Body.

The Meditation of yesterday filled my mind with so many doubts that it is no longer in my power to forget them. And yet I do not see in what manner I can resolve them; and, just as if I had all of a sudden fallen into very deep water, I am so disconcerted that I can neither make certain of setting my feet on the bottom, nor can I swim and so support myself on the surface. I shall nevertheless make an effort and follow anew the same path as that on which I yesterday entered, i.e. I shall proceed by setting aside all that in which the least doubt could be supposed to exist, just as if I had discovered that it was absolutely false; and I shall ever follow in this road until I have met with something which is certain, or at least, if I can do nothing else, until I have learned for certain that there is nothing in the world that is certain. Archimedes, in order that he might draw the terrestrial globe out of its place, and transport it elsewhere, demanded only that one point should be fixed and immovable; in the same way I shall have the right to conceive high hopes if I am happy enough to discover one thing only which is certain and indubitable.

I suppose, then, that all the things that I see are false; I persuade myself that nothing has ever existed of all that my fallacious memory represents to me. I consider that I possess no senses; I imagine that body, figure, extension, movement and place are but the fictions of my mind. What, then, can be esteemed as true? Perhaps nothing at all, unless that there is nothing in the world that is certain.

But how can I know there is not something different from those things that I have just considered, of which one cannot have the slightest doubt? Is there not some God, or some other being by whatever name we call it, who puts these reflections into my mind? That is not necessary, for is it not possible that I am capable of producing them myself? I myself, am I not at least something? But I have already denied that I had senses and body. Yet I hesitate, for what follows from that? Am I so dependent on body and senses that I cannot exist without these? But I was persuaded that there was nothing in all the world, that there was no heaven, no earth, that there were no minds, nor any bodies: was I not then likewise persuaded that I did not exist? Not at all; of a surety I myself did exist since I persuaded myself of something [or merely because I thought of something]. But there is some deceiver or other, very powerful and very cunning, who ever employs his ingenuity in deceiving me. Then without doubt I exist also if he deceives me, and let him deceive me as much as he will, he can never cause me to be nothing so long as I think that I am something. So that after having reflected well and carefully examined all things, we must come to the definite conclusion that this proposition: I am, I exist, is necessarily true each time that I pronounce it, or that I mentally conceive it.

But I do not yet know clearly enough what I am, I who am certain that I am; and hence I must be careful to see that I do not imprudently take some other object in place of myself, and thus that I do not go astray in respect of this knowledge that I hold to be the most certain and most evident of all I have formerly learned. That is why I shall now consider anew what I believed myself to be before I embarked upon these last reflections; and of my former opinions I shall withdraw all that might even in a small degree be invalidated by the reasons which I have just brought forward, in order that there may be nothing at all left beyond what is absolutely certain and indubitable.

What then did I formerly believe myself to be? Undoubtedly I believed myself to be a man. But what is a man? Shall I say a reasonable animal? Certainly not; for then I should have to inquire what an animal is, and what is reasonable; and thus from a single question I should insensibly fall into an infinitude of others more difficult; and I should not wish to waste the little time and leisure remaining to me in trying to unravel subtleties like these. But I shall rather stop here to consider the thoughts which of themselves spring up in my mind, and which were not inspired by anything beyond my own nature alone when I applied myself to the consideration of my being. In the first place, then, I considered myself as having a face, hands, arms, and all that system of members composed of bones and flesh as seen in a corpse which I designated by the name of body. In addition to this I considered that I was nourished, that I walked, that I felt, and that I thought, and I referred all these actions to the soul; but I did not stop to consider what the soul was, or if I did stop, I imagined that it was something extremely rare and subtle like a wind, a flame, or an ether, which was spread throughout my grosser parts. As to body I had no manner of doubt about its nature, but thought I had a very clear knowledge of it; and if I had desired to explain it according to the notions that I had then formed of it, I should have described it thus: By the body I understand all that which can be defined by a certain figure: something which can be confined in a certain place, and which can fill a given space in such a way that every other body will be excluded from it; which can be perceived either by touch, or by sight, or by hearing, or by taste, or by smell: which can be moved in many ways not, in truth, by itself, but by something which is foreign to it, by which it is touched [and from which it receives impressions]: for to have the power of self-movement, as also of feeling or of thinking, I did not consider to appertain to the nature of body: on the contrary, I was rather astonished to find that faculties similar to them existed in some bodies.

But what am I, now that I suppose that there is a certain genius which is extremely powerful, and, if I may say so, malicious, who employs all his powers in deceiving me? Can I affirm that I possess the least of all those things which I have just said pertain to the nature of body? I pause to consider, I revolve all these things in my mind, and I find none of which I can say that it pertains to me. It would be tedious to stop to enumerate them. Let us pass to the attributes of soul and see if there is any one which is in me? What of nutrition or walking [the first mentioned]? But if it is so that I have no body it is also true that I can neither walk nor take nourishment. Another attribute is sensation. But one cannot feel without body, and besides I have thought I perceived many things during sleep that I recognised in my waking moments as not having been experienced at all. What of thinking? I find here that thought is an attribute that belongs to me; it alone cannot be separated from me. I am, I exist, that is certain. But how often? Just when I think; for it might possibly be the case if I ceased entirely to think, that I should likewise cease altogether to exist. I do not now admit anything which is not necessarily true: to speak accurately I am not more than a thing which thinks, that is to say a mind or a soul, or an understanding, or a reason, which are terms whose significance was formerly unknown to me. I am, however, a real thing and really exist; but what thing? I have answered: a thing which thinks.

And what more? I shall exercise my imagination [in order to see if I am not something more]. I am not a collection of members which we call the human body: I am not a subtle air distributed through these members, I am not a wind, a fire, a vapour, a breath, nor anything at all which I can imagine or conceive; because I have assumed that all these were nothing. Without changing that supposition I find that I only leave myself certain of the fact that I am somewhat. But perhaps it is true that these same things which I supposed were non-existent because they are unknown to me, are really not different from the self which I know. I am not sure about this, I shall not dispute about it now; I can only give judgment on things that are known to me. I know that I exist, and I inquire what I am, I whom I know to exist. But it is very certain that the knowledge of my existence taken in its precise significance does not depend on things whose existence is not yet known to me; consequently it does not depend on those which I can feign in imagination. And indeed the very term *feign* in imagination proves to me my error, for I really do this if I image myself a something, since to imagine is nothing else than to contemplate the figure or image of a corporeal thing. But I already know for certain that I am, and that it may be that all these images, and, speaking generally, all things that relate to the nature of body are nothing but dreams [and chimeras]. For this reason I see clearly that I have as little reason to say, 'I shall stimulate my imagination in order to know more distinctly what I am,' than if I were to say, 'I am now awake, and I perceive somewhat that is real and true: but because I do not yet perceive it distinctly enough, I shall go to sleep of express purpose, so that my dreams may represent the perception with greatest truth and evidence.' And, thus, I know for certain that nothing of all that I can understand by means of my imagination belongs to this knowledge which I have of myself, and that it is necessary to recall the mind from this mode of thought with the utmost diligence in order that it may be able to know its own nature with perfect distinctness.

But what then am I? A thing which thinks. What is a thing which thinks? It is a thing which doubts, understands, [conceives], affirms, denies, wills, refuses, which also imagines and feels.

Certainly it is no small matter if all these things pertain to my nature. But why should they not so pertain? Am I not that being who now doubts nearly everything, who nevertheless understands certain things, who affirms that one only is true, who denies all the others, who desires to know more, is averse from being deceived, who imagines many things, sometimes indeed despite his will, and who perceives many likewise, as by the intervention of the bodily organs? Is there nothing in all this which is as true as it is certain that I exist, even though I should always sleep and though he who has given me being employed all his ingenuity in deceiving me? Is there likewise any one of these attributes which can be distinguished from my thought, or which might be said to be separated from myself? For it is so evident of itself that it is I who doubts, who understands, and who desires, that there is no reason here to add anything to explain it. And I have certainly the power of imagining likewise; for although it may happen (as I formerly supposed) that none of the things which I imagine are true, nevertheless this power of imagining does not cease to be really in use, and it forms part of my thought. Finally, I am the same who feels, that is to say, who perceives certain things, as by the organs of sense, since in truth I see light, I hear noise, I feel heat. But it will be said that these phenomena are false and that I am dreaming. Let it be so; still it is at least quite certain that it seems to me that I see light, that I hear noise and that I feel heat. That cannot be false; properly speaking it is what is in me called feeling; and used in this precise sense that is no other thing than thinking.

From this time I begin to know what I am with a little more clearness and distinction than before; but nevertheless it still seems to me, and I cannot prevent myself from thinking, that corporeal things, whose images are framed by thought, which are tested by the senses, are much more distinctly known than that obscure part of me which does not come under the imagination. Although really it is very strange to say that I know and understand more distinctly these things whose existence seems to me dubious, which are unknown to me, and which do not belong to me, than others of the truth of which I am convinced, which are known to me and which pertain to my real nature, in a word, than myself. But I see clearly how the case stands: my mind loves to wander, and cannot yet suffer itself to be retained within the just limits of truth. Very good, let us once more give it the freest rein, so that, when afterwards we seize the proper occasion for pulling up, it may the more easily be regulated and controlled.

Let us begin by considering the commonest matters, those which we believe to be the most distinctly comprehended, to wit, the bodies which we touch and see; not indeed bodies in general, for these general ideas are usually a little more confused, but let us consider one body in particular. Let us take, for example, this piece of wax: it has been taken quite freshly from the hive, and it has not yet lost the sweetness of the honey which it contains; it still retains somewhat of the odour of the flowers from which it has been culled; its colour, its figure, its size are apparent; it is hard, cold, easily handled, and if you strike it with the finger, it will emit a sound. Finally all the things which are requisite to cause us distinctly to recognise a body, are met with in it. But notice that while I speak and approach the fire what remained of the taste is exhaled, the smell evaporates, the colour alters, the figure is destroyed, the size increases, it becomes liquid, it heats, scarcely can one handle it, and when one strikes it, no sound is emitted. Does the same wax remain after this change? We must confess that it remains; none would judge otherwise. What then did I know so distinctly in this piece of wax? It could certainly be nothing of all that the senses brought to my notice, since all these things which fall under taste, smell, sight, touch, and hearing, are found to be changed, and yet the same wax remains.

Perhaps it was what I now think, viz. that this wax was not that sweetness of honey, nor that agreeable scent of flowers, nor that particular whiteness, not that figure, nor that sound, but simply a body which a little while before appeared to me as perceptible under these forms, and which is now perceptible under others. But what, precisely, is it that I imagine when I form such conceptions? Let us attentively consider this, and, abstracting from all that does not belong to the wax, let us see what remains. Certainly nothing remains excepting a certain extended thing which is flexible and movable. But what is the meaning of flexible and movable? Is it not that I imagine that this piece of wax being round is capable of becoming square and of passing from a square to a triangular figure?

No, certainly it is not that, since I imagine it admits of an infinitude of similar changes, and I nevertheless do not know how to compass the infinitude by my imagination, and consequently this conception which I have of the wax is not brought about by the faculty of imagination. What now is this extension? Is it not also unknown? For it becomes greater when the wax is melted, greater when it is boiled, and greater still when the heat increases; and I should not conceive [clearly] according to truth what wax is, if I did not think that even this piece that we are considering is capable of receiving more variations in extension than I have ever imagined. We must then grant that I could not even understand through the imagination what this piece of wax is, and that it is my mind alone which perceives it. I say this piece of wax in particular, for as to wax in general it is yet clearer. But what is this piece of wax which cannot be understood excepting by the [understanding or] mind? It is certainly the same that I see, touch, imagine, and finally it is the same which I have always believed it to be from the beginning. But what must particularly be observed is that its perception is neither an act of vision, nor of touch, nor of imagination, and has never been such although it may have appeared formerly to be so, but only an intuition of the mind, which may be imperfect and confused as it was formerly, or clear and distinct as it is at present, according as my attention is more or less directed to the elements which are found in it, and of which it is composed.

Yet in the meantime I am greatly astonished when I consider [the great feebleness of mind] and its proneness to fall [insensibly] into error; for although without giving expression to my thoughts I consider all this in my own mind, words often impede me and I am almost deceived by the terms of ordinary language. For we say that we see the same wax, if it is present, and not that we simply judge that it is the same from its having the same colour and figure. From this I should conclude that I knew the wax by means of vision and not simply by the intuition of the mind; unless by chance I remember that, when looking from a window and saying I see men who pass in the street, I really do not see them, but infer that what I see is men, just as I say that I see wax. And yet what do I see from the window but hats and coats which may cover automatic machines? Yet I judge these to be men. And similarly solely by the faculty of judgment which rests in my mind, I comprehend that which I believed I saw with my eyes.

A man who makes it his aim to raise his knowledge above the common should be ashamed to derive the occasion for doubting from the forms of speech invented by the vulgar; I prefer to pass on and consider whether I had a more evident and perfect conception of what the wax was when I first perceived it, and when I believed I knew it by means of the external senses or at least by the common sense as it is called, that is to say by the imaginative faculty, or whether my present conception is clearer now that I have most carefully examined what it is, and in what way it can be known. It would certainly be absurd to doubt as to this. For what was there in this first perception which was distinct? What was there which might not as well have been perceived by any of the animals? But when I distinguish the wax from its external forms, and when, just as if I had taken from it its vestments, I consider it quite naked, it is certain that although some error may still be found in my judgment, I can nevertheless not perceive it thus without a human mind.

But finally what shall I say of this mind, that is, of myself, for up to this point I do not admit in myself anything but mind? What then, I who seem to perceive this piece of wax so distinctly, do I not know myself, not only with much more truth and certainty, but also with much more distinctness and clearness? For if I judge that the wax is or exists from the fact that I see it, it certainly follows much more clearly that I am or that I exist myself from the fact that I see it. For it may be that what I see is not really wax, it may also be that I do not possess eyes with which to see anything; but it cannot be that when I see, or (for I no longer take account of the distinction) when I think I see, that I myself who think am nought. So if I judge that the wax exists from the fact that I touch it, the same thing will follow, to wit, that I am; and if I judge that my imagination, or some other cause, whatever it is, persuades me that the wax exists, I shall still conclude the same. And what I have here remarked of wax may be applied to all other things which are external to me [and which are met with outside of me]. And further, if the [notion or] perception of wax has seemed to me clearer and more distinct, not only after the sight or the touch, but also after many other causes have rendered it quite manifest to me, with how much more [evidence] and distinctness must it be said that I now know myself, since all the reasons which contribute to the knowledge of wax, or any other body whatever, are yet better proofs of the nature of my mind! And there are so many other things in the mind itself which may contribute to the elucidation of its nature, that those which depend on body such as these just mentioned, hardly merit being taken into account.

But finally here I am, having insensibly reverted to the point I desired, for, since it is now manifest to me that even bodies are not properly speaking known by the senses or by the faculty of imagination, but by the understanding only, and since they are not known from the fact that they are seen or touched, but only because they are understood, I see clearly that there is nothing which is easier for me to know than my mind. But because it is difficult to rid oneself so promptly of an opinion to which one was accustomed for so long, it will be well that I should halt a little at this point, so that by the length of my meditation I may more deeply imprint on my memory this new knowledge.

3

Defining Oneself
Through
Commitment

PEER GYNT

HENRIK IBSEN

(trans. by William and Charles Archer)

Henrik Ibsen (1828–1906) was a Norwegian playwright and poet who is inter-
nationally celebrated for his didactic dramas that expose what is shallow,
spurious, and hypocritical in human society and the individual. Ibsen's plays
range from poetic dramas such as *Peer Gynt* and *Brand,* to social dramas
such as *A Doll's House* and *Ghosts,* to works of a more psychological and
symbolic nature such as *Hedda Gabler* and *The Lady from the Sea.*

Ibsen's play *Peer Gynt* stresses the point that the individual self is defined
through commitments. Ibsen portrays Peer Gynt as a charming but worthless
rogue who has skittered across the surface of life, selfishly enjoying a variety
of experiences but never decisively committing himself to any specific type
of existence. He has always adhered to his motto "To thyself be enough,"
making sure that each way of life he followed could be easily discarded. Consequently, at the end of his life he is fit only for the "Button Molder's ladle"
where all unformed, characterless souls go to be melted down and eventually
recast. He had never found a meaning for his life, never dedicated himself to
anything, and therefore remained stunted and insignificant, a virtual nonen-
tity. As the philosopher George Santayana remarked with reference to another
restless spirit, Faust, "Man is constituted by his limitations, by his station
contrasted with all other stations, and his purposes chosen from amongst all
other purposes . . . to be at all you must be something in particular."

In the following selection Peer returns to his native Norway at the end of
a life spent traveling throughout the world. He was a slave trader in America,
sold idols, rum, and Bibles in the Orient, and became a prophet in Arabia.
Now he is an impoverished old man reduced to gathering wild onions for
food.

ACT V, SCENE V

PEER: Well, this is one standpoint. Where is the next?
One should try all things and choose the best.
Well, I have done so,—beginning from Caesar,
And downwards as far as to Nebuchadnezzar.
So I've had, after all, to go through Bible history;—
The old boy has come back to his mother again.
After all it is written: Of the earth art thou come.—
The main thing in life is to fill one's belly.
Fill it with onions? That's not much good;—
I must take to cunning, and set out snares.
There's water in the beck here; I shan't suffer thirst;
And I count as the first 'mong the beasts after all.
When my time comes to die—as most likely it will,—
I shall crawl in under a wind-fallen tree;
Like the bear, I will heap up a leaf-mound above me,
And I'll scratch in big print on the bark of the tree:
Here rests Peer Gynt, that decent soul
Kaiser o'er all of the other beasts.—
Kaiser?
       Laughs inwardly.
              Why, you old soothsayer's-dupe!
No Kaiser are you; you are nought but an onion.
I'm going to peel you now, my good Peer!
You won't escape either by begging or howling.
       Takes an onion and strips off one coat after another.
There lies the outermost layer, all torn;
That's the shipwrecked man on the jolly-boat's keel.
Here's the passenger layer, scanty and thin;—
And yet in its taste there's a tang of Peer Gynt.
Next underneath is the gold-digger ego;
The juice is all gone—if it ever had any.
This coarse-grained layer with the hardened skin
Is the peltry hunter by Hudson's Bay.
The next one looks like a crown;—oh, thanks!
We'll throw it away without more ado.
Here's the archaeologist, short but sturdy,
And here is the Prophet, juicy and fresh.
He stinks, as the Scripture has it, of lies,
Enough to bring the water to an honest man's eyes.
This layer that rolls itself softly together
Is the gentleman, living in ease and good cheer.
The next one seems sick. There are black streaks upon it;—
Black symbolises both parsons and niggers.
       Pulls off several layers at once.

What an enormous number of swathings!
Is not the kernel soon coming to light?
  Pulls the whole onion to pieces.
I'm blest if it is! To the innermost centre,
It's nothing but swathings—each smaller and smaller.—
Nature is witty!
  Throws the fragments away.

. . .

SCENE VII

THE BUTTON-MOULDER, *with a box of tools and a large casting-ladle,*
  comes from a side path.
THE BUTTON-MOULDER: Well met, old gaffer!
PEER: Good evening, friend!
THE BUTTON-MOULDER: The man's in a hurry. Why, where is he going?
PEER: To a grave-feast.
THE BUTTON-MOULDER: Indeed? My sight's not very good;—
  Excuse me,—your name doesn't chance to be Peer?
PEER: Peer Gynt, as the saying is.
THE BUTTON-MOULDER: That I call luck!
  It's precisely Peer Gynt I am sent for to-night.
PEER: You're sent for? What do you want?
THE BUTTON-MOULDER: Why, see here;
  I mould buttons; and you must go into my ladle.
PEER: What to do there?
THE BUTTON-MOULDER: To be melted up.
PEER: To be melted?
THE BUTTON-MOULDER: Here it is, empty and scoured.
Your grave is dug ready, your coffin bespoke.
The worms in your body will live at their ease;—
But I have orders, without delay,
On Master's behalf to fetch in your soul.
PEER: It can't be! Like this, without any warning——!
THE BUTTON-MOULDER: It's an old tradition at burials and births
To appoint in secret the day of the feast,
With no warning at all to the guest of honour.
PEER: Ay, ay, that's true. All my brain's awhirl.
You are——?
THE BUTTON-MOULDER: Why, I told you—a button-moulder.
PEER: I see! A pet child has many nicknames.
So that's it, Peer; it is there you're to harbour
But these, my good man, are most unfair proceedings!
I'm sure I deserve better treatment than this;—

I'm not nearly so bad as perhaps you think,—
Indeed I've done more or less good in the world;—
At worst you may call me a sort of a bungler,—
But certainly not an exceptional sinner.
THE BUTTON-MOULDER: Why that is precisely the rub, my man;
You're no sinner at all in the higher sense;
That's why you're excused all the torture-pangs,
And, like others, land in the casting-ladle.
PEER: Give it what name you please—call it ladle or pool;
Spruce ale and swipes, they are both of them beer.
Avaunt from me, Satan!
THE BUTTON-MOULDER: You can't be so rude
As to take my foot for a horse's hoof?
PEER: On horse's hoof or on fox's claws—
Be off; and be careful what you're about!
THE BUTTON-MOULDER: My friend, you're making a great mistake.
We're both in a hurry, and so, to save time,
I'll explain the reason of the whole affair.
You are, with your own lips you told me so,
No sinner on the so-called heroic scale,—
Scarce middling even——
PEER: Ah, now you're beginning
To talk common sense——
THE BUTTON-MOULDER: Just have patience a bit—
But to call you a good man were going too far.—
PEER: Well, you know I have never laid claim to that.
THE BUTTON-MOULDER: You're nor one thing nor t'other then, only so-so.
A sinner of really grandiose style
Is nowadays not to be met on the highways.
It wants much more than merely to wallow in mire;
For both vigour and earnestness go to a sin.
PEER: Ay, it's very true that remark of yours;
One has to lay on, like the old Berserkers.
THE BUTTON-MOULDER: You, friend, on the other hand, took your sin
    lightly.
PEER: Only outwardly, friend, like a splash of mud.
THE BUTTON-MOULDER: Ah, we'll soon be at one now. The sulphur pool
Is no place for you, who but plashed in the mire.
PEER: And in consequence, friend, I may go as I came?
THE BUTTON-MOULDER: No, in consequence, friend, I must melt you up.
PEER: What tricks are these that you've hit upon
At home here, while I've been in foreign parts?
THE BUTTON-MOULDER: The custom's as old as the Snake's creation;
It's designed to prevent loss of good material.
You've worked at the craft—you must know that often
A casting turns out, to speak plainly, mere dross;

The buttons, for instance, have sometimes no loop to them.
What did you do then?
PEER: Flung the rubbish away.
THE BUTTON-MOULDER: Ah, yes; Jon Gynt was well known for a waster,
So long as he'd aught left in wallet or purse.
But Master, you see, he is thrifty, he is;
And that is why he's so well-to-do.
He flings nothing away as entirely worthless
That can be made use of as raw material.
Now, you were designed for a shining button
On the vest of the world; but your loop gave way;
So into the waste-box you needs must go,
And then, as they phrase it, be merged in the mass.
PEER: You're surely not meaning to melt me up,
With Dick, Tom, and Hal, into something new?
THE BUTTON-MOULDER: That's just what I do mean, and nothing else.
We've done it already to plenty of folks.
At Kongsberg they do just the same with coin
That's been current so long that its impress is lost.
PEER: But this is the wretchedest miserliness!
My dear good friend, let me get off free;—
A loopless button, a worn out farthing,—
What is that to a man in your Master's position?
THE BUTTON-MOULDER: Oh, so long as, and seeing, the spirit is in you,
You always have value as so much metal.
PEER: No, I say! No! With both teeth and claws
I'll fight against this! Sooner anything else!
THE BUTTON-MOULDER: But what else? Come now, be reasonable.
You know you're not airy enough for heaven——
PEER: I'm not hard to content; I don't aim so high;—
But I won't be deprived of one doit of my Self.
Have me judged by the law in the old-fashioned way!
For a certain time place me with Him of the Hoof;—
Say a hundred years, come the worst to the worst;
That, now, is a thing that one surely can bear;
They say that the torment is moral no more,
So it can't be so pyramid-like after all.
It is, as 'tis written, a mere transition;
And as the fox said: One waits; there comes
An hour of deliverance; one lives in seclusion,
And hopes in the meantime for happier days.—
But this other notion—to have to be merged,
Like a mote, in the carcass of some outsider,—
This casting-ladle business, this Gynt-cessation,—
It stirs up my innermost soul in revolt!
THE BUTTON-MOULDER: Bless me, my dear Peer, there is surely no need

To get so wrought up about trifles like this.
Yourself you never have been at all;—
Then what does it matter, your dying right out?
PEER: Have *I* not been——? I could almost laugh!
Peer Gynt, then, has been something else, I suppose!
No, Button-moulder, you judge in the dark.
If you could but look into my very veins,
You'd find only Peer there, and Peer all through,—
Nothing else in the world, no, nor anything more.
THE BUTTON-MOULDER: It's impossible. Here I have got my orders.
Look, here it is written: Peer Gynt shalt thou summon.
He has set at defiance his life's design;
Clap him into the ladle with other spoilt goods.
PEER: What nonsense! They must mean some other person.
Is it really Peer? It's not Rasmus, or Jon?
THE BUTTON-MOULDER: It is many a day since I melted them.
So come quietly now, and don't waste my time.
PEER: I'll be damned if I do! Ay, 'twould be a fine thing
If it turned out to-morrow some one else was meant.
You'd better take care what you're at, my good man!
Think of the onus you're taking upon you——
THE BUTTON-MOULDER: I have it in writing——
PEER: At least give me time
THE BUTTON-MOULDER: What good would that do you?
PEER: I'll use it to prove
That I've been myself all the days of my life:
And that's the question that's in dispute.
THE BUTTON-MOULDER: You'll prove it? And how?
PEER: Why, by vouchers and witnesses.
THE BUTTON-MOULDER: I'm sadly afraid Master will not accept them.
PEER: Impossible! However, enough for the day—!
My dear man, allow me a loan of myself;
I'll be back again shortly. One is born only once,
And one's self, as created, one fain would stick to.
Come, are we agreed?
THE BUTTON-MOULDER: Very well then, so be it.
But remember, we meet at the next cross-roads.
  PEER GYNT *runs off.*

                    SCENE VIII

  A *further point on the heath.*
PEER: (*Running hard.*) Time is money, as the Scripture says.
If I only knew where the cross-roads are;—
They may be near and they may be far.

The earth burns beneath me like red-hot iron.
A witness! A witness! Oh, where shall I find one?
It's almost unthinkable here in the forest.
The world is a bungle! A wretched arrangement,
When a right must be proved that is patent as day!
 An OLD MAN, *bent with age, with a staff in his hand and a bag on his*
  back, is trudging in front of him.
THE OLD MAN: (*Stops.*) Dear, kind sir—a trifle to a houseless soul!
PEER: Excuse me; I've got no small change in my pocket——
THE OLD MAN: Prince Peer! Oh, to think we should meet again——!
PEER: Who are you?
THE OLD MAN: You forget the Old Man in the Rondë?
PEER: Why, you're never——?
THE OLD MAN: The King of the Dovrë,[1] my boy!
PEER: The Dovrë-King? Really? The Dovrë-King? Speak!
THE OLD MAN: Oh, I've come terribly down in the world——!
PEER: Ruined?
THE OLD MAN: Ay, plundered of every stiver.
Here am I tramping it, starved as a wolf.
PEER: Hurrah! Such a witness doesn't grow on the trees.
THE OLD MAN: My Lord Prince, too, has grizzled a bit since we met.
PEER: My dear father-in-law, the years gnaw and wear one.—
Well well, a truce to all private affairs,—
And pray, above all things, no family jars.
I was then a sad madcap——
THE OLD MAN: Oh yes; oh yes;—
His Highness was young; and what won't one do then?
But his Highness was wise in rejecting his bride
He saved himself thereby both worry and shame
For since then she's utterly gone to the bad——
PEER: Indeed!
THE OLD MAN: She has led a deplorable life;
And, just think,—she and Trond are now living together.
PEER: Which Trond?
THE OLD MAN: Of the Valfjeld.
PEER: It's he! Aha;
It was he I cut out with the saeter-girls.
THE OLD MAN: But my grandson has shot up both stout and tall,
And has flourishing children all over the land——
PEER: Now, my dear man, spare us this flow of words;—
I've something quite different troubling my mind.—
I've got into rather a ticklish position,
And am greatly in need of a witness or voucher;—
That's how you could help me best, father-in-law,

1 Dovrë: trolls.

And I'll find you a trifle to drink my health.
THE OLD MAN: You don't say so; can I be of use to his Highness?
You'll give me a character, then, in return?
PEER: Most gladly. I'm somewhat hard pressed for cash,
And must cut down expenses in every direction.
Now hear what's the matter. No doubt you remember
That night when I came to the Rondë a-wooing——
THE OLD MAN: Why, of course, my Lord Prince!
PEER: Oh, no more of the Prince!
But no matter. You wanted, by sheer brute force,
To bias my sight, with a slit in the lens,
And to change me about from Peer Gynt to a troll.
What did *I* do then? I stood out against it,—
Swore I would stand on no feet but my own;
Love, power, and glory at once I renounced,
And all for the sake of remaining myself.
Now this fact, you see, you must swear to in Court——
THE OLD MAN: No, I'm blest if I can.
PEER: Why, what nonsense is this?
THE OLD MAN: You surely don't want to compel me to lie?
You pulled on the troll-breeches, don't you remember,
And tasted the mead——
PEER: Ay, you lured me seductively;—
But I flatly declined the decisive test,
And that is the thing you must judge your man by.
It's the end of the ditty that all depends on.
THE OLD MAN: But it ended, Peer, just in the opposite way.
PEER: What rubbish is this?
THE OLD MAN: When you left the Rondë,
You inscribed my motto upon your escutcheon.
PEER: What motto?
THE OLD MAN: The potent and sundering word.
PEER: The word?
THE OLD MAN: That which severs the whole race of men
From the troll-folk: Troll! To thyself be enough!
PEER: (*Recoils a step.*) Enough!
THE OLD MAN: And with every nerve in your body,
You've been living up to it ever since.
PEER: What, I? Peer Gynt?
THE OLD MAN: (*Weeps.*) It's ungrateful of you!
You've lived as a troll, but have still kept it secret.
The word I taught you has shown you the way
To swing yourself up as a man of substance;—
And now you must needs come and turn up your nose
At me and the word you've to thank for it all.

PEER: Enough! A hill-troll! An egoist!
This must be all rubbish; that's perfectly certain.

. . .

SCENE IX

At *a cross-road.*
PEER GYNT: Now comes the pinch, Peer, as never before!
This Dovrish Enough has passed judgment upon you.
The vessel's a wreck; one must float with the spars.
All else; but to go to the scrap-heap—no, no!
THE BUTTON-MOULDER: (*At the cross-road.*) Well now, Peer Gynt, have
    you found your voucher?
PEER: Is this, then, the cross-road? Well, that is short work!
THE BUTTON-MOULDER: I can see on your face, as it were on a signboard,
The gist of the paper before I have read it.
PEER: I got tired of the hunt;—one might lose one's way——
THE BUTTON-MOULDER: Yes; and what does it lead to, after all?
PEER: True enough; in the wood, and by night as well——
THE BUTTON-MOULDER: There's an old man, though, trudging. Shall we
    call him here?
PEER: No, let him go. He is drunk, my dear fellow!
THE BUTTON-MOULDER: But perhaps he might——
PEER: Hush; no—let him alone!
THE BUTTON-MOULDER: Well, shall we begin then?
PEER: One question—just one:
What is it, at bottom, this "being oneself"?
THE BUTTON-MOULDER: A singular question, most odd in the mouth
Of a man who but now——
PEER: Come, a straightforward answer.
THE BUTTON-MOULDER: To be oneself is: to slay oneself.
But on you that answer is doubtless lost;
And therefore we'll say: to stand forth everywhere
With Master's intention displayed like a signboard.
PEER: But suppose a man never has come to know
What Master meant with him?
THE BUTTON-MOULDER: He must divine it.
PEER: But how oft are divinings beside the mark,——
Then one's carried "ad undas" in middle career.
THE BUTTON-MOULDER: That is certain, Peer Gynt; in default of divining
The cloven-hoofed gentleman finds his best hook.
PEER: This matter's excessively complicated.——
See here! I no longer plead being myself;—
It might not be easy to get it proven.

That part of my case I must look on as lost.
But just now, as I wandered alone o'er the heath,
I felt my conscience-shoe pinching me;
I said to myself: After all, you're a sinner——
THE BUTTON-MOULDER: You seem bent on beginning all over again——
PEER: No, very far from it; a great one I mean;
Not only in deeds, but in words and desires.
I've lived a most damnable life abroad——
THE BUTTON-MOULDER: Perhaps; I must ask you to show me the schedule!
PEER: Well well, give me time; I will find out a parson,
Confess with all speed, and then bring you his voucher.
THE BUTTON-MOULDER: Ay, if you can bring me that, then it is clear
You may yet escape from the casting-ladle.
But Peer, I'd my orders——
PEER: The paper is old;
It dates no doubt from a long past period;—
At one time I lived with disgusting slackness,
Went playing the prophet, and trusted in Fate.
Well, may I try?
THE BUTTON-MOULDER: But——!
PEER: My dear, good man,
I'm sure you can't have so much to do.
Here, in this district, the air is so bracing,
It adds an ell to the people's ages.
Recollect what the Justedal parson wrote:
"It's seldom that any one dies in this valley."
THE BUTTON-MOULDER: To the next cross-roads then; but not a step further.
PEER: A priest I must catch, if it be with the tongs.
He starts running.

SCENE X

A *heather-clad hillside with a path following the windings of the ridge.*
PEER: This may come in useful in many ways,
Said Esben as he picked up a magpie's wing.
Who could have thought one's account of sins
Would come to one's aid on the last night of all?
Well, whether or no, it's a ticklish business;
A move from the frying-pan into the fire;—
But then there's a proverb of well-tried validity
Which says that as long as there's life there is hope.
A LEAN PERSON *in a priest's cassock, kilted-up high, and with a birding-net over his shoulder, comes hurrying along the ridge.*
PEER: Who goes there? A priest with a fowling-net!
Hei, hop! I'm the spoilt child of fortune indeed!

Good evening, Herr Pastor! the path is bad——

THE LEAN ONE: Ah yes; but what wouldn't one do for a soul?

PEER: Aha! then there's some one bound heavenwards?

THE LEAN ONE: No; I hope he is taking a different road.

PEER: May I walk with Herr Pastor a bit of the way?

THE LEAN ONE: With pleasure; I'm partial to company.

PEER: I should like to consult you——

THE LEAN ONE: *Heraus!* Go ahead!

PEER: You see here before you a good sort of man.
The laws of the state I have strictly observed,
Have made no acquaintance with fetters or bolts;—
But it happens at times that one misses one's footing
And stumbles——

THE LEAN ONE: Ah yes; that occurs to the best of us.

PEER: Now these trifles you see——

THE LEAN ONE: Only trifles?

PEER: Yes; from sinning *en gros* I have ever refrained.

THE LEAN ONE: Oh then, my dear fellow, pray leave me in peace;—
I'm not the person you seem to think me.—
You look at my fingers? What see you in them?

PEER: A nail-system somewhat extremely developed.

THE LEAN ONE: And now? You are casting a glance at my feet?

PEER: (*Pointing.*) That's a natural hoof?

THE LEAN ONE: So I flatter myself.

PEER: (*Raises his hat.*) I'd have taken my oath you were simply a parson;
And I find I've the honour——. Well, best is best;—
When the hall door stands wide,—shun the kitchen way;
When the king's to be met with,—avoid the lackey.

THE LEAN ONE: Your hand! You appear to be free from prejudice.
Say on then, my friend; in what way can I serve you?
Now you mustn't ask me for wealth or power;
I couldn't supply them although I should hang for it.
You can't think how slack the whole business is;—
Transactions have dwindled most pitiably.
Nothing doing in souls; only now and again
A stray one——

PEER: The race has improved so remarkably?

THE LEAN ONE: No, just the reverse; it's sunk shamefully low;—
The majority end in a casting-ladle.

PEER: Ah yes—I have heard that ladle mentioned;
In fact, 'twas the cause of my coming to you.

THE LEAN ONE: Speak out!

PEER: If it were not too much to ask,
I should like——

THE LEAN ONE: A harbour of refuge? eh?

PEER: You've guessed my petition before I have asked.
You tell me the business is going awry;
So I daresay you will not be over-particular.
THE LEAN ONE: But, my dear——
PEER: My demands are in no way excessive.
I shouldn't insist on a salary;
But treatment as friendly as things will permit.
THE LEAN ONE: A fire in your room?
PEER: Not too much fire;—and chiefly
The power of departing in safety and peace,—
The right, as the phrase goes, of freely withdrawing
Should an opening offer for happier days.
THE LEAN ONE: My dear friend, I vow I'm sincerely distressed;
But you cannot imagine how many petitions
Of similar purport good people send in,
When they're quitting the scene of their earthly activity.
PEER: But now that I think of my past career,
I feel I've an absolute claim to admission——
THE LEAN ONE: 'Twas but trifles, you said——
PEER: In a certain sense;—
But, now I remember, I've trafficked in slaves——
THE LEAN ONE: There are men that have trafficked in wills and souls,
But who bungled it so that they failed to get in.
PEER: I've shipped Bramah-figures in plenty to China.
THE LEAN ONE: Mere wish-wash again! Why, we laugh at such things.
There are people that ship off far gruesomer figures
In sermons, in art, and in literature,
Yet have to stay out in the cold——
PEER: Ah, but then,
Do you know—I once went and set up as a prophet!
THE LEAN ONE: In foreign parts? Humbug! Why most people's *Sehen
Ins Blaue* ends in the casting-ladle.
If you've no more than that to rely upon,
With the best of good will, I can't possibly house you.
PEER: But hear this: In a shipwreck—I clung to a boat's keel,—
And it's written: A drowning man grasps at a straw,—
Furthermore it is written: You're nearest yourself,—
So I half-way divested a cook of his life.
THE LEAN ONE: It were all one to me if a kitchen-maid
You had half-way divested of something else.
What sort of stuff is this half-way jargon,
Saving your presence? Who, think you, would care
To throw away dearly-bought fuel, in times
Like these, on such spiritless rubbish as this?
There now, don't be enraged; 'twas your sins that I scoffed at;

And excuse my speaking my mind so bluntly.—
Come, my dearest friend, banish this stuff from your head,
And get used to the thought of the casting-ladle.
What would you gain if I lodged you and boarded you?
Consider; I know you're a sensible man.
Well, you'd keep your memory; that's so far true;—
But the retrospect o'er recollection's domain
Would be, both for heart and for intellect,
What the Swedes call "Mighty poor sport" indeed.
You have nothing either to howl or to smile about;
No cause for rejoicing nor yet for despair;
Nothing to make you feel hot or cold;
Only a sort of a something to fret over.
PEER: It is written: It's never so easy to know
Where the shoe is tight that one isn't wearing.
THE LEAN ONE: Very true; I have—praise be to so-and-so!—
No occasion for more than a single odd shoe.
But it's lucky we happened to speak of shoes;
It reminds me that I must be hurrying on;—
I'm after a roast that I hope will prove fat;
So I really mustn't stand gossiping here.—
PEER: And may one inquire, then, what sort of sin-diet
The man has been fattened on?
THE LEAN ONE: I understand
He has been himself both by night and by day,
And that, after all, is the principal point.
PEER: Himself? Then do such folks belong to your parish?
THE LEAN ONE: That depends; the door, at least, stands ajar for them.
Remember, in two ways a man can be
Himself—there's a right and wrong side to the jacket.
You know they have lately discovered in Paris
A way to take portraits by help of the sun.
One can either produce a straightforward picture,
Or else what is known as a negative one.
In the latter the lights and the shades are reversed,
And they're apt to seem ugly to commonplace eyes;
But for all that the likeness is latent in them,
And all you require is to bring it out.
If, then, a soul shall have pictured itself
In the course of its life by the negative method,
The plate is not therefore entirely cashiered,—
But without more ado they consign it to me.
For ulterior treatment I take it in hand,
And by suitable methods effect its development.
I steam it, I dip it, I burn it, I scour it,
With sulphur and other ingredients like that,

Till the image appears which the plate was designed for,—
That, namely, which people call positive.
But for one who, like you, has smudged himself out,
Neither sulphur nor potash avails in the least.

. . .

[The Devil leaves and PEER remains on the ridge, reflecting on his state. He
sees a shooting star and nods after it.]

Greet all friends from Peer Gynt, Brother Starry-Flash!
To flash forth, to go out, and be naught at a gulp—
   Pulls himself together as though in terror, and goes deeper in among the
     mists; stillness for awhile; then he cries:
Is there no one, no one in all the whirl,—
In the void no one, and no one in heaven—!
   He comes forward again further down, throws his hat upon the ground,
     and tears at his hair. By degrees a stillness comes over him.
So unspeakably poor, then, a soul can go
Back to nothingness, into the grey of the mist.
Thou beautiful earth, be not angry with me
That I trampled thy grasses to no avail.
Thou beautiful sun, thou hast squandered away
Thy glory of light in an empty hut.
There was no one within it to hearten and warm;—
The owner, they tell me, was never at home.
Beautiful sun and beautiful earth,
You were foolish to bear and give light to my mother.
The spirit is niggard and nature lavish;
And dearly one pays for one's birth with one's life—
I will clamber up high, to the dizziest peak;
I will look once more on the rising sun,
Gaze till I'm tired o'er the promised land;
Then try to get snowdrifts piled up over me.
They can write above them: "Here No One lies buried";
And afterwards,—then——! Let things go as they can.

. . .

TRAGIC SENSE OF LIFE

MIGUEL DE UNAMUNO

(trans. by J. E. Crawford Flitch)

Miguel de Unamuno (1864–1936) was a Spanish writer and philosopher who is best known for his highly personal, philosophic work *The Tragic Sense of Life* and for his short novel *St. Emmanuel the Good, Martyr*. In all of his writings he is mainly concerned with themes of unbelief, compassion, the longing for immortality, and the significance of the individual.

The Tragic Sense of Life conveys the message that we are not spectators but participants in life. In order to exist at all, we cannot remain distanced at some abstract level of being but must involve ourselves in life's concrete struggles, accepting its mutability and tragic dimension. To Unamuno, the individual cannot be equated with mankind but is a particular embodied self, whose heart rather than his mind is in close touch with reality.

The man we have to do with is the man of flesh and bone—I, you, reader of mine, the other man yonder, all of us who walk solidly on the earth.

And this concrete man, this man of flesh and bone, is at once the subject and the supreme object of all philosophy, whether certain self-styled philosophers like it or not.

In most of the histories of philosophy that I know, philosophic systems are presented to us as if growing out of one another spontaneously, and their authors, the philosophers, appear only as mere pretexts. The inner biography of the philosophers, of the men who philosophized, occupies a secondary place. And yet it is precisely this inner biography that explains for us most things.

It behoves us to say, before all, that philosophy lies closer to poetry than to science. All philosophic systems which have been constructed as a supreme concord of the final results of the individual sciences have in every age possessed much less consistency and life than those which expressed the integral spiritual yearning of their authors.

And, though they concern us so greatly, and are, indeed, indispensable for our life and thought, the sciences are in a certain sense more foreign to us than philosophy. They fulfill a more objective end—that is to say, an end more external to ourselves. They are fundamentally a matter of economics. A new scientific discovery, of the kind called theoretical, is, like a mechanical discovery—that of the steam-engine, the telephone, the phonograph, or the aeroplane—a thing which is useful for something else. Thus the telephone may be useful to us in enabling us to communicate at a distance with the woman we love. But she, wherefore is she useful to us? A man takes an electric tram to go to hear an opera, and asks himself, Which, in this case, is the more useful, the tram or the opera?

Philosophy answers to our need of forming a complete and unitary conception of the world and of life, and as a result of this conception, a feeling which gives birth to an inward attitude and even to outward action. But the fact is that this feeling, instead of being a consequence of this conception, is the cause of it. Our philosophy—that is, our mode of understanding or not understanding the world and life—springs from our feeling towards life itself. And life, like everything affective, has roots in subconsciousness, perhaps in unconsciousness.

It is not usually our ideas that make us optimists or pessimists, but it is our optimism or our pessimism, of physiological or perhaps pathological origin, as much the one as the other, that makes our ideas.

Man is said to be a reasoning animal. I do not know why he has not been defined as an affective or feeling animal. Perhaps that which differentiates him from other animals is feeling rather than reason. More often I have seen a cat reason than laugh or weep. Perhaps it weeps or laughs inwardly—but then perhaps, also inwardly, the crab resolves equations of the second degree.

And thus, in a philosopher, what must needs most concern us is the man.

Take Kant, the man Immanuel Kant, who was born and lived at Königsberg, in the latter part of the eighteenth century and the beginning of the nineteenth. In the philosophy of this man Kant, a man of heart and head—that is to say, a man—there is a significant somersault, as Kierkegaard, another man—and what a man!—would have said, the somersault from the *Critique of Pure Reason* to the *Critique of Practical Reason*. He reconstructs in the latter what he destroyed in the former, in spite of what those may say who do not see the man himself. After having examined and pulverized with his analysis the traditional proofs of the existence of God, of the Aristotelian God, who is the God corresponding to the ζῷον πολιτικόν, the abstract God, the unmoved prime Mover, he reconstructs God anew; but the God of the conscience, the Author of the moral order—the Lutheran God, in short. This transition of Kant exists already in embryo in the Lutheran notion of faith.

The first God, the rational God, is the projection to the outward infinite of man as he is by definition—that is to say, of the abstract man, of the man no-man; the other God, the God of feeling and volition, is the projection to the inward infinite of man as he is by life, of the concrete man, the man of flesh and bone.

Kant reconstructed with the heart that which with the head he had overthrown. And we know, from the testimony of those who knew him and from his testimony in his letters and private declarations, that the man Kant, the more or less selfish old bachelor who professed philosophy at Königsberg at the end of the century of the Encyclopedia and the goddess of Reason, was a man much preoccupied with the problem—I mean with the only real vital problem, the problem that strikes at the very root of our being, the problem of our individual and personal destiny, of the immortality of the soul. The man Kant was not resigned to die utterly. And because he was not resigned to die utterly he made that leap, that immortal somersault,[1] from the one Critique to the other.

Whosoever reads the *Critique of Practical Reason* carefully and without blinkers will see that, in strict fact, the existence of God is therein deduced from the immortality of the soul, and not the immortality of the soul from the existence of God. The categorical imperative leads us to a moral postulate which necessitates in its turn, in the teleological or rather eschatological order, the immortality of the soul, and in order to sustain this immortality God is introduced. All the rest is the jugglery of the professional of philosophy.

The man Kant felt that morality was the basis of eschatology, but the professor of philosophy inverted the terms.

Another professor, the professor and man William James, has somewhere said that for the generality of men God is the provider of immortality. Yes, for the generality of men, including the man Kant, the man James, and the man who writes these lines which you, reader, are reading.

Talking to a peasant one day, I proposed to him the hypothesis that there might indeed be a God who governs heaven and earth, a Consciousness [2] of the Universe, but that for all that the soul of every man may not be immortal in the traditional and concrete sense. He replied: "Then wherefore God?" So answered, in the secret tribunal of their consciousness, the man Kant and the man James. Only in their capacity as professors they were compelled to justify rationally an attitude in itself so little rational. Which does not mean, of course, that the attitude is absurd.

Hegel made famous his aphorism that all the rational is real and all the real rational; but there are many of us who, unconvinced by Hegel, continue to believe that the real, the really real, is irrational, that reason builds upon irrationalities. Hegel, a great framer of definitions, attempted with definitions to reconstruct the universe, like that artillery sergeant who said that cannon were made by taking a hole and enclosing it with steel.

Another man, the man Joseph Butler, the Anglican bishop who lived at the beginning of the eighteenth century and whom Cardinal Newman declared to be the greatest man in the Anglican Church, wrote, at the conclusion of the first chapter of his great work, *The Analogy of Religion*, the chapter which treats of a future life, these pregnant words: "This credibility of a future life, which has been here insisted upon, how little soever it may satisfy our curiosity, seems to answer all the purposes of religion, in like manner as a demonstrative proof would. Indeed a proof, even a demonstrative one, of a future life, would not be a proof of religion. For, that we are to live hereafter, is just as reconcilable with the scheme of atheism, and as well to be accounted for by it, as that we are now alive is:

---

[1] *"Salto inmortal."* There is a play here upon the term *salto mortal,* used to denote the dangerous aerial somersault of the acrobat, which cannot be rendered in English [J. E. C. F.]
[2] *"Conciencia."* The same word is used in Spanish to denote both consciousness and conscience. If the latter is specifically intended, the qualifying adjective *"moral"* or *"religiosa"* is commonly added. [J. E. C. F.]

and therefore nothing can be more absurd than to argue from that scheme that there can be no future state."

The man Butler, whose works were perhaps known to the man Kant, wished to save the belief in the immortality of the soul, and with this object he made it independent of belief in God. The first chapter of his *Analogy* treats, as I have said, of the future life, and the second of the government of God by rewards and punishments. And the fact is that, fundamentally, the good Anglican bishop deduces the existence of God from the immortality of the soul. And as this deduction was the good Anglican bishop's starting-point, he had not to make that somersault which at the close of the same century the good Lutheran philosopher had to make. Butler, the bishop, was one man and Kant, the professor, another man.

To be a man is to be something concrete, unitary, and substantive; it is to be a thing—*res*. Now we know what another man, the man Benedict Spinoza, that Portuguese Jew who was born and lived in Holland in the middle of the seventeenth century, wrote about the nature of things. The sixth proposition of Part III. of his *Ethic* states: *unaquæque res, quatenus in se est, in suo esse perseverare conatur*—that is, Everything, in so far as it is in itself, endeavours to persist in its own being. Everything in so far as it is in itself—that is to say, in so far as it is substance, for according to him substance is *id quod in se est et per se concipitur*—that which is in itself and is conceived by itself. And in the following proposition, the seventh, of the same part, he adds: *conatus, quo unaquæque res in suo esse perseverare conatur, nihil est præter ipsius rei actualem essentiam*—that is, the endeavour wherewith everything endeavours to persist in its own being is nothing but the actual essence of the thing itself. This means that your essence, reader, mine, that of the man Spinoza, that of the man Butler, of the man Kant, and of every man who is a man, is nothing but the endeavour, the effort, which he makes to continue to be a man, not to die. And the other proposition which follows these two, the eighth, says: *conatus, quo unaquæque res in suo esse perseverare conatur, nullum tempus finitum, sed indefinitum involvit*—that is, The endeavour whereby each individual thing endeavours to persist involves no finite time but indefinite time. That is to say that you, I, and Spinoza wish never to die and that this longing of ours never to die is our actual essence. Nevertheless this poor Portuguese Jew, exiled in the mists of Holland, could never attain to believing in his own personal immortality, and all his philosophy was but a consolation which he contrived for his lack of faith. Just as other men have a pain in hand or foot, heart-ache or head-ache, so he had God-ache. Unhappy man! And unhappy fellow-men!

And man, this thing, is he a thing? How absurd soever the question may appear, there are some who have propounded it. Not long ago there went abroad a certain doctrine called Positivism, which did much good and much ill. And among other ills that it wrought was the introduction of a method of analysis whereby facts were pulverized, reduced to a dust of facts. Most of the facts labelled as such by Positivism were really only fragments of facts. In psychology its action was harmful. There were even scholastics meddling in literature—I will not say philosophers meddling in poetry, because poet and philosopher are twin brothers, if not even one and the same—who carried this Positivist psychological analysis into the novel and the drama, where the main business is to give act and motion to concrete men, men of flesh and bone, and by dint of studying states of consciousness, consciousness itself disappeared. The same thing happened to them which is said often to happen in the examination and testing of certain complicated, organic, living chemical compounds, when the reagents destroy the very body which it was proposed to examine and all that is obtained is the products of its decomposition.

Taking as their starting-point the evident fact that contradictory states pass through our consciousness, they did not succeed in envisaging consciousness itself, the "I." To ask a man about his "I" is like asking him about his body. And note that in speaking of the "I," I speak of the concrete and personal "I," not of the "I" of Fichte, but of Fichte himself, the man Fichte.

That which determines a man, that which makes him one man, one and not another, the man he is and not the man he is not, is a principle of unity and a principle of continuity. A principle of unity firstly in space, thanks to the body, and next in action and intention. When we walk, one foot does not go forward and the other backward, nor, when we look, if we are normal, does one eye look towards the north and the other towards the south. In each moment of our life we entertain some purpose, and to this purpose the synergy of our actions is directed. Notwithstanding the next moment we may change our purpose. And in a certain sense a man is so much the more a man the more unitary his action. Some there are who throughout their whole life follow but one single purpose, be it what it may.

Also a principle of continuity in time. Without entering upon a discussion—an unprofitable discussion—as to whether I am or am not he who I was twenty years ago, it appears to me to be indisputable that he who I am to-day derives, by a continuous series of states of consciousness, from him who was in my body twenty years ago. Memory is the basis of individual personality, just as tradition is the basis of the collective personality of a people. We live in memory and by memory, and our spiritual life is at bottom simply the effort of our memory to persist, to transform itself into hope, the effort of our past to transform itself into our future.

All this, I know well, is sheer platitude; but in going about in the world one meets men who seem to have no feeling of their own personality. One of my best friends with whom I have walked and talked every day for many years, whenever I spoke to him of this sense of one's own personality, used to say: "But I have no sense of myself; I don't know what that is."

On a certain occasion this friend remarked to me: "I should like to be

So-and-so" (naming someone), and I said: "That is what I shall never be able to understand—that one should want to be someone else. To want to be someone else is to want to cease to be he who one is. I understand that one should wish to have what someone else has, his wealth or his knowledge; but to be someone else, that is a thing I cannot comprehend." It has often been said that every man who has suffered misfortunes prefers to be himself, even with his misfortunes, rather than to be someone else without them. For unfortunate men, when they preserve their normality in their misfortune—that is to say, when they endeavour to persist in their own being—prefer misfortune to non-existence. For myself I can say that as a youth, and even as a child, I remained unmoved when shown the most moving pictures of hell, for even then nothing appeared to me quite so horrible as nothingness itself. It was a furious hunger of being that possessed me, an appetite for divinity, as one of our ascetics has put it.[3]

To propose to a man that he should be someone else, that he should become someone else, is to propose to him that he should cease to be himself. Everyone defends his own personality, and only consents to a change in his mode of thinking or of feeling in so far as this change is able to enter into the unity of his spirit and become involved in its continuity; in so far as this change can harmonize and integrate itself with all the rest of his mode of being, thinking and feeling, and can at the same time knit itself with his memories. Neither of a man nor of a people— which is, in a certain sense, also a man—can a change be demanded which breaks the unity and continuity of the person. A man can change greatly, almost completely even, but the change must take place within his continuity.

It is true that in certain individuals there occur what are called changes of personality; but these are pathological cases, and as such are studied by alienists. In these changes of personality, memory, the basis of consciousness, is completely destroyed, and all that is left to the sufferer as the substratum of his individual continuity, which has now ceased to be personal, is the physical organism. For the subject who suffers it, such an infirmity is equivalent to death—it is not equivalent to death only for those who expect to inherit his fortune, if he possesses one! And this infirmity is nothing less than a revolution, a veritable revolution.

A disease is, in a certain sense, an organic dissociation; it is a rebellion of some element or organ of the living body which breaks the vital synergy and seeks an end distinct from that which the other elements coordinated with it seek. Its end, considered in itself—that is to say, in the abstract—may be more elevated, more noble, more anything you like; but it is different. To fly and breathe in the air may be better than to swim and breathe in the water; but if the fins of a fish aimed at converting themselves into wings, the fish, as a fish, would perish. And it is useless to say that it would end by becoming a bird, if in this becoming there was not a

3 San Juan de los Angeles.

process of continuity. I do not precisely know, but perhaps it may be possible for a fish to engender a bird, or another fish more akin to a bird than itself; but a fish, this fish, cannot itself and during its own lifetime become a bird.

Everything in me that conspires to break the unity and continuity of my life conspires to destroy me and consequently to destroy itself. Every individual in a people who conspires to break the spiritual unity and continuity of that people tends to destroy it and to destroy himself as a part of that people. What if some other people is better than our own? Very possibly, although perhaps we do not clearly understand what is meant by better or worse. Richer? Granted. More cultured? Granted likewise. Happier? Well, happiness . . . but still, let it pass! A conquering people (or what is called conquering) while we are conquered? Well and good. All this is good—but it is something different. And that is enough. Because for me the becoming other than I am, the breaking of the unity and continuity of my life, is to cease to be he who I am—that is to say, it is simply to cease to be. And that—no! Anything rather than that!

Another, you say, might play the part that I play as well or better? Another might fulfill my function in society? Yes, but it would not be I.

"I, I, I, always I!" some reader will exclaim; "and who are you?" I might reply in the words of Obermann, that tremendous man Obermann: "For the universe, nothing—for myself, everything"; but no, I would rather remind him of a doctrine of the man Kant—to wit, that we ought to think of our fellow-men not as means but as ends. For the question does not touch me alone, it touches you also, grumbling reader, it touches each and all. Singular judgments have the value of universal judgments, the logicians say. The singular is not particular, it is universal.

Man is an end, not a means. All civilization addresses itself to man, to each man, to each I. What is that idol, call it Humanity or call it what you like, to which all men and each individual man must be sacrificed? For I sacrifice myself for my neighbours, for my fellow-countrymen, for my children, and these sacrifice themselves in their turn for theirs, and theirs again for those that come after them, and so on in a never-ending series of generations. And who receives the fruit of this sacrifice?

Those who talk to us about this fantastic sacrifice, this dedication without an object, are wont to talk to us also about the right to live. What is this right to live? They tell me I am here to realize I know not what social end; but I feel that I, like each one of my fellows, am here to realize myself, to live.

Yes, yes, I see it all!—an enormous social activity, a mighty civilization, a profuseness of science, of art, of industry, of morality, and afterwards, when we have filled the world with industrial marvels, with great factories, with roads, museums, and libraries, we shall fall exhausted at the foot of it all, and it will subsist—for whom? Was man made for science or was science made for man?

"Why!" the reader will exclaim again, "we are coming back to what the Catechism says: '*Q*. For whom did God create the world? A. For man.'" Well, why not?—so ought the man who is a man to reply. The ant, if it took account of these matters and were a person, would reply "For the ant," and it would reply rightly. The world is made for consciousness, for each consciousness.

A human soul is worth all the universe, someone—I know not whom—has said and said magnificently. A human soul, mind you! Not a human life. Not this life. And it happens that the less a man believes in the soul—that is to say in his conscious immortality, personal and concrete—the more he will exaggerate the worth of this poor transitory life. This is the source from which springs all that effeminate, sentimental ebullition against war. True, a man ought not to wish to die, but the death to be renounced is the death of the soul. "Whosoever will save his life shall lose it," says the Gospel; but it does not say "whosoever will save his soul," the immortal soul—or, at any rate, which we believe and wish to be immortal.

And what all the objectivists do not see, or rather do not wish to see, is that when a man affirms his "I," his personal consciousness, he affirms man, man concrete and real, affirms the true humanism—the humanism of man, not of the things of man—and in affirming man he affirms consciousness. For the only consciousness of which we have consciousness is that of man.

The world is for consciousness. Or rather this *for*, this notion of finality, and feeling rather than notion, this teleological feeling, is born only where there is consciousness. Consciousness and finality are fundamentally the same thing.

If the sun possessed consciousness it would think, no doubt, that it lived in order to give light to the worlds; but it would also and above all think that the worlds existed in order that it might give them light and enjoy itself in giving them light and so live. And it would think well.

And all this tragic fight of man to save himself, this immortal craving for immortality which caused the man Kant to make that immortal leap of which I have spoken, all this is simply a fight for consciousness. If consciousness is, as some inhuman thinker has said, nothing more than a flash of light between two eternities of darkness, then there is nothing more execrable than existence.

Some may espy a fundamental contradiction in everything that I am saying, now expressing a longing for unending life, now affirming that this earthly life does not possess the value that is given to it. Contradiction? To be sure! The contradiction of my heart that says Yes and of my head that says No! Of course there is contradiction. Who does not recollect those words of the Gospel, "Lord, I believe, help thou my unbelief"? Contradiction! Of course! Since we only live in and by contradictions, since life is tragedy and the tragedy is perpetual struggle, without victory or the hope of victory, life is contradiction.

The values we are discussing are, as you see, values of the heart, and against values of the heart reasons do not avail. For reasons are only reasons—that is to say, they are not even truths. There is a class of pedantic label-mongers, pedants by nature and by grace, who remind me of that man who, purposing to console a father whose son has suddenly died in the flower of his years, says to him, "Patience, my friend, we all must die!" Would you think it strange if this father were offended at such an impertinence? For it is an impertinence. There are times when even an axiom can become an impertinence. How many times may it not be said—

> *Para pensar cual tú, sólo es preciso*
> *no tener nada mas que inteligencia.*[4]

There are, in fact, people who appear to think only with the brain, or with whatever may be the specific thinking organ; while others think with all the body and all the soul, with the blood, with the marrow of the bones, with the heart, with the lungs, with the belly, with the life. And the people who think only with the brain develop into definition-mongers; they become the professionals of thought. And you know what a professional is? You know what a product of the differentiation of labour is?

Take a professional boxer. He has learnt to hit with such economy of effort that, while concentrating all his strength in the blow, he only brings into play just those muscles that are required for the immediate and definite object of his action—to knock out his opponent. A blow given by a non-professional will not have so much immediate, objective efficiency; but it will more greatly vitalize the striker, causing him to bring into play almost the whole of his body. The one is the blow of a boxer, the other that of a man. And it is notorious that the Hercules of the circus, the athletes of the ring, are not, as a rule, healthy. They knock out their opponents, they lift enormous weights, but they die of phthisis or dyspepsia.

If a philosopher is not a man, he is anything but a philosopher; he is above all a pedant, and a pedant is a caricature of a man. The cultivation of any branch of science—of chemistry, of physics, of geometry, of philology—may be a work of differentiated specialization, and even so only within very narrow limits and restrictions; but philosophy, like poetry, is a work of integration and synthesis, or else it is merely pseudophilosophical erudition.

All knowledge has an ultimate object. Knowledge for the sake of knowledge is, say what you will, nothing but a dismal begging of the question. We learn something either for an immediate practical end, or in order to complete the rest of our knowledge. Even the knowledge that appears to us to be most theoretical—that is to say, of least immediate application to the non-intellectual necessities of life—answers to a neces-

---

[4] To be lacking in everything but intelligence is the necessary qualification for thinking like you.

sity which is no less real because it is intellectual, to a reason of economy in thinking, to a principle of unity and continuity of consciousness. But just as a scientific fact has its finality in the rest of knowledge, so the philosophy that we would make our own has also its extrinsic object—it refers to our whole destiny, to our attitude in face of life and the universe. And the most tragic problem of philosophy is to reconcile intellectual necessities with the necessities of the heart and the will. For it is on this rock that every philosophy that pretends to resolve the eternal and tragic contradiction, the basis of our existence, breaks to pieces. But do all men face this contradiction squarely?

Little can be hoped from a ruler, for example, who has not at some time or other been preoccupied, even if only confusedly, with the first beginning and the ultimate end of all things, and above all of man, with the "why" of his origin and the "wherefore" of his destiny.

And this supreme preoccupation cannot be purely rational, it must involve the heart. It is not enough to think about our destiny: it must be felt. And the would-be leader of men who affirms and proclaims that he pays no heed to the things of the spirit, is not worthy to lead them. By which I do not mean, of course, that any ready-made solution is to be required of him. Solution? Is there indeed any?

So far as I am concerned, I will never willingly yield myself, nor entrust my confidence, to any popular leader who is not penetrated with the feeling that he who orders a people orders men, men of flesh and bone, men who are born, suffer, and, although they do not wish to die, die; men who are ends in themselves, not merely means; men who must be themselves and not others; men, in fine, who seek that which we call happiness. It is inhuman, for example, to sacrifice one generation of men to the generation which follows, without having any feeling for the destiny of those who are sacrificed, without having any regard, not for their memory, not for their names, but for them themselves.

All this talk of a man surviving in his children, or in his works, or in the universal consciousness, is but vague verbiage which satisfies only those who suffer from affective stupidity, and who, for the rest, may be persons of a certain cerebral distinction. For it is possible to possess great talent, or what we call great talent, and yet to be stupid as regards the feelings and even morally imbecile. There have been instances.

These clever-witted, affectively stupid persons are wont to say that it is useless to seek to delve in the unknowable or to kick against the pricks. It is as if one should say to a man whose leg has had to be amputated that it does not help him at all to think about it. And we all lack something; only some of us feel the lack and others do not. Or they pretend not to feel the lack, and then they are hypocrites.

A pedant who beheld Solon weeping for the death of a son said to him, "Why do you weep thus, if weeping avails nothing?" And the sage answered him, "Precisely for that reason—because it does not avail." It is manifest that weeping avails something, even if only the alleviation of distress; but the deep sense of Solon's reply to the impertinent questioner is plainly seen. And I am convinced that we should solve many things if we all went out into the streets and uncovered our griefs, which perhaps would prove to be but one sole common grief, and joined together in beweeping them and crying aloud to the heavens and calling upon God. And this, even though God should hear us not; but He would hear us. The chiefest sanctity of a temple is that it is a place to which men go to weep in common. A *miserere* sung in common by a multitude tormented by destiny has as much value as a philosophy. It is not enough to cure the plague: we must learn to weep for it. Yes, we must learn to weep! Perhaps that is the supreme wisdom. Why? Ask Solon.

BIBLIOGRAPHY

A. PHILOSOPHIC WORKS

Anderson, Alan Ross. *Minds and Machines*. Englewood Cliffs, N.J.: Prentice-Hall, 1964.

Anscombe, G. E. M. *Intention*. Oxford: Basil Blackwell, 1957.

Aristotle. *de Anima*. In *The Works of Aristotle*, edited by W. D. Ross. Oxford: Clarendon Press, 1908–52.

Armstrong, D. M. *A Materialist Theory of Mind*. New York: Humanities Press, 1968.

Ayer, A. J. *The Concept of a Person*. New York: St. Martin's Press, 1963.

Borst, Clive V., ed. *The Mind-Brain Identity Theory*. New York: St. Martin's Press, 1970.

Broad, C. D. *The Mind and Its Place in Nature*. New York: Harcourt Brace Jovanovich, Inc., 1925.

Campbell, C. A. *Selfhood and Godhood*. New York: Macmillan, 1957.

Castell, A. *The Self in Philosophy*. New York: Macmillan, 1965.

Chappell, V. C., ed. *The Philosophy of Mind*. Englewood Cliffs, N.J.: Prentice-Hall, 1962.

Chisholm, Roderick. *Person and Object*. London: Allen and Unwin, 1976.

Coval, S. *Scepticism and the First Person*. London: Methuen, 1966.

Ducasse, Curt J. *Nature, Mind and Death*. La Salle, Ill.: Open Court, 1951.

Evans, C. O. *Subject of Consciousness*. New York: Humanities Press, 1970.

Feigl, H. *The "Mental" and the "Physical."* Minneapolis: University of Minnesota, 1967.

Geach, Peter. *Mental Acts*. London: Routledge and K. Paul, 1960.

Hampshire, Stuart, ed. *Philosophy of Mind*. New York: Harper and Row, 1966.

———. *Thought and Action*. New York: Viking Press, 1960.

Harding, Mary Esther. *The I and the Not-I*. New York: Pantheon Press, 1965.

Hume, David. *A Treatise of Human Nature*, Bk. I, Part 4, Sec. 6. Edited by L. A. Selby-Bigge. Oxford: Clarendon Press, 1928.

Husserl, Edmund. *Cartesian Meditations*. The Hague: M. Nijhoff, 1960.

James, William. *Principles of Psychology*. New York: Dover, 1918.

Johnstone, Henry W., Jr. *The Problem of the Self*. University Park, Pa.: Pennsylvania State University, 1970.

Jourard, Sidney M., ed. *To Be or Not to Be*. Gainesville, Fla.: University of Florida, 1967.

Kierkegaard, Soren. *The Sickness Unto Death*. Translated by W. Lowrie. Princeton: Princeton University Press, 1941.

Kohut, H. *The Analysis of the Self*. New York: International Universities Press, 1971.

Laird, John. *Problems of the Self*. London: Macmillan, 1917.

Lewis, H. D. *The Elusive Mind*. New York: Humanities Press, 1969.

Locke, John. *An Essay Concerning Human Understanding*, Bk. 2, Ch. 27. Edited by A. S. Pringle-Pattison. Oxford: Clarendon Press, 1924.

Lovejoy, Arthur. *The Revolt Against Dualism*. New York: Norton, 1930.

Mayo, Bernard. *The Logic of Personality*. London: Jonathan Cape, 1952.

Mead, G. H. *Mind, Self and Society*. Edited by C. W. Morris. Chicago: University of Chicago, 1934.

Melden, A. I. *Free Action*. New York: Humanities Press, 1964.

Mischel, Theodore, ed. *The Self: Psychological and Philosophical Issues*. Totowa, N.J.: Rowan and Littlefield, 1977.

Moustakas, C. E., ed. *The Self*. New York: Harper and Row, 1956.

Myers, Gerald E. *Self, Religion and Metaphysics*. New York: Macmillan, 1961.

Popper, K. and Eccles, John. *The Self and Its Brain*. New York: Springer International, 1977.

Presley, C. F., ed. *The Identity Theory of Mind*. St. Lucia, Brisbane: University of Queensland, 1967.

Reid, Thomas. *Essays on the Intellectual Powers of Man*, Essay III, Chs. 4, 6. In *The Works of Thomas Reid*, edited by W. Hamilton. London: Longmans, Green, 1895.

Russell, Bertrand. *The Analysis of Mind.* New York: Macmillan, 1921.

Ryle, Gilbert. *The Concept of Mind.* London: Hutchinson's University Library, 1949.

Sartre, Jean-Paul. *Being and Nothingness.* Translated by H. Barnes. New York: Philosophical Library, 1956.

Shoemaker, Sydney. *Self-Knowledge and Self-Identity.* Ithaca, N.Y.: Cornell University, 1963.

Smart, J. J. C. *Philosophy and Scientific Realism.* New York: Humanities Press, 1963.

Strawson, P. F. *Individuals.* London: Methuen, 1959.

Vesey, Godfrey, ed. *Body and Mind.* London: Allen and Unwin, 1964.

———. *Personal Identity.* London: Macmillan, 1974.

White, Alan R. *The Philosophy of Mind.* New York: Random House, 1967.

Williams, Bernard. *Problems of the Self.* Cambridge: Cambridge University, 1973.

Wisdom, John. *Other Minds.* New York: Philosophical Library, 1952.

Wittgenstein, Ludwig. *Philosophical Investigations.* New York: Macmillan, 1973.

B. LITERARY WORKS

Albee, Edward. *The American Dream.* New York: Coward-McCann, 1961.

Arnold, Matthew. "Self Dependence." In *The Poems of Matthew Arnold.* London: Oxford University, 1913.

Balzac, Honoré de. *Le Père Goriot.* Translated by J. M. Sedgwick. New York: Rinehart, 1950.

Borges, Jorge Luis. *Form of the Sword* and *Theme of the Traitor and Hero.* In *Ficciones,* translated by Emercé Editores. New York: Grove Press, 1962.

Brecht, Bertolt. *A Man's a Man.* In *Seven Plays,* edited by E. Bentley. New York: Grove Press, 1961.

Camus, Albert. *The Fall.* Translated by J. O'Brien. New York: Knopf, 1957.

Capek, Karel. *R. U. R.* Translated by P. Selver. Garden City, N.Y.: Doubleday, Page, 1923.

Chekhov, Anton. *The Seagull.* In *Best Plays,* translated by S. Young. New York: Modern Library, 1956.

Conrad, Joseph. *Lord Jim.* Garden City, N.Y.: Doubleday, Doran, 1920.

———. *The Secret Sharer.* In *The Shadow Line and Two Other Tales,* edited by M. W. Zabel. Garden City, N.Y.: Doubleday, 1959.

Cummings, E. E. "Him." In *Complete Poems, 1913–62.* New York: Harcourt Brace Jovanovich, Inc., 1972.

Daudet, Alphonse. *Sapho.* New York: Boni and Liveright, 1919.

Dennis, Nigel. *Cards of Identity.* New York: Vanguard Press, 1955.

Dostoevsky, Fedor. *The Double.* Translated by G. Bird. Bloomington: Indiana University, 1958.

Du Maurier, George. *Trilby.* New York: Harper, 1894,

Goethe, Johann Wolfgang von. *Wilhelm Meister.* Translated by T. Carlyle. New York: Dutton, 1912.

Huxley, Aldous. *Brave New World.* Garden City, N.Y.: Doubleday, Doran, 1932.

Ibsen, Henrik. *Peer Gynt.* Translated by R. F. Sharp. New York: Dutton, 1925.

Joyce, James. *Portrait of the Artist as a Young Man.* New York: Viking, 1925.

Kafka, Franz. *The Metamorphosis.* Translated by A. I. Loyd. New York: Vanguard, 1946.

Lagerlöf, Selma. *The Story of Gösta Berling.* Translated by P. B. Flach. Garden City, N.Y.: Doubleday, Page, 1923.

Mann, Thomas. *Death in Venice.* Translated by K. Burke. New York: Knopf, 1965.

Maupassant, Guy de. *Une Vie.* Translated by E. Boyd. New York: Modern Library, 1923.

Meredith, George. *The Egoist.* London: Oxford University, 1947.

Miller, Arthur. *Death of a Salesman.* Edited by G. Weales. New York: Viking Press, 1967.

Musil, Robert. *The Man Without Qualities.* Translated by E. Wilkins and E. Kaiser. New York: Capricorn, 1965.

Nietzsche, Friedrich. *Thus Spoke Zarathustra.* Translated by W. Kaufmann. New York: Viking Press, 1966.

Orwell, George. *Nineteen Eighty-Four*. New York: Harcourt Brace Jovanovich, Inc., 1949.

Pinter, Harold. *The Birthday Party*. New York: Grove Press, 1961.

Pirandello, Luigi. *As You Desire Me*. In *Modern Continental Dramas*, edited by H. Hatcher. New York: Harcourt Brace Jovanovich, Inc., 1941.

Rattigan, Terence. *The Browning Version*. In *Collected Plays*. London: H. Hamilton, 1953–64.

Shakespeare, William. *Hamlet*. In *The Works of William Shakespeare*, edited by W. G. Clark and W. A. Wright. New York: St. Martin's Press, 1956.

Shaw, George Bernard. *Pygmalion*. In *The Collected Works of Bernard Shaw*, edited by A. St. Lawrence. New York: W. H. Wise, 1930.

Thoreau, Henry David. "Independence." In *Collected Poems*, edited by C. Bode. Baltimore, Md.: Johns Hopkins, 1964.

———. *Walden*. Edited by O. Thomas. New York: Norton, 1966.

Wells, H. G. *The Story of the Late Mr. Elvesham*. In *The Works of H. G. Wells*. London: T. F. Unwin, 1924–27.

Whitman, Walt. "Song of Myself." In *The Works of Walt Whitman*. New York: Funk and Wagnalls, 1968.

Wilde, Oscar. *The Picture of Dorian Gray*. New York: Harper and Row, 1965.

Woolf, Virginia. *Jacob's Room*. New York: Harcourt Brace Jovanovich, Inc., 1929.

TWO

THE PROBLEM OF EVIL

According to the Judeo-Christian concept, God is a personal being who is infinitely loving, wise, and powerful, a deity who has existed for all eternity, and who created man and the world out of the void. Given this description of God, however, certain logical questions arise as to why he introduced or permitted natural evil as part of his creation. If God is wholly good, supremely intelligent, and almighty, why are there natural evils such as hurricanes, volcanic eruptions, avalanches, tidal waves, earthquakes, and floods? Why should there be lions, sharks, and cobras, arctic wastes and barren deserts, disease, sickness, and death? In short, if God is good, why is man's earthly home filled with so many sources of pain and suffering?

This is the problem of evil that has puzzled philosophers and plagued theologians for several hundred years. Why should a benevolent father permit harm to come to his children? The suffering that people inflict upon each other in wars or violent crimes can be explained within a theological system, but the suffering that human beings experience because of the natural environment is more difficult to justify. With regard to man's inhumanity to man, it can be argued that God wants human beings to possess free will and that entails the ability to perform good or evil actions. Since free will is an important

73

element in the life of man (and a necessary ingredient for moral responsibility), a good God would want people to have freedom of choice even though they could choose cruelty and destructiveness. Therefore man was created "sufficient to have stood, though free to fall" as Milton writes in *Paradise Lost*. But why would a God of perfect love permit natural disasters to occur and, above all, allow children to suffer the pain of terrible illnesses?

If one does not believe in God's existence, of course, the problem of evil does not arise. For then all natural events, whether helpful or harmful to man, are thought to happen accidentally, without any reason or ultimate purpose behind them. Although explanations may be offered in terms of physical laws governing the behavior of energy and matter, there can be no meaning to events and no possible account can be given of their purpose. Catastrophes are not meant to occur; they simply happen as part of the natural order of the world and no one is responsible for the human misery that occurs as a result.

In the same way, if God is thought to exist but to be limited with regard to attributes of power and love, then the problem of evil is easily resolved. For God could then be viewed as lacking either the ability to prevent evil from occurring (perhaps because the forces of evil are too powerful for him to combat), or to be less than wholly loving toward humanity. Both alternatives, however, have been unacceptable to most theologians who view omnipotence and absolute love as essential characteristics of God. Hence the existence of evil remains a problem for the believer. As the philosopher David Hume writes, paraphrasing Epicurus, "Is [God] willing to prevent evil, but not able? then he is impotent. Is he able, but not willing? then is he malevolent. Is he both able and willing? whence then is evil?"

Various answers have been offered to this question within the field of *theodicy*—an area of theology devoted to a defense of God's treatment of man in the light of natural evil. One recurring explanation is the claim that evil functions to punish people for their sins. In order for the universe to operate fairly, it is argued, people must be punished for their transgressions just as they must be rewarded for their virtues. For the sake of justice, therefore, God makes the wicked suffer by visiting natural evils upon them, not only in hell but on earth as well. This is the explanation offered in scripture for the destruction of Sodom and Gomorrah, and for the Flood that drowned everyone on earth except for the virtuous Noah and his family. It is also the explanation that is often invoked when disasters occur in everyday life, for people frequently ask themselves what they have done to deserve such punishment, thereby assuming that all suffering is caused by wrongdoing.

Although this kind of "retributive" thinking may be natural and prevalent, a moment's reflection will show that it cannot be a valid explanation for natural evil. For good people seem to experience as many natural calamities as awful people; sinners alone are not singled out for suffering. When an earthquake devastates a city, good and bad alike are buried beneath the wreckage, and when ships capsize in hurricanes, it is not just the wicked who are drowned. Patients in hospitals are not all depraved, and people with fine characters are not spared the misery of excruciating illnesses. In short, the human misery that exists as a result of natural evil cannot be correlated with the sinfulness of the individuals. Not only is the distribution of evils askew, but the degree of suffering is often grossly out of proportion to the guilt or innocence of the sufferer. This is most evident in the case of children who may barely have had time to sin before they are afflicted with poliomyelitis or leukemia.

Quite obviously, then, this explanation for natural evil is not justified by the facts. Most theologians find it as unacceptable as Job did in the Old Testament when he protested against the suffering he underwent even though he was "blameless and upright." Job finally declared, "I call aloud, but there is no justice."

Another solution that has been proposed to the problem of evil centers around the idea that contrasts are necessary for appreciation. That is, unless we experienced evil we would be unable to value the good. God therefore allows a variety of negative events to occur so that we can appreciate the positive blessings in life. The discomfort of sickness enables us to enjoy good health, storms and cold temperatures make us value fine weather, and hunger enables us to relish the joy of eating well. In other words, God permits natural evil in order to provide human beings with a base for comparison so they can thereby appreciate the pleasures of the earth. It is sometimes added to this argument that unless the world were somewhat hellish, people would lack the incentive to strive for heaven.

Upon analysis, however, the logic of this proposal is also found to be questionable. It is not at all certain that contrasts are necessary for appreciation; a child might well enjoy the taste of strawberries without ever having eaten sour or bitter foods. Furthermore, even if contrasts should be necessary, *opposites* certainly would not be. That is, we may need partly sunny days to appreciate brilliantly sunny ones, but we do not need blizzards or torrential rains that precipitate floods. More precisely, contrasts can occur between various shades of good; there is no necessity for having gradations of bad. The natural evils that occur, therefore, are hardly needed to accomplish the end of appreciation.[1]

---

[1] It has been argued that our blessings are appreciated more when disasters have been experienced, but this argument stresses only the greater degree of appreciation and tacitly assumes that opposites are not needed for appreciation *per se*. Furthermore, most people would happily settle for less appreciation if the sufferings due to natural evil could be eliminated.

Still another alleged solution claims that both good and evil must exist so that we can have genuine choice. If good were the only available option in the world, our freedom would be rendered meaningless; it would become a latent capacity that could never be actualized. If real choice is to occur, then the alternatives of good and evil must be present.

But the argument is something of a straw man. Not only are natural evils compounded far beyond what is required to ensure the existence of options, but in most cases, natural evils do not permit any choices to be made. The avalanche or tidal wave, shark or poisonous snake strikes down its victim without providing alternatives. The survivors, admittedly, may have the option of deciding whether or not to combat the destructive forces in nature, but surely we cannot applaud a scheme that secures freedom of choice for some by the suffering and death of others. God, with all possibilities at his disposal, could be expected to devise a more humane system.

A somewhat more persuasive claim is that natural evil is justified as a catalyst to the development of fine character. The argument asserts that people who undergo severe or prolonged suffering develop dimensions to their personalities that individuals living in continual comfort can never hope to attain. Pain is purifying and disciplining. It refines the individual's emotional capacities, orders his will, and encourages a more reflective attitude of mind. Soft conditions, on the other hand, tend to produce soft people who are complacent and self-satisfied. The race as a whole has progressed by overcoming natural adversities—winter cold, predatory animals, and plagues—and throughout history civilization has thrived in environments that were somewhat harsh. Languishing in Tennyson's "Land of the Lotus Eaters" we would never have developed our potentialities, individually or collectively. Just as athletes and artists can only achieve success by prolonged and painful effort, human achievement as a whole must always be preceded by struggle. God, in his wisdom, has provided us with the necessary challenges in our environment so that by surmounting obstacles, we can refine our characters and the species as a whole can continually improve.

However, many victims of hurricanes, tornadoes, volcanic eruptions, and so on, never survive to have their characters improved; babies that die of disease have no chance to develop any character. Furthermore, even though some individuals may find severe hardship a stimulus to development and creativity, most people are demeaned by suffering. For every Helen Keller, there are hundreds of similarly afflicted individuals who lead miserable lives. A final consideration is that many great people in history seem to have developed outstanding characters without having endured great suffering, which implies that experiencing natural evil is not a necessary condition for building character.

Faced with all of these difficulties, some theologians have declared that we simply must have faith in God's goodness despite appearances. Perhaps the evil we see is only apparent, not real; in the overall scheme of the universe it may well be good. With our finite understanding we are not able to comprehend the true purpose of human suffering, but in the infinitude of God's wisdom it may have a necessary place.

But blind faith is a poor substitute for lucid reasons, and if the appeal to faith is to have any validity it cannot simply ignore damaging arguments. Genuine faith carries the believer beyond the point where the logical evidence leaves off; it does not fly in the face of the facts. The world does contain natural evil, and the believer must either reconcile this fact with God's goodness or modify his beliefs accordingly. Robert Browning wrote that when "God's in His heaven, all's right with the world," which suggests that when all's not right with the world, perhaps God's not in His heaven. At least before we accept the claims of religion we can expect to be given some justification for human suffering in a world governed by a benevolent God.

1

Human Suffering
as Incompatible
with God's Goodness

THE BROTHERS KARAMAZOV
("The Grand Inquisitor")

FEDOR DOSTOEVSKY

(trans. by Constance Garnett)

Fedor Dostoevsky (1821–1881) was a Russian novelist who, as the author of works such as *Crime and Punishment, The Idiot, The Possessed,* and *The Brothers Karamazov,* is universally acknowledged to be one of the world's most profound writers. In all of his novels, Dostoevsky stresses man's inherent sinfulness, perversity, and passional will, which make it impossible to have a utopia of rationality and benevolence on earth.

In the following section from *The Brothers Karamazov,* Dostoevsky depicts Ivan Karamazov as rebelling against a God who permits the innocent to suffer—particularly innocent children. Even if the harmony of the universe in some incomprehensible way requires earthly pain, Ivan cannot accept the scheme; too high a price is asked. Ivan would rather return his passport to heaven than condone an inhumane system. When his brother Alyosha counters in an indirect way by claiming that Christ has the power to forgive the torturers of the innocent, Ivan introduces his parable of The Grand Inquisitor. The parable apparently condemns Christ for bringing men freedom rather than happiness, but Ivan actually feels that freedom is of greater importance, and as this becomes apparent his opposition to Christ loses its point. However, Ivan does succeed in exploring the problem of evil with great dramatic force in passages that have become classic expositions of the problem of evil.

At this point in the narrative, Ivan expresses his outrage at the unjust suffering in the world, and cites several cases in which innocent children were cruelly treated while God apparently remained indifferent.

"Listen! I took the case of children only to make my case clearer. Of the other tears of humanity with which the earth is soaked from its crust to its centre, I will say nothing. I have narrowed my subject on purpose. I am a bug, and I recognise in all humility that I cannot understand why the world is arranged as it is. Men are themselves to blame, I suppose; they were given paradise, they wanted freedom, and stole fire from heaven, though they knew they would become unhappy, so there is no need to pity them. With my pitiful, earthly, Euclidian understanding, all I know is that there is suffering and that there are none guilty; that cause follows effect, simply and directly; that everything flows and finds its level—but that's only Euclidian nonsense, I know that, and I can't consent to live by it! What comfort is it to me that there are none guilty and that cause follows effect simply and directly, and that I know it—I must have justice, or I will destroy myself. And not justice in some remote infinite time and space, but here on earth, and that I could see myself. I have believed in it. I want to see it, and if I am dead by then, let me rise again, for if it all happens without me, it will be too unfair. Surely I haven't suffered, simply that I, my crimes and my sufferings, may manure the soil of the future harmony for somebody else. I want to see with my own eyes the hind lie down with the lion and the victim rise up and embrace his murderer. I want to be there when every one suddenly understands what it has all been for. All the religions of the world are built on this longing, and I am a believer. But then there are the children, and what am I to do about them? That's a question I can't answer. For the hundredth time I repeat, there are numbers of questions, but I've only taken the children, because in their case what I mean is so unanswerably clear. Listen! If all must suffer to pay for the eternal harmony, what have children to do with it, tell me, please? It's beyond all comprehension why they should suffer, and why they should pay for the harmony. Why should they, too, furnish material to enrich the soil for the harmony of the future? I understand solidarity in sin among men. I understand solidarity in retribution, too; but there can be no such solidarity with children. And if it is really true that they must share responsibility for all their fathers' crimes, such a truth is not of this world and is beyond my comprehension. Some jester will say, perhaps, that the child would have grown up and have sinned, but you see he didn't grow up, he was torn to pieces by the dogs, at eight years old. Oh, Alyosha, I am not blaspheming! I understand, of course, what an upheaval of the universe it will be, when everything in heaven and earth blends in one hymn of praise and everything that lives and has lived cries aloud: 'Thou art just, O Lord, for Thy ways are revealed.' When the mother embraces the fiend who threw her child to the dogs, and all three cry aloud with tears, 'Thou art just, O Lord!' then, of course, the crown of knowledge will be reached and all will be made clear. But what pulls me up here is that I can't accept that harmony. And while I am on earth, I make haste to take my own measures. You see, Alyosha, perhaps it really may happen that if I live to that moment, or rise again to see it, I, too, perhaps, may cry aloud with the rest, looking at the mother embracing the child's torturer, 'Thou art just, O Lord!' but I don't want to cry aloud then. While there is still time, I hasten to protect myself and so I renounce the higher harmony altogether. It's not worth the tears of that one tortured child who beat itself on the breast with its little fist and prayed in its stinking outhouse, with its unexpiated tears to 'dear, kind God'! It's not worth it, because those tears are unatoned for. They must be atoned for, or there can be no harmony. But how? How are you going to atone for them? Is it possible? By their being avenged? But what do I care for avenging them? What do I care for a hell for oppressors? What good can hell do, since those children have already been tortured? And what becomes of harmony, if there is hell? I want to forgive. I want to embrace. I don't want more suffering. And if the sufferings of children go to swell the sum of sufferings which was necessary to pay for truth, then I protest that the truth is not worth such a price. I don't want the mother to embrace the oppressor who threw her son to the dogs! She dare not forgive him! Let her forgive him for herself, if she will, let her forgive the torturer for the immeasurable suffering of her mother's heart. But the sufferings of her tortured child she has no right to forgive; she dare not forgive the torturer, even if the child were to forgive him! And if that is so, if they dare not forgive, what becomes of harmony? Is there in the whole world a being who would have the right to forgive and could forgive? I don't want harmony. From love for humanity I don't want it. I would rather be left with the unavenged suffering. I would rather remain with my unavenged suffering and unsatisfied indignation, *even if I were wrong*. Besides, too high a price is asked for harmony; it's beyond our means to pay so much to enter on it. And so I hasten to give back my entrance ticket, and if I am an honest man I am bound to give it back as soon as possible. And that I am doing. It's not God that I don't accept, Alyosha, only I most respectfully return Him the ticket."

"That's rebellion," murmured Alyosha, looking down.

"Rebellion? I am sorry you call it that," said Ivan earnestly. "One can hardly live in rebellion, and I want to live. Tell me yourself, I challenge you—answer. Imagine that you are creating a fabric of human destiny with the object of making men happy in the end, giving them peace and rest at last, but that it was essential and inevitable to torture to death only one tiny creature—that baby beating its breast with its fist, for instance—and to found that edifice on its unavenged tears, would you consent to be the architect on those conditions? Tell me, and tell the truth."

"No, I wouldn't consent," said Alyosha softly.

"And can you admit the idea that men for whom you are building it would agree to accept their happiness on the foundation of the unexpiated blood of a little victim? And accepting it would remain happy for ever?"

"No, I can't admit it. Brother," said Alyosha suddenly, with flashing eyes, "you said just now, is there a being in the whole world who would have the right to forgive and could forgive? But there is a Being and He can forgive everything, all and for all, because He gave His innocent blood for all and everything. You have forgotten Him, and on Him is built the edifice, and it is to Him they cry aloud, 'Thou art just, O Lord, for Thy ways are revealed!' "

"Ah! the One without sin and His blood! No, I have not forgotten Him; on the contrary I've been wondering all the time how it was you did not bring Him in before, for usually all arguments on your side put Him in the foreground. Do you know, Alyosha—don't laugh! I made a poem about a year ago. If you can waste another ten minutes on me, I'll tell it to you."

"You wrote a poem?"

"Oh, no, I didn't write it," laughed Ivan, "and I've never written two lines of poetry in my life. But I made up this poem in prose and I remembered it. I was carried away when I made it up. You will be my first reader—that is, listener. Why should an author forego even one listener?" smiled Ivan. "Shall I tell it to you?"

"I am all attention," said Alyosha.

"My poem is called 'The Grand Inquisitor'; it's a ridiculous thing, but I want to tell it to you."

THE GRAND INQUISITOR

. . .

"My story is laid in Spain, in Seville, in the most terrible time of the Inquisition, when fires were lighted every day to the glory of God, and 'in the splendid *auto da fé* the wicked heretics were burnt.' Oh, of course, this was not the coming in which He will appear according to His promise at the end of time in all His heavenly glory, and which will be sudden 'as lightning flashing from east to west.' No, He visited His children only for a moment, and there where the flames were crackling round the heretics. In His infinite mercy He came once more among men in that human shape in which He walked among men for three years fifteen centuries ago. He came down to the 'hot pavement' of the southern town in which on the day before almost a hundred heretics had, *ad majorem gloriam Dei*, been burnt by the cardinal, the Grand Inquisitor, in a magnificent *auto da fé*, in the presence of the king, the court, the knights, the cardinals, the most charming ladies of the court, and the whole population of Seville.

"He came softly, unobserved, and yet, strange to say, every one recognised Him. That might be one of the best passages in the poem. I mean, why they recognised Him. The people are irresistibly drawn to Him, they surround Him, they flock about Him, follow Him. He moves silently in their midst with a gentle smile of infinite compassion. The sun of love burns in His heart, light and power shine from His eyes, and their radiance, shed on the people, stirs their hearts with responsive love. He holds out His hands to them, blesses them, and a healing virtue comes from contact with Him, even with His garments. An old man in the crowd,

blind from childhood, cries out, 'O Lord, heal me and I shall see Thee!'
and, as it were, scales fall from his eyes and the blind man sees Him.
The crowd weeps and kisses the earth under His feet. Children throw
flowers before Him, sing, and cry hosannah. 'It is He—it is He!' all
repeat. 'It must be He, it can be no one but Him!' He stops at the steps
of the Seville cathedral at the moment when the weeping mourners are
bringing in a little open white coffin. In it lies a child of seven, the only
daughter of a prominent citizen. The dead child lies hidden in flowers.
'He will raise your child,' the crowd shouts to the weeping mother. The
priest, coming to meet the coffin, looks perplexed, and frowns, but the
mother of the dead child throws herself at His feet with a wail. 'If it is
Thou, raise my child!' she cries, holding out her hands to Him. The
procession halts, the coffin is laid on the steps at His feet. He looks with
compassion, and His lips once more softly pronounce, 'Maiden, arise!'
and the maiden arises. The little girl sits up in the coffin and looks round,
smiling with wide-open wondering eyes, holding a bunch of white roses
they had put in her hand.

"There are cries, sobs, confusion among the people, and at that moment the cardinal himself, the Grand Inquisitor, passes by the cathedral.
He is an old man, almost ninety, tall and erect, with a withered face and
sunken eyes, in which there is still a gleam of light. He is not dressed in
his gorgeous cardinal's robes, as he was the day before, when he was
burning the enemies of the Roman Church—at that moment he was wearing his coarse, old, monk's cassock. At a distance behind him come his
gloomy assistants and slaves and the 'holy guard.' He stops at the sight of
the crowd and watches it from a distance. He sees everything; he sees
them set the coffin down at His feet, sees the child rise up, and his face
darkens. He knits his thick grey brows and his eyes gleam with a sinister
fire. He holds out his finger and bids the guards take Him. And such
is his power, so completely are the people cowed into submission and
trembling obedience to him, that the crowd immediately make way for
the guards, and in the midst of deathlike silence they lay hands on Him
and lead Him away. The crowd instantly bows down to the earth, like
one man, before the old inquisitor. He blesses the people in silence and
passes on. The guards lead their prisoner to the close, gloomy vaulted
prison in the ancient palace of the Holy Inquisition and shut Him in it.
The day passes and is followed by the dark, burning 'breathless' night of
Seville. The air is 'fragrant with laurel and lemon.' In the pitch darkness
the iron door of the prison is suddenly opened and the Grand Inquisitor
himself comes in with a light in his hand. He is alone; the door is closed
at once behind him. He stands in the doorway and for a minute or two
gazes into His face. At last he goes up slowly, sets the light on the table
and speaks.

" 'Is it Thou? Thou?' but receiving no answer, he adds at once, 'Don't
answer, be silent. What canst Thou say, indeed? I know too well what
Thou wouldst say. And Thou hast no right to add anything to what

Thou hadst said of old. Why, then, art Thou come to hinder us? For Thou hast come to hinder us, and Thou knowest that. But dost Thou know what will be to-morrow? I know not who Thou art and care not to know whether it is Thou or only a semblance of Him, but to-morrow I shall condemn Thee and burn Thee at the stake as the worst of heretics. And the very people who have to-day kissed Thy feet, to-morrow at the faintest sign from me will rush to heap up the embers of Thy fire. Knowest Thou that? Yes, maybe Thou knowest it,' he added with thoughtful penetration, never for a moment taking his eyes off the Prisoner."

"I don't quite understand, Ivan. What does it mean?" Alyosha, who had been listening in silence, said with a smile. "Is it simply a wild fantasy, or a mistake on the part of the old man—some impossible *quiproquo?*"

"Take it as the last," said Ivan, laughing, "if you are so corrupted by modern realism and can't stand anything fantastic. If you like it to be a case of mistaken identity, let it be so. It is true," he went on, laughing, "the old man was ninety, and he might well be crazy over his set idea. He might have been struck by the appearance of the Prisoner. It might, in fact, be simply his ravings, the delusion of an old man of ninety, over-excited by the *auto da fé* of a hundred heretics the day before. But does it matter to us after all whether it was a mistake of identity or a wild fantasy? All that matters is that the old man should speak out, should speak openly of what he has thought in silence for ninety years."

"And the Prisoner too is silent? Does He look at him and not say a word?"

"That's inevitable in any case," Ivan laughed again. "The old man has told Him He hasn't the right to add anything to what He has said of old. One may say it is the most fundamental feature of Roman Catholicism, in my opinion at least. 'All has been given by Thee to the Pope,' they say, 'and all, therefore, is still in the Pope's hands, and there is no need for Thee to come now at all. Thou must not meddle for the time, at least.' That's how they speak and write too—the Jesuits, at any rate. I have read it myself in the works of their theologians. 'Hast Thou the right to reveal to us one of the mysteries of that world from which Thou hast come?' my old man asks Him, and answers the question for Him. 'No, Thou hast not; that Thou mayest not add to what has been said of old and mayest not take from men the freedom which Thou didst exalt when Thou wast on earth. Whatsoever Thou revealest anew will encroach on men's freedom of faith; for it will be manifest as a miracle, and the freedom of their faith was dearer to Thee than anything in those days fifteen hundred years ago. Didst Thou not often say then, "I will make you free"? But now Thou hast seen "free" men,' the old man adds suddenly, with a pensive smile. 'Yes, we've paid dearly for it,' he goes on, looking sternly at Him, 'but at last we have completed that work in Thy name. For fifteen centuries we have been wrestling with Thy freedom, but now it is ended and over for good. Dost Thou not believe that it's over for good? Thou lookest meekly at me and deignest not even to be wroth with me. But let me tell Thee that now, to-day, people are more persuaded than ever that they have perfect freedom, yet they have brought their freedom to us and laid it humbly at our feet. But that has been our doing. Was this what Thou didst? Was this Thy freedom?' "

"I don't understand again," Alyosha broke in. "Is he ironical, is he jesting?"

"Not a bit of it! He claims it as a merit for himself and his Church that at last they have vanquished freedom and have done so to make men happy. 'For now' (he is speaking of the Inquisition, of course) 'for the first time it has become possible to think of the happiness of men. Man was created a rebel; and how can rebels be happy? Thou wast warned,' he says to Him. 'Thou hast had no lack of admonitions and warnings, but Thou didst not listen to those warnings; Thou didst reject the only way by which men might be made happy. But, fortunately, departing Thou didst hand on the work to us. Thou hast promised, Thou hast established by Thy word, Thou hast given to us the right to bind and to unbind, and now, of course, Thou canst not think of taking it away. Why, then, hast Thou come to hinder us?' "

"And what's the meaning of 'no lack of admonitions and warnings'?" asked Alyosha.

"Why, that's the chief part of what the old man must say."

" 'The wise and dread spirit, the spirit of self-destruction and non-existence,' the old man goes on, 'the great spirit talked with Thee in the wilderness, and we are told in the books that he "tempted" Thee. Is that so? And could anything truer be said than what he revealed to Thee in three questions and what Thou didst reject, and what in the books is called "the temptation"? And yet if there has ever been on earth a real stupendous miracle, it took place on that day, on the day of the three temptations. The statement of those three questions was itself the miracle. If it were possible to imagine simply for the sake of argument that those three questions of the dread spirit had perished utterly from the books, and that we had to restore them and to invent them anew, and to do so had gathered together all the wise men of the earth—rulers, chief priests, learned men, philosophers, poets—and had set them the task to invent three questions, such as would not only fit the occasion, but express in three words, three human phrases, the whole future history of the world and of humanity—dost Thou believe that all the wisdom of the earth united could have invented anything in depth and force equal to the three questions which were actually put to Thee then by the wise and mighty spirit in the wilderness? From those questions alone, from the miracle of their statement, we can see that we have here to do not with the fleeting human intelligence, but with the absolute and eternal. For in those three questions the whole subsequent history of mankind is, as it were, brought together into one whole, and foretold, and in them are united all the unsolved historical contradictions of human nature. At the time it could not be so clear, since the future was unknown; but now that fifteen hundred years have passed, we see that everything in those three questions was so justly divined and foretold, and has been so truly fulfilled, that nothing can be added to them or taken from them.

" 'Judge Thyself who was right—Thou or he who questioned Thee then? Remember the first question; its meaning, in other words, was this: "Thou wouldst go into the world, and art going with empty hands, with some promise of freedom which men in their simplicity and their natural unruliness cannot even understand, which they fear and dread—for nothing has ever been more insupportable for a man and a human society than freedom. But seest Thou these stones in this parched and barren wilderness? Turn them into bread, and mankind will run after Thee like a flock of sheep, grateful and obedient, though for ever trembling, lest Thou withdraw Thy hand and deny them Thy bread." But Thou wouldst not deprive man of freedom and didst reject the offer, thinking, what is that freedom worth, if obedience is bought with bread? Thou didst reply that man lives not by bread alone. But dost Thou know that for the sake of that earthly bread the spirit of the earth will rise up against Thee and will strive with Thee and overcome Thee, and all will follow him, crying, "Who can compare with this beast? He has given us fire from heaven!" Dost Thou know that the ages will pass, and humanity will proclaim by the lips of their sages that there is no crime, and therefore no sin; there is only hunger? "Feed men, and then ask of them virtue!" that's what they'll write on the banner, which they will raise against Thee, and with which they will destroy Thy temple. Where Thy temple stood will rise a new building; the terrible tower of Babel will be built again, and though, like the one of old, it will not be finished, yet Thou mightest have prevented that new tower and have cut short the sufferings of men for a thousand years; for they will come back to us after a thousand years of agony with their tower. They will seek us again, hidden underground in the catacombs, for we shall be again persecuted and tortured. They will find us and cry to us, "Feed us, for those who have promised us fire from heaven haven't given it!" And then we shall finish building their tower, for he finishes the building who feeds them. And we alone shall feed them in Thy name, declaring falsely that it is in Thy name. Oh, never, never can they feed themselves without us! No science will give them bread so long as they remain free. In the end they will lay their freedom at our feet, and say to us, "Make us your slaves, but feed us." They will understand themselves, at last, that freedom and bread enough for all are inconceivable together, for never, never will they be able to share between them! They will be convinced, too, that they can never be free, for they are weak, vicious, worthless and rebellious. Thou didst promise them the bread of Heaven, but, I repeat again, can it compare with earthly bread in the eyes of the weak, ever sinful and ignoble race of man? And if for the sake of the bread of Heaven thousands and tens of thousands shall follow Thee, what is to become of the millions and tens of thousands of millions of creatures who will not have the strength to forego the earthly bread for the sake of the heavenly? Or dost Thou care only for the tens of thousands of the great and strong, while the millions, numerous as the sands of the sea, who are weak but love Thee, must exist only for the sake of the great and strong? No, we care for the weak too. They are sinful and rebellious, but in the end they too will become obedient. They will marvel at us and look on us as gods, because we are ready to endure the freedom which they have found so dreadful and to rule over them—so awful it will seem to them to be free. But we shall tell them that we are Thy servants and rule them in Thy name. We shall deceive them again, for we will not let Thee come to us again. That deception will be our suffering, for we shall be forced to lie.

" 'This is the significance of the first question in the wilderness, and this is what Thou hast rejected for the sake of that freedom which Thou hast exalted above everything. Yet in this question lies hid the great secret of this world. Choosing "bread," Thou wouldst have satisfied the universal and everlasting craving of humanity—to find some one to worship. So long as man remains free he strives for nothing so incessantly and so painfully as to find some one to worship. But man seeks to worship what is established beyond dispute, so that all men would agree at once to worship it. For these pitiful creatures are concerned not only to find what one or the other can worship, but to find something that all would believe in and worship; what is essential is that all may be *together* in it. This craving for *community* of worship is the chief misery of every man individually and of all humanity from the beginning of time. For the sake of common worship they've slain each other with the sword. They have set up gods and challenged one another, "Put away your gods and come and worship ours, or we will kill you and your gods!" And so it will be to the end of the world, even when gods disappear from the earth; they will fall down before idols just the same. Thou didst know, Thou couldst not but have known, this fundamental secret of human nature, but Thou didst reject the one infallible banner which was offered Thee to make all men bow down to Thee alone—the banner of earthly bread; and Thou hast rejected it for the sake of freedom and the bread of Heaven. Behold what Thou didst further. And all again in the name of freedom! I tell Thee that man is tormented by no greater anxiety than to find some one quickly to whom he can hand over that gift of freedom with which the ill-fated creature is born. But only one who can appease their conscience can take over their freedom. In bread there was offered Thee an invincible banner; give bread, and man will worship Thee, for nothing is more certain than bread. But if some one else gains possession of his conscience—oh! then he will cast away Thy bread and follow after him who has ensnared his conscience. In that Thou wast right. For the secret of man's being is not only to live but to have something to live for. Without a stable conception of the object of life, man would not consent to go on living, and would rather destroy himself than remain on earth, though he had bread in abundance. That is true. But what happened? Instead of taking men's freedom from them, Thou didst make it greater than ever! Didst Thou forget that man prefers peace, and even death, to freedom of choice in the knowledge of good and evil? Nothing is more seductive for man than his freedom of conscience, but nothing is a greater cause of suffering. And behold, instead of giving a firm foundation for setting the conscience of man at rest for ever, Thou didst choose all that is exceptional, vague and enigmatic; Thou didst choose what was utterly beyond the strength of men, acting as though Thou didst not love them at all—Thou who didst come to give Thy life for them! Instead of taking possession of men's freedom, Thou didst increase it, and burdened the spiritual kingdom of mankind with its sufferings for ever. Thou didst desire man's free love, that he should follow Thee freely, enticed and taken captive by Thee. In place of the rigid ancient law, man must hereafter with free heart decide for himself what is good and what is evil, having only Thy image before him as his guide. But didst Thou not know he would at last reject even Thy image and Thy truth, if he is weighed down with the fearful burden of free choice? They will cry aloud at last that the truth is not in Thee, for they could not have been left in greater confusion and suffering than Thou hast caused, laying upon them so many cares and unanswerable problems.

" 'So that, in truth, Thou didst Thyself lay the foundation for the destruction of Thy kingdom, and no one is more to blame for it. Yet what was offered Thee? There are three powers, three powers alone, able to conquer and to hold captive for ever the conscience of these impotent rebels for their happiness—those forces are miracle, mystery and authority. Thou hast rejected all three and hast set the example for doing so. When the wise and dead spirit set Thee on the pinnacle of the temple and said to Thee, "If Thou wouldst know whether Thou art the Son of God then cast Thyself down, for it is written: the angels shall hold him up lest he fall and bruise himself, and Thou shalt know then whether Thou art the Son of God and shalt prove then how great is Thy faith in Thy Father." But Thou didst refuse and wouldst not cast Thyself down. Oh! of course, Thou didst proudly and well, like God; but the weak, unruly race of men, are they gods? Oh, Thou didst know then that in taking one step, in making one movement to cast Thyself down, Thou wouldst be tempting God and have lost all Thy faith in Him, and wouldst have been dashed to pieces against that earth which Thou didst come to save. And the wise spirit that tempted Thee would have rejoiced. But I ask again, are there many like Thee? And couldst Thou believe for one moment that men, too, could face such a temptation? Is the nature of men such, that they can reject miracle, and at the great moments of their life, the moments of their deepest, most agonising spiritual difficulties, cling only to the free verdict of the heart? Oh, Thou didst know that Thy deed would be recorded in books, would be handed down to remote times and the utmost ends of the earth, and Thou didst hope that man, following Thee, would cling to God and not ask for a miracle. But Thou didst not know that when man rejects miracle he rejects God too; for man seeks not so much God as the miraculous. And as man cannot bear to be without the miraculous, he will create new miracles of his own for himself, and will worship deeds of sorcery and witchcraft, though he might be a hundred times over a rebel, heretic and infidel. Thou didst not come down from the Cross when they shouted to Thee, mocking and reviling Thee, "Come down from the cross and we will believe that Thou art He." Thou didst not come down, for again Thou wouldst not enslave man by a miracle, and didst crave faith given freely, not based on miracle. Thou didst crave for free love and not the base raptures of the slave before the might that has overawed him for ever. But Thou didst think too highly of men therein, for they are slaves, of course, though rebellious by nature. Look round and judge; fifteen centuries have passed, look upon them. Whom hast Thou raised up to Thyself? I swear, man is weaker and baser by nature than Thou hast believed him! Can he, can he do what Thou didst? By showing him so much respect, Thou didst, as it were, cease to feel for him, for Thou didst ask far too much from him—Thou who hast loved him more than Thyself! Respecting him less, Thou wouldst have asked less of him. That would have been more like love, for his burden would have been lighter. He is weak and vile. What though he is everywhere now rebelling against our power, and proud of his rebellion? It is the pride of a child and a schoolboy. They are little children rioting and barring out the teacher at school. But their childish delight will end; it will cost them dear. They will cast down temples and drench the earth with blood. But they will see at last, the foolish children, that, though they are rebels, they are impotent rebels, unable to keep up their own rebellion. Bathed in their foolish tears, they will recognise at last that He who created them rebels must have meant to mock at them. They will say this in despair, and their utterance will be a blasphemy which will make them more unhappy still, for man's nature cannot bear blasphemy, and in the end always avenges it on itself. And so unrest, confusion and unhappiness—that is the present lot of man after Thou didst bear so much for their freedom! Thy great prophet tells in vision and in image, that he saw all those who took part in the first resurrection and that there were of each tribe twelve thousand. But if there were so many of them, they must have been not men but gods. They had borne Thy cross, they had endured scores of years in the barren, hungry wilderness, living upon locusts and roots—and Thou mayest indeed point with pride at those children of freedom, of free love, of free and splendid sacrifice for Thy name. But remember that they were only some thousands; and what of the rest? And how are the other weak ones to blame, because they could not endure what the strong have endured? How is the weak soul to blame that it is unable to receive such terrible gifts? Canst Thou have simply come to the elect and for the elect? But if so, it is a mystery and we cannot understand it. And if it is a mystery, we too have a right to preach a mystery, and to teach them that it's not the free judgment of their hearts, not love that matters, but a mystery which they must follow blindly, even against their conscience. So we have done. We have corrected Thy work and have founded it upon *miracle, mystery* and *authority*. And men rejoiced that they were again led like sheep, and that the terrible gift that had brought them such suffering, was, at last, lifted from their hearts. Were we right teaching them this? Speak! Did we not love mankind, so meekly acknowledging their feebleness, lovingly lightening their burden, and permitting their weak nature even sin with our sanction? Why hast Thou come now to hinder us? And why dost Thou look silently and searchingly at me with Thy mild eyes? Be angry. I don't want Thy love, for I love Thee not. And what use is it for me to hide anything from Thee? Don't I know to Whom I am speaking? All that I can say is known to Thee already. And is it for me to conceal from Thee our mystery? Perhaps it is Thy will to hear it from my lips. Listen, then. We are not working with Thee, but with *him*—that is our mystery. It's long—eight centuries—since we have been on *his* side and not on Thine. Just eight centuries ago, we took from him what Thou didst reject with scorn, that last gift he offered Thee, showing Thee all the kingdoms of the earth. We took from him Rome and the sword of Cæsar, and proclaimed ourselves sole rulers of the earth, though hitherto we have not been able to complete our work. But whose fault is that? Oh, the work is only beginning, but it has begun. It has long to await completion and the earth has yet much to suffer, but we shall triumph and shall be Cæsars, and then we shall plan the universal happiness of man. But Thou mightest have taken even then the sword of Cæsar. Why didst Thou reject that last gift? Hadst Thou accepted that last counsel of the mighty spirit, Thou wouldst have accomplished all that man seeks on earth—that is, some one to worship, some one to keep his conscience, and some means of uniting all in one unanimous and harmonious ant-heap, for the craving for universal unity is the third and last anguish of men. Mankind as a whole has always striven to organise a universal state. There have been many great nations with great histories, but the more highly they were developed the more unhappy they were, for they felt more acutely than other people the craving for worldwide union. The great conquerors, Timours and Ghenghis-Khans, whirled like hurricanes over the face of the earth striving to subdue its people, and they too were but the unconscious expression of the same craving for universal unity. Hadst Thou taken the world and Cæsar's purple, Thou wouldst have founded the universal state and have given universal peace. For who can rule men if not he who holds their conscience and their bread in his hands? We have taken the sword of Cæsar, and in taking it, of course, have rejected Thee and followed *him*. Oh, ages are yet to come of the confusion of free thought, of their science and cannibalism. For having begun to build their tower of Babel without us, they will end, of course, with cannibalism. But then the beast will crawl to us and lick our feet and spatter them with tears of blood. And we shall sit upon the beast and raise the cup, and on it will be written, "Mystery." But then, and only then, the reign of peace and happiness will come for men. Thou art proud of Thine elect, but Thou hast only the elect, while we give rest to all. And besides, how many of those elect, those mighty ones who could become elect, have grown weary waiting for Thee, and have transferred and will transfer the powers of their spirit and the warmth of their heart to the other camp, and end by raising their *free* banner against Thee. Thou didst Thyself lift up that banner. But with us all will be happy and will no more rebel nor destroy one another as under Thy freedom. Oh, we shall persuade them that they will only become free when they renounce their freedom to us and submit to us. And shall we be right or shall we be lying? They will be convinced that we are right, for they will remember the horrors of slavery and confusion to which Thy freedom brought them. Freedom, free thought and science, will lead them into such straits and will bring them face to face with such marvels and insoluble mysteries, that some of them, the fierce and rebellious, will destroy themselves, others, rebellious but weak, will destroy one another, while the rest, weak and unhappy, will crawl fawning to our feet and whine to us: "Yes, you were right, you alone possess His mystery, and we come back to you, save us from ourselves!"

" 'Receiving bread from us, they will see clearly that we take the bread made by their hands from them, to give it to them, without any miracle. They will see that we do not change the stones to bread, but in truth they will be more thankful for taking it from our hands than for the bread itself! For they will remember only too well that in old days, without our help, even the bread they made turned to stones in their hands, while since they have come back to us, the very stones have turned to bread in their hands. Too, too well they know the value of complete submission! And until men know that, they will be unhappy. Who is most to blame for their not knowing it, speak? Who scattered the flock and sent it astray on unknown paths? But the flock will come together again and will submit once more, and then it will be once for all. Then we shall give them the quiet humble happiness of weak creatures such as they are by nature. Oh, we shall persuade them at last not to be proud, for Thou didst lift them up and thereby taught them to be proud. We shall show them that they are weak, that they are only pitiful children, but that childlike happiness is the sweetest of all. They will become timid and will look to us and huddle close to us in fear, as chicks to the hen. They will marvel at us and will be awestricken before us, and will be proud at our being so powerful and clever, that we have been able to subdue such a turbulent flock of thousands of millions. They will tremble impotently before our wrath, their minds will grow fearful, they will be quick to shed tears like women and children, but they will be just as ready at a sign from us to pass to laughter and rejoicing, to happy mirth and childish song. Yes, we shall set them to work, but in their leisure hours we shall make their life like a child's game, with children's songs and innocent dance. Oh, we shall allow them even sin, they are weak and helpless, and they will love us like children because we allow them to sin. We shall tell them that every sin will be expiated, if it is done with our permission, that we allow them to sin because we love them, and the punishment for these sins we take upon ourselves. And we shall take it upon ourselves, and they will adore us as their saviours who have taken on themselves their sins before God. And they will have no secrets from us. We shall allow or forbid them to live with their wives and mistresses, to have or not to have children—according to whether they have been obedient or disobedient—and they will submit to us gladly and cheerfully. The most painful secrets of their conscience, all, all they will bring to us, and we shall have an answer for all. And they will be glad to believe our answer, for it will save them from the great anxiety and terrible agony they endure at present in making a free decision for themselves. And all will be happy, all the millions of creatures except the hundred thousand who rule over them. For only we, we who guard the mystery, shall be unhappy. There will be thousands of millions of happy babes, and a hundred thousand sufferers who have taken upon themselves the curse of the knowledge of good and evil. Peacefully they will die, peacefully they will expire in Thy name, and beyond the grave they will find nothing but death. But we shall keep the secret, and for their happiness we shall allure them with the reward of heaven and eternity. Though if there were anything in the other world, it certainly would not be for such as they. It is prophesied that Thou wilt come again in victory, Thou wilt come with Thy chosen, the proud and strong, but we will say that they have only saved themselves, but we have saved all. We are told that the harlot who sits upon the beast, and holds in her hands the *mystery*, shall be put to shame, that the weak will rise up again, and will rend her royal purple and will strip naked her loathsome body. But then I will stand up and point out to Thee the thousand millions of happy children who have known no sin. And we who have taken their sins upon us for their happiness will stand up before Thee and say: "Judge us if Thou canst and darest." Know that I fear Thee not. Know that I too have been in the wilderness, I too have lived on roots and locusts, I too prized the freedom with which Thou hast blessed men, and I too was striving to stand among Thy elect, among the strong and powerful, thirsting "to make up the number." But I awakened and would not serve madness. I turned back and joined the ranks of those *who have corrected Thy work.* I left the proud and went back to the humble, for the happiness of the humble. What I say to Thee will come to pass, and our dominion will be built up. I repeat, to-morrow Thou shalt see that obedient flock who at a sign from me will hasten to heap up the hot cinders about the pile on which I shall burn Thee for coming to hinder us. For if any one has ever deserved our fires, it is Thou. To-morrow I shall burn Thee. Dixi.' "

Ivan stopped. He was carried away as he talked and spoke with excitement; when he had finished, he suddenly smiled.

Alyosha had listened in silence; towards the end he was greatly moved and seemed several times on the point of interrupting, but restrained himself. Now his words came with a rush.

"But . . . that's absurd!" he cried, flushing. "Your poem is in praise of Jesus, not in blame of Him—as you meant it to be. And who will believe you about freedom? Is that the way to understand it? That's not the idea of it in the Orthodox Church . . . That's Rome, and not even the whole of Rome, it's false—those are the worst of the Catholics, the Inquisitors, the Jesuits! . . . And there could not be such a fantastic creature as your Inquisitor. What are these sins of mankind they take on themselves? Who are these keepers of the mystery who have taken some curse upon themselves for the happiness of mankind? When have they been seen? We know the Jesuits, they are spoken ill of, but surely they are not what you describe? They are not that at all, not at all. . . . They are simply the Romish army for the earthly sovereignty of the world in the future, with the Pontiff of Rome for Emperor . . . that's their ideal, but there's no sort of mystery or lofty melancholy about it. . . . It's simple lust of power, of filthy earthly gain, of domination—something like a universal serfdom with them as masters—that's all they stand for. They don't even believe in God perhaps. Your suffering inquisitor is a mere fantasy."

"Stay, stay," laughed Ivan, "how hot you are! A fantasy you say, let it be so! Of course it's a fantasy. But allow me to say: do you really think that the Roman Catholic movement of the last centuries is actually nothing but the lust of power, of filthy earthly gain? Is that Father Païssy's teaching?"

"No, no, on the contrary, Father Païssy did once say something rather the same as you . . . but of course it's not the same, not a bit the same," Alyosha hastily corrected himself.

"A precious admission, in spite of your 'not a bit the same.' I ask you why your Jesuits and Inquisitors have united simply for vile material gain? Why can there not be among them one martyr oppressed by great sorrow and loving humanity? You see, only suppose that there was one such man among all those who desire nothing but filthy material gain—if there's only one like my old inquisitor, who had himself eaten roots in the desert and made frenzied efforts to subdue his flesh to make himself free and perfect. But yet all his life he loved humanity, and suddenly his eyes were opened, and he saw that it is no great moral blessedness to attain perfection and freedom, if at the same time one gains the conviction that millions of God's creatures have been created as a mockery, that they will never be capable of using their freedom, that these poor rebels can never turn into giants to complete the tower, that it was not for such geese that the great idealist dreamt his dream of harmony. Seeing all that he turned back and joined—the clever people. Surely that could have happened?"

"Joined whom, what clever people?" cried Alyosha, completely carried

away. "They have no such great cleverness and no mysteries and secrets.
. . . Perhaps nothing but Atheism, that's all their secret. Your inquisitor
does not believe in God, that's his secret!"

"What if it is so! At last you have guessed it. It's perfectly true that
that's the whole secret, but isn't that suffering, at least for a man like
that, who has wasted his whole life in the desert and yet could not shake
off his incurable love of humanity? In his old age he reached the clear
conviction that nothing but the advice of the great dread spirit could build
up any tolerable sort of life for the feeble, unruly, 'incomplete, empirical
creatures created in jest.' And so, convinced of this, he sees that he must
follow the counsel of the wise spirit, the dread spirit of death and
destruction, and therefore accept lying and deception, and lead men
consciously to death and destruction, and yet deceive them all the way
so that they may not notice where they are being led, that the poor blind
creatures may at least on the way think themselves happy. And note, the
deception is in the name of Him in Whose ideal the old man had so
fervently believed all his life long. Is not that tragic? And if only one
such stood at the head of the whole army 'filled with the lust of power
only for the sake of filthy gain'—would not one such be enough to make
a tragedy? More than that, one such standing at the head is enough to
create the actual leading idea of the Roman Church with all its armies and
Jesuits, its highest idea. I tell you frankly that I firmly believe that there
has always been such a man among those who stood at the head of the
movement. Who knows, there may have been some such even among
the Roman Popes. Who knows, perhaps the spirit of that accursed old
man who loves mankind so obstinately in his own way, is to be found
even now in a whole multitude of such old men, existing not by chance
but by agreement, as a secret league formed long ago for the guarding of
the mystery, to guard it from the weak and the unhappy, so as to make
them happy. No doubt it is so, and so it must be indeed. I fancy that
even among the Masons there's something of the same mystery at the
bottom, and that that's why the Catholics so detest the Masons as their
rivals breaking up the unity of the idea, while it is so essential that there
should be one flock and one shepherd. . . . But from the way I defend
my idea I might be an author impatient of your criticism. Enough of
it."

"You are perhaps a Mason yourself!" broke suddenly from Alyosha.
"You don't believe in God," he added, speaking this time very sorrowfully. He fancied besides that his brother was looking at him ironically.
"How does your poem end?" he asked, suddenly looking down. "Or was it
the end?"

"I meant to end it like this. When the Inquisitor ceased speaking he
waited some time for his Prisoner to answer him. His silence weighed
down upon him. He saw that the Prisoner had listened intently all the
time, looking gently in his face and evidently not wishing to reply. The
old man longed for Him to say something, however bitter and terrible.

But He suddenly approached the old man in silence and softly kissed him on his bloodless aged lips. That was all his answer. The old man shuddered. His lips moved. He went to the door, opened it, and said to Him: 'Go, and come no more. . . . come not at all, never, never!' And he let Him out into the dark alleys of the town. The Prisoner went away."

"And the old man?"

"The kiss glows in his heart, but the old man adheres to his idea."

DIALOGUES CONCERNING NATURAL RELIGION

(Parts X and XI)

DAVID HUME

David Hume (1711–1776) was a British philosopher, historian, and economist who concerned himself principally with the application of the empirical method to questions of the nature of man and the theory of knowledge. *A Treatise of Human Nature* and *An Enquiry Concerning Human Understanding* constitute his major philosophic works. His *History of England* and *Political Discourses* established him as a first-rank historian.

In the *Dialogues Concerning Natural Religion,* Hume explores various facets and implications of the problem of evil in the form of a philosophic dialogue. He ranges over such questions as whether evil can be denied, whether it can be subsumed under the perfection of the whole, and what inferences may be drawn to the intention of a creator. Hume's own opinion is hidden, and there has been considerable scholarly debate as to which participant in the dialogue, especially Philo or Cleanthes, may be said to represent him. Nevertheless, the *Dialogues* remain one of the best sources of the development of this philosophic issue.

PART X

It is my opinion, I own, replied DEMEA, that each man feels, in a manner, the truth of religion within his own breast; and from a consciousness of his imbecility and misery, rather than from any reasoning, is led to seek protection from that Being, on whom he and all nature is dependent. So anxious or so tedious are even the best scenes of life, that futurity is still the object of all our hopes and fears. We incessantly look forward, and endeavour, by prayers, adoration, and sacrifice, to appease those unknown powers, whom we find, by experience, so able to afflict and oppress us. Wretched creatures that we are! What resource for us amidst the innumerable ills of life, did not religion suggest some methods of atonement, and appease those terrors, with which we are incessantly agitated and tormented?

I am indeed persuaded, said PHILO, that the best and indeed the only method of bringing every one to a due sense of religion is by just representations of the misery and wickedness of men. And for that purpose a talent of eloquence and strong imagery is more requisite than that of reasoning and argument. For is it necessary to prove, what every one feels within himself? It is only necessary to make us feel it, if possible, more intimately and sensibly.

The people, indeed, replied DEMEA, are sufficiently convinced of this great and melancholy truth. The miseries of life, the unhappiness of man, the general corruptions of our nature, the unsatisfactory enjoyment of pleasures, riches, honours; these phrases have become almost proverbial in all languages. And who can doubt of what all men declare from their own immediate feeling and experience?

In this point, said PHILO, the learned are perfectly agreed with the vulgar; and in all letters, *sacred* and *profane*, the topic of human misery has been insisted on with the most pathetic eloquence that sorrow and melancholy could inspire. The poets, who speak from sentiment, without a system, and whose testimony has therefore the more authority, abound in images of this nature. From HOMER down to Dr. YOUNG, the whole inspired tribe have ever been sensible, that no other representation of things would suit the feeling and observation of each individual.

As to authorities, replied DEMEA, you need not seek them. Look round this library of CLEANTHES. I shall venture to affirm, that, except authors of particular sciences, such as chemistry or botany, who have no occasion to treat of human life, there scarce is one of those innumerable writers, from whom the sense of human misery has not, in some passage or other, extorted a complaint and confession of it. At least, the chance is entirely on that side; and no one author has ever, so far as I can recollect, been so extravagant as to deny it.

There you must excuse me, said PHILO: LEIBNITZ has denied it; and is perhaps the first,[1] who ventured upon so bold and paradoxical an opinion; at least, the first, who made it essential to his philosophical system.

And by being the first, replied DEMEA, might he not have been sensible of his error? For is this a subject in which philosophers can propose to make discoveries, especially in so late an age? And can any man hope by a simple denial (for the subject scarcely admits of reasoning) to bear down the united testimony of mankind, founded on sense and consciousness?

And why should man, added he, pretend to an exemption from the lot of all other animals? The whole earth, believe me, PHILO, is cursed and polluted. A perpetual war is kindled amongst all living creatures. Necessity, hunger, want, stimulate the strong and courageous: Fear, anxiety, terror, agitate the weak and infirm. The first entrance into life gives anguish to the new-born infant and to its wretched parent: Weakness, impotence, distress, attend each stage of that life: And it is at last finished in agony and horror.

Observe too, says PHILO, the curious artifices of nature, in order to embitter the life of every living being. The stronger prey upon the weaker, and keep them in perpetual terror and anxiety. The weaker too, in their turn, often prey upon the stronger, and vex and molest them without relaxation. Consider that innumerable race of insects, which either are bred on the body of each animal, or flying about infix their stings in him. These insects have others still less than themselves, which torment them. And thus on each hand, before and behind, above and below, every

---

[1] That sentiment had been maintained by Dr. King [*De Origine Mali*, 1702] and some few others, before LEIBNITZ, though by none of so great fame as that German philosopher. [N. K. Smith.]

animal is surrounded with enemies, which incessantly seek his misery and destruction.

Man alone, said DEMEA, seems to be, in part, an exception to this rule. For by combination in society, he can easily master lions, tigers, and bears, whose greater strength and agility naturally enable them to prey upon him.

On the contrary, it is here chiefly, cried PHILO, that the uniform and equal maxims of nature are most apparent. Man, it is true, can, by combination, surmount all his *real* enemies, and become master of the whole animal creation: But does he not immediately raise up to himself *imaginary* enemies, the dæmons of his fancy, who haunt him with superstitious terrors, and blast every enjoyment of life? His pleasure, as he imagines, becomes, in their eyes, a crime: His food and repose give them umbrage and offence: His very sleep and dreams furnish new materials to anxious fear: And even death, his refuge from every other ill, presents only the dread of endless and innumerable woes. Nor does the wolf molest more the timid flock, than superstition does the anxious breast of wretched mortals.

Besides, consider, DEMEA; this very society, by which we surmount those wild beasts, our natural enemies; what new enemies does it not raise to us? What woe and misery does it not occasion? Man is the greatest enemy of man. Oppression, injustice, contempt, contumely, violence, sedition, war, calumny, treachery, fraud; by these they mutually torment each other: And they would soon dissolve that society which they had formed, were it not for the dread of still greater ills, which must attend their separation.

But though these external insults, said DEMEA, from animals, from men, from all the elements, which assault us, form a frightful catalogue of woes, they are nothing in comparison of those, which arise within ourselves, from the distempered condition of our mind and body. How many lie under the lingering torment of diseases? Hear the pathetic enumeration of the great poet.

> Intestine stone and ulcer, colic-pangs,
> Daemoniac frenzy, moping melancholy,
> And moon-struck madness, pining atrophy,
> Marasmus and wide-wasting pestilence.
> Dire was the tossing, deep the groans: DESPAIR
> Tended the sick, busiest from couch to couch.
> And over them triumphant DEATH his dart
> Shook, but delay'd to strike, tho' oft invok'd
> With vows, as their chief good and final hope.[2]

The disorders of the mind, continued DEMEA, though more secret, are not perhaps less dismal and vexatious. Remorse, shame, anguish, rage,

2 [Milton: *Paradise Lost*, XI]

disappointment, anxiety, fear, dejection, despair; who has ever passed through life without cruel inroads from these tormentors? How many have scarcely ever felt any better sensations? Labour and poverty, so abhorred by every one, are the certain lot of the far greater number: And those few privileged persons, who enjoy ease and opulence, never reach contentment or true felicity. All the goods of life united would not make a very happy man: But all the ills united would make a wretch indeed; and any one of them almost (and who can be free from every one), nay often the absence of one good (and who can possess all) is sufficient to render life ineligible.

Were a stranger to drop, in a sudden, into this world, I would show him, as a specimen of its ills, an hospital full of diseases, a prison crowded with malefactors and debtors, a field of battle strowed with carcases, a fleet floundering in the ocean, a nation languishing under tyranny, famine, or pestilence. To turn the gay side of life to him, and give him a notion of its pleasures; whither should I conduct him? to a ball, to an opera, to court? He might justly think, that I was only showing him a diversity of distress and sorrow.

There is no evading such striking instances, said PHILO, but by apologies, which still farther aggravate the charge. Why have all men, I ask, in all ages, complained incessantly of the miseries of life? . . . They have no just reason, says one: These complaints proceed only from their discontented, repining, anxious disposition . . . And can there possibly, I reply, be a more certain foundation of misery, than such a wretched temper?

But if they were really as unhappy as they pretend, says my antagonist, why do they remain in life? . . .

Not satisfied with life, afraid of death.

This is the secret chain, say I, that holds us. We are terrified, not bribed to the continuance of our existence.

It is only a false delicacy, he may insist, which a few spirits indulge, and which has spread these complaints among the whole race of mankind. . . . And what is this delicacy, I ask, which you blame? Is it any thing but a greater sensibility to all the pleasures and pains of life? and if the man of a delicate, refined temper, by being so much more alive than the rest of the world, is only so much more unhappy; what judgment must we form in general of human life?

Let men remain at rest, says our adversary; and they will be easy. They are willing artificers of their own misery. . . . No! reply I; an anxious languor follows their repose: Disappointment, vexation, trouble, their activity and ambition.

I can observe something like what you mention in some others, replied CLEANTHES: But I confess, I feel little or nothing of it in myself; and hope that it is not so common as you represent it.

If you feel not human misery yourself, cried DEMEA, I congratulate you on so happy a singularity. Others, seemingly the most prosperous, have not been ashamed to vent their complaints in the most melancholy strains. Let us attend to the great, the fortunate Emperor, CHARLES V, when, tired with human grandeur, he resigned all his extensive dominions into the hands of his son. In the last harangue, which he made on that memorable occasion, he publicly avowed, *that the greatest prosperities which he had ever enjoyed, had been mixed with so many adversities, that he might truly say he had never enjoyed any satisfaction or contentment.* But did the retired life, in which he sought for shelter, afford him any greater happiness? If we may credit his son's account, his repentance commenced the very day of his resignation.

CICERO's fortune, from small beginnings, rose to the greatest lustre and renown; yet what pathetic complaints of the ills of life do his familiar letters, as well as philosophical discourses, contain? And suitably to his own experience, he introduces CATO, the great, the fortunate CATO, protesting in his old age, that, had he a new life in his offer, he would reject the present.

Ask yourself, ask any of your acquaintance, whether they would live over again the last ten or twenty years of their life. No! but the next twenty, they say, will be better:

> And from the dregs of life, hope to receive
> What the first sprightly running could not give.[3]

Thus at last they find (such is the greatness of human misery; it reconciles even contradictions) that they complain, at once, of the shortness of life, and of its vanity and sorrow.

And it is possible, CLEANTHES, said PHILO, that after all these reflections, and infinitely more, which might be suggested, you can still persevere in your anthropomorphism, and assert the moral attributes of the Deity, his justice, benevolence, mercy, and rectitude, to be of the same nature with these virtues in human creatures? His power we allow infinite: Whatever he wills is executed: But neither man nor any other animal are happy: Therefore he does not will their happiness. His wisdom is infinite: He is never mistaken in choosing the means to any end: But the course of nature tends not to human or animal felicity: Therefore it is not established for that purpose. Through the whole compass of human knowledge, there are no inferences more certain and infallible than these. In what respect, then, do his benevolence and mercy resemble the benevolence and mercy of men?

EPICURUS's old questions are yet unanswered. Is he willing to prevent evil, but not able? then is he impotent. Is he able, but not willing? then is he malevolent. Is he both able and willing? whence then is evil?

You ascribe, CLEANTHES (and I believe justly) a purpose and intention

---

3 Dryden, *Aurengzebe*, Act IV, sc. I. Hume has written "hope" for "think." [N. K. Smith.]

to nature. But what, I beseech you, is the object of that curious artifice and machinery, which she has displayed in all animals? The preservation alone of individuals and propagation of the species. It seems enough for her purpose, if such a rank be barely upheld in the universe, without any care or concern for the happiness of the members that compose it. No resource for this purpose: No machinery, in order merely to give pleasure or ease: No fund of pure joy and contentment: No indulgence without some want or necessity accompanying it. At least, the few phenomena of this nature are overbalanced by opposite phenomena of still greater importance.

Our sense of music, harmony, and indeed beauty of all kinds, gives satisfaction, without being absolutely necessary to the preservation and propagation of the species. But what racking pains, on the other hand, arise from gouts, gravels, megrims, tooth-aches, rheumatisms; where the injury to the animal-machinery is either small or incurable? Mirth, laughter, play, frolic, seem gratuitous satisfactions, which have no farther tendency: Spleen, melancholy, discontent, superstition, are pains of the same nature. How then does the divine benevolence display itself in the sense of you anthropomorphites? None but we mystics, as you were pleased to call us, can account for this strange mixture of phenomena, by deriving it from attributes, infinitely perfect, but incomprehensible.

And have you at last, said CLEANTHES smiling, betrayed your intentions, PHILO? Your long agreement with DEMEA did indeed a little surprise me; but I find you were all the while erecting a concealed battery against me. And I must confess, that you have now fallen upon a subject worthy of your noble spirit of opposition and controversy. If you can make out the present point, and prove mankind to be unhappy or corrupted, there is an end at once of all religion. For to what purpose establish the natural attributes of the Deity, while the moral are still doubtful and uncertain?

You take umbrage very easily, replied DEMEA, at opinions the most innocent, and the most generally received even amongst the religious and devout themselves: And nothing can be more surprising than to find a topic like this, concerning the wickedness and misery of man, charged with no less than atheism and profaneness. Have not all pious divines and preachers, who have indulged their rhetoric on so fertile a subject; have they not easily, I say, given a solution of any difficulties which may attend it? This world is but a point in comparison of the universe: This life but a moment in comparison of eternity. The present evil phenomena, therefore, are rectified in other regions, and in some future period of existence. And the eyes of men, being then opened to larger views of things, see the whole connection of general laws, and trace, with adoration, the benevolence and rectitude of the Deity, through all the mazes and intricacies of his providence.

No! replied CLEANTHES, No! These arbitrary suppositions can never be admitted, contrary to matter of fact, visible and uncontroverted. Whence can any cause be known but from its known effects? Whence can any hypothesis be proved but from the apparent phenomena? To establish one hypothesis upon another is building entirely in the air; and the utmost we ever attain, by these conjectures and fictions, is to ascertain the bare possibility of our opinion; but never can we, upon such terms, establish its reality.

The only method of supporting divine benevolence (and it is what I willingly embrace) is to deny absolutely the misery and wickedness of man. Your representations are exaggerated: Your melancholy views mostly fictitious: Your inferences contrary to fact and experience. Health is more common than sickness: Pleasure than pain: Happiness than misery. And for one vexation which we meet with, we attain, upon computation, a hundred enjoyments.

Admitting your position, replied PHILO, which yet is extremely doubtful, you must, at the same time, allow, that, if pain be less frequent than pleasure, it is infinitely more violent and durable. One hour of it is often able to outweigh a day, a week, a month of our common insipid enjoyments: And how many days, weeks, and months are passed by several in the most acute torments? Pleasure, scarcely in one instance, is ever able to reach ecstasy and rapture: And in no one instance can it continue for any time at its highest pitch and altitude. The spirits evaporate; the nerves relax; the fabric is disordered; and the enjoyment quickly degenerates into fatigue and uneasiness. But pain often, Good God, how often! rises to torture and agony; and the longer it continues, it becomes still more genuine agony and torture. Patience is exhausted; courage languishes; melancholy seizes us; and nothing terminates our misery but the removal of its cause, or another event, which is the sole cure of all evil, but which, from our natural folly, we regard with still greater horror and consternation.

But not to insist upon these topics, continued PHILO, though most obvious, certain, and important; I must use the freedom to admonish you, CLEANTHES, that you have put this controversy upon a most dangerous issue, and are unawares introducing a total scepticism into the most essential articles of natural and revealed theology. What! no method of fixing a just foundation for religion, unless we allow the happiness of human life, and maintain a continued existence even in this world, with all our present pains, infirmities, vexations, and follies, to be eligible and desirable! But this is contrary to every one's feeling and experience: It is contrary to an authority so established as nothing can subvert: No decisive proofs can ever be produced against this authority; nor is it possible for you to compute, estimate, and compare all the pains and all the pleasures in the lives of all men and of all animals: And thus by your resting the whole system of religion on a point, which, from its very nature, must for ever be uncertain, you tacitly confess, that that system is equally uncertain.

But allowing you, what never will be believed; at least, what you never possibly can prove, that animal, or at least, human happiness, in this life, exceeds its misery; you have yet done nothing: For this is not, by any means, what we expect from infinite power, infinite wisdom, and infinite goodness. Why is there any misery at all in the world? Not by chance surely. From some cause then. Is it from the intention of the Deity? But he is perfectly benevolent. Is it contrary to his intention? But he is almighty. Nothing can shake the solidity of this reasoning, so short, so clear, so decisive; except we assert, that these subjects exceed all human capacity, and that our common measures of truth and falsehood are not applicable to them; a topic, which I have all along insisted on, but which you have, from the beginning, rejected with scorn and indignation.

But I will be contented to retire still from this intrenchment: For I deny that you can ever force me in it: I will allow, that pain or misery in man is *compatible* with infinite power and goodness in the Deity, even in your sense of these attributes: What are you advanced by all these concessions? A mere possible compatibility is not sufficient. You must *prove* these pure, unmixed, and uncontrollable attributes from the present mixed and confused phenomena, and from these alone. A hopeful undertaking! Were the phenomena ever so pure and unmixed, yet being finite, they would be insufficient for that purpose. How much more, were they also so jarring and discordant?

Here, CLEANTHES, I find myself at ease in my argument. Here I triumph. Formerly, when we argued concerning the natural attributes of intelligence and design, I needed all my sceptical and metaphysical subtilty to elude your grasp. In many views of the universe, and of its parts, particularly the latter, the beauty and fitness of final causes strike us with such irresistible force, that all objections appear (what I believe they really are) mere cavils and sophisms; nor can we then imagine how it was ever possible for us to repose any weight on them. But there is no view of human life, or of the condition of mankind, from which, without the greatest violence, we can infer the moral attributes, or learn that infinite benevolence, conjoined with infinite power and infinite wisdom, which we must discover by the eyes of faith alone. It is your turn now to tug the labouring oar, and to support your philosophical subtilties against the dictates of plain reason and experience.

PART XI

I scruple not to allow, said CLEANTHES, that I have been apt to suspect the frequent repetition of the word, *infinite*, which we meet with in all theological writers, to savour more of panegyric than of philosophy, and that any purposes of reasoning, and even of religion, would be better served, were we to rest contented with more accurate and more moderate expressions. The terms, *admirable, excellent, superlatively great, wise*, and *holy*; these sufficiently fill the imaginations of men; and any thing beyond, besides that it leads into absurdities, has no influence on the affections or sentiments. Thus, in the present subject, if we abandon all human analogy, as seems your intention, DEMEA, I am afraid we abandon all religion, and retain no conception of the great object of our adoration. If we preserve human analogy, we must for ever find it impossible to reconcile any mixture of evil in the universe with infinite attributes; much less, can we ever prove the latter from the former. But supposing the Author of nature to be finitely perfect, though far exceeding mankind; a satisfactory account may then be given of natural and moral evil, and every untoward phenomenon be explained and adjusted. A less evil may then be chosen, in order to avoid a greater: Inconveniences be submitted to, in order to reach a desirable end: And in a word, benevolence, regulated by wisdom, and limited by necessity, may produce just such a world as the present. You, PHILO, who are so prompt at starting views, and reflections, and analogies; I would gladly hear, at length, without interruption, your opinion of this new theory; and if it deserve our attention, we may afterwards, at more leisure, reduce it into form.

My sentiments, replied PHILO, are not worth being made a mystery of; and therefore, without any ceremony, I shall deliver what occurs to me with regard to the present subject. It must, I think, be allowed, that, if a very limited intelligence, whom we shall suppose utterly unacquainted with the universe, were assured, that it were the production of a very good, wise, and powerful Being, however finite, he would, from his conjectures, form *beforehand* a different notion of it from what we find it to be by experience; nor would he ever imagine, merely from these attributes of the cause, of which he is informed, that the effect could be so full of vice and misery and disorder, as it appears in this life. Supposing now, that this person were brought into the world, still assured, that it was the workmanship of such a sublime and benevolent Being; he might, perhaps, be surprised at the disappointment; but would never retract his former belief, if founded on any very solid argument; since such a limited intelligence must be sensible of his own blindness and ignorance, and must allow, that there may be many solutions of those phenomena, which will for ever escape his comprehension. But supposing, which is the real case with regard to man, that this creature is not antecedently convinced of a supreme intelligence, benevolent, and powerful, but is left to gather such a belief from the appearances of things; this entirely alters the case, nor will he ever find any reason for such a conclusion. He may be fully convinced of the narrow limits of his understanding; but this will not help him in forming an inference concerning the goodness of superior powers, since he must form that inference from what he knows, not from what he is ignorant of. The more you exaggerate his weakness and ignorance, the more diffident you render him, and give him the greater suspicion, that such subjects are beyond the reach of his faculties. You are obliged, therefore, to reason with him merely from the known phenomena, and to drop every arbitrary supposition or conjecture.

Did I show you a house or palace, where there was not one apartment convenient or agreeable; where the windows, doors, fires, passages, stairs, and the whole œconomy of the building were the source of noise, confusion, fatigue, darkness, and the extremes of heat and cold; you would certainly blame the contrivance, without any farther examination. The architect would in vain display his subtilty, and prove to you, that if this door or that window were altered, greater ills would ensue. What he says, may be strictly true: The alteration of one particular, while the other parts of the building remain, may only augment the inconveniences. But still you would assert in general, that, if the architect had had skill and good intentions, he might have formed such a plan of the whole, and might have adjusted the parts in such a manner, as would have remedied all or most of these inconveniences. His ignorance, or even your own ignorance of such a plan, will never convince you of the impossibility of it. If you find many inconveniences and deformities in the building, you will always, without entering into any detail, condemn the architect.

In short, I repeat the question: Is the world considered in general, and as it appears to us in this life, different from what a man or such a limited being would, *beforehand*, expect from a very powerful, wise, and benevolent Deity? It must be strange prejudice to assert the contrary. And from thence I conclude, that, however consistent the world may be, allowing certain suppositions and conjectures, with the idea of such a Deity, it can never afford us an inference concerning his existence. The consistence is not absolutely denied, only the inference. Conjectures, especially where infinity is excluded from the divine attributes, may, perhaps, be sufficient to prove a consistence; but can never be foundations for any inference.

There seem to be *four* circumstances, on which depend all, or the greatest part of the ills, that molest sensible creatures; and it is not impossible but all these circumstances may be necessary and unavoidable. We know so little beyond common life, or even of common life, that, with regard to the œconomy of a universe, there is no conjecture, however wild, which may not be just; nor any one, however plausible, which may not be erroneous. All that belongs to human understanding, in this deep ignorance and obscurity, is to be sceptical, or at least cautious; and not to admit of any hypothesis, whatever; much less, of any which is supported by no appearance of probability. Now this I assert to be the case with regard to all the causes of evil, and the circumstances on which it depends. None of them appear to human reason, in the least degree, necessary or unavoidable; nor can we suppose them such, without the utmost licence of imagination.

The *first* circumstance which introduces evil, is that contrivance or œconomy of the animal creation, by which pains, as well as pleasures, are employed to excite all creatures to action, and make them vigilant in the great work of self-preservation. Now pleasure alone, in its various degrees, seems to human understanding sufficient for this purpose. All animals might be constantly in a state of enjoyment; but when urged by any of the necessities of nature, such as thirst, hunger, weariness; instead of pain, they might feel a diminution of pleasure, by which they might be prompted to seek that object, which is necessary to their subsistence. Men pursue pleasure as eagerly as they avoid pain; at least, might have been so constituted. It seems, therefore, plainly possible to carry on the business of life without any pain. Why then is any animal ever rendered susceptible of such a sensation? If animals can be free from it an hour, they might enjoy a perpetual exemption from it; and it required as particular a contrivance of their organs to produce that feeling, as to endow them with sight, hearing, or any of the senses. Shall we conjecture, that such a contrivance was necessary, without any appearance of reason? And shall we build on that conjecture as on the most certain truth?

But a capacity of pain would not alone produce pain, were it not for the *second* circumstance, viz. the conducting of the world by general laws; and this seems nowise necessary to a very perfect Being. It is true; if every thing were conducted by particular volitions, the course of nature would be perpetually broken, and no man could employ his reason in the conduct of life. But might not other particular volitions remedy this inconvenience? In short, might not the Deity exterminate all ill, wherever it were to be found; and produce all good, without any preparation or long progress of causes and effects?

Besides, we must consider, that, according to the present œconomy of the world, the course of nature, though supposed exactly regular, yet to us appears not so, and many events are uncertain, and many disappoint our expectations. Health and sickness, calm and tempest, with an infinite number of other accidents, whose causes are unknown and variable, have a great influence both on the fortunes of particular persons and on the prosperity of public societies: And indeed all human life, in a manner, depends on such accidents. A Being, therefore, who knows the secret springs of the universe, might easily, by particular volitions, turn all these accidents to the good of mankind, and render the whole world happy, without discovering himself in any operation. A fleet, whose purposes were salutary to society, might always meet with a fair wind: Good princes enjoy sound health and long life: Persons born to power and authority, be framed with good tempers and virtuous dispositions. A few such events as these, regularly and wisely conducted, would change the face of the world; and yet would no more seem to disturb the course of nature or confound human conduct, than the present œconomy of things, where the causes are secret, and variable, and compounded. Some small touches, given to CALIGULA's brain in his infancy, might have converted him into a TRAJAN: One wave, a little higher than the rest, by burying CÆSAR and his fortune in the bottom of the ocean, might have restored liberty to a considerable part of mankind. There may, for aught we know, be good reasons, why providence interposes not in this manner; but they are unknown to us: And though the mere supposition, that such reasons exist, may be sufficient to *save* the conclusion concerning the divine attributes, yet surely it can never be sufficient to *establish* that conclusion.

If every thing in the universe be conducted by general laws, and if animals be rendered susceptible of pain, it scarcely seems possible but some ill must arise in the various shocks of matter, and the various concurrence and opposition of general laws: But this ill would be very rare, were it not for the *third* circumstance, which I proposed to mention, viz. the great frugality with which all powers and faculties are distributed to every particular being. So well adjusted are the organs and capacities of all animals, and so well fitted to their preservation, that, as far as history or tradition reaches, there appears not to be any single species which has yet been extinguished in the universe.[4] Every animal has the requisite endowments; but these endowments are bestowed with so scrupulous an œconomy, that any considerable diminution must entirely destroy the creature. Wherever one power is increased, there is a proportional abatement in the others. Animals, which excel in swiftness, are commonly defective in force. Those, which possess both, are either imperfect in some of their senses, or are oppressed with the most craving wants. The human species, whose chief excellency is reason and sagacity, is of all others the most necessitous, and the most deficient in bodily advantages; without clothes, without arms, without food, without lodging, without any convenience of life, except what they owe to their own skill and industry. In short, nature seems to have formed an exact calculation of the necessities of her creatures; and like a *rigid master*, has afforded them little more powers or endowments, than what are strictly sufficient to supply those necessities. An *indulgent parent* would have bestowed a large stock, in order to guard against accidents, and secure the happiness and welfare of the creature, in the most unfortunate concurrence of circumstances. Every course of life would not have been so surrounded with precipices, that the least departure from the true path, by mistake or necessity, must involve us in misery and ruin. Some reserve, some fund would have been provided to ensure happiness; nor would the powers and the necessities have been adjusted with so rigid an œconomy. The Author of nature is inconceivably powerful: His force is supposed great, if not altogether inexhaustible: Nor is there any reason, as far as we can judge, to make him observe this strict frugality in his dealings with his creatures. [It would have been better, were his power extremely limited, to have created fewer animals, and to have endowed these with more faculties for their happiness and preservation. A builder is never esteemed prudent, who undertakes a plan, beyond what his stock will enable him to finish.]

[In order to cure most of the ills of human life, I require not that man should have the wings of the eagle, the swiftness of the stag, the force of the ox, the arms of the lion, the scales of the crocodile or rhinoceros; much

---

[4] *In Hume's manuscript there is here the following note, scored out:* CAESAR, speaking of the woods in Germany, mentions some animals as subsisting there, which are now utterly extinct. *De Bello Gall:* lib. 6. These, and some few more instances, may be exceptions to the proposition here delivered. STRABO (lib. 4) quotes from POLYBIUS an account of an animal about the Tyrol, which is not now to be found, If POLYBIUS was not deceived, which is possible, the animal must have been then very rare, since STRABO cites but one authority, and speaks doubtfully. [N. K. Smith.]

less do I demand the sagacity of an angel or cherubim. I am contented to take an increase in one single power of faculty of his soul. Let him be endowed with a greater propensity to industry and labour; a more vigorous spring and activity of mind; a more constant bent to business and application. Let the whole species possess naturally an equal diligence with that which many individuals are able to attain by habit and reflection; and the most beneficial consequences, without any allay of ill, is the immediate and necessary result of this endowment. Almost all the moral, as well as natural evils of human life arise from idleness; and were our species, by the original constitution of their frame, exempt from this vice or infirmity, the perfect cultivation of land, the improvement of arts and manufactures, the exact execution of every office and duty, immediately follow; and men at once may fully reach that state of society, which is so imperfectly attained by the best-regulated government. But as industry is a power, and the most valuable of any, nature seems determined, suitably to her usual maxims, to bestow it on men with a very sparing hand; and rather to punish him severely for his deficiency in it, than to reward him for his attainments. She has so contrived his frame, that nothing but the most violent necessity can oblige him to labour; and she employs all his other wants to overcome, at least in part, the want of diligence, and to endow him with some share of a faculty, of which she has thought fit naturally to bereave him. Here our demands may be allowed very humble, and therefore the more reasonable. If we required the endowments of superior penetration and judgment, of a more delicate taste of beauty, of a nicer sensibility to benevolence and friendship; we might be told, that we impiously pretend to break the order of nature, that we want to exalt ourselves into a higher rank of being, that the presents which we require, not being suitable to our state and condition, would only be pernicious to us. But it is hard; I dare to repeat it, it is hard, that being placed in a world so full of wants and necessities; where almost every being and element is either our foe or refuses us their assistance; we should also have our own temper to struggle with, and should be deprived of that faculty which can alone fence against these multiplied evils.]

The *fourth* circumstance, whence arises the misery and ill of the universe, is the inaccurate workmanship of all the springs and principles of the great machine of nature. It must be acknowledged, that there are few parts of the universe, which seem not to serve some purpose, and whose removal would not produce a visible defect and disorder in the whole. The parts hang all together; or can one be touched without affecting the rest, in a greater or less degree. But at the same time, it must be observed, that none of these parts or principles, however useful, are so accurately adjusted, as to keep precisely within those bounds in which their utility consists; but they are, all of them, apt, on every occasion, to run into the one extreme or the other. One would imagine, that this grand production has not received the last hand of the maker; so little finished is every part, and so coarse are the strokes, with which it is executed. Thus, the winds are requisite to convey the vapours along the surface of the globe, and to assist men in navigation: But how oft, rising up to tempests and hurricanes, do they become pernicious? Rains are necessary to nourish all the plants and animals of the earth: But how often are they defective? how often excessive? Heat is requisite to all life and vegetation; but is not always found in the due proportion. On the mixture and secretion of the humours and juices of the body depend the health and prosperity of the animal: But the parts perform not regularly their proper function. What more useful than all the passions of the mind, ambition, vanity, love, anger? But how oft do they break their bounds, and cause the greatest convulsions in society? There is nothing so advantageous in the universe, but what frequently becomes pernicious, by its excess or defect; nor has nature guarded, with the requisite accuracy, against all disorder or confusion. The irregularity is never, perhaps, so great as to destroy any species; but is often sufficient to involve the individuals in ruin and misery.

On the concurrence, then, of these *four* circumstances does all or the greatest part of natural evil depend. Were all living creatures incapable of pain, or were the world administered by particular volitions, evil never could have found access into the universe: And were animals endowed with a large stock of powers and faculties, beyond what strict necessity requires; or were the several springs and principles of the universe so accurately framed as to preserve always the just temperament and medium; there must have been very little ill in comparison of what we feel at present. What then shall we pronounce on this occasion? Shall we say, that these circumstances are not necessary, and that they might easily have been altered in the contrivance of the universe? This decision seems too presumptuous for creatures so blind and ignorant. Let us be more modest in our conclusions. Let us allow, that, if the goodness of the Deity (I mean a goodness like the human) could be established on any tolerable reasons *a priori*, these phenomena, however untoward, would not be sufficient to subvert that principle; but might easily, in some unknown manner, be reconcilable to it. But let us still assert, that as this goodness is not antecedently established, but must be inferred from the phenomena, there can be no grounds for such an inference, while there are so many ills in the universe, and while these ills might so easily have been remedied, as far as human understanding can be allowed to judge on such a subject. I am sceptic enough to allow, that the bad appearances, notwithstanding all my reasonings, may be compatible with such attributes as you suppose: But surely they can never prove these attributes. Such a conclusion cannot result from scepticism; but must arise from the phenomena, and from our confidence in the reasonings which we deduce from these phenomena.

[Look round this universe. What an immense profusion of beings, animated and organized, sensible and active! You admire this prodigious variety and fecundity. But inspect a little more narrowly these living existences, the only beings worth regarding. How hostile and destructive to each other! How insufficient all of them for their own happiness! How contemptible or odious to the spectator! The whole presents nothing but the idea of a blind nature, impregnated by a great vivifying principle, and pouring forth from her lap, without discernment or parental care, her maimed and abortive children.]

Here the Manichæan system occurs as a proper hypothesis to solve the difficulty: And no doubt, in some respects, it is very specious, and has more probability than the common hypothesis, by giving a plausible account of the strange mixture of good and ill which appears in life. But if we consider, on the other hand, the perfect uniformity and agreement of the parts of the universe, we shall not discover in it any marks of the combat of a malevolent with a benevolent Being. There is indeed an opposition of pains and pleasures in the feelings of sensible creatures: But are not all the operations of nature carried on by an opposition of principles, of hot and cold, moist and dry, light and heavy? The true conclusion is, that the original source of all things is entirely indifferent to all these principles, and has no more regard to good above ill than to heat above cold, or to drought above moisture, or to light above heavy.

There may *four* hypotheses be framed concerning the first causes of the universe: *that* they are endowed with perfect goodness, *that* they have perfect malice, *that* they are opposite and have both goodness and malice, *that* they have neither goodness nor malice. Mixed phenomena can never prove the two former unmixed principles. And the uniformity and steadiness of general laws seem to oppose the third. The fourth, therefore, seems by far the most probable.

What I have said concerning natural evil will apply to moral, with little or no variation; and we have no more reason to infer, that the rectitude of the supreme Being resembles human rectitude than that his benevolence resembles the human. Nay, it will be thought, that we have still greater cause to exclude from him moral sentiments, such as we feel them; since moral evil, in the opinion of many, is much more predominant above moral good than natural evil above natural good.

But even though this should not be allowed, and though the virtue, which is in mankind, should be acknowledged much superior to the vice; yet so long as there is any vice at all in the universe, it will very much puzzle you anthropomorphites, how to account for it. You must assign a cause for it, without having recourse to the first cause. But as every effect must have a cause, and that cause another; you must either carry on the progression *in infinitum,* or rest on that original principle, who is the ultimate cause of all things. . . . .

Hold! Hold! cried Demea: Whither does your imagination hurry you? I joined in alliance with you, in order to prove the incomprehensible nature of the divine Being, and refute the principles of Cleanthes, who would measure every thing by a human rule and standard. But I now find you running into all the topics of the greatest libertines and infidels; and betraying that holy cause, which you seemingly espoused. Are you secretly, then, a more dangerous enemy than Cleanthes himself?

And are you so late in perceiving it? replied CLEANTHES. Believe me, DEMEA; your friend PHILO, from the beginning, has been amusing himself at both our expence; and it must be confessed, that the injudicious reasoning of our vulgar theology has given him but too just a handle of ridicule. The total infirmity of human reason, the absolute incomprehensibility of the divine nature, the great and universal misery and still greater wickedness of men; these are strange topics surely to be so fondly cherished by orthodox divines and doctors. In ages of stupidity and ignorance, indeed, these principles may safely be espoused; and perhaps, no views of things are more proper to promote superstition, than such as encourage the blind amazement, the diffidence, and melancholy of mankind. But at present. . . .

Blame not so much, interposed PHILO, the ignorance of these reverend gentlemen. They know how to change their style with the times. Formerly it was a most popular theological topic to maintain, that human life was vanity and misery, and to exaggerate all the ills and pains which are incident to men. But of late years, divines, we find, begin to retract this position, and maintain, though still with some hesitation, that there are more goods than evils, more pleasures than pains, even in this life. When religion stood entirely upon temper and education, it was thought proper to encourage melancholy; as indeed, mankind never have recourse to superior powers so readily as in that disposition. But as men have now learned to form principles, and to draw consequences, it is necessary to change the batteries, and to make use of such arguments as will endure, at least some scrutiny and examination. . . .

2

Divine Justification in the Ultimate Design

THE DEATH OF IVAN ILYITCH
LEO TOLSTOY
(trans. by N. H. Dole)

Leo Tolstoy (1828–1910) was a Russian novelist and short story writer who created two of the greatest novels in world literature—*War and Peace* and *Anna Karenina*. In all of his works, Tolstoy seeks to demonstrate that God's hand is at work behind the scenes, both in human history and in the life of every person.

Tolstoy's short story *The Death of Ivan Ilyitch* deals with an individual's experience of dying, but it does not treat the phenomenon as an irredeemable evil. Rather, Tolstoy shows how dying can be a time for profound reflection on the significance of one's life, whether one has lived well or badly, and where one stands in relation to God and one's fellow man. Through suffering and isolation in his suffering, Ivan Ilyitch comes to certain realizations about the sham, hypocrisy, and empty conventionality of the society of which he had been a part, and at the last moment repents and asks forgiveness of God. Tolstoy is demonstrating that even death has a place in the grand cosmic scheme, bringing men to an awareness of fundamental values and the purpose of life on earth, which is to serve God through love for all mankind.

CHAPTER II

The past history of Ivan Ilyitch's life was most simple and uneventful, and yet most terrible.

Ivan Ilyitch died at the age of forty-five, a member of the Court of Justice. He was the son of a functionary who had followed, in various ministries and departments at Petersburg, a career such as brings men into a position from which, on account of their long service and their rank, they are never turned adrift, even though it is plainly manifest that their actual usefulness is at an end; and consequently they obtain imaginary, fictitious places, and from six to ten thousand that are not fictitious, on which they live till a good old age.

Such had been Ilya Yefimovitch Golovin, privy councilor, a useless member of various useless commissions.

He had three sons; Ivan Ilyitch was the second. The eldest had followed the same career as his father's, but in a different ministry, and was already nearing that period of his service in which inertia carries a man into emoluments. The third son had been a failure. He had completely gone to pieces in several positions, and he was now connected with railways; and his father and his brothers and especially their wives not only disliked to meet him, but, except when it was absolutely necessary, even forgot that he existed.

A sister was married to Baron Gref, who, like his father-in-law, was a Petersburg chinovnik. Ivan Ilyitch had been *le phénix de la famille*,[1] as they used to say. He was neither so chilling and formal as the eldest brother, nor so unpromising as the youngest. He was the mean between them,—an intelligent, lively, agreeable, and polished man. He had studied at the law school with his younger brother, who did not graduate but was expelled from the fifth class; Ivan Ilyitch, however, finished his course creditably. At the law-school he showed the same characteristics by which he was afterward distinguished all his life: he was capable, good-natured even to gayety, and sociable, but strictly fulfilling all that he considered to be his duty; duty, in his opinion, was all that is considered to be such by men in the highest station. He was not one to curry favor, either as a boy, or afterward in manhood; but from his earliest years he had been attracted by men in the highest station in society, just as a fly is by the light; he adopted their ways, their views of life, and entered into relations of friendship with them. All the passions of childhood and youth had passed away, not leaving serious traces. He had yielded to sensuality and vanity, and, toward the last of his life, to the higher forms of liberalism, but all within certain limits which his nature faithfully prescribed for him.

While at the law-school, he had done some things which hitherto had seemed to him very shameful, and which while he was engaged in them aroused in him deep scorn for himself. But afterward, finding that these things were also done by men of high position, and were not considered by them disgraceful, he came to regard them, not indeed as worthy, but as something to put entirely out of his mind, and he was not in the least troubled by the recollection of them.

When Ivan Ilyitch had graduated from the law-school with the tenth rank, and received from his father some money for his uniform, he ordered a suit of Scharmer, added to his trinkets the little medal with the legend *respice finem*, bade the prince and principal farewell, ate a dinner with his classmates at Donon's and, furnished with new and stylish trunk, linen, uniform, razors, and toilet articles, and a plaid, ordered or bought at the very best shops, he departed for the province, as chinovnik and private secretary to the governor—a place which his father procured for him.

---

[1] the paragon of the family

In the province, Ivan Ilyitch at once got himself into the same sort of easy and agreeable position as his position in the law-school had been. He attended to his duties, pressed forward in his career, and at the same time enjoyed life in a cheerful and circumspect manner. From time to time, delegated by his chief, he visited the districts, bore himself with dignity toward both his superiors and subordinates, and, without overweening conceit, fulfilled with punctuality and incorruptible integrity the duties imposed upon him, preëminently in the affair of the dissenters.

Notwithstanding his youth, and his tendency to be gay and easy-going, he was, in matters of State, thoroughly discreet, and carried his official reserve even to sternness. But in society he was often merry and witty, and always good-natured, polite, and *bon enfant,* as he was called by his chief and his chief's wife, at whose house he was intimate.

While he was in the province, he had maintained relations with one of those ladies who are ready to fling themselves into the arms of an elegant young lawyer. There was also a dressmaker; and there were occasional sprees with visiting flügel-adjutants, and visits to some out-of-the-way street after supper; he had also the favor of his chief and even of his chief's wife, but everything of this sort was attended with such a high tone of good-breeding that it could not be qualified by hard names; it all squared with the rubric of the French expression, *Il faut que jeunesse se passe.*[2]

All was done with clean hands, with clean linen, with French words, and, above all, in company with the very highest society, and therefore with the approbation of those high in rank.

In this way Ivan Ilyitch served five years, and a change was instituted in the service. The new tribunals were established; new men were needed.

And Ivan Ilyitch was chosen as one of the new men.

He was offered the position of examining magistrate; and accepted it, notwithstanding the fact that this place was in another government, and that he would be obliged to give up the connections he had formed, and form new ones.

Ivan Ilyitch's friends saw him off. They were photographed in a group, they presented him a silver cigarette-case, and he departed for his new post.

As an examining magistrate, Ivan Ilyitch was just as *comme il faut,*[3] just as circumspect, and careful to sunder the obligations of his office from his private life, and as successful in winning universal consideration, as when he was a chinovnik with special functions. The office of magistrate itself was vastly more interesting and attractive to Ivan Ilyitch than his former position had been.

To be sure, it used to be agreeable to him, in his former position, to pass with free and easy gait, in his Scharmer-made uniform, in front of

---

2 A man must sow his wild oats.
3 proper; correct

trembling petitioners and petty officials, waiting for an interview, and
envying him, as he went without hesitation into his chief's private room,
and sat down with him to drink a cup of tea, and smoke a cigarette; but
the men who had been directly dependent on his pleasure were few,—
merely police captains and dissenters, if he were sent out with special
instructions. And he liked to meet these men, dependent on him, not only
politely, but even on terms of comradeship; he liked to make them feel
that he, who had the power to crush them, treated them simply, and like
friends. Such men at that time were few.

But now, as examining magistrate, Ivan Ilyitch felt that all, all without
exception, even men of importance, of distinction, all were in his hands,
and that all he had to do was to write such and such words on a piece of
paper and a heading, and this important, distinguished man would be
brought to him in the capacity of accused or witness, and, unless he
wished to ask him to sit down, he would have to stand in his presence, and
submit to his questions. Ivan Ilyitch never took undue advantage of this
power; on the contrary, he tried to temper the expression of it. But the
consciousness of this power, and the possibility of tempering it, furnished
for him the chief interest and attractiveness of his new office.

In the office itself, especially in investigations, Ivan Ilyitch was very
quick to master the process of eliminating all circumstances extraneous
to the case, and of disentangling the most complicated details in such a
manner that the case would be presented on paper only in its essentials,
and absolutely shorn of his own personal opinion, and, last and not least,
that every necessary formality would be fulfilled. This was a new mode of
doing things. And he was one of the first to be engaged in putting into
operation the code of 1864.

When he took up his residence in the new city, as examining magistrate, Ivan Ilyitch made new acquaintances and ties; he put himself on a
new footing, and adopted a somewhat different tone. He held himself
rather aloof from the provincial authorities, and took up with a better
circle among the judges and wealthy nobles living in the city; and he
adopted a tone of easy-going criticism of the government, together with a
moderate form of liberalism and "civilized citizenship." At the same
time, though Ivan Ilyitch in no wise diminished the elegance of his toilet,
yet he ceased to shave his chin, and allowed his beard to grow as it
would.

Ivan Ilyitch's life in the new city also passed very agreeably. The society which *fronded* against the government was good and friendly; his
salary was larger than before; and, while he had no less zest in life, he
had the additional pleasure of playing whist, a game in which, as he enjoyed playing cards, he quickly learned to excel, so that he was always on
the winning side.

After two years of service in the new city Ivan Ilyitch met the lady
who became his wife. Praskovia Feodorovna Mikhel was the most fasci-
nating, witty, brilliant young girl in the circle where Ivan Ilyitch moved.

In the multitude of other recreations, and as a solace from the labors of his office, Ivan Ilyitch established sportive, easy-going relations with Praskovia Feodorovna.

At the time when Ivan Ilyitch was a chinovnik with special functions, he had been a passionate lover of dancing; but now that he was examining magistrate, he danced only as an occasional exception. He now danced with the idea that, "though I am an advocate of the new order of things, and belong to the fifth class, still, as far as the question of dancing goes, I can at least show that in this respect I am better than the rest."

Thus, it frequently happened that, toward the end of a party, he danced with Praskovia Feodorovna; and it was principally at the time of these dances, that he made the conquest of Praskovia Feodorovna. She fell in love with him. Ivan Ilyitch had no clearly decided intention of getting married; but when the girl fell in love with him, he asked himself this question: "In fact, why should I not get married?" said he to himself.

The young lady, Praskovia Feodorovna, came of a good family belonging to the nobility, far from ill-favored, had a small fortune. Ivan Ilyitch might have aspired to a more brilliant match, but this was an excellent one. Ivan Ilyitch had his salary; she, he hoped, would have as much more. She was of good family; she was sweet, pretty, and a thoroughly well-bred woman. To say that Ivan Ilyitch got married because he was in love with his betrothed, and found in her sympathy with his views of life, would be just as incorrect as to say that he got married because the men of his set approved of the match.

Ivan Ilyitch took a wife for two reasons: he gave himself a pleasure in taking such a wife; and, at the same time, the people of the highest rank considered such an act proper.

And so Ivan Ilyitch got married.

The wedding ceremony itself, and the first few days of their married life with its connubial caresses, their new furniture, their new plate, their new linen, everything, even the prospects of an increasing family, were all that could be desired. So that Ivan Ilyitch began to think that marriage not only was not going to disturb his easy-going, pleasant, gay, and always respectable life, so approved by society, and which Ivan Ilyitch considered a perfectly natural characteristic of life in general, but was also going to add to it. But from the first months of his wife's pregnancy, there appeared something new, unexpected, disagreeable, hard, and trying, which he could not have foreseen, and from which it was impossible to escape.

His wife, without any motive, as it seemed to Ivan Ilyitch, *de gaité de cœur,*[4] as he said to himself, began to interfere with the pleasant and decent current of his life; without any cause she grew jealous of him, demanded attentions from him, found fault with everything, and caused him disagreeable and stormy scenes.

At first Ivan Ilyitch hoped to free himself from this unpleasant state of

---

4 frivolously; gratuitously; out of sheer wantonness

things by the same easy-going and respectable acceptation of life which had helped him in days gone by. He tried to ignore his wife's disposition, and continued to live as before in an easy and pleasant way. He invited his friends, he gave card-parties, he attempted to make his visits to the club or to friends; but his wife began one time to abuse him with rough and energetic language, and continued persistently to scold him each time that he failed to fulfil her demands, having evidently made up her mind not to cease berating him until he was completely subjected to her authority,—in other words, until he would stay at home, and be just as deeply in the dumps as she herself,—a thing which Ivan Ilyitch dreaded above all.

He learned that married life, at least as far as his wife was concerned, did not always add to the pleasantness and decency of existence, but, on the contrary, disturbed it, and that, therefore, it was necessary to protect himself from such interference. And Ivan Ilyitch tried to devise means to this end. His official duties were the only thing that had an imposing effect upon Praskovia Feodorovna; and Ivan Ilyitch, by means of his office, and the duties arising from it, began the struggle with his wife, for the defense of his independent life.

When the child was born, and in consequence of the various attempts and failures to have it properly nursed, and the illnesses, real and imaginary, of both mother and child, wherein Ivan Ilyitch's sympathy was demanded, but which were absolutely foreign to him, the necessity for him to secure a life outside of his family became still more imperative.

According as his wife grew more irritable and exacting, so Ivan Ilyitch transferred the center of his life's burdens more and more into his office. He began to love his office more and more, and became more ambitious than he had ever been.

Very soon, not longer than a year after his marriage, Ivan Ilyitch came to the conclusion that married life, while affording certain advantages, was in reality a very complicated and burdensome thing, in relation to which, if one would fulfil his duty, that is, live respectably and with the approbation of society, one must work out a certain system, just as in public office.

And such a system Ivan Ilyitch secured in his matrimonial life. He demanded of family life only such conveniences in the way of home dinners, a housekeeper, a bed, as it could furnish him, and, above all, that respectability in external forms which was in accordance with the opinions of society. As for the rest, he was anxious for pleasant amenities; and if he found them, he was very grateful. On the other hand, if he met with opposition and complaint, then he immediately took refuge in the far-off world of his official duties, which alone offered him delight.

Ivan Ilyitch was regarded as an excellent magistrate, and at the end of three years he was appointed deputy-prokuror. His new functions, their importance, the power vested in him of arresting and imprisoning any one, the publicity of his speeches, his success obtained in this field,—all this still more attached him to the service.

Children came; his wife kept growing more irritable and ill-tempered; but the relations which Ivan Ilyitch maintained toward family life made him almost proof against her temper.

After seven years of service in one city, Ivan Ilyitch was promoted to the office of prokuror in another government. They moved; they had not much money, and the place where they went did not suit his wife. Although his salary was larger than before, yet living was more expensive; moreover, two of their children died; and thus family life became still more distasteful to Ivan Ilyitch.

Praskovia Feodorovna blamed her husband for all the misfortunes that came on them in their new place of abode. Most of the subjects of conversation between husband and wife, especially the education of their children, led to questions which were productive of quarrels, so that quarrels were always ready to break out. Only at rare intervals came those periods of affection which distinguish married life, but they were not of long duration. These were little islands in which they rested for a time; but then again they pushed out into the sea of secret animosity, which expressed itself by driving them farther and farther apart.

This alienation might have irritated Ivan Ilyitch, if he had not considered that it was inevitable; but he now began to look on this situation not merely as normal, but even as the goal of his activity in the family. This goal consisted in withdrawing as far as possible from these unpleasantnesses, or of giving them a character of innocence and respectability; and he attained this end by spending less and less time with his family; but when he was to do so, then he endeavored to guarantee his position by the presence of strangers.

But Ivan Ilyitch's chief resource was his office. In the world of his duties was concentrated all his interest in life. And this interest wholly absorbed him. The consciousness of his power of ruining any one whom he might wish to ruin; the importance of his position manifested outwardly when he came into court or met his subordinates; his success with superiors and subordinates; and, above all, his skill in the conduct of affairs,—and he was perfectly conscious of it,—all this delighted him, and, together with conversations with his colleagues, dinners and whist, filled all his life. Thus, for the most part, Ivan Ilyitch's life continued to flow in its even tenor as he considered that it ought to flow,—pleasantly and respectably.

Thus he lived seven years longer. His eldest daughter was already sixteen years old; still another little child had died; and there remained a lad, the one who was in school, the object of their wrangling. Ivan Ilyitch wanted to send him to the law-school; but Praskovia, out of spite toward him, selected the gymnasium. The daughter studied at home, and made good progress; the lad also was not at all backward in his studies.

(Ivan Ilyitch receives an advance in rank and a consequent increase in salary which enables him to live on an even grander scale. By all social standards he is an extremely successful man and he himself looks upon his life as a fortunate one, but a shadow falls over his happiness. One day while climbing a

ladder he slips and injures his side. The bruise seems minor, but gradually
he begins to feel pain internally, and his suffering increases to a point where
he realizes that the injury is a serious one. The doctors differ in their diag-
noses and ultimately cannot offer any help; Ivan Ilyitch slowly accepts the
fact that he is dying.)

. . .

CHAPTER VIII

It was morning.

It was morning merely because Gerasim had gone, and Piotr, the
lackey, had come. He put out the candles, opened one curtain, and began
noiselessly to put things to rights. Whether it were morning, whether it
were evening, Friday or Sunday, all was a matter of indifference to him,
all was one and the same thing. The agonizing, shooting pain, never for an
instant appeased; the consciousness of a life hopelessly wasting away, but
not yet departed; the same terrible, cursed death coming nearer and nearer,
the one reality, and always the same lie,—what matter, then, here, of days,
weeks, and hours of the day?

"Will you not have me bring the tea?"

"He must follow form, and that requires masters to take tea in the
morning," he thought; and he said merely:—

"No."

"Wouldn't you like to go over to the divan?"

"He has to put the room in order, and I hinder him; I am uncleanness,
disorder!" he thought to himself, and said merely:—

"No; leave me!"

The lackey still bustled about a little. Ivan Ilyitch put out his hand.
Piotr officiously hastened to him:—

"What do you wish?"

"My watch."

Piotr got the watch, which lay near by, and gave it to him.

"Half-past eight. They aren't up yet?"

"No one at all. Vasili Ivanovitch"—that was his son—"has gone to
school, and Praskovia Feodorovna gave orders to wake her up if you asked
for her. Do you wish it?"

"No, it is not necessary.—Shall I not try the tea?" he asked himself.
"Yes . . . . tea . . . . bring me some."

Piotr started to go out. Ivan Ilyitch felt terror-stricken at being left
alone. "How can I keep him? Yes, my medicine. Piotr, give me my medicine.—Why not? perhaps the medicine may help me yet."

He took the spoon, sipped it.

"No, there is no help. All this is nonsense and delusion," he said, as he
immediately felt the familiar, mawkish, hopeless taste.

"No, I cannot have any faith in it. But this pain, ... why this pain?
Would that it might cease for a minute!"

And he began to groan. Piotr came back.

"Nothing. . . . go! Bring the tea."

Piotr went out. Ivan Ilyitch, left alone, began to groan, not so much from the pain, although it was horrible, as from mental anguish.

"Always the same thing, and the same thing; all these endless days and nights. Would it might come very soon! What very soon? Death, blackness? No, no! Anything rather than death!"

When Piotr came back with the tea on a tray, Ivan Ilyitch stared long at him in bewilderment, not comprehending who he was, what he was. Piotr was abashed at this gaze; and when Piotr showed his confusion, Ivan Ilyitch came to himself.

"Oh, yes," said he, "the tea; very well, set it down. Only help me to wash, and to put on a clean shirt."

And Ivan Ilyitch began to perform his toilet. With resting spells he washed his hands and face, cleaned his teeth, began to comb his hair, and looked into the mirror. It seemed frightful, perfectly frightful, to him, to see how his hair lay flat upon his pale brow.

While he was changing his shirt, he knew that it would be still more frightful if he gazed at his body; and so he did not look at himself. But now it was done. He put on his khalat, wrapped himself in his plaid, and sat down in his easy-chair to take his tea. For a single moment he felt refreshed; but as soon as he began to drink the tea, again that same taste, that same pain. He compelled himself to drink it all, and lay down, stretching out his legs. He lay down, and let Piotr go.

Always the same thing. Now a drop of hope gleaming, then a sea of despair rising up, and always pain, always melancholy, and always the same monotony. It was terribly melancholy to the lonely man; he longed to call in some one, but he knew in advance that it is still worse when others are present.

"Even morphine again . . . . to get a little sleep! . . . . I will tell him, tell the doctor, to find something else. It is impossible, impossible so."

One hour, two hours, would pass in this way. But there! the bell in the corridor. Perhaps it is the doctor. Exactly: it is the doctor, fresh, hearty, portly, jovial, with an expression as if he said, "You may feel apprehension of something or other, but we will immediately straighten things out for you."

The doctor knows that this expression is not appropriate here; but he has already put it on once for all, and he cannot rid himself of it—like a man who has put on his dress-coat in the morning, and gone to make calls.

The doctor rubs his hands with an air of hearty assurance.

"I am cold. A healthy frost. Let me get warm a little," says he, with just the expression that signifies that all he needs is to wait until he gets warmed a little, and, when he is warmed, then he will straighten things out.

"Well, now, how goes it?"

Ivan Ilyitch feels that the doctor wants to say, "How go your little affairs?" but that he feels that it is impossible to say so; and he says, "What sort of a night did you have?"

Ivan Ilyitch would look at the doctor with an expression which seemed to ask the question, "Are you never ashamed of lying?"

But the doctor has no desire to understand his question.

And Ivan Ilyitch *says:*—

"It was just horrible! The pain does not cease, does not disappear. If you could only give me something for it!"

"That is always the way with you sick folks! Well, now, it seems to me I am warm enough; even the most particular Praskovia Feodorovna would not find anything to take exception to in my temperature. Well, now, how are you really?"

And the doctor shakes hands with him.

And, laying aside his former jocularity, the doctor begins with serious mien to examine the sick man, his pulse and temperature, and he renews the tappings and the auscultation.

Ivan Ilyitch knew for a certainty, and beyond peradventure, that all this was nonsense and foolish deception; but when the doctor, on his knees, leaned over toward him, applying his ear, now higher up, now lower down, and with most sapient mien performed various gymnastic evolutions on him, Ivan Ilyitch succumbed to him, as once he succumbed to the discourses of the lawyers, even when he knew perfectly well that they were deceiving him, and why they were deceiving him.

The doctor, still on his knees on the divan, was still performing the auscultation, when at the door were heard the rustle of Praskovia Feodorovna's silk dress, and her words of blame to Piotr because he had not informed her of the doctor's visit.

She came in, kissed her husband, and immediately began to explain that she had been up a long time; and only through a misunderstanding she had not been there when the doctor came.

Ivan Ilyitch looked at her, observed her from head to foot, and felt a secret indignation at her fairness and her plumpness, and the cleanliness of her hands, her neck, her glossy hair, and the brilliancy of her eyes, brimming with life. He hated her with all the strength of his soul, and her touch made him suffer an actual paroxysm of hatred of her.

Her attitude toward him and his malady was the same as before. Just as the doctor had formulated his treatment of his patient and could not change it, so she had formulated her treatment of him, making him feel that he was not doing what he ought to do, and was himself to blame; and she liked to reproach him for this, and she could not change her attitude toward him.

"Now, just see! he does not heed, he does not take his medicine regularly; and, above all, he lies in a position that is surely bad for him— his feet up."

She related how he made Gerasim hold his legs.

The doctor listened with a disdainfully good-natured smile, as much as to say:—

"What is to be done about it, pray? These sick folks are always conceiving some such foolishness. But you must let it go."

When the examination was over, the doctor looked at his watch; and then Praskovia Feodorovna declared to Ivan Ilyitch that, whether he was willing or not, she was going that very day to call in the celebrated doctor to come and have an examination and consultation with Mikhaïl Danilovitch—that was the name of their ordinary doctor.

"Now, don't oppose it, please. I am doing this for my own self," she said ironically, giving him to understand that she did it all for him, and only on this account did not allow him the right to oppose her.

He said nothing, and frowned. He felt that this lie surrounding him was so complicated that it was now hard to escape from it.

She did all this for him, only in her own interest; and she said that she was doing it for him, while she was in reality doing it for herself, as some incredible thing, so that he was forced to take it in its opposite sense.

The celebrated doctor, in fact, came about half-past eleven. Once more they had auscultations; and learned discussions took place before him, or in the next room, about his kidney, about the blind intestine, and questions and answers in such a learned form that again the place of the real question of life and death, which now alone faced him, was driven away by the question of the kidney and the blind intestine, which were not acting as became them, and on which Mikhaïl Danilovitch and the celebrity were to fall instantly and compel to attend to their duties.

The famous doctor took leave with a serious but not hopeless expression. And in reply to the timid question which Ivan Ilyitch's eyes, shining with fear and hope, asked of him, whether there was a possibility of his getting well, it replied that it could not vouch for it, but there was a possibility.

The look of hope with which Ivan Ilyitch followed the doctor was so pathetic that Praskovia Feodorovna, seeing it, even wept, as she went out of the library door in order to give the celebrated doctor his honorarium.

The raising of his spirits, caused by the doctor's hopefulness, was but temporary. Again the same room, the same pictures, curtains, wall-paper, vials, and his aching, pain-broken body. And Ivan Ilyitch began to groan. They gave him a subcutaneous injection, and he fell asleep.

When he woke up it was beginning to grow dusky. They brought him his dinner. He forced himself to eat a little *bouillon*. And again the same monotony, and again the advancing night.

About seven o'clock, after dinner, Praskovia Feodorovna came into his room, dressed as for a party, with her exuberant bosom swelling in her stays, and with traces of powder on her face. She had already that morning told him that they were going to the theater. Sarah Bernhardt had come to town, and they had a box which he had insisted on their taking.

Now he had forgotten about that, and her toilet offended him. But he concealed his vexation when he recollected that he himself had insisted on their taking a box, and going, on the ground that it would be an instructive, esthetic enjoyment for the children.

Praskovia Feodorovna came in self-satisfied, but, as it were, feeling a little to blame. She sat down, asked after his health, as he saw, only for the sake of asking, and not so as to learn, knowing that there was nothing to learn, and began to say what was incumbent on her to say,—that she would not have gone for anything, but that they had taken the box; and that Elen and her daughter and Petrishchef—the examining magistrate, her daughter's betrothed—were going, and it was impossible to let them go alone, but that it would have been more agreeable to her to stay at home with him. Only he should be sure to follow the doctor's prescriptions in her absence.

"Yes—and Feodor Petrovitch"—the betrothed—"wanted to come in. May he? And Liza!"

"Let them come."

The daughter came in, in evening dress, with her fair young body,—her body that made his anguish more keen. But she paraded it before him, strong, healthy, evidently in love, and irritated against the disease, the suffering, and death which stood in the way of her happiness.

Feodor Petrovitch also entered, in his dress-coat, with curly hair *à la Capoul*, with long, sinewy neck tightly incased in a white standing collar, with a huge white bosom, and his long, muscular legs in tight black trousers, with a white glove on one hand, and with an opera hat.

Immediately behind him, almost unnoticed, came the gymnasium scholar, in his new uniform, poor little fellow, with gloves on, and with that terrible blue circle under the eyes, the meaning of which Ivan Ilyitch understood.

He always felt a pity for his son. And terrible was his timid and compassionate glance. With the exception of Gerasim, Vasya alone, it seemed to Ivan Ilyitch, understood and pitied him.

All sat down; again they asked after his health. Silence ensued. Liza asked her mother if she had the opera-glasses. A dispute arose between mother and daughter as to who had mislaid them. It was a disagreeable episode.

Feodor Petrovitch asked Ivan Ilyitch if he had seen Sarah Bernhardt. Ivan Ilyitch did not at first understand his question, but in a moment he said:—

"No . . . . why, have you seen her yet?"

"Yes, in 'Adrienne Lecouvreur.'"

Praskovia Feodorovna said that she was especially good in that. The daughter disagreed with her. A conversation arose about the grace and realism of her acting,—the same conversation, which is always and forever one and the same thing.

In the midst of the conversation, Feodor Petrovitch glanced at Ivan Ilyitch, and grew silent. The others glanced at him, and grew silent. Ivan Ilyitch was looking straight ahead with gleaming eyes, evidently indignant at them. Some one had to extricate them from their embarrassment, but there seemed to be no way out of it. No one spoke; and a panic seized them all, lest suddenly this ceremonial lie should somehow be shattered, and the absolute truth become manifest to all.

Liza was the first to speak. She broke the silence. She wished to hide what all felt, but she betrayed it.

"One thing is certain,—*if we are going*, it is time," she said, glancing at her watch, her father's gift; and giving the young man a sign, scarcely perceptible, and yet understood by him, she smiled, and arose in her rustling dress.

All arose, said good-by, and went.

When they had gone, Ivan Ilyitch thought that he felt easier: the lying was at an end; it had gone with them; but the pain remained. Always this same pain, always this same terror, made it hard as hard could be. There was no easing of it. It grew ever worse, always worse.

Again minute after minute dragged by, hour after hour, forever the same monotony, and forever endless, and forever more terrible—the inevitable end.

"Yes, send me Gerasim," was his reply to Piotr's question.

CHAPTER IX

Late at night his wife returned. She came in on her tiptoes, but he heard her; he opened his eyes, and quickly closed them again. She wanted to send Gerasim away, and sit with him herself. He opened his eyes, and said:—

"No, go away."

"You suffer very much."

"It makes no difference."

"Take some opium."

He consented, and drank it. She went.

Until three o'clock he was in a painful sleep. It seemed to him that they were forcing him cruelly into a narrow sack, black and deep; and they kept crowding him down, but could not force him in. And this performance, horrible for him, was accompanied with anguish. And he was afraid, and yet wished to get in, and struggled against it, and yet tried to help.

And here suddenly he broke through, and fell . . . . and awoke.

There was Gerasim still sitting at his feet on the bed, dozing peacefully, patiently.

But he was lying there with his emaciated legs in stockings resting on his shoulders, the same candle with its shade, and the same never ending pain.

"Go away, Gerasim," he whispered.

"It's nothing; I will sit here a little while."

"No, go away."

He took down his legs, lay on his side on his arm, and began to pity himself. He waited only until Gerasim had gone into the next room, and then he no longer tried to control himself, but wept like a child. He wept over his helplessness, over his terrible loneliness, over the cruelty of men, over the cruelty of God, over the absence of God.

"Why hast Thou done this? Why didst Thou place me here? Why, why dost Thou torture me so horribly?"

He expected no reply; and he wept because there was none, and could be none. The pain seized him again; but he did not stir, did not call. He said to himself:—

"There, now again, now strike! But why? What have I done to Thee? Why is it?"

Then he became silent; ceased not only to weep, ceased to breathe, and became all attention: as it were, he heard, not a voice speaking with sounds, but the voice of his soul, the tide of his thoughts, arising in him.

"What dost thou need?" was the first clear concept possible to be expressed in words which he heard.

" 'What dost thou need? What dost thou need?' " he said to himself. "What? Freedom from suffering. To live," he replied.

And again he gave his attention, with such effort that already he did not even notice his pain.

"To live? how live?" asked the voice of his soul.

"Yes, to live as I used to live—well, pleasantly."

"How didst thou live before when thou didst live well and pleasantly?" asked the voice.

And he began to call up in his imagination the best moments of his pleasant life. But, strangely enough, all these best moments of his pleasant life seemed to him absolutely different from what they had seemed then, —all, except the earliest remembrances of his childhood. There, in childhood, was something really pleasant, which would give new zest to life if it were to return. But the person who had enjoyed that pleasant existence was no more; it was as if it were the remembrance of some one else.

As soon as the period began which had produced the present *he*, Ivan Ilyitch, all the pleasures which seemed such then, now in his eyes dwindled away, and changed into something of no account, and even disgusting.

And the farther he departed from infancy, and the nearer he came to the present, so much the more unimportant and dubious were the pleasures.

This began in the law-school. There was still something even then which was truly good; then there was gayety, there was friendship, there were hopes. But in the upper classes these good moments became rarer.

Then, in the time of his first service at the governor's, again appeared good moments; these were the recollections of love for a woman. Then all this became confused, and the happy time grew less. The nearer he came to the present, the worse it grew, and still worse and worse it grew.

"My marriage . . . . so unexpected, and disillusionment and my wife's breath, and sensuality, hypocrisy! And this dead service, and these labors for money; and thus one year, and two, and ten, and twenty,— and always the same thing. And the longer it went, the more dead it became.

"It is as if all the time I were going down the mountain, while thinking that I was climbing it. So it was. According to public opinion, I was climbing the mountain; and all the time my life was gliding away from under my feet. . . . And here it is already . . . . die!

"What is this? Why? It cannot be! It cannot be that life has been so irrational, so disgusting. But even if it is so disgusting and irrational, still, why die, and die in such agony? There is no reason.

"Can it be that I did not live as I ought?" suddenly came into his head. "But how can that be, when I have done all that it was my duty to do?" he asked himself. And immediately he put away this sole explanation of the enigma of life and death as something absolutely impossible.

"What dost thou wish now?—To live? To live how? To live as thou livest in court when the usher proclaims, 'The court is coming! the court is coming'?

"The court is coming—the court," he repeated to himself. "Here it is, the court. Yes; but I am not guilty," he cried with indignation. "What for?"

And he ceased to weep; and, turning his face to the wall, he began to think about that one thing, and that alone. "Why, wherefore, all this horror?"

But, in spite of all his thoughts, he received no answer. And when the thought occurred to him, as it had often occurred to him, that all this came from the fact that he had not lived as he should, he instantly remembered all the correctness of his life, and he drove away this strange thought.

CHAPTER X

Thus two weeks longer passed. Ivan Ilyitch no longer got up from the divan. He did not wish to lie in bed, and he lay on the divan. And, lying almost all the time with his face to the wall, he still suffered in solitude the same inexplicable sufferings, and still thought in solitude the same inexplicable thought.

"What is this? Is it true that this is death?"

And an inward voice responded:—

"Yes, it is true."

"Why these torments?"

And the voice responded:—

"But it is so. There is no why."

Farther and beyond this, there was nothing.

From the very beginning of his malady, from the time when Ivan Ilyitch for the first time went to the doctor, his life was divided into two conflicting tendencies, alternately succeeding each other. Now it was despair, and the expectation of an incomprehensible and frightful death; now it was hope, and the observation of the functional activity of his body, so full of interest for him. Now before his eyes was the kidney, or the intestine, which, for the time being, failed to fulfil its duty. Then it was that incomprehensible, horrible death, from which it was impossible for any one to escape.

These two mental states, from the very beginning of his illness, kept alternating with one another. But the farther the illness progressed, the more dubious and fantastical became his ideas about the kidney, and the more real his consciousness of approaching death.

He had but to call to mind what he had been three months before, and what he was now, to call to mind with what regularity he had been descending the mountain; and that was sufficient for all possibility of hope to be dispelled.

During the last period of this solitude through which he was passing, as he lay with his face turned to the back of the divan,—a solitude amid a populous city, and amid his numerous circle of friends and family,—a solitude deeper than which could not be found anywhere, either in the depths of the sea, or in the earth,—during the last period of this terrible solitude, Ivan Ilyitch lived only by imagination in the past.

One after another, the pictures of his past life arose before him. They always began with the time nearest to the present, and went back to the very remotest,—to his childhood, and there they rested.

If Ivan Ilyitch remembered the stewed prunes which they had given him to eat that very day, then he remembered the raw, puckery French prunes of his childhood, their peculiar taste, and the abundant flow of saliva caused by the stone. And in connection with these recollections of taste, started a whole series of recollections of that time,—his nurse, his brother, his toys.

"I must not think about these things; it is too painful," said Ivan Ilyitch to himself. And again he transported himself to the present,—the button on the back of the divan, and the wrinkles of the morocco. "Morocco is costly, not durable. There was a quarrel about it. But there was some other morocco, and some other quarrel, when we tore father's portfolio and got punished, and mamma brought us some tarts."

And again his thoughts reverted to childhood; and again it was painful to Ivan Ilyitch, and he tried to avoid it, and think of something else.

And again, together with this current of recollections, there passed through his mind another current of recollections about the progress and rise of his disease. Here, also, according as he went back, there was more and more of life. There was more, also, of excellence in life, and more of life itself. And the two were confounded.

"Just as this agony goes from worse to worse, so also all my life has gone from worse to worse," he thought. "One shining point, there back in the distance, at the beginning of life; and then all growing blacker and blacker, swifter and swifter, in inverse proportion to the square of the distance from death," thought Ivan Ilyitch.

And the comparison of a stone falling with accelerating rapidity occurred to his mind. Life, a series of increasing tortures, always speeding swifter and swifter to the end,—the most horrible torture.

"I am falling." . . .

He shuddered, he tossed, he wished to resist it. But he already knew that it was impossible to resist; and again, with eyes weary of looking, but still not able to resist looking at what was before him, he stared at the back of the divan, and waited, waited for this frightful fall, shock, and destruction.

"It is impossible to resist," he said to himself. "But can I not know the wherefore of it? Even that is impossible. It might be explained by saying that I had not lived as I ought. But it is impossible to acknowledge that," he said to himself, recollecting all the legality, the uprightness, the propriety of his life.

"It is impossible to admit that," he said to himself, with a smile on his lips, as if some one were to see that smile of his, and be deceived by it.

"No explanation! torture, death . . . . why?"

CHAPTER XI

Thus passed two weeks. In these weeks, there occurred an event desired by Ivan Ilyitch and his wife. Petrishchef made a formal proposal. This took place in the evening. On the next day, Praskovia Feodorovna went to her husband, meditating in what way to explain to him Feodor Petrovitch's proposition; but that very same night, a change for the worse had taken place in Ivan Ilyitch's condition. Praskovia Feodorovna found him on the same divan, but in a new position. He was lying on his back; he was groaning, and looking straight up with a fixed stare.

She began to speak about medicines. He turned his eyes on her. She did not finish saying what she had begun, so great was the hatred against her expressed in that look.

"For Christ's sake, let me die in peace!" said he.

She was about to go out; but just at this instant the daughter came in, and came near to wish him good-morning. He looked at his daughter as he had looked at his wife, and, in reply to her questions about his health, told her dryly that he would quickly relieve them all of his presence. Neither mother nor daughter said anything more; but they sat for a few moments longer, and then went out.

"What are we to blame for?" said Liza to her mother. "As if we had made him so! I am sorry for papa, but why should he torment us?"

At the usual time the doctor came. Ivan Ilyitch answered "yes," "no," not taking his angry eyes from him; and at last he said:—

"Now see here, you know that you don't help any, so leave me!"

"We can appease your sufferings," said the doctor.

"You cannot even do that; leave me!"

The doctor went into the drawing-room, and advised Praskovia Feodorovna that it was very serious, and that there was only one means— opium—of appeasing his sufferings, which must be terrible.

The doctor said that his physical sufferings were terrible, and this was true; but more terrible than his physical sufferings were his moral sufferings, and in this was his chief torment.

His moral sufferings consisted in the fact that that very night, as he looked at Gerasim's sleepy, good-natured face, with its high cheek-bones, it had suddenly come into his head:—

"But how is it if in reality my whole life, my conscious life, has been wrong?"

It came into his head that what had shortly before presented itself to him as an absolute impossibility—that he had not lived his life as he ought —might be true. It came into his head that the scarcely recognizable desires to struggle against what men highest in position considered good,— desires scarcely recognizable, which he had immediately banished,— might be true, and all the rest might be wrong. And his service, and his course of life, and his family, and these interests of society and office—all this might be wrong.

He endeavored to defend all this before himself. And suddenly he realized all the weakness of what he was defending. And there was nothing to defend.

"But if this is so," he said to himself, "and I am departing from life with the consciousness that I have wasted all that was given me, and that it is impossible to rectify it, what then?"

He lay flat on his back, and began entirely anew to examine his whole life.

When in the morning he saw the lackey, then his wife, then his daughter, then the doctor, each one of their motions, each one of their words, confirmed for him the terrible truth which had been disclosed to him that night. He saw in them himself, all that for which he had lived; and he saw clearly that all this was wrong, all this was a terrible, monstrous lie, concealing both life and death.

This consciousness increased his physical sufferings, added tenfold to them. He groaned and tossed, and threw off the clothes. It seemed to him that they choked him, and loaded him down.

And that was why he detested them.

They gave him a great dose of opium; he became unconscious, but at dinner-time the same thing began again. He drove them from him, and threw himself from place to place.

His wife came to him, and said:—

"Jean, darling, do this for me (*for me!*). It cannot do any harm, and sometimes it helps. Why, it is a mere nothing. And often well people try it."

He opened his eyes wide.

"What? Take the sacrament? Why? It's not necessary. But, however . . . ."

She burst into tears.

"Will you, my dear? I will get our priest. He is so sweet!"

"Excellent! very good," he continued.

When the priest came, and confessed him, he became calmer, felt, as it were, an alleviation of his doubts, and consequently of his sufferings; and there came a moment of hope. He again began to think about the blind intestine and the possibility of curing it. He took the sacrament with tears in his eyes.

When they put him to bed after the sacrament, he felt comfortable for the moment, and once more hope of life appeared. He began to think of the operation which they had proposed.

"I want to live, to live," he said to himself.

His wife came to congratulate him. She said the customary words, and added:—

"You feel better, don't you?"

Without looking at her, he said:—

"Yes."

Her hope, her temperament, the expression of her face, the sound of her voice, all said to him one thing:—

"Wrong! all that for which thou hast lived, and thou livest, is falsehood, deception, hiding from thee life and death."

And as soon as he expressed this thought, his exasperation returned, and, together with his exasperation, the physical, tormenting agony; and, with the agony, the consciousness of inevitable death close at hand. Something new took place: a screw seemed to turn in him, twinging pain to show through him, and his breathing was constricted.

The expression of his face, when he said "yes," was terrible. After he had said that "yes," he looked straight into her face, and then, with extraordinary quickness for one so weak, he threw himself on his face and cried:—

"Go away! go away! leave me!"

CHAPTER XII

From that moment began that shriek that did not cease for three days, and was so terrible that, when it was heard two rooms away, it was impossible to hear it without terror. At the moment that he answered his wife, he felt that he was lost, and there was no return, that the end had come, absolutely the end, and the question was not settled, but remained a question.

"U! uu! u!" he cried in varying intonations. He began to shriek, "*N'ye khotchu*—I won't;" and thus he kept up the cry on the letter *u*.

Three whole days, during which for him there was no time, he struggled in that black sack into which an invisible, invincible power was thrusting him. He fought as one condemned to death fights in the hands of the hangman, knowing that he cannot save himself, and at every moment he felt that, notwithstanding all the violence of his struggle, he was nearer and nearer to that which terrified him. He felt that his suffering consisted, both in the fact that he was being thrust into that black hole, and still more that he could not make his way through into it. What hindered him from making his way through was the confession that his life had been good. This justification of his life caught him and did not let him advance, and more than all else tormented him.

Suddenly some force knocked him in the breast, in the side, still more forcibly compressed his breath; he was hurled through the hole, and there at the bottom of the hole some light seemed to shine on him. It happened to him as it sometimes does on a railway carriage when you think that you are going forward, but are really going backward, and suddenly recognize the true direction.

"Yes, all was wrong," he said to himself; "but that is nothing. I might, I might have done right. What is right?" he asked himself, and suddenly stopped.

This was at the end of the third day, two hours before his death. At this very same time the little student noiselessly stole into his father's room, and approached his bed. The moribund was continually shrieking desperately, and tossing his arms. His hand struck upon the little student's head. The little student seized it, pressed it to his lips, and burst into tears.

It was at this very same time that Ivan Ilyitch fell through, saw the light, and it was revealed to him that his life had not been as it ought, but that still it was possible to repair it. He was just asking himself, "What is right?" and stopped to listen.

Then he felt that some one was kissing his hand. He opened his eyes, and looked at his son. He felt sorry for him. His wife came to him. He looked at her. With open mouth, and with her nose and cheeks wet with tears, with an expression of despair, she was looking at him. He felt sorry for her.

"Yes, I am a torment to them," he thought. "I am sorry for them, but they will be better off when I am dead."

He wanted to express this, but he had not the strength to say it. "However, why should I say it? I must do it."

He pointed out his son to his wife by a glance, and said:—

"Take him away . . . . I am sorry . . . . and for thee."

He wanted to say also, "*Prosti*—Forgive," but he said, "*Propusti*—Let it pass;" and, not having the strength to correct himself, he waved his hand, knowing that he would comprehend who had the right.

And suddenly it became clear to him that what oppressed him, and was hidden from him, suddenly was lighted up for him all at once, and on two sides, on ten sides, on all sides.

He felt sorry for them; he felt that he must do something to make it less painful for them. To free them, and free himself, from these torments, "How good and how simple!" he thought.

"But the pain," he asked himself, "where is it?—Here, now, where art thou, pain?"

He began to listen.

"Yes, here it is! Well, then, do your worst, pain!"

"And death? where is it?"

He tried to find his former customary fear of death, and could not. "Where is death? What is it?"

There was no fear, because there was no death.

In place of death was light!

"Here is something like!" he suddenly said aloud. "What joy!"

For him all this passed in a single instant, and the significance of this instant did not change.

For those who stood by his side, his death-agony was prolonged two hours more. In his breast something bubbled up, his emaciated body shuddered. Then more and more rarely came the bubbling and the rattling.

"It is all over," said some one above him.

He heard these words, and repeated them in his soul.

"It is over! death!" he said to himself. "It does not exist more."

He drew in one more breath, stopped in the midst of it, stretched himself, and died.

AN ESSAY ON MAN
(Epistle I)
ALEXANDER POPE

Alexander Pope (1688–1744) was an English poet celebrated for his satirical poems such as *The Rape of the Lock* and *The Dunciad,* and for his verse translations of Classical writings, most notably the *Iliad* and the *Odyssey.* Pope is also known for his *Essay on Man,* which was written to "vindicate the ways of God to man," the *Epistle to Dr. Arbuthnot,* which defends the aims of satire, and *An Essay on Criticism,* which contains the epigrams "a little learning is a dangerous thing" and "to err is human, to forgive divine."

The *Essay on Man* presents an argument in poetic form for the necessary wisdom of God's ultimate design. Pope argues that it would be arrogant for man, with his paltry understanding, to presume to criticize the works of God. We are children in relation to the divine wisdom and must simply affirm that all events occur for some ultimate good. Despite appearances to the contrary Pope declares, "Whatever is, is right."

EPISTLE I

AWAKE, my St. John! leave all meaner things
To low ambition, and the pride of Kings.
Let us (since Life can little more supply
Than just to look about us and to die)
Expatiate free o'er all this scene of Man;
A mighty maze! but not without a plan;
A Wild, where weeds and flowers promiscuous shoot;
Or Garden, tempting with forbidden fruit.
Together let us beat this ample field,
Try what the open, what the covert yield;
The latent tracts, the giddy heights, explore
Of all who blindly creep, or sightless soar;
Eye Nature's walks, shoot Folly as it flies,
And catch the Manners living as they rise;
Laugh where we must, be candid where we can;
But vindicate the ways of God to Man.

I. Say first, of God above, or Man below,
What can we reason, but from what we know?
Of Man, what see we but his station here,
From which to reason, or to which refer?
Through worlds unnumbered though the God be known,
'Tis ours to trace him only in our own.
He, who through vast immensity can pierce,
See worlds on worlds compose one universe,

Observe how system into system runs,
What other planets circle other suns,
What varied Being peoples every star,
May tell why Heaven has made us as we are.
But of this frame the bearings, and the ties,
The strong connexions, nice dependencies,
Gradations just, has thy pervading soul
Looked through? or can a part contain the whole?
　　Is the great chain, that draws all to agree,
And drawn supports, upheld by God, or thee?

　　II. Presumptuous Man! the reason wouldst thou find,
Why formed so weak, so little, and so blind?
First, if thou canst, the harder reason guess,
Why formed no weaker, blinder, and no less?
Ask of thy mother earth, why oaks are made
Taller or stronger than the weeds they shade?
Or ask of yonder argent fields above,
Why JOVE'S satellites are less than JOVE?
　　Of Systems possible, if 'tis confest
That Wisdom infinite must form the best,
Where all must full or not coherent be,
And all that rises, rise in due degree;
Then, in the scale of reas'ning life, 'tis plain,
There must be, somewhere, such a rank as Man:
And all the question (wrangle e'er so long)
Is only this, if God has placed him wrong?
　　Respecting Man, whatever wrong we call,
May, must be right, as relative to all.
In human works, though laboured on with pain,
A thousand movements scarce one purpose gain;
In God's, one single can its end produce;
Yet serves to second too some other use.
So Man, who here seems principal alone,
Perhaps acts second to some sphere unknown,
Touches some wheel, or verges to some goal;
'Tis but a part we see, and not a whole.
　　When the proud steed shall know why Man restrains
His fiery course, or drives him o'er the plains:
When the dull Ox, why now he breaks the clod,
Is now a victim, and now Egypt's God:
Then shall Man's pride and dullness comprehend
His actions', passions', being's, use and end;
Why doing, suffering, checked, impelled; and why
This hour a slave, the next a deity.

Then say not Man's imperfect, Heaven in fault;
Say rather, Man's as perfect as he ought:
His knowledge measured to his state and place;
His time a moment, and a point his space.
If to be perfect in a certain sphere,
What matter, soon or late, or here or there?
The blest to day is as completely so,
As who began a thousand years ago.

III. Heaven from all creatures hides the book of Fate,
All but the page prescribed, their present state:
From brutes what men, from men what spirits know:
Or who could suffer Being here below?
The lamb thy riot dooms to bleed to-day,
Had he thy Reason, would he skip and play?
Pleased to the last, he crops the flowery food,
And licks the hand just raised to shed his blood.
Oh blindness to the future! kindly given,
That each may fill the circle marked by Heaven:
Who sees with equal eye, as God of all,
A hero perish, or a sparrow fall,
Atoms or systems into ruin hurled,
And now a bubble burst, and now a world.
Hope humbly then; with trembling pinions soar;
Wait the great teacher Death; and God adore.
What future bliss, he gives not thee to know,
But gives that Hope to be thy blessing now.
Hope springs eternal in the human breast:
Man never Is, but always To be blest:
The soul, uneasy and confined from home,
Rests and expatiates in a life to come.
Lo, the poor Indian! whose untutored mind
Sees God in clouds, or hears him in the wind;
His soul, proud Science never taught to stray
Far as the solar walk, or milky way;
Yet simple Nature to his hope has given,
Behind the cloud-topt hill, an humbler heaven;
Some safer world in depth of woods embraced,
Some happier island in the watery waste,
Where slaves once more their native land behold,
No fiends torment, no Christians thirst for gold.
To Be, contents his natural desire,
He asks no Angel's wing, no Seraph's fire;
But thinks, admitted to that equal sky,
His faithful dog shall bear him company.

IV. Go, wiser thou! and, in thy scale of sense,
Weigh thy Opinion against Providence;
Call imperfection what thou fanciest such,
Say, here he gives too little, there too much:
Destroy all Creatures for thy sport or gust,
Yet cry, If Man's unhappy, God's unjust;
If Man alone engross not Heaven's high care,
Alone made perfect here, immortal there:
Snatch from his hand the balance and the rod,
Re-judge his justice, be the God of God.
In Pride, in reas'ning Pride, our error lies;
All quit their sphere, and rush into the skies.
Pride still is aiming at the blest abodes,
Men would be Angels, Angels would be Gods.
Aspiring to be Gods, if Angels fell,
Aspiring to be Angels, Men rebel:
And who but wishes to invert the laws
Of Order, sins against th' Eternal Cause.

V. Ask for what end the heavenly bodies shine,
Earth for whose use? Pride answers, " 'Tis for mine:
For me kind Nature wakes her genial Power,
Suckles each herb, and spreads out every flower;
Annual for me, the grape, the rose renew
The juice nectareous, and the balmy dew;
For me, the mine a thousand treasures brings;
For me, health gushes from a thousand springs;
Seas roll to waft me, suns to light me rise;
My foot-stool earth, my canopy the skies."
But errs not Nature from this gracious end,
From burning suns when livid deaths descend,
When earthquakes swallow, or when tempests sweep
Towns to one grave, whole nations to the deep?
"No," ('tis replied) "the first Almighty Cause
Acts not by partial, but by gen'ral laws;
Th' exceptions few; some change since all began:
And what created perfect?" —Why then Man?
If the great end be human Happiness,
Then Nature deviates; and can Man do less?
As much that end a constant course requires
Of showers and sun-shine, as of Man's desires;
As much eternal springs and cloudless skies,
As Men for ever temp'rate, calm, and wise.
If plagues or earthquakes break not Heaven's design,
Why then a Borgia, or a Catiline?

Who knows but he, whose hand the lightning forms,
Who heaves old Ocean, and who wings the storms;
Pours fierce Ambition in a Caesar's mind,
Or turns young Ammon loose to scourge mankind?
From pride, from pride, our very reasoning springs;
Account for moral, as for natural things:
Why charge we Heaven in those, in these acquit?
In both, to reason right is to submit.
    Better for Us, perhaps, it might appear,
Were there all harmony, all virtue here;
That never air or ocean felt the wind;
That never passion discomposed the mind.
But ALL subsists by elemental strife;
And Passions are the elements of Life.
The gen'ral ORDER, since the whole began,
Is kept in Nature, and is kept in Man.

    VI. What would this Man? Now upward will he soar,
And little less than Angel, would be more;
Now looking downwards, just as grieved appears
To want the strength of bulls, the fur of bears.
Made for his use all creatures if he call,
Say what their use, had he the powers of all?
Nature to these, without profusion, kind,
The proper organs, proper powers assigned;
Each seeming want compensated of course,
Here with degrees of swiftness, there of force;
All in exact proportion to the state;
Nothing to add, and nothing to abate.
Each beast, each insect, happy in its own:
Is heaven unkind to Man, and Man alone?
Shall he alone, whom rational we call,
Be pleased with nothing, if not blessed with all?
    The bliss of Man (could Pride that blessing find)
Is not to act or think beyond mankind;
No powers of body or of soul to share,
But what his nature and his state can bear.
Why has not Man a microscopic eye?
For this plain reason, Man is not a Fly.
Say what the use, were finer optics given,
T'inspect a mite, not comprehend the heaven?
Or touch, if tremblingly alive all o'er,
To smart and agonize at every pore? .
Or quick effluvia darting through the brain,
Die of a rose in aromatic pain?

If nature thundered in his opening ears,
And stunned him with the music of the spheres,
How would he wish that Heaven had left him still
The whisp'ring Zephyr, and the purling rill?
Who finds not Providence all good and wise,
Alike in what it gives, and what denies?

    VII. Far as Creation's ample range extends,
The scale of sensual, mental powers ascends:
Mark how it mounts, to Man's imperial race,
From the green myriads in the peopled grass:
What modes of sight betwixt each wide extreme,
The mole's dim curtain, and the lynx's beam:
Of smell, the headlong lioness between,
And hound sagacious on the tainted green:
Of hearing, from the life that fills the Flood,
To that which warbles through the vernal wood:
The spider's touch, how exquisitely fine!
Feels at each thread, and lives along the line:
In the nice bee, what sense so subtly true
From pois'nous herbs extracts the healing dew?
How Instinct varies in the grov'iling swine,
Compared, half-reas'ning elephant, with thine!
'Twixt that, and Reason, what a nice barrier,
For ever sep'rate, yet for ever near!
Remembrance and Reflection how allied;
What thin partitions Sense from Thought divide:
And Middle natures, how they long to join,
Yet never pass th' insuperable line!
Without this just gradation, could they be
Subjected, these to those, or all to thee?
The powers of all subdued by thee alone,
Is not thy Reason all these powers in one?

    VIII. See, through this air, this ocean, and this earth,
All matter quick, and bursting into birth.
Above, how high, progressive life may go!
Around, how wide! how deep extend below!
Vast chain of Being! which from God began,
Natures ethereal, human, angel, man,
Beast, bird, fish, insect, what no eye can see,
No glass can reach; from Infinite to thee,
From thee to Nothing.—On superior powers
Were we to press, inferior might on ours:
Or in the full creation leave a void,
Where, one step broken, the great scale's destroyed:

From Nature's chain whatever link you strike,
Tenth or ten thousandth, breaks the chain alike.
     And, if each system in gradation roll
Alike essential to th' amazing Whole,
The least confusion but in one, not all
That system only, but the Whole must fall.
Let Earth unbalanced from her orbit fly,
Planets and Suns run lawless through the sky;
Let ruling Angels from their spheres be hurled,
Being on Being wrecked, and world on world;
Heaven's whole foundations to their centre nod,
And Nature tremble to the throne of God.
All this dread ORDER break—for whom? for thee?
Vile worm!—Oh Madness! Pride! Impiety!

     IX. What if the foot, ordained the dust to tread,
Or hand, to toil, aspired to be the head?
What if the head, the eye, or ear repined
To serve mere engines to the ruling Mind?
Just as absurd for any part to claim
To be another, in this gen'ral frame:
Just as absurd, to mourn the tasks or pains,
The great directing MIND of ALL ordains.
     All are but parts of one stupendous whole,
Whose body Nature is, and God the soul;
That, changed through all, and yet in all the same;
Great in the earth, as in th' ethereal frame;
Warms in the sun, refreshes in the breeze,
Glows in the stars, and blossoms in the trees,
Lives through all life, extends through all extent,
Spreads undivided, operates unspent;
Breathes in our soul, informs our mortal part,
As full, as perfect, in a hair as heart:
As full, as perfect, in vile Man that mourns,
As the rapt Seraph that adores and burns:
To him no high, no low, no great, no small;
He fills, he bounds, connects, and equals all.

     X. Cease then, nor ORDER Imperfection name:
Our proper bliss depends on what we blame.
Know thy own point: This kind, this due degree
Of blindness, weakness, Heaven bestows on thee.
Submit.—In this, or any other sphere,
Secure to be as blest as thou canst bear:
Safe in the hand of one disposing Power,
Or in the natal, or the mortal hour.

All Nature is but Art, unknown to thee;
All Chance, Direction, which thou canst not see;
All Discord, Harmony not understood;
All partial Evil, universal Good:
And, spite of Pride, in erring Reason's spite,
One truth is clear, whatever is, is RIGHT.

DISCOURSE ON METAPHYSICS
GOTTFRIED WILHELM LEIBNIZ
(trans. by George R. Montgomery)

Gottfried Wilhelm Leibniz (1646–1716) was a German philosopher who is most notable for his theory of "monads," simple substances without parts which he identified as the basic constituents of the universe. Leibniz is also known for his work in symbolic logic and calculus, but his main contribution to philosophy lies in the area of metaphysics as contained in the *Monadology* and *Discourse on Metaphysics.*

In the following section of the *Discourse,* Leibniz argues for the ideal character of this world from the necessary perfection of God. As in the *Theodicy,* he presents a dogmatic argument reminiscent of medieval theology, which begins with a definition of God as an absolutely perfect being and deduces that therefore the universe has been created in the most desirable way. Man lives in "the best of all possible worlds," Leibniz's famous dictum states, one that ex *hypothesi* could not conceivably be better than it is. In effect, Leibniz is denying the evidence of our senses and the judgment that certain events are genuinely bad.

In answer to this we could argue that if we cannot judge evil for what it is, then we cannot judge good for what it is either. If judgment is undermined, then God certainly cannot be blamed, but, equally well, he cannot be praised; the argument is a double-edged sword that cuts both ways. Nevertheless, Leibniz's theory may be taken as an outstanding example of an argument from the benevolent nature of God to the essential goodness of his creation.

I. *Concerning the divine perfection and that God does everything in the most desirable way.*

The conception of God which is the most common and the most full of meaning is expressed well enough in the words: God is an absolutely perfect being. The implications, however, of these words fail to receive sufficient consideration. For instance, there are many different kinds of perfection, all of which God possesses, and each one of them pertains to him in the highest degree.

We must also know what perfection is. One thing which can surely be affirmed about it is that those forms or natures which are not susceptible of it to the highest degree, say the nature of numbers or of figures, do not permit of perfection. This is because the number which is the greatest of all (that is, the sum of all the numbers), and likewise the greatest of all figures, imply contradictions. The greatest knowledge, however, and omnipotence contain no impossibility. Consequently power and knowledge do admit of perfection, and in so far as they pertain to God they have no limits.

Whence it follows that God who possesses supreme and infinite wisdom acts in the most perfect manner not only metaphysically, but also from the moral standpoint. And with respect to ourselves it can be said that the more we are enlightened and informed in regard to the works of God the more will we be disposed to find them excellent and conforming entirely to that which we might desire.

II. *Against those who hold that there is in the works of God no goodness, or that the principles of goodness and beauty are arbitrary.*

Therefore I am far removed from the opinion of those who maintain that there are no principles of goodness or perfection in the nature of things, or in the ideas which God has about them, and who say that the works of God are good only through the formal reason that God has made them. If this position were true, God, knowing that he is the author of things, would not have to regard them afterwards and find them good, as the Holy Scripture witnesses. Such anthropological expressions are used only to let us know that excellence is recognized in regarding the works themselves, even if we do not consider their evident dependence on their author. This is confirmed by the fact that it is in reflecting upon the works that we are able to discover the one who wrought. They must therefore bear in themselves his character. I confess that the contrary opinion seems to me extremely dangerous and closely approaches that of recent innovators who hold that the beauty of the universe and the goodness which we attribute to the works of God are chimeras of human beings who think of God in human terms. In saying, therefore, that things are not good according to any standard of goodness, but simply by the will of God, it seems to me that one destroys, without realizing it, all the love of God and all his glory; for why praise him for what he has done, if he would be equally praiseworthy in doing the contrary? Where will be his justice and his wisdom if he has only a certain despotic power, if arbitrary will takes the place of reasonableness, and if in accord with the definition of tyrants, justice consists in that which is pleasing to the most powerful? Besides it seems that every act of willing supposes some reason for the willing and this reason, of course, must precede the act. This is why, accordingly, I find so strange those expressions of certain philosophers who say that the eternal truths of metaphysics and Geometry, and consequently the principles of goodness, of justice, and of perfection, are effects only of the will of God. To me it seems that all these follow from his understanding, which does not depend upon his will any more than does his essence.

III. *Against those who think that God might have made things better than he has.*

No more am I able to approve of the opinion of certain modern writers who boldly maintain that that which God has made is not perfect in the highest degree, and that he might have done better. It seems to me that the consequences of such an opinion are wholly inconsistent with the glory of God. *Uti minus malum habet rationem boni, ita minus bonum habet rationem mali.*[1] I think that one acts imperfectly if he acts with less perfection than he is capable of. To show that an architect could have done better is to find fault with his work. Furthermore this opinion is contrary to the Holy Scriptures when they assure us of the goodness of God's work. For if comparative perfection were sufficient, then in whatever way God had accomplished his work, since there is an infinitude of possible imperfections, it would always have been good in comparison with the less perfect; but a thing is little praiseworthy when it can be praised only in this way.

I believe that a great many passages from the divine writings and from the holy fathers will be found favoring my position, while hardly any will be found in favor of that of these modern thinkers. Their opinion is, in my judgment, unknown to the writers of antiquity and is a deduction based upon the too slight acquaintance which we have with the general harmony of the universe and with the hidden reasons for God's conduct. In our ignorance, therefore, we are tempted to decide audaciously that many things might have been done better.

These modern thinkers insist upon certain hardly tenable subtleties, for they imagine that nothing is so perfect that there might not have been something more perfect. This is an error. They think, indeed, that they are thus safeguarding the liberty of God. As if it were not the highest liberty to act in perfection according to the sovereign reason. For to think that God acts in anything without having any reason for his willing, even if we overlook the fact that such action seems impossible, is an opinion which conforms little to God's glory. For example, let us suppose that God chooses between A and B, and that he takes A without any reason for preferring it to B. I say that this action on the part of God is at least not praiseworthy, for all praise ought to be founded upon reason which *ex hypothesi* is not present here. My opinion is that God does nothing for which he does not deserve to be glorified.

IV. *That love for God demands on our part complete satisfaction with and acquiescence in that which he has done.*

The general knowledge of this great truth that God acts always in the most perfect and most desirable manner possible, is in my opinion the basis of the love which we owe to God in all things; for he who loves seeks his satisfaction in the felicity or perfection of the object loved and in the perfection of his actions. *Idem velle et idem nolle vera amicitia est.*[2] I believe that it is difficult to love God truly when one, having the power to change his disposition, is not disposed to wish for that which God desires.

---

1 [Editor's note: Just as the worse may have good reasons, so the less good may have bad reasons.]
2 [Editor's note: Having the same likes and dislikes makes the best friendships.]

In fact those who are not satisfied with what God does seem to me like dis-satisfied subjects whose attitude is not very different from that of rebels. I hold therefore, that on these principles, to act conformably to the love of God it is not sufficient to force oneself to be patient, we must be really satisfied with all that comes to us according to his will. I mean this acquiescence in regard to the past; for as regards the future one should not be a quietist with the arms folded, open to ridicule, awaiting that which God will do; according to the sophism which the ancients called λόγον ἀεργον, the lazy reason. It is necessary to act conformably to the pre-sumptive will of God as far as we are able to judge of it, trying with all our might to contribute to the general welfare and particularly to the orna-mentation and the perfection of that which touches us, or of that which is nigh and so to speak at our hand. For if the future shall perhaps show that God has not wished our good intention to have its way, it does not follow that he has not wished us to act as we have; on the contrary, since he is the best of all masters, he ever demands only the right intentions, and it is for him to know the hour and the proper place to let good de-signs succeed.

V. *In what the principles of the divine perfection consist, and that the simplicity of the means counterbalances the richness of the effects.*

It is sufficient therefore to have this confidence in God, that he has done everything for the best and that nothing will be able to injure those who love him. To know in particular, however, the reasons which have moved him to choose this order of the universe, to permit sin, to dispense his salutary grace in a certain manner,—this passes the capacity of a finite mind, above all when such a mind has not come into the joy of the vision of God. Yet it is possible to make some general remarks touching the course of providence in the government of things. . . .

XXX. *How God inclines our souls without necessitating them; that there are no grounds for complaint; that we must not ask why Judas sinned because this free act is contained in his concept, the only question being why Judas the sinner is admitted to existence, preferably to other possible persons; concerning the original imper-fection or limitation before the fall and concerning the different degrees of grace.*

Regarding the action of God upon the human will there are many quite different considerations which it would take too long to investigate here. Nevertheless the following is what can be said in general. God in co-operating with ordinary actions only follows the laws which he has established, that is to say, he continually preserves and produces our being so that the ideas come to us spontaneously or with freedom in that order which the concept of our individual substance carries with itself. In this concept they can be foreseen for all eternity. Furthermore, by virtue of the decree which God has made that the will shall always seek the apparent good in certain particular respects (in regard to which this apparent good always has in it something of reality expressing or imitating God's will), he, without at all necessitating our choice, determines it by that which appears most desirable. For absolutely speaking, our will as contrasted with necessity, is in a state of indifference, being able to act otherwise, or wholly to suspend its action, either alternative being and remaining possible. It therefore devolves upon the soul to be on guard against appearances, by means of a firm will, to reflect and to refuse to act or decide in certain circumstances, except after mature deliberation. It is, however, true and has been assured from all eternity that certain souls will not employ their power upon certain occasions.

But who could do more than God has done, and can such a soul complain of anything except itself? All these complaints after the deed are unjust, inasmuch as they would have been unjust before the deed. Would this soul a little before committing the sin have had the right to complain of God as though he had determined the sin. Since the determinations of God in these matters cannot be foreseen, how would the soul know that it was preordained to sin unless it had already committed the sin? It is merely a question of wishing to or not wishing to, and God could not have set an easier or juster condition. Therefore all judges without asking the reasons which have disposed a man to have an evil will, consider only how far this will is wrong. But, you object, perhaps it is ordained from all eternity that I will sin. Find your own answer. Perhaps it has not been. Now then, without asking for what you are unable to know and in regard to which you can have no light, act according to your duty and your knowledge. But, some one will object; whence comes it then that this man will assuredly do this sin? The reply is easy. It is that otherwise he would not be a man. For God foresees from all time that there will be a certain Judas, and in the concept or idea of him which God has, is contained this future free act. The only question, therefore, which remains is why this certain Judas, the betrayer who is possible only because of the idea of God, actually exists. To this question, however, we can expect no answer here on earth excepting to say in general that it is because God has found it good that he should exist notwithstanding that sin which he foresaw. This evil will be more than overbalanced. God will derive a greater good from it, and it will finally turn out that this series of events in which is included the existence of this sinner, is the most perfect among all the possible series of events. An explanation in every case of the admirable economy of this choice cannot be given while we are sojourners on earth. It is enough to know the excellence without understanding it. It is here that must be recognized *altitudinem divitiarum*, the unfathomable depth of the divine wisdom, without hesitating at a detail which involves an infinite number of considerations. It is clear, however, that God is not the cause of ill. For not only after the loss of innocence by men, has original sin possessed the soul, but even before that there was an original limitation or imperfection in the very nature of all creatures, which rendered them open to sin and able to fall. There is, therefore, no more difficulty in the supralapsarian view than there is in the other views of sin. To this also, it seems to me can be reduced the opinion of Saint Augustine and of other authors: that the root of evil is in the negativity, that is to say, in the lack or limitation of creatures which God graciously remedies by whatever degree of perfection it pleases him to give. This grace of God, whether ordinary or extraordinary has its degrees and its measures. It is always efficacious in itself to produce a certain proportionate effect and furthermore it is always sufficient not only to keep one from sin but even to effect his salvation, provided that the man co-operates with that which is in him. It has not always, however, sufficient power to overcome the inclination, for, if it did, it would no longer be limited in any way, and this superiority to limitations is reserved to that unique grace which is absolutely efficacious. This grace is always victorious whether through its own self or through the congruity of circumstances.

XXXI. *Concerning the motives of election; concerning faith foreseen and the absolute decree and that it all reduces to the question why God has chosen and resolved to admit to existence just such a possible person, whose concept includes just such a sequence of free acts and of free gifts of grace. This at once puts an end to all difficulties.*

Finally, the grace of God is wholly unprejudiced and creatures have no claim upon it. Just as it is not sufficient in accounting for God's choice in his dispensations of grace to refer to his absolute or conditional prevision of men's future actions, so it is also wrong to imagine his decrees as absolute with no reasonable motive. As concerns foreseen faith and good works, it is very true that God has elected none but those whose faith and charity he foresees, *quos se fide donaturum praescivit.* The same question, however, arises again as to why God gives to some rather than to others the grace of faith or of good works. As concerns God's ability to foresee not only the faith and good deeds, but also their material and predisposition, or that which a man on his part contributes to them (since there are as truly diversities on the part of men as on the part of grace, and a man although he needs to be aroused to good and needs to become converted, yet acts in accordance with his temperament),—as regards his ability to foresee there are many who say that God, knowing what a particular man will do without grace, that is without his extraordinary assistance, or knowing at least what will be the human contribution, resolves to give grace to those whose natural dispositions are the best, or at any rate are the least imperfect and evil. But if this were the case then the natural dispositions in so far as they were good would be like gifts of grace, since God would have given advantages to some over others; and therefore, since he would well know that the natural advantages which he had given would serve as motives for his grace or for his extraordinary assistance, would not everything be reduced to his mercy? I think, therefore, that since we do not know how much and in what way God regards natural dispositions in the dispensations of his grace, it would be safest and most exact to say, in accordance with our principles and as I have already remarked, that there must needs be among possible beings the person Peter or John whose concept or idea contains all that particular sequence of ordinary and extraordinary manifestations of grace together with the rest of the accompanying events and circumstances, and that it has pleased God to choose him among an infinite number of persons equally possible for actual existence. When we have said this there seems nothing left to ask, and all difficulties vanish. For in regard to that great and ultimate question why it has pleased God to choose him among so great a number of possible persons, it is surely unreasonable to demand more than the general reasons which we have given. The reasons in detail surpass our ken. Therefore, instead of postulating an absolute decree, which being without reason would be unreasonable, and instead of postulating reasons which do not succeed in solving the difficulties and in turn have need themselves of reasons, it will be best to say with St. Paul that there are for God's choice certain great reasons of wisdom and congruity which he follows, which reasons, however, are unknown to mortals and are founded upon the general order, whose goal is the greatest perfection of the world. This is what is meant when the motives of God's glory and of the manifestation of his justice are spoken of, as well as when men speak of his mercy, and his perfection in general; that immense vastness of wealth, in fine, with which the soul of the same St. Paul was so thrilled.

3
Evil as a Reality
to Be
Overcome

CANDIDE
VOLTAIRE
(trans. by Richard Aldington)

Voltaire (François Marie Arouet) (1694–1778) was a French dramatist, novelist, and historian of worldwide reputation who throughout his life continually advocated the ideal of humanitarian progress. In his critical and creative writings, he is known for his use of profound wit and irony to drive his points home. Plays such as *Zaïre and Alzire* were extremely popular in eighteenth-century France, and his novel *Candide* has become a classic in satirical litera-ture. Voltaire's philosophic ideas are cryptically presented in his *Philosophic Letters*.

The following selections from *Candide* illustrate the way in which Voltaire deflated the optimistic philosophy of Leibniz (and Alexander Pope) who main-tained that the world was created in an ideal form. Rather than attacking this notion by means of logical arguments, Voltaire employed a *reductio ad absurdum* approach in which he showed that human experience contradicts the view that everything happens for some good purpose.

Voltaire demonstrates his point by describing the adventures of a gullible young man named Candide (meaning sincere, naive, candid) who travels through many parts of the world and finds suffering and misery almost every-where. Candide is puzzled by his experience, because his former tutor, Pangloss (a thinly disguised caricature of German metaphysicians in general and Leibniz in particular) had taught him that everything is for the best. The facts do not fit the theory, he finds if this is the best of all possible worlds what can the worst be like? Finally, after witnessing every variety of horror from war to earthquake to *auto-da-fé* (the burning of heretics by the Inquisi-tion), Candide is led to define optimism as "the mania of maintaining that everything is well when we are wretched."

Voltaire's conclusion, however, is not a pessimistic one. The world is neither good nor bad but tolerable, and man's task is to improve the condi-tions of life through realistic action on an individual scale. "Il faut cultiver notre jardin," Voltaire advises us, and by cultivating our garden we will be opposing the evils of raw nature. The world can never be improved, however, if we deny that evil exists and assume that life on earth is perfect already.

CHAPTER I

*How Candide was brought up in a noble castle, and how he was
expelled from the same*

In the castle of Baron Thunder-ten-tronckh in Westphalia there lived
a youth, endowed by Nature with the most gentle character. His face
was the expression of his soul. His judgment was quite honest and he was
extremely simple-minded; and this was the reason, I think, that he was
named Candide. Old servants in the house suspected that he was the son
of the Baron's sister and a decent honest gentleman of the neighbourhood,
whom this young lady would never marry because he could only prove
seventy-two quarterings, and the rest of his genealogical tree was lost,
owing to the injuries of time.

The Baron was one of the most powerful lords in Westphalia, for his
castle possessed a door and windows. His Great Hall was even decorated
with a piece of tapestry. The dogs in his stable-yards formed a pack of
hounds when necessary; his grooms were his huntsmen; the village curate
was his Grand Almoner. They all called him "My Lord," and laughed
heartily at his stories.

The Baroness weighed about three hundred and fifty pounds, was
therefore greatly respected, and did the honours of the house with a
dignity which rendered her still more respectable. Her daughter Cunegonde, aged seventeen, was rosy-cheeked, fresh, plump and tempting. The
Baron's son appeared in every respect worthy of his father. The tutor
Pangloss was the oracle of the house, and little Candide followed his lessons with all the candour of his age and character.

Pangloss taught metaphysico-theologo-cosmolo-nigology. He proved ad-
mirably that there is no effect without a cause and that, in this best of all
possible worlds, My Lord the Baron's castle was the best of castles and his
wife the best of all possible Baronesses.

" 'Tis demonstrated," said he, "that things cannot be otherwise; for,
since everything is made for an end, everything is necessarily for the best
end. Observe that noses were made to wear spectacles; and so we have
spectacles. Legs were visibly instituted to be breeched, and we have
breeches. Stones were formed to be quarried and to build castles; and My
Lord has a very noble castle; the greatest Baron in the province should
have the best house; and as pigs were made to be eaten, we eat pork all
the year round; consequently, those who have asserted that all is well[1]
talk nonsense; they ought to have said that all is for the best."

Candide listened attentively and believed innocently; for he thought
Miss Cunegonde extremely beautiful, although he was never bold
enough to tell her so. He decided that after the happiness of being born
Baron of Thunder-ten-tronckh, the second degree of happiness was to be
Miss Cunegonde; the third, to see her every day; and the fourth to listen

---

[1] *Tout est bien,* all is well, said Rousseau in his famous attack on Voltaire's poem about
the Lisbon earthquake. [Richard Aldington.]

to Doctor Pangloss, the greatest philosopher of the province and there-fore of the whole world.

One day when Cunegonde was walking near the castle, in a little wood which was called The Park, she observed Doctor Pangloss in the bushes, giving a lesson in experimental physics to her mother's waiting-maid, a very pretty and docile brunette. Miss Cunegonde had a great inclination for science and watched breathlessly the reiterated experiments she wit-nessed; she observed clearly the Doctor's sufficient reason, the effects and the causes, and returned home very much excited, pensive, filled with the desire of learning, reflecting that she might be the sufficient reason of young Candide and that he might be hers.

On her way back to the castle she met Candide and blushed; Candide also blushed. She bade him good-morning in a hesitating voice; Candide replied without knowing what he was saying. Next day, when they left the table after dinner, Cunegonde and Candide found themselves behind a screen; Cunegonde dropped her handkerchief, Candide picked it up; she innocently held his hand; the young man innocently kissed the young lady's hand with remarkable vivacity, tenderness and grace; their lips met, their eyes sparkled, their knees trembled, their hands wandered. Baron Thunder-ten-tronckh passed near the screen, and, observing this cause and effect, expelled Candide from the castle by kicking him in the back-side frequently and hard. Cunegonde swooned; when she recovered her senses, the Baroness slapped her in the face; and all was in consternation in the noblest and most agreeable of all possible castles.

CHAPTER II

What happened to Candide among the Bulgarians

Candide, expelled from the earthly paradise, wandered for a long time without knowing where he was going, turning up his eyes to Heaven, gazing back frequently at the noblest of castles which held the most beautiful of young Baronesses; he lay down to sleep supperless between two furrows in the open fields; it snowed heavily in large flakes. The next morning the shivering Candide, penniless, dying of cold and exhaustion, dragged himself towards the neighbouring town, which was called Wald-berghoff-trarbk-dikdorff. He halted sadly at the door of an inn. Two men dressed in blue noticed him.

"Comrade," said one, "there's a well-built young man of the right height."

They went up to Candide and very civilly invited him to dinner.

"Gentlemen," said Candide with charming modesty, "you do me a great honour, but I have no money to pay my share."

"Ah, sir," said one of the men in blue, "persons of your figure and merit never pay anything; are you not five feet five tall?"

"Yes, gentlemen," said he, bowing, "that is my height."

"Ah, sir, come to table; we will not only pay your expenses, we will never allow a man like you to be short of money; men were only made to help each other."

"You are in the right," said Candide, "that is what Doctor Pangloss was always telling me, and I see that everything is for the best."

They begged him to accept a few crowns, he took them and wished to give them an IOU; they refused to take it and all sat down to table.

"Do you not love tenderly . . ."

"Oh, yes," said he. "I love Miss Cunegonde tenderly."

"No," said one of the gentlemen. "We were asking if you do not tenderly love the King of the Bulgarians."

"Not a bit," said he, "for I have never seen him."

"What! He is the most charming of kings, and you must drink his health."

"Oh, gladly, gentlemen."

And he drank.

"That is sufficient," he was told. "You are now the support, the aid, the defender, the hero of the Bulgarians; your fortune is made and your glory assured."

They immediately put irons on his legs and took him to a regiment. He was made to turn to the right and left, to raise the ramrod and return the ramrod, to take aim, to fire, to double up, and he was given thirty strokes with a stick; the next day he drilled not quite so badly, and received only twenty strokes; the day after, he only had ten and was looked on as a prodigy by his comrades.

Candide was completely mystified and could not make out how he was a hero. One fine spring day he thought he would take a walk, going straight ahead, in the belief that to use his legs as he pleased was a privilege of the human species as well as of animals. He had not gone two leagues when four other heroes, each six feet tall, fell upon him, bound him and dragged him back to a cell. He was asked by his judges whether he would rather be thrashed thirty-six times by the whole regiment or receive a dozen lead bullets at once in his brain. Although he protested that men's wills are free and that he wanted neither one nor the other, he had to make a choice; by virtue of that gift of God which is called *liberty*, he determined to run the gauntlet thirty-six times and actually did so twice. There were two thousand men in the regiment. That made four thousand strokes which laid bare the muscles and nerves from his neck to his backside. As they were about to proceed to a third turn, Candide, utterly exhausted, begged as a favour that they would be so kind as to smash his head; he obtained this favour; they bound his eyes and he was made to kneel down. At that moment the King of the Bulgarians came by and inquired the victim's crime; and as this King was possessed of a vast genius, he perceived from what he learned about Candide that he was a young metaphysician very ignorant in worldly matters, and therefore pardoned him with a clemency which will be praised in all newspapers and all ages. An honest surgeon healed Candide in three weeks with the ointments recommended by Dioscorides.[2] He had already regained a little skin and could walk when the King of the Bulgarians went to war with the King of the Abares.[3]

CHAPTER III

How Candide escaped from the Bulgarians and what became of him

Nothing could be smarter, more splendid, more brilliant, better drawn up than the two armies. Trumpets, fifes, hautboys, drums, cannons formed a harmony such as has never been heard even in hell. The cannons first of all laid flat about six thousand men on each side; then the musketry removed from the best of worlds some nine or ten thousand blackguards who infested its surface. The bayonet also was the sufficient reason for the death of some thousands of men. The whole might amount to thirty thousand souls. Candide, who trembled like a philosopher, hid himself as well as he could during this heroic butchery.

At last, while the two kings each commanded a Te Deum in his camp, Candide decided to go elsewhere to reason about effects and causes. He clambered over heaps of dead and dying men and reached a neighbouring village, which was in ashes; it was an Abare village which the Bulgarians had burned in accordance with international law. Here, old men dazed with blows watched the dying agonies of their murdered wives who clutched their children to their bleeding breasts; there, disembowelled girls who had been made to satisfy the natural appetites of heroes gasped their last sighs; others, half-burned, begged to be put to death. Brains were scattered on the ground among dismembered arms and legs.

Candide fled to another village as fast as he could; it belonged to the Bulgarians, and Abarian heroes had treated it in the same way. Candide, stumbling over quivering limbs or across ruins, at last escaped from the theatre of war, carrying a little food in his knapsack, and never forgetting Miss Cunegonde. His provisions were all gone when he reached Holland; but, having heard that everyone in that country was rich and a Christian, he had no doubt at all but that he would be as well treated as he had been in the Baron's castle before he had been expelled on account of Miss Cunegonde's pretty eyes.

He asked an alms of several grave persons, who all replied that if he continued in that way he would be shut up in a house of correction to teach him how to live.

He then addressed himself to a man who had been discoursing on

[2] A Greek author of the time of Nero. [Richard Aldington.]
[3] The Bulgarians are the Prussians and the Abares the French. The King of vast genius is Frederick the Great, whose recruiting methods are glanced at in this chapter. [Richard Aldington.]

charity in a large assembly for an hour on end. This orator, glancing at him askance, said:

"What are you doing here? Are you for the good cause?"

"There is no effect without a cause," said Candide modestly. "Everything is necessarily linked up and arranged for the best. It was necessary that I should be expelled from the company of Miss Cunegonde, that I ran the gauntlet, and that I beg my bread until I can earn it; all this could not have happened differently."

"My friend," said the orator, "do you believe that the Pope is Anti-Christ?"

"I had never heard so before," said Candide, "but whether he is or isn't, I am starving."

"You don't deserve to eat," said the other. "Hence, rascal; hence, you wretch; and never come near me again."

The orator's wife thrust her head out of the window and seeing a man who did not believe that the Pope was Anti-Christ, she poured on his head a full . . . O Heavens! To what excess religious zeal is carried by ladies!

A man who had not been baptised, an honest Anabaptist named Jacques, saw the cruel and ignominious treatment of one of his brothers, a featherless two-legged creature with a soul; he took him home, cleaned him up, gave him bread and beer, presented him with two florins, and even offered to teach him to work at the manufacture of Persian stuffs which are made in Holland. Candide threw himself at the man's feet, exclaiming:

"Doctor Pangloss was right in telling me that all is for the best in this world, for I am vastly more touched by your extreme generosity than by the harshness of the gentleman in the black cloak and his good lady."

The next day when he walked out he met a beggar covered with sores, dull-eyed, with the end of his nose fallen away, his mouth awry, his teeth black, who talked huskily, was tormented with a violent cough and spat out a tooth at every cough.

CHAPTER IV

How Candide met his old master in philosophy, Doctor Pangloss, and what happened

Candide, moved even more by compassion than by horror, gave this horrible beggar the two crowns he had received from the honest Anabaptist, Jacques. The phantom gazed fixedly at him, shed tears and threw its arms round his neck. Candide recoiled in terror.

"Alas!" said the wretch to the other wretch, "don't you recognise your dear Pangloss?"

"What do I hear? You, my dear master! You, in this horrible state! What misfortune has happened to you? Why are you no longer in the noblest of castles? What has become of Miss Cunegonde, the pearl of young ladies, the masterpiece of Nature?"

"I am exhausted," said Pangloss. Candide immediately took him to the Anabaptist's stable, where he gave him a little bread to eat; and when Pangloss had recovered:

"Well!" said he, "Cunegonde?"

"Dead," replied the other.

At this word Candide swooned; his friend restored him to his senses with a little bad vinegar which happened to be in the stable. Candide opened his eyes.

"Cunegonde dead! Ah! best of worlds, where are you? But what illness did she die of? Was it because she saw me kicked out of her father's noble castle?"

"No," said Pangloss. "She was disembowelled by Bulgarian soldiers, after having been raped to the limit of possibility; they broke the Baron's head when he tried to defend her; the Baroness was cut to pieces; my poor pupil was treated exactly like his sister; and as to the castle, there is not one stone standing on another, not a barn, not a sheep, not a duck, not a tree; but we were well avenged, for the Abares did exactly the same to a neighbouring barony which belonged to a Bulgarian Lord."

At this, Candide swooned again; but, having recovered and having said all that he ought to say, he inquired the cause and effect, the sufficient reason which had reduced Pangloss to so piteous a state.

"Alas!" said Pangloss, " 'tis love; love, the consoler of the human race, the preserver of the universe, the soul of all tender creatures, gentle love."

"Alas!" said Candide, "I am acquainted with this love, this sovereign of hearts, this soul of our soul; it has never brought me anything but one kiss and twenty kicks in the backside. How could this beautiful cause produce in you so abominable an effect?"

Pangloss replied as follows:

"My dear Candide! You remember Paquette, the maid-servant of our august Baroness; in her arms I enjoyed the delights of Paradise which have produced the tortures of Hell by which you see I am devoured; she was infected and perhaps is dead. Paquette received this present from a most learned monk, who had it from the source; for he received it from an old countess, who had it from a cavalry captain, who owed it to a marchioness, who derived it from a page, who had received it from a Jesuit, who, when a novice, had it in a direct line from one of the companions of Christopher Columbus. For my part, I shall not give it to anyone, for I am dying."

"O Pangloss!" exclaimed Candide, "this is a strange genealogy! Wasn't the devil at the root of it?"

"Not at all," replied that great man. "It was something indispensable in this best of worlds, a necessary ingredient; for, if Columbus in an island of America had not caught this disease, which poisons the source of generation, and often indeed prevents generation, we should not have chocolate and cochineal; it must also be noticed that hitherto in our continent this disease is peculiar to us, like theological disputes. The Turks, the Indians, the Persians, the Chinese, the Siamese and the Japanese are not yet familiar with it; but there is a sufficient reason why they in their turn should become familiar with it in a few centuries. Meanwhile, it has made marvellous progress among us, and especially in those large armies composed of honest, well-bred stipendiaries who decide the destiny of States; it may be asserted that when thirty thousand men fight a pitched battle against an equal number of troops, there are about twenty thousand with the pox on either side."

"Admirable!" said Candide. "But you must get cured."

"How can I?" said Pangloss. "I haven't a sou, my friend, and in the whole extent of this globe, you cannot be bled or receive an enema without paying or without someone paying for you."

This last speech determined Candide; he went and threw himself at the feet of his charitable Anabaptist, Jacques, and drew so touching a picture of the state to which his friend was reduced that the good easy man did not hesitate to succour Pangloss; he had him cured at his own expense. In this cure Pangloss only lost one eye and one ear. He could write well and knew arithmetic perfectly. The Anabaptist made him his bookkeeper. At the end of two months he was compelled to go to Lisbon on business and took his two philosophers on the boat with him. Pangloss explained to him how everything was for the best. Jacques was not of this opinion.

"Men," said he, "must have corrupted nature a little, for they were not born wolves, and they have become wolves. God did not give them twenty-four-pounder cannons or bayonets, and they have made bayonets and cannons to destroy each other. I might bring bankruptcies into the account and Justice which seizes the goods of bankrupts in order to deprive the creditors of them."

"It was all indispensable," replied the one-eyed doctor, "and private misfortunes make the public good, so that the more private misfortunes there are, the more everything is well."

While he was reasoning, the air grew dark, the winds blew from the four quarters of the globe and the ship was attacked by the most horrible tempest in sight of the port of Lisbon.

CHAPTER V

Storm, shipwreck, earthquake, and what happened to Dr. Pangloss, to Candide and the Anabaptist Jacques

Half the enfeebled passengers, suffering from that inconceivable anguish which the rolling of a ship causes in the nerves and in all the humours of bodies shaken in contrary directions, did not retain strength enough even to trouble about the danger. The other half screamed and prayed;

the sails were torn, the masts broken, the vessel was leaking. Those worked who could, no one co-operated, no one commanded. The Anabaptist tried to help the crew a little; he was on the main-deck; a furious sailor struck him violently and stretched him on the deck; but the blow he delivered gave him so violent a shock that he fell head-first out of the ship. He remained hanging and clinging to part of the broken mast. The good Jacques ran to his aid, helped him to climb back, and from the effort he made was flung into the sea in full view of the sailor, who allowed him to drown without condescending even to look at him. Candide came up, saw his benefactor reappear for a moment and then be engulfed for ever. He tried to throw himself after him into the sea; he was prevented by the philosopher Pangloss, who proved to him that the Lisbon roads had been expressly created for the Anabaptist to be drowned in them. While he was proving this *a priori*, the vessel sank, and everyone perished except Pangloss, Candide and the brutal sailor who had drowned the virtuous Anabaptist; the blackguard swam successfully to the shore and Pangloss and Candide were carried there on a plank.

When they had recovered a little, they walked toward Lisbon; they had a little money by the help of which they hoped to be saved from hunger after having escaped the storm.

Weeping the death of their benefactor, they had scarcely set foot in the town when they felt the earth tremble under their feet; the sea rose in foaming masses in the port and smashed the ships which rode at anchor. Whirlwinds of flame and ashes covered the streets and squares; the houses collapsed, the roofs were thrown upon the foundations, and the foundations were scattered; thirty thousand inhabitants of every age and both sexes were crushed under the ruins. Whistling and swearing, the sailor said:

"There'll be something to pick up here."

"What can be the sufficient reason for this phenomenon?" said Pangloss.

"It is the last day!" cried Candide.

The sailor immediately ran among the debris, dared death to find money, found it, seized it, got drunk, and having slept off his wine, purchased the favours of the first woman of good-will he met on the ruins of the houses and among the dead and dying. Pangloss, however, pulled him by the sleeve.

"My friend," said he, "this is not well, you are disregarding universal reason, you choose the wrong time."

"Blood and 'ounds!" he retorted, "I am a sailor and I was born in Batavia; four times have I stamped on the crucifix during four voyages to Japan;[4] you have found the right man for your universal reason!"

---

[4] After a conspiracy of Christians in Japan, all foreigners were expelled. The Dutch, who had revealed the plot to the Emperor of Japan, alone were permitted to remain, on condition that they gave up all signs of Christianity and stamped on the crucifix. [Richard Aldington.]

Candide had been hurt by some falling stones; he lay in the street covered with debris. He said to Pangloss:

"Alas! Get me a little wine and oil; I am dying."

"This earthquake is not a new thing," replied Pangloss. "The town of Lima felt the same shocks in America last year; similar causes produce similar effects; there must certainly be a train of sulphur underground from Lima to Lisbon."

"Nothing is more probable," replied Candide; "but, for God's sake, a little oil and wine."

"What do you mean, probable?" replied the philosopher; "I maintain that it is proved."

Candide lost consciousness, and Pangloss brought him a little water from a neighbouring fountain.

Next day they found a little food as they wandered among the ruins and regained a little strength. Afterwards they worked like others to help the inhabitants who had escaped death. Some citizens they had assisted gave them as good a dinner as could be expected in such a disaster; true, it was a dreary meal; the hosts watered their bread with their tears, but Pangloss consoled them by assuring them that things could not be otherwise.

"For," said he, "all this is for the best; for, if there is a volcano at Lisbon, it cannot be anywhere else; for it is impossible that things should not be where they are; for all is well."

A little, dark man, a familiar of the Inquisition, who sat beside him, politely took up the conversation, and said:

"Apparently you do not believe in original sin; for, if everything is for the best, there was neither fall nor punishment."

"I most humbly beg your excellency's pardon," replied Pangloss still more politely, "for the fall of man and the curse necessarily entered into the best of all possible worlds."

"Then you do not believe in free-will?" said the familiar.

"Your excellency will pardon me," said Pangloss; "free-will can exist with absolute necessity; for it was necessary that we should be free; for in short, limited will . . ."

Pangloss was in the middle of his phrase when the familiar nodded to his armed attendant who was pouring out port or Oporto wine for him.

CHAPTER VI

How a splendid auto-da-fé was held to prevent earthquakes, and how Candide was flogged

After the earthquake which destroyed three-quarters of Lisbon, the wise men of that country could discover no more efficacious way of preventing a total ruin than by giving the people a splendid *auto-da-fé*. It was decided by the university of Coimbre that the sight of several persons being slowly burned in great ceremony is an infallible secret for preventing earthquakes.

Consequently they had arrested a Biscayan convicted of having married his fellow-godmother, and two Portuguese who, when eating a chicken, had thrown away the bacon; after dinner they came and bound Dr. Pangloss and his disciple Candide, one because he had spoken and the other because he had listened with an air of approbation; they were both carried separately to extremely cool apartments, where there was never any discomfort from the sun; a week afterwards each was dressed in a sanbenito and their heads were ornamented with paper mitres; Candide's mitre and sanbenito were painted with flames upside down and with devils who had neither tails nor claws; but Pangloss's devils had claws and tails, and his flames were upright.

Dressed in this manner they marched in procession and listened to a most pathetic sermon, followed by lovely plain-song music. Candide was flogged in time to the music, while the singing went on; the Biscayan and the two men who had not wanted to eat bacon were burned, and Pangloss was hanged, although this is not the custom. The very same day, the earth shook again with a terrible clamour.

Candide, terrified, dumbfounded, bewildered, covered with blood, quivering from head to foot, said to himself:

"If this is the best of all possible worlds, what are the others? Let it pass that I was flogged, for I was flogged by the Bulgarians, but, O my dear Pangloss! The greatest of philosophers! Must I see you hanged without knowing why! O my dear Anabaptist! The best of men! Was it necessary that you should be drowned in port! O Miss Cunegonde! The pearl of women! Was it necessary that your belly should be slit!" . . .

(Candide discovers that Miss Cunegonde is alive and sets off with a companion, Martin, to find her.)

CHAPTER XX

What happened to Candide and Martin at sea

So the old man, who was called Martin, embarked with Candide for Bordeaux. Both had seen and suffered much; and if the ship had been sailing from Surinam to Japan by way of the Cape of Good Hope they would have been able to discuss moral and physical evil during the whole voyage.

However, Candide had one great advantage over Martin, because he still hoped to see Miss Cunegonde again, and Martin had nothing to hope for; moreover, he possessed gold and diamonds; and, although he had lost a hundred large red sheep laden with the greatest treasures on earth, although he was still enraged at being robbed by the Dutch captain, yet when he thought of what he still had left in his pockets and when he talked of Cunegonde, especially at the end of a meal, he still inclined towards the system of Pangloss.

"But what do you think of all this, Martin?" said he to the man of letters. "What is your view of moral and physical evil?"

"Sir," replied Martin, "my priests accused me of being a Socinian; but the truth is I am a Manichæan."[5]

"You are poking fun at me," said Candide, "there are no Manichæans left in the world."

"I am one," said Martin. "I don't know what to do about it, but I am unable to think in any other fashion."

"You must be possessed by the devil," said Candide.

"He takes so great a share in the affairs of this world," said Martin, "that he might well be in me, as he is everywhere else; but I confess that when I consider this globe, or rather this globule, I think that God has abandoned it to some evil creature—always excepting Eldorado. I have never seen a town which did not desire the ruin of the next town, never a family which did not wish to exterminate some other family. Everywhere the weak loathe the powerful before whom they cower and the powerful treat them like flocks of sheep whose wool and flesh are to be sold. A million drilled assassins go from one end of Europe to the other murdering and robbing with discipline in order to earn their bread, because there is no honester occupation; and in the towns which seem to enjoy peace and where the arts flourish men are devoured by more envy, troubles and worries than the afflictions of a besieged town. Secret griefs are even more cruel than public miseries. In a word, I have seen so much and endured so much that I have become a Manichæan."

"Yet there is some good," replied Candide.

"There may be," said Martin, "but I do not know it."

In the midst of this dispute they heard the sound of cannon. The noise increased every moment. Everyone took his telescope. About three miles away they saw two ships engaged in battle; and the wind brought them so near the French ship that they had the pleasure of seeing the fight at their ease. At last one of the two ships fired broadside so accurately and so low down that the other ship began to sink. Candide and Martin distinctly saw a hundred men on the main deck of the sinking ship; they raised their hands to Heaven and uttered frightful shrieks; in a moment all were engulfed.

"Well!" said Martin, "that is how men treat each other."

"It is certainly true," said Candide, "that there is something diabolical in this affair."

As he was speaking, he saw something of a brilliant red swimming near the ship. They launched a boat to see what it could be; it was one of his

---

[5] [Editor's note: Manicheanism was a third-century sect based on Zoroastrianism, Gnosticism, Buddhism, and so on, which believed in a cosmic dualism: good or light was attributed to Mazda, and evil or darkness to Ahriman. The religion was vigorously attacked by St. Augustine.]

sheep. Candide felt more joy at recovering his sheep than grief at losing a hundred all laden with large diamonds from Eldorado.

The French captain soon perceived that the captain of the remaining ship was a Spaniard and that the sunken ship was a Dutch pirate; the captain was the very same who had robbed Candide. The immense wealth this scoundrel had stolen was swallowed up with him in the sea and only a sheep was saved.

"You see," said Candide to Martin, "that crime is sometimes punished; this scoundrel of a Dutch captain has met the fate he deserved."

"Yes," said Martin, "but was it necessary that the other passengers on his ship should perish too? God punished the thief, and the devil punished the others."

Meanwhile the French and Spanish ships continued on their way and Candide continued his conversation with Martin. They argued for a fortnight, and at the end of the fortnight they had got no further than at the beginning. But after all, they talked, they exchanged ideas, they consoled each other. Candide stroked his sheep.

"Since I have found you again," said he, "I may very likely find Cunegonde."

CHAPTER XXI

Candide and Martin approach the coast of France and argue

At last they sighted the coast of France.

"Have you ever been to France, Mr. Martin?" said Candide.

"Yes," said Martin, "I have traversed several provinces. In some half the inhabitants are crazy, in others they are too artful, in some they are usually quite gentle and stupid, and in others they think they are clever; in all of them the chief occupation is making love, the second scandal-mongering and the third talking nonsense."

"But, Mr. Martin, have you seen Paris?"

"Yes, I have seen Paris; it is a mixture of all these species; it is a chaos, a throng where everybody hunts for pleasure and hardly anybody finds it, at least so far as I could see. I did not stay there long; when I arrived there I was robbed of everything I had by pickpockets at Saint-Germain's fair; they thought I was a thief and I spent a week in prison; after which I became a printer's reader to earn enough to return to Holland on foot. I met the scribbling rabble, the intriguing rabble and the fanatical rabble. We hear that there are very polite people in the town; I am glad to think so."

"For my part, I have not the least curiosity to see France," said Candide. "You can easily guess that when a man has spent a month in Eldorado he cares to see nothing else in the world but Miss Cunegonde.[6]

6 [Editor's note: Candide has since learned that Cunegonde was not killed but only wounded.]

I shall go and wait for her at Venice; we will go to Italy by way of France; will you come with me?"

"Willingly," said Martin. "They say that Venice is only for the Venetian nobles, but that foreigners are nevertheless well received when they have plenty of money; I have none, you have plenty, I will follow you anywhere."

"Apropos," said Candide, "do you think the earth was originally a sea, as we are assured by that large book[7] belonging to the captain?"

"I don't believe it in the least," said Martin, "any more than all the other whimsies we have been pestered with recently!"

"But to what end was this world formed?" said Candide.

"To infuriate us," replied Martin.

"Are you not very much surprised," continued Candide, "by the love those two girls of the country of the Oreillons had for those two monkeys, whose adventure I told you?"

"Not in the least," said Martin. "I see nothing strange in their passion; I have seen so many extraordinary things that nothing seems extraordinary to me."

"Do you think," said Candide, "that men have always massacred each other, as they do to-day? Have they always been liars, cheats, traitors, brigands, weak, flighty, cowardly, envious, gluttonous, drunken, grasping and vicious, bloody, backbiting, debauched, fanatical, hypocritical and silly?"

"Do you think," said Martin, "that sparrow-hawks have always eaten the pigeons they came across?"

"Yes, of course," said Candide.

"Well," said Martin, "if sparrow-hawks have always possessed the same nature, why should you expect men to change theirs? . . ."

CHAPTER XXVIII

"Well! my dear Pangloss," said Candide, "when you were hanged, dissected, stunned with blows and made to row in the galleys, did you always think that everything was for the best in this world?"

"I am still of my first opinion," replied Pangloss, "for after all I am a philosopher; and it would be unbecoming for me to recant, since Leibnitz could not be in the wrong and pre-established harmony is the finest thing imaginable like the plenum and subtle matter."

[7] [Editor's note: The Bible.]

NATURE
JOHN STUART MILL

John Stuart Mill (1806–1873) was an English philosopher who is famous for his studies in logic, ethics, and political philosophy. His main work in these three areas is contained in *A System of Logic, Utilitarianism,* and *Essay on Liberty,* respectively. As a political reformer Mill championed various liberal causes, actively supporting movements for the rights of women and the working class.

In his essay *Nature,* Mill echoes the sentiments of Voltaire in maintaining that the natural order contains a great deal of destructiveness. In fact, Mill asserts, every crime which men abhor is commonplace in the physical world. Therefore, rather than using nature as a model, as is sometimes suggested, human beings must introduce standards of justice and kindness in place of the mindless brutality that exists in the natural environment. Not only should we improve the given world, but we must repress a number of our own natural impulses, including our propensity toward destructiveness, cruelty, and the domination of our fellow man.

In effect, Mill contends that the natural is not necessarily good, and that if we were to judge the Creator from His works, we could not reach a favorable verdict as to God's moral character.

No one, indeed, asserts it to be the intention of the Creator that the spontaneous order of the creation should not be altered, or even that it should not be altered in any new way. But there still exists a vague notion that though it is very proper to control this or the other natural phenomenon, the general scheme of nature is a model for us to imitate: that with more or less liberty in details, we should on the whole be guided by the spirit and general conception of nature's own ways: that they are God's work, and as such perfect; that man cannot rival their unapproachable excellence, and can best show his skill and piety by attempting, in however imperfect a way, to reproduce their likeness; and that if not the whole, yet some particular parts of the spontaneous order of nature, selected according to the speaker's predilections, are in a peculiar sense, manifestations of the Creator's will; a sort of finger posts pointing out the direction which things in general, and therefore our voluntary actions, are intended to take. Feelings of this sort, though repressed on ordinary occasions by the contrary current of life, are ready to break out whenever custom is silent, and the native promptings of the mind have nothing opposed to them but reason: and appeals are continually made to them by rhetoricians, with the effect, if not of convincing opponents, at least of making those who already hold the opinion which the rhetorician desires to recommend, better satisfied with it. For in the present day it probably seldom happens that any one is persuaded to approve any course of action because it appears to him to bear an analogy to the divine government of the world, though the argument tells on him with great force, and is felt by him to be a great support, in behalf of anything which he is already inclined to approve. . . .

For, how stands the fact? That next to the greatness of these cosmic forces, the quality which most forcibly strikes every one who does not avert his eyes from it, is their perfect and absolute recklessness. They go straight to their end, without regarding what or whom they crush on the road. Optimists, in their attempts to prove that "whatever is, is right," are obliged to maintain, not that Nature ever turns one step from her path to avoid trampling us into destruction, but that it would be very unreasonable in us to expect that she should. Pope's "Shall gravitation cease when you go by?" may be a just rebuke to any one who should be so silly as to expect common human morality from nature. But if the question were between two men, instead of between a man and a natural phenomenon, that triumphant apostrophe would be thought a rare piece of impudence. A man who should persist in hurling stones or firing cannon when another man "goes by," and having killed him should urge a similar plea in exculpation, would very deservedly be found guilty of murder.

In sober truth, nearly all the things which men are hanged or imprisoned for doing to one another, are nature's every day performances. Killing, the most criminal act recognized by human laws, Nature does once to every being that lives; and in a large proportion of cases, after protracted tortures such as only the greatest monsters whom we read of ever purposely inflicted on their living fellow-creatures. If, by an arbitrary reservation, we refuse to account anything murder but what abridges a certain term supposed to be allotted to human life, nature also does this to all but a small percentage of lives, and does it in all the modes, violent or insidious, in which the worst human beings take the lives of one another. Nature impales men, breaks them as if on the wheel, casts them to be devoured by wild beasts, burns them to death, crushes them with stones like the first christian martyr, starves them with hunger, freezes them with cold, poisons them by the quick or slow venom of her exhalations, and has hundreds of other hideous deaths in reserve, such as the ingenious cruelty of a Nabis or a Domitian never surpassed. All this, Nature does with the most supercilious disregard both of mercy and of justice, emptying her shafts upon the best and noblest indifferently with the meanest and worst; upon those who are engaged in the highest and worthiest enterprises, and often as the direct consequence of the noblest acts; and it might almost be imagined as a punishment for them. She mows down those on whose existence hangs the well-being of a whole people, perhaps the prospects of the human race for generations to come, with as little compunction as those whose death is a relief to themselves, or a blessing to those under their noxious influence. Such are Nature's dealings with life. Even when she does not intend to kill, she inflicts the same tortures in apparent wantonness. In the clumsy provision which she has made for that perpetual renewal of animal life, rendered necessary by the prompt termination she puts to it in every individual instance, no human being ever comes into the world but another human being is literally stretched on the rack for hours or days, not unfrequently issuing in death. Next to taking life (equal to it according to a high authority) is taking the means by which we live; and Nature does this too on the largest scale and with the most callous indifference. A single hurricane destroys the hopes of a season; a flight of locusts, or an inundation, desolates a district; a trifling chemical change in an edible root, starves a million of people. The waves of the sea, like banditti seize and appropriate the wealth of the rich and the little all of the poor with the same accompaniments of stripping, wounding, and killing as their human antitypes. Everything in short, which the worst men commit either against life or property is perpetrated on a larger scale by natural agents. Nature has Noyades more fatal than those of Carrier;[1] her explosions of fire damp are as destructive as human artillery; her plague and cholera far surpass the poison cups of the Borgias. Even the love of "order" which is thought to be a following of the ways of Nature, is in fact a contradiction of them. All which people are accustomed to deprecate as "disorder" and its consequences, is precisely a counterpart of Nature's ways. Anarchy and the Reign of Terror are overmatched in injustice, ruin, and death, by a hurricane and a pestilence.

But, it is said, all these things are for wise and good ends. On this I must first remark that whether they are so or not, is altogether beside the point. Supposing it true that contrary to appearances these horrors when perpetrated by Nature, promote good ends, still as no one believes that good ends would be promoted by our following the example, the course of Nature cannot be a proper model for us to imitate. Either it is right that we should kill because nature kills; torture because nature tortures; ruin and devastate because nature does the like; or we ought not to consider at all what nature does, but what it is good to do. If there is such a thing as a *reductio ad absurdum*, this surely amounts to one. If it is a sufficient reason for doing one thing, that nature does it, why not another thing? If not all things, why anything? The physical government of the world being full of things which when done by men are deemed the greatest enormities, it cannot be religious or moral in us to guide our actions by the analogy of the course of nature. This proposition remains true, whatever occult quality of producing good may reside in those facts of nature which to our perceptions are most noxious, and which no one considers it other than a crime to produce artificially.

But, in reality, no one consistently believes in any such occult quality. The phrases which ascribe perfection to the course of nature can only be considered as the exaggerations of poetic or devotional feeling, not intended to stand the test of a sober examination. No one, either religious or irreligious, believes that the hurtful agencies of nature, considered as a whole, promote good purposes, in any other way than by inciting human rational creatures to rise up and struggle against them. If we be-

---

[1] [Editor's note: Carrier executed people by drowning (Noyades) in Nantes in 1794.]

lieved that those agencies were appointed by a benevolent Providence as the means of accomplishing wise purposes which could not be compassed if they did not exist, then everything done by mankind which tends to chain up these natural agencies or to restrict their mischievous operation, from draining a pestilential marsh down to curing the toothache, or putting up an umbrella, ought to be accounted impious; which assuredly nobody does account them, notwithstanding an undercurrent of sentiment setting in that direction which is occasionally perceptible. On the contrary, the improvements on which the civilized part of mankind most pride themselves, consist in more successfully warding off those natural calamities which if we really believed what most people profess to believe, we should cherish as medicines provided for our earthly state by infinite wisdom. Inasmuch too as each generation greatly surpasses its predecessors in the amount of natural evil which it succeeds in averting, our condition, if the theory were true, ought by this time to have become a terrible manifestation of some tremendous calamity, against which the physical evils we have learnt to overmaster, had previously operated as a preservative. Any one, however, who acted as if he supposed this to be the case, would be more likely, I think, to be confined as a lunatic, than reverenced as a saint. . . .

This brief survey is amply sufficient to prove that the duty of man is the same in respect to his own nature as in respect to the nature of all other things, namely not to follow but to amend it. . . .

With regard to this particular hypothesis, that all natural impulses, all propensities sufficiently universal and sufficiently spontaneous to be capable of passing for instincts, must exist for good ends, and ought to be only regulated, not repressed; this is of course true of the majority of them, for the species could not have continued to exist unless most of its inclinations had been directed to things needful or useful for its preservation. But unless the instincts can be reduced to a very small number indeed, it must be allowed that we have also bad instincts which it should be the aim of education not simply to regulate but to extirpate, or rather (what can be done even to an instinct) to starve them by disuse. Those who are inclined to multiply the number of instincts, usually include among them one which they call destructiveness: an instinct to destroy for destruction's sake. I can conceive no good reason for preserving this, no more than another propensity which if not an instinct is very like one, what has been called the instinct of domination; a delight in exercising despotism, in holding other beings in subjection to our will. The man who takes pleasure in the mere exertion of authority, apart from the purpose for which it is to be employed, is the last person in whose hands one would willingly entrust it. Again, there are persons who are cruel by character, or, as the phrase is, naturally cruel; who have a real pleasure in inflicting, or seeing the infliction of pain. This kind of cruelty is not mere hardheartedness, absence of pity or remorse; it is a positive thing; a particular kind of voluptuous excitement. The East, and Southern Europe, have afforded, and probably still afford, abundant examples of this hateful propensity. I suppose it will be granted that this is not one of the natural inclinations which it would be wrong to suppress. The only question would be whether it is not a duty to suppress the man himself along with it.

But even if it were true that every one of the elementary impulses of human nature has its good side, and may by a sufficient amount of artificial training be made more useful than hurtful; how little would this amount to, when it must in any case be admitted that without such training all of them, even those which are necessary to our preservation, would fill the world with misery, making human life an exaggerated likeness of the odious scene of violence and tyranny which is exhibited by the rest of the animal kingdom, except in so far as tamed and disciplined by man. There, indeed, those who flatter themselves with the notion of reading the purposes of the Creator in his works, ought in consistency to have seen grounds for inferences from which they have shrunk. If there are any marks at all of special design in creation, one of the things most evidently designed is that a large proportion of all animals should pass their existence in tormenting and devouring other animals. They have been lavishly fitted out with the instruments necessary for that purpose; their strongest instincts impel them to it, and many of them seem to have been constructed incapable of supporting themselves by any other food. If a tenth part of the pains which have been expended in finding benevolent adaptations in all nature, had been employed in collecting evidence to blacken the character of the Creator, what scope for comment would not have been found in the entire existence of the lower animals, divided, with scarcely an exception, into devourers and devoured, and a prey to a thousand ills from which they are denied the faculties necessary for protecting themselves! If we are not obliged to believe the animal creation to be the work of a demon, it is because we need not suppose it to have been made by a Being of infinite power. But if imitation of the Creator's will as revealed in nature, were applied as a rule of action in this case, the most atrocious enormities of the worst men would be more than justified by the apparent intention of Providence that throughout all animated nature the strong should prey upon the weak.

4

The Answer
of Absolute Faith

J.B.

ARCHIBALD MACLEISH

Archibald MacLeish (1892–   ), is an American poet and winner of the Pulitzer Prize; he has also served in several government posts including an appointment as Librarian of Congress. MacLeish's writings have ranged from intense subjectivity (*The Hamlet of MacLeish*) to half-imitations of Ezra Pound and T. S. Eliot (*The Happy Marriage, The Pot of Earth*) to social commentary (*Fall of the City, Air Raid*) to religious themes (*J.B.*). He is known for his mastery of cadence and rhythm and his condensed, incisive style.

MacLeish's play, *J.B.*, like the Biblical story of Job on which it is closely patterned, rejects the common theory that blessings are rewards for virtue and evils are punishments for sin.[1] To ask the infinite God for reasons for events is in itself sinful; it is both presumptuous and ignorant because it fails to appreciate that everything the earth contains is freely given by God irrespective of man's merit. Therefore, instead of demanding a just explanation as to why we deserve our lot, we must be grateful for what we receive and trust God in all circumstances.

The action of the play shifts between the events of J.B.'s life and the conversations between Zuss and Nickles in which J.B.'s prosperity, suffering, and religious response are passionately analyzed. Both Zuss and Nickles are failed actors working as circus vendors, and when they come upon a stage arranged for a performance of *J.B.* they cannot resist playing the parts of God and Satan—Zuss, of course, playing God. From this position they enter into the play within a play, often stepping out of character to comment on the events that are magically enacted before them. A tuneless song that Nickles sings to himself seated on the rung of a ladder makes a fitting beginning for this excerpt; immediately following is a scene in which J.B. is having Thanksgiving dinner with his wife Sarah and their five children, David, Rebecca, Jonathan, Mary, and Ruth.

---

[1] In Robert Frost's play, *A Masque of Reason*, God says to Job:

> I've had you on my mind a thousand years
> To thank you someday for the way you helped me
> Establish once for all the principle
> There's no connection man can reason out
> Between his just desserts and what he gets
> Virtue may fail and wickedness succeed.

THE PROLOGUE

NICKLES: I heard upon his dry dung heap
              That man cry out who cannot sleep:
              "If God is God He is not good,
              If God is good He is not God;
              Take the even, take the odd,
              I would not sleep here if I could
              Except for the little green leaves in the wood
              And the wind on the water."

SCENE ONE

. . .

SARAH: *gently*   God doesn't give all this for nothing:
              A good home, good food,
              Father, mother, brothers, sisters.
              We too have our part to play.
              If we do our part He does His,
              He always has. If we forget Him
              He will forget. Forever. In everything.
              David!

David raises his head reluctantly.

              Did you think of God?

David does not reply.

              Did you think, when you woke in your beds this morning,
              Any one of you, of Him?

Silence.

J.B.: *uncomfortable*
              Of course they did. They couldn't have helped it . . .

              Bit of the breast for you, Rebecca?

SARAH: Please, Job. I want them to answer me.

J.B.:   How can they answer things like that?

              Gravy? That's the girl . . .

                             They know though.

              Gift of waking, grace of light,
              You and the world brought back together,
              You from sleep, the world from night,
              By God's great goodness and mercy . . .

Wing for Mary? Wing for Mary! . . .

They know all that. It's hard to talk about.

SARAH: *flushed, an edge to her voice*
Even if it's hard we have to.
We can't just take, eat, just—relish!
Children aren't animals.

J.B.: *he goes on with his serving*   Sweet Sal! Sweet Sal!
Children know the grace of God
Better than most of us. They see the world
The way the morning brings it back to them,
New and born and fresh and wonderful . . .

Ruth? She's always ravenous . . .

                                        I remember . . .

Jonathan? He never is . . .

                                        . . . when I was
Ten I used to stand behind
The window watching when the light began,
Hidden and watching.

                    That's for David—
Dark and thin.

MARY: Why? Why hidden?

J.B.:   Hidden from the trees of course.
I must have thought the trees would see me
Peeking at them and turn back.

REBECCA: Back where?

J.B.:   Back where they came from, baby.

That's for your mother: crisp and gold.

RUTH: Father, you'd be cold. You didn't.

SARAH: *the edge still there*
He still does. He lies there watching
Long before I see the light—
Can't bear to miss a minute of it:
Sun at morning, moon at night,
The last red apple, the first peas!
I've never seen the dish he wouldn't
Taste and relish and want more of:
People either!

J.B.: *serving himself with heaping spoons*
                                 Come on, Sal!
                    Plenty of people I don't like.

He sits down. Pours himself a glass of wine.

                    I like their being people though . . .

Sips his wine.

                    Trying to be.

SARAH: You're hungry for them—
                    Any kind. People and vegetables:
                    Any vegetables so long as
                    Leaves come out on them. He loves leaves!

J.B.:   You love them too. You love them better.
                    Just because you know their names
                    You think you choose among your flowers:
                    Well, you don't. You love the lot of them.

SARAH: I can't take them as a gift though:
                    I owe for them. We do. We *owe*.

J.B.:   Owe for the greening of the leaves?

SARAH: Please!
                    Please, Job. I want the children
                    Somehow to understand this day, this . . .
                    Feast . . .

Her voice breaks.

J.B.:   Forgive me, Sal. I'm sorry—but they
                    Do. They understand. A little.
                    Look at me, all of you.

                                 Ruth, you answer:
                    Why do we eat all this, these dishes,
                    All this food?

Ruth twists her napkin.

                             You say, Rebecca.
                    You're the littlest of us all.
                    Why?

REBECCA: Because it's good?

SARAH: Baby!
                    Ah, my poor baby!

J.B.:   Why your poor baby?
                    She's right, isn't she? It is. It's good.

SARAH: Good—and God has sent it to us!

J.B.:   She knows that.

SARAH: Does she?

She raises her head sharply.

                                        Job! . . .

                                        do *you?*

Their eyes meet; hers drop.

                    Oh, I think you do . . .

                                        but sometimes—

                    Times like this when we're together—
                    I get frightened, Job . . .

                                        we have so

          Much!

J.B.: *dead serious*   You ought to think I do.
                    Even if no one else should, you should.
                    Never since I learned to tell
                    My shadow from my shirt, not once,
                    Not for a watch-tick, have I doubted
                    God was on my side, was good to me.
                    Even young and poor I knew it.
                    People called it luck: it wasn't.
                    I never thought so from the first
                    Fine silver dollar to the last
                    Controlling interest in some company
                    I couldn't get—and got. It isn't
                    Luck.

MARY: That's in the story.

JONATHAN: Tell the
                    Story.

RUTH: Tell the lucky story.

REBECCA: Lucky, lucky, tell the lucky.

J.B.: *getting to his feet again to carve*
                    Tell the story?

                              Drumstick, David?

Man enough to eat a drumstick?
You too, Jonathan?

REBECCA: Story, story.

J.B.:   Fellow came up to me once in a restaurant:
"J.B.," he says—I knew him . . .

Mary, want the other wing?

"Why do you get the best of the rest of us?"
Fellow named Foley, I think, or Sullivan:
New-come man he was in town.

MARY: Your turn, Mother.

SARAH: Patrick Sullivan.

J.B. AND THE CHILDREN: *together in a shouted chant*
Patrick Sullivan, that's the man!

J.B.:   "Why do you get the best of the rest of us?
I've got as many brains as you.
I work as hard. I keep the lamp lit.
Luck! That's what it is," says Sullivan.
"Look!" I said. "Look out the window!"
"What do you see?" "The street," he tells me.

J.B. AND THE CHILDREN: *as before*
"The street?" says I. "The street," says he.

J.B.:   "What do you want me to call it?" he asks me.
"What do I want you to call it?" says I.
"A road," says I. "It's going somewhere."
"Where?" says he. "You say," I said to him.

J.B. AND THE CHILDREN:
"God knows!" says Mr. Sullivan.

J.B.:   "He does," says I. "That's where it's going.
That's where I go too. That's why."
"Why what?" says he. "I get the best of you:
It's God's country, Mr. Sullivan."

J.B. AND THE CHILDREN:
"God forbid!" says Mr. Sullivan.

J.B.:   I laughed till I choked. He only looked at me.
"Lucky so-and-so," he yells.

SARAH: Poor Mr. Sullivan.

J.B.: *soberly*   He was wrong.
It isn't luck when God is good to you.

> It's something more. It's like those dizzy
> Daft old lads who dowse for water.
> They feel the alder twig twist down
> And know they've got it and they have:
> They've got it. Blast the ledge and water
> Gushes at you. And they knew.
> It wasn't luck. They knew. They felt the
> Gush go shuddering through their shoulders, huge
> As some mysterious certainty of opulence.
> They couldn't hold it. I can't hold it.

He looks at Sarah.

> I've always known that God was with me.
> I've tried to show I knew it—not
> Only in words.

SARAH: *touched*   Oh, you have,
> I know you have. And it's ridiculous,
> Childish, and I shouldn't be afraid . . .
> Not even now when suddenly everything
> Fills to overflowing in me
> Brimming the fulness till I feel
> My happiness impending like a danger.
> If ever anyone deserved it, you do.

J.B.:   That's not true. I don't deserve it.
> It's not a question of deserving.

SARAH: Oh, it is. That's all the question.
> However could we sleep at night . . .

J.B.:   Nobody *deserves* it, Sarah:
> Not the world that God has given us.

There is a moment's strained silence, then J.B. is laughing.

J.B.:   But I believed in it, Sal. I trust in it.
> I trust my luck—my life—our life—
> God's goodness to me.

SARAH: *trying to control her voice*   Yes! You do!
> I know you do! And that's what frightens me!
> It's not so simple as all that. It's not.
> They mustn't think it is. God punishes.
> God rewards and God can punish.
> God is just.

J.B.: *easy again*   Of course He's just.
> He'll never change. A man can count on Him.

Look at the world, the order of it,
The certainty of day's return
And spring's and summer's: the leaves' green—
That never cheated expectation.

SARAH: *vehemently*

God can reward and God can punish.
Us He has rewarded. Wonderfully.
Given us everything. Preserved us.
Kept us from harm, each one—each one.
And why? Because of you . . .

J.B. *raises his head sharply.*

SARAH: No!

Let me say it! Let me say it!
I need to speak the words that say it—
I need to hear them spoken. Nobody,
Nobody knows of it but me.
You never let them know: not anyone—
Even your children. They don't know.

J.B. *heaves himself out of his chair, swings round the table, leans over
Sarah, his arms around her.*

J.B.:   Eat your dinner, Sal my darling.
We love our life because it's good:
It isn't good because we love it—
Pay for it—in thanks or prayers. The thanks are
Part of love and paid like love:
Free gift or not worth having.
You know that, Sal . . .

He kisses her.

                                        better than anyone.
Eat your dinner, girl! There's not a
Harpy on the roof for miles.

She reaches up to touch his cheek with her hand.

SARAH: Nevertheless it's true, Job. You
Can trust your luck because you've earned the
Right to trust it: earned the right
For all of us to trust it.

J.B.: *back at his own place, filling his glass again*
                                        Nonsense!
We get the earth for nothing, don't we?
It's given to us, gift on gift:

Sun on the floor, airs in the curtain.
We lie a whole day long and look at it
Crowing or crying in our cribs:
It doesn't matter—crow or cry
The sun shines, the wind blows . . .

Rebecca! Back for more already?

REBECCA: I want the wishbone please.

J.B.:   Whatever
        For?

REBECCA: To wish.

SARAH: For what, my baby?

REBECCA: For the wishbone.

SARAH: *pulling Rebecca into her lap*
                        Little pig!
        Wishing for wishes!

J.B.: *forking the wishbone onto Rebecca's plate*
                        That's my girl!

SARAH: She is! The spit and image of you!
        Thinking she can eat the world
        With luck and wishes and no thanks!

J.B.:   That isn't fair. We're thankful, both of us.

SARAH: *cuddling Rebecca*
        Both! And both the same! Just look at you!
        A child shows gratitude the way a woman
        Shows she likes a pretty dress—
        Puts it on and takes it off again—
        That's the way a child gives thanks:
        She tries the world on. So do you.

J.B.:   God understands that language, doesn't He?
        He should. He made the colts.

SCENE TWO

The Platform. As the platform light comes on, the figures fade from the canvas sky and Mr. Zuss and Nickles straighten up, lifting their masks off, stretching, yawning.

MR. ZUSS: Well, that's our pigeon.

NICKLES: Lousy actor.

MR. ZUSS: Doesn't really act at all.

NICKLES: Just eats.

MR. ZUSS: And talks.

NICKLES: The love of life!
Poisoning their little minds
With love of life! At that age!

MR. ZUSS: No!
Some of that, I thought, was beautiful.

NICKLES: Best thing you can teach your children
Next to never drawing breath
Is choking on it.

MR. ZUSS: Who said that?
Someone's spoiled philosophy, it sounds like:
Intellectual butter a long war
And too much talking have turned rancid.
I thought he made that small familiar
Feast a true thanksgiving . . . only . . .

NICKLES: Only what?

MR. ZUSS: Something went wrong.

NICKLES: That's what I've been telling you.

MR. ZUSS: He didn't
Act.

NICKLES: He can't. He's not an actor.

MR. ZUSS: I wonder if he knows?

NICKLES: Knows what?

MR. ZUSS: Knows that he's in it?

NICKLES: Is he?

MR. ZUSS: Certainly.

NICKLES: How can you tell?

MR. ZUSS: That's him. That's Job.
He has the wealth, the wife, the children,
Position in the world.

NICKLES: The piety!

MR. ZUSS: He loves God, if that's what you're saying.
A *perfect and an upright man.*

NICKLES: Piety's hard enough to take
              Among the poor who *have* to practice it.
              A rich man's piety stinks. It's insufferable.

MR. ZUSS: You're full of fatuous aphorisms, aren't you!
              A poor man's piety is hope of having:
              A rich man *has* his—and he's grateful.

NICKLES: Bought and paid for like a waiter's smirk!
              You know what talks when that man's talking?
              All that gravy on his plate—
              His cash—his pretty wife—his children!
              Lift the lot of them, he'd sing
              Another canticle to different music.

MR. ZUSS: That's what Satan says—but better.

NICKLES: It's obvious. No one needs to say it.

MR. ZUSS: You don't like him.

NICKLES: I don't have to.
              You're the one who has to like him.

MR. ZUSS: I thought you spoke of Job with sympathy.

NICKLES: Job on his dung hill, yes. That's human.
              That makes sense. But this world-master,
              This pious, flatulent, successful man
              Who feasts on turkey and thanks God!—
              He sickens me!

MR. ZUSS: Of course he sickens you,
              He trusts the will of God and loves—

*Mr. Zuss is swollen with indignation and rhetoric. He swoops his mask up
from the rail with a magnificent gesture, holds it.*

              Loves a woman who must sometime, somewhere,
              Later, sooner, leave him; fixes
              All his hopes on little children
              One night's fever or a running dog
              Could kill between the dark and day;
              Plants his work, his enterprise, his labor,
              Here where every planted thing
              Fails in its time but still he plants it . . .

NICKLES: *nastily*

              God will teach him better won't He?
              God will show him what the world is like—
              What man's like—the ignoble creature,
              Victim of the spinning joke!

MR. ZUSS: Teach him better than he knows!
                    God will show him God!

NICKLES: *shrugging*   It's the same
                    Thing. It hurts.

MR. ZUSS: *gathering momentum*   God will teach him!
                    God will show him what God *is*—
                    Enormous pattern of the steep of stars,
                    Minute perfection of the frozen crystal,
                    Inimitable architecture of the slow,
                    Cold, silent, ignorant sea-snail:
                    The unimaginable will of stone:
                    Infinite mind in midge of matter!

NICKLES: Infinite mush! Wait till your pigeon
                    Pecks at the world the way the rest do—
                    Eager beak to naked bum!

MR. ZUSS: You ought to have your tongue torn out!

NICKLES: All men should: to suffer silently.

MR. ZUSS: Get your mask back on! I tell you
                    Nothing this good man might suffer,
                    Nothing at all, would make him yelp
                    As you do. He'd praise God no matter.

NICKLES: *whispering*
                    Why must he suffer then?

The question catches Mr. Zuss with his mask halfway to his face. He lowers it slowly, staring into it as though the answer might be written inside.

MR. ZUSS: *too loud*   To praise!

NICKLES: *softly*
                    He praises now. Like a canary.

Mr. Zuss lifts his mask again.

MR. ZUSS: Well, will you put it on or won't you?

NICKLES: Shall I tell you why?
            violently   To learn!
                    Every human creature born
                    Is born into the bright delusion
                    Beauty and loving-kindness care for him.
                    Suffering teaches! Suffering's good for us!
                    Imagine men and women dying
                    Still believing that the cuddling arms

> Enclosed them! They would find the worms
> Peculiar nurses, wouldn't they? Wouldn't they?

He breaks off; picks his mask up; goes on in a kind of jigging chant half to himself.

> What once was cuddled must learn to kiss
> The cold worm's mouth. That's all the mystery.
> That's the whole muddle. Well, we learn it.
> God is merciful and we learn it . . .
> We learn to wish we'd never lived!

MR. ZUSS: This man will not.

NICKLES: Won't he? Won't he?
> Shall I tell you how it ends?
> Shall I prophesy? I see our
> Smug world-master on his dung heap,
> Naked, miserable, and alone,
> Pissing the stars. Ridiculous gesture!—
> Nevertheless a gesture—meaning
> All there is on earth to mean:
> Man's last word . . . and worthy of him!

MR. ZUSS: This man will not. He trusts God.
> No matter how it ends, he trusts Him.

NICKLES: Even when God tests him?—tortures him?

MR. ZUSS: Would God permit the test unless
> He knew the outcome of the testing?

NICKLES: Then why test him if God knows?

MR. ZUSS: So Job can see.

NICKLES: See what?

MR. ZUSS: See God.

NICKLES: A fine sight from an ash heap, certainly!

MR. ZUSS: Isn't there anything you understand?
> It's from the ash heap God is seen
> Always! Always from the ashes.
> Every saint and martyr knew that.

NICKLES: And so he suffers to see God:
> Sees God because he suffers. Beautiful!

MR. ZUSS: Put on your mask. I'd rather look at . . .

NICKLES: I should think you would! A human
> Face would shame the mouth that said that!

*They put their masks on fiercely, standing face to face. The platform light
fades out. The spotlight catches them, throwing the two masked shadows
out and up. The voices are magnified and hollow, the gestures formal, as
at the end of the Prologue.*

GODMASK: Hast thou considered my servant Job
                  That there is none like him on the earth,
                  A perfect and an upright man, one
                  That feareth God and escheweth evil?

SATANMASK: *sardonic*
                  Doth Job fear God for naught?

The God-shadow turns away in a gesture of anger.

SATANMASK: *deprecatingly*
                  Hast thou not made an hedge about him
                  And about his house
                  And about all that he hath on every side?
                  Thou hast blessed the work of his hands
                  And his substance is increased.

The voice drops

                  But put forth thine hand now and touch
                  All that he hath . . .

The voice becomes a hissing whisper.

                                  and he will
                  Curse thee to thy face!

GODMASK: *in a furious, great voice, arm thrown out in a gesture of
         contemptuous commitment*
                  Behold!
                  All that he hath is in thy power!

*The Satan-shadow bows mockingly; raises its two arms, advancing until the
shadows become one shadow. The light fades. Suddenly, out of the darkness the Distant Voice of the Prologue.*

THE DISTANT VOICE:
                  Only . . .

Silence.

GODMASK: Only
                  Upon himself
                  Put not forth thy hand!

Darkness. The crash of a drum; a single stroke. Silence.

(As a consequence of the pact between God and Satan, all of Job's children are killed in various, awful ways; his bank and factory are destroyed, reducing him to poverty; and he contracts a torturous skin disease, which makes him repulsive to others and to himself. Finally, he sits in rags amidst debris surrounded by comforters/tormentors, asking why his suffering has been so great.)

SCENE NINE

.   .   .

A long silence. The Three Comforters squat smoking and waiting. At length J.B. pulls himself painfully up to kneel on his table, his face raised.

J.B.: *a whisper*

God! My God! My God! What have I
Done?

Silence.

BILDAD: *removing his cigarette*

Fair question, Big Boy.
Anyone answer you yet? No answer?

ZOPHAR: *removing his cigar*

That was answered long ago—
Long ago.

ELIPHAZ: *knocking out his pipe*

In dreams are answers.
How do your dreams go, Big Boy? Tell!

J.B.: *peering*

Is someone there? Where? I cannot
See you in this little light
My eyes too fail me . . .

Silence.

Who is there?

Silence.

I know how ludicrous I must look,
Covered with rags, my skin pustulent . . .

Silence.

I know . . .

Silence.

I know how others see me.

A long silence.

Why have you come?

BILDAD: *a coarse laugh*   For comfort, Big Boy.
                 Didn't you ring?

ZOPHAR: *a fat laugh*   That's it: for comfort!

ELIPHAZ: *a thin laugh*
                 All the comfort you can find.

BILDAD: All the kinds of.

ELIPHAZ: *All* the comforts.

ZOPHAR: You called us and we came.

J.B.:   I called
                 God.

BILDAD: Didn't you!

ELIPHAZ: Didn't you just!

ZOPHAR: Why should God reply to *you*
                 From the blue depths of His Eternity?

ELIPHAZ: Blind depths of His Unconsciousness?

BILDAD: Blank depths of His Necessity?

ZOPHAR: God is far above in Mystery.

ELIPHAZ: God is far below in Mindlessness.

BILDAD: God is far within in History—
                 Why should God have time for you?

J.B.:   The hand of God has touched me. Look at me!
                 Every hope I ever had,
                 Every task I put my mind to,
                 Every work I've ever done
                 Annulled as though I had not done it.
                 My trace extinguished in the land,
                 My children dead, my father's name
                 Obliterated in the sunlight everywhere . . .

                 Love too has left me.

BILDAD: Love!
           a great guffaw
                 What's love to Him? One man's misery!

J.B.: *hardly daring*
                 If I am innocent . . . ?

BILDAD: *snort of jeering laughter*   Innocent! Innocent!
                        Nations shall perish in their innocence.
                        Classes shall perish in their innocence.
                        Young men in slaughtered cities
                        Offering their silly throats
                        Against the tanks in innocence shall perish.
                        What's your innocence to theirs?
                        God is History. If you offend Him
                        Will not History dispense with you?
                        History has no time for innocence.

J.B.:   God is just. We are not squeezed
                        Naked through a ridiculous orifice
                        Like bulls into a blazing ring
                        To blunder there by blindfold laws
                        We never learn or can, deceived by
                        Stratagems and fooled by feints,
                        For sport, for nothing, till we fall
                        We're pricked so badly.

BILDAD: *all park-bench orator*   Screw your justice!
                        History is justice—time
                        Inexorably turned to truth!—
                        Not for one man. For humanity.
                        One man's life won't measure on it.
                        One man's suffering won't count, no matter
                        What his suffering; but All will.
                        At the end there will be justice!—
                        Justice for All! Justice for everyone!
              subsiding
                        On the way—it doesn't matter.

J.B.:   Guilt matters. Guilt must always matter.
                        Unless guilt matters the whole world is
                        Meaningless. God too is nothing.

BILDAD: *losing interest*
                        You may be guiltier than Hell
                        As History counts guilt and not
                        One smudging thumbprint on your conscience.
                        Guilt is a sociological accident:
                        Wrong class—wrong century—
                        You pay for your luck with your licks, that's all.

*Eliphaz has been fidgeting. Now he breaks in like a professor in a seminar,
poking a forefinger at the air.*

ELIPHAZ: Come! Come! Come! Guilt is a
                        Psychophenomenal situation—

An illusion, a disease, a sickness:
That filthy feeling at the fingers,
Scent of dung beneath the nails . . .

ZOPHAR: *outraged, flushed, head thrown back*
Guilt is illusion? Guilt is reality!—
The one reality there is!
All mankind are guilty always!

BILDAD: *jeering*
The Fall of Man it felled us all!

*J.B.'s voice breaks through the squabbling with something of its old
authority.*

J.B.:
No doubt ye are the people
And wisdom shall die with you! I am
Bereaved, in pain, desperate, and you mock me!
There was a time when men found pity
Finding each other in the night:
Misery to walk with misery—
Brother in whose brother-guilt
Guilt could be conceived and recognized.
We have forgotten pity.

ELIPHAZ: No.
We have surmounted guilt. It's quite,
Quite different, isn't it? You see the difference.
Science knows now that the sentient spirit
Floats like the chambered nautilus on a sea
That drifts it under skies that drive:
Beneath, the sea of the subconscious;
Above, the winds that wind the world.
Caught between that sky, that sea,
Self has no will, cannot be guilty.
The sea drifts. The sky drives.
The tiny, shining bladder of the soul
Washes with wind and wave or shudders
Shattered between them.

ZOPHAR: Blasphemy!

BILDAD: Bullshit!

ELIPHAZ: *oblivious*
There is no guilt, my man. We all are
Victims of our guilt, not guilty.
We kill the king in ignorance: the voice
Reveals: we blind ourselves. At our
Beginning, in the inmost room,

Each one of us, disgusting monster
Changed by the chilling moon to child,
Violates his mother. Are we guilty?
Our guilt is underneath the Sybil's
Stone: not known.

J.B.: *violently*   I'd rather suffer
Every unspeakable suffering God sends,
Knowing it was I that suffered,
I that earned the need to suffer,
I that acted, I that chose,
Than wash my hands with yours in that
Defiling innocence. Can we be men
And make an irresponsible ignorance
Responsible for everything? I will not
Listen to you!

J.B. pulls his rags over his head.

ELIPHAZ: *shrugging*   But you will. You will.

ZOPHAR: Ah, my son, how well you said that!
How well you said it! Without guilt
What is a man? An animal, isn't he?
A wolf forgiven at his meat,
A beetle innocent in his copulation.
What divides us from the universe
Of blood and seed, conceives the soul in us,
Brings us to God, but guilt? The lion
Dies of death: we die of suffering.
The lion vanishes: our souls accept
Eternities of reparation.
But for our guilt we too would vanish,
Bundles of corrupting bones
Bagged in a hairless hide and rotting.
Happy the man whom God correcteth!
He tastes his guilt. His hope begins.
He is in league with the stones in certainty.

J.B. pulls his rags from his head, drags himself around toward the voice.

J.B.:   *Teach me and I will hold my tongue.*
Show me my transgression.

ZOPHAR: *gently*   No.
No, my son. You show *me*.

He hunches forward dropping his voice.

Search your inmost heart! Question it!
Guilt is a deceptive secret,
The labor often of years, a work
Conceived in infancy, brought to birth
In unpredictable forms years after:
At twelve the palpable elder brother;
At seventeen, perhaps, the servant
Seen by the lamp by accident . . .

J.B.: *urgently, the words forced from him*   My
Sin! Teach me my sin! My wickedness!
Surely iniquity that suffers
Judgment like mine cannot be secret.
Mine is no childish fault, no nastiness
Concealed behind a bathroom door,
No sin a prurient virtue practices
Licking the silence from its lips
Like sugar afterwards. Mine is flagrant,
Worthy of death, of many deaths,
Of shame, loss, hurt, indignities
Such as these! Such as these!
Speak of the sin I must have sinned
To suffer what you see me suffer.

ZOPHAR: Do we need to name our sins
To know the need to be forgiven?
Repent, my son! Repent!

J.B.: *an agony of earnestness*   I sit here
Such as you see me. In my soul
I suffer what you guess I suffer.
Tell me the wickedness that justifies it.
Shall I repent of sins I have not
Sinned to understand it? Till I
Die I will not violate my integrity.

ZOPHAR: *a fat chuckle*
Your integrity! Your integrity!
What integrity have you? —
A man, a miserable, mortal, sinful,
Venal man like any other.
You squat there challenging the universe
To tell you what your crime is called,
Thinking, because your life was virtuous,
It can't be called. It can. Your sin is
Simple. You were born a man!

J.B.:   What is my fault? What have I done?

ZOPHAR: *thundering*
                               What is your fault? Man's heart is evil!
                               What have you done? Man's will is evil.
                               Your fault, your sin, are heart and will:
                               The worm at heart, the wilful will
                               Corrupted with its foul imagining.

J.B. crouches lower in his rags. Silence.

J.B.:   Yours is the cruelest comfort of them all,
                               Making the Creator of the Universe
                               The miscreator of mankind—
                               A party to the crimes He punishes . . .

                               Making my sin . . .
                                              a horror . . .
                                                      a deformity . . .

ZOPHAR: *collapsing into his own voice*
                               If it were otherwise we could not bear it . . .
                               Without the fault, without the Fall,
                               We're madmen: all of us are madmen . . .

He sits staring at his hands, then repeats the phrase:

                               Without the Fall
                                  We're madmen all.
                               We watch the stars
                                  That creep and crawl . . .

BILDAD: Like dying flies
                                  Across the wall
                               Of night . . .

ELIPHAZ: and shriek . . .
                               And that is all.

ZOPHAR: Without the Fall . . .

A long silence. Out of the silence at last J.B.'s voice, barely audible.

J.B.:   *God, my God, my God, answer me!*

Silence.

His voice rises.

                               I cry out of wrong but I am not heard . . .
                               I cry aloud but there is no judgment.

Silence.

violently

> Though He slay me, yet will I trust in Him . . .

Silence.

His voice drops.

> But I will maintain my own ways before Him . . .

Silence.

The ancient human cry.

> Oh, that I knew where I might find Him!—
> That I might come even to His seat!
> I would order my cause before Him
> And fill my mouth with arguments.

There is a rushing sound in the air.

> Behold,
> I go forward but He is not there,
> Backward, but I cannot perceive Him . . .

Out of the rushing sound, the Distant Voice; J.B. cowers as he hears it, his rags over his head.

THE DISTANT VOICE:

> Who is this that darkeneth counsel
> By words without knowledge? . . .

> Where wast thou
> When I laid the foundations of the earth . . .

> When the morning stars sang together
> And all the sons of God shouted for
> Joy?

> Hast thou commanded the morning?

> Hast thou entered into the springs of the sea
> Or hast thou walked in the search of the depth?

> Have the gates of death been opened unto thee?

> Where is the way where light dwelleth?
> And as for darkness, where is the place thereof?

> Hast thou entered into the treasures of the snow?

> By what way is the light parted
> Which scattereth the east wind upon the earth?

> Can'st thou bind the sweet influences of the
> Pleiades?

Hast thou given the horse strength?
Hast thou clothed his neck with thunder?

He saith among the trumpets, Ha, ha;
He smelleth the battle afar off,
The thunder of the captains and the shouting.

Doth the eagle mount up at thy command?

Her eyes behold afar off.
Her young ones also suck up blood:
And where the slain are, there is she . . .

The rushing sound dies away. The Three Comforters stir uneasily, peering up into the darkness. One by one they rise.

BILDAD: The wind's gone round.

ZOPHAR: It's cold.

BILDAD: I told you.

ELIPHAZ: I hear the silence like a sound.

ZOPHAR: Wait for me!

BILDAD: The wind's gone round.

They go out as they came. Silence. J.B. sits motionless, his head covered. The rushing sound returns like the second, stronger gust of a great storm. The Voice rises above it.

THE DISTANT VOICE:
          Shall he that contendeth with the Almighty instruct
          Him? . . .

The rushing sound dies away again. The women sit up, huddle together.

JOLLY ADAMS: *screaming*
                    Mother! Mother! what was
          That?

MRS. ADAMS: The wind, child. Only the wind.
          Only the wind.

JOLLY ADAMS: I heard a word.

MRS. ADAMS: You heard the thunder in the wind.

JOLLY ADAMS: *drowsy*
          Under the wind there was a word . . .

Mrs. Adams picks her up. The women gather their newspapers and blankets and stumble out into the darkness through the door. For the third time the rushing sound returns.

THE DISTANT VOICE:
>He that reproveth God, let him answer it!

J.B.:
>Behold, I am vile; what shall I answer thee?
>I will lay mine hand upon my mouth.

THE DISTANT VOICE:
>Gird up thy loins like a man:
>I will demand of thee, and declare thou unto me.

J.B. pulls himself painfully to his knees.
>Wilt thou disannul my judgment?

J.B. does not answer.

>Wilt thou condemn
>Me that thou mayest be righteous?

>Hast thou an arm like God? Or canst thou
>Thunder with a voice like Him?

>Deck thyself now with majesty and excellency
>And array thyself with glory and beauty . . .

>Then will I also confess unto thee
>That thine own right hand can save thee.

J.B. raises his bowed head.

J.B.: *gently*   I know that thou canst do everything . . .

The rushing sound dies away.

>And that no thought can be withholden from thee.
>Who is he that hideth counsel without knowledge?
>Therefore have I uttered that I understood not:
>Things too wonderful for me, which I knew not.

>Hear, I beseech thee, and I will speak: . . .

Silence.

>I have heard of thee by the hearing of the ear . . .
>But now . . .

His face is drawn in agony.

>mine eye seeth thee!

He bows his head. His hands wring each other.

>Wherefore
>I abhor myself . . . and repent . . .

The light fades.

SCENE TEN

The Platform. As the lights come on the two actors turn violently away from each other, tearing their masks off. Nickles, with a gesture of disgust, skims his into a corner.

NICKLES: Well, that's that!

MR. ZUSS: That's . . . that!

Silence. After a time Nickles looks cautiously around at Mr. Zuss.

NICKLES: What's the matter with you?

MR. ZUSS: Nothing.

NICKLES: You don't look pleased.

MR. ZUSS: Should I?

NICKLES: Well,
You were right weren't you?

MR. ZUSS: *too loud*   Of course I was right.

NICKLES: *too soft*
Anyway, you were magnificent.

MR. ZUSS: Thank you.

He looks at the mask in his hands: puts it down as though it had stung him. Silence. Mr. Zuss pretends to be busy with a shoelace.

MR. ZUSS: Why did you say that?

NICKLES: What did I say?

MR. ZUSS: Why did you say it like that?

NICKLES: Like what?

MR. ZUSS: *imitating*
"Anyway!" . . .
        "*Anyway*, you were magnificent!"

NICKLES: You know. "Anyway." Regardless.

MR. ZUSS: Regardless of
What?

NICKLES: Now, wait a minute! Wait a
Minute! You were magnificent. I said so.

MR. ZUSS: Go on. Finish it.

NICKLES: Finish what?

MR. ZUSS: Regardless of . . . ?

NICKLES: . . . being right, of course.

            What's got into you, my friend? What's eating you?
            Being magnificent and being right
            Don't go together in this universe.
            It's being wrong—a desperate stubbornness
            Fighting the inextinguishable stars—
            Excites imagination. You were
            Right. And knew it. And were admirable.
            Notwithstanding!
snickering   anyway!
a snarl   regardless!

MR. ZUSS: I knew you noticed.

NICKLES: Of course I noticed.
            What lover of the art could fail to!

Something in Mr. Zuss's expression stops him.

                           Noticed
            What?

MR. ZUSS: That tone! That look he gave me!

NICKLES: He misconceived the part entirely.

MR. ZUSS: Misconceived the world! Buggered it!

NICKLES: Giving in like that! Whimpering!

MR. ZUSS: Giving in! You call that arrogant,
            Smiling, supercilious humility
            Giving in to God?

NICKLES: Arrogant!
            His suppurating flesh—his children—
            Let's not talk about those children—
            Everything he ever had!
            And all he asks is answers of the universe:
            All he asks is reasons why—
            Why? Why? And God replies to him:
            God comes whirling in the wind replying—
            What? That God knows more than he does.
            That God's more powerful than he!—
            Throwing the whole creation at him!
            Throwing the Glory and the Power!
            What's the Power to a broken man
            Trampled beneath it like a toad already?

What's the Glory to a skin that stinks!
And this ham actor!—what does *he* do?
How does he play Job to that?

attitude

"Thank you!" "I'm a worm!" "Take two!"

Plays the way a sheep would play it—
Pious, contemptible, goddam sheep
Without the spunk to spit on Christmas!

PENSÉES
BLAISE PASCAL
(trans. by W. F. Trotter)

Blaise Pascal (1623–1662) was a French theologian, scientist, and philosopher best known for his *Pensées* but equally celebrated for his writings on mathematics and physics. He formulated what is known as Pascal's Law in hydrostatics and Pascal's Triangle in mathematics, as well as a calculus of probabilities.

Pascal was always torn between an intellectual and a spiritual approach to life, finally embracing Christianity toward the end of his short life. His final position, as expressed in the *Pensées* or *Thoughts* is that the heart not the mind experiences God; faith is God felt within oneself. Although Pascal does accept faith over reason he never fully discards rational argumentation, as evidenced by his "wager" argument for God's existence.

43

. . . Let man then contemplate the whole of nature in her full and grand majesty, and turn his vision from the low objects which surround him. Let him gaze on that brilliant light, set like an eternal lamp to illumine the universe; let the earth appear to him a point in comparison with the vast circle described by the sun; and let him wonder at the fact that this vast circle is itself but a very fine point in comparison with that described by the stars in their revolution round the firmament. But if our view be arrested there, let our imagination pass beyond; it will sooner exhaust the power of conception than nature that of supplying material for conception. The whole visible world is only an imperceptible atom in the ample bosom of nature. No idea approaches it. We may enlarge our conceptions beyond all imaginable space; we only produce atoms in comparison with the reality of things. It is an infinite sphere, the centre of which is everywhere, the circumference nowhere. In short it is the greatest sensible mark of the almighty power of God, that imagination loses itself in that thought.

Returning to himself, let man consider what he is in comparison with all existence; let him regard himself as lost in this remote corner of nature; and from the little cell in which he finds himself lodged, I mean the universe, let him estimate at their true value the earth, kingdoms, cities, and himself. What is a man in the Infinite?

But to show him another prodigy equally astonishing, let him examine the most delicate things he knows. Let a mite be given him, with its minute body and parts incomparably more minute, limbs with their joints, veins in the limbs, blood in the veins, humours in the blood, drops in the humours, vapours in the drops. Dividing these last things again, let him exhaust his powers of conception, and let the last object at which he can arrive be now that of our discourse. Perhaps he will think that here is the smallest point in nature. I will let him see therein a new abyss. I will paint for him not only the visible universe, but all that he can conceive of nature's immensity in the womb of this abridged atom. Let him see therein an infinity of universes, each of which has its firmament, its planets, its earth, in the same proportion as in the visible world; in each earth animals, and in the last mites, in which he will find again all that the first had, finding still in these others the same thing without end and without cessation. Let him lose himself in wonders as amazing in their littleness as the others in their vastness. For who will not be astounded at the fact that our body, which a little ago was imperceptible in the universe, itself imperceptible in the bosom of the whole, is now a colossus, a world, or rather a whole, in respect of the nothingness which we cannot reach? He who regards himself in this light will be afraid of himself, and observing himself sustained in the body given him by nature between those two abysses of the Infinite and Nothing, will tremble at the sight of these marvels; and I think that, as his curiosity changes into admiration, he will be more disposed to contemplate them in silence than to examine them with presumption.

For in fact what is man in nature? A Nothing in comparison with the Infinite, an All in comparison with the Nothing, a mean between nothing and everything. Since he is infinitely removed from comprehending the extremes, the end of things and their beginning are hopelessly hidden from him in an impenetrable secret; he is equally incapable of seeing the Nothing from which he was made, and the Infinite in which he is swallowed up. . . .

194

. . . Let them at least learn what is the religion they attack, before attacking it. If this religion boasted of having a clear view of God, and of possessing it open and unveiled, it would be attacking it to say that we see nothing in the world which shows it with this clearness. But since, on the contrary, it says that men are in darkness and estranged from God, that He has hidden Himself from their knowledge, that this is in fact the name which He gives Himself in the Scriptures, *Deus absconditus*,[1] and finally, if it endeavours equally to establish these two things: that God has set up in the Church visible signs to make Himself known to those who should seek Him sincerely, and that He has nevertheless so disguised them that He will only be perceived by those who seek Him with all their heart; what advantage can they obtain, when, in the negligence with which they make profession of being in search of the truth, they cry out that nothing reveals it to them; and since that darkness in which they are, and with which they upbraid the Church, establishes only one of the things which

---

[1] "A hidden God" *Isaiah* xiv, 15.

she affirms, without touching the other, and, very far from destroying, proves her doctrine?

In order to attack it, they should have protested that they had made every effort to seek Him everywhere, and even in that which the Church proposes for their instruction, but without satisfaction. If they talked in this manner, they would in truth be attacking one of her pretensions. But I hope here to show that no reasonable person can speak thus, and I venture even to say that no one has ever done so. We know well enough how those who are of this mind behave. They believe they have made great efforts for their instruction, when they have spent a few hours in reading some book of Scripture, and have questioned some priest on the truths of the faith. After that, they boast of having made vain search in books and among men. But, verily, I will tell them what I have often said, that this negligence is insufferable. We are not here concerned with the trifling interest of some stranger, that we should treat it in this fashion; the matter concerns ourselves and our all.

The immortality of the soul is a matter which is of so great consequence to us, and which touches us so profoundly, that we must have lost all feeling to be indifferent as to knowing what it is. All our actions and thoughts must take such different courses, according as there are or are not eternal joys to hope for, that it is impossible to take one step with sense and judgment, unless we regulate our course by our view of this point which ought to be our ultimate end.

Thus our first interest and our first duty is to enlighten ourselves on this subject, whereon depends all our conduct. Therefore among those who do not believe, I make a vast difference between those who strive with all their power to inform themselves, and those who live without troubling or thinking about it.

I can have only compassion for those who sincerely bewail their doubt, who regard it as the greatest of misfortunes, and who, sparing no effort to escape it, make of this inquiry their principal and most serious occupation.

But as for those who pass their life without thinking of this ultimate end of life, and who, for this sole reason that they do not find within themselves the lights which convince them of it, neglect to seek them elsewhere, and to examine thoroughly whether this opinion is one of those which people receive with credulous simplicity, or one of those which, although obscure in themselves, have nevertheless a solid and immovable foundation, I look upon them in a manner quite different.

This carelessness in a matter which concerns themselves, their eternity, their all, moves me more to anger than pity; it astonishes and shocks me; it is to me monstrous. I do not say this out of the pious zeal of a spiritual devotion. I expect, on the contrary, that we ought to have this feeling from principles of human interest and self-love; for this we need only see what the least enlightened persons see.

We do not require great education of the mind to understand that here is no real and lasting satisfaction; that our pleasures are only vanity;

that our evils are infinite; and, lastly, that death, which threatens us every moment, must infallibly place us within a few years under the dreadful necessity of being for ever either annihilated or unhappy.

There is nothing more real than this, nothing more terrible. Be as heroic as we like, that is the end which awaits the noblest life in the world. Let us reflect on this, and then say whether it is not beyond doubt that there is no good in this life but in the hope of another; that we are happy only in proportion as we draw near it; and that, as there are no more woes for those who have complete assurance of eternity, so there is no more happiness for those who have no insight into it. . . .

199

Let us imagine a number of men in chains, and all condemned to death, where some are killed each day in the sight of the others, and those who remain see their own fate in that of their fellows, and wait their turn, looking at each other sorrowfully and without hope. It is an image of the condition of men.

205

When I consider the short duration of my life, swallowed up in the eternity before and after, the little space which I fill, and even can see, engulfed in the infinite immensity of spaces of which I am ignorant, and which know me not, I am frightened, and am astonished at being here rather than there; for there is no reason why here rather than there, why now rather than then. Who has put me here? By whose order and direction have this place and time been alloted to me? . . .

206

The eternal silence of these infinite spaces frightens me.

233

. . . If there is a God, He is infinitely incomprehensible, since, having neither parts nor limits, He has no affinity to us. We are then incapable of knowing either what He is or if He is. This being so, who will dare to undertake the decision of the question? Not we, who have no affinity to Him.

Who then will blame Christians for not being able to give a reason for their belief, since they profess a religion for which they cannot give a reason? They declare, in expounding it to the world, that it is a foolishness, *stultitiam*; and then you complain that they do not prove it! If they proved it, they would not keep their word; it is in lacking proofs, that they are not lacking in sense. "Yes, but although this excuses those who offer it as such, and takes away from them the blame of putting it forward without reason, it does not excuse those who receive it." Let us then examine this point, and say, "God is, or He is not." But to which side shall we incline? Reason can decide nothing here. There is an infinite chaos which separates us. A game is being played at the extremity of this infinite distance where heads or tails will turn up. What will you wager? According to reason, you can do neither the one thing nor the other; according to reason, you can defend neither of the propositions.

Do not then reprove for error those who have made a choice; for you know nothing about it. "No, but I blame them for having made, not this choice, but a choice; for again both he who chooses heads and he who chooses tails are equally at fault, they are both in the wrong. The true course is not to wager at all."

—Yes; but you must wager. It is not optional. You are embarked. Which will you choose then? Let us see. Since you must choose, let us see which interests you least. You have two things to lose, the true and the good; and two things to stake, your reason and your will, your knowledge and your happiness; and your nature has two things to shun, error and misery. Your reason is no more shocked in choosing one rather than the other, since you must of necessity choose. This is one point settled. But your happiness? Let us weigh the gain and the loss in wagering that God is. Let us estimate these two chances. If you gain, you gain all; if you lose, you lose nothing. Wager then without hesitation that He is. . . .

The end of this discourse.—Now what harm will befall you in taking this side? You will be faithful, honest, humble, grateful, generous, a sincere friend, truthful. Certainly you will not have those poisonous pleasures, glory and luxury; but will you not have others? I will tell you that you will thereby gain in this life, and that, at each step you take on this road, you will see so great certainty of gain, so much nothingness in what you risk, that you will at last recognize that you have wagered for something certain and infinite, for which you have given nothing.

"Ah! This discourse transports me, charms me," &c.

If this discourse pleases you and seems impressive, know that it is made by a man who has knelt, both before and after it, in prayer to that Being, infinite and without parts, before whom he lays all he has, for you also to lay before Him all you have for your own good and for His glory, that so strength may be given to lowliness.

277

The heart has its reasons, which reason does not know. We feel it in a thousand things. I say that the heart naturally loves the Universal Being, and also itself naturally, according as it gives itself to them; and it hardens itself against one or the other at its will. You have rejected the one, and kept the other. Is it by reason that you love yourself?

278

It is the heart which experiences God, and not the reason. This, then, is faith: God felt by the heart, not by the reason.

BIBLIOGRAPHY

A. PHILOSOPHIC WORKS

Ahern, M. B. *The Problem of Evil.* London: Routledge and K. Paul, 1971.

Augustine, St. *The City of God.* Cambridge: Harvard University, 1957–72.

Berdyaev, Nicholas. *The Divine and the Human.* Translated by R. M. French. London: G. Bles, 1949.

Bible. "Book of Job." "Ecclesiastes."

Brightman, E. S. *A Philosophy of Religion.* New York: Prentice-Hall, 1940.

———. *The Problem of God.* New York: Abingdon Press, 1930.

Buber, Martin. *Good and Evil.* Translated by M. Bullock. New York: Scribner, 1953.

Burgh, W. G. de. *From Morality to Religion.* London: Macdonald and Evans, 1938.

Ferre, Nels F. S. *Evil and the Christian Faith.* New York: Harper, 1947.

Flew, Antony, and MacIntyre, Alasdair, eds. *New Essays in Philosophical Theology.* New York: Macmillan, 1964.

Hick, John. *Evil and the God of Love.* London: Macmillan, 1966.

———. *Faith and the Philosophers.* New York: St. Martin's Press, 1964.

Joad, Cyril E. *God and Evil.* Freeport, N.Y.: Books for Libraries Press, 1972.

Laird, John. *Mind and Deity.* London: Allen and Unwin, 1941.

Leibniz, G. W. *The Theodicy.* Translated by E. M. Huggard. London: Routledge and K. Paul, 1952.

Lewis, C. S. *The Problem of Pain.* New York: Macmillan, 1945.

McTaggart, John. *Some Dogmas of Religion.* London: Arnold, 1930.

Maimonides, Moses. *Guide for the Perplexed.* New York: Hutchinson, 1948.

Mill, John Stuart. "Nature." In *Three Essays on Religion.* New York: Greenwood Press, 1909.

Mitchell, Basil, ed. *Faith and Logic.* Boston: Beacon Press, 1957.

Niebuhr, Reinhold. *Moral Man and Immoral Society.* New York: Scribner's Sons, 1932.

Petit, Francois. *The Problem of Evil.* Translated by C. Williams. New York: Hawthorne, 1959.

Plato. "Euthyphro." In *The Dialogues of Plato,* translated by B. Jowett. Oxford: Clarendon Press, 1871.

Rashdall, Hastings. *The Theory of Good and Evil,* vol. 2. Oxford: Clarendon Press, 1907.

Ricoeur, Paul. *Symbolism of Evil.* Translated by E. Buchanan. New York: Harper and Row, 1967.

Ross, F. H. *Personalism and the Problem of Evil.* New Haven: Yale University, 1940.

Royce, Josiah. *The Religious Aspect of Philosophy.* Boston: Houghton Mifflin, 1885.

———. *Studies of Good and Evil.* New York: D. Appleton, 1898.

Russell, Bertrand. *Mysticism and Logic.* New York: Longmans, Green, 1921.

Siwek, Paul. *The Philosophy of Evil.* New York: Ronald, 1951.

Spinoza, Benedict. *Ethics.* Translated by W. H. White. New York: Hafner, 1949.

Temple, William. *Nature, Man and God.* London: Macmillan, 1935.

Tennant, F. R. *Philosophical Theology,* vol. 2. Cambridge: Cambridge University, 1928–30.

Tsanoff, Radoslav. *The Nature of Evil.* New York: Macmillan, 1931.

Williams, Norman P. *The Ideas of the Fall and of Original Sin.* New York: Longmans, Green, 1927.

B. LITERARY WORKS

Aeschylus. *Prometheus Bound.* In *Aeschylus,* translated by H. W. Smyth, New York: Putnam, 1922–26.

Arnold, Matthew. "Dover Beach." In *The Poetical Works of Matthew Arnold.* Oxford: University Press, 1942.

Bernanos, Georges. *Joy.* Translated by L. Varèse. London: Bodley Head, 1949.

Capek, Karel and Josef. *Adam the Creator.* Translated by D. Round. New York: R. R. Smith, 1929.

Chaucer, Geoffrey. "The Friar's Tale." In *Canterbury Tales,* edited by D. Wright. New York: Random House, 1965.

Dostoevsky, Fedor. *The Brothers Kara-mazov*. Translated by C. Garnett. New York: Modern Library, 1937.

Frost, Robert. "Design." In *Collected Poems of Robert Frost*. New York: Henry Holt, 1930.

———. *A Masque of Reason*. New York: Henry Holt, 1945.

Gorky, Maxim. *The Lower Depths*. In *Twenty Five Modern Plays*, edited by S. M. Tucker. New York: Harper, 1948.

Hamsun, Knut. *Growth of the Soil*. Translated by W. W. Worster. New York: Knopf, 1921.

Hardy, Thomas. "Convergence of the Twain." In *Collected Poems of Thomas Hardy*. New York: Macmillan, 1926.

Hugo, Victor. *The Hunchback of Notre Dame*. New York: Modern Library, 1941.

Mann, Thomas. *Doctor Faustus*. Translated by H. T. Lowe-Porter. New York: Knopf, 1948.

Manzoni, Alessandro. *The Betrothed*. Translated by A. Colquhour. New York: Dutton, 1961.

Marlowe, Christopher. *The Tragical History of Dr. Faustus*. Edited by P. H. Kocher. New York: Appleton-Century-Crofts, 1950.

Melville, Herman. *Moby Dick*. New York: Dutton, 1907.

Milton, John. "Paradise Lost." In *The Works of John Milton*. New York: Columbia University, 1931–38.

Shakespeare, William. *King Lear*. In *The Works of William Shakespeare*, edited by W. G. Clark and W. A. Wright. New York: St. Martin's Press, 1956.

Shelley, Percy Bysshe. "Prometheus Unbound." In *The Complete Poetical Works*, edited by T. Hutchinson. London: Oxford University, 1935.

Stephens, James. "The Whisperers." In *Collected Poems of James Stephens*. New York: Macmillan, 1926.

Strindberg, August. *The Father* and *The Spook Sonata*. In *Eight Famous Plays*, translated by E. Björkman and N. Erichsen. New York: Scribner, 1949.

Wilder, Thornton. *The Bridge of San Luis Rey*. New York: A. and C. Bonic, 1928.

THREE

FREE WILL AND DETERMINISM

The issue between the determinist and the advocate of free will (sometimes labeled an indeterminist or libertarian) is whether human beings have the freedom to choose between alternative courses of action. The determinist takes the absolute position that all actions, including those men think they deliberately choose, are the inevitable result of prior factors; consequently, all choices have already been made for people. The factors that are operative may be internal or external, but they completely govern human actions in accordance with natural laws. Once these laws are fully known, all behavior will be predictable; it is only because of incomplete knowledge that we cannot predict conduct with complete accuracy at present.

The libertarian admits that people often do behave in predictable ways and that statistical probabilities are possible, but he claims people are not forced to act as they do and are always free to behave differently. In brief, the libertarian maintains that the causes of human choice lie with the human being, or that reasons for decisions cannot be reduced to causes.

Thus the lines are drawn, and various arguments are used by the two sides to support their positions.

DETERMINISM

The determinist, first of all, admits that decisions are usually thought to be free, but he claims that this is a false assumption due to ignorance. Once we scientifically analyze the mechanics of action and understand the full range of factors lying behind our choices, then the true nature of our situation becomes apparent. Freedom is seen as a delusion, a popular misconception that must give way to the scientific truth of determination.

Among the causal factors cited by the determinist is our genetic inheritance, including our body type, nervous system, skeletal structure, brain capacity, glandular secretions, and so forth. Each of these biological factors affects the way we live. Our body type, for example, determines whether we choose sedentary or energetic activities, and our brain capacity determines the type of occupation we decide to follow. In addition to genetic factors, the determinist also points to geographic and climatic conditions that exert an influence on our behavior. People who live in mountainous regions are not the same as those who live on the plains, and cold climates produce different individuals than those found in warm weather areas. Even more important than these factors, the determinist claims, are the effects of a person's social environment. For, each society determines the character of its members by the customs and mores that it holds, its religious and philosophical ideas, the social, economic, and political structures that it embodies. As a consequence, the Chinese differ from the French, and the Africans from the South Americans. Other factors that are said to determine an individual's personality and decisions are his family upbringing, formal and informal education, and the unique experiences he has undergone in his particular life.

The list could be extended, but the point that the determinist makes is that once all of these factors are taken into account, the causes of a person's actions are revealed; we can then see why a person had to act as he did. What's more, the better we know someone the more confident we become that the person will behave in certain consistent ways. Social interaction is predicated upon this dependability, and when someone disappoints us, we conclude that we did not know the person as thoroughly as we had assumed. Knowing someone, then, means being aware of his motivational and behavioral patterns, that is, having knowledge of the determining factors and the conduct that follows from them.

Determinists further argue that science is founded upon the assumption of an orderly and rationally comprehensible universe, shot throughout with causal principles and natural laws. Surely human actions are embraced within this universal scheme and cannot be exempted as unique events carrying special status. Psychology, that branch of science specifically concerned with human behavior, assumes that conduct has causal determinants by its use of the stimulus-response model—a model that has been employed with considerable success in analyzing and predicting behavior. As a result of psychological research, we now know that choices are responses to given stimuli; when other stimuli are present, different choices are made. The conclusion must be that causal conditions lie behind human actions, that all events occur according to deterministic laws.

LIBERTARIANISM

The libertarian responds to the determinist's indictment by first arguing that factors of biology, climate, geography, and so on, only affect the individual until they are brought to the level of consciousness; at that point, they become influences not determinants. Once an individual is aware of the forces operating upon him, he is free to respond positively or negatively to their influence. That is, the individual is always free to choose his influences once he is conscious of them.

Furthermore, knowing an individual and having confidence in him does not mean knowing what he is forced to do, but having knowledge of the choices he consistently makes. We depend upon a person in the sense that we know what he does do, not what he must do. Freedom of the will, then, is perfectly consistent with the ability to predict someone's behavior. To say that people are free does not mean that they behave capriciously and unpredictably, but only that their choices, while falling into a pattern, are decided by themselves.

With regard to the scientific assumption of universal causation, the libertarian maintains that perhaps man is an unusual organism, uniquely capable of reflection and conscious deliberation prior to action. Heisenberg, in his principle of indeterminacy, indicated that cause and effect laws may not be applicable to nuclear physics; if exceptions exist there, man may well be an exception also. But even within the causal framework, belief in free will can be maintained, for the libertarian argues that the individual himself is the cause of his actions. Various forces may play upon him, but it is he who makes the final choice. In other words, a person's decision is the ultimate causal factor. This position, of course, usually depends upon a nonphysical conception of self (as described in Part I).

The libertarian also takes the offensive and levels some criticisms against the determinist theory. He maintains, for example, that determinism renders moral and legal obligations meaningless by assuming that the individual is not responsible for his actions. For, if all behavior is determined and events could never have been otherwise, then the individual is not accountable for what happens; he can neither be praised nor blamed. As Kant taught us, "ought implies can." In order to recommend that an action *ought* to be performed, we must logically presuppose that the person *can* do that which is prescribed. If an individual has no choice but is compelled in his behavior by forces beyond his control, then moral prescriptions become futile. In the same way, moral judgments of the person are then inappropriate, and no legal responsibility can be assigned. Courts and prisons should therefore close, for the criminal is a victim, not a free agent, and cannot be held responsible for his crimes. The force of this criticism is that since these consequences of determinism are unacceptable (that is, they conflict with our ethical assumptions about responsibility), the theory cannot be regarded as valid.

Finally, the libertarian charges the determinist with contradicting himself. For, the determinist claims that all decisions are caused by factors beyond the individual's control, yet by arguing for the truth of this claim, the determinist is assuming that people are free to accept or reject the determinist theory. In other words, if people are considered capable of affirming or denying determinism, then they cannot be regarded as determined. Therefore, the more the determinist tries to convince others to accept determinism, the more apparent it becomes that determinism should be rejected.

To be consistent, the determinist could not argue his point, but would maintain that he has been determined to believe in determinism just as the libertarian has been determined to believe in free will. All arguments would be thought futile since people must believe as they do. But the moment the determinist presents a case for determinism, he gives the game away, for he then presupposes that people are free to change their minds. For anyone to be convinced of the truth of determinism means that determinism cannot be true.

These are some of the principal arguments used on both sides. Yet, the libertarian does not necessarily have the last word. With regard to legal punishment, for example, the determinist sometimes argues that criminals can still be imprisoned even if they are not thought to be responsible for their crimes. Prison can simply function to condition the criminal against performing future crimes, and, at the same time, to deter any potential criminals in the society. In a determinist system we cannot blame someone for what he has done, but we can administer punishment to keep him from doing it again. The determinist also defends himself against the charge of self-contradiction by claiming that if the libertarian changes his mind in response to determinist arguments, it will not be because he has made a free decision to do so but because he could not do otherwise; the determinist arguments forced him to agree and served as the determinants involved. The entire process, therefore, is further proof of determinism, for, the strongest causal factors always win.

The libertarian has counterarguments to these points, but we must leave the matter here and pass on to literary and philosophic examples of the two positions which will deepen our understanding of the issue. Having explored some of the main areas of controversy between the determinist and libertarian, we are now in a position to deal with the problem in a more sophisticated way and, perhaps, to arrive at an adequate solution.

1

The Predeterminism
of Destiny

OEDIPUS, KING OF THEBES

SOPHOCLES

(trans. by Gilbert Murray)

Sophocles (c. 495–406 B.C.) was a Greek poet who can be grouped with
Aeschylus and Euripides as one of the three great ancient dramatists. *Oedipus,
King of Thebes, Oedipus at Colonus, Antigone,* and *Electra* are probably his
best-known plays, but all seven of his surviving dramas exhibit a remarkable
standard in the spoken verse. He is also justly celebrated for the power of
his plots and the imaginative creation of sympathetic characters.

Sophocles' *Oedipus* typifies Greek drama insofar as the events among men
are referred upwards to the dictates of the gods, or, more fundamentally, to
moira (or fate), which predetermines the life of men and gods. (Similar themes
of predestination occur in Sophocles' *Oedipus at Colonus* and *Philoctetes,*
and in the conclusions of Euripides' plays *Alcestis, Helena, Andromache,* and
The Bacchae.) To some extent, Oedipus' downfall is punishment for the sin
of hubris—his excessive pride in insisting upon knowing the truth despite
repeated warnings, but by and large he is in the grip of destiny and the
prophecies of patricide and incest must be fulfilled.

Oedipus, who previously was given the throne (as well as Queen Jocasta)
for saving Thebes by answering the riddle of the sphinx, is again called upon
to rescue the city by discovering who killed old King Laius; the oracle at
Delphi had declared that the unavenged murder was causing the pestilence
in the city. At the start of this excerpt, the seer Tiresias has been summoned
by Oedipus to help discover the murderer.

TIRESIAS (*to himself*).

Ah me!
A fearful thing is knowledge, when to know
Helpeth no end. I knew this long ago,
But crushed it dead. Else had I never come.

OEDIPUS.

What means this? Comest thou so deep in gloom?

TIRESIAS.

Let me go back! Thy work shall weigh on thee
The less, if thou consent, and mine on me.

OEDIPUS.

Prophet, this is not lawful; nay, nor kind
To Thebes, who feeds thee, thus to veil thy mind.

TIRESIAS.

'Tis that I like not thy mind, nor the way
It goeth. Therefore, lest I also stray . . .
        [He moves to go off. OEDIPUS *bars his road.*

OEDIPUS.

Thou shalt not, knowing, turn and leave us! See,
We all implore thee, all, on bended knee.

TIRESIAS.

Ye have no knowledge. What is mine I hold
For ever dumb, lest what is thine be told.

OEDIPUS.

What wilt thou? Know and speak not? In my need
Be false to me, and let thy city bleed?

TIRESIAS.

I will not wound myself nor thee. Why seek
To trap and question me? I will not speak.

OEDIPUS.

Thou devil!
       [Movement of LEADER *to check him.*
      Nay; the wrath of any stone
Would rise at him. It lies with thee to have done
And speak. Is there no melting in thine eyes!

TIRESIAS.

Naught lies with me! With thee, with thee there lies,
I warrant, what thou ne'er hast seen nor guessed.

OEDIPUS (*to* LEADER, *who tries to calm him*).

How can I hear such talk?—he maketh jest
Of the land's woe—and keep mine anger dumb?

TIRESIAS.

Howe'er I hold it back, 'twill come, 'twill come.

OEDIPUS.

The more shouldst thou declare it to thy King.

TIRESIAS.

I speak no more. For thee, if passioning
Doth comfort thee, on, passion to thy fill!
[*He moves to go.*

OEDIPUS.

'Fore God, I am in wrath; and speak I will,
Nor stint what I see clear. 'Twas thou, 'twas thou,
Didst plan this murder; aye, and, save the blow,
Wrought it.—I know thou art blind; else I could swear
Thou, and thou only, art the murderer.

TIRESIAS (*returning*).

So?—I command thee by thine own word's power,
To stand accurst, and never from this hour
Speak word to me, nor yet to these who ring
Thy throne. Thou art thyself the unclean thing.

OEDIPUS.

Thou front of brass, to fling out injury
So wild! Dost think to bate me and go free?

TIRESIAS.

I am free. The strong truth is in this heart.

OEDIPUS.

What prompted thee? I swear 'twas not thine art.

TIRESIAS.

'Twas thou. I spoke not, save for thy command.

OEDIPUS.

Spoke what? What was it? Let me understand.

TIRESIAS.

Dost tempt me? Were my words before not plain!

OEDIPUS.

Scarce thy full meaning. Speak the words again.

TIRESIAS.

Thou seek'st this man of blood: Thyself art he.

OEDIPUS.

'Twill cost thee dear, twice to have stabbed at me!

TIRESIAS.

Shall I say more, to see thee rage again?

OEDIPUS.

Oh, take thy fill of speech: 'twill all be vain.

TIRESIAS.

Thou livest with those near to thee in shame
Most deadly, seeing not thyself nor them.

OEDIPUS.

Thou think'st 'twill help thee, thus to speak and speak?

TIRESIAS.

Surely, until the strength of Truth be weak.

OEDIPUS.

'Tis weak to none save thee. Thou hast no part
In truth, thou blind man, blind eyes, ears and heart.

TIRESIAS.

More blind, more sad thy words of scorn, which none
Who hears but shall cast back on thee: soon, soon.

OEDIPUS.

Thou spawn of Night, not I nor any free
And seeing man would hurt a thing like thee.

TIRESIAS.

God is enough.—'Tis not my doom to fall
By thee. He knows and shall accomplish all.

OEDIPUS (*with a flash of discovery*).

Ha! Creon!—Is it his or thine, this plot?

TIRESIAS.

'Tis thyself hates thee. Creon hates thee not.

OEDIPUS.

O wealth and majesty, O skill all strife
Surpassing on the fevered roads of life,
What is your heart but bitterness, if now
For this poor crown Thebes bound upon my brow,
A gift, a thing I sought not—for this crown
Creon the stern and true, Creon mine own
Comrade, comes creeping in the dark to ban
And slay me; sending first this magic-man
And schemer, this false beggar-priest, whose eye

Is bright for gold and blind for prophecy.
Speak, thou. When hast thou ever shown thee strong
For aid? The She-Wolf of the woven song
Came, and thy art could find no word, no breath,
To save thy people from her riddling death.
'Twas scarce a secret, that, for common men
To unravel. There was need of Seer-craft then.
And thou hadst none to show. No fowl, no flame,
No God revealed it thee. 'Twas I that came,
Rude Oedipus, unlearned in wizard's lore,
And read her secret, and she spoke no more.
Whom now thou thinkest to hunt out, and stand
Foremost in honour at King Creon's hand.
I think ye will be sorry, thou and he
That shares thy sin-hunt. Thou dost look to me
An old man; else, I swear this day should bring
On thee the death thou plottest for thy King.

LEADER.

Lord Oedipus, these be but words of wrath,
All thou hast spoke and all the Prophet hath.
Which skills not. We must join, for ill or well,
In search how best to obey God's oracle.

TIRESIAS.

King though thou art, thou needs must bear the right
Of equal answer. Even in me is might
For thus much, seeing I live no thrall of thine,
But Lord Apollo's; neither do I sign
Where Creon bids me.
           I am blind, and thou
Hast mocked my blindness. Yea, I will speak now.
Eyes hast thou, but thy deeds thou canst not see
Nor where thou art, nor what things dwell with thee.
Whence art thou born? Thou know'st not; and unknown,
On quick and dead, on all that were thine own,
Thou hast wrought hate. For that across thy path
Rising, a mother's and a father's wrath,
Two-handed, shod with fire, from the haunts of men
Shall scourge thee, in thine eyes now light, but then
Darkness. Aye, shriek! What harbour of the sea,
What wild Kithairon shall not cry to thee
In answer, when thou hear'st what bridal song,
What wind among the torches, bore thy strong
Sail to its haven, not of peace but blood.
Yea, ill things multitude on multitude

Thou seest not, which so soon shall lay thee low,
Low as thyself, low as thy children.—Go,
Heap scorn on Creon and my lips withal:
For this I tell thee, never was there fall
Of pride, nor shall be, like to thine this day.

OEDIPUS.

To brook such words from this thing? Out, I say!
Out to perdition! Aye, and quick, before . . .
[*The* LEADER *restrains him.*
Enough then!—Turn and get thee from my door.

TIRESIAS.

I had not come hadst thou not called me here.

OEDIPUS.

I knew thee not so dark a fool. I swear
'Twere long before I called thee, had I known.

TIRESIAS.

Fool, say'st thou? Am I truly such an one?
The two who gave thee birth, they held me wise.

OEDIPUS.

Birth? . . . Stop! Who were they? Speak thy prophecies.

TIRESIAS.

This day shall give thee birth and blot thee out.

OEDIPUS.

Oh, riddles everywhere and words of doubt!

TIRESIAS.

Aye. Thou wast their best reader long ago.

OEDIPUS.

Laugh on. I swear thou still shalt find me so.

TIRESIAS.

That makes thy pride and thy calamity.

OEDIPUS.

I have saved this land, and care not if I die.

TIRESIAS.

Then I will go.—Give me thine arm, my child.

OEDIPUS.

Aye, help him quick.—To see him there makes wild
My heart. Once gone, he will not vex me more.

TIRESIAS (*turning again as he goes*).

I fear thee not; nor will I go before
That word be spoken which I came to speak.
How canst thou ever touch me?—Thou dost seek
With threats and loud proclaim the man whose hand
Slew Laïus. Lo, I tell thee, he doth stand
Here. He is called a stranger, but these days
Shall prove him Theban true, nor shall he praise
His birthright. Blind, who once had seeing eyes,
Beggared, who once had riches, in strange guise,
His staff groping before him, he shall crawl
O'er unknown earth, and voices round him call:
"Behold the brother-father of his own
Children, the seed, the sower and the sown,
Shame to his mother's blood, and to his sire
Son, murderer, incest-worker."
Cool thine ire
With thought of these, and if thou find that aught
Faileth, then hold my craft a thing of naught.
   [*He goes out.* OEDIPUS *returns to the* Palace.

CHORUS.

[*They sing of the unknown murderer,*
What man, what man is he whom the voice of Delphi's cell
Hath named of the bloody hand, of the deed no tongue may tell?
     Let him fly, fly, for his need
     Hath found him; oh, where is the speed
That flew with the winds of old, the team of North-Wind's spell?
  For feet there be that follow. Yea, thunder-shod
  And girt with fire he cometh, the Child of God;
And with him are they that fail not, the Sin-Hounds risen from Hell.

For the mountain hath spoken, a voice hath flashed from amid the snows,
That the wrath of the world go seek for the man whom no man knows.
     Is he fled to the wild forest,
     To caves where the eagles nest?
O angry bull of the rocks, cast out from thy herdfellows!
  Rage in his heart, and rage across his way,
  He toileth ever to beat from his ears away
The word that floateth about him, living, where'er he goes.
[*And of the Prophet's strange accusation.*
Yet strange, passing strange, the wise augur and his lore;

And my heart it cannot speak; I deny not nor assent,
But float, float in wonder at things after and before;
   Did there lie between their houses some old wrath unspent,
That Corinth against Cadmus should do murder by the way?
   No tale thereof they tell, nor no sign thereof they show;
Who dares to rise for vengeance and cast Oedipus away
          For a dark, dark death long ago!

Ah, Zeus knows, and Apollo, what is dark to mortal eyes;
   They are Gods. But a prophet, hath he vision more than mine?
Who hath seen? Who can answer? There be wise men and unwise.
   I will wait, I will wait, for the proving of the sign. . . .

JOCASTA.

Husband, in God's name, say what hath ensued
Of ill, that thou shouldst seek so dire a feud.

OEDIPUS.

I will, wife. I have more regard for thee
Than these.—Thy brother plots to murder me.

JOCASTA.

Speak on. Make all thy charge. Only be clear.

OEDIPUS.

He says that I am Laïus' murderer.

JOCASTA.

Says it himself? Says he hath witnesses?

OEDIPUS.

Nay, of himself he ventures nothing. 'Tis
This priest, this hellish seer, makes all the tale.

JOCASTA.

The seer?—Then tear thy terrors like a veil
And take free breath. A seer? No human thing
Born on the earth hath power for conjuring
Truth from the dark of God.

                    Come, I will tell
An old tale. There came once an oracle
To Laïus: I say not from the God
Himself, but from the priests and seers who trod
His sanctuary: if ever son were bred
From him and me, by that son's hand, it said,
Laïus must die. And he, the tale yet stays

Among us, at the crossing of three ways
Was slain by robbers, strangers. And my son—
God's mercy!—scarcely the third day was gone
When Laïus took, and by another's hand
Out on the desert mountain, where the land
Is rock, cast him to die. Through both his feet
A blade of iron they drove. Thus did we cheat
Apollo of his will. My child could slay
No father, and the King could cast away
The fear that dogged him, by his child to die
Murdered.—Behold the fruits of prophecy!
Which heed not thou! God needs not that a seer
Help him, when he would make his dark things clear.

OEDIPUS.

Woman, what turmoil hath thy story wrought
Within me! What up-stirring of old thought!

JOCASTA.

What thought? It turns thee like a frightened thing.

OEDIPUS.

'Twas at the crossing of three ways this King
Was murdered? So I heard or so I thought.

JOCASTA.

That was the tale. It is not yet forgot.

OEDIPUS.

The crossing of three ways! And in what land?

JOCASTA.

Phokis 'tis called. A road on either hand
From Delphi comes and Daulia, in a glen.

OEDIPUS.

How many years and months have passed since then?

JOCASTA.

'Twas but a little time before proclaim
Was made of thee for king, the tidings came.

OEDIPUS.

My God, what hast thou willed to do with me?

JOCASTA.

Oedipus, speak! What is it troubles thee?

OEDIPUS.

Ask me not yet. But say, what build, what height
Had Laïus? Rode he full of youth and might?

JOCASTA.

Tall, with the white new gleaming on his brow
He walked. In shape just such a man as thou.

OEDIPUS.

God help me! I much fear that I have wrought
A curse on mine own head, and knew it not.

JOCASTA.

How sayst thou? O my King, I look on thee
And tremble.

OEDIPUS (*to himself*).

Horror, if the blind can see!
Answer but one thing and 'twill all be clear.

JOCASTA.

Speak. I will answer though I shake with fear.

OEDIPUS.

Went he with scant array, or a great band
Of armèd followers, like a lord of land?

JOCASTA.

Four men were with him, one a herald; one
Chariot there was, where Laïus rode alone.

OEDIPUS.

Aye me! 'Tis clear now.
Woman, who could bring
To Thebes the story of that manslaying?

JOCASTA.

A house-thrall, the one man they failed to slay.

OEDIPUS.

The one man . . . ? Is he in the house to-day?

JOCASTA.

Indeed no. When he came that day, and found
Thee on the throne where once sat Laïus crowned,
He took my hand and prayed me earnestly
To send him to the mountain heights, to be

A herdsman, far from any sight or call
Of Thebes. And there I sent him. 'Twas a thrall
Good-hearted, worthy a far greater boon.

OEDIPUS.

Canst find him? I would see this herd, and soon.

JOCASTA.

'Tis easy. But what wouldst thou with the herd?

OEDIPUS.

I fear mine own voice, lest it spoke a word
Too much; whereof this man must tell me true.

JOCASTA.

The man shall come.—My lord, methinks I too
Should know what fear doth work thee this despite.

OEDIPUS.

Thou shalt. When I am tossed to such an height
Of dark foreboding, woman, when my mind
Faceth such straits as these, where should I find
A mightier love than thine?
                                        My father—thus
I tell thee the whole tale—was Polybus,
In Corinth King; my mother Meropê
Of Dorian line. And I was held to be
The proudest in Corinthia, till one day
A thing befell: strange was it, but no way
Meet for such wonder and such rage as mine.
A feast it was, and some one flushed with wine
Cried out at me that I was no true son
Of Polybus. Oh, I was wroth! That one
Day I kept silence, but the morrow morn
I sought my parents, told that tale of scorn
And claimed the truth; and they rose in their pride
And smote the mocker. . . . Aye, they satisfied
All my desire; yet still the cavil gnawed
My heart, and still the story crept abroad.
   At last I rose—my father knew not, nor
My mother—and went forth to Pytho's floor
To ask. And God in that for which I came
Rejected me, but round me, like a flame,
His voice flashed other answers, things of woe,
Terror, and desolation. I must know
My mother's body and beget thereon

A race no mortal eye durst look upon,
And spill in murder mine own father's blood.
   I heard, and, hearing, straight from where I stood,
No landmark but the stars to light my way,
Fled, fled from the dark south where Corinth lay,
To lands far off, where never I might see
My doom of scorn fulfilled. On bitterly
I strode, and reached the region where, so saith
Thy tale, that King of Thebes was struck to death. . . .
Wife, I will tell thee true. As one in daze
I walked, till, at the crossing of three ways,
A herald, like thy tale, and o'er his head
A man behind strong horses charioted
Met me. And both would turn me from the path,
He and a thrall in front. And I in wrath
Smote him that pushed me—'twas a groom who led
The horses. Not a word the master said,
But watched, and as I passed him on the road
Down on my head his iron-branchèd goad
Stabbed. But, by heaven, he rued it! In a flash
I swung my staff and saw the old man crash
Back from his car in blood. . . . Then all of them
I slew.
       Oh, if that man's unspoken name
Had aught of Laïus in him, in God's eye
What man doth move more miserable than I,
More dogged by the hate of heaven! No man, kin
Nor stranger, any more may take me in;
No man may greet me with a word, but all
Cast me from out their houses. And withal
'Twas mine own self that laid upon my life
These curses.—And I hold the dead man's wife
In these polluting arms that spilt his soul. . . .
Am I a thing born evil? Am I foul
In every vein? Thebes now doth banish me,
And never in this exile must I see
Mine ancient folk of Corinth, never tread
The land that bore me; else my mother's bed
Shall be defiled, and Polybus, my good
Father, who loved me well, be rolled in blood.
If one should dream that such a world began
In some slow devil's heart, that hated man,
Who should deny him?—God, as thou art clean,
Suffer not this, oh, suffer not this sin
To be, that e'er I look on such a day!
Out of all vision of mankind away

To darkness let me fall ere such a fate
Touch me, so unclean and so desolate! . . .

(A messenger arrives from Corinth announcing the death of the king, Polybus,
and subsequently discloses to Oedipus that he is not the king's blood son but
was given to Polybus as a baby by a shepherd. Oedipus immediately sends for
the shepherd and questions him about the child.)

OEDIPUS.

In what way
Came it to thee? Was it thine own child, or
Another's?

SHEPHERD.

Nay, it never crossed my door:
Another's.

OEDIPUS.

Whose? What man, what house, of these
About thee?

SHEPHERD.

In the name of God who sees,
Ask me no more!

OEDIPUS.

If once I ask again,
Thou diest.

SHEPHERD.

From the folk of Laïus, then,
It came.

OEDIPUS.

A slave, or born of Laïus' blood?

SHEPHERD.

There comes the word I dread to speak, O God!

OEDIPUS.

And I to hear: yet heard it needs must be.

SHEPHERD.

Know then, they said 'twas Laïus' child. But she
Within, thy wife, best knows its fathering.

OEDIPUS.

'Twas she that gave it?

SHEPHERD.

It was she, O King.

OEDIPUS.

And bade you . . . what?

SHEPHERD.

Destroy it.

OEDIPUS.

Her own child? . . .

Cruel!

SHEPHERD.

Dark words of God had made her wild.

OEDIPUS.

What words?

SHEPHERD.

The babe must slay his father; so
'Twas written.

OEDIPUS.

Why didst thou, then, let him go
With this old man?

SHEPHERD.

O King, my heart did bleed.
I thought the man would save him, past all need
Of fear, to his own distant home. . . . And he
Did save him, to great evil. Verily
If thou art he whom this man telleth of,
Know, to affliction thou art born.

OEDIPUS.

Enough!
All will come true. . . . Thou Light, never again
May I behold thee, I in the eyes of men
Made naked, how from sin my being grew,
In sin I wedded and in sin I slew!
           [He rushes into the Palace. The SHEPHERD is led away by the
              thralls.

CHORUS.

[Strophe.

Nothingness, nothingness,

Ye Children of Man, and less
    I count you, waking or dreaming!
And none among mortals, none,
Seeking to live, hath won
More than to seem, and to cease
    Again from his seeming.
While ever before mine eyes
One fate, one example, lies—
Thine, thine, O Oedipus, sore
    Of God oppressèd—
What thing that is human more
    Dare I call blessèd?

                          [*Antistrophe.*

Straight his archery flew
To the heart of living; he knew
    Joy and the fulness of power,
O Zeus, when the riddling breath
Was stayed and the Maid of Death
Slain, and we saw him through
    The death-cloud, a tower!

For that he was called my king;
Yea, every precious thing
Wherewith men are honoured, down
    We cast before him,
And great Thebes brought her crown
    And kneeled to adore him.

                        [*Strophe.*

But now, what man's story is such bitterness to speak?
  What life hath Delusion so visited, and Pain,
        And swiftness of Disaster?
        O great King, our master,
  How oped the one haven to the slayer and the slain?
And the furrows of thy father, did they turn not nor shriek,
  Did they bear so long silent thy casting of the grain?

                    [*Antistrophe.*

'Tis Time, Time, desireless, hath shown thee what thou art;
  The long monstrous mating, it is judged and all its race.
        O child of him that sleepeth,
        Thy land weepeth, weepeth,
  Unfathered. . . . Would God, I had never seen thy face!
From thee in great peril fell peace upon my heart,
  In thee mine eye clouded and the dark is come apace.

            [A MESSENGER *rushes out from the Palace.*

MESSENGER.

O ye above this land in honour old
Exalted, what a tale shall ye be told,
What sights shall see, and tears of horror shed,
If still your hearts be true to them that led
Your sires! There runs no river, well I ween,
Not Phasis nor great Ister, shall wash clean
This house of all within that hideth—nay,
Nor all that creepeth forth to front the day,
Of purposed horror. And in misery
That woundeth most which men have willed to be.

LEADER.

No lack there was in what we knew before
Of food for heaviness. What bring'st thou more?

MESSENGER.

One thing I bring thee first. . . . 'Tis quickly said.
Jocasta, our anointed queen, is dead.

LEADER.

Unhappy woman! How came death to her?

MESSENGER.

By her own hand. . . . Oh, of what passed in there
Ye have been spared the worst. Ye cannot see.
Howbeit, with that which still is left in me
Of mind and memory, ye shall hear her fate.
    Like one entranced with passion, through the gate
She passed, the white hands flashing o'er her head,
Like blades that tear, and fled, unswerving fled,
Toward her old bridal room, and disappeared
And the doors crashed behind her. But we heard
Her voice within, crying to him of old,
Her Laïus, long dead; and things untold
Of the old kiss unforgotten, that should bring
The lover's death and leave the loved a thing
Of horror, yea, a field beneath the plough
For sire and son: then wailing bitter-low
Across that bed of births unreconciled,
Husband from husband born and child from child.
And, after that, I know not how her death
Found her. For sudden, with a roar of wrath,
Burst Oedipus upon us. Then, I ween,
We marked no more what passion held the Queen,
But him, as in the fury of his stride,

"A sword! A sword! And show me here," he cried,
"That wife, no wife, that field of bloodstained earth
Where husband, father, sin on sin, had birth,
Polluted generations!" While he thus
Raged on, some god—for sure 'twas none of us—
Showed where she was; and with a shout away,
As though some hand had pointed to the prey,
He dashed him on the chamber door. The straight
Door-bar of oak, it bent beneath his weight,
Shook from its sockets free, and in he burst
To the dark chamber.
                                There we saw her first
Hanged, swinging from a noose, like a dead bird.
He fell back when he saw her. Then we heard
A miserable groan, and straight he found
And loosed the strangling knot, and on the ground
Laid her.—Ah, then the sight of horror came!
The pin of gold, broad-beaten like a flame,
He tore from off her breast, and, left and right,
Down on the shuddering orbits of his sight
Dashed it: "Out! Out! Ye never more shall see
Me nor the anguish nor the sins of me.
Ye looked on lives whose like earth never bore,
Ye knew not those my spirit thirsted for:
Therefore be dark for ever!"
                                Like a song
His voice rose, and again, again, the strong
And stabbing hand fell, and the massacred
And bleeding eyeballs streamed upon his beard,
Wild rain, and gouts of hail amid the rain.
    Behold affliction, yea, afflictions twain
From man and woman broken, now made one
In downfall. All the riches yester sun
Saw in this house were rich in verity.
What call ye now our riches? Agony,
Delusion, Death, Shame, all that eye or ear
Hath ever dreamed of misery, is here.

LEADER.

And now how fares he? Doth the storm abate?

MESSENGER.

He shouts for one to open wide the gate
And lead him forth, and to all Thebes display
His father's murderer, his mother's. . . . Nay,
Such words I will not speak. And his intent

Is set, to cast himself in banishment
Out to the wild, not walk 'mid human breed
Bearing the curse he bears. Yet sore his need
Of strength and of some guiding hand. For sure
He hath more burden now than man may endure.
   But see, the gates fall back, and that appears
Which he who loathes shall pity—yea, with tears.
     [OEDIPUS *is led in, blinded and bleeding.*
       The Old Men bow down and hide their faces; some of
       them weep.

CHORUS.

Oh, terrible! Oh, sight of all
   This life hath crossed, most terrible!
   Thou man more wronged than tongue can tell,
What madness took thee? Do there crawl
   Live Things of Evil from the deep
   To leap on man? Oh, what a leap
Was His that flung thee to thy fall!

THE DISCOURSES
EPICTETUS

(trans. by Thomas Higginson)

Epictetus (c. A.D. 55–135) was a Roman philosopher who, together with Seneca and Marcus Aurelius, is identified as one of the founders of Stoicism. His *Discourses* and *Encheiridion* (or *Manual*), which contain lectures and conversations recorded by Arrian, together constitute the principal sources for Stoic morals. The philosophy of Stoicism in general exerted considerable influence on ancient thought and early Christianity.

Epictetus is a typical Stoic in his belief that all physical events, including every human action, are *predestined* to occur. He believed that the way of wisdom then, is not merely to accept what happens but to cheerfully assent to the inevitable since we cannot change it. As his writings point out, we have no power over events but we can control our reactions to them, maintaining our optimism and equanimity even in the face of catastrophe.

Stoicism appeals to us as a doctrine during times of great difficulty when we feel impotent to alter the conditions of our lives and consequently turn inward for tranquility and some measure of happiness. If we believe that all events are inevitable this can lead to peace of mind.

OF THE THINGS WHICH ARE, AND THE THINGS WHICH ARE NOT IN OUR OWN POWER

Of human faculties in general, you will find that each is unable to contemplate itself, and therefore to approve or disapprove itself. How far does the proper sphere of grammar extend? As far as the judging of language. Of music? As far as the judging of melody. Does either of them contemplate itself, then? By no means.

Thus, for instance, when you are to write to your friend, grammar will tell you what to write; but whether you are to write to your friend at all, or no, grammar will not tell you. Thus music, with regard to tunes; but whether it be proper or improper, at any particular time, to sing or play, music will not tell you.

What will tell, then?

That faculty which contemplates both itself and all other things.

And what is that?

The Reasoning Faculty; for that alone is found able to place an estimate upon itself,—what it is, what are its powers, what its value and likewise all the rest. For what is it else that says, gold is beautiful? since the gold itself does not speak. Evidently, that faculty which judges of the appearances of things. What else distinguishes music, grammar, the other faculties, proves their uses, and shows their proper occasions?

Nothing but this.

As it was fit, then, this most excellent and superior faculty alone, a right use of the appearances of things, the gods have placed in our own power; but all other matters they have not placed in our power. What, was it because they would not? I rather think that, if they could, they had granted us these too; but they certainly could not. For, placed upon earth, and confined to such a body and to such companions, how was it possible that, in these respects, we should not be hindered by things outside of us?

But what says Zeus? "O Epictetus, if it had been possible, I had made this little body and property of thine free, and not liable to hindrance. But now do not mistake; it is not thy own, but only a finer mixture of clay. Since, then, I could not give thee this, I have given thee a certain portion of myself; this faculty of exerting the powers of pursuit and avoidance, of desire and aversion, and, in a word, the use of the appearances of things. Taking care of this point, and making what is thy own to consist in this, thou wilt never be restrained, never be hindered; thou wilt not groan, wilt not complain, wilt not flatter any one. How, then? Do all these advantages seem small to thee? Heaven forbid! Let them suffice thee, then, and thank the gods."

But now, when it is in our power to take care of one thing, and to apply ourselves to one, we choose rather to take care of many, and to encumber ourselves with many,—body, property, brother, friend, child, and slave,—and, by this multiplicity of encumbrances, we are burdened and weighed down. Thus, when the weather does not happen to be fair for sailing, we sit in distress and gaze out perpetually. Which way is the wind? North. What good will that do us? When will the west blow? When it pleases, friend, or when Æolus pleases; for Zeus has not made you dispenser of the winds, but Æolus.

What, then, is to be done?

To make the best of what is in our power, and take the rest as it occurs.

And how does it occur?

As it pleases God.

What, then, must I be the only one to lose my head?

Why, would you have all the world, then, lose their heads for your consolation? Why are not you willing to stretch out your neck, like Lateranus,[1] when he was commanded by Nero to be beheaded? For, shrinking a little after receiving a weak blow, he stretched it out again. And before this, when Epaphroditus,[2] the freedman of Nero, interrogated him about the conspiracy, "If I have a mind to say anything," replied he, "I will tell it to your master."

What resource have we, then, upon such occasions? Why, what else but to distinguish between what is *ours*, and what not *ours*,—what is right, and what is wrong? I must die, and must I die groaning too? I must be fettered; must I be lamenting too? I must be exiled; and what hinders me, then, but that I may go smiling, and cheerful, and serene? "Betray a

---

1 Plautius Lateranus, a consul elect, was put to death by the command of Nero, for being privy to the conspiracy of Piso. [Thomas Higginson.]

2 Epaphroditus was the master of requests and freedman of Nero, and the master of Epictetus. He assisted Nero in killing himself, for which he was condemned to death by Domitian. [Thomas Higginson.]

secret." I will not betray it, for this is in my own power. "Then I will fetter you." What do you say, man? Fetter me? You will fetter my leg, but not Zeus himself can get the better of my free will. "I will throw you into prison; I will behead that paltry body of yours." Did I ever tell you that I alone had a head not liable to be cut off? These things ought philosophers to study; these ought they daily to write, and in these to exercise themselves.

Thraseas[3] used to say, "I had rather be killed today than banished tomorrow." But how did Rufus[4] answer him? "If you prefer it as a heavier misfortune, how foolish a preference! If as a lighter, who has put it in your power? Why do you not study to be contented with what is allotted you?"

Well, and what said Agrippinus[5] upon this account? "I will not be a hindrance to myself." Word was brought him, "Your cause is pending in the senate." "Good luck attend it; but it is eleven o'clock" (the hour when he used to exercise before bathing),—"let us go to our exercise." This being over, a messenger tells him, "You are condemned." "To banishment," says he, "or to death?" "To banishment." "What of my estate?" "It is not taken away." "Well, then, let us go as far as Aricia,[6] and dine there."

This it is to have studied what ought to be studied; to have placed our desires and aversions above tyranny and above chance. I must die,—if instantly, I will die instantly; if in a short time, I will dine first, and when the hour comes, then will I die. How? As becomes one who restores what is not his own. . . .

OF PROGRESS

He who is entering on a state of progress, having learned from the philosophers that good should be sought and evil shunned, and having learned, too, that prosperity and peace are no otherwise attainable by man than in not missing what he seeks, nor incurring what he shuns,—such a one totally extirpates and banishes all wayward desire, and shuns only those things over which he can have control. For if he should attempt to shun those things over which he has no control, he knows that

---

3 Thraseas Pætus, a Stoic philosopher put to death by Nero. He was husband of Arria, so well known by that beautiful epigram in Martial. The expression of Tacitus concerning him is remarkable: "After the murder of so many excellent persons, Nero at last formed a desire of cutting off virtue itself, by the execution of Thraseas Pætus and Bareas Soranus." [Thomas Higginson.]

4 Rufus was a Tuscan, of the equestrian order, and a Stoic philosopher. [Thomas Higginson.]

5 Agrippinus was banished by Nero, for no other crime than the unfortunate death of his father, who had been causelessly killed by the command of Tiberius; and this had furnished a pretence for accusing him of hereditary disloyalty. [Thomas Higginson.]

6 Aricia, a town about sixteen miles from Rome, the first stage in his road to banishment. [Thomas Higginson.]

he must sometimes incur that which he shuns, and be unhappy. Now if virtue promises happiness, prosperity, and peace, then progress in virtue is certainly progress in each of these. For to whatever point the perfection of anything absolutely brings us, progress is always an approach towards it.

How happens it, then, that when we confess virtue to be such, yet we seek, and make an ostentatious show of progress in other things! What is the business of virtue?

A life truly prosperous.

Who is in a state of progress, then? He who has best studied Chrysippus?[7] Why, does virtue consist in having read Chrysippus through? If so, progress is confessedly nothing else than understanding a great deal of Chrysippus; otherwise we confess virtue to consist in one thing, and declare progress, which is an approach to it, to be quite another thing.

This person, they say, is already able to understand Chrysippus, by himself. "Certainly, sir, you have made a vast improvement!" What improvement? Why do you delude him? Why do you withdraw him from a sense of his real needs? Why do not you show him the real function of virtue, that he may know where to seek progress? Seek it there, O unfortunate, where your work lies. And where does your work lie? In learning what to seek and what to shun, that you may neither be disappointed of the one nor incur the other; in practising how to pursue and how to avoid, that you may not be liable to fail; in practising intellectual assent and doubt, that you may not be liable to be deceived. These are the first and most necessary things. But if you merely seek, in trembling and lamentation, to keep away all possible ills, what real progress have you made?

Show me then your progress in this point. As if I should say to a wrestler, Show me your muscle; and he should answer me, "See my dumb-bells." Your dumb-bells are your own affair; I desire to see the effect of them.

"Take the treatise on the active powers, and see how thoroughly I have perused it."

I do not inquire into this, O slavish man, but how you exert those powers, how you manage your desires and aversions, your intentions and purposes, how you meet events,—whether in accordance with nature's laws or contrary to them. If in accordance, give me evidence of that, and I will say you improve; if the contrary, you may go your way, and not only comment on these treatises, but write such yourself; and yet what service will it do you? Do not you know that the whole volume is sold for five denarii? Does he who comments upon it, then, value himself at more than that sum? Never make your life to lie in one thing and yet seek progress in another.

---

[7] Chrysippus was regarded as the highest authority among the later Stoics; but not one of his seven hundred volumes has come down to posterity. [Thomas Higginson.]

Where is progress, then?

If any of you, withdrawing himself from externals, turns to his own will, to train, and perfect, and render it conformable to nature,—noble, free, unrestrained, unhindered, faithful, humble;—if he has learned, too, that whoever desires or shuns things beyond his own power can neither be faithful nor free, but must necessarily take his chance with them, must necessarily too be subject to others, to such as can procure or prevent what he desires or shuns; if, rising in the morning, he observes and keeps to these rules; bathes regularly, eats frugally, and to every subject of action applies the same fixed principles,—if a racer to racing, if an orator to oratory,—this is he who truly makes progress; this is he who has not labored in vain. But if he is wholly intent on reading books, and has labored that point only, and travelled for that, I bid him go home immediately and do his daily duties; since that which he sought is nothing.

The only real thing is to study how to rid life of lamentation, and complaint, and *Alas!* and *I am undone*, and misfortune, and failure; and to learn what death, what exile, what a prison, what poison is; that he may be able to say in a prison, like Socrates, "My dear Crito, if it thus pleases the gods, thus let it be;" and not, "Wretched old man, have I kept my gray hairs for this!" [Do you ask] who speaks thus? Do you think I quote some mean and despicable person? Is it not Priam who says it? Is it not Œdipus? Nay, how many kings say it? For what else is tragedy but the dramatized sufferings of men, bewildered by an admiration of externals? If one were to be taught by fictions that things beyond our will are nothing to us, I should rejoice in such a fiction, by which I might live prosperous and serene. But what your own aims are, it is your business to consider. . . .

OF CONTENTMENT

Concerning the gods, some affirm that there is no deity; others, that he indeed exists, but is slothful, negligent, and without providential care; a third class admits both his being and his providence, but only in respect to great and heavenly objects, not earthly; a fourth recognizes him both in heaven and earth, but only in general, not individual matters; a fifth, like Odysseus and Socrates, says, "I cannot be hid from thee in any of my motions."

It is, before all things, necessary to examine each of these opinions; which is, and which is not rightly spoken. Now, if there are no gods, wherefore serve them? If there are, but they take no care of anything, how is the case bettered? Or, if they both are, and take care; yet, if there is nothing communicated from them to men, and therefore certainly nothing to me, how much better is it? A wise and good man, after examining these things, submits his mind to Him who administers the whole, as good citizens do to the laws of the commonwealth.

He, then, who comes to be instructed, ought to come with this aim: "How may I in everything follow the gods? How may I acquiesce in the divine administration? And how may I be free?" For he is free to whom all happens agreeably to his desire, and whom no one can unduly restrain.

"What, then, is freedom mere license?"

By no means; for madness and freedom are incompatible.

"But I would have that happen which appears to me desirable, however it comes to appear so."

You are mad; you have lost your senses. Do not you know that freedom is a very beautiful and valuable thing? But for me to choose at random, and for things to happen agreeably to such a choice, may be so far from a beautiful thing, as to be of all things the most undesirable. For how do we proceed in writing? Do I choose to write the name of Dion (for instance) as I will? No, but I am taught to be willing to write it as it ought to be written. And what is the case in music? The same. And what in every other art or science? Otherwise, it would be of no purpose to learn anything if it were to be adapted to each one's particular humor. Is it, then, only in the greatest and principal matter, that of freedom, permitted me to desire at random? By no means; but true instruction is this, —learning to desire that things should happen as they do. And how do they happen? As the appointer of them hath appointed. He hath appointed that there should be summer and winter, plenty and dearth, virtue and vice, and all such contrarieties, for the harmony of the whole. To each of us he has given a body and its parts, and our several possessions and companions. Mindful of this appointment, we should enter upon a course of education and instruction, not in order to change the constitution of things,—a gift neither practicable nor desirable,—but that, things being as they are with regard to us, we may have our minds accommodated to the facts. Can we, for instance, flee from mankind? How is that possible? Can we, by conversing with them, transform them? Who has given us such a power? What, then, remains, or what method is there to be found, for such a commerce with them that, while they act according to the appearances in their own minds, we may nevertheless be affected conformably to nature?

But you are wretched and discontented. If you are alone, you term it a desert; and if with men, you call them cheats and robbers. You find fault too with your parents, and children, and brothers, and neighbors. Whereas you ought, if you live alone, to call that repose and freedom, and to esteem yourself as resembling the gods; and when you are in company, not to call it a crowd, and a tumult, and a trouble, but an assembly, and a festival,—and thus to take all things contentedly. What, then, is the punishment of those who do not so accept them? To be—as they are. Is any one discontented with being alone? Let him remain in his desert.

Discontented with his parents? Let him be a bad son; and let him mourn. Discontented with his children? Let him be a bad father. Shall we throw him into prison? What prison? Where he already is; for he is in a situation against his will, and wherever any one is against his will, that is to him a prison,—just as Socrates was not truly in prison, for he was willingly there.

"What, then, must my leg be lame?"

And is it for one paltry leg, wretch, that you accuse the universe? Can you not forego that, in consideration of the whole? Can you not give up something? Can you not gladly yield it to him who gave it? And will you be angry and discontented with the decrees of Zeus,—which he, with the Fates, who spun in his presence the thread of your birth, ordained and appointed? Do not you know how very small a part you are of the whole? —that is, as to body; for, as to reason, you are neither worse nor less than divine. For reason is not measured by size or height, but by principles. Will you not, therefore, place your good there where you share with the gods?

"But how wretched am I, in such a father and mother!"

What, then, was it granted you to come beforehand, and make your own terms, and say, "Let such and such persons, at this hour, be the authors of my birth"? It was not granted; for it was necessary that your parents should exist before you, and so you be born afterwards. Of whom? Of just such as they were. What, then, since they are such, is there no remedy afforded you? Surely, you would be wretched and miserable if you knew not the use of sight, and shut your eyes in presence of colors; and are not you more wretched and miserable in being ignorant that you have within you the needful nobleness and manhood wherewith to meet these accidents? Events proportioned to your reason are brought before you; but you turn your mind away, at the very time when you ought to have it the most open and discerning. Why do not you rather thank the gods that they have made you superior to those events which they have not placed within your own control, and have rendered you accountable for that only which is within your own control? They discharge you from all responsibility for your parents, for your brothers, for your body, possessions, death, life. For what, then, have they made you responsible? For that which is alone in your own power,—a right use of things as they appear. Why, then, should you draw those cares upon yourself for which you are not accountable? This is giving one's self vexation without need.

2

Economic and Material Factors as Determinants

GERMINAL
ÉMILE ZOLA
(trans. by L. W. Tancock)

Emile Zola (1840–1902) was a French novelist and critic who is usually credited with founding the naturalist movement in literature. He is chiefly remembered for the vast Rougon-Macquart cycle of nineteen novels, among them *The Dramshop* and *Nana*.

In general, naturalistic writers such as Zola, William Faulkner, John Steinbeck, Theodore Dreiser, and Honoré de Balzac assume that their "slice of life" reveals the individual as a puppet manipulated by social forces of a vast and overpowering kind. In *Germinal*, Emile Zola assumes that it is economic forces in particular that determine the lives of men, whether workers, managers, or owners. In Zola's notes for this novel about mining he wrote:

> The miner must be shown crushed, starving, a victim of ignorance, suffering with his children in a hell on earth—but not persecuted, for the bosses are not deliberately vindictive—he is simply overwhelmed by the social situation as it exists. . . . The worker is the victim of the facts of existence—capital, competition, industrial crises.

Maheu was furious; more bad luck—now he had gone and lost one of his haulage girls with no hope of replacing her yet awhile! He worked on a contract system—four colliers together on the face, himself, Zacharie, Levaque, and Chaval. With only Catherine left to move the stuff, the job would be slowed down. Suddenly he cried:

'Half a minute! What about that chap who was looking for a job?'

Dansaert happened to be passing the locker-room. Maheu told him what had happened and asked permission to take the man on, using as an argument the Company's policy to replace haulage girls by men, as at Anzin. The overman's first reaction was a smile, for as a rule the miners objected to the plan to exclude women from underground work, being much more concerned about jobs for their daughters than about hygiene and morality. But after a moment's hesitation he gave his permission, subject to ratification by Monsieur Négrel, the engineer.

'Anyhow, if he's still running he will be miles away by now,' said Zacharie.

'No,' said Catherine, 'I saw him stop by the boilers.'

'Go along, look sharp!' said Maheu.

She rushed off, while a wave of miners moved on up to the cages, leaving their places by the fire to others. Without waiting for his father, Jeanlin went and got his lamp, with Bébert, a great ninny of a boy, and Lydie, a puny girl of ten. Mouquette had set off in front, and she was screaming in the dark stairway, calling them dirty little brats and threatening to clout them if they pinched her.

In the boiler-house Étienne was talking to the stoker shovelling coal into the furnace, for the thought of having to go back into the night chilled him to the bone. He was making up his mind to move on when he felt a hand on his shoulder.

'Come this way,' said Catherine; 'there's something for you.'

At first he did not understand. Then he seized her hand and shook it violently in an outburst of joy.

'Thanks, chum! You're a good sort, and no mistake!'

As she looked at him in the red glare of the furnaces she began to laugh, for it seemed so funny that he should take her for a boy, though certainly she was still slight and her hair was hidden under her cap. He on his part was laughing with relief, and there they stood for a moment, cheeks aglow, laughing at each other.

In the locker-room, Maheu was crouching in front of his locker, taking off his clogs and thick woollen stockings. When Étienne arrived everything was fixed up in a few words: thirty sous a day, hard work but easy to pick up. The collier advised him to keep his boots on and lent him an old round leather cap to protect the head—a precaution he and his children scorned. Tools were taken out, including Fleurance's spade, and when he had locked up his clogs and stockings, together with Étienne's bundle, Maheu suddenly burst out in a rage:

'What's up with that bloody Chaval? One more girl upended on a heap of stones, I suppose! We're half an hour late today.'

Zacharie and Levaque calmly went on toasting their shoulders, but in the end Zacharie said:

'You waiting for Chaval? He got here before us and went straight down.'

'What! You knew that and didn't tell me? Come on! Come on! Get a move on!'

Catherine was warming her hands, but had to fall in behind the rest. Étienne let her go in front and followed after. Once again he found himself in a maze of stairs and dark passages, in which the miners' bare feet made a flopping sound like old slippers. They came to the lamp-room, a glasshouse full of racks, with hundreds of Davy lamps in rows one above the other. They had all been cleaned and inspected the day before, and the whole place was ablaze like a *chapelle ardente*.[1] Each man, as he passed the window, took his own lamp, stamped with his number, examined it and closed it himself, and the timekeeper at his table entered the time in his book. Maheu had to apply for a lamp for his new man. As a final precaution everybody had to pass a checker who saw that lamps were properly closed.

'Lumme! it's none too hot,' said Catherine, shivering.

Étienne only nodded back. Once again he was by the shaft, in the middle of the huge draughty shed. He thought he was brave enough, but what with the rumbling trucks, bumping signals, megaphones bellowing indistinctly and cables ceaselessly flying past as the drums wound and unwound at full speed, a nasty feeling seemed to grip him by the throat. The cages slid up and down stealthily like beasts of the night, and went on swallowing men as though the pit were a mouth gulping them down. As his turn came he felt very cold, and his silent tension called forth a sneer from Zacharie and Levaque, for neither of them approved of taking this stranger on—particularly Levaque, who was offended at not having been consulted. So Catherine was glad to hear her father explaining things to the young man.

'You see, up above the cages there is a safety catch; iron hooks catch the guides if the cable breaks. It works . . . well, sometimes. . . . Yes, the shaft is divided vertically by planking into three compartments: the middle one has the cages, on the left is the well for ladders. . . .' But he broke off to grumble, though not too loud:

'What the hell are we doing here, anyway? Keeping us standing about freezing like this!'

Richomme, the deputy, was on his way down too, his open lamp fixed by a nail to his leather cap, and heard him complaining; being an ex-collier himself whose sympathies were still with his old friends, he muttered paternally: 'Careful! You never know who's listening. Besides, the unloading has got to be done. . . . Well, here we are! Get your lot in.'

The cage was waiting for them, resting on its keeps. It was fitted with fine wire netting, reinforced with strips of sheet-iron. Maheu, Zacharie, Levaque, and Catherine slipped into a tub on the further side, and as there was supposed to be room for five Étienne went in too. But the best places had gone and he had to squeeze in beside Catherine, one of whose elbows stuck into his stomach. His lamp got in his way and he was advised to hook it into a buttonhole in his coat, but he did not hear and went on holding it in his hand, clumsily. The loading went on above and below; it was like shovelling in a lot of livestock pell-mell. Still no move! What was the matter? He seemed to have been fuming there for minutes on end. At length he felt a jerk, everything turned over, the things round

---

[1] [Editor's note: Mortuary chapel.]

him flew away and a sickening sensation of falling tugged at his bowels. This lasted as long as there was any light, while they were passing the two pithead landings and their flying beams. Then, in the darkness of the pit, he was stunned and lost any clear idea of his sensations.

'Here we go!' casually remarked Maheu.

They were all quite calm. He wondered at times whether he was going down or up. There were moments when there was a sort of stillness —that was when the cage dropped sheer, without touching the guides. Then there would be sudden tremors as it bobbed about between the beams, and he was terrified of a disaster. In any case, he could not see the walls of the shaft although his face was glued to the netting. At his feet the huddled bodies were hardly visible, so dim were the lamps, but the open lamp of the deputy in the next tub shone out like a solitary beacon.

But Maheu was going on with his instructions: 'This one is four metres in diameter. It's high time it was re-lined—water is coming in everywhere. We are getting down to that level now; can't you hear it?'

Étienne was already wondering what the noise was. It was like pouring rain. First a few heavy drops had pattered on the cage roof, like the beginning of a shower, but now the rain was streaming down faster and faster, turning into a real deluge. The roofing must have been faulty, for a trickle of water on his shoulder went through to the skin. It was intensely cold; they were sinking into wet blackness. Suddenly they went through a blaze of light: in a flash there was a vision of a cave with men moving about. And then the void again.

'That was the first level,' Maheu was saying. 'We are three hundred and twenty metres down. Look at the speed.'

He held up his lamp and shone it on to one of the guidebeams which was flying past like a rail under an express train, but apart from that nothing could be seen. Three other levels went by in glimpses of light, and the deafening rain lashed in the blackness.

'What a depth!' murmered Étienne.

The plunge must have been going on for hours. He had taken up an awkward position and did not dare to move, and this was particularly painful because Catherine's elbow was sticking into him. She said nothing, but he could feel her warm against him. When at last the cage stopped at the bottom, five hundred and fifty-four metres below ground, he was amazed to learn that the descent had taken exactly one minute. But the clang of the bolts and the feel of solid ground beneath him suddenly cheered him up, and he light-heartedly chipped Catherine:

'What have you got under your skin to make you so warm? I've got your elbow in my stomach. . . .'

What a donkey he was to go on taking her for a boy! Had he got his eyes bunged up, or what? She burst out:

'I'll tell you where you've got my elbow—in your eye.'

At this there was a general storm of laughter which quite mystified the young man.

The cage was emptying and the men crossed the bottom landing, a hall hewn out of the rock, with the roof reinforced with masonry, and lit by three large open-flame lamps. Onsetters were hurrying loaded tubs along the iron floor. The walls exuded a smell of cellars: a cold saltpetre smell mingled with the warmer breath of the stables nearby. Four galleries yawned in front of them.

'This way!' said Maheu. 'You're not there yet; we've got two good kilometres to do.'

The miners separated into groups and disappeared into the black holes. Some fifteen of them had made their way into the one to the left, and Étienne brought up the rear, behind Maheu, who was behind Catherine, Zacharie, and Levaque. It was a good haulage-road, running through such firm rock that it had needed timbering only here and there. They went on and on in single file by the light of their little lamps, and uttering never a word. At every step the young man stumbled and tripped over the rails. He had been puzzled for some little time by a dull roar like the rumbling of a storm, distant at first but, he thought, growing in violence, and coming from the bowels of the earth. Was it the thunder of a fall, which would bring crashing down on their heads the enormous mass between them and the light of day? The blackness was suddenly broken by a light, the rock trembled; he flattened himself against the wall like his mates. A big white horse went by, close to his face, pulling a train of tubs. Bébert was sitting on the first, holding the reins, whilst Jeanlin was running along barefoot, holding on to the last one.

They resumed their tramp. Further on they came to a junction where two new galleries opened out. The party divided up again as the miners gradually spread themselves out over all the workings of the pit. The road was now timbered, the roof supported by oak stays and the loose rocks lined with planking, between which could be seen strata of shale, sparkling with mica, and the duller masses of rugged sandstone. Trains of full or empty tubs were continually passing him and passing each other, and their thunderous rumbling was borne away into the darkness by phantom animals, trotting along unseen. On a siding a stationary train was slumbering like a long black serpent. The horse snorted; it was wrapped in such deep shadow that you would have taken its vague outline for a block of stone fallen from the roof. Ventilation traps slowly opened and closed. As they went on, the gallery became narrower and lower and the roof more and more irregular, so that they had to keep their backs bent.

Étienne gave his head a nasty bang. But for the leather helmet his skull would have been split open. And yet he was imitating even the slightest movement of Maheu in front of him, whose dark shape stood out in the glimmer of the lamps. None of the others ever hit anything; doubtless they knew every bump, every knot in the timbers, every bulging rock by heart. To add to his troubles, the slippery floor was getting wetter and wetter: sometimes he walked through real pools, which could only be descried by the churned-up mud all round. The most surprising thing of all was the sudden changes of temperature. At pit-bottom it was very cold, and along the main tram-road, which ventilated the whole mine, the confined space between the walls had turned the icy wind into a hurricane. But further on, now that they were penetrating into other roads which had only a small share of the ventilation, the wind had dropped and the heat was increasing, a suffocating heat, as heavy as lead.

Maheu had not said another word. He now turned to the right along a new gallery, simply calling back, without turning his head:

'The Guillaume seam.'

The face they were working on was in this seam. After the very first steps Étienne bruised his head and elbows. The sloping roof came so low that he had to walk bent double for twenty or thirty metres at a time, and always ankle-deep in water. They did two hundred metres in this way, when suddenly Levaque, Zacharie, and Catherine vanished. They seemed to have melted away into a narrow crack in front of him.

'We have to climb,' said Maheu. 'Hang your lamp to a button-hole and grab the beams.' And then he disappeared too.

Étienne had to follow. The chimney was a private way left through the seam, by which miners could reach all the secondary roads. It was the same width as the coal seam, scarcely sixty centimetres, and it was as well that he was thin, for in his inexperience he hoisted himself up with needless waste of energy, pulling in his shoulders and haunches and moving up by sheer strength of arm as he clung to the timbers. The first gallery was fifteen metres up, but they had to go on further, as the face on which Maheu and his gang were working was the sixth—up in hell, they called it. The galleries, spaced one above the other at fifteen-metre intervals, seemed to go on for ever, and the climb up this narrow fissure was scraping the skin off his back and chest. He was gasping for breath as though the rocks were crushing his limbs beneath their weight, he felt as though his hands were being torn off and his legs were black and blue, while the lack of air made his blood seem ready to burst through his skin. In one of the galleries he dimly made out two creatures, one small and the other big, crouching as they pushed tubs along: it was Lydie and Mouquette, already at work. And two more faces to climb! Blinded with sweat, he despaired of keeping up with the others, whose agile limbs he could hear brushing along the rock.

'Cheer up, here we are!' said Catherine's voice.

And there he really was, when another voice called from further along the coal face:

'Well, what the hell? You don't seem to care a damn! I've got two kilometres to walk from Montsou and I'm here first!'

It was Chaval, angry at having been kept waiting. He was a man of twenty-five, tall, thin, bony, with strong features. When he saw Étienne, he asked with pained surprise:

'What's that supposed to be?' And when Maheu had explained the story be muttered:

'So the men pinch the girls' jobs now!'

In the glance that the two men exchanged there flared up one of those sudden instinctive hatreds. Although he had not quite understood, Étienne felt that an insult was intended. There was a silence and they all set to work. Gradually all the seams had filled with workers, and there was activity at every face on all levels, and right to the end of every road. The greedy pit had swallowed its daily ration of men; nearly seven hundred of them were now toiling in this immense ant-hill, burrowing in the earth, riddling it with holes like old, worm-eaten wood. In the heavy silence down in the deep seams, you could have put your ear to the rock and heard these human insects busily at work, from the flying cable raising and lowering the cage to the click of tools picking away at the workings.

As he turned round, Étienne once more found himself pressing against Catherine. But this time he became aware of the curve of her young breast, and suddenly understood.

'So you are a girl?' he murmured in amazement.

She replied in her gay, straightforward way:

'Yes, of course! What a time it has taken you to find out!'

. . .

The four colliers had spread themselves out, one above the other, to cover the whole coal face. Each one occupied about four metres of the seam, and there were hooked planks between them to catch the coal as it fell. The seam was so thin, hardly more than fifty centimetres through at this point, that they were flattened between roof and wall, dragging themselves along by their knees and elbows, unable to turn without grazing their shoulders. In order to get at the coal, they had to lie on one side with twisted neck, arms above their heads, and wield their short-handled picks slantways.

Zacharie was at the bottom, with Levaque and Chaval above him and Maheu at the top. Each cut into the bed of shale with his pick, then made two vertical slots in the coal and finally drove an iron wedge in at the top, thus loosening a block. The coal was soft, and in its fall the block broke up and rolled in pieces all over the men's stomachs and thighs. When these pieces, stopped by the planks, had collected beneath them, the men disappeared, immured in the narrow cleft.

Maheu had the worst of it. At the top, the temperature went up to ninety-five degrees, air could not circulate, and he was stifled to death. In order to see, he had to hang his lamp on a nail so near the top of his head that its heat set his blood on fire. But it was the wet that really tortured him, for the rock, only a few centimetres above his face, incessantly dripped fast and heavy drops with maddening regularity always on the same spot. Try as he might to twist his neck and bend his head backwards, the drops splashed relentlessly on his face, pit-a-pat. In a quarter of an hour he was soaked through, what with his own sweat as well, and steaming like a wash-tub. On this particular morning he was swearing because a drop was determined to go in his eye. He would not stop cutting, and the violent blows of his pick shook him, as he lay between the two rocks like a fly caught between the pages of a book, in danger of being flattened out.

Not a word was exchanged. They all hacked away, and all that could be heard was their irregular tapping, which sounded distant and muffled, for in this dead air sounds raised no echo but took on a harsh sonority. The darkness was mysterious in its blackness, thick with flying coal-dust and heavy with gases which pressed down upon the eyes. Only reddish points of light could be seen through the gauze covers of the lamps. The coal face was scarcely discernible; it went up slantwise like a broad, flat, sloping chimney, blackened with the impenetrable night of ten winters of soot, and in it ghostly forms moved about and an occasional gleam threw into momentary relief the shape of a man's haunch, a sinewy arm, a wild, dirty, criminal-looking face. Now and then blocks of coal shimmered as they came loose, their surfaces or edges glinted suddenly like crystal, and then all went black again, the picks tapped on dully, and the only other sounds were panting breath and groans of discomfort and fatigue in the heavy air and dripping water.

Zacharie had been out on the spree the day before and was not feeling strong in the arm. He soon gave up work, finding the excuse that some timbering needed doing. This gave him a chance to go off into a dream, whistling to himself and staring vaguely into space. Nearly three metres of the seam were cut away behind them, and they had not taken the precaution to prop up the rock. Fear of losing precious time made them heedless of danger.

'Here, you, the toff!' he called to Étienne. 'Pass me some wood.'

Étienne was being taught by Catherine how to wield his shovel, but he had to take some wood along. There was a little store left over from the previous day. Usually pieces of wood ready cut to the size of the seam were sent down every morning.

'Look sharp, you lazy devil!' Zacharie went on, watching the new haulage man clumsily hoisting himself up amid the coal, with his arms encumbered by four pieces of oak.

With his pick he nicked a hole in the roof and another in the wall, ramming in the ends of the wood which thus propped up the rock. Every afternoon the rippers cleared away the waste after the colliers and filled in the cavities in the seam, leaving the timbering covered in. Only the top and bottom galleries were left intact for haulage.

Maheu stopped groaning. He had got his block loose. Wiping his streaming face on his sleeve, he turned to find out what Zacharie had come up to do behind him.

'Leave that alone,' he said: 'we'll see about it after lunch. Better go on cutting if we want to make our right number of tubs.'

'Yes, but it's getting lower,' answered his son. 'Look! There's a crack here. I'm afraid it'll come down.'

His father only shrugged his shoulders. Come down! Never! Besides, it wouldn't be the first time; they'd get out of it somehow. He finished up by losing his temper and sending his son back to the cutting face.

As a matter of fact, they were all taking a bit of a rest. Levaque, still on his back, was cursing as he looked at his left thumb, which had been grazed by a fall of sandstone and was bleeding. Chaval was tearing off his shirt, stripping to the waist to keep cool. They were already black with coal, coated with fine dust which their sweat turned into a paste that ran in trickles and puddles. Maheu was the first to begin picking again, at a lower level, with his head right down on the rock. And now the drop of water was falling so mercilessly on his forehead that it seemed to be boring a hole through his skull.

'Don't take any notice,' explained Catherine. 'They always holler like that.'

She took up the lesson again like a kindly soul: each loaded tub reached pit-top exactly as it left the face, marked with a special counter so that the checker could credit it to the team. That was why you had to be so careful to fill it, and fill it with clean coal; otherwise it would be rejected.

The young man's eyes were now accustomed to the gloom, and he looked at her. Her skin still had a chlorotic pallor, and he could not have guessed her age, but put it at twelve because she seemed so small. And yet he felt that she must be older, with her boyish freedom of manner and candid cheekiness which he found a little disconcerting; no, he did not like her—her white Pierrot's face with the skull-cap effect of her headgear struck him as too roguish. But he was amazed at the child's strength, a nervous strength with much skill in it. She filled her tub quicker than he did, with fast, regular little movements of her shovel, then pushed it to the incline with a long, slow push without any hitch, passing easily under the low rocks. He, on the other hand, tore himself to shreds, ran off the rails and soon got stuck.

It certainly was not an easy road. From the coal face to the incline was about sixty metres, and the rippers had not yet widened the tunnel, which was a mere pipe with a very uneven roof, bulging at every moment. At some points a loaded tub would only just go through, and the haulage man had to flatten himself and push kneeling down so as not to smash his head. What was more, the timbers were already giving and snapping, and long, pale rents appeared as they gave in the middle, like crutches too weak for their job. You had to be careful not to scrape your skin off on this splintered wood, and as you crawled on your belly under the slowly sinking roof, which could snap oak props as thick as a man's thigh, you felt a haunting fear that suddenly you would hear your own spine crack.

. . .

Up in the bedroom, through the closed shutters, dawn had gradually thrown bars of grey light over the ceiling, like a fan, the air was close and heavy and everybody had resumed the night's sleep. Lénore and Henri lay in each other's arms, Alzire was propped up on her hump but her head

had lolled over, whilst Grandpa Bonnemort, now in sole possession of
Zacharie and Jeanlin's bed, snored away open-mouthed. Not a sound
came from the little room, where Maheude had dropped off again in the
middle of feeding Estelle, with her breast hanging over to one side and
the baby lying across her stomach, gorged with milk and fast asleep as
well, half suffocated in the soft cushion of her mother's bosom.

The cuckoo downstairs struck six. Doors could be heard banging
along the terraces of the village, and clogs clattered on the paving
stones. It was the screeners going on. Silence fell again until seven when
shutters flew back and yawns and coughs could be heard through the
walls. Somebody's coffee-mill went on squeaking for a long time before
anybody woke in the room.

But suddenly a distant sound of blows and shouting made Alzire sit
up. Realizing what the time was, she ran barefoot and gave her mother
a shake.

'Mummy! Mummy, it's late! You've got to go out. Mind! You are
squashing Estelle.' She rescued the baby, half smothered under its mother's
great pendulous breasts.

'Oh, what a hell of a life!' muttered Maheude, rubbing her eyes. 'I'm
so knocked up I could sleep all day. You dress Lénore and Henri, and
I'll take them with me while you mind Estelle. I don't want to cart her
about for fear she'll pick up a cold in this filthy weather.'

She washed hurriedly, slipped on an old blue skirt, her cleanest, and
a grey woollen jacket that she had patched in two places the day before.

'And the soup! Oh dear, oh dear, what a life!' And she muttered on
while she went downstairs, knocking everything over on her way, whilst
Alzire took Estelle back with her into the bedroom. The baby had begun
to yell, but she was used to her tantrums, and already, at the age of
eight, had recourse to a woman's tender wiles to calm her and distract
her attention. She gently laid her in her own warm bed and coaxed her
to sleep by giving her a finger to suck. It was high time, too, for a new
hubbub was beginning and she had to make peace between Lénore and
Henri who were at last waking up. These two scarcely ever got on together, and never put their arms round each other's neck except when
they were asleep. As soon as she got up in the morning the girl, who
was six, fell upon the boy, two years her junior, and rained blows on him
which he could not return. They both had the family head, too big,
looking as though it were inflated, and with tousled yellow hair. Alzire
had to pull her sister by the legs and threaten to skin her bottom for her.
Then there was a stamping scene over washing and each garment she
put on them. The blinds were left pulled so as not to disturb Grandpa
Bonnemort's sleep. He went on snoring away all through the appalling
hullabaloo.

'Ready!' shouted Maheude. 'How are you getting on up there?'

She had pushed back the shutters, given the fire a poke and put some
more coal on. She had hoped that the old man would not have swallowed

all the soup, but she found the saucepan wiped clean, and so she put a handful of vermicelli on to boil, having kept this in reserve for three days. They would have to eat it plain, without butter, for there could not possibly be any of yesterday's little bit left. To her surprise, she found that Catherine had performed the miracle of making the sandwiches and yet leaving a piece the size of a walnut. But now the cupboard really was bare: not a crust, not a scrap, not a single bone to gnaw, nothing at all. What was to become of them if Maigrat went on refusing credit and if the people at La Piolaine did not give her five francs? When the men and her daughter came home from the pit they would have to eat, though, for unfortunately nobody had yet invented a way of living without food.

'Come down, will you!' she shouted irritably; 'I ought to be gone by now!'

When Alzire and the children were down, she divided the vermicelli out on three plates, saying that she was not hungry herself. Although Catherine had already put water through yesterday's coffee-grounds, she did so again and drank two large glasses of a coffee so pale in colour that it looked like rusty water. But still, it would keep her going.

'Now listen,' she told Alzire; 'let Grandpa sleep on and mind Estelle doesn't bang her head. If she wakes up and hollers too much, look, here is some sugar you can melt and give her in a spoon. I know you are a good girl and won't eat it yourself.'

'What about school, Mummy?'

'School? Well, that will have to wait for another day. Today I want you.'

'What about the soup? Do you want me to make it if you are late getting back?'

'The soup? Let me see . . . no, wait till I come.'

Alzire evidently understood, for she asked no more questions. She knew all about soup-making; she had the precocious intelligence of the invalid child. By now the whole village was agog, and children were going off to school in twos and threes, shuffling along in their clogs. It struck eight, and from the Levaques' on the left the chatter of tongues grew louder and louder. The women's day was starting: they stood round the coffee-pots, hands on hips, tongues going round and round like millstones. An over-blown face, with thick lips and flat nose, was pressed against the window-pane and calling:

'Just a minute! I've got some news.'

'No, no, see you later,' replied Maheude; 'I've got to go out.'

And she hustled off Lénore and Henri, for fear of yielding to a proffered glass of hot coffee. Grandpa Bonnemort was still snoring up-stairs, with a regular snore that rocked the house.

When she was out in the street she was surprised to find that the wind had dropped. There had been a sudden thaw, the sky was the colour of the earth, the walls were sticky with greenish condensation and the streets thick with mud—a special mud peculiar to the coal country, as black as a solution of soot, but so thick and viscous that it nearly pulled her shoes off. She suddenly had to clout Lénore because the child was having a game with her clogs, using them like spades to dig up the mud. On leaving the village, she first skirted the slagheap and then followed the canal road, taking short cuts along abandoned roads, across tracts of waste ground marked off by moss-covered fences. Shed followed shed, and long factory buildings, with tall chimneys belching forth soot and blackening these desolate outskirts of an industrial town. Behind a clump of poplars rose the crumbling headgear of the Réquillart pit, with only its skeleton still standing. Turning to the right, she came out on the main road.

'Just you wait, you dirty little pig? I'll give you mud-pies, I will!'

This time it was Henri; he had picked up a handful of mud and was kneading it into a ball. The two children were cuffed indiscriminately and resumed an orderly progress, squinting down at the holes their feet made in the heaps of mud. They were already too tired to keep on pulling their feet out at each stride, and just paddled through it.

The road stretched ahead towards Marchiennes with its two leagues of cobblestones, running dead straight through the reddish earth like a greasy ribbon. But in the opposite direction it zigzagged down through Montsou, which was built on a slope of the great rolling plain. These roads in the Nord, running straight as a die from one manufacturing town to another, or with slight curves and gentle gradients, are gradually being built up, and the whole Department is turning into a single industrial city. The little brick houses, colour-washed to make up for the climate, some yellow, some blue, but others black (perhaps so as to reach the ultimate black with the least delay), ran downhill, twisting to right and left. Here and there the line of little huddled façades was broken by a large two-storeyed house, the home of some manager. A church, built of brick like everything else, looked like some new type of blast furnace, with its square tower already black with coal-dust. But what stood out most of all among the sugar refineries, rope-works and sawmills, was the immense number of dance-halls, bars, and pubs—there were over five hundred of them to a thousand houses.

On nearing the Company's yards, a vast series of workshops and sheds, Maheude decided to take Lénore and Henri by the hand, one on each side. Just beyond was the house of the managing director, Monsieur Hennebeau, a large chalet-like building standing back behind iron gates and a garden containing some scraggy trees. A carriage happened to be drawn up at the gate, setting down a gentleman wearing a ribbon in his buttonhole, and a lady in a fur coat, evidently guests from Paris who had come from Marchiennes station, for Madame Hennebeau, dimly visible in the doorway, was uttering a little scream of surprise and joy.

'Come on, lazybones!' growled their mother as she hauled along the two children who were just standing about in the mud.

She had reached Maigrat's and was feeling very apprehensive. Maigrat lived next door to the manager, from whose home his little house was separated only by a wall, and he kept a store, a long building, opening on to the road, like a shop without windows. He stocked everything: grocery, provisions, greengrocery; he sold bread, beer, and pots and pans. Formerly an inspector at Le Voreux, he had set up in business with a small canteen, and then, thanks to official protection, his trade had grown and grown until it had killed the small shops in Montsou. He combined everything under one roof, and his large number of customers from the industrial villages enabled him to undercut and give more credit. Incidentally he was still in the Company's power, for they had built his little house and shop for him.

'Here I am again, Monsieur Maigrat,' said Maheude humbly, finding him standing at his shop door.

He looked at her without speaking. He was a fat man, coldly polite in manner, and he prided himself on never going back on a decision.

'You won't turn me away like you did yesterday, will you? We must eat between now and Saturday. . . . I know we have owed you sixty francs for two years now. . . .'

And she tried to explain in awkward, short sentences. It was a long-standing debt that went back to the last strike. They had promised to pay it off a score of times, but could never manage to let him have his forty sous per fortnight. And then she had had more trouble the day before yesterday, when she had had to pay a cobbler twenty francs because he was threatening to put the bailiffs in. And that was why they hadn't a penny. Otherwise they would have managed until Saturday, same as the others.

But Maigrat stood there, arms folded over distended belly, answering each supplication with a shake of the head.

'Only two loaves, Monsieur Maigrat. I don't expect a lot, I am not asking for coffee. . . . Just two three-pound loaves a day!'

'No!' he shouted at the top of his voice.

His wife had appeared; she was a sickly creature, who spent the whole day poring over a ledger and not even daring to raise her head. The sight of this poor woman's pleading eyes terrified her, and she fled. It was said that she gave up her place in her husband's bed to haulage girls among the customers. It was a known fact that when a miner wanted more credit, all he had to do was to send along his daughter or wife, no matter whether she was pretty or plain so long as she was willing.

Maheude was still looking at Maigrat imploringly, but the lecherous flicker in his little eyes as he looked her up and down made her feel naked and ashamed. It angered her, too—there might have been some excuse for it when she was young, before she had had seven children. She dragged away Lénore and Henri, who were picking nutshells up from the gutter and examining them, and set off again.

'This won't do you any good, Monsieur Maigrat, you mark my words!'

The only thing left now was the people at La Piolaine. If they did not cough up five francs, then they could all go to bed and die. She had now turned left along the Joiselle road. The Offices were along there on a corner, a real palace of bricks and mortar where the big-wigs from Paris, generals and government gentlemen, came and had grand dinners every autumn. As she walked on, she was already laying out the five francs in her mind; first bread and coffee, then a quarter of butter, a bushel of potatoes for the morning soup and evening stew, and then perhaps a little brawn because Dad needed some meat.

The parish priest of Montsou, abbé Joire, came along, holding up his cassock like a dainty and well-fed cat, afraid of dirtying his frock. He was a gentle little man who affected to take no part in anything so as not to upset either workers or employers.

'Good morning, Monsieur le Curé.'

He hurried on without stopping, throwing a smile at the children and leaving her standing in the middle of the road. She was no churchgoer, but she had suddenly imagined that this priest was going to do something for her.

The tramp through the black, sticky mud began again. There were still two kilometres to be done and the children were not finding things so funny now, but were scared and dragging behind more and more. On either side, the same waste ground stretched on and on with its moss-covered fences, the same black and grimy factory buildings bristling with tall chimneys. Further away the land spread out in open fields, endlessly flat like a sea of brown clods with never a tree for a mast, on and on to the purple line of the forest of Vandame.

'Mummy, I want to be carried.'

She carried them in turns. The pot-holes were full of water, and she held up her skirt for fear of being too dirty when she got there. Three times she all but fell down, so slippery were the dratted cobblestones. When at long last they came out in front of the steps, two huge dogs leaped out, barking so loud that the children screamed in terror. The coachman had to take a whip to them.

'Leave your clogs here and come in,' said Honorine.

Mother and children stood motionless in the dining-room, dazed by the sudden warmth and overawed by this elderly gentleman and lady staring at them from the depths of their armchairs.

'My dear,' said the lady to her daughter, 'give your little presents.'

The Grégoires made Cécile distribute their charities; it was part of a ladylike education, they thought. One must be charitable, and they used to say that their house was the Lord's dwelling. But they flattered themselves that their charity was discriminating, and were continually haunted by the fear of being hoodwinked and so encouraging wickedness. Therefore they never gave money, never!—not ten sous, not even two sous, for it was a known fact that as soon as the poor had two sous they drank them. No, their charity was always in kind, especially warm clothing, distributed in the winter to necessitous children.

'Oh, poor little things!' cried Cécile. 'How peaky they look after that walk in the cold. . . . Honorine, go and fetch the parcel from the cupboard.'

The maids were also staring at these poor creatures, with that sympathy not unmixed with uneasiness displayed by the well-fed. Whilst the parlourmaid was going upstairs, cook put the remains of the brioche down on the table, and stood there gaping and empty-handed.

'Yes,' Cécile went on, 'I happen to have two woollen frocks and some shawls left. Think how they will keep the poor little things warm!'

At last Maheude found her tongue and managed to say:

'Thank you very much, Mademoiselle. . . . You are all very kind.'

Her eyes filled with tears, and she felt confident of getting the five francs—only she was a bit worried about the best way to ask for them if they were not forthcoming. The maid had not reappeared, and there was an awkward silence. The two children clung to their mother's skirts and stared wide-eyed at the brioche.

'You have only these two?' asked Madame Grégoire, by way of breaking the silence.

'Oh, no, Madame! I have seven.'

At this Monsieur Grégoire, who had taken up his paper again, jumped with outraged surprise.

'Seven children! But why, in Heaven's name?'

'Not very prudent,' murmured his wife.

Maheude made a vaguely apologetic gesture. That's how it was, you didn't give it a thought and then they just came along naturally. But then when they grew up they brought in money and kept the home going. Now they, for instance, would have managed all right if it hadn't been for grandfather getting so stiff, and out of the whole bunch of them only the two boys and her eldest girl were old enough to go down the mine. You see, you still had to feed the little ones who did nothing at all.

'So you have been working in the mines a long time?'

Maheude's sallow face lit up in a grin.

'Oh yes, oh yes! I was down there till I was twenty. When I had my second baby, the doctor warned me I would stay down for good because something was misplaced in my innards, it seemed. . . . But in any case, I got married just then and I had enough to do at home. But on my husband's side they've been down for ages. It goes back to grandfather's grandfather, in fact nobody knows when—right to the start, when they first began to sink Réquillart.'

Monsieur Grégoire gazed reflectively at the mother and her pitiful children, at their wax-like flesh, colourless hair, their look of stunted degeneration, wasted by anaemia, and the miserable ugliness of the underfed. There was another silence, only broken by the spurting of gas from the burning coal. The warm room was full of that heavy feeling of well-being in which cosy bourgeois love to settle themselves down to slumber.

'What *is* she up to?' exclaimed Cécile in annoyance. 'Mélanie, go up and tell her that the parcel is at the bottom of the cupboard, on the left.'

Monsieur Grégoire continued aloud the thoughts inspired by the sight of these starving creatures:

'Yes, there is a lot of suffering in this world, it is true; but, my good woman, we must also admit that the workers are not very sensible. Instead of putting a little on one side as the peasants do, the miners drink, run into debt, and end up by being unable to support their families.'

'You are quite right, Sir,' answered Maheude, smugly serious; 'they don't always keep to the right path. That's what I always say to ne'er-do-wells when they complain. Now I am fortunate, my husband doesn't drink. Of course, he does sometimes have a little too much on holiday Sundays, but it never goes beyond that. And that is all the nicer of him because before we were married he drank like a swine, begging your pardon. And yet, you see, his being so moderate doesn't seem to do us much good. There are days like today when you could turn out all the drawers in the house and never find a brass farthing.'

She was trying to convey the idea of a five-franc piece to them, and went on in her soft voice to explain the fatal debt, modest at first, but soon swelling to overwhelming proportions. You paid up regularly for fortnights on end, but one day you got late and that was that; you never caught up again. The gap got wider and the men couldn't see the point of working if they couldn't ever pay their way. Then, God help you, you were in the soup until Kingdom come. Besides, you had to try and understand: a miner needed a half-pint to wash the dust out of his tubes. That's how it began, and then when things got difficult, he sat in the pub all day. Perhaps, without complaining about anybody in particular, it might be that the workers really did not earn enough.

'But I thought the Company gave you accommodation and fuel?' said Madame Grégoire.

Maheude gave a sidelong glance at the coal blazing in the grate.

'Oh, yes, we are given coal of a sort, though it does burn, I suppose. . . . As for the rent, it is only six francs a month, which doesn't sound anything at all, but it's often jolly hard to find. Now look at me today— you could cut me up into little pieces and never find a halfpenny. Where there's nothing, there's nothing.'

The lady and gentleman sat silent in their comfortable armchairs, for this exhibition of poverty was beginning to upset them and get on their nerves. Maheude was afraid she had offended them, and so went on in her calm, fair, and practical way:

'Oh, I don't mean to complain. That's how things are and we have to accept them, especially as however much we struggled we probably shouldn't be able to alter anything. So the best thing, Monsieur and Madame, is to try to do your job properly in the place God has put you, isn't it?'

Monsieur Grégoire emphatically agreed:

'With such sentiments, my good woman, one is proof against misfortune.'

At last Honorine and Mélanie came in with the parcel. Cécile undid it and took out the two frocks, to which she added shawls and even stockings and mittens. Yes, they would all fit beautifully, and she made haste to get the servants to pack them up; for her music-mistress had just arrived, and she bundled mother and children towards the door.

'We are very hard up,' stammered Maheude; 'if only we had a five-franc piece. . . .'

The words struck in her throat, for the Maheus were proud and did not beg. Cécile glanced anxiously at her father, but he refused point-blank with the air of doing a painful duty.

'No, it is not our custom. It can't be done.'

Cécile was touched by the mother's tragic face and wished to do all she could for the children. They were still staring at the brioche. She cut two pieces and gave them one each.

'Look! this is for you.'

Then she took them back and asked for an old newspaper.

'Wait a minute, you can share them with your brothers and sisters.'

She managed to push them out of the room, while her parents fondly looked on. The poor, starving brats went off, respectfully holding the pieces of brioche in their numbed little fists.

THE COMMUNIST MANIFESTO

(Part I)

KARL MARX AND FRIEDRICH ENGELS

Karl Marx (1818–1883) and Friedrich Engels (1820–1895) were German political theorists who collaborated in formulating the major tenets of Communism
as contained in *The Communist Manifesto*. They interpreted human history
as proceeding in a dialectic or triadic pattern with economic (material) factors
as the most basic, driving force. Ultimately and inevitably a society will be
created in which wealth is equally distributed and all class distinctions that
divide men are finally obliterated. Marx defended and documented his theory
more fully in his classic work *Capital*.

In the following selection from *The Communist Manifesto* Marx and
Engels argue that a society's mode of economic production and exchange,
and its consequent social organization, determine not only the political and
intellectual history of that society but its moral, religious, and cultural character as well. Whether, in the face of this analysis, Marx and Engels are then
justified in exhorting the proletariat to change the existing order is a moot
point; perhaps men do not possess the freedom to do so. Be that as it may,
The Communist Manifesto presents a persuasive case for economic factors as
the determinants of society.

A spectre is haunting Europe—the spectre of Communism. All the
Powers of old Europe have entered into a holy alliance to exorcise this
spectre; Pope and Czar, Metternich and Guizot, French Radicals and
German police-spies.

Where is the party in opposition that has not been decried as com-
munistic by its opponents in power? Where the Opposition that has not
hurled back the branding reproach of Communism, against the more advanced opposition parties, as well as against its re-actionary adversaries?

Two things result from this fact.

I. Comunism is already acknowledged by all European Powers to be
itself a Power.

II. It is high time that Communists should openly, in the face of the
whole world, publish their views, their aims, their tendencies, and meet
this nursery tale of the Spectre of Communism with a Manifesto of the
party itself.

To this end, Communists of various nationalities have assembled in
London, and sketched the following manifesto, to be published in the
English, French, German, Italian, Flemish and Danish languages.

I.

BOURGEOIS AND PROLETARIANS

The history of all hitherto existing society is the history of class
struggles.

Freeman and slave, patrician and plebeian, lord and serf, guild-master and journeyman, in a word, oppressor and oppressed, stood in constant opposition to one another, carried on an uninterrupted, now hidden, now open fight, a fight that each time ended, either in a revolutionary re-constitution of society at large, or in the common ruin of the contending classes.

In the earlier epochs of history, we find almost everywhere a compli-cated arrangement of society into various orders, a manifold gradation of social rank. In ancient Rome we had patricians, knights, plebeians, slaves; in the middle ages, feudal lords, vassals, guild-masters, journeymen, apprentices, serfs; in almost all of these classes, again, subordinate grada-tions.

The modern bourgeois society that has sprouted from the ruins of feudal society, has not done away with class antagonisms. It has but established new classes, new conditions of oppression, new forms of struggle in place of the old ones.

Our epoch, the epoch of the bourgeoisie, possesses, however, this distinctive feature; it has simplified the class antagonisms. Society as a whole is more and more splitting up into two great hostile camps, into two great classes directly facing each other: Bourgeoisie and Proletariat.

From the serf of the middle ages sprang the chartered burghers of the earliest towns. From these burgesses the first elements of the bourgeoisie were developed.

The discovery of America, the rounding of the Cape, opened up fresh ground for the rising bourgeoisie. The East-Indian and Chinese markets, the colonisation of America, trade with the colonies, the increase in the means of exchange and in commodities generally, gave to commerce, to navigation, to industry, an impulse never before known, and thereby, to the revolutionary element in the tottering feudal society, a rapid development.

The feudal system of industry, under which industrial production was monopolised by closed guilds, now no longer sufficed for the growing wants of the new markets. The manufacturing system took its place. The guild-masters were pushed on one side by the manufacturing middle-class; division of labour between the different corporate guilds vanished in the face of division of labour in each single workshop.

Meantime the markets kept ever growing, the demand ever rising. Even manufacture no longer sufficed. Thereupon, steam and machinery revolutionised industrial production. The place of manufacture was taken by the giant, Modern Industry, the place of the industrial middle-class, by industrial millionaires, the leaders of whole industrial armies, the modern bourgeois.

Modern Industry has established the world-market, for which the dis-covery of America paved the way. This market has given an immense development to commerce, to navigation, to communication by land. This development has, in its turn, reacted on the extension of industry; and in proportion as industry, commerce, navigation, railways extended, in the same proportion the bourgeoisie developed, increased its capital, and pushed into the background every class handed down from the Middle Ages.

We see, therefore, how the modern bourgeoisie is itself the product of a long course of development, of a series of revolutions in the modes of production and of exchange.

Each step in the development of the bourgeoisie was accompanied by a corresponding political advance of that class. An oppressed class under the sway of the feudal nobility, an armed and self-governing association in the mediaeval commune, here independent urban republic (as in Italy and Germany), there taxable "third estate" of the monarchy (as in France), afterwards, in the period of manufacture proper, serving either the semi-feudal or the absolute monarchy as a counterpoise against the nobility, and, in fact, corner stone of the great monarchies in general, the bourgeoisie has at last, since the establishment of Modern Industry and of the world-market, conquered for itself, in the modern representative State, exclusive political sway. The executive of the modern State is but a committee for managing the common affairs of the whole bourgeoisie.

The bourgeoisie, historically, has played a most revolutionary part.

The bourgeoisie, wherever it has got the upper hand, has put an end to all feudal, patriarchal, idyllic relations. It has pitilessly torn asunder the motley feudal ties that bound man to his "natural superiors," and has left remaining no other nexus between man and man than naked self-interest, than callous "cash payment." It has drowned the most heavenly ecstacies of religious fervour, of chivalrous enthusiasm, of philistine sentimentalism, in the icy water of egotistical calculation. It has resolved personal worth into exchange value, and in the place of the numberless indefeasible chartered freedoms, has set up that single, unconscionable freedom—Free Trade. In one word, for exploitation, veiled by religious and political illusions, it has substituted naked, shameless, direct, brutal exploitation.

The bourgeoisie has stripped of its halo every occupation hitherto honoured and looked up to with reverent awe. It has converted the physician, the lawyer, the priest, the poet, the man of science, into its paid wage-labourers.

The bourgeoisie has torn away from the family its sentimental veil, and has reduced the family relation to a mere money relation.

The bourgeoisie has disclosed how it came to pass that the brutal display of vigour in the Middle Ages, which Reactionists so much admire, found its fitting complement in the most slothful indolence. It has been the first to show what man's activity can bring about. It has accomplished wonders far surpassing Egyptian pyramids, Roman aqueducts, and Gothic cathedrals; it has conducted expeditions that put in the shade all former Exoduses of nations and crusades.

The bourgeoisie cannot exist without constantly revolutionising the instruments of production, and thereby the relations of production, and with them the whole relations of society. Conservation of the old modes of production in unaltered form, was, on the contrary, the first condition of existence for all earlier industrial classes. Constant revolutionising of production, uninterrupted disturbance of all social conditions, everlasting uncertainty and agitation distinguish the bourgeois epoch from all earlier ones. All fixed, fast-frozen relations, with their train of ancient and venerable prejudices and opinions, are swept away, all new-formed ones become antiquated before they can ossify. All that is solid melts into air, all that is holy is profaned, and man is at last compelled to face with sober senses, his real conditions of life, and his relations with his kind.

The need of a constantly expanding market for its products chases the bourgeoisie over the whole surface of the globe. It must nestle everywhere, settle everywhere, establish connexions everywhere.

The bourgeoisie has through its exploitation of the world-market given a cosmopolitan character to production and consumption in every country. To the great chagrin of Re-actionists, it has drawn from under the feet of industry the national ground on which it stood. All old-established national industries have been destroyed or are daily being destroyed. They are dislodged by new industries, whose introduction becomes a life and death question for all civilised nations, by industries that no longer work up indigenous raw material, but raw material drawn from the remotest zones; industries whose products are consumed, not only at home, but in every quarter of the globe. In place of the old wants, satisfied by the productions of the country, we find new wants, requiring for their satisfaction the products of distant lands and climes. In place of the old local and national seclusion and self-sufficiency, we have intercourse in every direction, universal inter-dependence of nations. And as in material, so also in intellectual production. The intellectual creations of individual nations become common property. National one-sidedness and narrow-mindedness become more and more impossible, and from the numerous national and local literatures, there arises a world-literature.

The bourgeoisie, by the rapid improvement of all instruments of production, by the immensely facilitated means of communication, draws all, even the most barbarian, nations into civilisation. The cheap prices of its commodities are the heavy artillery with which it batters down all Chinese walls, with which it forces the barbarians' intensely obstinate hatred of foreigners to capitulate. It compels all nations, on pain of ex-tinction, to adopt the bourgeois mode of production; it compels them to introduce what it calls civilisation into their midst, *i.e.*, to become bourgeois themselves. In one word, it creates a world after its own image.

The bourgeoisie has subjected the country to the rule of the towns. It has created enormous cities, has greatly increased the urban population as compared with the rural, and has thus rescued a considerable part of the population from the idiocy of rural life. Just as it has made the country dependent on the towns, so it has made barbarian and semi-barbarian countries dependent on the civilised ones, nations of peasants on nations of bourgeois, the East on the West.

The bourgeoisie keeps more and more doing away with the scattered state of the population, of the means of production, and of property. It has agglomerated population, centralised means of production, and has concentrated property in a few hands. The necessary consequence of this was political centralisation. Independent, or but loosely connected provinces, with separate interests, laws, governments and systems of taxation, became lumped together into one nation, with one government, one code of laws, one national class-interest, one frontier and one customs-tariff.

The bourgeoisie, during its rule of scarce one hundred years, has created more massive and more colossal productive forces than have all preceding generations together. Subjection of Nature's forces to man, machinery, application of chemistry to industry and agriculture, steam-navigation, railways, electric telegraphs, clearing of whole continents for cultivation, canalization of rivers, whole populations conjured out of the ground—what earlier century had even a presentiment that such productive forces slumbered in the lap of social labour?

We see then: the means of production and of exchange on whose foundation the bourgeoisie built itself up, were generated in feudal society. At a certain stage in the development of these means of production and of exchange, the conditions under which feudal society produced and exchanged, the feudal organisation of agriculture and manufacturing industry, in one word, the feudal relations of property became no longer compatible with the already developed productive forces; they became so many fetters. They had to be burst asunder; they were burst asunder.

Into their place stepped free competition, accompanied by a social and political constitution adapted to it, and by the economical and political sway of the bourgeois class.

A similar movement is going on before our own eyes. Modern bourgeois society with its relations of production, of exchange and of property, a society that has conjured up such gigantic means of production and of exchange, is like the sorcerer, who is no longer able to control the powers of the nether world whom he has called up by his spells. For many a decade past the history of industry and commerce is but the history of the revolt of modern productive forces against modern conditions of production, against the property relations that are the conditions for the existence of the bourgeoisie and of its rule. It is enough to mention the commercial crises that by their periodical return put on its trial, each time more threateningly, the existence of the entire bourgeois society. In these crises a great part not only of the existing products, but also of the previously created productive forces, are periodically destroyed. In these crises there breaks out an epidemic that, in all earlier epochs, would have seemed an absurdity—the epidemic of over-production. Society suddenly finds itself put back into a state of momentary barbarism; it appears as if a famine, a universal war of devastation had cut off the supply of every means of subsistence; industry and commerce seem to be destroyed; and why? Because there is too much civilisation, too much means of subsistence, too much industry, too much commerce. The productive forces at the disposal of society no longer tend to further the development of the conditions of bourgeois property; on the contrary, they have become too powerful for these conditions, by which they are fettered, and so soon as they overcome these fetters, they bring disorder into the whole of bourgeois society, endanger the existence of bourgeois property. The conditions of bourgeois society are too narrow to comprise the wealth created by them. And how does the bourgeoisie get over these crises? On the one hand by enforced destruction of a mass of productive forces; on the other, by the conquest of new markets, and by more thorough exploitation of the old ones. That is to say, by paving the way for more extensive and more destructive crises, and by diminishing the means whereby crises are prevented.

The weapons with which the bourgeoisie felled feudalism to the ground are now turned against the bourgeoisie itself.

But not only has the bourgeoisie forged the weapons that bring death to itself; it has also called into existence the men who are to wield those weapons—the modern working-class—the proletarians.

In proportion as the bourgeoisie, *i.e.*, capital, is developed, in the same proportion is the proletariat, the modern working-class, developed, a class of labourers, who live only so long as they find work, and who find work only so long as their labour increases capital. These labourers, who must sell themselves piecemeal, are a commodity, like every other article of commerce, and are consequently exposed to all the vicissitudes of competition, to all the fluctuations of the market.

Owing to the extensive use of machinery and to division of labour, the work of the proletarians has lost all individual character, and, consequently, all charm for the workman. He becomes an appendage of the machine, and it is only the most simple, most monotonous, and most easily acquired knack, that is required of him. Hence, the cost of production of a workman is restricted, almost entirely, to the means of subsistence that he requires for his maintenance, and for the propagation of his race. But the price of a commodity, and therefore also of labour, is equal to its cost of production. In proportion, therefore, as the repulsiveness of the work increases, the wage decreases. Nay more, in proportion as the use of machinery and division of labour increases, in the same proportion the burden of toil also increases, whether by prolongation of the working hours, by increase of the work exacted in a given time, or by increased speed of the machinery, etc.

Modern industry has converted the little workshop of the patriarchal master, into the great factory of the industrial capitalist. Masses of labourers, crowded into the factory, are organised like soldiers. As privates of the industrial army they are placed under the command of a perfect hierarchy of officers and sergeants. Not only are they slaves of the bourgeois class, and of the bourgeois State, they are daily and hourly enslaved by the machine, by the over-looker, and, above all, by the individual bourgeois manufacturer himself. The more openly this despotism proclaims gain to be its end and aim, the more petty, the more hateful and the more embittering it is.

The less the skill and exertion of strength implied in manual labour, in other words, the more modern industry becomes developed, the more is the labour of men superseded by that of women. Differences of age and sex have no longer any distinctive social validity for the working class. All are instruments of labour, more or less expensive to use according to their age and sex.

No sooner is the exploitation of the labourer by the manufacturer, so far, at an end, that he receives his wages in cash, than he is set upon by the other portions of the bourgeoisie, the landlord, the shopkeeper, the pawnbroker, etc.

The lower strata of the Middle class—the small tradespeople, shop-keepers, and retired tradesmen generally, the handicraftsmen and peasants —all these sink gradually into the proletariat, partly because their diminutive capital does not suffice for the scale on which Modern Industry is carried on, and is swamped in the competition with the large capitalists, partly because their specialised skill is rendered worthless by new methods of production. Thus the proletariat is recruited from all classes of the population.

The proletariat goes through various stages of development. With its birth begins its struggle with the bourgeoisie. At first the contest is carried on by individual labourers, then by the workpeople of a factory, then by the operatives of one trade, in one locality, against the individual bourgeois who directly exploits them. They direct their attacks not against the bourgeois conditions of production, but against the instruments of production themselves; they destroy imported wares that compete with their labour, they smash to pieces machinery, they set factories ablaze, they seek to restore by force the vanished status of the workman of the Middle Ages.

At this stage the labourers still form an incoherent mass scattered over the whole country, and broken up by their mutual competition. If anywhere they unite to form more compact bodies, this is not yet the consequence of their own active union, but of the union of the bourgeoisie, which class, in order to attain its own political ends, is compelled to set the whole proletariat in motion, and is moreover yet, for a time, able to do so. At this stage, therefore, the proletarians do not fight their enemies, but the enemies of their enemies, the remnants of absolute monarchy, the landowners, the non-industrial bourgeois, the petty bourgeoisie. Thus the whole historical movement is concentrated in the hands of the bourgeoisie; every victory so obtained is a victory for the bourgeoisie.

But with the development of industry the proletariat not only increases in number; it becomes concentrated in greater masses, its strength grows, and it feels that strength more. The various interests and conditions of life within the ranks of the proletariat are more and more equalised, in proportion as machinery obliterates all distinctions of labour, and nearly everywhere reduces wages to the same low level. The growing competition among the bourgeois, and the resulting commercial crises, make the wages of the workers ever more fluctuating. The unceasing improvement of machinery, ever more rapidly developing, makes their livelihood more and more precarious; the collisions between individual workmen and individual bourgeois take more and more the character of collisions between two classes. Thereupon the workers begin to form combinations (Trades' Unions) against the bourgeois; they club together in order to keep up the rate of wages; they found permanent associations in order to make provisions beforehand for these occasional revolts. Here and there the contest breaks out into riots.

Now and then the workers are victorious, but only for a time. The real fruit of their battles lies, not in the immediate result, but in the ever expanding union of the workers. This union is helped on by the improved means of communication that are created by modern industry, and that place the workers of different localities in contact with one another. It was just this contact that was needed to centralise the numerous local struggles, all of the same character, into one national struggle between classes. But every class struggle is a political struggle. And that union, to attain which the burghers of the Middle Ages, with their miserable highways, required centuries, the modern proletarians, thanks to railways, achieve in a few years.

This organisation of the proletarians into a class, and consequently into a political party, is continually being upset again by the competition between the workers themselves. But it ever rises up again, stronger, firmer, mightier. It compels legislative recognition of particular interests of the workers, by taking advantage of the divisions among the bourgeoisie itself. Thus the ten-hour's-bill in England was carried.

Altogether collisions between the classes of the old society further, in many ways, the course of development of the proletariat. The bourgeoisie finds itself involved in a constant battle. At first with the aristocracy; later on, with those portions of the bourgeoisie itself, whose interests have become antagonistic to the progress of industry; at all times, with the bourgeoisie of foreign countries. In all these battles it sees itself compelled to appeal to the proletariat, to ask for its help, and thus, to drag it into the political arena. The bourgeoisie itself, therefore, supplies the proletariat with its own elements of political and general education, in other words, it furnishes the proletariat with weapons for fighting the bourgeoisie.

Further, as we have already seen, entire sections of the ruling classes are, by the advance of industry, precipitated into the proletariat, or are at least threatened in their conditions of existence. These also supply the proletariat with fresh elements of enlightenment and progress.

Finally, in times when the class-struggle nears the decisive hour, the process of dissolution going on within the ruling class, in fact within the whole range of old society, assumes such a violent, glaring character, that a small section of the ruling class cuts itself adrift, and joins the revolutionary class, the class that holds the future in its hands. Just as, therefore, at an earlier period, a section of the nobility went over to the bourgeoisie, so now a portion of the bourgeoisie goes over to the proletariat, and in particular, a portion of the bourgeois ideologists, who have raised themselves to the level of comprehending theoretically the historical movement as a whole.

Of all the classes that stand face to face with the bourgeoisie today, the proletariat alone is a really revolutionary class. The other classes decay and finally disappear in the face of modern industry; the proletariat is its special and essential product.

The lower middle-class, the small manufacturer, the shopkeeper, the artisan, the peasant, all these fight against the bourgeoisie, to save from extinction their existence as fractions of the middle-class. They are therefore not revolutionary, but conservative. Nay more, they are reactionary, for they try to roll back the wheel of history. If by chance they are revolutionary, they are so, only in view of their impending transfer into the proletariat, they thus defend not their present, but their future interests, they desert their own standpoint to place themselves at that of the proletariat.

The "dangerous class," the social scum, that passively rotting mass thrown off by the lowest layers of old society, may, here and there, be swept into the movement by a proletarian revolution; its conditions of life, however, prepare it far more for the part of a bribed tool of reactionary intrigue.

In the conditions of the proletariat, those of old society at large are already virtually swamped. The proletarian is without property; his relation to his wife and children has no longer anything in common with the bourgeois family-relations; modern industrial labour, modern subjection to capital, the same in England as in France, in America as in Germany, has stripped him of every trace of national character. Law, morality, religion, are to him so many bourgeois prejudices, behind which lurk in ambush just as many bourgeois interests.

All the preceding classes that got the upper hand, sought to fortify their already acquired status by subjecting society at large to their conditions of appropriation. The proletarians cannot become masters of the productive forces of society, except by abolishing their own previous mode of appropriation, and thereby also every other previous mode of appropriation. They have nothing of their own to secure and to fortify; their mission is to destroy all previous securities for, and insurances of, individual property.

All previous historical movements were movements of minorities, or in the interest of minorities. The proletarian movement is the self-conscious, independent movement of the immense majority, in the interest of the immense majority. The proletariat, the lowest stratum of our present society, cannot stir, cannot raise itself up, without the whole super-incumbent strata of official society being sprung into the air.

Though not in substance, yet in form, the struggle of the proletariat with the bourgeoisie is at first a national struggle. The proletariat of each country must, of course, first of all settle matters with its own bourgeoisie.

In depicting the most general phases of the development of the proletariat, we traced the more or less veiled civil war, raging within existing society, up to the point where that war breaks out into open revolution, and where the violent overthrow of the bourgeoisie, lays the foundation for the sway of the proletariat.

Hitherto, every form of society has been based, as we have already seen, on the antagonism of oppressing and oppressed classes. But in order to oppress a class, certain conditions must be assured to it under which it can, at least, continue its slavish existence. The serf, in the period of serfdom, raised himself to membership in the commune, just as the petty bourgeois, under the yoke of feudal absolutism, managed to develop into a bourgeois. The modern labourer, on the contrary, instead of rising with the progress of industry, sinks deeper and deeper below the conditions of existence of his own class. He becomes a pauper, and pauperism develops more rapidly than population and wealth. And here it becomes evident, that the bourgeoisie is unfit any longer to be the ruling class in society, and to impose its conditions of existence upon society as an over-riding law. It is unfit to rule because it is incompetent to assure an existence to its slave within his slavery, because it cannot help letting him sink into such a state, that it has to feed him, instead of being fed by him. Society can no longer live under this bourgeoisie, in other words, its existence is no longer compatible with society.

The essential condition for the existence, and for the sway of the bourgeois class, is the formation and augmentation of capital; the condition for capital is wage-labour. Wage-labour rests exclusively on competition between the labourers. The advance of industry, whose involuntary promoter is the bourgeoisie, replaces the isolation of the labourers, due to competition, by their revolutionary combination, due to association. The development of Modern Industry, therefore, cuts from under its feet the very foundation on which the bourgeoisie produces and appropriates products. What the bourgeoisie therefore produces, above all, are its own grave-diggers. Its fall and the victory of the proletariat are equally inevitable.

3

Psychological Laws
and
Human Control

BRAVE NEW WORLD
(Chapter II)
ALDOUS HUXLEY

Aldous Huxley (1894–1963) was a British novelist who is best known for his futuristic novel *Brave New World,* but is also celebrated for such works as *Crome Yellow, Antic Hay,* and *Point Counter Point,* which are clever, urbane, and outrageously comical. In his later years he wrote *The Perennial Philosophy,* a serious study strongly influenced by Hindu and mystical thought, *The Doors of Perception,* dealing with the hallucinogenic drug mescalin, and *Island,* a utopian novel which contrasts sharply with his earlier pessimistic vision.

Huxley styled himself a "Pyrrhonic aesthete" who was merely amused by the direction the world was taking, but it is difficult to see only detachment and not censure in his writings. In *Brave New World,* a chapter of which appears below, Huxley portrays the insidious process of psychological conditioning that molds human behavior; in the society depicted it is used as a deliberate political device.

Mr. Foster was left in the Decanting Room. The D.H.C. and his students stepped into the nearest lift and were carried up to the fifth floor.

INFANT NURSERIES. NEO-PAVLOVIAN CONDITIONING ROOMS, announced the notice board.

The Director opened a door. They were in a large bare room, very bright and sunny; for the whole of the southern wall was a single window. Half a dozen nurses, trousered and jacketed in the regulation white viscose-linen uniform, their hair aseptically hidden under white caps, were engaged in setting out bowls of roses in a long row across the floor. Big bowls, packed tight with blossom. Thousands of petals, ripe-blown and silkily smooth, like the cheeks of innumerable little cherubs, but of cherubs, in that bright light, not exclusively pink and Aryan, but also luminously Chinese, also Mexican, also apoplectic with too much blowing of celestial trumpets, also pale as death, pale with the posthumous white-ness of marble.

The nurses stiffened to attention as the D.H.C. came in.

"Set out the books," he said curtly.

In silence the nurses obeyed his command. Between the rose bowls the books were duly set out—a row of nursery quartos opened invitingly each at some gaily coloured image of beast or fish or bird.

"Now bring in the children."

They hurried out of the room and returned in a minute or two, each pushing a kind of tall dumbwaiter laden, on all its four wire-netted shelves, with eight-month-old-babies, all exactly alike (a Bokanovsky Group, it was evident) and all (since their caste was Delta) dressed in khaki.

"Put them down on the floor."

The infants were unloaded.

"Now turn them so that they can see the flowers and books."

Turned, the babies at once fell silent, then began to crawl towards those clusters of sleek colours, those shapes so gay and brilliant on the white pages. As they approached, the sun came out of a momentary eclipse behind a cloud. The roses flamed up as though with a sudden passion from within; a new and profound significance seemed to suffuse the shining pages of the books. From the ranks of the crawling babies came little squeals of excitement, gurgles and twitterings of pleasure.

The Director rubbed his hands. "Excellent!" he said. "It might almost have been done on purpose."

The swiftest crawlers were already at their goal. Small hands reached out uncertainly, touched, grasped, unpetaling the transfigured roses, crum-pling the illuminated pages of the books. The Director waited until all were happily busy. Then, "Watch carefully," he said. And, lifting his hand, he gave the signal.

The Head Nurse, who was standing by a switchboard at the other end of the room, pressed down a little lever.

There was a violent explosion. Shriller and ever shriller, a siren shrieked. Alarm bells maddeningly sounded.

The children started, screamed; their faces were distorted with terror.

"And now," the Director shouted (for the noise was deafening), "now we proceed to rub in the lesson with a mild electric shock."

He waved his hand again, and the Head Nurse pressed a second lever. The screaming of the babies suddenly changed its tone. There was some-thing desperate, almost insane, about the sharp spasmodic yelps to which they now gave utterance. Their little bodies twitched and stiffened; their limbs moved jerkily as if to the tug of unseen wires.

"We can electrify that whole strip of floor," bawled the Director in ex-planation. "But that's enough," he signalled to the nurse.

The explosions ceased, the bells stopped ringing, the shriek of the siren died down from tone to tone into silence. The stiffly twitching bodies relaxed, and what had become the sob and yelp of infant maniacs broadened out once more into a normal howl of ordinary terror.

"Offer them the flowers and the books again."

The nurses obeyed; but at the approach of the roses, at the mere sight of those gaily-coloured images of pussy and cock-a-doodle-doo and baa-baa black sheep, the infants shrank away in horror; the volume of their howling suddenly increased.

"Observe," said the Director triumphantly, "observe."

Books and loud noises, flowers and electric shocks—already in the infant mind these couples were compromisingly linked; and after two hundred repetitions of the same or a similar lesson would be wedded indissolubly. What man has joined, nature is powerless to put asunder.

"They'll grow up with what the psychologists used to call an 'instinctive' hatred of books and flowers. Reflexes unalterably conditioned. They'll be safe from books and botany all their lives." The Director turned to his nurses. "Take them away again."

Still yelling, the khaki babies were loaded on to their dumb-waiters and wheeled out, leaving behind them the smell of sour milk and a most welcome silence.

One of the students held up his hand; and though he could see quite well why you couldn't have the lower-caste people wasting the Community's time over books, and that there was always the risk of their reading something which might undesirably decondition one of their reflexes, yet . . . well, he couldn't understand about the flowers. Why go to the trouble of making it psychologically impossible for Deltas to like flowers?

Patiently the D.H.C. explained. If the children were made to scream at the sight of a rose, that was on grounds of high economic policy. Not so very long ago (a century or thereabouts), Gammas, Deltas, even Epsilons, had been conditioned to like flowers—flowers in particular and wild nature in general. The idea was to make them want to be going out into the country at every available opportunity, and so compel them to consume transport.

"And didn't they consume transport?" asked the student.

"Quite a lot," the D.H.C. replied. "But nothing else."

Primroses and landscapes, he pointed out, have one grave defect: they are gratuitous. A love of nature keeps no factories busy. It was decided to abolish the love of nature, at any rate among the lower classes; to abolish the love of nature, but *not* the tendency to consume transport. For of course it was essential that they should keep on going to the country, even though they hated it. The problem was to find an economically sounder reason for consuming transport than a mere affection for primroses and landscapes. It was duly found.

"We condition the masses to hate the country," concluded the Director. "But simultaneously we condition them to love all country sports.

At the same time, we see to it that all country sports shall entail the use of elaborate apparatus. So that they consume manufactured articles as well as transport. Hence those electric shocks."

"I see," said the student, and was silent, lost in admiration.

There was a silence; then, clearing his throat, "Once upon a time," the Director began, "while our Ford was still on earth, there was a little boy called Reuben Rabinovitch. Reuben was the child of Polish-speaking parents." The Director interrupted himself. "You know what Polish is, I suppose?"

"A dead language."

"Like French and German," added another student, officiously showing off his learning.

"And 'parent'?" questioned the D.H.C.

There was an uneasy silence. Several of the boys blushed. They had not yet learned to draw the significant but often very fine distinction between smut and pure science. One, at last, had the courage to raise a hand.

"Human beings used to be . . ." he hesitated; the blood rushed to his cheeks. "Well, they used to be viviparous."

"Quite right." The Director nodded approvingly.

"And when the babies were decanted . . ."

" 'Born'," came the correction.

"Well, then they were the parents—I mean, not the babies, of course; the other ones." The poor boy was overwhelmed with confusion.

"In brief," the Director summed up, "the parents were the father and the mother." The smut that was really science fell with a crash into the boys' eye-avoiding silence. "Mother," he repeated loudly rubbing in the science; and, leaning back in his chair, "These," he said gravely, "are unpleasant facts; I know it. But then most historical facts *are* unpleasant."

He returned to Little Reuben—to Little Reuben, in whose room, one evening, by an oversight, his father and mother (crash, crash!) happened to leave the radio turned on.

("For you must remember that in those days of gross viviparous reproduction, children were always brought up by their parents and not in State Conditioning Centres.")

While the child was asleep, a broadcast programme from London suddenly started to come through; and the next morning, to the astonishment of his crash and crash (the more daring of the boys ventured to grin at one another), Little Reuben woke up repeating word for word a long lecture by that curious old writer ("one of the very few whose works have been permitted to come down to us"), George Bernard Shaw, who was speaking, according to a well-authenticated tradition, about his own genius. To Little Reuben's wink and snigger, this lecture was, of course, perfectly incomprehensible and, imagining that their child had suddenly gone mad, they sent for a doctor. He, fortunately, understood English, recognized the discourse as that which Shaw had broadcasted the previous evening, realized the significance of what had happened, and sent a letter to the medical press about it.

"The principle of sleep-teaching, or hypnopædia, had been discovered." The D.H.C. made an impressive pause.

The principle had been discovered; but many, many years were to elapse before that principle was usefully applied.

"The case of Little Reuben occurred only twenty-three years after Our Ford's first T-Model was put on the market." (Here the Director made a sign of the T on his stomach and all the students reverently followed suit.) "And yet . . ."

Furiously the students scribbled. *"Hypnopædia, first used officially in A.F. 214. Why not before? Two reasons. (a) . . ."*

"These early experimenters," the D.H.C. was saying, "were on the wrong track. They thought that hypnopædia could be made an instrument of intellectual education . . ."

(A small boy asleep on his right side, the right arm stuck out, the right hand hanging limp over the edge of the bed. Through a round grating in the side of a box a voice speaks softly.

"The Nile is the longest river in Africa and the second in length of all the rivers of the globe. Although falling short of the length of the Mississippi-Missouri, the Nile is at the head of all rivers as regards the length of its basin, which extends through 35 degrees of latitude . . ."

At breakfast the next morning, "Tommy," some one says, "do you know which is the longest river in Africa?" A shaking of the head. "But don't you remember something that begins: The Nile is the . . ."

"The - Nile - is - the - longest - river - in - Africa - and - the - second - in - length - of - all - the - rivers - of - the - globe . . ." The words come rushing out. "Although - falling - short - of . . ."

"Well now, which is the longest river in Africa?"

The eyes are blank. "I don't know."

"But the Nile, Tommy."

"The - Nile - is - the - longest - river - in - Africa - and - second . . ."

"Then which river is the longest, Tommy?"

Tommy bursts into tears. "I don't know," he howls.)

That howl, the Director made it plain, discouraged the earliest investigators. The experiments were abandoned. No further attempt was made to teach children the length of the Nile in their sleep. Quite rightly. You can't learn a science unless you know what it's all about.

"Whereas, if they'd only started on *moral* education," said the Director, leading the way towards the door. The students followed him, desperately scribbling as they walked and all the way up in the lift. "Moral education, which ought never, in any circumstances, to be rational."

"Silence, silence," whispered a loud speaker as they stepped out at the fourteenth floor, and "Silence, silence," the trumpet mouths indefatigably repeated at intervals down every corridor. The students and even the Director himself rose automatically to the tips of their toes. They were Alphas, of course; but even Alphas have been well conditioned. "Silence, silence." All the air of the fourteenth floor was sibilant with the categorical imperative.

Fifty yards of tiptoeing brought them to a door which the Director cautiously opened. They stepped over the threshold into the twilight of a shuttered dormitory. Eighty cots stood in a row against the wall. There was a sound of light regular breathing and a continuous murmur, as of very faint voices remotely whispering.

A nurse rose as they entered and came to attention before the Director.

"What's the lesson this afternoon?" he asked.

"We had Elementary Sex for the first forty minutes," she answered. "But now it's switched over to Elementary Class Consciousness."

The Director walked slowly down the long line of cots. Rosy and relaxed with sleep, eighty little boys and girls lay softly breathing. There was a whisper under every pillow. The D.H.C. halted and, bending over one of the little beds, listened attentively.

"Elementary Class Consciousness, did you say? Let's have it repeated a little louder by the trumpet."

At the end of the room a loud speaker projected from the wall. The Director walked up to it and pressed a switch.

". . . all wear green," said a soft but very distinct voice, beginning in the middle of a sentence, "and Delta Children wear khaki. Oh no, I don't want to play with Delta children. And Epsilons are still worse. They're too stupid to be able to read or write. Besides they wear black, which is such a beastly colour. I'm *so* glad I'm a Beta."

There was a pause; then the voice began again.

"Alpha children wear grey. They work much harder than we do, because they're so frightfully clever. I'm really awfully glad I'm a Beta, because I don't work so hard. And then we are much better than the Gammas and Deltas. Gammas are stupid. They all wear green, and Delta children wear khaki. Oh no, I *don't* want to play with Delta children. And Epsilons are still worse. They're too stupid to be able . . ."

The Director pushed back the switch. The voice was silent. Only its thin ghost continued to mutter from beneath the eighty pillows.

"They'll have that repeated forty or fifty times more before they wake; then again on Thursday, and again on Saturday. A hundred and twenty times three times a week for thirty months. After which they go on to a more advanced lesson."

Roses and electric shocks, the khaki of Deltas and a whiff of asafœtida —wedded indissolubly before the child can speak. But wordless conditioning is crude and wholesale; cannot bring home the finer distinctions, cannot inculcate the more complex courses of behaviour. For that there must be words, but words without reason. In brief, hypnopædia.

"The greatest moralizing and socializing force of all time."

The students took it down in their little books. Straight from the horse's mouth.

Once more the Director touched the switch.

". . . so frightfully clever," the soft, insinuating, indefatigable voice was saying. "I'm really awfully glad I'm a Beta, because . . ."

Not so much like drops of water, though water, it is true, can wear holes in the hardest granite; rather, drops of liquid sealing-wax, drops that adhere, incrust, incorporate themselves with what they fall on, till finally the rock is all one scarlet blob.

"Till at last the child's mind *is* these suggestions, and the sum of the suggestions *is* the child's mind. And not the child's mind only. The adult's mind too—all his life long. The mind that judges and desires and decides —made up of these suggestions. But all these suggestions are *our* suggestions!" The Director almost shouted in his triumph. "Suggestions from the State." He banged the nearest table. "It therefore follows . . ."

A noise made him turn round.

"Oh, Ford!" he said in another tone, "I've gone and woken the children."

SCIENCE AND HUMAN BEHAVIOR

B. F. SKINNER

B. F. Skinner (1904–   ) is an American psychologist, novelist, and educator, and the leading exponent of behaviorism, the psychological movement that explains human conduct in terms of physiological responses of the organism to environmental stimuli.

Walden II, Skinner's most popular book, describes an ideal community constructed according to the principles of behavioral engineering. There are interesting comparisons to be made between Skinner's vision of utopia and that of Francis Bacon, Thomas More, and especially Edward Bellamy, H. G. Wells, and Henry David Thoreau.

In *Science and Human Behavior* Skinner accepts as fact that increased control of the conditions governing behavior will be exercised in modern society. After rebutting the objections to a science of behavior, he analyzes the "variables" involved in manipulating the responses of individual organisms.

THE PRACTICAL ISSUE

Our current practices do not represent any well-defined theoretical position. They are, in fact, thoroughly confused. At times we appear to regard a man's behavior as spontaneous and responsible. At other times we recognize that inner determination is at least not complete, that the individual is not always to be held to account. We have not been able to reject the slowly accumulating evidence that circumstances beyond the individual are relevant. We sometimes exonerate a man by pointing to "extenuating circumstances." We no longer blame the uneducated for their ignorance or call the unemployed lazy. We no longer hold children wholly accountable for their delinquencies. "Ignorance of the law" is no longer wholly inexcusable: "Father, forgive them; for they know not what they do." The insane have long since been cleared of responsibility for their condition, and the kinds of neurotic or psychotic behavior to which we now apply this extenuation are multiplying.

But we have not gone all the way. We regard the common man as the product of his environment; yet we reserve the right to give personal credit to great men for their achievements. (At the same time we take a certain delight in proving that part of the output of even such men is due to the "influence" of other men or to some trivial circumstance in their personal history.) We want to believe that right-minded men are moved by valid principles even though we are willing to regard wrong-minded men as victims of erroneous propaganda. Backward peoples may be the fault of a poor culture, but we want to regard the elite as something more than the product of a good culture. Though we observe that Moslem children in general become Moslems while Christian children in general become Christians, we are not willing to accept an accident of birth as a basis for belief. We dismiss those who disagree with us as victims of ignorance, but we regard the promotion of our own religious beliefs as something more than the arrangement of a particular environment.

All of this suggests that we are in transition. We have not wholly abandoned the traditional philosophy of human nature; at the same time we are far from adopting a scientific point of view without reservation. We have accepted the assumption of determinism in part; yet we allow our sympathies, our first allegiances, and our personal aspirations to rise to the defense of the traditional view. We are currently engaged in a sort of patchwork in which new facts and methods are assembled in accordance with traditional theories.

If this were a theoretical issue only, we would have no cause for alarm; but theories affect practices. A scientific conception of human behavior dictates one practice, a philosophy of personal freedom another. Confusion in theory means confusion in practice. The present unhappy condition of the world may in large measure be traced to our vacillation. The principal issues in dispute between nations, both in peaceful assembly and on the battlefield, are intimately concerned with the problem of human freedom and control. Totalitarianism or democracy, the state or the individual, planned society or laissez-faire, the impression of cultures upon alien peoples, economic determinism, individual initiative, propaganda, education, ideological warfare—all concern the fundamental nature of human behavior. We shall almost certainly remain ineffective in solving these problems until we adopt a consistent point of view. . . .

SOME OBJECTIONS TO A SCIENCE OF BEHAVIOR

The report of a single event raises no theoretical problems and comes into no conflict with philosophies of human behavior. The scientific laws or systems which express uniformities are likely to conflict with theory because they claim the same territory. When a science of behavior reaches the point of dealing with lawful relationships, it meets the resistance of those who give their allegiance to prescientific or extrascientific conceptions. The resistance does not always take the form of an overt rejection of science. It may be transmuted into claims of limitations, often expressed in highly scientific terms.

It has sometimes been pointed out, for example, that physical science has been unable to maintain its philosophy of determinism, particularly at the subatomic level. The Principle of Indeterminacy states that there are circumstances under which the physicist cannot put himself in possession of all relevant information: if he chooses to observe one event, he must relinquish the possibility of observing another. In our present state of knowledge, certain events therefore appear to be unpredictable. It does not follow that these events are free or capricious. Since human behavior is enormously complex and the human organism is of limited dimensions, many acts may involve processes to which the Principle of Indeterminacy applies. It does not follow that human behavior is free, but only that it may be beyond the range of a predictive or controlling science. Most students of behavior, however, would be willing to settle for the degree of prediction and control achieved by the physical sciences in spite of this limitation. A final answer to the problem of lawfulness is to be sought, not in the limits of any hypothetical mechanism within the organism, but in our ability to demonstrate lawfulness in the behavior of the organism as a whole.

A similar objection has a logical flavor. It is contended that reason cannot comprehend itself or—in somewhat more substantial terms—that the behavior required in understanding one's own behavior must be something beyond the behavior which is understood. It is true that knowledge is limited by the limitations of the knowing organism. The number of things in the world which might be known certainly exceeds the number of possible different states in all possible knowers. But the laws and systems of science are designed to make a knowledge of particular events unimportant. It is by no means necessary that one man should understand all the facts in a given field, but only that he should understand all the *kinds* of facts. We have no reason to suppose that the human intellect is incapable of formulating or comprehending the basic principles of human behavior—certainly not until we have a clearer notion of what those principles are.

The assumption that behavior is a lawful scientific datum sometimes meets with another objection. Science is concerned with the general, but the behavior of the individual is necessarily unique. The "case history" has a richness and flavor which are in decided contrast with general principles. It is easy to convince oneself that there are two distinct worlds and that one is beyond the reach of science. This distinction is not peculiar to the study of behavior. It can always be made in the early stages of any science, when it is not clear what we may deduce from a general principle with respect to a particular case. What the science of physics has to say about the world is dull and colorless to the beginning student when compared with his daily experience, but he later discovers that it is actually a more incisive account of even the single instance. When we wish to deal effectively with the single instance, we turn to science for help. The argument will lose cogency as a science of behavior progresses and as the implications of its general laws become clear. A comparable argument against the possibility of a science of medicine has already lost its significance. In *War and Peace*, Tolstoy wrote of the illness of a favorite character as follows:

> Doctors came to see Natasha, both separately and in consultation. They said a great deal in French, in German, and in Latin. They criticised one another, and prescribed the most diverse remedies for all the diseases they were familiar with. But it never occurred to one of them to make the simple reflection that they could not understand the disease

from which Natasha was suffering, as no single disease can be fully understood in a living person; for every living person has his individual peculiarities and always has his own peculiar, new, complex complaints unknown to medicine—not a disease of the lungs, of the kidneys, of the skin, of the heart, and so on, as described in medical books, but a disease that consists of one out of the innumerable combinations of ailments of those organs.

Tolstoy was justified in calling every sickness a unique event. Every action of the individual is unique, as well as every event in physics and chemistry. But his objection to a science of medicine in terms of uniqueness was unwarranted. The argument was plausible enough at the time; no one could then contradict him by supplying the necessary general principles. But a great deal has happened in medical science since then, and today few people would care to argue that a disease cannot be described in general terms or that a single case cannot be discussed by referring to factors common to many cases. The intuitive wisdom of the old-style diagnostician has been largely replaced by the analytical procedures of the clinic, just as a scientific analysis of behavior will eventually replace the personal interpretation of unique instances.

A similar argument is leveled at the use of statistics in a science of behavior. A prediction of what the *average* individual will do is often of little or no value in dealing with a particular individual. The actuarial tables of life-insurance companies are of no value to a physician in predicting the death or survival of a particular patient. This issue is still alive in the physical sciences, where it is associated with the concepts of causality and probability. It is seldom that the science of physics deals with the behavior of individual molecules, atoms, or subatomic particles. When it is occasionally called upon to do so, all the problems of the particular event arise. In general a science is helpful in dealing with the individual only insofar as its laws refer to individuals. A science of behavior which concerns only the behavior of groups is not likely to be of help in our understanding of the particular case. But a science may also deal with the behavior of the individual, and its success in doing so must be evaluated in terms of its achievements rather than any a priori contentions.

The extraordinary complexity of behavior is sometimes held to be an added source of difficulty. Even though behavior may be lawful, it may be too complex to be dealt with in terms of law. Sir Oliver Lodge once asserted that "though an astronomer can calculate the orbit of a planet or comet or even a meteor, although a physicist can deal with the structure of atoms, and a chemist with their possible combinations, neither a biologist nor any scientific man can calculate the orbit of a common fly." This is a statement about the limitations of scientists or about their aspirations, not about the suitability of a subject matter. Even so, it is wrong. It may be said with some assurance that if no one has calculated the orbit of a fly, it is only because no one has been sufficiently interested in doing so. The tropistic movements of many insects are now fairly well understood, but the instrumentation needed to record the flight of a fly and to give an account of all the conditions affecting it would cost more than the importance of the subject justifies. There is, therefore, no reason to conclude, as the author does, that "an incalculable element of self-determination thus makes its appearance quite low down the animal scale." Self-determination does not follow from complexity. Difficulty in calculating the orbit of the fly does not prove capriciousness, though it may make it impossible to prove anything else. The problems imposed by the complexity of a subject matter must be dealt with as they arise. Apparently hopeless cases often become manageable in time. It is only recently that any sort of lawful account of the weather has been possible. We often succeed in reducing complexity to a reasonable degree by simplifying conditions in the laboratory; but where this is impossible, a statistical analysis may be used to achieve an inferior, but in many ways acceptable, prediction. Certainly no one is prepared to say now what a science of behavior can or cannot accomplish eventually. Advance estimates of the limits of science have generally proved inaccurate. The issue is in the long run pragmatic: we cannot tell until we have tried.

Still another objection to the use of scientific method in the study of human behavior is that behavior is an anomalous subject matter because a prediction made about it may alter it. If we tell a friend that he is going to buy a particular kind of car, he may react to our prediction by buying a different kind. The same effect has been used to explain the failures of public opinion polls. In the presidential election of 1948 it was confidently predicted that a majority of the voters would vote for a candidate who, as it turned out, lost the election. It has been asserted that the electorate reacted to the prediction in a contrary way and that the published prediction therefore had an effect upon the predicted event. But it is by no means necessary that a prediction of behavior be permitted to affect the behaving individual. There may have been practical reasons why the results of the poll in question could not be withheld until after the election, but this would not be the case in a purely scientific endeavor.

There are other ways in which observer and observed interact. Study distorts the thing studied. But there is no special problem here peculiar to human behavior. It is now accepted as a general principle in scientific method that it is necessary to interfere in some degree with any phenomenon in the act of observing it. A scientist may have an effect upon behavior in the act of observing or analyzing it, and he must certainly take this effect into account. But behavior may also be observed with a minimum of interaction between subject and scientist, and this is the case with which one naturally tries to begin.

A final objection deals with the practical application of a scientific analysis. Even if we assume that behavior is lawful and that the methods of science will reveal the rules which govern it, we may be unable to make any technological use of these rules unless certain conditions can be brought under control. In the laboratory many conditions are simplified and irrelevant conditions often eliminated. But of what value are laboratory studies if we must predict and control behavior where a comparable simplification is impossible? It is true that we can gain control over behavior only insofar as we can control the factors responsible for it. What a scientific study does is to enable us to make optimal use of the control we possess. The laboratory simplification reveals the relevance of factors which we might otherwise overlook.

We cannot avoid the problems raised by a science of behavior by simply denying that the necessary conditions can be controlled. In actual fact there is a considerable degree of control over many relevant conditions. In penal institutions and military organizations the control is extensive. We control the environment of the human organism in the nursery and in institutions which care for those to whom the conditions of the nursery remain necessary in later life. Fairly extensive control of conditions relevant to human behavior is maintained in industry in the form of wages and conditions of work, in schools in the form of grades and conditions of work, in commerce by anyone in possession of goods or money, by governmental agencies through the police and military, in the psychological clinic through the consent of the controllee, and so on. A degree of effective control, not so easily identified, rests in the hands of entertainers, writers, advertisers, and propagandists. These controls, which are often all too evident in their practical application, are more than sufficient to permit us to extend the results of a laboratory science to the interpretation of human behavior in daily affairs—for either theoretical or practical purposes. Since a science of behavior will continue to increase the effective use of this control, it is now more important than ever to understand the processes involved and to prepare ourselves for the problems which will certainly arise. . . .

Direct information about many of the chemical and electrical processes in the nervous system is now available. Statements about the nervous system are no longer necessarily inferential or fictional. But there is still a measure of circularity in much physiological explanation, even in the writings of specialists. In World War I a familiar disorder was called "shell shock." Disturbances in behavior were explained by arguing that violent explosions had damaged the structure of the nervous system, though no direct evidence of such damage was available. In World War II the same disorder was classified as "neuropsychiatric." The prefix seems to show a continuing unwillingness to abandon explanations in terms of hypothetical neural damage.

Eventually a science of the nervous system based upon direct observation rather than inference will describe the neural states and events which immediately precede instances of behavior. We shall know the precise neurological conditions which immediately precede, say, the response, "No, thank you." These events in turn will be found to be preceded by other neurological events, and these in turn by others. This series will lead us back to events outside the nervous system and, eventually, outside the organism. . . .

THE VARIABLES OF WHICH BEHAVIOR IS A FUNCTION

The practice of looking inside the organism for an explanation of behavior has tended to obscure the variables which are immediately available for a scientific analysis. These variables lie outside the organism, in its immediate environment and in its environmental history. They have a physical status to which the usual techniques of science are adapted, and they make it possible to explain behavior as other subjects are explained in science. These independent variables are of many sorts and their relations to behavior are often subtle and complex, but we cannot hope to give an adequate account of behavior without analyzing them.

Consider the act of drinking a glass of water. This is not likely to be an important bit of behavior in anyone's life, but it supplies a convenient example. We may describe the topography of the behavior in such a way that a given instance may be identified quite accurately by any qualified observer. Suppose now we bring someone into a room and place a glass of water before him. Will he drink? There appear to be only two possibilities: either he will or he will not. But we speak of the *chances* that he will drink, and this notion may be refined for scientific use. What we want to evaluate is the *probability* that he will drink. This may range from virtual certainly that drinking will occur to virtual certainty that it will not. The very considerable problem of how to measure such a probability will be discussed later. For the moment, we are interested in how the probability may be increased or decreased.

Everyday experience suggests several possibilities, and laboratory and clinical observations have added others. It is decidedly not true that a horse may be led to water but cannot be made to drink. By arranging a history of severe deprivation we could be "absolutely sure" that drinking would occur. In the same way we may be sure that the glass of water in our experiment will be drunk. Although we are not likely to arrange them experimentally, deprivations of the necessary magnitude sometimes occur outside the laboratory. We may obtain an effect similar to that of deprivation by speeding up the excretion of water. For example, we may induce sweating by raising the temperature of the room or by forcing heavy exercise, or we may increase the excretion of urine by mixing salt or urea in food taken prior to the experiment. It is also well known that loss of blood, as on a battlefield, sharply increases the probability of drinking. On the other hand, we may set the probability at virtually zero by inducing or forcing our subject to drink a large quantity of water before the experiment.

If we are to predict whether or not our subject will drink, we must know as much as possible about these variables. If we are to induce him to drink, we must be able to manipulate them. In both cases, moreover, either for accurate prediction or control, we must investigate the effect of each variable quantitatively with the methods and techniques of a laboratory science.

Other variables may, of course, affect the result. Our subject may be "afraid" that something has been added to the water as a practical joke or for experimental purposes. He may even "suspect" that the water has been poisoned. He may have grown up in a culture in which water is drunk only when no one is watching. He may refuse to drink simply to prove that we cannot predict or control his behavior. These possibilities do not disprove the relations between drinking and the variables listed in the preceding paragraphs; they simply remind us that other variables may have to be taken into account. We must know the history of our subject with respect to the behavior of drinking water, and if we cannot eliminate social factors from the situation, then we must know the history of his personal relations to people resembling the experimenter. Adequate prediction in any science requires information about all relevant variables, and the control of a subject matter for practical purposes makes the same demands.

Other types of "explanation" do not permit us to dispense with these requirements or to fulfill them in any easier way. It is of no help to be told that our subject will drink provided he was born under a particular sign of the zodiac which shows a preoccupation with water or provided he is the lean and thirsty type or was, in short, "born thirsty." Explanations in terms of inner states or agents, however, may require some further comment. To what extent is it helpful to be told, "He drinks because he is thirsty"? If to be thirsty means nothing more than to have a tendency to drink, this is mere redundancy. If it means that he drinks because of a state of thirst, an inner causal event is invoked. If this state is purely inferential—if no dimensions are assigned to it which would make direct observation possible—it cannot serve as an explanation. But if it has physiological or psychic properties, what role can it play in a science of behavior?

The physiologist may point out that several ways of raising the probability of drinking have a common effect: they increase the concentration of solutions in the body. Through some mechanism not yet well understood, this may bring about a corresponding change in the nervous system which in turn makes drinking more probable. In the same way, it may be argued that all these operations make the organism "feel thirsty" or "want a drink" and that such a psychic state also acts upon the nervous system in some unexplained way to induce drinking. In each case we have a causal chain consisting of three links: (1) an operation performed upon the organism from without—for example, water deprivation; (2) an inner condition—for example, physiological or psychic thirst; and (3) a kind of behavior—for example, drinking. Independent information about the second link would obviously permit us to predict the third without recourse to the first. It would be a preferred type of variable because it would be nonhistoric; the first link may lie in the past history of the organism, but the second is a current condition. Direct information about the second link is, however, seldom, if ever, available. Sometimes we infer the second link from the third: an animal is judged to be thirsty if it drinks. In that case, the explanation is spurious. Sometimes we infer the second link from the first: an animal is said to be thirsty if it has not drunk for a long time. In that case, we obviously cannot dispense with the prior history.

The second link is useless in the *control* of behavior unless we can manipulate it. At the moment, we have no way of directly altering neural processes at appropriate moments in the life of a behaving organism, nor has any way been discovered to alter a psychic process. We usually set up the second link through the first: we make an animal thirsty, in either the physiological or the psychic sense, by depriving it of water, feeding it salt, and so on. In that case, the second link obviously does not permit us to dispense with the first. Even if some new technical discovery were to enable us to set up or change the second link directly, we should still have to deal with those enormous areas in which human behavior is controlled through manipulation of the first link. A technique of operating upon the second link would increase our control of behavior, but the techniques which have already been developed would still remain to be analyzed.

The most objectionable practice is to follow the causal sequence back only as far as a hypothetical second link. This is a serious handicap both in a theoretical science and in the practical control of behavior. It is no help to be told that to get an organism to drink we are simply to "make it thirsty" unless we are also told how this is to be done. When we have obtained the necessary prescription for thirst, the whole proposal is more complex than it need be. Similarly, when an example of maladjusted behavior is explained by saying that the individual is "suffering from anxiety," we have still to be told the cause of the anxiety. But the external conditions which are then invoked could have been directly related to the maladjusted behavior. Again, when we are told that a man stole a loaf of bread because "he was hungry," we have still to learn of the external conditions responsible for the "hunger." These conditions would have sufficed to explain the theft.

The objection to inner states is not that they do not exist, but that they are not relevant in a functional analysis. We cannot account for the behavior of any system while staying wholly inside it; eventually we must turn to forces operating upon the organism from without. Unless there is a weak spot in our causal chain so that the second link is not lawfully determined by the first, or the third by the second, then the first and third links must be lawfully related. If we must always go back beyond the second link for prediction and control, we may avoid many tiresome and exhausting digressions by examining the third link as a function of the first. Valid information about the second link may throw light upon this relationship but can in no way alter it.

A FUNCTIONAL ANALYSIS

The external variables of which behavior is a function provide for what may be called a causal or functional analysis. We undertake to predict and control the behavior of the individual organism. This is our "dependent variable"—the effect for which we are to find the cause. Our "independent variables"—the causes of behavior—are the external conditions of which behavior is a function. Relations between the two—the "cause-and-effect relationships" in behavior—are the laws of a science. A synthesis of these laws expressed in quantitative terms yields a comprehensive picture of the organism as a behaving system.

This must be done within the bounds of a natural science. We cannot assume that behavior has any peculiar properties which require unique methods or special kinds of knowledge. It is often argued that an act is not so important as the "intent" which lies behind it, or that it can be described only in terms of what it "means" to the behaving individual or to others whom it may affect. If statements of this sort are useful for scientific purposes, they must be based upon observable events, and we may confine ourselves to such events exclusively in a functional analysis. We shall see later that although such terms as "meaning" and "intent" appear to refer to properties of behavior, they usually conceal references to independent variables. This is also true of "aggressive," "friendly," "disorganized," "intelligent," and other terms which appear to describe properties of behavior but in reality refer to its controlling relations.

The independent variables must also be described in physical terms. An effort is often made to avoid the labor of analyzing a physical situation by guessing what it "means" to an organism or by distinguishing between the physical world and a psychological world of "experience." This practice also reflects a confusion between dependent and independent variables. The events affecting an organism must be capable of description in the language of physical science. It is sometimes argued that certain "social forces" or the "influences" of culture or tradition are exceptions. But we cannot appeal to entities of this sort without explaining how they can affect both the scientist and the individual under observation. The physical events which must then be appealed to in such an explanation will supply us with alternative material suitable for a physical analysis.

By confining ourselves to these observable events, we gain a considerable advantage, not only in theory, but in practice. A "social force" is no more useful in manipulating behavior than an inner state of hunger, anxiety, or skepticism. Just as we must trace these inner events to the manipulable variables of which they are said to be functions before we may put them to practical use, so we must identify the physical events through which a "social force" is said to affect the organism before we can manipulate it for purposes of control. In dealing with the directly observable data we need not refer to either the inner state or the outer force.

The material to be analyzed in a science of behavior comes from many sources:

(1) Our *casual observations* are not to be dismissed entirely. They are especially important in the early stages of investigation. Generalizations based upon them, even without explicit analysis, supply useful hunches for further study.

(2) In *controlled field observation*, as exemplified by some of the methods of anthropology, the data are sampled more carefully and conclusions stated more explicitly than in casual observation. Standard instruments and practices increase the accuracy and uniformity of field observation.

(3) *Clinical observation* has supplied extensive material. Standard practices in interviewing and testing bring out behavior which may be easily measured, summarized, and compared with the behavior of others. Although it usually emphasizes the disorders which bring people to clinics, the clinical sample is often unusually interesting and of special value when the exceptional condition points up an important feature of behavior.

(4) Extensive observations of behavior have been made under more rigidly controlled conditions in *industrial, military, and other institutional research*. This work often differs from field or clinical observation in its greater use of the experimental method.

(5) *Laboratory studies of human behavior* provide especially useful material. The experimental method includes the use of instruments which improve our contact with behavior and with the variables of which it is a function. Recording devices enable us to observe behavior over long periods of time, and accurate recording and measurement make effective quantitative analysis possible. The most important feature of the laboratory method is the deliberate manipulation of variables: the importance of a given condition is determined by changing it in a controlled fashion and observing the result.

Current experimental research on human behavior is sometimes not so comprehensive as one might wish. Not all behavioral processes are easy to set up in the laboratory, and precision of measurement is sometimes obtained only at the price of unreality in conditions. Those who are primarily concerned with the everyday life of the individual are often impatient with these artificialities, but insofar as relevant relationships can be brought under experimental control, the laboratory offers the best chance of obtaining the quantitative results needed in a scientific analysis.

(6) The extensive results of *laboratory studies of the behavior of*

animals below the human level are also available. The use of this material often meets with the objection that there is an essential gap between man and the other animals, and that the results of one cannot be extrapolated to the other. To insist upon this discontinuity at the beginning of a scientific investigation is to beg the question. Human behavior is distinguished by its complexity, its variety, and its greater accomplishments, but the basic processes are not therefore necessarily different. Science advances from the simple to the complex; it is constantly concerned with whether the processes and laws discovered at one stage are adequate for the next. It would be rash to assert at this point that there is no essential difference between human behavior and the behavior of lower species; but until an attempt has been made to deal with both in the same terms, it would be equally rash to assert that there is. A discussion of human embryology makes considerable use of research on the embryos of chicks, pigs, and other animals. Treatises on digestion, respiration, circulation, endocrine secretion, and other physiological processes deal with rats, hamsters, rabbits, and so on, even though the interest is primarily in human beings. The study of behavior has much to gain from the same practice.

We study the behavior of animals because it is simpler. Basic processes are revealed more easily and can be recorded over longer periods of time. Our observations are not complicated by the social relation between subject and experimenter. Conditions may be better controlled. We may arrange genetic histories to control certain variables and special life histories to control others—for example, if we are interested in how an organism learns to see, we can raise an animal in darkness until the experiment is begun. We are also able to control current circumstances to an extent not easily realized in human behavior—for example, we can vary states of deprivation over wide ranges. These are advantages which should not be dismissed on the a priori contention that human behavior is inevitably set apart as a separate field. . . .

The effect of a social environment upon the behavior of the individual may be inferred point for point from an analysis of that environment. Let us consider an individual at the age of thirty. To what extent may his behavior reasonably be traced to the cultural variables with which he has come into contact?

Work level. In the sense that particular parts of our subject's repertoire show given probabilities as the result of reinforcement, we say that he shows a given level of interest, enthusiasm, or freedom from "mental fatigue." We are likely to find a high level of relevant behavior if the physical environment includes a favorable climate, an adequate food supply, and other resources. It is also important that abundant positive reinforcement is supplied by the family, the group as a whole, and various subgroups, as well as by governmental, religious, psychotherapeutic, economic, and educational agencies.

Motivation. Whether an individual is frequently hungry will depend, not only upon the availability of food in the nonsocial environment, but upon cultural practices which control what he eats, when he eats it, whether he observes periods of fasting, and so on. His sexual behavior will depend, not only upon the availability of members of the opposite sex, but upon the ethical control of sexual relations, upon governmental and religious restrictions, upon sex education, and so on. Other kinds of deprivation and satiation are also controlled by both social and nonsocial conditions.

Emotional dispositions. The social environment is mainly responsible for the fact that our subject may have grown up in an atmosphere of love, hate, anger, or resentment, and that various emotional patterns may therefore characterize his behavior.

Repertoire. The inanimate world builds an elaborate repertoire of practical responses. It may also set up behavior which is effective in extending such a repertoire: our subject will show a strong "curiosity about nature" if exploratory responses have frequently been reinforced, and special skills in research and invention if self-manipulative behavior . . . has been conditioned. But the comparable repertoire generated by the culture is usually much more extensive. Verbal problem-solving and the social skills employed in personal control are important examples. All controlling agencies are concerned in part with the creation of behavior of this sort, although it is the special concern, of course, of education. The competence of the individual in dealing with things, as well as men, will depend largely upon the extent to which such agencies have characterized the social environment.

Self-control. The inanimate environment may establish some degree of self-control—for example, the individual may learn not to eat a delicious but indigestible food—but by far the greater part of self-control is culturally determined, particularly by ethical, religious, and governmental agencies. The amoral individual who escapes this influence shows the effect of too little control, while the completely "inhibited" or restrained individual stands at the other extreme. Whether our subject conspicuously displays the other effects of his culture which we have just considered will often depend upon this one effect. For example, he may behave readily in an emotional fashion or show a stoical restraint depending upon the extent to which his emotional behavior has been reinforced or punished as right or wrong, legal or illegal, or pious or sinful.

Self-knowledge. Discriminative responses to one's own behavior and to the variables of which it is a function appear to be the exclusive product of the social environment. Whether or not our subject will be self-conscious and introspective depends upon the extent to which the group has insisted upon answers to questions such as "What are you doing?" or "Why did you do that?"

Neurotic behavior. A purely physical environment could no doubt generate behavior which was so ineffective, disadvantageous, or dangerous that it would be called neurotic. By far the greater source of trouble, however, is social. Whether or not our subject is well balanced, in good contact with the environment, or free of crippling emotional reactions will depend mainly upon the controlling practices of the group into which he was born.

4

The Affirmation
of
Free Will

NOTES FROM UNDERGROUND

(Part I)

FEDOR DOSTOEVSKY

(trans. by Ralph Matlaw)

Fedor Dostoevsky (1821–1881). For notes on Dostoevsky see page 78.

Dostoevsky's *Notes from Underground* asserts the reality and value of free will, even in a scientific society in which choices (theoretically) can be calculated in advance. Even if a man's self-interest were made clear to him, Dostoevsky writes, he could still choose to ignore it and, through perverseness or irrationality, choose what is less advantageous to him. Moreover, if that resistance too could be predicted, man would then go mad just to be free from natural laws and to prove to himself that he is a human being and not a mechanical object.

I

I am a sick man . . . I am a spiteful man. I am an unpleasant man. I think my liver is diseased. However, I don't know beans about my disease, and I am not sure what is bothering me. I don't treat it and never have, though I respect medicine and doctors. Besides, I am extremely superstitious, let's say sufficiently so to respect medicine. (I am educated enough not to be superstitious, but I am.) No, I refuse to treat it out of spite. You probably will not understand that. Well, but *I* understand it. Of course, I can't explain to you just whom I am annoying in this case by my spite. I am perfectly well aware that I cannot "get even" with the doctors by not consulting them. I know better than anyone that I thereby injure only myself and no one else. But still, if I don't treat it, it is out of spite. My liver is bad, well then—let it get even worse!

I have been living like that for a long time now—twenty years. I am forty now. I used to be in the civil service, but no longer am. I was a spiteful official. I was rude and took pleasure in being so. After all, I did not accept bribes, so I was bound to find a compensation in that, at least.

(A bad joke but I will not cross it out. I wrote it thinking it would sound very witty; but now that I see myself that I only wanted to show off in a despicable way, I will purposely not cross it out!) When petitioners would come to my desk for information I would gnash my teeth at them, and feel intense enjoyment when I succeeded in distressing some one. I was almost always successful. For the most part they were all timid people —of course, they were petitioners. But among the fops there was one officer in particular I could not endure. He simply would not be humble, and clanked his sword in a disgusting way. I carried on a war with him for eighteen months over that sword. At last I got the better of him. He left off clanking it. However, that happened when I was still young. But do you know, gentlemen, what the real point of my spite was? Why, the whole trick, the real vileness of it lay in the fact that continually, even in moments of the worst spleen, I was inwardly conscious with shame that I was not only not spiteful but not even an embittered man, that I was simply frightening sparrows at random and amusing myself by it. I might foam at the mouth, but bring me some kind of toy, give me a cup of tea with sugar, and I would be appeased. My heart might even be touched, though probably I would gnash my teeth at myself afterward and lie awake at night with shame for months after. That is the way I am.

I was lying when I said just now that I was a spiteful official. I was lying out of spite. I was simply indulging myself with the petitioners and with the officer, but I could never really become spiteful. Every moment I was conscious in myself of many, very many elements completely opposite to that. I felt them positively teeming in me, these opposite elements. I knew that they had been teeming in me all my life, begging to be let out; but I would not let them, would not let them, purposely would not let them out. They tormented me till I was ashamed; they drove me to convulsions, and finally, they bored me, how they bored me! Well, are you not imagining, gentlemen, that I am repenting for something now, that I am asking your forgiveness for something? I am sure you are imagining that. However, I assure you it does not matter to me if you are.

Not only could I not become spiteful, I could not even become anything: neither spiteful nor kind, neither a rascal nor an honest man, neither a hero nor an insect. Now, I am living out my life in my corner, taunting myself with the spiteful and useless consolation that an intelligent man cannot seriously become anything and that only a fool can become something. Yes, an intelligent man in the nineteenth century must and morally ought to be pre-eminently a characterless creature; a man of character, an active man, is pre-eminently a limited creature. That is the conviction of my forty years. I am forty years old now, and forty years, after all, is a whole lifetime; after all, that is extreme old age. To live longer than forty years is bad manners; it is vulgar, immoral. Who does live beyond forty? Answer that, sincerely and honestly. I will tell you who do: fools and worthless people do. I tell all old men that to their face, all those respectable old men, all those silver-haired and reverend old men! I tell the whole world that to its face. I have a right to say so, for I'll go on living to sixty myself. I'll live till seventy! Till eighty! Wait, let me catch my breath.

No doubt you think, gentlemen, that I want to amuse you. You are mistaken in that, too. I am not at all such a merry person as you imagine, or as you may imagine; however, if irritated by all this babble (and I can feel that you are irritated) you decide to ask me just who I am—then my answer is, I am a certain low-ranked civil servant. I was in the service in order to have something to eat (but only for that reason), and when last year a distant relation left me six thousand roubles in his will I immediately retired from the service and settled down in my corner. I used to live in this corner before, but now I have settled down in it. My room is a wretched, horrid one on the outskirts of town. My servant is an old country-woman, spiteful out of stupidity, and, moreover, she always smells bad. I am told that the Petersburg climate is bad for me, and that with my paltry means it is very expensive to live in Petersburg. I know all that better than all these sage and experienced counsellors and monitors. But I am going to stay in Petersburg. I will not leave Petersburg! I will not leave because . . . Bah, after all it does not matter in the least whether I leave or stay.

But incidentally, what can a decent man speak about with the greatest pleasure?

Answer: About himself.

Well, then. I will talk about myself.

II

Now I want to tell you, gentlemen, whether you care to hear it or not, why I could not even become an insect. I tell you solemnly that I wanted to become an insect many times. But I was not even worthy of that. I swear to you, gentlemen, that to be hyperconscious is a disease, a real positive disease. Ordinary human consciousness would be too much for man's everyday needs, that is, half or a quarter of the amount which falls to the lot of a cultivated man of our unfortunate nineteenth century, especially one who has the particular misfortune to inhabit Petersburg, the most abstract and intentional city in the whole world. (There are intentional and unintentional cities.) It would have been quite enough, for instance, to have the consciousness by which all so-called straight-forward persons and men of action live. I'll bet you think I am writing all this to show off, to be witty at the expense of men of action; and what is more, that out of ill-bred showing-off, I am clanking a sword, like my officer. But, gentlemen, whoever can pride himself on his diseases and even show off with them?

However, what am I talking about? Everyone does that. They do pride themselves on their diseases, and I, perhaps, more than any one. There is no doubt about it: my objection was absurd. Yet just the same, I am firmly convinced not only that a great deal of consciousness, but that any consciousness is a disease. I insist on it. Let us drop that, too, for a minute. Tell me this: why did it happen that at the very, yes, at the very moment when I was most capable of recognizing every refinement of "all the sublime and beautiful," as we used to say at one time, I would, as though purposely, not only feel but do such hideous things, such that—well, in short, such as everyone probably does but which, as though purposely, occurred to me at the very time when I was most conscious that they ought not to be done. The more conscious I was of goodness, and of all that "sublime and beautiful," the more deeply I sank into my mire and the more capable I became of sinking into it completely. But the main thing was that all this did not seem to occur in me accidentally, but as though it had to be so. As though it were my most normal condition, and not in the least disease or depravity, so that finally I even lost the desire to struggle against this depravity. It ended by my almost believing (perhaps actually believing) that probably this was really my normal condition. But at first, in the beginning, that is, what agonies I suffered in that struggle! I did not believe that others went through the same things, and therefore I hid this fact about myself as a secret all my life. I was ashamed (perhaps I am even ashamed now). I reached the point of feeling a sort of secret abnormal, despicable enjoyment in returning home to my corner on some disgusting Petersburg night, and being acutely conscious that that day I had again done something loathsome, that what was done could never be undone, and secretly, inwardly gnaw, gnaw at myself for it, nagging and consuming myself till at last the bitterness turned into a sort of shameful accursed sweetness, and finally into real positive enjoyment! Yes, into enjoyment, into enjoyment! I insist upon that. And that is why I have started to speak, because I keep wanting to know for a fact whether other people feel such an enjoyment. Let me explain: the enjoyment here consisted precisely in the hyperconsciousness of one's own degradation; it was from feeling oneself that one had reached the last barrier, that it was nasty, but that it could not be otherwise; that you no longer had an escape; that you could never become a different person; that even if there remained enough time and faith for you to change into something else you probably would not want to change; or if you did want to, even then you would do nothing; because perhaps in reality there was nothing for you to change into. And the worst of it, and the root of it all, was that it all proceeded according to the normal and fundamental laws of hyperconsciousness, and with the inertia that was the direct result of those laws, and that consequently one could not only not change but one could do absolutely nothing. Thus it would follow, as the result of hyperconsciousness, that one is not to blame for being a scoundrel, as though that were any consolation to the scoundrel once he himself has come to realize that he actually is a scoundrel. But enough. Bah, I have talked a lot of nonsense, but what have I explained? Can this enjoyment be explained? But I will explain it! I will get to the bottom of it! That is why I have taken up my pen.

To take an instance, I am terribly vain. I am as suspicious and touchy as a hunchback or a dwarf. But to tell the truth, there have been moments when if someone had happened to slap my face I would, perhaps, have even been glad of that. I say, very seriously, that I would probably have been able to discover a peculiar sort of enjoyment even in that—the enjoyment, of course, of despair; but in despair occur the most intense enjoyments, especially when one is very acutely conscious of one's hopeless position. As for the slap in the face—why then the consciousness of being beaten to a pulp would positively overwhelm one. The worst of it is, no matter how I tried, it still turned out that I was always the most to blame in everything, and what is most humiliating of all, to blame for no fault of my own but, so to say, through the laws of nature. In the first place, to blame because I am cleverer than any of the people surrounding me. (I have always considered myself cleverer than any of the people surrounding me, and sometimes, would you believe it, I have even been ashamed of that. At any rate, all my life, I have, as it were, looked away and I could never look people straight in the eye.) To blame, finally, because even if I were magnanimous, I would only have suffered more from the consciousness of all its uselessness. After all, I would probably never have been able to do anything with my magnanimity—neither to forgive, for my assailant may have slapped me because of the laws of nature, and one cannot forgive the laws of nature; nor to forget, for even if it were the laws of nature, it is insulting all the same. Finally, even if I had wanted to be anything but magnanimous, had desired on the contrary to revenge myself on the man who insulted me, I could not have revenged myself on anyone for anything because I would certainly never have made up my mind to do anything, even if I had been able to. Why would I not have made up my mind? I want to say a few words about that in particular.

III

After all, people who know how to revenge themselves and to take care of themselves in general, how do they do it? After all, when they are possessed, let us suppose, by the feeling of revenge, then for the time there is nothing else but that feeling left in their whole being. Such a man simply rushes straight toward his object like an infuriated bull with its horns down, and nothing but a wall will stop him. (By the way: facing the wall, such people—that is, the straightforward persons and men of action—are genuinely nonplussed. For them a wall is not an evasion, as for example for us people who think and consequently do nothing; it is not an excuse for turning aside, an excuse for which our kind is always very glad, though we scarcely believe in it ourselves, usually. No, they are nonplussed in all sincerity. The wall has for them something tranquilizing, morally soothing, final—maybe even something mysterious . . . but of the wall later.) Well, such a direct person I regard as the real normal man, as his tender mother nature wished to see him when she graciously brought him into being on the earth. I envy such a man till I am green in the face. He is stupid. I am not disputing that, but perhaps the normal man should be stupid, how do you know? Perhaps it is very beautiful, in fact. And I am all the more convinced of that suspicion, if one can call it so, by the fact that if, for instance, you take the antithesis of the normal man, that is, the hyperconscious man, who has come, of course, not out of the lap of nature but out of a retort (this is almost mysticism, gentlemen, but I suspect this, too), this retort-made man is sometimes so nonplussed in the presence of his antithesis that with all his hyperconsciousness he genuinely thinks of himself as a mouse and not a man. It may be a hyperconscious mouse, yet it is a mouse, while the other is a man, and therefore, etc. And the worst is, he himself, his very own self, looks upon himself as a mouse. No one asks him to do so. And that is an important point. Now let us look at this mouse in action. Let us suppose, for instance, that it feels insulted, too (and it almost always does feel insulted), and wants to revenge itself too. There may even be a greater accumulation of spite in it than in *l'homme de la nature et de la vérité*.[1] The base, nasty desire to repay with spite whoever has offended it, rankles perhaps even more nastily in it than in *l'homme de la nature et de la vérité*, because *l'homme de la nature et de la vérité* through his innate stupidity looks upon his revenge as justice pure and simple; while in consequence of his hyper-consciousness the mouse does not believe in the justice of it. To come at last to the deed itself, to the very act of revenge. Apart from the one fundamental nastiness the unfortunate mouse succeeds in creating around it so many other nastinesses in the form of doubts and questions, adds to the one question so many unsettled questions, that there inevitably works up around it a sort of fatal brew, a stinking mess, made up of its doubts, agitations and lastly of the contempt spat upon it by the straightforward men of action who stand solemnly about it as judges and arbitrators, laughing at it till their healthy sides ache. Of course the only thing left for it is to dismiss all that with a wave of its paw, and, with a smile of assumed contempt in which it does not even believe itself, creep igno-miniously into its mouse-hole. There, in its nasty, stinking, underground home our insulted, crushed and ridiculed mouse promptly becomes ab-sorbed in cold, malignant and, above all, everlasting spite. For forty years together it will remember its injury down to the smallest, most shameful detail, and every time will add, of itself, details still more shameful, spitefully teasing and irritating itself with its own imagination. It will be ashamed of its own fancies, but yet it will recall everything, it will go over it again and again, it will invent lies against itself pretending that those things might have happened, and will forgive nothing. Maybe it will begin to revenge itself, too, but, as it were, piecemeal, in trivial ways, from behind the stove, incognito, without believing either in its own right to ven-

[1] [Editor's note: The honest man in a state of nature.]

geance, or in the success of its revenge, knowing beforehand that from all its efforts at revenge it will suffer a hundred times more than he on whom it revenges itself, while he, probably will not even feel it. On its deathbed it will recall it all over again, with interest accumulated over all the years. But it is just in that cold, abominable half-despair, half-belief, in that conscious burying oneself alive for grief in the underworld for forty years, in that hyperconsciousness and yet to some extent doubtful hopelessness of one's position, in that hell of unsatisfied desires turned inward, in that fever of oscillations, of resolutions taken for ever and regretted again a minute later—that the savor of that strange enjoyment of which I have spoken lies. It is so subtle, sometimes so difficult to analyze consciously, that somewhat limited people, or simply people with strong nerves, will not understand anything at all in it. "Possibly," you will add on your own account with a grin, "people who have never received a slap in the face will not understand it either," and in that way you will politely hint to me that I, too, perhaps, have been slapped in the face in my life, and so I speak as an expert. I'll bet that you are thinking that. But set your minds at rest, gentlemen, I have not received a slap in the face, though it doesn't matter to me at all what you may think about it. Possibly, I even myself regret that I have given so few slaps in the face during my life. But enough, not another word on the subject of such extreme interest to you.

I will continue calmly about people with strong nerves who do not understand a certain refinement of enjoyment. Though in certain circumstances these gentlemen bellow their loudest like bulls, though this, let us suppose, does them the greatest honor, yet, as I have already said, confronted with the impossible they at once resign themselves. Does the impossible mean the stone wall? What stone wall? Why, of course, the laws of nature, the conclusions of natural science, of mathematics. As soon as they prove to you, for instance, that you are descended from a monkey, then it is no use scowling, accept it as a fact. When they prove to you that in reality one drop of your own fat must be dearer to you than a hundred thousand of your fellow creatures, and that this conclusion is the final solution of all so-called virtues and duties and all such ravings and prejudices, then you might as well accept it, you can't do anything about it, because two times two is a law of mathematics. Just try refuting it.

"But really," they will shout at you, "there is no use protesting; it is a case of two times two makes four! Nature does not ask your permission, your wishes, and whether you like or dislike her laws does not concern her. You are bound to accept her as she is, and consequently also all her conclusions. A wall, you see, is a wall—etc. etc." Good God! but what do I care about the laws of nature and arithmetic, when, for some reason, I dislike those laws and the fact that two times two makes four? Of course I cannot break through a wall by battering my head against it if I really do not have the strength to break through it, but I am not going to resign myself to it simply because it is a stone wall and I am not strong enough.

As though such a stone wall really were a consolation, and really did contain some word of conciliation, if only because it is as true as two times two makes four. Oh, absurdity of absurdities! How much better it is to understand it all, to be conscious of it all, all the impossibilities and the stone walls, not to resign yourself to a single one of those impossibilities and stone walls if it disgusts you to resign yourself; to reach, through the most inevitable, logical combinations, the most revolting conclusions on the everlasting theme that you are yourself somehow to blame even for the stone wall, though again it is as clear as day you are not to blame in the least, and therefore grinding your teeth in silent impotence sensuously to sink into inertia, brooding on the fact that it turns out that there is even no one for you to feel vindictive against, that you have not, and perhaps never will have, an object for your spite, that it is a sleight-of-hand, a bit of juggling, a card-sharper's trick, that it is simply a mess, no knowing what and no knowing who, but in spite of all these uncertainties, and jugglings, still there is an ache in you, and the more you do not know, the worse the ache.

IV

"Ha, ha, ha! Next you will find enjoyment in a toothache," you cry with a laugh.

"Well? So what? There is enjoyment even in a toothache," I answer. I had a toothache for a whole month and I know there is. In that case, of course, people are not spiteful in silence, they moan; but these are not sincere moans, they are malicious moans, and the maliciousness is the whole point. The sufferer's enjoyment finds expression in those moans; if he did not feel enjoyment in them he would not moan. It is a good example, gentlemen, and I will develop it. The moans express in the first place all the aimlessness of your pain, which is so humiliating to your consciousness; the whole legal system of Nature on which you spit disdainfully, of course, but from which you suffer all the same while she does not. They express the consciousness that you have no enemy, but that you do have a pain; the consciousness that in spite of all the dentists in the world you are in complete slavery to your teeth; that if someone wishes it, your teeth will leave off aching, and if he does not, they will go on aching another three months; and that finally if you still disagree and still protest, all that is left you for your own gratification is to thrash yourself or beat your wall with your fist as hard as you can, and absolutely nothing more. Well then, these mortal insults, these jeers on the part of someone unknown, end at last in an enjoyment which sometimes reaches the highest degree of sensuality. I beg you, gentlemen, to listen sometimes to the moans of an educated man of the nineteenth century who is suffering from a toothache, particularly on the second or third day of the attack, when he has already begun to moan not as he moaned on the first day, that is, not simply because he has a toothache, not just as any coarse peasant might moan, but as a man affected by progress and European civilization, a man who is "divorced from the soil and the national principles," as they call it these days. His moans become nasty, disgustingly spiteful, and go on for whole days and nights. And, after all, he himself knows that he does not benefit at all from his moans; he knows better than anyone that he is only lacerating and irritating himself and others in vain; he knows that even the audience for whom he is exerting himself and his whole family now listen to him with loathing, do not believe him for a second, and that deep down they understand that he could moan differently, more simply, without trills and flourishes, and that he is only indulging himself like that out of spite, out of malice. Well, sensuality exists precisely in all these consciousnesses and infamies. "It seems I am troubling you, I am lacerating your hearts, I am keeping everyone in the house awake. Well, stay awake then, you, too, feel every minute that I have a toothache. I am no longer the hero to you now that I tried to appear before, but simply a nasty person, a scoundrel. Well, let it be that way, then! I am very glad that you see through me. Is it nasty for you to hear my foul moans? Well, let it be nasty. Here I will let you have an even nastier flourish in a minute. . . ." You still do not understand, gentlemen? No, it seems our development and our consciousness must go further to understand all the intricacies of this sensuality. You laugh? I am delighted. My jokes, gentlemen, are of course in bad taste, uneven, involved, lacking self-confidence. But of course that is because I do not respect myself. Can a man with consciousness respect himself at all?

V

Come, can a man who even attempts to find enjoyment in the very feeling of self-degradation really have any respect for himself at all? I am not saying this now from any insipid kind of remorse. And, indeed, I could never endure to say, "Forgive me, Daddy, I won't do it again," not because I was incapable of saying it, but, on the contrary, perhaps just because I was too capable of it, and in what a way, too! As though on purpose I used to get into trouble on occasions when I was not to blame in the faintest way. That was the nastiest part of it. At the same time I was genuinely touched and repentant, I used to shed tears and, of course, tricked even myself, though it was not acting in the least and there was a sick feeling in my heart at the time. For that one could not even blame the laws of nature, though the laws of nature have offended me continually all my life more than anything. It is loathsome to remember it all, but it was loathsome even then. Of course, in a minute or so I would realize with spite that it was all a lie, a lie, an affected, revolting lie, that is, all this repentance, all these emotions, these vows to reform. And if you ask why I worried and tortured myself that way, the answer is because it was very dull to twiddle one's thumbs, and so one began cutting capers. That is really it. Observe yourselves more carefully, gentlemen, then you will understand that that's right! I invented adventures for myself and made up a life, so as to live at least in some way. How many times it has happened to me—well, for instance, to take offence at nothing, simply on purpose; and one knows oneself, of course, that one is offended at nothing, that one is pretending, but yet one brings oneself, at last, to the point of really being offended. All my life I have had an impulse to play such pranks, so that in the end, I could not control it in myself. Another time, twice, in fact, I tried to force myself to fall in love. I even suffered, gentlemen, I assure you. In the depth of my heart I did not believe in my suffering, there was a stir of mockery, but yet I did suffer, and in the real, regular way I was jealous, I was beside myself, and it was all out of boredom, gentlemen, all out of boredom; inertia overcame me. After all, the direct, legitimate, immediate fruit of consciousness is inertia, that is, conscious thumb twiddling. I have referred to it already, I repeat, I repeat it emphatically: all straightforward persons and men of action are active just because they are stupid and limited. How can that be explained? This way: as a result of their limitation they take immediate and secondary causes for primary ones, and in that way persuade themselves more quickly and easily than other people do that they have found an infallible basis for their activity, and their minds are at ease and that, you know, is the most important thing. To begin to act, you know, you must first have your mind completely at ease and without a trace of doubt left in it. Well, how am I, for example, to set my mind at rest? Where are the primary causes on which I am to build? Where are my bases? Where am I to get them from? I exercise myself in the process of thinking, and consequently with me every primary cause at once draws after itself another still more primary, and so on to infinity. That is precisely the essence of every sort of consciousness and thinking. It must be a case of the laws of nature again. In what does it finally result? Why, just the same. Remember I spoke just now of vengeance. (I am sure you did not grasp that.) I said that a man revenges himself because he finds justice in it. Therefore he has found a primary cause, found a basis, to wit, justice. And so he is completely set at rest, and consequently he carries out his revenge calmly and successfully, as he is convinced that he is doing a just and honest thing. But, after all, I see no justice in it, I find no sort of virtue in it either, and consequently if I attempt to revenge myself, it would only be out of spite. Spite, of course, might overcome everything, all my doubts, and could consequently serve quite successfully in a place of a primary cause, precisely because it is not a cause. But what can be done if I do not even have spite (after all, I began with that just now)? Again, in consequence of those accursed laws of consciousness, my spite is subject to chemical disintegration. You look into it, the object flies off into air, your reasons evaporate, the criminal is not to be found, the insult becomes fate rather than an insult, something like the toothache, for which no one is to blame, and consequently there is only the same outlet left again—that is, to beat the wall as hard as you can. So you give it up as hopeless because you have not found a fundamental cause. And try letting yourself be carried away by your feelings, blindly, without reflection, without a primary cause, repelling consciousness at least for a time; hate or love, if only not to sit and twiddle your thumbs. The day after tomorrow, at the latest, you will begin despising yourself for having knowingly deceived yourself. The result—a soap-bubble and inertia. Oh, gentlemen, after all, perhaps I consider myself an intelligent man only because all my life I have been able neither to begin nor to finish anything. Granted, granted I am a babbler, a harmless annoying babbler, like all of us. But what is to be done if the direct and sole vocation of every intelligent man is babble, that is, the intentional pouring of water through a sieve?

VI

Oh, if I had done nothing simply out of laziness! Heavens, how I would have respected myself then. I would have respected myself because I would at least have been capable of being lazy; there would at least have been in me one positive quality, as it were, in which I could have believed myself. Question: Who is he? Answer: A loafer. After all, it would have been pleasant to hear that about oneself! It would mean that I was positively defined, it would mean that there was something to be said about me. "Loafer"—why, after all, it is a calling and an appointment, it is a career, gentlemen. Do not joke, it is so. I would then, by rights, be a member of the best club, and would occupy myself only in continually respecting myself. I knew a gentleman who prided himself all his life on being a connoisseur of Lafitte. He considered this as his positive virtue, and never doubted himself. He died, not simply with a tranquil but with a triumphant conscience, and he was completely right. I should have chosen a career for myself then too: I would have been a loafer and a glutton, not a simple one, but, for instance, one in sympathy with everything good and beautiful. How do you like that? I have long had visions of it. That "sublime and beautiful" weighs heavily on my mind at forty. But that is when I am forty, while then—oh, then it would have been different! I would have found myself an appropriate occupation, namely, to drink to the health of everything sublime and beautiful. I would have seized every opportunity to drop a tear into my glass and then to drain it to all that is sublime and beautiful. I would then have turned everything into the sublime and the beautiful; I would have sought out the sublime and the beautiful in the nastiest, most unquestionable trash. I would have become as tearful as a wet sponge. An artist, for instance, paints Ge's picture.[2] At once I drink to the health of the artist who painted Ge's picture, because I love all that is "sublime and beautiful." An author writes "Whatever You Like"[3]; at once I drink to the health of "Whatever You

---

2 N. N. Ge exhibited his "Last Supper" in 1863. Dostoyevsky thought it a faulty conception. [Ralph Matlaw.]
3 An article on improving man written by Shchedrin, in 1863. [Ralph Matlaw.]

Like" because I love all that is "sublime and beautiful." I would demand respect for doing so, I would persecute anyone who would not show me respect. I would live at ease, I would die triumphantly—why, after all, it is charming, perfectly charming! And what a belly I would have grown, what a triple chin I would have established, what a red nose I would have produced for myself, so that every passer-by would have said, looking at me: "Here is an asset! Here is something really positive!" And, after all, say what you like, it is very pleasant to hear such remarks about oneself in this negative age, gentlemen.

VII

But these are all golden dreams. Oh, tell me, who first declared, who first proclaimed, that man only does nasty things because he does not know his own real interests; and that if he were enlightened, if his eyes were opened to his real normal interests, man would at once cease to do nasty things, would at once become good and noble because, being enlightened and understanding his real advantage, he would see his own advantage in the good and nothing else, and we all know that not a single man can knowingly act to his own disadvantage. Consequently, so to say, he would begin doing good through necessity. Oh, the babe! Oh, the pure, innocent child! Why, in the first place, when in all these thousands of years has there ever been a time when man has acted only for his own advantage? What is to be done with the millions of facts that bear witness that men, *knowingly*, that is, fully understanding their real advantages, have left them in the background and have rushed headlong on another path, to risk, to chance, compelled to this course by nobody and by nothing, but, as it were, precisely because they did not want the beaten track, and stubbornly, willfully, went off on another difficult, absurd way seeking it almost in the darkness. After all, it means that this stubbornness and willfulness were more pleasant to them than any advantage. Advantage! What is advantage? And will you take it upon yourself to define with perfect accuracy in exactly what the advantage of man consists of? And what if it so happens that a man's advantage *sometimes* not only may, but even must, consist exactly in his desiring under certain conditions what is harmful to himself and not what is advantageous. And if so, if there can be such a condition then the whole principle becomes worthless. What do you think—are there such cases? You laugh; laugh away, gentlemen, so long as you answer me: have man's advantages been calculated with perfect certainty? Are there not some which not only have been included but cannot possibly be included under any classification? After all, you, gentlemen, so far as I know, have taken your whole register of human advantages from the average of statistical figures and scientific-economic formulas. After all, your advantages are prosperity, wealth, freedom, peace—and so on, and so on. So that a man who, for instance, would openly and knowingly oppose that whole list would, to your thinking, and indeed to mine too, of course, be an obscurantist or an absolute madman, would he not? But, after all, here is something amazing: why does it happen that all these statisticians, sages and lovers of humanity, when they calculate human advantages invariably leave one out? They don't even take it into their calculation in the form in which it should be taken, and the whole reckoning depends upon that. There would be no great harm to take it, this advantage, and to add it to the list. But the trouble is, that this strange advantage does not fall under any classification and does not figure in any list. For instance, I have a friend. Bah, gentlemen! But after all he is your friend, too; and indeed there is no one, no one, to whom he is not a friend! When he prepares for any undertaking this gentleman immediately explains to you, pompously and clearly, exactly how he must act in accordance with the laws of reason and truth. What is more, he will talk to you with excitement and passion of the real normal interests of man; with irony he will reproach the short-sighted fools who do not understand their own advantage, for the true significance of virtue; and, within a quarter of an hour, without any sudden outside provocation, but precisely through that something internal which is stronger than all his advantages, he will go off on quite a different tack— that is, act directly opposite to what he has just been saying himself, in opposition to the laws of reason, in opposition to his own advantage—in fact, in opposition to everything. I warn you that my friend is a compound personality, and therefore it is somehow difficult to blame him as an individual. The fact is, gentlemen, it seems that something that is dearer to almost every man than his greatest advantages must really exist, or (not to be illogical) there is one most advantageous advantage (the very one omitted of which we spoke just now) which is more important and more advantageous than all other advantages, for which, if necessary, a man is ready to act in opposition to all laws, that is, in opposition to reason, honor, peace, prosperity—in short, in opposition to all those wonderful and useful things if only he can attain that fundamental, most advantageous advantage which is dearer to him than all.

"Well, but it is still advantage just the same," you will retort. But excuse me, I'll make the point clear, and it is not a case of a play on words, but what really matters is that this advantage is remarkable from the very fact that it breaks down all our classifications, and continually shatters all the systems evolved by lovers of mankind for the happiness of mankind. In short, it interferes with everything. But before I mention this advantage to you, I want to compromise myself personally, and therefore I boldly declare that all these fine systems—all these theories for explaining to mankind its real normal interests, so that inevitably striving to obtain these interests, it may at once become good and noble—are, in my opinion, so far, mere logical exercises! Yes, logical exercises. After all, to maintain even this theory of the regeneration of mankind by means of its own advantage, is, after all, to my mind almost the same thing as—as to claim, for instance, with Buckle, that through civilization mankind becomes softer, and consequently less blood-thirsty, and less fitted for warfare. Logically it does not seem to follow from his arguments. But man is so fond of systems and abstract deductions that he is ready to distort the truth intentionally, he is ready to deny what he can see and hear just to justify his logic. I take this example because it is the most glaring instance of it. Only look about you: blood is being spilled in streams, and in the merriest way, as though it were champagne. Take the whole of the nineteenth century in which Buckle lived. Take Napoleon—both the Great and the present one. Take North America—the eternal union. Take farcical Schleswig-Holstein. And what is it that civilization softens in us? Civilization only produces a greater variety of sensations in man— and absolutely nothing more. And through the development of this variety, man may even come to find enjoyment in bloodshed. After all, it has already happened to him. Have you noticed that the subtlest slaughterers have almost always been the most civilized gentlemen, to whom the various Attilas and Stenka Razins could never hold a candle, and if they are not so conspicuous as the Attilas and Stenka Razins it is precisely because they are so often met with, are so ordinary and have become so familiar to us. In any case if civilization has not made man more bloodthirsty, it has at least made him more abominably, more loathsomely bloodthirsty than before. Formerly he saw justice in bloodshed and with his conscience at peace exterminated whomever he thought he should. And now while we consider bloodshed an abomination, we nevertheless engage in this abomination and even more than ever before. Which is worse? Decide that for yourselves. It is said that Cleopatra (pardon the example from Roman history) was fond of sticking gold pins into her slave-girls' breasts and derived enjoyment from their screams and writhing. You will say that that occurred in comparatively barbarous times; that these are barbarous times too, because (also comparatively speaking) pins are stuck in even now; that even though man has now learned to see more clearly occasionally than in barbarous times, he is still far from having *accustomed* himself to act as reason and science would dictate. But all the same you are fully convinced that he will inevitably accustom himself to it when he gets completely rid of certain old bad habits, and when common sense and science have completely re-educated human nature and turned it in a normal direction. You are confident that man will then refrain from erring *intentionally*, and will, so to say, willy-nilly, not want to set his will against his normal interests. More than that: then, you say, science itself will teach man (though to my mind that is a luxury) that he does not really have either caprice or will of his own and that he has never had it, and that he himself is something like a piano key or an organ stop, and that, moreover, laws of nature exist in this world, so that everything he does is not done by his will at all, but is done by itself, according to the laws of nature. Consequently we have only to discover these laws of nature, and man will no longer be responsible for his actions and life will become exceedingly easy for him. All human actions will then, of course, be tabulated according to these laws, mathematically, like tables of logarithms up to 108,000, and entered in a table; or, better still, there would be published certain edifying works like the present encyclopedic lexicons, in which everything will be so clearly calculated and designated that there will be no more incidents or adventures in the world.

Then—it is still you speaking—new economic relations will be established, all ready-made and computed with mathematical exactitude, so that every possible question will vanish in a twinkling, simply because every possible answer to it will be provided. Then the crystal palace will be built. Then—well, in short, those will be halcyon days. Of course there is no guaranteeing (this is my comment now) that it will not be, for instance, terribly boring then (for what will one have to do when everything is calculated according to the table?) but on the other hand everything will be extraordinarily rational. Of course boredom may lead you to anything. After all, boredom even sets one to sticking gold pins into people, but all that would not matter. What is bad (this is my comment again) is that for all I know people will be thankful for the gold pins then. After all, man is stupid, phenomenally stupid. Or rather he is not stupid at all, but he is so ungrateful that you could not find another like him in all creation. After all, it would not surprise me in the least, if, for instance, suddenly for no reason at all, general rationalism in the midst of the future, a gentleman with an ignoble, or rather with a reactionary and ironical, countenance were to arise and, putting his arms akimbo, say to us all: "What do you think, gentlemen, hadn't we better kick over all that rationalism at one blow, scatter it to the winds; just to send these logarithms to the devil, and to let us live once more according to our own foolish will!" That again would not matter; but what is annoying is that after all he would be sure to find followers—such is the nature of man. And all that for the most foolish reason, which, one would think, was hardly worth mentioning: that is, that man everywhere and always, whoever he may be, has preferred to act as he wished and not in the least as his reason and advantage dictated. Why, one may choose what is contrary to one's own interests, and sometimes one *positively ought* (that is my idea). One's own free unfettered choice, one's own fancy, however wild it may be, one's own fancy worked up at times to frenzy—why that is that very "most advantageous advantage" which we have overlooked, which comes under no classification and through which all systems and theories are continually being sent to the devil. And how do these sages know that man must necessarily need a rationally advantageous choice? What man needs is simply *independent* choice, whatever that independence may cost and wherever it may lead. Well, choice, after all, the devil only knows . . .

VIII

"Ha! ha! ha! But after all, if you like, in reality, there is no such thing as choice," you will interrupt with a laugh. "Science has even now succeeded in analyzing man to such an extent that we know already that choice and what is called freedom of will are nothing other than—"

Wait, gentlemen, I meant to begin with that myself. I admit that I was even frightened. I was just going to shout that after all the devil only knows what choice depends on, and that perhaps that was a very good thing, but I remembered the teaching of science—and pulled myself up. And here you have begun to speak. After all, really, well, if some day they truly discover a formula for all our desires and caprices—that is, an explanation of what they depend upon, by what laws they arise, just how they develop, what they are aiming at in one case or another and so on, and so on, that is, a real mathematical formula—then, after all, man would most likely at once stop to feel desire, indeed, he will be certain to. For who would want to choose by rule? Besides, he will at once be transformed from a human being into an organ stop or something of the sort; for what is a man without desire, without free will and without choice, if not a stop in an organ? What do you think? Let us consider the probability—can such a thing happen or not?

"H'm!" you decide. "Our choice is usually mistaken through a mistaken notion of our advantage. We sometimes choose absolute nonsense because in our stupidity we see in that nonsense the easiest means for attaining an advantage assumed beforehand. But when all that is explained and worked out on paper (which is perfectly possible, for it is contemptible and senseless to assume in advance that man will never understand some laws of nature), then, of course, so-called desires will not exist. After all, if desire should at any time come to terms completely with reason, we shall then, of course, reason and not desire, simply because, after all, it will be impossible to retain reason and *desire* something senseless, and in that way knowingly act against reason and desire to injure ourselves. And as all choice and reasoning can really be calculated, because some day they will discover the laws of our so-called free will—so joking aside, there may one day probably be something like a table of desires so that we really shall choose in accordance with it. After all, if, for instance, some day they calculate and prove to me that I stuck my tongue out at someone because I could not help sticking my tongue out at him and that I had to do it in that particular way, what sort of *freedom* is left me, especially if I am a learned man and have taken my degree somewhere? After all, then I would be able to calculate my whole life for thirty years in advance. In short, if that comes about, then, after all, we could do nothing about it. We would have to accept it just the same.

And, in fact, we ought to repeat to ourselves incessantly that at such and such a time and under such and such circumstances, Nature does not ask our leave; that we must accept her as she is and not as we imagine her to be, and if we really aspire to tables and indices and well, even—well, let us say to the chemical retort, then it cannot be helped. We must accept the retort, too, or else it will be accepted without our consent."

Yes, but here I come to a stop! Gentlemen, you must excuse me for philosophizing; it's the result of forty years underground! Allow me to indulge my fancy for a minute. You see, gentlemen, reason, gentlemen, is an excellent thing, there is no disputing that, but reason is only reason and can only satisfy man's rational faculty, while will is a manifestation of all life, that is, of all human life including reason as well as all impulses. And although our life, in this manifestation of it, is often worthless, yet it is life nevertheless and not simply extracting square roots. After all, here I, for instance, quite naturally want to live, in order to satisfy all my faculties for life, and not simply my rational faculty, that is, not simply one-twentieth of all my faculties for life. What does reason know? Reason only knows what it has succeeded in learning (some things it will perhaps never learn; while this is nevertheless no comfort, why not say so frankly?) and human nature acts as a whole, with everything that is in it, consciously or unconsciously, and, even if it goes wrong, it lives. I suspect, gentlemen, that you are looking at me with compassion; you repeat to me that an enlightened and developed man, such, in short, as the future man will be, cannot knowingly desire anything disadvantageous to himself, that this can be proved mathematically. I thoroughly agree, it really can—by mathematics. But I repeat for the hundredth time, there is one case, one only, when man may purposely, consciously, desire what is injurious to himself, what is stupid, very stupid—simply in order *to have the right* to desire for himself even what is very stupid and not to be bound by an obligation to desire only what is rational. After all, this very stupid thing, after all, this caprice of ours, may really be more advantageous for us, gentlemen, than anything else on earth, especially in some cases. And in particular it may be more advantageous than any advantages even when it does us obvious harm, and contradicts the soundest conclusions of our reason about our advantage—because in any case it preserves for us what is most precious and most important—that is, our personality, our individuality. Some, you see, maintain that this really is the most precious thing for man; desire can, of course, if it desires, be in agreement with reason; particularly if it does not abuse this practice but does so in moderation, it is both useful and sometimes even praiseworthy. But very often, and even most often, desire completely and stubbornly opposes reason, and . . . and . . . and do you know that that, too, is useful and sometimes even praiseworthy? Gentlemen, let us suppose that man is not stupid. (Indeed, after all, one cannot say that about him anyway, if only for the one consideration that, if man is stupid, then, after all, who is wise?) But if he is not stupid, he is just the same monstrously ungrateful! Phenomenally ungrateful. I even believe that the best definition of man is—a creature that walks on two legs and is ungrateful. But that is not all, that is not his worst defect; his worst defect is his perpetual immorality, perpetual—from the days of the Flood to the Schleswig-Holstein period of human destiny. Immorality, and consequently lack of good sense; for it has long been accepted that lack of good sense is due to no other cause than immorality. Try it, and cast a look upon the history of mankind. Well, what will you see? Is it a grand spectacle? All right, grand, if you like. The Colossus of Rhodes, for instance, that is worth something. Mr. Anaevsky may well testify that some say it is the work of human hands, while others maintain that it was created by Nature herself. Is it variegated? Very well, it may be variegated too. If one only took the dress uniforms, military and civilian, of all peoples in all ages—that alone is worth something, and if you take the undress uniforms you will never get to the end of it; no historian could keep up with it. Is it monotonous? Very well. It may be monotonous, too; they fight and fight; they are fighting now, they fought first and they fought last—you will admit that it is almost too monotonous. In short, one may say anything about the history of the world—anything that might enter the most disordered imagination. The only thing one cannot say is that it is rational. The very word sticks in one's throat. And, indeed, this is even the kind of thing that continually happens. After all, there are continually turning up in life moral and rational people, sages, and lovers of humanity, who make it their goal for life to live as morally and rationally as possible, to be, so to speak, a light to their neighbors, simply in order to show them that it is really possible to live morally and rationally in this world. And so what? We all know that those very people sooner or later toward the end of their lives have been false to themselves, playing some trick, often a most indecent one. Now I ask you: What can one expect from man since he is a creature endowed with such strange qualities? Shower upon him every earthly blessing, drown him in bliss so that nothing but bubbles would dance on the surface of his bliss, as on a sea; give him such economic prosperity that he would have nothing else to do but sleep, eat cakes and busy himself with ensuring the continuation of world history and even then man, out of sheer ingratitude, sheer libel, would play you some loathsome trick. He would even risk his cakes and would deliberately desire the most fatal rubbish, the most uneconomical absurdity, simply to introduce into all this positive rationality his fatal fantastic element. It is just his fantastic dreams, his vulgar folly, that he will desire to retain, simply in order to prove to himself (as though that were so necessary) that men still are men and not piano keys, which even if played by the laws of nature themselves threaten to be controlled so completely that soon one will be able to desire nothing but by the calendar. And, after all, that is not all: even if man really were nothing but a piano key, even if this were proved to him by natural science and mathematics, even then he would not become reasonable, but would purposely do something perverse out of sheer ingratitude, simply to have his own way. And if he does not find any means he will devise destruction and chaos, will devise sufferings of all sorts, and will thereby have his own way. He will launch a curse upon the world, and, as only man can curse (it is his privilege, the primary distinction between him and other animals) then, after all, perhaps only by his curse will he attain his object, that is, really convince himself that he is a man and not a piano key! If you say that all this, too, can be calculated and tabulated, chaos and darkness and curses, so that the mere possibility of calculating it all beforehand would stop it all, and reason would reassert itself—then man would purposely go mad in order to be rid of reason and have his own way! I believe in that, I vouch for it, because, after all, the whole work of man seems really to consist in nothing but proving to himself continually that he is a man and not an organ stop. It may be at the cost of his skin! But he has proved it; he may become a caveman, but he will have proved it. And after that can one help sinning, rejoicing that it has not yet come, and that desire still depends on the devil knows what!

You will shout at me (that is, if you will still favor me with your shout) that, after all, no one is depriving me of my will, that all they are concerned with is that my will should somehow of itself, of its own free will, coincide with my own normal interests, with the laws of nature and arithmetic.

Bah, gentlemen, what sort of free will is left when we come to tables and arithmetic, when it will all be a case of two times two makes four? Two times two makes four even without my will. As if free will meant that!

THE SELF: ITS BODY AND FREEDOM
(Chapter III)

WILLIAM ERNEST HOCKING

William Ernest Hocking (1873–1966) was an American philosopher identified together with Josiah Royce as an advocate of Idealism, which claims that the mental or spiritual aspects of the world are fundamental. His most important works are *The Meaning of God in Human Experience* and *Human Nature and Its Remaking*.

In the following selection from Hocking's book *The Self: Its Body and Freedom*, he arrives at an endorsement of free will from a systematic metaphysical theory. Hocking links freedom to selfhood, and argues that since every self has hope, every self is free. Rather than being pushed from behind by stimuli or mechanical causes, we are drawn forward to choose various goals—provided that we reflect upon our present self and the ideal self we want to become. Leading an unthinking life of habit we are within the grip of causation, but we free ourselves when the course of our existence is directed by purpose and meaning.[1]

10. FREEDOM FROM WITHIN

In ancient Arabia, Mamun, son of Harun al Rashid, inherited a city. When he came to take possession, he found it in disorder and on the verge of ruin. Persian traders, falling into dispute with the citizens in the markets, had found them weak and had beome emboldened to pillage and violence.

The young prince was advised to set forth a new code of law and enforce it. This he did; but with the result that disputes multiplied, the lawyers enriched themselves, the citizens were impoverished, and traders began to avoid the city. In despair, Mamun bethought himself of a device. He secretly brought together certain foreign craftsmen, and enjoined them to work out in ivory and precious woods the image of a surpassingly beautiful city, whose design he gave them. When it was finished, he rewarded them richly and sent them away; and bore the image by night to the chief mosque, concealing it behind a curtain.

Mamun then issued an edict that every traveler and trader entering the gates must first be brought to this mosque to worship, and be pledged to silence. The image was there revealed to them; and it became evident to the citizens by the altered demeanor of these strangers that they had seen a noble vision of which they could not or dared not speak. They demanded to see it also—which was what Mamun had desired: they were accordingly admitted, one by one, on the same conditions.

Now it began to appear that the ruler of the artists was more successful than the ruler of the law-makers; for, changed by the sight of the

---

[1] Cf. Rollo May's *Love and Will* for a similar analysis of will, using William James's *Principles of Psychology* as a launching point.

image, the people carried out their business in peace. Order, gaiety, and wealth returned silently to the place. And in its rebuilding, the city which Mamun inherited resembled the city of his dream.

For our purposes, this city may represent a self, the citizens its instincts and habits, and the traders the lines of natural causation that run into it and out of it. Without these citizens and traders, no city. Without their laws, no city. But together, these elements are incapable of providing unity or common life. This life depends on the hope, or vision, which is the source from which meaning descends to the parts. And freedom is represented in the fact that, when that hope is active, the *detail of behavior is different* from what it would otherwise have been. It is behavior which belongs to that hope or meaning, and not primarily to the causal laws which it observes.

Since there is no self without its hope, there is no self which is not free. Freedom is not an attribute of the will; it is the essence of selfhood. As the meaning descends into all parts, freedom pervades the entire self of behavior. It is not that the mind, as purposive, is free, while the body, as causal, is determined; it is I as a whole that am free. What my body does, I do. All the determining influences that would pass to the control of my muscles must stop at the source of meaning and receive its stamp.

This meaning itself has no earthly source: it is the self as artist that has produced it. For the self is a new fact in the world; its perception of good is its own; and the hierarchy of control which it establishes has its apex in a unique perception of possible value.

The prince in the allegory set up his image and left it to do its work. But the self is always destroying its old images and making new ones, with an endless train of foreign suggestions passing through its workshop. The identity of its hope is not destroyed in this process of growth. But as the self expands, the material swept into its organization of behavior becomes greater; and a new chaos furnishes the theme for a new construction. It belongs to selfhood to increase without limit the mastery of meaning; hence it belongs to selfhood to grow without limit in material depth and rootage. It requires an infinite material universe to open the future to the infinite appetite of freedom.

In the cycles of causation we were studying, the appearance of initiative with the mind proves to have been a true appearance. The threshold of consent marks the entry of meaning into that circuit, and the submission of the whole process to the ownership of the self.

Though every act of a living self is a free act, there are special occasions in which freedom is realized from within in contrast to a course of behavior relatively unfree. These occasions are the acts of *reflexion*. Reflexion is an experience in which the self turns and looks at itself, makes itself an object of contemplation, and becomes more or less aware of the difference between the self as observed and the self it desires to be.

When the self thus observes itself, it is to some extent *detached from what it sees*. A degree of independence is established between the self observing and the self observed; so that what the self judges the self to be is at once true and untrue. Let us say that in the order of nature I am a lazy man. Then I remain a lazy man, thoroughly subject to the causal laws of inheritance of habit, until such time as it may occur to me to observe my own laziness. But let me, in a moment of reflexion, recognize this trait, and judge "I am lazy." The judgment is true: yet it is not the whole truth. For I am also a man who observes and criticizes his laziness. This criticism is possible because of some standard, belonging to my hope—some standard of what a man might well be. In this moment of reflexion, or self-judgment, the self has in its power the beginning of a departure from laziness. Reflexion is a beginning of freedom.

The fact that the knowing mind, the subject, has or acquires a certain independence of what it observes, its object, has been recognized in various currents of thought, as by the realists of to-day. The realists are prone to insist that the object known is completely independent of the knower, even (one must suppose) when the object is one's self. We need not go to this extent: it is enough to see that when we judge ourselves we continue to make the usual distinction between the self judging and the object judged. This is particularly true when we "stop to consider" or contemplate our object as in a picture: for as mankind from Aristotle to Schopenhauer has repeatedly observed, the contemplator (whether as artist or enjoyer) is detached in will and being from what he considers.

The implications of this detachment are far-reaching. When I perceive myself as defective or limited in any respect, I am in that act somewhat beyond this defect and limitation: to be somewhat beyond it is a condition of being able to observe it. Then I am a shade beyond any limit that I can discover: and there is, in this capacity of reflexion, a promise of indefinite growth. Infinitude is on the side of the self which knows itself to be finite. And for the self which knows itself to be caused, *causation has ceased to be the whole truth*.

Now there is nothing in the field of natural causation entering into me upon which I may not thus reflect. And to discover a cause in the act of affecting me is to be upon my guard against its action. Hence any series of natural consequences which flows up to me becomes distinct from me when I discover it. If I find that my body is the last term in some evolutionary series, I cease to be that last term. *I am never merely the last term of any series which I observe.* The clock strikes twelve: to the physical order, the last stroke is the last, and no other. To me who listen it is "twelve"; for I am keeping the others in mind with it. I am *with* the other strokes while I am with the last stroke: so that what is true of the last term of such a series is never all the truth about *me*.

So the description of a man as a set of reactions becomes untrue when he becomes aware that he is being so described. Whenever anyone knows what reaction a given stimulus is supposed to produce, he has a new motive for not acting that way. In certain writings on the psychology of advertising, I am told that the picture of a domestic scene will tend to soften the purchaser's heart and so to loosen his purse strings: when next I see this domestic scene in an advertising page, my heart hardens, and I inwardly refuse to buy.

Because of this trait of freeing himself by reflexion from every causal series he discovers, it is never possible to know all the reactions of any man. If any psychologist or friend thinks that he knows all the reactions of any individual, he has only to tell him so, and he will get a new one! Let anyone discover that he is behaving in any situation like a reaction-mechanism and he will feel toward that behavior perhaps an excess of repudiation, for very fear of resemblance to that which he most dreads, the inanimate machine.

Hence any program, which like that of the behavioristic psychology, aims through the scientific knowledge of human nature to "predict and control" our behavior, as agriculture hopes to predict and control the response of crops to different fertilizers and soils, can only succeed so long as it is kept a profound secret. You can only "manage" men through "stimuli" so long as they do not know that you are managing them! There is no more futile undertaking in the world than that of "applying" a cause-and-effect psychology. Books on applied psychology, on being published, begin the process of defeating their own aim. As a law of history becomes untrue by being known and stated, so does every alleged law of conscious behavior.

In contrast with this spurious and self-defeating management of men by way of stimuli and causation, there is the honest management which follows the reverse procedure. Instead of trying to control the man by way of his physical situation, it controls the physical situation by way of the man's conscious choice. . . .

In sum: the nature which is known as an object of thought can never reduce the self to a link in its own chains of causation. *Reflexion* upon the self-in-nature situation automatically provides the self with *another alternative* than the uniquely determined causal outcome. With the one space-and-nature before it as object, it can conceive possible others, and choose among them. The self is free from the single-series determination of whatever it makes its object. . . .

12. DEGREES OF FREEDOM

The nature of freedom will be clearer to us if we remember that freedom is a matter of degree.

Freedom runs down daily. We are more mechanical at the end of a

day's work than at the beginning. We make more mistakes in our thinking and behaving. Fatigue, strained attention, hunger—a hundred causes
limit our elasticity, restrict the range of our vision, block our access to
more liberal alternatives of mood and meaning. We approach the condition of a mechanical manikin.

At its limit, freedom might be considered as reduced to zero. With its
disappearance, conscious direction would vanish also. Habit might be
regarded as operating the machine without the intrusion of living interest.
There are abnormal states of human nature which suggest such a picture. "Asylums are full of pitiful economic persons who, lost to the laws of
social life, continue as automatons to follow an unmodified instinct in
picking up and hoarding pins, leaves, scraps of food, paper." [2] We are
all aware of bordering at times on some similar stage of unfreedom, as
when our very smiles, in a long-drawn-out social function, become mechanical responses-to-stimuli, uncharged with the personal perceptions
whose fountain has run dry.

When freedom is at zero, the self is perfectly inserted in nature.
The cycle of causation is complete; its original impulses come wholly
from the outer mechanisms of the world. If the mind awakes, meaning
begins to have a share in directing the course of events, and events are
different because of this direction. The cycle still remains complete, and
no external observer can detect the fact that the self is no longer perfect
in its insertion. But a subtle change has taken place in the sources of motion: energy is being sent into the circuit, as it were, through its pores.
The self is holding before itself now an object-good which is its own, not
a mere projection of the results of nature and habit: reason, instead of
being controlled by impulse, or passively lending itself to "rationalize" an
irrational motive-force, is building the *meaning* of every impulse or passion
into the body of its hope; and the courses of outgoing action are being
turned into channels in which they promise to promote that hope.

The degree of freedom is measured by the liveliness of that hope, the
unstraining tension of the self toward it, and the consequent irradiation
of the several activities of the self by that will-object. Whatever renews
one's effortless grasp of his hope—such as rest, play, worship—increases the
degree of freedom. Worship may be described as the deliberate effort to
restore or increase freedom by renewing the relation of the self to its ultimate hope. [3]

Our ultimate freedom lies in the fact that we are free to control the
degree of our freedom, through these various natural arts of recreation.
The last crime against our own natures is the choice, itself a free choice,
to drift into that state of helpless control by habit and impulse in which it
becomes literally true that we "have no choice."

---

[2] Carleton H. Parker, *Motives in Economic Life.*
[3] This view is developed in an article by the author, "The Illicit Naturalizing of Religion,"
in *The Journal of Religion,* November, 1923.

BIBLIOGRAPHY

A. PHILOSOPHIC WORKS

Anscombe, G. E. M. *Intention.* Ithaca, N.Y.: Cornell University, 1963.

Augustine, St. *On Free Choice of the Will.* Translated by A. S. Benjamin and L. H. Hackstaff. Indianapolis: Bobbs-Merrill, 1964.

Ayer, A. J. *Philosophical Essays,* Ch. 12. London: Macmillan, 1954.

Ayers, M. R. *The Refutation of Determinism.* London: Methuen, 1968.

Bergson, Henri. *Time and Free Will.* Translated by F. L. Pogson. London: Allen and Unwin, 1950.

Berofsky, Bernard. *Determinism.* Princeton: University Press, 1971.

————, ed. *Free Will and Determinism.* New York: Harper and Row, 1966.

Bowes, Pratima. *Consciousness and Freedom: Three Views.* London: Methuen, 1971.

Calvin, John. *The Institutes of the Christian Religion,* Bk. III. Translated by H. Beveridge. London: J. Clarke, 1962.

Campbell, C. A. *In Defense of Free Will.* London: Allen and Unwin, 1967.

Cicero, Marcus Tullius. *On Fate.* In *The Treatises of M. T. Cicero,* edited by C. D. Yonge. London: Bell, 1876.

Compton, Arthur H. *The Freedom of Man.* New York: Greenwood Press, 1969.

Descartes, René. *Meditations,* IV. Translated by J. Veitch. La Salle, Ill.: Open Court, 1966.

————. *Principles of Philosophy,* Part 1. In *The Method, Meditations, and Selections.* Translated by J. Veitch. Edinburgh: Blackwood, 1913.

Edwards, Jonathan. *Freedom of the Will.* Edited by P. Ramsey. New Haven: Yale University, 1957.

Enteman, Willard, ed. *The Problem of Free Will.* New York: Scribner, 1967.

Farrer, Austin. *The Freedom of the Will.* London: A. and C. Black, 1963.

Franklin, R. L. *Freewill and Determinism.* New York: Humanities Press, 1968.

Hampshire, Stuart. *Freedom of the Individual.* Princeton: University Press, 1975.

Hare, R. M. *Freedom and Reason.* Oxford: University Press, 1965.

Hobbes, Thomas. *The Questions Concerning Liberty, Necessity and Chance.* In *The English Works of Thomas Hobbes,* edited by W. Molesworth. London: J. Bohn, 1839–45.

Honderich, T., ed. *Essays on Freedom of Action.* Boston: Routledge and K. Paul, 1973.

Hook, Sidney, ed. *Determinism and Freedom in the Age of Modern Science.* New York: Macmillan, 1969.

Hume, David. *Enquiry Concerning Human Understanding,* Sec. 8. La Salle, Ill.: Open Court, 1966.

James, William. *The Dilemma of Determinism.* In *The Will to Believe.* New York: Dover, 1956.

Kant, Immanuel. *Critique of Practical Reason.* Translated by L. W. Beck. Chicago: University Press, 1949.

————. *Critique of Pure Reason,* "Transcendental Dialectic." Translated by F. M. Müller. New York: Macmillan, 1896.

Koestler, Arthur. *The Ghost in the Machine.* New York: Macmillan, 1968.

Laird, John. *On Human Freedom.* New York: Humanities Press, 1947.

Lamont, Corliss. *Freedom of Choice Affirmed.* New York: Horizon Press, 1967.

Lehrer, Keith, ed. *Freedom and Determinism.* New York: Random House, 1966.

Locke, John. *An Essay Concerning Human Understanding,* Bk. 2, Ch. 21. Edited by P. H. Nidditch. Oxford: University Press, 1975.

Lucas, J. R. *The Freedom of the Will.* Oxford: University Press, 1970.

Luther, Martin. *The Bondage of the Will.* Translated by J. I. Packer and O. R. Johnston. Old Tappan, N.J.: Revell, 1970.

Melden, A. I. *Free Action.* New York: Humanities Press, 1961.

Morgenbesser, S. and Walsh, J., eds. *Free Will.* Englewood Cliffs, N.J.: Prentice-Hall, 1962.

Pears, D. F., ed. *Freedom and the Will.* New York: St. Martin's Press, 1963.

Pontifex, Mark. *Freedom and Providence*. New York: Hawthorn Books, 1960.

Rankin, K. W. *Choice and Chance*. New York: Humanities Press, 1961.

Reid, Thomas. *Essays on the Intellectual and Active Powers of Man*. Philadelphia: William Young, 1793.

Russell, Bertrand. *The Analysis of Mind*, esp. Lecture 5. New York: Macmillan, 1921.

——. *On the Notion of Cause*. In *Mysticism and Logic*. Garden City, N.Y.: Doubleday, 1957.

Ryle, Gilbert. *It Was To Be*. In *Dilemmas*. Cambridge: University Press, 1954.

Sartre, Jean-Paul. *Being and Nothingness*, esp. "Being and Doing: Freedom." Translated by Hazel Barnes. New York: Citadel Press, 1969.

Schopenhauer, Arthur. *Essay on the Freedom of the Will*. Translated by K. Kolenda. New York: Liberal Arts Press, 1960.

Skinner, B. F. *Beyond Freedom and Dignity*. New York: Knopf, 1971.

Taylor, R. *Action and Purpose*. Englewood Cliffs, N.J.: Prentice-Hall, 1966.

Weiss, Paul. *Man's Freedom*. New Haven: Yale University, 1950.

Wright, G. H. von. *Causality and Determinism*. New York: Columbia University, 1974.

B. LITERARY WORKS

Balzac, Honoré de. *Eugenie Grandet*. Translated by K. P. Wormeley. Boston: Little, Brown, 1913.

Butler, Samuel. *The Way of All Flesh*. New York: Macmillan, 1928.

Cervantes, Miguel de. *Don Quixote*. Translated by P. Motteux. London: J. M. Dent, 1936.

Conrad, Joseph. *Chance*. New York: Doubleday, 1957.

Corneille, Pierre. *Horace*. In *Le Cid, Horace, and Polyeucte*, edited by W. A. Nitze. New York: Henry Holt, 1924.

Dreiser, Theodor. *An American Tragedy*. Cleveland: World Publishing Co., 1953.

Euripides. *Alcestis, Iphigenia*, and *Medea*. In *Euripides*, translated by A. S. Way. Cambridge: Harvard University, 1959–65.

Gary, Romain. *A European Education*. New York: Simon and Schuster, 1960.

Golding, William. *Free Fall*. New York: Harcourt Brace Jovanovich, Inc., 1959.

Hardy, Thomas. *The Dynasts*. New York: Macmillan, 1936.

Hemingway, Ernest. *The Killers*. In *The Short Stories of Ernest Hemingway*. New York: Charles Scribner's Sons, 1953.

Homer. *The Iliad*. Translated by A. T. Murray. Cambridge: Harvard University, 1960.

——. *The Odyssey*. Translated by A. T. Murray. Cambridge: Harvard University, 1946.

Hugo, Victor. *Les Miserables*. Translated by C. E. Wilbour. New York: Modern Library, 1931.

Mallarmé, Stéphane. *Dice Thrown Never Will Annul Chance*. Translated by B. Coffey. Chester Springs, Pa.: Dufour Editions, 1967.

Mann, Thomas. *Buddenbrooks*. Translated by H. T. Lowe-Porter. New York: Knopf, 1964.

O'Neill, Eugene. *The Hairy Ape*. In *Plays*. New York: Boni and Liveright, 1925.

Pope, Alexander. "The Universal Prayer." In *Poems*. Edited by J. Butt. New Haven: Yale University, 1963.

Pushkin, Alexander. *The Captain's Daughter*. In *Selected Works*, translated by E. E. Turner. Moscow: Progress Publishers, 1974.

Racine, Jean Baptiste. *Phaedra*. In *Five Plays*, translated by S. Solomon. New York: Random House, 1967.

Schiller, Johann C. F. *Wilhelm Tell*. In *The Works of Friedrich von Schiller*, translated by T. Martin. New York: The Aldus Press, 1902.

Shakespeare, William. *Henry VI*, and *Richard III*. In *The Works of William Shakespeare*, edited by W. G. Clark and W. A. Wright. New York: St. Martin's Press, 1956.

Sholokhov, Mikhail. *And Quiet Flows the Don*. Translated by S. Garry. New York: Knopf, 1946.

Skinner, B. F. *Walden Two*. New York: Macmillan, 1948.

Solzhenitsyn, Alexander. *The Gulag Archi-*

pelago. Translated by T. P. Whitney. New York: Harper and Row, 1974.

Sophocles. *Three Theban Plays*. Translated by T. H. Banks. New York: Oxford University, 1956.

Tolstoy, Leo. *War and Peace*. Translated by L. and A. Maude. New York: Simon and Schuster, 1942.

Warren, Robert Penn. *All the King's Men*. New York: Harcourt Brace Jovanovich, Inc., 1946.

Wilder, Thornton. *Our Town*. New York: Coward McCann, 1938.

Zola, Emile. *Nana*. Translated by F. J. Viztelly. New York: Limited Editions, 1948.

———. *Theresa*. New York: French, 1947.

FOUR

ETHICAL IDEALS: THE GOOD LIFE

Ethics, or more broadly, moral philosophy, constitutes one of the major branches of philosophy and includes questions such as the following: Why should people ever do what is not to their own advantage? Should we judge actions in terms of their consequences, their intrinsic merit, or the intentions of the person? Are all values relative to a society or are they established objectively? Is it always right to tell the truth, keep promises, and help others; and is it always wrong to kill, steal, and exploit others? Do we derive our knowledge of morality from reasoning, experience with life, our conscience, or authorities such as books, traditional beliefs, parents, teachers, or religious leaders? What things are good to pursue and attain, that is, worth striving for? All of these questions are vital to ethics, but we will here confine ourselves to the last, which is the very central problem of what is good.

Philosophers often distinguish between "right" and "wrong" on the one hand, which refer to the ethical quality of actions or conduct, and "good" and "bad" on the other, which refer to goals or aims, the purposes or ends of human existence. The two sets of concepts can be compatible, but "good" is the more inclusive concept since it is concerned with man's ultimate purpose for living, that state or condition without which life loses its attraction and meaning. I might add that the moral philosopher is not concerned with what people *do* desire but with what they *ought* to desire in life, that is, the goals that are worthy of being attained—the ethically *desirable*.

Ultimately, each person must decide the question for himself, which does not mean that one person's opinion is as good as another's. The person who can consciously adopt a goal after critical examination and the consideration of alternative theories is more likely to hold a valid answer as to what is good than the person who unreflectively accepts the popular notions of his time. Let us therefore survey, in a very general way, some of the major theories of the nature of the good life.

Aristotle declared happiness to be the "one ultimate End, that at which all things aim." To his mind there seemed to be almost universal consensus on this point which lent weight to the contention without necessarily proving it (for ethical questions are not decided by counting heads). Aristotle realized that human beings differ in the way they define happiness, some assuming it to be the satisfaction of appetites, some honor, some moneymaking, some contemplation, but he maintained that everyone agrees that the good is happiness of some kind. Aristotle also pointed out that happiness is self-sufficient (that is, when we are happy we lack nothing), and that it is always chosen "for its own sake and never as a means to something else." For this endorsement of happiness as the good in life (expressed in the *Nicomachean Ethics*) Aristotle has been labeled a *hedonist,* although other passages from the *Ethics* make the label "rationalist" or "self-realizationist" appropriate also.

Two other philosophers of antiquity, Aristippus and Epicurus, endorsed a kindred theory of hedonism, each in his particular way. Both affirmed happiness or pleasure as the good; this was interpreted by Aristippus the Cyrenaic as pleasure of an intense, immediate, brief, and sensual kind, and by Epicurus as passive, extended, and tranquil happiness of a mental kind. Epicurus is the more philosophically interesting since the Cyrenaics in general were rather short-sighted, preferring to enjoy themselves today despite the penalties tomorrow, and unwilling to endure discomfort now for the sake of greater pleasures later. Epicurus developed hedonism more intelligently, and in one of the surviving fragments of his works he wrote: "I know not how I can conceive the good, if I withdraw the pleasures of taste, and withdraw the pleasures of love, and withdraw the pleasures of hearing, and withdraw the pleasurable emotions caused to sight by beautiful form." Perhaps Epicurus is only making pleasure a part of the good and not the whole of it, but his words convey a joy and celebration of living which is hard to resist. They are reminiscent of Homer's cry: "Dear to us ever is the banquet and the harp and the dance and changes of raiment and the warm bath and love and sleep."

Jeremy Bentham and John Stuart Mill in the nineteenth century reaffirmed the primacy of happiness. However, because of their social consciences, they rejected individualistic hedonism in favor of a universalistic doctrine—a Utilitarianism which promoted the maximum pleasure for the maximum number of persons in the community. Bentham states categorically: "Pleasure is in *itself* a good—nay even, setting aside immunity from pain, the only good; pain is in itself an evil—and, indeed without exception, the only evil." (His reference to immunity from pain harks back to the Epicureans, who valued avoiding pain above seeking pleasure—an attitude for which the walled garden of Epicurus is a fitting symbol; it walled out trouble rather than walling in enjoyment, rather like a Medieval city.) [1] Bentham recognized differences in amount but not in kind with regard to pleasure, and constructed a calculus for the precise measurement of the pleasure that would be derived from any given action. In this way it could be scientifically determined which act yielded more pleasure for more people and consequently was more moral.

Mill endorsed universalistic hedonism in turn but rejected Bentham's idea that only the quantity of pleasure matters. He maintained that qualitative distinctions between pleasures were necessary as refinements of the Utilitarian doctrine and basic to the establishment of an ethic which was consistent with the dignity of man. It is the higher, human pleasures, Mill thought, which constitute the good and should be maximized for mankind. As Mill said: "It is better to be a human being dissatisfied than a pig satisfied; better to be Socrates dissatisfied than a fool satisfied."

Unfortunately, this "corrective" weakens rather than strengthens the theory that happiness or pleasure is the good. For "better" and "worse" are difficult to determine without using some standard outside of hedonism, and this standard would then replace pleasure as the criterion for the good. For example, if higher pleasures were interpreted to mean spiritual ones, then ultimately the spiritual life is being endorsed, even though it may not yield pleasure. Mill himself displayed this defect when he wrote that it is better to be a human being dissatisfied than a pig satisfied. Humanness, evidently, is better than satisfaction, and that is a non-hedonistic notion of the good.

All hedonists encounter this problem when they try to refine their

---

[1] The negativism of Epicurus, arising as it does from distress, has a parallel in Old Testament attitudes such as "Do not do unto others what you would not have them do unto you." The Christian version is positive, of course, which is not to say superior. It is an open question whether helping people is better than leaving them in peace.

doctrine and differentiate between higher and lower pleasures. Yet, without this refinement, hedonism remains a vulgar philosophy endorsing a life of animal pleasures for human beings.

A rival theory of the good life, which is diametrically opposed to hedonism, is the ideal of *duty*. The eighteenth-century German philosopher Immanuel Kant is usually taken as representative of this theory which maintains that people should always act in terms of generalizable rules of conduct. A good life, according to Kant, is one in which we recognize our duty to behave morally toward all humanity and act accordingly.

More specifically, Kant takes as the fundamental moral rule of life that we should "act so that the maxim for our actions could become a universal law." That is, whenever we think about performing an action we must ask ourselves whether that action could be subsumed under a moral principle that is binding upon all people at all times. For, conduct that is right is universally right, and is capable of being placed under a categorical rule of behavior.

It is important to notice what Kant excludes from his concept of a worthwhile existence. He excludes hedonism or any related theory that attempts to justify action in terms of the end that is produced. Whether an act yields pleasure or any other state is irrelevant to its moral worth, for it is the nature of action that makes it worthwhile not the consequence. That which can be supported by a moral principle is justified and should always be done, whereas that which is immoral should never be done, regardless of the benefits that may accrue from it.

Kant also rejects the idea that actions done from humanitarian impulses are good, because he does not regard emotional inclinations as a safe basis for morality. If an act is grounded in universal rules then it is sure to be sound, but feelings are too fickle and their moral value cannot be tested. Actions based on principle, on the other hand, can always be measured by asking whether we could will that everyone behave in the same way.

Kant's ideal of duty while being very pure strikes many people as unusually severe, and his theory has been formally criticized on various counts. For example, it has been pointed out that we would much rather be surrounded by people who have good dispositions and are not just good on principle. In addition, the consequences of action do not seem to be morally irrelevant in judging how to behave, for we would not want to do what is correct in principle but which would be harmful in its effect. Telling the truth may be the proper thing to do, but we should not tell a disturbing truth to someone with a weak heart, or inform a potential murderer as to the whereabouts of his intended victim. Kant is so opposed to the doctrine of the end justifying the means that he makes the equal mistake of thinking that the means justify the ends; both positions, however, are extreme.

Philosophers have pointed out other difficulties in the Kantian ethic, for instance, the problem of finding any principles that are universal. Nevertheless, the ideal of duty is very appealing. It makes an interesting alternative to the theory of happiness as a goal in life, and very often we cannot both follow principles and achieve happiness. One must be sacrificed to the other, and in these cases we must decide which is more important.

These choices as to what is good, however, are not the only ones. Some philosophers endorse the ideal of *self-realization,* which is a theory that has appeared at various times in the history of ideas. England and the United States appear to have provided the most fertile breeding ground for this theory and the nineteenth century the most favorable climate. F. H. Bradley, T. H. Green, Josiah Royce, W. C. Hocking and even G. W. F. Hegel all propounded a form of the self-realization ethic. Although these men frequently disagreed, their quarrels were more like denominational feuds than religious wars and pointed up the similarities in their positions more than the differences. Contemporary forms of self-realization can be found in the writings of psychologists such as Carl Rogers, Erich Fromm, and Abraham Maslow.

In their respective ways, each of these individuals criticized the ethical theories that had been proposed, especially the common belief in hedonism. Something could be pleasurable but not good and good but not pleasurable, they argued; therefore, hedonism was considered inadequate. They maintained that when pleasurable states are called good it is by virtue of a wider value than pleasure. It is not enjoyment, then, which is the supreme good in life, but something more inclusive that can be identified with the individual's overall welfare. The good, it was decided, has to be a state in which a person fully develops his various capacities, actualizes the potentialities of the self, and becomes all that he is capable of becoming. This means not only fulfilling his physical drives for food, sex, and property, which often seem to be the primary concerns of hedonism, but realizing the richer tendencies of his nature as well. For example, man's social tendency should be realized, including his desire for the respect of others and his capacity for compassion. Also included in man's nature is an intellectual capacity, which is expressed in the search for knowledge, a capacity for religious experience (including awe, reverence, and solemnity before the universe), and an ability to appreciate beauty, realizable in aesthetic contemplation and creation. All these powers are inherent in the self and constitute what we term our human nature as opposed to our animal nature.[2]

[2] In an effort to isolate the essential fact of human nature, philosophers have described man variously as the political or social animal, the rational being, the tool-using animal, the only dissatisfied animal, the creature who destroys his own kind, the language-using animal, the self-conscious organism and so on. The characterizations stress either man's unique abilities or his outstanding ones.

The self-realizationist believes that people can freely select between competing impulses rather than being at the mercy of a stimulus-
response mechanism. Consequently, they are able to adjust the various
impulses to each other in the interest of the harmonious development
of their personalities. Lesser impulses can be subordinated to greater
ones, the trivial to the profound, and life activities can be chosen
that contribute to the end of complete self-realization. An ideal self
can be imagined that gives purpose and direction to one's life, and
if a person is deliberate and fortunate, he will be able to maximize his
selfhood even if he cannot actualize his ideal being.

Some theorists, such as T. H. Green, link the realization of the self
to a concept of deity. God is that totality and completeness of being
that the human spirit aspires toward, the perfectly realized entity.
Therefore, to approach one's ideal self is to approach the divine. Full
realization means participation in eternal consciousness; God and man
are united as in an apotheosis. This is a predictable extension of the
theory once the notion of an ideal self is introduced, for a perfect
spiritual being is its ultimate goal.

Self-realization is an appealing theory, but there are problems connected with it as well. One essential problem consists in the dis-
crepancy that can exist between a realized self and what is good. For
not all of man's tendencies are good, and a kind of self may be
realized that is not worthwhile at all. Even if Genghis Khan were fully
developed, we would be hard pressed to praise the result. If it were
argued that he developed his *animal* nature rather than his *human* nature, and that only the latter is good, this would be hard to prove;
relishing another man's suffering is as human as enjoying his good
luck. Only some human tendencies are good, and only some good
tendencies are human.

The self-realizationist consequently faces a dilemma. Either he
maintains that man's nature should be realized, in which case good is
not necessarily brought about, or he opts for the good, which means
an abandonment of the ideal of self-realization. He cannot modify his
theory to read "realize that which it is good to realize" for he has
defined good as complete self-realization; his argument would then be
circular. Like Mill, the self-realizationist stumbles over a necessary
refinement with regard to better and worse states, which points beyond the theory itself for standards.

Evolutionism is an additional theory as to what constitutes a good
life, and it posits a particular aspect of nature as the model for human conduct. Rather than apologizing for man's natural tendencies,
it conceives of the good as conformity to the natural order of which
man is a part. Whether natural forces are operating primarily within
man or outside of him, immanently or transcendently, their influence
is considered helpful not harmful to human existence. In order to

maintain this position, of course, certain assumptions are made concerning the character of nature.

More specifically, evolutionism as an ethical theory claims that the type of evolutionary development operative throughout the universe furnishes a moral model for mankind. Good is defined as that end toward which the process is moving; consequently, man's task and moral obligation consist in furthering the goal of complete evolutionary development. Man must mime nature in her operations by creating a civilization that, according to Herbert Spencer at least, embodies the virtues of self-preservation, protection of the young, and social cooperation—"the greatest totality of life in self, in off-spring, and in fellowman." Other evolutionary theorists, such as Sir Leslie Stephen, the Huxleys, and Peter Kropotkin, present different versions but they also maintain that the most evolved is ethically the most desirable.

Evolutionism and other nature theories are attractive in that they link man to the natural world in an intimate way and conceive of his ethic as integral to his natural environment. However, it is precisely this grounding of ethics in nature that brings down the strongest criticism. Evolutionism commits what is called the "naturalistic fallacy," which is the fallacy of deriving a value system from descriptive facts. No amount of information as to how the natural world operates entitles us to conclude that life should operate that way. What *ought* to be the case cannot be decided in terms of what *is* the case. Natural facts cannot be taken as the basis for how people should behave.

For this reason, nature theories are generally in disrepute among philosophers. People will sometimes say "we must be philosophical" meaning naturally stoical, or "it is survival of the fittest in this world" thereby citing the example of nature, but these tend to be little more than slogans. The appeal to "survival of the fittest," in fact, is usually an attempt to rationalize a person's selfishness or the exploitation of another human being. The natural is not always good.

There are many other theories of the good beside those of hedonism, duty, self-realization, and evolutionism; we have merely touched on a few. Two additional theories, in fact, are developed in the philosophic and literary selections in this chapter: dedication to God, and furthering the progress of mankind. But the foregoing analysis should provide a launching point for evaluating the various ethical alternatives by indicating the kinds of considerations that are important.

1

Pursuing Happiness
or
Following Principles

ANTIGONE
JEAN ANOUILH

(trans. by Lewis Galantiére)

Jean Anouilh (1910–   ) is a French playwright first celebrated for his *Antigone*, which was interpreted as both a parable of the German Occupation and a statement of existentialism. Anouilh's other works, notably *Point of Departure*, *Becket*, and *Waltz of the Toreadors*, range from historical to surrealistic to comic, but the common element in all of his plays is a political pessimism and a pervasive metaphysical despair.

The conflict between the good and the right, previously described, provides the dramatic force in Jean Anouilh's *Antigone*. For Creon the king is committed to securing the maximum good for his country despite the violence done to decency, justice, honesty, and family love, whereas Antigone, his niece, is primarily motivated by personal integrity and pure principles despite the futility of her stand and the threat of death. The moral conflict that occurs is much more subtle than a mere clash between altruism and egoism because both characters appear altruistic in their behavior. Antigone does what she feels she must do, uncompromisingly and courageously, and Creon takes the necessary steps to promote the well-being of the society when, initially, he never wished to be king. But in spite of the fact that they are equally unselfish, they operate on two fundamentally different levels and cannot communicate. Creon presents arguments showing the fruitlessness of Antigone's conduct, which is of course irrelevant to her, and Antigone criticizes Creon's lies and self-betrayal, which is beside the point when one is working for beneficial ends. Since Creon cannot yield in the direction of right any more than Antigone can modify her position relative to the good, the outcome is decided by power and Antigone is killed. However, the moral dilemma remains unresolved.

In the following section of the play Antigone's views clash with Creon's specifically when she attempts to bury the body of her brother Polynices. Creon had decreed that the body was to remain exposed upon a hill because Polynices had died a traitor. He had led a revolt against his brother Eteocles, thus precipitating a bloody civil war in which the two brothers had killed

314

one another. When Creon ascended to the throne he declared Eteocles a national hero and Polynices anathema; his body was to be left above ground to decay as a gesture of detestation and an awful warning to potential revolutionaries.

CREON: Why did you try to bury your brother?

ANTIGONE: I owed it to him.

CREON: I had forbidden it.

ANTIGONE: I owed it to him. Those who are not buried wander eternally and find no rest. If my brother were alive, and he came home weary after a long day's hunting, I should kneel down and unlace his boots, I should fetch him food and drink, I should see that his bed was ready for him. Polynices is home from the hunt. I owe it to him to unlock the house of the dead in which my father and my mother are waiting to welcome him. Polynices has earned his rest.

CREON: Polynices was a rebel and a traitor, and you know it.

ANTIGONE: He was my brother.

CREON: You heard my edict. It was proclaimed throughout Thebes. You read my edict. It was posted up on the city walls.

ANTIGONE: Of course I did.

CREON: You knew the punishment I decreed for any person who attempted to give him burial.

ANTIGONE: Yes, I knew the punishment.

CREON: Did you by any chance act on the assumption that a daughter of Oedipus, a daughter of Oedipus' stubborn pride, was above the law?

ANTIGONE: No, I did not act on that assumption.

CREON: Because if you had acted on that assumption, Antigone, you would have been deeply wrong. Nobody has a more sacred obligation to obey the law than those who make the law. You are a daughter of lawmakers, a daughter of kings, Antigone. You must observe the law.

ANTIGONE: Had I been a scullery maid washing my dishes when that law was read aloud to me, I should have scrubbed the greasy water from my arms and gone out in my apron to bury my brother.

CREON: What nonsense! If you had been a scullery maid, there would have been no doubt in your mind about the seriousness of that edict. You would have known that it meant death; and you would have been satisfied to weep for your brother in your kitchen. But you! You thought that because you come of the royal line, because you were my niece and were going to marry my son, I shouldn't dare have you killed.

ANTIGONE: You are mistaken. Quite the contrary. I never doubted for an instant that you would have me put to death.

(*A pause, as* CREON *stares fixedly at her*)

CREON: The pride of Oedipus! Oedipus and his headstrong pride all over again. I can see your father in you—and I believe you. Of course you thought that I should have you killed! Proud as you are, it seemed to you a natural climax in your existence. Your father was like that. For him as for you human happiness was meaningless; and mere human misery was not enough to satisfy his passion for torment. (*He sits on a stool behind the table*) You come of people for whom the human vestment is a kind of strait jacket: it cracks at the seams. You spend your lives wriggling to get out of it. Nothing less than a cosy tea party with death and destiny will quench your thirst. The happiest hour of your father's life came when he listened greedily to the story of how, unknown to himself, he had killed his own father and dishonored the bed of his own mother. Drop by drop, word by word, he drank in the dark story that the gods had destined him, first to live and then to hear. How avidly men and women drink the brew of such a tale when their names are Oedipus—and Antigone! And it is so simple, afterward, to do what your father did, to put out one's eyes and take one's daughter begging on the highways.

Let me tell you, Antigone: those days are over for Thebes. Thebes has a right to a king without a past. My name, thank God, is only Creon. I stand here with both feet firm on the ground; with both hands in my pockets; and I have decided that so long as I am king—being less ambitious than your father was—I shall merely devote myself to introducing a little order into this absurd kingdom; if that is possible.

Don't think that being a king seems to me romantic. It is my trade; a trade a man has to work at every day; and like every other trade, it isn't all beer and skittles. But since it is my trade, I take it seriously. And if, tomorrow, some wild and bearded messenger walks in from some wild and distant valley—which is what happened to your dad— and tells me that he's not quite sure who my parents were, but thinks that my wife Eurydice is actually my mother, I shall ask him to do me the kindness to go back where he came from; and I shan't let a little matter like that persuade me to order my wife to take a blood test and the police to let me know whether or not my birth certificate was forged. Kings, my girl, have other things to do than to surrender themselves to their private feelings. (*He looks at her and smiles*) Hand *you* over to be killed! (*He rises, moves to end of table and sits on the top of table*) I have other plans for you. You're going to marry Haemon; and I want you to fatten up a bit so that you can give him a sturdy boy. Let me assure you that Thebes needs that boy a good deal more than it needs your death. You will go to your room, now, and do as you have been told; and you won't say a word about this to anybody. Don't fret about the guards: I'll see that their mouths are shut. And don't annihilate me with those eyes. I know that you think I am a brute, and I'm sure you must consider me very prosaic. But the fact is, I have always been fond of you, stubborn though you always were. Don't forget that the first doll you ever had came from me. (*A pause.* ANTIGONE *says nothing, rises and crosses slowly below the table toward the arch.* CREON *turns and watches her; then*) Where are you going?

ANTIGONE (*Stops downstage. Without any show of rebellion*): You know very well where I am going.

CREON (*After a pause*): What sort of game are you playing?

ANTIGONE: I am not playing games.

CREON: Antigone, do you realize that if, apart from those three guards, a single soul finds out what you have tried to do, it will be impossible for me to avoid putting you to death? There is still a chance that I can save you; but only if you keep this to yourself and give up your crazy purpose. Five minutes more, and it will be too late. You understand that?

ANTIGONE: I must go and bury my brother. Those men uncovered him.

CREON: What good will it do? You know that there are other men standing guard over Polynices. And even if you did cover him over with earth again, the earth would again be removed.

ANTIGONE: I know all that. I know it. But that much, at least, I can do. And what a person can do, a person ought to do.

(*Pause*)

CREON: Tell me, Antigone, do you believe all that flummery about religious burial? Do you really believe that a so-called shade of your brother is condemned to wander for ever homeless if a little earth is not flung on his corpse to the accompaniment of some priestly abracadabra? Have you ever listened to the priests of Thebes when they were mumbling their formula? Have you ever watched those dreary bureaucrats while they were preparing the dead for burial—skipping half the gestures required by the ritual, swallowing half their words, hustling the dead into their graves out of fear that they might be late for lunch?

ANTIGONE: Yes, I have seen all that.

CREON: And did you never say to yourself as you watched them, that if someone you really loved lay dead under the shuffling, mumbling ministrations of the priests, you would scream aloud and beg the priests to leave the dead in peace?

ANTIGONE: Yes, I've thought all that.

CREON: And you still insist upon being put to death—merely because I refuse to let your brother go out with that grotesque passport; because I refuse his body the wretched consolation of that mass-production jibber-jabber, which you would have been the first to be embarrassed by if I had allowed it. The whole thing is absurd!

ANTIGONE: Yes, it's absurd.

CREON: Then why, Antigone, why? For whose sake? For the sake of them that believe in it? To raise them against me?

ANTIGONE: No.

CREON: For whom then if not for them and not for Polynices either?

ANTIGONE: For nobody. For myself.

(*A pause as they stand looking at one another*)

CREON: You must want very much to die. You look like a trapped animal.

ANTIGONE: Stop feeling sorry for me. Do as I do. Do your job. But if you are a human being, do it quickly. That is all I ask of you. I'm not going to be able to hold out for ever.

CREON (*Takes a step toward her*): I want to save you, Antigone.

ANTIGONE: You are the king, and you are all-powerful. But that you cannot do.

CREON: You think not?

ANTIGONE: Neither save me nor stop me.

CREON: Prideful Antigone! Little Oedipus!

ANTIGONE: Only this can you do: have me put to death.

CREON: Have you tortured, perhaps?

ANTIGONE: Why would you do that? To see me cry? To hear me beg for mercy? Or swear whatever you wish, and then begin over again?

(*A pause*)

CREON: You listen to me. You have cast me for the villain in this little play of yours, and yourself for the heroine. And you know it, you damned little mischief-maker! But don't you drive me too far! If I were one of your preposterous little tyrants that Greece is full of, you would be lying in a ditch this minute with your tongue pulled out and your body drawn and quartered. But you can see something in my face that makes me hesitate to send for the guards and turn you over to them. Instead, I let you go on arguing; and you taunt me, you take the offensive. (*He grasps her left wrist*) What are you driving at, you she-devil?

ANTIGONE: Let me go. You are hurting my arm.

CREON (*Gripping her tighter*): I will not let you go.

ANTIGONE (*Moans*): Oh!

CREON: I was a fool to waste words. I should have done this from the beginning. (*He looks at her*) I may be your uncle—but we are not a particularly affectionate family. Are we, eh? (*Through his teeth, as he twists*) Are we? (CREON *propels* ANTIGONE *round below him to his side*) What fun for you, eh? To be able to spit in the face of a king who has all the power in the world; a man who has done his own killing in his day; who has killed people just as pitiable as you are— and who is still soft enough to go to all this trouble in order to keep you from being killed.

(*A pause*)

ANTIGONE: Now you are squeezing my arm too tightly. It doesn't hurt any more.

(CREON *stares at her, then drops her arm*)

CREON: I shall save you yet. (*He goes below the table to the chair at end of table, takes off his coat and places it on the chair*) God knows, I have things enough to do today without wasting my time on an insect like you. There's plenty to do, I assure you, when you've just put down a revolution. But urgent things can wait. I am not going to let politics be the cause of your death. For it is a fact that this whole business is nothing but politics: the mournful shade of Polynices, the decomposing corpse, the sentimental weeping and the hysteria that you mistake for heroism—nothing but politics.

Look here. I may not be soft, but I'm fastidious. I like things clean, ship-shape, well scrubbed. Don't think that I am not just as offended as you are by the thought of that meat rotting in the sun. In the evening, when the breeze comes in off the sea, you can smell it in the palace, and it nauseates me. But I refuse even to shut my window. It's vile; and I can tell you what I wouldn't tell anybody else: it's stupid, monstrously stupid. But the people of Thebes have got to have their noses rubbed into it a little longer. My God! If it was up to me, I should have had them bury your brother long ago as a mere matter of public hygiene. I admit that what I am doing is childish. But if the featherheaded rabble I govern are to understand what's what, that stench has got to fill the town for a month!

ANTIGONE (*Turns to him*): You are a loathsome man!

CREON: I agree. My trade forces me to be. We could argue whether I ought or ought not to follow my trade; but once I take on the job, I must do it properly.

ANTIGONE: Why do you do it at all?

CREON: My dear, I woke up one morning and found myself King of Thebes. God knows, there were other things I loved in life more than power.

ANTIGONE: Then you should have said no.

CREON: Yes, I could have done that. Only, I felt that it would have been cowardly. I should have been like a workman who turns down a job that has to be done. So I said yes.

ANTIGONE: So much the worse for you, then. I didn't say yes. I can say no to anything I think vile, and I don't have to count the cost. But because you said yes, all that you can do, for all your crown and your trappings, and your guards—all that you can do is to have me killed.

CREON: Listen to me.

ANTIGONE: If I want to. I don't have to listen to you if I don't want to. You've said your *yes*. There is nothing more you can tell me that I don't know. You stand there, drinking in my words. (*She moves behind chair*) Why is it that you don't call your guards? I'll tell you why. You want to hear me out to the end; that's why.

CREON: You amuse me.

ANTIGONE: Oh, no, I don't. I frighten you. That is why you talk about saving me. Everything would be so much easier if you had a docile, tongue-tied little Antigone living in the palace. I'll tell you something, Uncle Creon: I'll give you back one of your own words. You are too fastidious to make a good tyrant. But you are going to have to put me to death today, and you know it. And that's what frightens you. God! Is there anything uglier than a frightened man!

CREON: Very well. I am afraid, then. Does that satisfy you? I am afraid that if you insist upon it, I shall have to have you killed. And I don't want to.

ANTIGONE: I don't have to do things that I think are wrong. If it comes to that, you didn't really want to leave my brother's body unburied, did you? Say it! Admit that you didn't.

CREON: I have said it already.

ANTIGONE: But you did it just the same. And now, though you don't want to do it, you are going to have me killed. And you call that being a king!

CREON: Yes, I call that being a king.

ANTIGONE: Poor Creon! My nails are broken, my fingers are bleeding, my arms are covered with the welts left by the paws of your guards—but I am a queen!

CREON: Then why not have pity on me, and live? Isn't your brother's corpse, rotting there under my windows, payment enough for peace and order in Thebes? My son loves you. Don't make me add your life to the payment. I've paid enough.

ANTIGONE: No, Creon! You said yes, and made yourself king. Now you will never stop paying.

CREON: But God in Heaven! Won't you try to understand me! I'm trying hard enough to understand you! There had to be one man who said yes. Somebody had to agree to captain the ship. She had sprung a hundred leaks; she was loaded to the water-line with crime, ignorance, poverty. The wheel was swinging with the wind. The crew refused to work and were looting the cargo. The officers were building a raft, ready to slip overboard and desert the ship. The mast was splitting, the wind was howling, the sails were beginning to rip. Every man jack on board was about to drown—and only because the only thing they thought of was their own skins and their cheap little day-to-day traffic. Was that a time, do you think, for playing with words like yes and no? Was that a time for a man to be weighing the pros and cons, wondering if he wasn't going to pay too dearly later on; if he wasn't going to lose his life, or his family, or his touch with other men? You grab the wheel, you right the ship in the face of a mountain of water. You shout an order, and if one man refuses to obey, you shoot straight into the mob. Into the mob, I say! The beast as nameless as the wave that crashes down upon your deck; as nameless as the whipping wind. The thing that drops when you shoot may be someone who poured you a drink the night before; but it has no name. And you, braced at the wheel, you have no name, either. Nothing has a name—except the ship, and the storm. (*A pause as he looks at her*) Now do you understand?

ANTIGONE: I am not here to understand. That's all very well for you. I am here to say no to you, and die.

CREON: It is easy to say no.

ANTIGONE: Not always.

CREON: It is easy to say no. To say yes, you have to sweat and roll up your sleeves and plunge both hands into life up to the elbows. It is easy to say no, even if saying no means death. All you have to do is to sit still and wait. Wait to go on living; wait to be killed. That is the coward's part. *No* is one of your man-made words. Can you imagine a world in which trees say *no* to the sap? In which beasts say *no* to hunger or to propagation? Animals are good, simple, tough. They move in droves, nudging one another onward, all traveling the same road. Some of them keel over; but the rest go on; and no matter how many may fall by the wayside, there are always those few left which go on bringing their young into the world, traveling the same road with the same obstinate will, unchanged from those who went before.

ANTIGONE: Animals, eh, Creon! What a king you could be if only men were animals!

(*A pause.* CREON *turns and looks at her*)

CREON: You despise me, don't you? (ANTIGONE *is silent.* CREON *goes on, as if to himself*) Strange. Again and again, I have imagined myself holding this conversation with a pale young man I have never seen in the flesh. He would have come to assassinate me, and would have failed. I would be trying to find out from him why he wanted to kill me. But with all my logic and all my powers of debate, the only thing I could get out of him would be that he despised me. Who would have thought that the white-faced boy would turn out to be you? And that the debate would arise out of something so meaningless as the burial of your brother?

ANTIGONE (*Repeats contemptuously*): Meaningless!

CREON (*Earnestly, almost desperately*): And yet, you must hear me out. My part is not an heroic one, but I shall play my part. I shall have you put to death. Only, before I do, I want to make one last appeal. I want to be sure that you know what you are doing as well as I know what I am doing. Antigone, do you know what you are dying for? Do you know the sordid story to which you are going to sign your name in blood, for all time to come?

ANTIGONE: What story?

CREON: The story of Eteocles and Polynices, the story of your brothers. You think you know it, but you don't. Nobody in Thebes knows that story but me. And it seems to me, this afternoon, that you have a right to know it too. (*A pause as* ANTIGONE *moves to chair and sits*) It's not a pretty story. (*He turns, gets stool from behind the table and places it between the table and the chair*) You'll see. (*He looks at her for a moment*) Tell me, first. What do you remember about your brothers? They were older than you, so they must have looked down on you. And I imagine that they tormented you—pulled your pigtails, broke your dolls, whispered secrets to each other to put you in a rage.

ANTIGONE: They were big and I was little.

CREON: And later on, when they came home wearing evening clothes, smoking cigarettes, they would have nothing to do with you; and you thought they were wonderful.

ANTIGONE: They were boys and I was a girl.

CREON: You didn't know why, exactly, but you knew that they were making your mother unhappy. You saw her in tears over them; and your father would fly into a rage because of them. You heard them come in, slamming doors, laughing noisily in the corridors—insolent, spineless, unruly, smelling of drink.

ANTIGONE (*Staring outward*): Once, it was very early and we had just got up. I saw them coming home, and hid behind a door. Polynices was very pale and his eyes were shining. He was so handsome in his evening clothes. He saw me, and said: "Here, this is for you"; and he gave me a big paper flower that he had brought home from his night out.

CREON: And of course you still have that flower. Last night, before you crept out, you opened a drawer and looked at it for a time, to give yourself courage.

ANTIGONE: Who told you so?

CREON: Poor Antigone! With her night-club flower. Do you know what your brother was?

ANTIGONE: Whatever he was, I know that you will say vile things about him.

CREON: A cheap, idiotic bounder, that is what he was. A cruel, vicious little voluptuary. A little beast with just wit enough to drive a car faster and throw more money away than any of his pals. I was with your father one day when Polynices, having lost a lot of money gambling, asked him to settle the debt; and when your father refused, the boy raised his hand against him and called him a vile name.

ANTIGONE: That's a lie!

CREON: He struck your father in the face with his fist. It was pitiful. Your father sat at his desk with his head in his hands. His nose was bleeding. He was weeping with anguish. And in a corner of your father's study, Polynices stood sneering and lighting a cigarette.

ANTIGONE: That's a lie.

(A *pause*)

CREON: When did you last see Polynices alive? When you were twelve years old. *That's* true, isn't it?

ANTIGONE: Yes, that's true.

CREON: Now you know why. Oedipus was too chicken-hearted to have the boy locked up. Polynices was allowed to go off and join the Argive army. And as soon as he reached Argos, the attempts upon your father's life began—upon the life of an old man who couldn't make up his mind to die, couldn't bear to be parted from his kingship. One after another, men slipped into Thebes from Argos for the purpose of assassinating him, and every killer we caught always ended by confessing who had put him up to it, who had paid him to try it. And it wasn't only Polynices. That is really what I am trying to tell you. I want you to know what went on in the back room, in the kitchen of politics; I want you to know what took place in the wings of this drama in which you are burning to play a part.

Yesterday, I gave Eteocles a State funeral, with pomp and honors. Today, Eteocles is a saint and a hero in the eyes of all Thebes. The whole city turned out to bury him. The schoolchildren emptied their savings boxes to buy wreaths for him. Old men, orating in quavering, hypocritical voices, glorified the virtues of the great-hearted brother, the devoted son, the loyal prince. I made a speech myself; and every temple priest was present with an appropriate show of sorrow and solemnity in his stupid face. And military honors were accorded the dead hero.

Well, what else could I have done? People had taken sides in the civil war. Both sides couldn't be wrong; that would be too much. I couldn't have made them swallow the truth. Two gangsters was more of a luxury than I could afford. (*He pauses for a moment*) And this is the whole point of my story. Eteocles, that virtuous brother, was just as rotten as Polynices. That great-hearted son had done his best, too, to procure the assassination of his father. That loyal prince had also offered to sell out Thebes to the highest bidder. Funny, isn't it? Polynices lies rotting in the sun while Eteocles is given a hero's funeral and will be housed in a marble vault. Yet I have absolute proof that everything that Polynices did, Eteocles had plotted to do. They were a pair of blackguards—both engaged in selling out Thebes, and both engaged in selling out each other; and they died like the cheap gangsters they were, over a division of the spoils.

But, as I told you a moment ago, I had to make a martyr of one of them. I sent out to the holocaust for their bodies; they were found clasped in one another's arms—for the first time in their lives, I imagine. Each had been spitted on the other's sword, and the Argive cavalry had trampled them down. They were mashed to a pulp, Antigone. I had the prettier of the two carcases brought in, and gave it a State funeral; and I left the other to rot. I don't know which was which. And I assure you, I don't care. (*Long silence, neither looking at the other*)

ANTIGONE (*In a mild voice*): Why do you tell me all this?

CREON: Would it have been better to let you die a victim to that obscene story?

ANTIGONE: It might have been. I had my faith.

CREON: What are you going to do now?

ANTIGONE (*Rises to her feet in a daze*): I shall go up to my room.

CREON: Don't stay alone. Go and find Haemon. And get married quickly.

ANTIGONE (*In a whisper*): Yes.

CREON: All this is really beside the point. You have your whole life ahead of you—and life is a treasure.

ANTIGONE: Yes.

CREON: And you were about to throw it away. Don't think me fatuous if I say that I understand you; and that at your age I should have done the same thing. A moment ago, when we were quarreling, you said I was drinking in your words. I was. But it wasn't you I was listening to; it was a lad named Creon who lived here in Thebes many years ago. He was thin and pale, as you are. His mind, too, was filled with thoughts of self-sacrifice. Go and find Haemon. And get married quickly, Antigone. Be happy. Life flows like water, and you young people let it run away through your fingers. Shut your hands; hold on to it, Antigone. Life is not what you think it is. Life is a child playing round your feet, a tool you hold firmly in your grip, a bench you sit down upon in the evening, in your garden. People will tell you that that's not life, that life is something else. They will tell you that because they need your strength and your fire, and they will want to make use of you. Don't listen to them. Believe me, the only poor consolation that we have in our old age is to discover that what I have said to you is true. Life is nothing more than the happiness that you get out of it.

ANTIGONE (*Murmurs, lost in thought*): Happiness . . .

CREON (*Suddenly a little self-conscious*): Not much of a word, is it?

ANTIGONE (*Quietly*): What kind of happiness do you foresee for me? Paint me the picture of your happy Antigone. What are the unimportant little sins that I shall have to commit before I am allowed to sink my teeth into life and tear happiness from it? Tell me: to whom shall I have to lie? Upon whom shall I have to fawn? To whom must I sell myself? Whom do you want me to leave dying, while I turn away my eyes?

CREON: Antigone, be quiet.

ANTIGONE: Why do you tell me to be quiet when all I want to know is what I have to do to be happy? This minute; since it is this very minute that I must make my choice. You tell me that life is so wonderful. I want to know what I have to do in order to be able to say that myself.

CREON: Do you love Haemon?

ANTIGONE: Yes, I love Haemon. The Haemon I love is hard and young, faithful and difficult to satisfy, just as I am. But if what I love in Haemon is to be worn away like a stone step by the tread of the thing you call life, the thing you call happiness; if Haemon reaches the point where he stops growing pale with fear when I grow pale, stops thinking that I must have been killed in an accident when I am five minutes late, stops feeling that he is alone on earth when I laugh and he doesn't know why—if he too has to learn to say yes to everything—why, no, then, no! I do not love Haemon!

CREON: You don't know what you are talking about!

ANTIGONE: I do know what I am talking about! Now it is you who have stopped understanding. I am too far away from you now, talking to you from a kingdom you can't get into, with your quick tongue and your hollow heart. (*Laughs*) I laugh, Creon, because I see you suddenly as you must have been at fifteen: the same look of impotence in your face and the same inner conviction that there was nothing you couldn't do. What has life added to you, except those lines in your face, and that fat on your stomach?

CREON: Be quiet, I tell you!

ANTIGONE: Why do you want me to be quiet? Because you know that I am right? Do you think I can't see in your face that what I am saying is true? You can't admit it, of course; you have to go on growling and defending the bone you call happiness.

CREON: It is your happiness, too, you little fool!

ANTIGONE: I spit on your happiness! I spit on your idea of life—that life that must go on, come what may. You are all like dogs that lick everything they smell. You with your promise of a humdrum happiness—provided a person doesn't ask too much of life. I want everything of life, I do; and I want it now! I want it total, complete: otherwise I reject it! I will *not* be moderate. I will *not* be satisfied with the bite of cake you offer me if I promise to be a good little girl. I want to be sure of everything this very day; sure that everything will be as beautiful as when I was a little girl. If not, I want to die!

UTILITARIANISM
(Chapter II)

JOHN STUART MILL

John Stuart Mill (1806–1873). For notes on Mill see page 161.

John Stuart Mill's *Utilitarianism* develops the theory of universalistic hedonism as previously described, and can be said to offer a philosophic justification for a position such as that of Creon. In fact, Creon explicitly states that life is nothing more than the happiness you get out of it, and he is primarily concerned to provide happiness for the society by introducing order in place of chaos.

WHAT UTILITARIANISM IS

A passing remark is all that needs be given to the ignorant blunder of supposing that those who stand up for utility as the test of right and wrong, use the term in that restricted and merely colloquial sense in which utility is opposed to pleasure. An apology is due to the philosophical opponents of utilitarianism, for even the momentary appearance of confounding them with any one capable of so absurd a misconception; which is the more extraordinary, inasmuch as the contrary accusation, of referring everything to pleasure, and that too in its grossest form, is another of the common charges against utilitarianism: and, as has been pointedly remarked by an able writer, the same sort of persons, and often the very same persons, denounce the theory "as impracticably dry when the word utility precedes the word pleasure, and as too practicably voluptuous when the word pleasure precedes the word utility." Those who know anything about the matter are aware that every writer, from Epicurus to Bentham, who maintained the theory of utility, meant by it, not something to be contradistinguished from pleasure, but pleasure itself, together with exemption from pain; and instead of opposing the useful to the agreeable or the ornamental, have always declared that the useful means these, among other things. Yet the common herd, including the herd of writers, not only in newspapers and periodicals, but in books of weight and pretension, are perpetually falling into this shallow mistake. Having caught up the word utilitarian, while knowing nothing whatever about it but its sound, they habitually express by it the rejection, or the neglect, of pleasure in some of its forms; of beauty, or ornament, or of amusement. Nor is the term thus ignorantly misapplied solely in disparagement, but occasionally in compliment; as though it implied superiority to frivolity and the mere pleasures of the moment. And this perverted use is the only one in which the word is popularly known, and the one from which the new generation are acquiring their sole notion of its meaning. Those who introduced the word, but who had for many years discontinued it as a distinctive appellation, may well feel themselves called upon to resume it, if by doing so they can hope to contribute anything towards rescuing it from this utter degradation.[1]

The creed which accepts as the foundation of morals, Utility, or the Greatest Happiness Principle, holds that actions are right in proportion as they tend to promote happiness, wrong as they tend to produce the reverse of happiness. By happiness is intended pleasure, and the absence of pain; by unhappiness, pain, and the privation of pleasure. To give a clear view of the moral standard set up by the theory, much more requires to be said; in particular, what things it includes in the ideas of pain and pleasure; and to what extent this is left an open question. But these supplementary explanations do not affect the theory of life on which this theory of morality is grounded—namely, that pleasure, and freedom from pain, are the only things desirable as ends; and that all desirable things (which are as numerous in the utilitarian as in any other scheme) are desirable either for the pleasure inherent in themselves, or as means to the promotion of pleasure and the prevention of pain.

Now, such a theory of life excites in many minds, and among them in some of the most estimable in feeling and purpose, inveterate dislike. To suppose that life has (as they express it) no higher end than pleasure— no better and nobler object of desire and pursuit—they designate as utterly mean and grovelling; as a doctrine worthy only of swine, to whom the followers of Epicurus were, at a very early period, contemptuously likened; and modern holders of the doctrine are occasionally made the subject of equally polite comparisons by its German, French, and English assailants.

When thus attacked, the Epicureans have always answered, that it is not they, but their accusers, who represent human nature in a degrading light; since the accusation supposes human beings to be capable of no pleasures except those of which swine are capable. If this supposition were true, the charge could not be gainsaid, but would then be no longer an imputation; for if the sources of pleasure were precisely the same to human beings and to swine, the rule of life which is good enough for the one would be good enough for the other. The comparison of the Epicurean life to that of beasts is felt as degrading, precisely because a beast's pleasures do not satisfy a human being's conceptions of happiness. Human beings have faculties more elevated than the animal appetites, and when once made conscious of them, do not regard anything as happiness which does not include their gratification. I do not, indeed, consider the Epicureans to have been by any means faultless in drawing out their scheme of consequences from the utilitarian principle. To do this in any sufficient

---

[1] The author of this essay has reason for believing himself to be the first person who brought the word utilitarian into use. He did not invent it, but adopted it from a passing expression in Mr. Galt's *Annals of the Parish*. After using it as a designation for several years, he and others abandoned it from a growing dislike to anything resembling a badge or watchword of sectarian distinction. But as a name for one single opinion, not a set of opinions—to denote the recognition of utility as a standard, not any particular way of applying it—the term supplies a want in the language, and offers, in many cases, a convenient mode of avoiding tiresome circumlocution.

manner, many Stoic, as well as Christian elements require to be included. But there is no known Epicurean theory of life which does not assign to the pleasures of the intellect, of the feelings and imagination, and of the moral sentiments, a much higher value as pleasures than to those of mere sensation. It must be admitted, however, that utilitarian writers in general have placed the superiority of mental over bodily pleasures chiefly in the greater permanency, safety, uncostliness, etc., of the former—that is, in their circumstantial advantages rather than in their intrinsic nature. And on all these points utilitarians have fully proved their case; but they might have taken the other, and, as it may be called, higher ground, with entire consistency. It is quite compatible with the principle of utility to recognise the fact, that some *kinds* of pleasure are more desirable and more valuable than others. It would be absurd that while, in estimating all other things, quality is considered as well as quantity, the estimation of pleasures should be supposed to depend on quantity alone.

If I am asked, what I mean by difference of quality in pleasures, or what makes one pleasure more valuable than another, merely as a pleasure, except its being greater in amount, there is but one possible answer. Of two pleasures, if there be one to which all or almost all who have experience of both give a decided preference, irrespective of any feeling of moral obligation to prefer it, that is the more desirable pleasure. If one of the two is, by those who are competently acquainted with both, placed so far above the other that they prefer it, even though knowing it to be attended with a greater amount of discontent, and would not resign it for any quantity of the other pleasure which their nature is capable of, we are justified in ascribing to the preferred enjoyment a superiority in quality, so far outweighing quantity as to render it, in comparison, of small account.

Now it is an unquestionable fact that those who are equally acquainted with, and equally capable of appreciating and enjoying, both, do give a most marked preference to the manner of existence which employs their higher faculties. Few human creatures would consent to be changed into any of the lower animals, for a promise of the fullest allowance of a beast's pleasures; no intelligent human being would consent to be a fool, no instructed person would be an ignoramus, no person of feeling and conscience would be selfish and base, even though they should be persuaded that the fool, the dunce, or the rascal is better satisfied with his lot than they are with theirs. They would not resign what they possess more than he for the most complete satisfaction of all the desires which they have in common with him. If they ever fancy they would, it is only in cases of unhappiness so extreme, that to escape from it they would exchange their lot for almost any other, however undesirable in their own eyes. A being of higher faculties requires more to make him happy, is capable probably of more acute suffering, and certainly accessible to it at more points, than one of an inferior type; but in spite of these liabilities, he can never really wish to sink into what he feels to be a lower grade of existence. We may give what explanation we please of this unwillingness; we may attribute it to pride, a name which is given indiscriminately to some of the most and to some of the least estimable feelings of which mankind are capable: we may refer it to the love of liberty and personal independence, an appeal to which was with the Stoics one of the most effective means for the inculcation of it; to the love of power, or to the love of excitement, both of which do really enter into and contribute to it: but its most appropriate appellation is a sense of dignity, which all human beings possess in one form or other, and in some, though by no means in exact, proportion to their higher faculties, and which is so essential a part of the happiness of those in whom it is strong, that nothing which conflicts with it could be, otherwise than momentarily, an object of desire to them. Whoever supposes that this preference takes place at a sacrifice of happiness—that the superior being, in anything like equal circumstances, is not happier than the inferior—confounds the two very different ideas, of happiness, and content. It is indisputable that the being whose capacities of enjoyment are low, has the greatest chance of having them fully satisfied; and a highly endowed being will always feel that any happiness which he can look for, as the world is constituted, is imperfect. But he can learn to bear its imperfections, if they are at all bearable; and they will not make him envy the being who is indeed unconscious of the imperfections, but only because he feels not at all the good which those imperfections qualify. It is better to be a human being dissatisfied than a pig satisfied; better to be Socrates dissatisfied than a fool satisfied. And if the fool, or the pig, are of a different opinion, it is because they only know their own side of the question. The other party to the comparison knows both sides.

It may be objected, that many who are capable of the higher pleasures, occasionally, under the influence of temptation, postpone them to the lower. But this is quite compatible with a full appreciation of the intrinsic superiority of the higher. Men often, from infirmity of character, make their election for the nearer good, though they know it to be the less valuable; and this no less when the choice is between two bodily pleasures, than when it is between bodily and mental. They pursue sensual indulgences to the injury of health, though perfectly aware that health is the greater good. It may be further objected, that many who begin with youthful enthusiasm for everything noble, as they advance in years sink into indolence and selfishness. But I do not believe that those who undergo this very common change, voluntarily choose the lower description of pleasures in preference to the higher. I believe that before they devote themselves exclusively to the one, they have already become incapable of the other. Capacity for the nobler feelings is in most natures a very tender plant, easily killed, not only by hostile influences, but by mere want of sustenance; and in the majority of young persons it speedily dies away if the occupations to which their position in life has devoted them, and the society into which it has thrown them, are not favourable to keeping that higher capacity in exercise. Men lose their high aspirations as they lose their intellectual tastes, because they have not time or opportunity for indulging them; and they addict themselves to inferior pleasures, not because they deliberately prefer them, but because they are either the only ones to which they have access, or the only ones which they are any longer capable of enjoying. It may be questioned whether any one who has remained equally susceptible to both classes of pleasures, ever knowingly and calmly preferred the lower; though many, in all ages, have broken down in an ineffectual attempt to combine both.

From this verdict of the only competent judges, I apprehend there can be no appeal. On a question which is the best worth having of two pleasures, or which of two modes of existence is the most grateful to the feelings, apart from its moral attributes and from its consequences, the judgment of those who are qualified by knowledge of both, or, if they differ, that of the majority among them, must be admitted as final. And there needs be the less hesitation to accept this judgment respecting the quality of pleasures, since there is no other tribunal to be referred to even on the question of quantity. What means are there of determining which is the acutest of two pains, or the intensest of two pleasurable sensations, except the general suffrage of those who are familiar with both? Neither pains nor pleasures are homogeneous, and pain is always heterogeneous with pleasure. What is there to decide whether a particular pleasure is worth purchasing at the cost of a particular pain, except the feelings and judgment of the experienced? When, therefore, those feelings and judgment declare the pleasures derived from the higher faculties to be preferable *in kind*, apart from the question of intensity, to those of which the animal nature, disjoined from the higher faculties, is susceptible, they are entitled on this subject to the same regard.

I have dwelt on this point, as being a necessary part of a perfectly just conception of Utility or Happiness, considered as the directive rule of human conduct. But it is by no means an indispensable condition to the acceptance of the utilitarian standard; for that standard is not the agent's own greatest happiness, but the greatest amount of happiness altogether; and if it may possibly be doubted whether a noble character is always the happier for its nobleness, there can be no doubt that it makes other people happier, and that the world in general is immensely a gainer by it. Utilitarianism, therefore, could only attain its end by the general cultivation of nobleness of character, even if each individual were only benefited by the nobleness of others, and his own, so far as happiness is concerned, were a sheer deduction from the benefit. But the bare enunciation of such an absurdity as this last, renders refutation superfluous.

According to the Greatest Happiness Principle, as above explained, the ultimate end, with reference to and for the sake of which all other things are desirable (whether we are considering our own good or that of other people), is an existence exempt as far as possible from pain, and as rich as possible in enjoyments, both in point of quantity and quality; the test of quality, and the rule for measuring it against quantity, being the preference felt by those who in their opportunities of experience, to which must be added their habits of self-consciousness and self-observation, are best furnished with the means of comparison. This, being, according to the utilitarian opinion, the end of human action, is necessarily also the standard of morality; which may accordingly be defined, the rules and precepts for human conduct, by the observance of which an existence such as has been described might be, to the greatest extent possible, secured to all mankind; and not to them only, but, so far as the nature of things admits, to the whole sentient creation.

Against this doctrine, however, arises another class of objectors, who say that happiness, in any form, cannot be the rational purpose of human life and action; because, in the first place, it is unattainable: and they contemptuously ask, what right hast thou to be happy? a question which Mr. Carlyle clenches by the addition, What right, a short time ago, hadst thou even *to be?* Next, they say, that men can do *without* happiness; that all noble human beings have felt this, and could not have become noble but by learning the lesson of Entsagen, or renunciation; which lesson, thoroughly learnt and submitted to, they affirm to be the beginning and necessary condition of all virtue.

The first of these objections would go to the root of the matter were it well founded; for if no happiness is to be had at all by human beings, the attainment of it cannot be the end of morality, or of any rational conduct. Though, even in that case, something might still be said for the utilitarian theory; since utility includes not solely the pursuit of happiness, but the prevention or mitigation of unhappiness; and if the former aim be chimerical, there will be all the greater scope and more imperative need for the latter, so long at least as mankind think fit to live, and do not take refuge in the simultaneous act of suicide recommended under certain conditions by Novalis. When, however, it is thus positively asserted to be impossible that human life should be happy, the assertion, if not something like a verbal quibble, is at least an exaggeration. If by happiness be meant a continuity of highly pleasurable excitement, it is evident enough that this is impossible. A state of exalted pleasure lasts only moments, or in some cases, and with some intermissions, hours or days, and is the occasional brilliant flash of enjoyment, not its permanent and steady flame. Of this the philosophers who have taught that happiness is the end of life were as fully aware as those who taunt them. The happiness which they meant was not a life of rapture; but moments of such, in an existence made up of few and transitory pains, many and various pleasures, with a decided predominance of the active over the passive, and having as the foundation of the whole, not to expect more from life than it is capable of bestowing. A life thus composed, to those who have been fortunate enough to obtain it, has always appeared worthy of the name of happiness. And such an existence is even now the lot of many, during some considerable portion of their lives. The present wretched education, and wretched social arrangements, are the only real hindrance to its being attainable by almost all.

The objectors perhaps may doubt whether human beings, if taught to consider happiness as the end of life, would be satisfied with such a moderate share of it. But great numbers of mankind have been satisfied with much less. The main constituents of a satisfied life appear to be two, either of which by itself is often found sufficient for the purpose: tranquillity, and excitement. With much tranquillity, many find that they can be content with very little pleasure: with much excitement, many can reconcile themselves to a considerable quantity of pain. There is assuredly no inherent impossibility in enabling even the mass of mankind to unite both; since the two are so far from being incompatible that they are in natural alliance, the prolongation of either being a preparation for, and exciting a wish for, the other. It is only those in whom indolence amounts to a vice, that do not desire excitement after an interval of repose: it is only those in whom the need of excitement is a disease, that feel the tranquillity which follows excitement dull and insipid, instead of pleasurable in direct proportion to the excitement which preceded it. When people who are tolerably fortunate in their outward lot do not find in life sufficient enjoyment to make it valuable to them, the cause generally is, caring for nobody but themselves. To those who have neither public nor private affections, the excitements of life are much curtailed, and in any case dwindle in value as the time approaches when all selfish interests must be terminated by death: while those who leave after them objects of personal affection, and especially those who have also cultivated a fellow-feeling with the collective interests of mankind, retain as lively an interest in life on the eve of death as in the vigour of youth and health. Next to selfishness, the principal cause which makes life unsatisfactory is want of mental cultivation. A cultivated mind—I do not mean that of a philosopher, but any mind to which the fountains of knowledge have been opened, and which has been taught, in any tolerable degree, to exercise its faculties—finds sources of inexhaustible interest in all that surrounds it; in the objects of nature, the achievements of art, the imaginations of poetry, the incidents of history, the ways of mankind, past and present, and their prospects in the future. It is possible, indeed, to become indifferent to all this, and that too without having exhausted a thousandth part of it; but only when one has had from the beginning no moral or human interest in these things, and has sought in them only the gratification of curiosity.

Now there is absolutely no reason in the nature of things why an amount of mental culture sufficient to give an intelligent interest in these objects of contemplation, should not be the inheritance of every one born in a civilised country. As little is there an inherent necessity that any human being should be a selfish egotist, devoid of every feeling or care but those which centre in his own miserable individuality. Something far superior to this is sufficiently common even now, to give ample earnest of what the human species may be made. Genuine private affections, and a sincere interest in the public good, are possible, though in unequal degrees, to every rightly brought up human being. In a world in which there is so much to interest, so much to enjoy, and so much also to correct and improve, every one who has this moderate amount of moral and intellectual requisites is capable of an existence which may be called enviable; and unless such a person, through bad laws, or subjection to the will of others, is denied the liberty to use the sources of happiness within his reach, he will not fail to find this enviable existence, if he escape the positive evils of life, the great sources of physical and mental suffering— such as indigence, disease, and the unkindness, worthlessness, or premature loss of objects of affection. The main stress of the problem lies, therefore, in the contest with these calamities, from which it is a rare good fortune entirely to escape; which, as things now are, cannot be obviated, and often cannot be in any material degree mitigated. Yet no one whose opinion deserves a moment's consideration can doubt that most of the great positive evils of the world are in themselves removable, and will, if human affairs continue to improve, be in the end reduced within narrow limits. Poverty, in any sense implying suffering, may be completely extinguished by the wisdom of society, combined with the good sense and providence of individuals. Even that most intractable of enemies, disease, may be indefinitely reduced in dimensions by good physical and moral education, and proper control of noxious influences; while the progress of science holds out a promise for the future of still more direct conquests over this detestable foe. And every advance in that direction relieves us from some, not only of the chances which cut short our own lives, but, what concerns us still more, which deprive us of those in whom our happiness is wrapt up. As for vicissitudes of fortune, and other disappointments connected with worldly circumstances, these are principally the effect either of gross imprudence, of ill-regulated desires, or of bad or imperfect social institutions. All the grand sources, in short, of human suffering are in a great degree, many of them almost entirely, conquerable by human care and effort; and though their removal is grievously slow—though a long succession of generations will perish in the breach before the conquest is completed, and this world becomes all that, if will and knowledge were not wanting, it might easily be made—yet every mind sufficiently intelligent and generous to bear a part, however small and unconspicuous, in the endeavour, will draw a noble enjoyment from the contest itself, which he would not for any bribe in the form of selfish indulgence consent to be without.

And this leads to the true estimation of what is said by the objectors concerning the possibility, and the obligation, of learning to do without happiness. Unquestionably it is possible to do without happiness; it is done involuntarily by nineteen-twentieths of mankind, even in those parts of our present world which are least deep in barbarism; and it often has to be done voluntarily by the hero or the martyr, for the sake of something which he prizes more than his individual happiness. But this something, what is it, unless the happiness of others, or some of the requisites of happiness? It is noble to be capable of resigning entirely one's own portion of happiness, or chances of it: but, after all, this self-sacrifice must be for some end; it is not its own end; and if we are told that its end is not happiness, but virtue, which is better than happiness, I ask, would the sacrifice be made if the hero or martyr did not believe that it would earn for others immunity from similar sacrifices? Would it be made if he thought that his renunciation of happiness for himself would produce no fruit for any of his fellow creatures, but to make their lot like his, and place them also in the condition of persons who have renounced happiness? All honour to those who can abnegate for themselves the personal enjoyment of life, when by such renunciation they contribute worthily to increase the amount of happiness in the world; but he who does it, or professes to do it, for any other purpose, is no more deserving of admiration than the ascetic mounted on his pillar. He may be an inspiriting proof of what men *can* do, but assuredly not an example of what they *should*.

Though it is only in a very imperfect state of the world's arrangements that any one can best serve the happiness of others by the absolute sacrifice of his own, yet so long as the world is in that imperfect state, I fully acknowledge that the readiness to make such a sacrifice is the highest virtue which can be found in man. I will add, that in this condition of the world, paradoxical as the assertion may be, the conscious ability to do without happiness gives the best prospect of realising such happiness as is attainable. For nothing except that consciousness can raise a person above the chances of life, by making him feel that, let fate and fortune do their worst, they have not power to subdue him: which, once felt, frees him from excess of anxiety concerning the evils of life, and enables him, like many a Stoic in the worst times of the Roman Empire, to cultivate in tranquillity the sources of satisfaction accessible to him, without concerning himself about the uncertainty of their duration, any more than about their inevitable end.

Meanwhile, let utilitarians never cease to claim the morality of self devotion as a possession which belongs by as good a right to them, as either to the Stoic or to the Transcendentalist. The utilitarian morality does recognise in human beings the power of sacrificing their own greatest good for the good of others. It only refuses to admit that the sacrifice is itself a good. A sacrifice which does not increase, or tend to increase, the sum total of happiness, it considers as wasted. The only self-renunciation which it applauds, is devotion to the happiness, or to some of the means of happiness, of others; either of mankind collectively, or of individuals within the limits imposed by the collective interests of mankind.

I must again repeat, what the assailants of utilitarianism seldom have the justice to acknowledge, that the happiness which forms the utilitarian standard of what is right in conduct, is not the agent's own happiness, but that of all concerned. As between his own happiness and that of others, utilitarianism requires him to be as strictly impartial as a disinterested and benevolent spectator. In the golden rule of Jesus of Nazareth, we read the complete spirit of the ethics of utility. To do as you would be done by, and to love your neighbour as yourself, constitute the ideal perfection of utilitarian morality. As the means of making the nearest approach to this ideal, utility would enjoin, first, that laws and social arrangements should place the happiness, or (as speaking practically it may be called) the interest, of every individual, as nearly as possible in harmony with the interest of the whole; and secondly, that education and opinion, which have so vast a power over human character, should so use that power as to establish in the mind of every individual an indissoluble association between his own happiness and the good of the whole; especially between his own happiness and the practice of such modes of conduct, negative and positive, as regard for the universal happiness prescribes; so that not only he may be unable to conceive the possibility of happiness to himself, consistently with conduct opposed to the general good, but also that a direct impulse to promote the general good may be in every individual one of the habitual motives of action, and the sentiments connected therewith may fill a large and prominent place in every human being's sentient existence. If the impugners of the utilitarian morality represented it to their own minds in this its true character, I know not what recommendation possessed by any other morality they could possibly affirm to be wanting to it; what more beautiful or more exalted developments of human nature any other ethical system can be supposed to foster, or what springs of action, not accessible to the utilitarian, such systems rely on for giving effect to their mandates.

The objectors to utilitarianism cannot always be charged with representing it in a discreditable light. On the contrary, those among them who entertain anything like a just idea of its disinterested character, sometimes find fault with its standard as being too high for humanity. They say it is exacting too much to require that people shall always act from the inducement of promoting the general interests of society. But this is to mistake the very meaning of a standard of morals, and confound the rule of action with the motive of it. It is the business of ethics to tell us what are our duties, or by what test we may know them; but no system of ethics requires that the sole motive of all we do shall be a feeling of duty; on the contrary, ninety-nine hundredths of all our actions are done from other motives, and rightly so done, if the rule of duty does not condemn them. It is the more unjust to utilitarianism that this particular misapprehension should be made a ground of objection to it, inasmuch as utilitarian moralists have gone beyond almost all others in affirming that the motive has nothing to do with the morality of the action, though much with the worth of the agent. He who saves a fellow creature from drowning does what is morally right, whether his motive be duty, or the hope of being paid for his trouble; he who betrays the friend that trusts him, is guilty of a crime, even if his object be to serve another friend to whom he is under greater obligations. But to speak only of actions done from the motive of duty, and in direct obedience to principle: it is a misapprehension of the utilitarian mode of thought, to conceive it as implying that people should fix their minds upon so wide a generality as the world, or society at large. The great majority of good actions are intended not for the benefit of the world, but for that of individuals, of which the good of the world is made up; and the thoughts of the most virtuous man need not on these occasions travel beyond the particular persons concerned, except so far as is necessary to assure himself that in benefiting them he is not violating the rights, that is, the legitimate and authorised expectations, of any one else. The multiplication of happiness is, according to the utilitarian ethics, the object of virtue: the occasions on which any person (except one in a thousand) has it in his power to do this on an extended scale, in other words to be a public benefactor, are but exceptional; and on these occasions alone is he called on to consider public utility; in every other case, private utility, the interest or happiness of some few persons, is all he has to attend to. Those alone the influence of whose actions extends to society in general, need concern themselves habitually about so large an object. In the case of abstinences indeed—of things which people forbear to do from moral considerations, though the consequences in the particular case might be beneficial—it would be unworthy of an intelligent agent not to be consciously aware that the action is of a class which, if practised generally, would be generally injurious, and that this is the ground of the obligation to abstain from it. The amount of regard for the public interest implied in this recognition, is no greater than is demanded by every system of morals, for they all enjoin to abstain from whatever is manifestly pernicious to society.

The same considerations dispose of another reproach against the doctrine of utility, founded on a still grosser misconception of the purpose of a standard of morality, and of the very meaning of the words right and wrong. It is often affirmed that utilitarianism renders men cold and unsympathising; that it chills their moral feelings towards individuals; that it makes them regard only the dry and hard consideration of the consequences of actions, not taking into their moral estimate the qualities from which those actions emanate. If the assertion means that they do not allow their judgment respecting the rightness or wrongness of an action to be influenced by their opinion of the qualities of the person who does it, this is a complaint not against utilitarianism, but against having any standard of morality at all; for certainly no known ethical standard decides an action to be good or bad because it is done by a good or a bad man, still less because done by an amiable, a brave, or a benevolent man, or the contrary. These considerations are relevant, not to the estimation of actions, but of persons; and there is nothing in the utilitarian theory inconsistent with the fact that there are other things which interest us in persons besides the rightness and wrongness of their actions. The Stoics, indeed, with the paradoxical misuse of language which was part of their system, and by which they strove to raise themselves above all concern about anything but virtue, were fond of saying that he who has that has everything; that he, and only he, is rich, is beautiful, is a king. But no claim of this description is made for the virtuous man by the utilitarian doctrine. Utilitarians are quite aware that there are other desirable possessions and qualities besides virtue, and are perfectly willing to allow to all of them their full worth. They are also aware that a right action does not necessarily indicate a virtuous character, and that actions which are blamable, often proceed from qualities entitled to praise. When this is apparent in any particular case, it modifies their estimation, not certainly of the act, but of the agent. I grant that they are, notwithstanding, of opinion, that in the long run the best proof of a good character is good actions; and resolutely refuse to consider any mental disposition as good, of which the predominant tendency is to produce bad conduct. This makes them unpopular with many people; but it is an unpopularity which they must share with every one who regards the distinction between right and wrong in a serious light; and the reproach is not one which a conscientious utilitarian need be anxious to repel.

If no more be meant by the objection than that many utilitarians look on the morality of actions, as measured by the utilitarian standard, with too exclusive a regard, and do not lay sufficient stress upon the other beauties of character which go towards making a human being lovable or admirable, this may be admitted. Utilitarians who have cultivated their moral feelings, but not their sympathies nor their artistic perceptions, do fall into this mistake; and so do all other moralists under the same conditions. What can be said in excuse for other moralists is equally available for them, namely, that, if there is to be any error, it is better that it should be on that side. As a matter of fact, we may affirm that among utilitarians as among adherents of other systems, there is every imaginable degree of rigidity and of laxity in the application of their standard: some are even puritanically rigorous, while others are as indulgent as can possibly be desired by sinner or by sentimentalist. But on the whole, a doctrine which brings prominently forward the interest that mankind have in the repression and prevention of conduct which violates the moral law, is likely to be inferior to no other in turning the sanctions of opinion against such violations. It is true, the question, What does violate the moral law? is one on which those who recognise different standards of morality are likely now and then to differ. But difference of opinion on moral questions was not first introduced into the world by utilitarianism, while that doctrine does supply, if not always an easy, at all events a tangible and intelligible mode of deciding such differences.

It may not be superfluous to notice a few more of the common misapprehensions of utilitarian ethics, even those which are so obvious and gross that it might appear impossible for any person of candour and intelligence to fall into them; since persons, even of considerable mental endowments, often give themselves so little trouble to understand the bearings of any opinion against which they entertain a prejudice, and men are in general so little conscious of this voluntary ignorance as a defect, that the vulgarest misunderstandings of ethical doctrines are continually met with in the deliberate writings of persons of the greatest pretensions both to high principle and to philosophy. We not uncommonly hear the doctrine of utility inveighed against as a *godless* doctrine. If it be necessary to say anything at all against so mere an assumption, we may say that the question depends upon what idea we have formed of the moral character of the Deity. If it be a true belief that God desires, above all things, the happiness of his creatures, and that this was his purpose in their creation, utility is not only not a godless doctrine, but more profoundly religious than any other. If it be meant that utilitarianism does not recognise the revealed will of God as the supreme law of morals, I answer, that a utilitarian who believes in the perfect goodness and wisdom of God, necessarily believes that whatever God has thought fit to reveal on the subject of morals, must fulfil the requirements of utility in a supreme degree. But others besides utilitarians have been of opinion that the Christian revelation was intended, and is fitted, to inform the hearts and minds of mankind with a spirit which should enable them to find for themselves what is right, and incline them to do it when found, rather than to tell them, except in a very general way, what it is; and that we need a doctrine of ethics, carefully followed out, to *interpret* to us the will of God. Whether this opinion is correct or not, it is superfluous here to discuss; since whatever aid religion, either natural or revealed, can afford to ethical investigation, is as open to the utilitarian moralist as to any other. He can use it as the testimony of God to the usefulness or hurtfulness of any given course of action, by as good a right as others can use it for the indication of a transcendental law, having no connection with usefulness or with happiness.

Again, Utility is often summarily stigmatised as an immoral doctrine by giving it the name of Expediency, and taking advantage of the popular use of that term to contrast it with Principle. But the Expedient, in the sense in which it is opposed to the Right, generally means that which is expedient for the particular interest of the agent himself; as when a minister sacrifices the interests of his country to keep himself in place. When it means anything better than this, it means that which is expedient for some immediate object, some temporary purpose, but which violates a rule whose observance is expedient in a much higher degree. The Expedient, in this sense, instead of being the same thing with the useful, is a branch of the hurtful. Thus, it would often be expedient, for the purpose of getting over some momentary embarrassment, or attaining some object immediately useful to ourselves or others, to tell a lie. But inasmuch as the cultivation in ourselves of a sensitive feeling on the subject of veracity, is one of the most useful, and the enfeeblement of that feeling one of the most hurtful, things to which our conduct can be instrumental; and inasmuch as any, even unintentional, deviation from truth, does that much towards weakening the trustworthiness of human assertion, which is not only the principal support of all present social well-being, but the insufficiency of which does more than any one thing that can be named to keep back civilisation, virtue, everything on which human happiness on the largest scale depends; we feel that the violation, for a present advantage, of a rule of such transcendant expediency, is not expedient, and that he who, for the sake of a convenience to himself or to some other individual, does what depends on him to deprive mankind of the good, and inflict upon them the evil, involved in the greater or less reliance which they can place in each other's word, acts the part of one of their worst enemies. Yet that even this rule, sacred as it is, admits of possible exceptions, is acknowledged by all moralists; the chief of which is when the withholding of some fact (as of information from a malefactor, or of bad news from a person dangerously ill) would save an individual (especially an individual other than oneself) from great and unmerited evil, and when the withholding can only be effected by denial. But in order that the exception may not extend itself beyond the need, and may have the least possible effect in weakening reliance on veracity, it ought to be recognised, and, if possible, its limits defined; and if the principle of utility is good for anything, it must be good for weighing these conflicting utilities against one another, and marking out the region within which one or the other preponderates.

Again, defenders of utility often find themselves called upon to reply to such objections as this—that there is not time, previous to action, for calculating and weighing the effects of any line of conduct on the general happiness. This is exactly as if any one were to say that it is impossible to guide our conduct by Christianity, because there is not time, on every occasion on which anything has to be done, to read through the Old and New Testaments. The answer to the objection is, that there has been ample time, namely, the whole past duration of the human species. During all that time, mankind have been learning by experience the tendencies of actions; on which experience all the prudence, as well as all the morality of life, are dependent. People talk as if the commencement of this course of experience had hitherto been put off, and as if, at the moment when some man feels tempted to meddle with the property or life of another, he had to begin considering for the first time whether murder and theft are injurious to human happiness. Even then I do not think that he would find the question very puzzling; but, at all events, the matter is now done to his hand. It is truly a whimsical supposition that, if mankind were agreed in considering utility to be the test of morality, they would remain without any agreement as to what *is* useful, and would take no measures for having their notions on the subject taught to the young, and enforced by law and opinion. There is no difficulty in proving any ethical standard whatever to work ill, if we suppose universal idiocy to be conjoined with it;

but on any hypothesis short of that, mankind must by this time have acquired positive beliefs as to the effects of some actions on their happiness; and the beliefs which have thus come down are the rules of morality for the multitude, and for the philosopher until he has succeeded in finding better. That philosophers might easily do this, even now, on many subjects; that the received code of ethics is by no means of divine right; and that mankind have still much to learn as to the effects of actions on the general happiness, I admit, or rather, earnestly maintain. The corollaries from the principle of utility, like the precepts of every practical art, admit of indefinite improvement, and, in a progressive state of the human mind, their improvement is perpetually going on. But to consider the rules of morality as improvable, is one thing; to pass over the intermediate generalisations entirely, and endeavour to test each individual action by the first principle, is another. It is a strange notion that the acknowledgment of a first principle is inconsistent with the admission of secondary ones. To inform a traveller respecting the place of his ultimate destination, is not to forbid the use of landmarks and direction-posts on the way. The proposition that happiness is the end and aim of morality, does not mean that no road ought to be laid down to that goal, or that persons going thither should not be advised to take one direction rather than another. Men really ought to leave off talking a kind of nonsense on this subject, which they would neither talk nor listen to on other matters of practical concernment. Nobody argues that the art of navigation is not founded on astronomy, because sailors cannot wait to calculate the Nautical Almanack. Being rational creatures, they go to sea with it ready calculated; and all rational creatures go out upon the sea of life with their minds made up on the common questions of right and wrong, as well as on many of the far more difficult questions of wise and foolish. And this, as long as foresight is a human quality, it is to be presumed they will continue to do. Whatever we adopt as the fundamental principle of morality, we require subordinate principles to apply it by; the impossibility of doing without them, being common to all systems, can afford no argument against any one in particular; but gravely to argue as if no such secondary principles could be had, and as if mankind had remained till now, and always must remain, without drawing any general conclusions from the experience of human life, is as high a pitch, I think, as absurdity has ever reached in philosophical controversy.

The remainder of the stock arguments against utilitarianism mostly consist in laying to its charge the common infirmities of human nature, and the general difficulties which embarrass conscientious persons in shaping their course through life. We are told that a utilitarian will be apt to make his own particular case an exception to moral rules, and, when under temptation, will see a utility in the breach of a rule, greater than he will see in its observance. But is utility the only creed which is able to furnish us with excuses for evil doing, and means of cheating our own conscience? They are afforded in abundance by all doctrines which recognise as a fact in morals the existence of conflicting considerations; which all doctrines do, that have been believed by sane persons. It is not the fault of any creed, but of the complicated nature of human affairs, that rules of conduct cannot be so framed as to require no exceptions, and that hardly any kind of action can safely be laid down as either always obligatory or always condemnable. There is no ethical creed which does not temper the rigidity of its laws, by giving a certain latitude, under the moral responsibility of the agent, for accommodation to peculiarities of circumstances; and under every creed, at the opening thus made, self-deception and dishonest casuistry get in. There exists no moral system under which there do not arise unequivocal cases of conflicting obligation. These are the real difficulties, the knotty points both in the theory of ethics, and in the conscientious guidance of personal conduct. They are overcome practically, with greater or with less success, according to the intellect and virtue of the individual; but it can hardly be pretended that any one will be the less qualified for dealing with them, from possessing an ultimate standard to which conflicting rights and duties can be referred. If utility is the ultimate source of moral obligations, utility may be invoked to decide between them when their demands are incompatible. Though the application of the standard may be difficult, it is better than none at all: while in other systems, the moral laws all claiming independent authority, there is no common umpire entitled to interfere between them; their claims to precedence one over another rest on little better than sophistry, and unless determined, as they generally are, by the unacknowledged influence of considerations of utility, afford a free scope for the action of personal desires and partialities. We must remember that only in these cases of conflict between secondary principles is it requisite that first principles should be appealed to. There is no case of moral obligation in which some secondary principle is not involved; and if only one, there can seldom be any real doubt which one it is, in the mind of any person by whom the principle itself is recognised.

GROUNDWORK OF THE METAPHYSIC OF MORALS

(Chapter I)

IMMANUEL KANT

(trans. by H. J. Paton)

Immanuel Kant (1724–1804) was a German philosopher acknowledged as one of the greatest minds in the history of philosophy. His main concerns were epistemology, metaphysics, and ethics, in that order. His principal work, the *Critique of Pure Reason,* deals with epistemic problems, or the theory of knowledge, and attempts a synthesis of rationalism and empiricism, the two main streams of thought as to how reliable knowledge is achieved.

Kant's *Groundwork of the Metaphysic of Morals* is concerned with establishing a foundation for ethical conduct. Instead of Mill's Principle of Utility—that actions are right in proportion to the happiness promoted—Kant offers his Categorical Imperative, which states that we should act so that the maxim for our actions could become a universal law. That is, if we can rationally apprehend that our conduct is an instance of a universal rule of conduct, then we are assured of its moral propriety. It is the essential nature of the act, then, that makes it ethically obligatory. This type of thinking is eminently compatible with Antigone's position.

PASSAGE FROM ORDINARY RATIONAL KNOWLEDGE OF MORALITY TO PHILOSOPHICAL

[*The good will*]

It is impossible to conceive anything at all in the world, or even out of it, which can be taken as good without qualification, except a *good will.* Intelligence, wit, judgement, and any other *talents* of the mind we may care to name, or courage, resolution, and constancy of purpose, as qualities of *temperament,* are without doubt good and desirable in many respects; but they can also be extremely bad and hurtful when the will is not good which has to make use of these gifts of nature, and which for this reason has the term '*character*' applied to its peculiar quality. It is exactly the same with *gifts of fortune.* Power, wealth, honour, even health and that complete well-being and contentment with one's state which goes by the name of '*happiness*', produce boldness, and as a consequence often overboldness as well, unless a good will is present by which their influence on the mind—and so too the whole principle of action—may be corrected and adjusted to universal ends; not to mention that a rational and impartial spectator can never feel approval in contemplating the uninterrupted prosperity of a being graced by no touch of a pure and good will, and that consequently a good will seems to constitute the indispensable condition of our very worthiness to be happy.

Some qualities are even helpful to this good will itself and can make its task very much easier. They have none the less no inner unconditioned worth, but rather presuppose a good will which sets a limit to the esteem in which they are rightly held and does not permit us to regard them as absolutely good. Moderation in affections and passions, self-control, and sober reflexion are not only good in many respects: they may even seem to constitute part of the *inner* worth of a person. Yet they are far from being properly described as good without qualification (however unconditionally they have been commended by the ancients). For without the principles of a good will they may become exceedingly bad; and the very coolness of a scoundrel makes him, not merely more dangerous, but also immediately more abominable in our eyes than we should have taken him to be without it.

[*The good will and its results*]

A good will is not good because of what it effects or accomplishes—because of its fitness for attaining some proposed end: it is good through its willing alone—that is, good in itself. Considered in itself it is to be esteemed beyond comparison as far higher than anything it could ever bring about merely in order to favour some inclination or, if you like, the sum total of inclinations. Even if, by some special disfavour of destiny or by the niggardly endowment of step-motherly nature, this will is entirely lacking in power to carry out its intentions; if by its utmost effort it still accomplishes nothing, and only good will is left (not, admittedly, as a mere wish, but as the straining of every means so far as they are in our control); even then it would still shine like a jewel for its own sake as something which has its full value in itself. Its usefulness or fruitfulness can neither add to, nor subtract from, this value. Its usefulness would be merely, as it were, the setting which enables us to handle it better in our ordinary dealings or to attract the attention of those not yet sufficiently expert, but not to commend it to experts or to determine its value.

[*The function of reason*]

Yet in this Idea of the absolute value of a mere will, all useful results being left out of account in its assessment, there is something so strange that, in spite of all the agreement it receives even from ordinary reason, there must arise the suspicion that perhaps its secret basis is merely some high-flown fantasticality, and that we may have misunderstood the purpose of nature in attaching reason to our will as its governor. We will therefore submit our Idea to an examination from this point of view.

In the natural constitution of an organic being—that is, of one contrived for the purpose of life—let us take it as a principle that in it no organ is to be found for any end unless it is also the most appropriate to that end and the best fitted for it. Suppose now that for a being possessed of reason and a will the real purpose of nature were his *preservation*, his *welfare*, or in a word his *happiness*. In that case nature would have hit on a very bad arrangement by choosing reason in the creature to carry out this purpose. For all the actions he has to perform with this end in view, and the whole rule of his behaviour, would have been mapped out for him far more accurately by instinct; and the end in question could have been maintained far more surely by instinct than it ever can be by reason. If reason should have been imparted to this favoured creature as well, it would have had to serve him only for contemplating the happy disposition of his nature, for admiring it, for enjoying it, and for being grateful to its beneficent Cause—not for subjecting his power of appetition to such feeble and defective guidance or for meddling incompetently with the purposes of nature. In a word, nature would have prevented reason from striking out into a *practical use* and from presuming, with its feeble vision, to think out for itself a plan for happiness and for the means to its attainment. Nature would herself have taken over the choice, not only of ends, but also of means, and would with wise precaution have entrusted both to instinct alone.

In actual fact too we find that the more a cultivated reason concerns itself with the aim of enjoying life and happiness, the farther does man get away from true contentment. This is why there arises in many, and that too in those who have made most trial of this use of reason, if they are only candid enough to admit it, a certain degree of *misology*—that is, a hatred of reason; for when they balance all the advantage they draw, I will not say from thinking out all the arts of ordinary indulgence, but even from science (which in the last resort seems to them to be also an indulgence of the mind), they discover that they have in fact only brought more trouble on their heads than they have gained in the way of happiness. On this account they come to envy, rather than to despise, the more common run of men, who are closer to the guidance of mere natural instinct, and who do not allow their reason to have much influence on their conduct. So far we must admit that the judgement of those who seek to moderate—and even to reduce below zero—the conceited glorification of such advantages as reason is supposed to provide in the way of happiness and contentment with life is in no way soured or ungrateful to the goodness with which the world is governed. These judgements rather have as their hidden ground the Idea of another and much more worthy purpose of existence, for which, and not for happiness, reason is quite properly designed, and to which, therefore, as a supreme condition the private purposes of man must for the most part be subordinated.

For since reason is not sufficiently serviceable for guiding the will safely as regards its objects and the satisfaction of all our needs (which it in part even multiplies)—a purpose for which an implanted natural instinct would have led us much more surely; and since none the less reason has been imparted to us as a practical power—that is, as one which is to have influence on the *will*; its true function must be to produce a *will* which is *good*, not as a *means* to some further end, but *in itself*; and for this function reason was absolutely necessary in a world where nature, in distributing her aptitudes, has everywhere else gone to work in a purposive manner. Such a will need not on this account be the sole and complete good, but it must be the highest good and the condition of all the rest, even of all our demands for happiness. In that case we can easily reconcile with the wisdom of nature our observation that the cultivation of reason which is required for the first and unconditioned purpose may in many ways, at least in this life, restrict the attainment of the second purpose—namely, happiness—which is always conditioned; and indeed that it can even reduce happiness to less than zero without nature proceeding contrary to its purpose; for reason, which recognises as its highest practical function the establishment of a good will, in attaining this end is capable only of its own peculiar kind of contentment—contentment in fulfilling a purpose which in turn is determined by reason alone, even if this fulfilment should often involve interference with the purposes of inclination.

[The good will and duty]

We have now to elucidate the concept of a will estimable in itself and good apart from any further end. This concept, which is already present in a sound natural understanding and requires not so much to be taught as merely to be clarified, always holds the highest place in estimating the total worth of our actions and constitutes the condition of all the rest. We will therefore take up the concept of *duty*, which includes that of a good will, exposed, however, to certain subjective limitations and obstacles. These, so far from hiding a good will or disguising it, rather bring it out by contrast and make it shine forth more brightly.

I will here pass over all actions already recognised as contrary to duty, however useful they may be with a view to this or that end; for about these the question does not even arise whether they could have been done *for the sake of duty* inasmuch as they are directly opposed to it. I will also set aside actions which in fact accord with duty, yet for which men have *no immediate inclination*, but perform them because impelled to do so by some other inclination. For there it is easy to decide whether the action which accords with duty has been done *from duty* or from some purpose of self-interest. This distinction is far more difficult to perceive when the action accords with duty and the subject has in addition an *immediate* inclination to the action. For example, it certainly accords with duty that a grocer should not overcharge his inexperienced customer; and where there is much competition a sensible shopkeeper refrains from so doing and keeps to a fixed and general price for everybody so that a child can buy from him just as well as anyone else. Thus people are served *honestly*; but this is not nearly enough to justify us in believing that the shopkeeper has acted in this way from duty or from principles of fair dealing; his interest required him to do so. We cannot assume him to have in addition an immediate inclination towards his customers, leading him, as it were out of love, to give no man preference over another in the matter of price. Thus the action was done neither from duty nor from immediate inclination, but solely from purposes of self-interest.

On the other hand, to preserve one's life is a duty, and besides this every one has also an immediate inclination to do so. But on account of this the often anxious precautions taken by the greater part of mankind for this purpose have no inner worth, and the maxim of their action is without moral content. They do protect their lives *in conformity with duty*, but not *from the motive of duty*. When on the contrary, disappointments and hopeless misery have quite taken away the taste for life; when a wretched man, strong in soul and more angered at his fate than faint-hearted or cast down, longs for death and still preserves his life without loving it—not from inclination or fear but from duty; then indeed his maxim has a moral content.

To help others where one can is a duty, and besides this there are many spirits of so sympathetic a temper that, without any further motive of vanity or self-interest, they find an inner pleasure in spreading happiness around them and take delight in the contentment of others as their own work. Yet I maintain that in such a case an action of this kind, however right and however amiable it may be, has still no genuinely moral worth. It stands on the same footing as other inclinations—for example, the inclination for honour, which if fortunate enough to hit on something beneficial and right and consequently honourable, deserves praise and encouragement, but not esteem; for its maxim lacks moral content, namely, the performance of such actions, not from inclination, but *from duty*. Suppose then that the mind of this friend of man were overclouded by sorrows of his own which extinguished all sympathy with the fate of others, but that he still had power to help those in distress, though no longer stirred by the need of others because sufficiently occupied with his own; and suppose that, when no longer moved by any inclination, he tears himself out of this deadly insensibility and does the action without any inclination for the sake of duty alone; then for the first time his action has its genuine moral worth. Still further: if nature had implanted little sympathy in this or that man's heart; if (being in other respects an honest fellow) he were cold in temperament and indifferent to the sufferings of others—perhaps because, being endowed with the special gift of patience and robust endurance in his own sufferings, he assumed the like in others or even demanded it; if such a man (who would in truth not be the worst product of nature) were not exactly fashioned by her to be a philanthropist, would he not still find in himself a source from which he might draw a worth far higher than any that a good-natured temperament can have? Assuredly he would. It is precisely in this that the worth of character begins to show—a moral worth and beyond all comparison the highest— namely, that he does good, not from inclination, but from duty.

To assure one's own happiness is a duty (at least indirectly); for discontent with one's state, in a press of cares and amidst unsatisfied wants, might easily become a great *temptation to the transgression of duty*. But here also, apart from regard to duty, all men have already of themselves the strongest and deepest inclination towards happiness, because precisely in this Idea of happiness all inclinations are combined into a sum total. The prescription for happiness is, however, often so constituted as greatly to interfere with some inclinations, and yet men cannot form under the name of 'happiness' any determinate and assured conception of the satisfaction of all inclinations as a sum. Hence it is not to be wondered at that a single inclination which is determinate as to what it promises and as to the time of its satisfaction may outweigh a wavering Idea; and that a man, for example, a sufferer from gout, may choose to enjoy what he fancies and put up with what he can—on the ground that on balance he has here at least not killed the enjoyment of the present moment because of some possibly groundless expectations of the good fortune supposed to attach to soundness of health. But in this case also, when the universal inclination towards happiness has failed to determine his will, when good health, at least for him, has not entered into his calculations as so necessary, what remains over, here as in other cases, is a law—the law of furthering his happiness, not from inclination, but from duty; and in this for the first time his conduct has a real moral worth.

It is doubtless in this sense that we should understand too the passages from Scripture in which we are commanded to love our neighbour and even our enemy. For love out of inclination cannot be commanded; but kindness done from duty—although no inclination impels us, and even although natural and unconquerable disinclination stands in our way— is *practical*, and not *pathological*, love, residing in the will and not in the propensions of feeling, in principles of action and not of melting compassion; and it is this practical love alone which can be an object of command.

[The formal principle of duty]

Our second proposition is this: An action done from duty has its moral worth, *not in the purpose* to be attained by it, but in the maxim according with which it is decided upon; it depends therefore, not on the realisation of the object of the action, but solely on the *principle* of *volition* in accordance with which, irrespective of all objects of the faculty of desire, the action has been performed. That the purposes we may have in our actions, and also their effects considered as ends and motives of the will, can give to actions no unconditioned and moral worth is clear from what has gone before. Where then can this worth be found if we are not to find it in the will's relation to the effect hoped for from the action? It can be found nowhere but *in the principle of the will*, irrespective of the ends which can be brought about by such an action; for between its *a priori* principle, which is formal, and its *a posteriori* motive, which is material, the will stands, so to speak, at a parting of the ways; and since it must be determined by some principle, it will have to be determined by the formal principle of volition when an action is done from duty, where, as we have seen, every material principle is taken away from it.

[Reverence for the law]

Our third proposition, as an inference from the two preceding, I would express thus: *Duty is the necessity to act out of reverence for the law.* For an object as the effect of my proposed action I can have an *inclination*, but *never reverence*, precisely because it is merely the effect, and not the activity, of a will. Similarly for inclination as such, whether my own or that of another, I cannot have reverence: I can at most in the first case approve, and in the second case sometimes even love—that is, regard it as favourable to my own advantage. Only something which is conjoined with my will solely as a ground and never as an effect—something which does not serve my inclination, but outweighs it or at least leaves it entirely out of account in my choice—and therefore only bare law for its own sake, can be an object of reverence and therewith a command. Now an action done from duty has to set aside altogether the influence of inclination, and along with inclination every object of the will; so there is nothing left able to determine the will except objectively the *law* and subjectively *pure reverence* for this practical law, and therefore the maxim[1] of obeying this law even to the detriment of all my inclinations.

Thus the moral worth of an action does not depend on the result expected from it, and so too does not depend on any principle of action that needs to borrow its motive from this expected result. For all these results (agreeable states and even the promotion of happiness in others) could have been brought about by other causes as well, and consequently their production did not require the will of a rational being, in which, however, the highest and unconditioned good can alone be found. Therefore nothing but the *idea of the law* in itself, *which admittedly is present only in a rational being*—so far as it, and not an expected result, is the ground determining the will—can constitute that pre-eminent good which we call moral, a good which is already present in the person acting on this idea and has not to be awaited merely from the result.[2]

---

[1] A *maxim* is the subjective principle of a volition: an objective principle (that is, one which would also serve subjectively as a practical principle for all rational beings if reason had full control over the faculty of desire) is a practical *law*. [H. J. Paton.]

[2] It might be urged against me that I have merely tried, under cover of the word '*reverence*', to take refuge in an obscure feeling instead of giving a clearly articulated answer to the question by means of a concept of reason. Yet although reverence is a feeling, it is not a feeling *received* through outside influence, but one *self-produced* by a rational concept, and therefore specifically distinct from feelings of the first kind, all of which can be reduced to inclination or fear. What I recognise immediately as law for me, I recognise with reverence, which means merely consciousness of the *subordination* of my will to a law without the mediation of external influences on my senses. Immediate determination of the will by the law and consciousness of this determination is called '*reverence*', so that reverence is regarded as the *effect* of the law on the subject and not as the *cause*

[*The categorical imperative*]

But what kind of law can this be the thought of which, even without regard to the results expected from it, has to determine the will if this is to be called good absolutely and without qualification? Since I have robbed the will of every inducement that might arise for it as a consequence of obeying any particular law, nothing is left but the conformity of actions to universal law as such, and this alone must serve the will as its principle. That is to say, I ought never to act except in such a way *that I can also will that my maxim should become a universal law*. Here bare conformity to universal law as such (without having as its base any law prescribing particular actions) is what serves the will as its principle, and must so serve it if duty is not to be everywhere an empty delusion and a chimerical concept. The ordinary reason of mankind also agrees with this completely in its practical judgements and always has the aforesaid principle before its eyes.

Take this question, for example. May I not, when I am hard pressed, make a promise with the intention of not keeping it? Here I readily distinguish the two senses which the question can have—Is it prudent, or is it right, to make a false promise? The first no doubt can often be the case. I do indeed see that it is not enough for me to extricate myself from present embarrassment by this subterfuge: I have to consider whether from this lie there may not subsequently accrue to me much greater inconvenience than that from which I now escape, and also—since, with all my supposed *astuteness*, to foresee the consequences is not so easy that I can be sure there is no chance, once confidence in me is lost, of this proving far more disadvantageous than all the ills I now think to avoid—whether it may not be a *more prudent* action to proceed here on a general maxim and make it my habit not to give a promise except with the intention of keeping it. Yet it becomes clear to me at once that such a maxim is always founded solely on fear of consequences. To tell the truth for the sake of duty is something entirely different from doing so out of concern for inconvenient results; for in the first case the concept of the action already contains in itself a law for me, while in the second case I have first of all to look around elsewhere in order to see what effects may be bound up with it for me. When I deviate from the principle of duty, this is quite

---

of the law. Reverence is properly awareness of a value which demolishes my self-love. Hence there is something which is regarded neither as an object of inclination nor as an object of fear, though it has at the same time analogy with both. The *object* of reverence is the *law* alone—that law which we impose *on ourselves* but yet as necessary in itself. Considered as a law, we are subject to it without any consultation of self-love; considered as self-imposed it is a consequence of our will. In the first respect it is analogous to fear, in the second to inclination. All reverence for a person is properly only reverence for the law (of honesty and so on) of which that person gives us an example. Because we regard the developments of our talents as a duty, we see too in a man of talent a sort of *example of the law* (the law of becoming like him by practice), and this is what constitutes our reverence for him. All moral *interest*, so-called, consists solely in *reverence* for the law. [H. J. Paton.]

certainly bad; but if I desert my prudential maxim, this can often be greatly to my advantage, though it is admittedly safer to stick to it. Suppose I seek, however, to learn in the quickest way and yet unerringly how to solve the problem 'Does a lying promise accord with duty?' I have then to ask myself 'Should I really be content that my maxim (the maxim of getting out of a difficulty by a false promise) should hold as a universal law (one valid both for myself and others)? And could I really say to myself that every one may make a false promise if he finds himself in a difficulty from which he can extricate himself in no other way?' I then become aware at once that I can indeed will to lie, but I can by no means will a universal law of lying; for by such a law there could properly be no promises at all, since it would be futile to profess a will for future action to others who would not believe my profession or who, if they did so overhastily, would pay me back in like coin; and consequently my maxim, as soon as it was made a universal law, would be bound to annul itself.

Thus I need no far-reaching ingenuity to find out what I have to do in order to possess a good will. Inexperienced in the course of world affairs and incapable of being prepared for all the chances that happen in it, I ask myself only 'Can you also will that your maxim should become a universal law?' Where you cannot, it is to be rejected, and that not because of a prospective loss to you or even to others, but because it cannot fit as a principle into a possible enactment of universal law. For such an enactment reason compels my immediate reverence, into whose grounds (which the philosopher may investigate) I have as yet no *insight*, although I do at least understand this much: reverence is the assessment of a worth which far outweighs all the worth of what is commended by inclination, and the necessity for me to act out of *pure* reverence for the practical law is what constitutes duty, to which every other motive must give way because it is the condition of a will good *in itself*, whose value is above all else.

[Ordinary practical reason]

In studying the moral knowledge of ordinary human reason we have now arrived at its first principle. This principle it admittedly does not conceive thus abstractly in its universal form; but it does always have it actually before its eyes and does use it as a norm of judgement. It would be easy to show here how human reason, with this compass in hand, is well able to distinguish, in all cases that present themselves, what is good or evil, right or wrong—provided that, without the least attempt to teach it anything new, we merely make reason attend, as Socrates did, to its own principle; and how in consequence there is no need of science or philosophy for knowing what man has to do in order to be honest and good, and indeed to be wise and virtuous. It might even be surmised in advance that acquaintance with what every man is obliged to do, and so also to know, will be the affair of every man, even the most ordinary. Yet we cannot observe without admiration the great advantage which the power of practical judgement has over that of theoretical in the minds of ordinary men. In theoretical judgements, when ordinary reason ventures to depart from the laws of experience and the perceptions of sense, it falls into sheer unintelligibility and self-contradiction, or at least into a chaos of uncertainty, obscurity, and vacillation. On the practical side, however, the power of judgement first begins to show what advantages it has in itself when the ordinary mind excludes all sensuous motives from its practical laws. Then ordinary intelligence becomes even subtle—it may be in juggling with conscience or with other claims as to what is to be called right, or in trying to determine honestly for its own instruction the value of various actions; and, what is most important, it can in the latter case have as good hope of hitting the mark as any that a philosopher can promise himself. Indeed it is almost surer in this than even a philosopher, because he can have no principle different from that of ordinary intelligence, but may easily confuse his judgement with a mass of alien and irrelevant considerations and cause it to swerve from the straight path. Might it not then be more advisable in moral questions to abide by the judgement of ordinary reason and, at the most, to bring in philosophy only in order to set forth the system of morals more fully and intelligibly and to present its rules in a form more convenient for use (though still more so for disputation)—but not in order to lead ordinary human intelligence away from its happy simplicity in respect of action and to set it by means of philosophy on a new path of enquiry and instruction?

[The need for philosophy]

Innocence is a splendid thing, only it has the misfortune not to keep very well and to be easily misled. On this account even wisdom—which in itself consists more in doing and not doing than in knowing—does require science as well, not in order to learn from it, but in order to win acceptance and durability for its own prescriptions. Man feels in himself a powerful counterweight to all the commands of duty presented to him by reason as so worthy of esteem—the counterweight of his needs and inclinations, whose total satisfaction he grasps under the name of 'happiness'. But reason, without promising anything to inclination, enjoins its commands relentlessly, and therefore, so to speak, with disregard and neglect of these turbulent and seemingly equitable claims (which refuse to be suppressed by any command). From this there arises a *natural dialectic*—that is, a disposition to quibble with these strict laws of duty, to throw doubt on their validity or at least on their purity and strictness, and to make them, where possible, more adapted to our wishes and inclinations; that is, to pervert their very foundations and destroy their whole dignity—a result which in the end even ordinary human reason is unable to approve.

In this way the *common reason of mankind* is impelled, not by any need for speculation (which never assails it so long as it is content to be mere sound reason), but on practical grounds themselves, to leave its own sphere and take a step into the field of *practical philosophy*. It there seeks to acquire information and precise instruction about the source of its own principle, and about the correct function of this principle in comparison with maxims based on need and inclination, in order that it may escape from the embarrassment of antagonistic claims and may avoid the risk of losing all genuine moral principles because of the ambiguity into which it easily falls. Thus ordinary reason, when cultivated in its practical use, gives rise insensibly to a *dialectic* which constrains it to seek help in philosophy, just as happens in its theoretical use; and consequently in the first case as little as in the second will it anywhere else than in a full critique of our reason be able to find peace.

2

Dedication to God

MURDER IN THE CATHEDRAL
(Part I)
T. S. ELIOT

T. S. Eliot (1888–1965) was an American-born British poet, dramatist, and essayist whose poetic style and critical writings greatly influenced English poetry in the first half of the twentieth century. *The Lovesong of J. Alfred Prufrock, The Wasteland,* and the *Four Quartets* are his best-known poems; his major plays include *Murder in the Cathedral, The Cocktail Party,* and *The Confidential Clerk.*

Murder in the Cathedral clearly illustrates Eliot's ideal of pure dedication to the divine will. A provocative part of Eliot's play concerns the temptations that Thomas Becket suffers in trying to maintain the highest motivations in his actions. He successfully resists numerous enticements: sensuous enjoyment; political power that will yield glory and the opportunity for improving the order of the world; common cause with the people in a revolution against the king; and pride in defeating his enemies and winning the eternal gratitude of men for his saintliness. The last temptation is the most insidious since Becket's pride in his own high intentions is used to make him doubt his overall purpose.

The following section of the play begins where Becket, now Archbishop, has returned to Canterbury after a seven-year absence in France. His return signifies that for the sake of Christendom he is now prepared to oppose the power of King Henry, with all the personal risks entailed by the struggle.

As the scene opens, the Chorus of Women have expressed the wish that Thomas return to France and remain their spiritual leader in exile; then at least there would be peace; the priests try to quiet the women.

[*Enter* THOMAS.]
THOMAS: Peace. And let them be, in their exaltation.
They speak better than they know, and beyond your understanding.
They know and do not know, what it is to act or suffer.
They know and do not know, that acting is suffering
And suffering is action. Neither does the actor suffer
Nor the patient act. But both are fixed
In an eternal action, an eternal patience
To which all must consent that it may be willed

And which all must suffer that they may will it,
That the pattern may subsist, for the pattern is the action
And the suffering, that the wheel may turn and still
Be forever still.

SECOND PRIEST: O my Lord, forgive me, I did not see you coming,
Engrossed by the chatter of these foolish women.
Forgive us, my Lord, you would have had a better welcome
If we had been sooner prepared for the event.
But your Lordship knows that seven years of waiting,
Seven years of prayer, seven years of emptiness,
Have better prepared our hearts for your coming,
Than seven days could make ready Canterbury.
However, I will have fires laid in all your rooms
To take the chill off our English December,
Your Lordship now being used to a better climate.
Your Lordship will find your rooms in order as you left them.

THOMAS: And will try to leave them in order as I find them.
I am more than grateful for all your kind attentions.
These are small matters. Little rest in Canterbury
With eager enemies restless about us.
Rebellious bishops, York, London, Salisbury,
Would have intercepted our letters,
Filled the coast with spies and sent to meet me
Some who hold me in bitterest hate.
By God's grace aware of their prevision
I sent my letters on another day,
Had fair crossing, found at Sandwich
Broc, Warenne, and the Sheriff of Kent,
Those who had sworn to have my head from me.
Only John, the Dean of Salisbury,
Fearing for the King's name, warning against treason,
Made them hold their hands. So for the time
We are unmolested.

FIRST PRIEST: But do they follow after?

THOMAS: For a little time the hungry hawk
Will only soar and hover, circling lower,
Waiting excuse, pretence, opportunity.
End will be simple, sudden, God-given.
Meanwhile the substance of our first act
Will be shadows, and the strife with shadows.
Heavier the interval than the consummation.
All things prepare the event. Watch.

[*Enter* FIRST TEMPTER.]

FIRST TEMPTER: You see, my Lord, I do not wait upon ceremony:
Here I have come, forgetting all acrimony,
Hoping that your present gravity

Will find excuse for my humble levity
Remembering all the good time past.
Your Lordship won't despise an old friend out of favour?
Old Tom, gay Tom, Becket of London,
Your Lordship won't forget that evening on the river
When the King, and you and I were all friends together?
Friendship should be more than biting Time can sever.
What, my Lord, now that you recover
Favour with the King, shall we say that summer's over
Or that the good time cannot last?
Fluting in the meadows, viols in the hall,
Laughter and apple-blossom floating on the water,
Singing at nightfall, whispering in chambers,
Fires devouring the winter season,
Eating up the darkness, with wit and wine and wisdom!
Now that the King and you are in amity,
Clergy and laity may return to gaiety,
Mirth and sportfulness need not walk warily.

THOMAS: You talk of seasons that are past. I remember
Not worth forgetting.

TEMPTER: And of the new season.
Spring has come in winter. Snow in the branches
Shall float as sweet as blossoms. Ice along the ditches
Mirror the sunlight. Love in the orchard
Send the sap shooting. Mirth matches melancholy.

THOMAS: We do not know very much of the future
Except that from generation to generation
The same things happen again and again.
Men learn little from others' experience.
But in the life of one man, never
The same time returns. Sever
The cord, shed the scale. Only
The fool, fixed in his folly, may think
He can turn the wheel on which he turns.

TEMPTER: My Lord, a nod is as good as a wink.
A man will often love what he spurns.
For the good times past, that are come again
I am your man.

THOMAS: Not in this train.
Look to your behaviour. You were safer
Think of penitence and follow your master.

TEMPTER: Not at this gait!
If you go so fast, others may go faster.
Your Lordship is too proud!
The safest beast is not the one that roars most loud.
This was not the way of the King our master!

You were not used to be so hard upon sinners
When they were your friends. Be easy, man!
The easy man lives to eat the best dinners.
Take a friend's advice. Leave well alone,
Or your goose may be cooked and eaten to the bone.
THOMAS: You come twenty years too late.
TEMPTER: Then I leave you to your fate.
I leave you to the pleasures of your higher vices,
Which will have to be paid for at higher prices.
Farewell, my Lord, I do not wait upon ceremony,
I leave as I came, forgetting all acrimony,
Hoping that your present gravity
Will find excuse for my humble levity.
If you will remember me, my Lord, at your prayers,
I'll remember you at kissing-time below the stairs.
THOMAS: Leave-well-alone, the springtime fancy,
So one thought goes whistling down the wind.
The impossible is still temptation.
The impossible, the undesirable,
Voices under sleep, waking a dead world,
So that the mind may not be whole in the present.
[*Enter* SECOND TEMPTER.]
SECOND TEMPTER. Your Lordship has forgotten me, perhaps. I will remind
    you.
We met at Clarendon, at Northampton,
And last at Montmirail, in Maine. Now that I have recalled them,
Let us but set these not too pleasant memories
In balance against other, earlier
And weightier ones: those of the Chancellorship.
See how the late ones rise! The master of policy
Whom all acknowledged, should guide the state again.
THOMAS: Your meaning?
TEMPTER: The Chancellorship that you resigned
When you were made Archbishop—that was a mistake
On your part—still may be regained. Think, my Lord,
Power obtained grows to glory,
Life lasting, a permanent possession,
A templed tomb, monument of marble.
Rule over men reckon no madness.
THOMAS: To the man of God what gladness?
TEMPTER: Sadness
Only to those giving love to God alone.
Fare forward, shun two files of shadows:
Mirth merrymaking, melting strength in sweetness,
Fiddling to feebleness, doomed to disdain;
And godlovers' longings, lost in God.

> Shall he who held the solid substance
> Wander waking with deceitful shadows?
> Power is present. Holiness hereafter.

THOMAS: Who then?

TEMPTER: The Chancellor. King and Chancellor.
> King commands. Chancellor richly rules.
> This is a sentence not taught in the schools.
> To set down the great, protect the poor,
> Beneath the throne of God can man do more?
> Disarm the ruffian, strengthen the laws,
> Rule for the good of the better cause,
> Dispensing justice make all even,
> Is thrive on earth, and perhaps in heaven.

THOMAS: What means?

TEMPTER: Real Power
> Is purchased at price of a certain submission.
> Your spiritual power is earthly perdition.
> Power is present, for him who will wield.

THOMAS: Whose was it?

TEMPTER: His who is gone.

THOMAS: Who shall have it?

TEMPTER: He who will come.

THOMAS: What shall be the month?

TEMPTER: The last from the first.

THOMAS: What shall we give for it?

TEMPTER: Pretence of priestly power.

THOMAS: Why should we give it?

TEMPTER: For the power and the glory.

THOMAS: No!

TEMPTER: Yes! Or bravery will be broken,
> Cabined in Canterbury, realmless ruler,
> Self-bound servant of a powerless Pope,
> The old stag, circled with hounds.

THOMAS: No!

TEMPTER: Yes! men must manoeuvre. Monarchs also,
> Waging war abroad, need fast friends at home.
> Private policy is public profit;
> Dignity still shall be dressed with decorum.

THOMAS: You forget the bishops
> Whom I have laid under excommunication.

TEMPTER: Hungry hatred
> Will not strive against intelligent self-interest.

THOMAS: You forget the barons. Who will not forget
> Constant curbing of pretty privilege.

TEMPTER: Against the barons
> Is King's cause, churl's cause, Chancellor's cause.

THOMAS: No! shall I, who keep the keys
    Of heaven and hell, supreme alone in England,
    Who bind and loose, with power from the Pope,
    Descend to desire a punier power?
    Delegate to deal the doom of damnation,
    To condemn kings, not serve among their servants,
    Is my open office. No! Go.
TEMPTER: Then I leave you to your fate.
    Your sin soars sunward, covering kings' falcons.
THOMAS: Temporal power, to build a good world,
    To keep order, as the world knows order.
    Those who put their faith in worldly order
    Not controlled by the order of God,
    In confident ignorance, but arrest disorder,
    Make it fast, breed fatal disease,
    Degrade what they exalt. Power with the King—
    I *was* the King, his arm, his better reason.
    But what was once exaltation
    Would now be only mean descent.
    [*Enter* THIRD TEMPTER.]
THIRD TEMPTER: I am an unexpected visitor.
THOMAS: I expected you.
TEMPTER: But not in this guise, or for my present purpose.
THOMAS: No purpose brings surprise.
TEMPTER: Well, my Lord,
    I am no trifler, and no politician.
    To idle or intrigue at court
    I have no skill. I am no courtier.
    I know a horse, a dog, a wench;
    I know how to hold my estates in order,
    A country-keeping lord who minds his own business.
    It is we country lords who know the country
    And we who know what the country needs.
    It is our country. We care for the country.
    We are the backbone of the nation.
    We, not the plotting parasites
    About the King. Excuse my bluntness:
    I am a rough straightforward Englishman.
THOMAS: Proceed straight forward.
TEMPTER: Purpose is plain.
    Endurance of friendship does not depend
    Upon ourselves, but upon circumstance.
    But circumstance is not undetermined.
    Unreal friendship may turn to real
    But real friendship, once ended, cannot be mended.
    Sooner shall enmity turn to alliance.

The enmity that never knew friendship
Can sooner know accord.
THOMAS: For a countryman
You wrap your meaning in as dark generality
As any courtier.
TEMPTER: This is the simple fact!
You have no hope of reconciliation
With Henry the King. You look only
To blind assertion in isolation.
That is a mistake.
THOMAS: O Henry, O my King!
TEMPTER: Other friends
May be found in the present situation.
King in England is not all-powerful;
King is in France, squabbling in Anjou;
Round him waiting hungry sons.
We are for England. We are in England.
You and I, my Lord, are Normans.
England is a land for Norman
Sovereignty. Let the Angevin
Destroy himself, fighting in Anjou.
He does not understand us, the English barons.
We are the people.
THOMAS: To what does this lead?
TEMPTER: To a happy coalition
Of intelligent interests.
THOMAS: But what have you—
If you do speak for barons—
TEMPTER: For a powerful party
Which has turned its eyes in your direction—
To gain from you, your Lordship asks.
For us, Church favour would be an advantage,
Blessing of Pope powerful protection
In the fight for liberty. You, my Lord,
In being with us, would fight a good stroke
At once, for England and for Rome,
Ending the tyrannous jurisdiction
Of king's court over bishop's court,
Of king's court over baron's court.
THOMAS: Which I helped to found.
TEMPTER: Which you helped to found.
But time past is time forgotten.
We expect the rise of a new constellation.
THOMAS: And if the Archbishop cannot trust the King,
How can he trust those who work for King's undoing?
TEMPTER: Kings will allow no power but their own;

Church and people have good cause against the throne.
THOMAS: If the Archbishop cannot trust the Throne,
He has good cause to trust none but God alone.
It is not better to be thrown
To a thousand hungry appetites than to one.
At a future time this may be shown.
I ruled once as Chancellor
And men like you were glad to wait at my door.
Not only in the court, but in the field
And in the tilt-yard I made many yield.
Shall I who ruled like an eagle over doves
Now take the shape of a wolf among wolves?
Pursue your treacheries as you have done before:
No one shall say that I betrayed a king.
TEMPTER: Then, my Lord, I shall not wait at your door;
And I well hope, before another spring
The King will show his regard for your loyalty.
THOMAS: To make, then break, this thought has come before,
The desperate exercise of failing power.
Samson in Gaza did no more.
But if I break, I must break myself alone.
[*Enter* FOURTH TEMPTER.]
FOURTH TEMPTER: Well done, Thomas, your will is hard to bend.
And with me beside you, you shall not lack a friend.
THOMAS: Who are you? I expected
Three visitors, not four.
TEMPTER: Do not be surprised to receive one more.
Had I been expected, I had been here before.
I always precede expectation.
THOMAS: Who are you?
TEMPTER: As you do not know me, I do not need a name,
And, as you know me, that is why I come.
You know me, but have never seen my face.
To meet before was never time or place.
THOMAS: Say what you come to say.
TEMPTER: It shall be said at last.
Hooks have been baited with morsels of the past.
Wantonness is weakness. As for the King,
His hardened hatred shall have no end.
You know truly, the King will never trust
Twice, the man who has been his friend.
Borrow use cautiously, employ
Your services as long as you have to lend.
You would wait for trap to snap
Having served your turn, broken and crushed.
As for barons, envy of lesser men

Is still more stubborn than king's anger.
Kings have public policy, barons private profit,
Jealousy raging possession of the fiend.
Barons are employable against each other;
Greater enemies must kings destroy.

THOMAS: What is your counsel?

TEMPTER: Fare forward to the end.
All other ways are closed to you
Except the way already chosen.
But what is pleasure, kingly rule,
Or rule of men beneath a king,
With craft in corners, stealthy stratagem,
To general grasp of spiritual power?
Man oppressed by sin, since Adam fell—
You hold the keys of heaven and hell.
Power to bind and loose: bind, Thomas, bind,
King and bishop under your heel.
King, emperor, bishop, baron, king:
Uncertain mastery of melting armies,
War, plague, and revolution,
New conspiracies, broken pacts;
To be master or servant within an hour,
This is the course of temporal power.
The Old King shall know it, when at last breath,
No sons, no empire, he bites broken teeth.
You hold the skein: wind, Thomas, wind
The thread of eternal life and death.
You hold this power, hold it.

THOMAS: Supreme, in this land?

TEMPTER: Supreme, but for one.

THOMAS: That I do not understand.

TEMPTER: It is not for me to tell you how this may be so;
I am only here, Thomas, to tell you what you know.

THOMAS: How long shall this be?

TEMPTER: Save what you know already, ask nothing of me.
But think, Thomas, think of glory after death.
When king is dead, there's another king,
And one more king is another reign.
King is forgotten, when another shall come:
Saint and Martyr rule from the tomb.
Think, Thomas, think of enemies dismayed,
Creeping in penance, frightened of a shade;
Think of pilgrims, standing in line
Before the glittering jewelled shrine,
From generation to generation
Bending the knee in supplication.

Think of the miracles, by God's grace,
And think of your enemies, in another place.
THOMAS: I have thought of these things.
TEMPTER: That is why I tell you.
Your thoughts have more power than kings to compel you.
You have also thought, sometimes at your prayers,
Sometimes hesitating at the angles of stairs,
And between sleep and waking, early in the morning,
When the bird cries, have thought of further scorning.
That nothing lasts, but the wheel turns,
The nest is rifled, and the bird mourns;
That the shrine shall be pillaged, and the gold spent,
The jewels gone for light ladies' ornament,
The sanctuary broken, and its stores
Swept into the laps of parasites and whores.
When miracles cease, and the faithful desert you,
And men shall only do their best to forget you.
And later is worse, when men will not hate you
Enough to defame or to execrate you,
But pondering the qualities that you lacked
Will only try to find the historical fact.
When men shall declare that there was no mystery
About this man who played a certain part in history.
THOMAS: But what is there to do? what is left to be done?
Is there no enduring crown to be won?
TEMPTER: Yes, Thomas, yes; you have thought of that too.
What can compare with glory of Saints
Dwelling forever in presence of God?
What earthly glory, of king or emperor,
What earthly pride, that is not poverty
Compared with richness of heavenly grandeur?
Seek the way of martyrdom, make yourself the lowest
On earth, to be high in heaven.
And see far off below you, where the gulf is fixed,
Your persecutors, in timeless torment,
Parched passion, beyond expiation.
THOMAS: No!
Who are you, tempting with my own desires?
Others have come, temporal tempters,
With pleasure and power at palpable price.
What do you offer? what do you ask?
TEMPTER: I offer what you desire. I ask
What you have to give. Is it too much
For such a vision of eternal grandeur?
THOMAS: Others offered real goods, worthless
But real. You only offer

Dreams to damnation.
TEMPTER: You have often dreamt them.
THOMAS: Is there no way, in my soul's sickness,
   Does not lead to damnation in pride?
   I well know that these temptations
   Mean present vanity and future torment.
   Can sinful pride be driven out
   Only by more sinful? Can I neither act nor suffer
   Without perdition?
TEMPTER: You know and do not know, what it is to act or suffer.
   You know and do not know, that acting is suffering,
   And suffering action. Neither does the actor suffer
   Nor the patient act. But both are fixed
   In an eternal action, an eternal patience
   To which all must consent that it may be willed
   And which all must suffer that they may will it,
   That the pattern may subsist, that the wheel may turn and still
   Be forever still.
CHORUS: There is no rest in the house. There is no rest in the street.
   I hear restless movement of feet. And the air is heavy and thick.
   Thick and heavy the sky. And the earth presses up beneath my feet.
   What is the sickly smell, the vapour? the dark green light from a cloud
   on a withered tree? The earth is heaving to parturition of issue of
   hell. What is the sticky dew that forms on the back of my hand?
THE FOUR TEMPTERS: Man's life is a cheat and a disappointment;
   All things are unreal,
   Unreal or disappointing:
   The Catherine wheel, the pantomime cat,
   The prizes given at the children's party,
   The prize awarded for the English Essay,
   The scholar's degree, the stateman's decoration.
   All things become less real, man passes
   From unreality to unreality.
   This man is obstinate, blind, intent
   On self-destruction,
   Passing from deception to deception,
   From grandeur to grandeur to final illusion,
   Lost in the wonder of his own greatness,
   The enemy of society, enemy of himself.
THE THREE PRIESTS: O Thomas my Lord do not fight the intractable tide,
   Do not sail the irresistible wind; in the storm,
   Should we not wait for the sea to subside, in the night
   Abide the coming of day, when the traveller may find his way,
   The sailor lay course by the sun?
CHORUS, PRIESTS *and* TEMPTERS *alternately*:
   C. Is it the owl that calls, or a signal between the trees?

P. Is the window-bar made fast, is the door under lock and bolt?

T. Is it rain that taps at the window, is it wind that pokes at the door?

C. Does the torch flame in the hall, the candle in the room?

P. Does the watchman walk by the wall?

T. Does the mastiff prowl by the gate?

C. Death has a hundred hands and walks by a thousand ways.

P. He may come in the sight of all, he may pass unseen unheard.

T. Come whispering through the ear, or a sudden shock on the skull.

C. A man may walk with a lamp at night, and yet be drowned in a ditch.

P. A man may climb the stair in the day, and slip on a broken step.

T. A man may sit at meat, and feel the cold in his groin.

CHORUS: We have not been happy, my Lord, we have not been too happy.
We are not ignorant women, we know what we must expect and not expect.
We know of oppression and torture,
We know of extortion and violence,
Destitution, disease,
The old without fire in winter,
The child without milk in summer,
Our labour taken away from us,
Our sins made heavier upon us.
We have seen the young man mutilated,
The torn girl trembling by the mill-stream.
And meanwhile we have gone on living,
Living and partly living,
Picking together the pieces,
Gathering faggots at nightfall,
Building a partial shelter,
For sleeping, and eating and drinking and laughter.

God gave us always some reason, some hope; but now a new terror
has soiled us, which none can avert, none can avoid, flowing under
our feet and over the sky;
Under doors and down chimneys, flowing in at the ear and the mouth
and the eye.
God is leaving us, God is leaving us, more pang, more pain, than birth
or death.
Sweet and cloying through the dark air
Falls the stifling scent of despair;
The forms take shape in the dark air:
Puss-purr of leopard, footfall of padding bear,
Palm-pat of nodding ape, square hyaena waiting
For laughter, laughter, laughter. The Lords of Hell are here.
They curl round you, lie at your feet, swing and wing through the dark
air.

O Thomas Archbishop, save us, save us, save yourself that we may be
   saved;
Destroy yourself and we are destroyed.
THOMAS: Now is my way clear, now is the meaning plain:
   Temptation shall not come in this kind again.
   The last temptation is the greatest treason:
   To do the right deed for the wrong reason.
   The natural vigour in the venial sin
   Is the way in which our lives begin.
   Thirty years ago, I searched all the ways
   That lead to pleasure, advancement and praise.
   Delight in sense, in learning and in thought,
   Music and philosophy, curiosity,
   The purple bullfinch in the lilac tree,
   The tiltyard skill, the strategy of chess,
   Love in the garden, singing to the instrument,
   Were all things equally desirable.
   Ambition comes when early force is spent
   And when we find no longer all things possible.
   Ambition comes behind and unobservable.
   Sin grows with doing good. When I imposed the King's law
   In England, and waged war with him against Toulouse,
   I beat the barons at their own game. I
   Could then despise the men who thought me most contemptible,
   The raw nobility, whose manners matched their fingernails.
   While I ate out of the King's dish
   To become servant of God was never my wish.
   Servant of God has chance of greater sin
   And sorrow, than the man who serves a king.
   For those who serve the greater cause may make the cause serve them,
   Still doing right: and striving with political men
   May make that cause political, not by what they do
   But by what they are. I know
   What yet remains to show you of my history
   Will seem to most of you at best futility,
   Senseless self-slaughter of a lunatic,
   Arrogant passion of a fanatic.
   I know that history at all times draws
   The strangest consequence from remotest cause.
   But for every evil, every sacrilege,
   Crime, wrong, oppression and the axe's edge,
   Indifference, exploitation, you, and you,
   And you, must all be punished. So must you.
   I shall no longer act or suffer, to the sword's end.
   Now my good Angel, whom God appoints
   To be my guardian, hover over the swords' points.

THE CITY OF GOD
(Book XIX)

ST. AUGUSTINE
(trans. by G. Walsh, D. Zema, and G. Monahan)

St. Augustine (A.D. 354–430) was a major Christian theologian who synthesized New Testament religion with the Platonism of Greece. Augustine's *Confessions* stands as one of the world's great spiritual autobiographies, but his *magnum opus* is *The City of God*, which majestically describes the two radically separate realms of the universe, that of the elect and that of the damned.

To Augustine, the supreme good is to be found not in this life which is filled with evils and misery but in the life to come. All earthly values ultimately prove disappointing, Augustine believes, but if we direct our worldly virtues toward serving God we will find eternal peace in heaven. Those who are not of the City of God, of course, will experience suffering on earth and eternal punishment in hell.

CHAPTER 4

If I am asked what stand the City of God would take on the issues raised and, first, what this City thinks of the supreme good and ultimate evil, the answer would be: She holds that eternal life is the supreme good and eternal death the supreme evil, and that we should live rightly in order to obtain the one and avoid the other. Hence the Scriptural expression, 'the just man lives by faith'—by faith, for the fact is that we do not now behold our good and, therefore, must seek it by faith; nor can we of ourselves even live rightly, unless He who gives us faith helps us to believe and pray, for it takes faith to believe that we need His help.

Those who think that the supreme good and evil are to be found in this life are mistaken. It makes no difference whether it is in the body or in the soul or in both—or, specifically, in pleasure or virtue or in both—that they seek the supreme good. They seek in vain whether they look to serenity, to virtue, or to both; whether to pleasure plus serenity, or to virtue, or to all three; or to the satisfaction of our innate exigencies, or to virtue, or to both. It is in vain that men look for beatitude on earth or in human nature. Divine Truth, as expressed in the Prophet's words, makes them look foolish: 'The Lord knows the thoughts of men' or, as the text is quoted by St. Paul: 'The Lord knows the thoughts of the wise that they are vain.'

For, what flow of eloquence is sufficient to set forth the miseries of human life? Cicero did the best he could in his *Consolatio de morte filiae*,[1] but how little was his very best? As for the primary satisfactions of our nature, when or where or how can they be so securely possessed in this life

1 [Editor's note: *Consolation at the Death of a Daughter.*]

that they are not subject to the ups and downs of fortune? There is no pain of body, driving out pleasure, that may not befall the wise man, no anxiety that may not banish calm. A man's physical integrity is ended by the amputation or crippling of any of his limbs; his beauty is spoiled by deformity, his health by sickness, his vigor by weariness, his agility by torpor and sluggishness. There is not one of these that may not afflict the flesh even of a philosopher. Among our elementary requirements we reckon a graceful and becoming erectness and movement; but what happens to these as soon as some sickness brings on palsy or, still worse, a spinal deformity so severe that a man's hands touch the ground as though he were a four-footed beast? What is then left of any beauty or dignity in a man's posture or gait? Turn, now, to the primary endowments of the soul: senses to perceive and intelligence to understand the truth. How much sensation does a man have left if, for example, he goes deaf and blind? And where does the reason or intelligence go, into what strange sleep, when sickness unsettles the mind? We can hardly hold back our tears when mad men say or do extravagant things—things wholly unlike their customary behavior and normal goodness. To witness such things, even to recall them, makes a decent man weep. Still worse is the case of those possessed by demons. Their intelligence seems driven away, not to say destroyed, when an evil spirit according to its will makes use of their body and soul. And who can be sure that even a philosopher will not be such a victim at some time in his life?

Further, what is to be said of our perception of the truth, at the very best? What kind of truth and how much of it can we reach through our bodily senses? Do we not read in the truth-speaking Book of Wisdom: 'For the corruptible body is a load upon the soul, and the earthly habitation presseth down the mind that museth upon many things'?

And what of the urge and appetite for action—*hormé*, as the Greeks call it—which is reckoned among the primary goods of our nature? Is not this the root, too, of those restless energies of the madmen who fill us with tears and fears when their senses deceive them and their reason refuses to function?

So much for the elementary endowments of nature. Look, now, at virtue herself, which comes later with education and claims for herself the topmost place among human goods. Yet, what is the life of virtue save one unending war with evil inclinations, and not with solicitations of other people alone, but with evil inclinations that arise within ourselves and are our very own.

I speak especially of temperance—*sōphrosynē*, as the Greeks call it—which must bridle our fleshly lusts if they are not to drag our will to consent to abominations of every sort. The mere fact that, as St. Paul says, 'the flesh is at war with the spirit,' is no small flaw in our nature; and virtue is at war with this evil inclination when, in the same Apostle's words, 'the spirit lusts against the flesh.' These are opposed to each other to such a degree that 'we do not the things that we would.' And when we seek final rest in the supreme good, what do we seek save an end to this conflict between flesh and spirit, freedom from this propensity to evil against which the spirit is at war? Yet, will as we may, such liberty cannot be had in mortal life.

This much, however, we can do with the help of God—not yield by surrender of the spirit and be dragged into sin willingly. Meanwhile, we must not fondly imagine that, so long as we wage this inward war, we may achieve that longed-for beatitude which can be solely the prize of the victor. For there lives no man so perfected in wisdom as not to have some conflict with excessive desires.

Take, next, the virtue called prudence. Is not this virtue constantly on the lookout to distinguish what is good from what is evil, so that there may be no mistake made in seeking the one and avoiding the other? So it bears witness to the fact that we are surrounded by evil and have evil within us. This virtue teaches that it is evil to consent to desires leading to sin and good to resist them. And what prudence preaches temperance puts into practice. Yet, neither prudence nor temperance can rid this life of the evils that are their constant concern.

Finally, there is justice. Its task is to see that to each is given what belongs to each. And this holds for the right order within man himself, so that it is just for the soul to be subordinate to God, and the body to the soul, and thus for body and soul taken together to be subject to God. Is there not abundant evidence that this virtue is unremittingly struggling to effect this internal order—and is far from finished? For, the less a man has God in his thoughts, the less is his soul subject to God; the more the flesh lusts counter to the spirit, the less the flesh is subject to the soul. So long, then, as such weakness, such moral sickliness remains within us, how can we dare to say that we are out of danger; and, if not yet out of danger, how can we say that our happiness is complete?

Look, now, at the great virtue called fortitude. Is not its very function —to bear patiently with misfortune—overwhelming evidence that human life is beset with unhappiness, however wise a man may be? It is beyond my comprehension how the Stoics can boldly argue that such ills are not really ills, meanwhile allowing that, if a philosopher should be tried by them beyond his obligation or duty to bear, he may have no choice but to take the easy way out by committing suicide. So stultifying is Stoic pride that, all evidences to the contrary, these men still pretend to find the ultimate good in this life and to hold that they are themselves the source of their own happiness. Their kind of sage—an astonishing silly sage, indeed —may go deaf, dumb and blind, may be crippled, wracked with pain, visited with every imaginable affliction, driven at last to take his own life, yet have the colossal impertinence to call such an existence the happy life! Happy life, indeed, which employs death's aid to end it! If such a life is happy, then I say, live it! Why pretend that evils are not evils, when they not only overcome the virtue of fortitude and force it to yield to evil, but make a man so irrational as to call one and the same life both happy and unlivable? How can anyone be so blind as not to see that if life is happy it should not be shunned? Yet, the moment sickness opens her mouth they say one must choose a way out. If so, why do they not bow their stiff necks and admit life's unhappiness? Now, let me ask: Was it courage or cowardice that made their hero Cato kill himself? Certainly, he would not have done what he did had he not been too cowardly to endure the victory of Caesar. Where, then, was his fortitude? It was a fortitude that yielded, that surrendered, that was so beaten that Cato ran away, deserted, abandoned the happy life. Or, maybe it was no longer the happy life? In that case, it was unhappy. If so, how can anyone deny that the ills that made Cato's life unhappy and unlivable were real evils?

From this it follows that those who admit that such things are evils, so do the Aristotelians and those of the Old Academy whom Varro defends, are nearer the truth than the Stoics, even though Varro also makes the egregious mistake of maintaining that this life is still the happy life in spite of evils so grievous that, for one who suffers them, suicide becomes imperative. 'The pains and afflictions of the body,' Varro admits, 'are evils; and the worse the pains, the greater the evil. To escape them you should end your life.' I ask: Which life? He answers: 'This life which is made grievous by so many evils.' Life, then, is the happy life in the midst of evils which drive a man to escape from life? Is it, perhaps, the happy life precisely because you are allowed to escape its unhappiness by death? Suppose you should be bound by a divine law to remain in its evils and be permitted neither to die nor ever to be free from such misfortunes? Then, at least, you would have to say that such a life would be unhappy. And, surely, if you admit it would be unhappy if unending, you cannot say that it is not unhappy just because there is a quick way out. You cannot maintain that just because unhappiness is short-lived it is really not unhappiness at all; or, what is more preposterous, that because unhappiness is short-lived it deserves to be called happiness.

No, these ills of life must be very real indeed if they can drive even a sage of their type to take his life. For, these philosophers say—and rightly say—that the first and most fundamental command of nature is that a man should cherish his own human life and, by his very nature, shun death; that a man should be his own best friend, wanting and working with all his might and main to keep himself alive and to preserve the union of his body and soul. These ills must be very real indeed if they can subdue the very instinct of nature that struggles in every possible way to put death off; overwhelm it so utterly that death, once shunned, is now desired, sought, and, when all else fails, is self-inflicted. Yes, very real, when they can turn courage into a killer, if, indeed, there be any question of genuine courage, when this virtue, devised to support and steel a man, is so battered down by misfortune that—having failed to sustain him—it is driven, against its very function, to finish him off. It is true, of course, that a philosopher should face death as well as all other trials, with fortitude, but that means death coming upon him from without.

If then, as these philosophers held, even a wise man must yield to suicide, they ought logically to admit that there are evils—even insufferable evils—that account for this tragic compulsion; and that a life so burdensome, so exposed to fortune's ebb and flow, should not be called happy! Nor would those who talk of 'the happy life' ever have called life happy if they had yielded to the truth and the cogency of reason in their search for the happy life as readily as they yield to unhappiness and the weight of evils when they lose their life by suicide; and if, further, they had given up the idea that they could enjoy the supreme good in this mortal life. They would have realized that man's very virtues, his best and most useful possessions, are the most solid evidences of the miseries of life, precisely because their function is to stand by him in perils and problems and pains.

For, when virtues are genuine virtues—and that is possible only when men believe in God— they make no pretense of protecting their possessors from unhappiness, for that would be a false promise; but they do claim that human life, now compelled to feel the misery of so many grievous ills on earth, can, by the hope of heaven, be made both happy and secure. If we are asked how a life can be happy before we are saved, we have the answer of St. Paul: 'For in hope were we saved. But hope that is seen is not hope. For how can a man hope for what he sees? But if we hope for what we do not see, we wait for it with patience.'

Of course, the Apostle was not speaking of men lacking prudence, fortitude, temperance, and justice, but of men whose virtues were true virtues because the men were living by faith. Thus, as 'we are saved by hope,' so we are made happy by hope. Neither our salvation nor our beatitude is here present, but 'we wait for it' in the future, and we wait 'with patience,' precisely because we are surrounded by evils which patience must endure until we come to where all good things are sources of inexpressible happiness and where there will be no longer anything to endure. Such is to be our salvation in the hereafter, such our final blessedness. It is because the philosophers will not believe in this beatitude which they cannot see that they go on trying to fabricate here below an utterly fraudulent felicity built on virtue filled with pride and bound to fail them in the end. . . .

CHAPTER 11

Thus, we may say of peace what we have said of eternal life—that it is our highest good; more particularly because the holy Psalmist was addressing the City of God (the nature of which I am trying, with so much difficulty, to make clear) when he said: 'Praise the Lord, O Jerusalem; praise thy God, O Sion. Because he hath strengthened the bolts of thy gates, he hath blessed thy children within thee. He hath placed peace in thy borders.' For, when the bolts of that city's gates will have been strengthened, none will enter in and none will issue forth. Hence, its borders [*fines*] must be taken to mean that peace which I am trying to show is our final good. Note, too, that Jerusalem, the mystical name which symbolizes this City, means, as I have already mentioned, 'the vision of peace.'

However, the word 'peace' is so often applied to conditions here on earth, where life is not eternal, that it is better, I think, to speak of 'eternal life' rather than of 'peace' as the end or supreme good of the City of God. It is in this sense that St. Paul says: 'But now being made free from sin, and become servants of God, you have your fruit unto sanctification, and the end life everlasting.'

It would be simplest for all concerned if we spoke of 'peace in eternal life,' or of 'eternal' or of 'eternal life in peace,' as the end or supreme good of this City. The trouble with the expression 'eternal life' is that those unfamiliar with the Scriptures might take this phrase to apply also to the eternal loss of the wicked, either because, as philosophers, they accept the immortality of the soul, or even because, as Christians, they know by faith that the punishment of the wicked has no end and, therefore, that they could not be punished forever unless their life were eternal.

The trouble with 'peace' is that, even on the level of earthly and temporal values, nothing that we can talk about, long for, or finally get, is so desirable, so welcome, so good as peace. At any rate, I feel sure that if I linger a little longer on this topic of peace I shall tire very few of my readers. After all, peace is the end of this City which is the theme of this work; besides, peace is so universally loved that its very name falls sweetly on the ear.

CHAPTER 12

Any man who has examined history and human nature will agree with me that there is no such thing as a human heart that does not crave for joy and peace. One has only to think of men who are bent on war. What they want is to win, that is to say, their battles are but bridges to glory and to peace. The whole point of victory is to bring opponents to their knees—this done, peace ensues. Peace, then, is the purpose of waging war; and this is true even of men who have a passion for the exercise of military prowess as rulers and commanders.

What, then, men want in war is that it should end in peace. Even while waging a war every man wants peace, whereas no one wants war while he is making peace. And even when men are plotting to disturb the peace, it is merely to fashion a new peace nearer to the heart's desire; it is not because they dislike peace as such. It is not that they love peace less, but that they love their kind of peace more. And even when a secession is successful, its purpose is not achieved unless some sort of peace remains among those who plotted and planned the rebellion. Take even a band of highwaymen. The more violence and impunity they want in disturbing the peace of other men, the more they demand peace among themselves. Take even the case of a robber so powerful that he dispenses with partnership, plans alone, and single-handed robs and kills his victims. Even he maintains some kind of peace, however shadowy, with those he cannot kill and whom he wants to keep in the dark with respect to his crimes. Certainly in his own home he wants to be at peace with his wife and children and any other members of his household. Of course, he is delighted when his every nod is obeyed; if it is not obeyed, he rages, and scolds, and demands peace in his own home and, if need be, gets it by sheer brutality. He knows that the price of peace in domestic society is to have everyone subject in the home to some head—in this instance, to himself.

Suppose, now, a man of this type were offered the allegiance of a larger society, say of a city or of a nation, with the pledge that he would be obeyed as he looks to be obeyed under his own roof. In this case, he would no longer hide himself away in a darksome robber's den; he would show himself off as a high and mighty king—the same man, however, with all of his old greed and criminality. Thus it is that all men want peace in their own society, and all want it in their own way. When they go to war what they want is to make, if they can, their enemies their own, and then to impose on them the victor's will and call it peace.

Now let us imagine a man like the one that poetry and mythology tell us about, a being so wild and anti-social that it was better to call him half-human than fully a man. He was called Cacus, which is Greek for 'bad.' His kingdom was the solitude of a dreadful cave and it was his extraordinary wickedness that gave him his name. He had no wife to exchange soft words with him; no tiny children to play with; no bigger ones to keep in order; no friend whose company he could enjoy, not even his father, Vulcan—than whom he was at least this much luckier that he had never begotten a monster like himself! There was no one to whom he would give anything, but whenever and from whomsoever he could he would take whatever he wanted and whenever he wanted it.

Nevertheless, all alone as he was in a cave that was always 'warm with the blood of some recent victim,'[2] his sole longing was for peace in which no force would do him harm and no fear disturb his rest. Even with his own body he wanted to be at peace, and he was at ease only when peace was there. Even when he was bidding his members to obey him and was seizing, killing, and devouring his victims, his purpose was peace—the speediest possible peace with his mortal nature, driven by its needs to rebellion, and with his hunger, in sedition, clamoring for the breakup of the union of body and soul. Brutal and wild as he was and brutal and wild as were his ways, what he wanted was to have his life and limbs in peace. So much so that, had he been as willing to be at peace with his neighbors

2 Aeneid 8.195.

as he was active in procuring peace within himself and in his cave, no one would have called him wicked, nor a monster, nor even sub-human; or, at least, despite the shape of his body and the smoke and fire that issued from his mouth and kept all neighbors at a distance, people would have said that what looked like injustice, greed, and savagery were merely means to self-preservation. The truth is, of course, that there never existed any such being or, at least, none just like the foil the poets' fancy invented to glorify Hercules at the expense of Cacus. As is the case with most poetic inventions, we need not believe that any such creature, human or sub-human, ever lived.

I turn now to real wild beasts (from which category the animal part of the so-called half-beast,[3] Cacus, was borrowed). They, too, keep their own particular genus in a kind of peace. Their males and females meet and mate, foster and feed their young, even though many of them by nature are more solitary than gregarious, like lions, foxes, eagles, and owls—as contrasted with deer, pigeons, starlings, and bees. Even a tigress purrs over her cubs and curbs all her fierceness when she fondles them. Even a falcon which seems so lonely when hovering above its prey mates and builds a nest, helps to hatch the eggs and feed the young, and makes every effort to maintain with the mother falcon a peaceful domestic society.

It is even more so with man. By the very laws of his nature, he seems, so to speak, forced into fellowship and, as far as in him lies, into peace with every man. At any rate, even when wicked men go to war they want peace for their own society and would like, if possible, to make all men members of that society, so that everyone and everything might be at the service of one head. Of course, the only means such a conqueror knows is to have all men so fear or love him that they will accept the peace which he imposes. For, so does pride perversely copy God. Sinful man hates the equality of all men under God and, as though he were God, loves to impose his sovereignty on his fellow men. He hates the peace of God which is just and prefers his own peace which is unjust. However, he is powerless not to love peace of some sort. For, no man's sin is so unnatural as to wipe out all traces whatsoever of human nature. Anyone, then, who is rational enough to prefer right to wrong and order to disorder can see that the kind of peace that is based on injustice, as compared with that which is based on justice, does not deserve the name of peace.

Of course, even disorder, in whole or in part, must come to some kind of terms either with the situation in which it finds itself or with the elements out of which it takes its being—otherwise it would have no being at all.

Take a man hanging upside down. Certainly his members are in disorder and the posture of the body as a whole is unnatural. The parts

[3] Aeneid 8.267:semiferus.

which nature demands should be above and below have become topsy-turvy. Such a position disturbs the peace of the body and is therefore painful. Nevertheless, the soul remains at peace with the body and continues to work for its welfare. Otherwise, the man would not live to feel the agony. And even if the soul is driven from the body by excess of pain, nevertheless, so long as the limbs hold together, some kind of peace among these parts remains. Otherwise, there would be no corpse to go on dangling there. Further, the fact that by gravity the corpse, made out of earth, tends to fall to the ground and pulls at the noose that holds it up proves that there is some order in which it seeks peace, and that its weight is, as it were, crying out for a place where it can rest. Lifeless and insensible though the body now is, it does not renounce that appropriate peace in the order of nature which it either has or seeks to have.

So, too, when a corpse is treated to embalming, to prevent dissolution and decay, there is a kind of peace which holds the parts together while the whole is committed to the earth, its proper resting place, and, therefore, a place with which the body is at peace. If, on the other hand, embalming is omitted and nature is allowed to take its course, the corpse remains a battleground of warring exhalations (that attack our senses with the stench we smell) only until such time as they finally fall in with the elements of this world and, slowly, bit by bit, become indistinguishable in a common peace.

Even afterward, however, the law and ordering of the Creator who is supreme in the whole cosmos and the regulator of its peace are still in control. Even when tiny bacteria spring from the corpse of a larger animal, it is by the same law of the Creator that all these minute bodies serve in peace the organic wholes of which they are parts. Even when the flesh of dead animals is eaten by other animals, there is no change in the universal laws which are meant for the common good of every kind of life, the common good that is effected by bringing like into peace with like. It makes no difference what disintegrating forces are at work, or what new combinations are made, or even what changes or transformations are effected.

CHAPTER 13

The peace, then, of the body lies in the ordered equilibrium of all its parts; the peace of the irrational soul, in the balanced adjustment of its appetites; the peace of the reasoning soul, in the harmonious correspondence of conduct and conviction; the peace of body and soul taken together, in the well-ordered life and health of the living whole. Peace between a mortal man and his Maker consists in ordered obedience, guided by faith, under God's eternal law; peace between man and man consists in regulated fellowship. The peace of a home lies in the ordered harmony of authority and obedience between the members of a family living together. The peace of the political community is an ordered harmony of authority and obedience between citizens. The peace of the heavenly City lies in a perfectly ordered and harmonious communion of those who find their joy in God and in one another in God. Peace, in its final sense, is the calm that comes of order. Order is an arrangement of like and unlike things whereby each of them is disposed in its proper place.

This being so, those who are unhappy, in so far as they are unhappy, are not in peace, since they lack the calm of that Order which is beyond every storm; nevertheless, even in their misery they cannot escape from order, since their very misery is related to responsibility and to justice. They do not share with the blessed in their tranquility, but this very separation is the result of the law of order. Moreover, even the miserable can be momentarily free from anxiety and can reach some measure of adjustment to their surroundings and, hence, some tranquility of order and, therefore, some slender peace. However, the reason why they remain unhappy is that, although they *may* be momentarily free from worry and from pain, they are not in a condition where they *must* be free both from worry and pain. Their condition of misery is worse when such peace as they have is not in harmony with that law which governs the order of nature. Their peace can also be disturbed by pain and in proportion to their pain; yet, some peace will remain, so long as the pain is not too acute and their organism as a whole does not disintegrate.

Notice that there can be life without pain, but no pain without some kind of life. In the same way, there can be peace without any kind of war, but no war that does not suppose some kind of peace. This does not mean that war as war involves peace; but war, in so far as those who wage it or have it waged upon them are beings with organic natures, involves peace—for the simple reason that to be organic means to be ordered and, therefore, to be, in some sense, at peace.

Similarly, there can be a nature without any defect and, even, a nature in which there can be no kind of evil whatever, but there can be no nature completely devoid of good. Even the nature of the Devil, in so far as it is a nature, is not evil; it was perversity—not being true to itself—that made it bad. The Devil did not 'stand in the truth' and, therefore, did not escape the judgment of truth. He did not stand fast in the tranquility of order—nor did he, for all that, elude the power of the Ordainer. The goodness which God gave to his nature does not withdraw him from the justice of God by which that nature is subject to punishment. Yet, even in that punishment, God does not hound the good which He created, but only the evil which the Devil committed. So it is that God does not take back the whole of His original gift. He takes a part and leaves a part; He leaves a nature that can regret what God has taken back. Indeed, the very pain inflicted is evidence of both the good that is lost and the good that is left. For, if there were no good left, there would be no one to lament the good that has been lost.

A man who sins is just that much worse if he rejoices in the loss of holiness; but one who suffers pain, and does not benefit by it, laments, at least, the loss of his health. Holiness and health are both good things and, because the loss of any good is more a cause for grief than for gladness (unless there be some higher compensation—the soul's holiness, to be sure, is preferable to the body's health), it is more in accordance with nature that a sinner grieve over his punishment than that he rejoice over his offense. Consequently, just as a man's happiness in abandoning the good of wrongdoing betrays his bad will, so his sorrowing for the good he has lost when in pain bears witness to the good of his nature. For, anyone who grieves over the loss of peace to his nature does so out of some remnant of that peace wherewith his nature loves itself. This is what happens—deservedly, too—in eternal punishment. In the midst of their agonies the evil and the godless weep for the loss of their nature's goods, knowing, meanwhile, that God whose great generosity they contemned was perfectly just when He took these goods away.

God, the wise Creator and just Ordainer of all natures, has made the mortal race of man the loveliest of all lovely things on earth. He has given to men good gifts suited to their existence here below. Among these is temporal peace, according to the poor limits of mortal life, in health, security, and human fellowship; and other gifts, too, needed to preserve this peace or regain it, once lost—for instance, the blessings that lie all around us, so perfectly adapted to our senses: daylight, speech, air to breathe, water to drink, everything that goes to feed, clothe, cure, and beautify the body. These good gifts are granted, however, with the perfectly just understanding that whoever uses the goods which are meant for the mortal peace of mortal men, as these goods should be used, will receive more abundant and better goods—nothing less than immortal peace and all that goes with it, namely, the glory and honor of enjoying God and one's neighbor in God everlastingly; but that whoever misuses his gifts on earth will both lose what he has and never receive the better gifts of heaven. . . .

CHAPTER 27

The City of God, however, has a peace of its own, namely, peace with God in this world by faith and in the world to come by vision. Still, any peace we have on earth, whether the peace we share with Babylon or our own peace through faith, is more like a solace for unhappiness than the joy of beatitude. Even our virtue in this life, genuine as it is because it is referred to the true goal of every good, lies more in the pardoning of sins than in any perfection of virtues. Witness the prayer of God's whole City, wandering on earth and calling out to Him through all her members: 'Forgive us our debts as we also forgive our debtors.'

This prayer is effective, not on the lips of those whose faith without works is dead, but only on the lips of men whose faith works through charity. This prayer is necessary for the just because their reason, though submissive to God, has only imperfect mastery over their evil inclinations so long as they live in this world and in a corruptible body that 'is a load upon the soul.' Reason may give commands, but can exercise no control without a struggle. And, in this time of weakness, something will inevitably creep in to make the best of soldiers—whether in victory or still in battle with such foes—offend by some small slip of the tongue, some passing thought, if not by habitual actions. This explains why we can know no perfect peace so long as there are evil inclinations to master. Those which put up a fight are put down only in perilous conflict; those that are already overcome cannot be kept so if one relaxes, but only at the cost of vigilant control. These are the battles which Scripture sums up in the single phrase: 'The life of man upon earth is a warfare.'

Who, then, save a proud man, will presume that he can live without needing to ask God: 'Forgive us our debts'? Not a great man, you may be sure, but one blown up with the wind of self-reliance—one whom God in His justice resists while He grants His grace to the humble. Hence, it is written: 'God resists the proud, but gives grace to the humble.'

This, then, in this world, is the life of virtue. When God commands, man obeys; when the soul commands, the body obeys; when reason rules, our passions, even when they fight back, must be conquered or resisted; man must beg God's grace to win merit and the remission of his sins and must thank God for the blessings he receives.

But, in that final peace which is the end and purpose of all virtue here on earth, our nature, made whole by immortality and incorruption, will have no vices and experience no rebellion from within or without. There will be no need for reason to govern non-existent evil inclinations. God will hold sway over man, the soul over the body; and the happiness in eternal life and law will make obedience sweet and easy. And in each and all of us this condition will be everlasting, and we shall know it to be so. That is why the peace of such blessedness or the blessedness of such peace is to be our supreme good.

CHAPTER 28

On the other hand, the doom in store for those who are not of the City of God is an unending wretchedness that is called 'the second death,' because neither the soul, cut off from the life of God, nor the body, pounded by perpetual pain, can there be said to live at all. And what will make that second death so hard to bear is that there will be no death to end it.

Now, since unhappiness is the reverse of happiness, death of life, and war of peace, one may reasonably ask: If peace is praised and proclaimed as the highest good, what kind of warfare are we to think of as the highest evil? If this inquirer will reflect, he will realize that what is hurtful and destructive in warfare is mutual clash and conflict, and, hence, that no one can imagine a war more unbearably bitter than one in which the will and passions are at such odds that neither can ever win the victory, and in which violent pain and the body's very nature will so clash that neither will ever yield. When this conflict occurs on earth, either pain wins and death puts an end to all feeling, or nature wins and health removes the pain. But, in hell, pain permanently afflicts and nature continues to feel it, for neither ever comes to term, since the punishment must never end.

3

Furthering
the Progress
of Mankind

MAN AND SUPERMAN

("Don Juan in Hell")

GEORGE BERNARD SHAW

George Bernard Shaw (1856–1950) was a British playwright celebrated for his ironic comedies which combine polemicism with wit. Shaw believed in a variety of ideas, including Fabian socialism and a vitalistic evolutionism, which appear in varying combinations in plays such as *Arms and the Man*, *The Devil's Disciple, Man and Superman, Major Barbara, Pygmalion*, and *Saint Joan*. His overall formula for drama was "Find the right thing to say, and then say it with utmost levity."

In the section of his play *Man and Superman,* entitled "Don Juan in Hell," Shaw argues against a life of pleasure, which diverts man from his central purpose and leaves him intolerably bored. He also criticizes religion, which is painted as hypocritical, superstitious, and socially conventional. Instead of either alternative, he prescribes an honest and lucid existence in which man makes use of his intellectual capacity to further the progress of life. The evolutionary "life force" must be channeled through philosophic contemplation and earnest labor so that it advances intelligently. In that way human existence can be rendered wider, deeper, and more intense. For Shaw, to be in hell is to drift on a sea of pleasures, to be in heaven is to steer toward higher and higher development for the human race.

No light, no sound, no time nor space, utter void. Then somewhere the beginning of a pallor, and with it a faint throbbing buzz as of a ghostly violoncello palpitating on the same note endlessly. A couple of ghostly violins presently take advantage of this bass and therewith the pallor

379

reveals a man in the void, an incorporeal but visible man, seated, absurdly enough, on nothing. For a moment he raises his head as the music passes him by. Then, with a heavy sigh, he droops in utter dejection; and the violins, discouraged, retrace their melody in despair and at last give it up, extinguished by wailings from uncanny wind instruments, thus:—

It is all very odd. One recognizes the Mozartian strain; and on this hint, and by the aid of certain sparkles of violet light in the pallor, the man's costume explains itself as that of a Spanish nobleman of the XV–XVI century. Don Juan, of course; but where? why? how? Where on earth —or elsewhere—have we got to from the XX century and the Sierra?

Another pallor in the void, this time not violet, but a disagreeable smoky yellow. With it, the whisper of a ghostly clarinet turning this tune into infinite sadness:

The yellowish pallor moves: there is an old crone wandering in the void, bent and toothless; draped, as well as one can guess, in the coarse brown frock of some religious order. She wanders and wanders in her slow hope-less way, much as a wasp flies in its rapid busy way, until she blunders against the thing she seeks: companionship. With a sob of relief the poor old creature clutches at the presence of the man and addresses him in her dry unlovely voice, which can still express pride and resolution as well as suffering.

THE OLD WOMAN: Excuse me; but I am so lonely; and this place is so awful.

DON JUAN: A new comer?

THE OLD WOMAN: Yes: I suppose I died this morning. I confessed; I had extreme unction; I was in bed with my family about me and my eyes fixed on the cross. Then it grew dark; and when the light came back it was this light by which I walk seeing nothing. I have wandered for hours in horrible loneliness.

DON JUAN [*sighing*]: Ah! you have not yet lost the sense of time. One soon does, in eternity.

THE OLD WOMAN: Where are we?

DON JUAN: In hell.

THE OLD WOMAN [*proudly*]: Hell! I in hell! How dare you?

DON JUAN [*unimpressed*]: Why not, Señora?

THE OLD WOMAN: You do not know to whom you are speaking. I am a lady, and a faithful daughter of the Church.

DON JUAN: I do not doubt it.

THE OLD WOMAN: But how then can I be in hell? Purgatory, perhaps: I have not been perfect: who has? But hell! oh, you are lying.

DON JUAN: Hell, Señora, I assure you; hell at its best: that is, its most solitary—though perhaps you would prefer company.

THE OLD WOMAN: But I have sincerely repented; I have confessed—

DON JUAN: How much?

THE OLD WOMAN: More sins than I really committed. I loved confession.

DON JUAN: Ah, that is perhaps as bad as confessing too little. At all events, Señora, whether by oversight or intention, you are certainly damned, like myself; and there is nothing for it now but to make the best of it.

THE OLD WOMAN [*indignantly*]: Oh! and I might have been so much wickeder! All my good deeds wasted! It is unjust.

DON JUAN: No: you were fully and clearly warned. For your bad deeds, vicarious atonement, mercy without justice. For your good deeds, justice without mercy. We have many good people here.

THE OLD WOMAN: Were you a good man?

DON JUAN: I was a murderer.

THE OLD WOMAN: A murderer! Oh, how dare they send me to herd with murderers! I was not as bad as that: I was a good woman. There is some mistake: where can I have it set right?

DON JUAN: I do not know whether mistakes can be corrected here. Probably they will not admit a mistake even if they have made one.

THE OLD WOMAN: But whom can I ask?

DON JUAN: I should ask the Devil, Señora: he understands the ways of this place, which is more than I ever could.

THE OLD WOMAN: The Devil! I speak to the Devil!

DON JUAN: In hell, Señora, the Devil is the leader of the best society.

THE OLD WOMAN: I tell you, wretch, I know I am not in hell.

DON JUAN: How do you know?

THE OLD WOMAN: Because I feel no pain.

DON JUAN: Oh, then there is no mistake: you are intentionally damned.

THE OLD WOMAN: Why do you say that?

DON JUAN: Because hell, Señora, is a place for the wicked. The wicked are quite comfortable in it: it was made for them. You tell me you feel no pain. I conclude you are one of those for whom Hell exists.

THE OLD WOMAN: Do you feel no pain?

DON JUAN: I am not one of the wicked, Señora; therefore it bores me, bores me beyond description, beyond belief.

THE OLD WOMAN: Not one of the wicked! You said you were a murderer.

DON JUAN: Only a duel. I ran my sword through an old man who was trying to run his through me.

THE OLD WOMAN: If you were a gentleman, that was not a murder.

DON JUAN: The old man called it murder, because he was, he said, defending his daughter's honor. By this he meant that because I foolishly fell in love with her and told her so, she screamed; and he tried to assassinate me after calling me insulting names.

THE OLD WOMAN: You were like all men. Libertines and murderers all, all, all!

DON JUAN: And yet we meet here, dear lady.

THE OLD WOMAN: Listen to me. My father was slain by just such a wretch as you, in just such a duel, for just such a cause. I screamed: it was my duty. My father drew on my assailant: his honor demanded it. He fell: that was the reward of honor. I am here: in hell, you tell me: that is the reward of duty. Is there justice in heaven?

DON JUAN: No; but there is justice in hell: heaven is far above such idle human personalities. You will be welcome in hell, Señora. Hell is the home of honor, duty, justice, and the rest of the seven deadly virtues. All the wickedness on earth is done in their name: where else but in hell should they have their reward? Have I not told you that the truly damned are those who are happy in hell?

THE OLD WOMAN: And are you happy here?

DON JUAN [*springing to his feet*]: No; and that is the enigma on which I ponder in darkness. Why am I here? I, who repudiated all duty, trampled honor underfoot, and laughed at justice!

THE OLD WOMAN: Oh, what do I care why you are here? Why am *I* here? I, who sacrificed all my inclinations to womanly virtue and propriety!

DON JUAN: Patience, lady: you will be perfectly happy and at home here. As saith the poet, "Hell is a city much like Seville."

THE OLD WOMAN: Happy! here! where I am nothing! where I am nobody!

DON JUAN: Not at all: you are a lady; and wherever ladies are is hell. Do not be surprised or terrified: you will find everything here that a lady can desire, including devils who will serve you from sheer love of servitude, and magnify your importance for the sake of dignifying their service—the best of servants.

THE OLD WOMAN: My servants will be devils!

DON JUAN: Have you ever had servants who were not devils?

THE OLD WOMAN: Never: they were devils, perfect devils, all of them. But that is only a manner of speaking. I thought you meant that my servants here would be real devils.

DON JUAN: No more real devils than you will be a real lady. Nothing is real here. That is the horror of damnation.

THE OLD WOMAN: Oh, this is all madness. This is worse than fire and the worm.

DON JUAN: For you, perhaps, there are consolations. For instance: how old were you when you changed from time to eternity?

THE OLD WOMAN: Do not ask me how old I was—as if I were a thing of the past. I am 77.

DON JUAN: A ripe age, Señora. But in hell old age is not tolerated. It is too real. Here we worship Love and Beauty. Our souls being entirely damned, we cultivate our hearts. As a lady of 77, you would not have a single acquaintance in hell.

THE OLD WOMAN: How can I help my age, man?

DON JUAN: You forget that you have left your age behind you in the realm of time. You are no more 77 than you are 7 or 17 or 27.

THE OLD WOMAN: Nonsense!

DON JUAN: Consider, Señora: was not this true even when you lived on earth? When you were 70, were you really older underneath your wrinkles and your grey hairs than when you were 30?

THE OLD WOMAN: No, younger: at 30 I was a fool. But of what use is it to feel younger and look older?

DON JUAN: You see, Señora, the look was only an illusion. Your wrinkles lied, just as the plump smooth skin of many a stupid girl of 17, with heavy spirits and decrepit ideas, lies about her age. Well, here we have no bodies: we see each other as bodies only because we learnt to think about one another under that aspect when we were alive; and we still think in that way, knowing no other. But we can appear to one another at what age we choose. You have but to will any of your old looks back, and back they will come.

THE OLD WOMAN: It cannot be true.

DON JUAN: Try.

THE OLD WOMAN: Seventeen!

DON JUAN: Stop. Before you decide, I had better tell you that these things are a matter of fashion. Occasionally we have a rage for 17; but it does not last long. Just at present the fashionable age is 40—or say 37; but there are signs of a change. If you were at all good-looking at 27, I should suggest your trying that, and setting a new fashion.

THE OLD WOMAN: I do not believe a word you are saying. However, 27 be it. [*Whisk! the old woman becomes a young one, and so handsome that in the radiance into which her dull yellow halo has suddenly lightened one might almost mistake her for Ann Whitefield*].

DON JUAN: Doña Ana de Ulloa!

ANA: What? You know me!

DON JUAN: And you forget me!

ANA: I cannot see your face. [*He raises his hat*]. Don Juan Tenorio! Monster! You who slew my father! even here you pursue me.

DON JUAN: I protest I do not pursue you. Allow me to withdraw [*going*].

ANA [*seizing his arm*]: You shall not leave me alone in this dreadful place.

DON JUAN: Provided my staying be not interpreted as pursuit.

ANA [*releasing him*]: You may well wonder how I can endure your presence. My dear, dear father!

DON JUAN: Would you like to see him?

ANA: My father here! ! !

DON JUAN: No: he is in heaven.

ANA: I knew it. My noble father! He is looking down on us now. What must he feel to see his daughter in this place, and in conversation with his murderer!

DON JUAN: By the way, if we should meet him—

ANA: How can we meet him? He is in heaven.

DON JUAN: He condescends to look in upon us here from time to time. Heaven bores him. So let me warn you that if you meet him he will be mortally offended if you speak of me as his murderer! He maintains that he was a much better swordsman than I, and that if his foot had not slipped he would have killed me. No doubt he is right: I was not a good fencer. I never dispute the point; so we are excellent friends.

ANA: It is no dishonor to a soldier to be proud of his skill in arms.

DON JUAN: You would rather not meet him, probably.

ANA: How dare you say that?

DON JUAN: Oh, that is the usual feeling here. You may remember that on earth—though of course we never confessed it—the death of anyone we knew, even those we liked best, was always mingled with a certain satisfaction at being finally done with them.

ANA: Monster! Never, never.

DON JUAN [*placidly*]: I see you recognize the feeling. Yes: a funeral was always a festivity in black, especially the funeral of a relative. At all events, family ties are rarely kept up here. Your father is quite accustomed to this: he will not expect any devotion from you.

ANA: Wretch: I wore mourning for him all my life.

DON JUAN: Yes: it became you. But a life of mourning is one thing: an eternity of it quite another. Besides, here you are as dead as he. Can anything be more ridiculous than one dead person mourning for another? Do not look shocked, my dear Ana; and do not be alarmed: there is plenty of humbug in hell (indeed there is hardly anything else); but the humbug of death and age and change is dropped because here we are all dead and all eternal. You will pick up our ways soon.

ANA: And will all the men call me their dear Ana?

DON JUAN: No. That was a slip of the tongue. I beg your pardon.

ANA [*almost tenderly*]: Juan: did you really love me when you behaved so disgracefully to me?

DON JUAN [*impatiently*]: Oh, I beg you not to begin talking about love. Here they talk of nothing else but love—its beauty, its holiness, its spirituality, its devil knows what!—excuse me; but it does so bore me.

They don't know what they're talking about. I do. They think they have achieved the perfection of love because they have no bodies. Sheer imaginative debauchery! Faugh!

ANA: Has even death failed to refine your soul, Juan? Has the terrible judgment of which my father's statue was the minister taught you no reverence?

DON JUAN: How is that very flattering statue, by the way? Does it still come to supper with naughty people and cast them into this bottomless pit?

ANA: It has been a great expense to me. The boys in the monastery school would not let it alone: the mischievous ones broke it; and the studious ones wrote their names on it. Three new noses in two years, and fingers without end. I had to leave it to its fate at last; and now I fear it is shockingly mutilated. My poor father!

DON JUAN: Hush! Listen! [*Two great chords rolling on syncopated waves of sound break forth: D minor and its dominant: a sound of dreadful joy to all musicians*]. Ha. Mozart's statue music. It is your father. You had better disappear until I prepare him. [*She vanishes*].

From the void comes a living statue of white marble, designed to represent a majestic old man. But he waives his majesty with infinite grace; walks with a feather-like step; and makes every wrinkle in his war worn visage brim over with holiday joyousness. To his sculptor he owes a perfectly trained figure, which he carries erect and trim; and the ends of his moustache curl up, elastic as watchsprings, giving him an air which, but for its Spanish dignity, would be called jaunty. He is on the pleasantest terms with Don Juan. His voice, save for a much more distinguished intonation, is so like the voice of Roebuck Ramsden that it calls attention to the fact that they are not unlike one another in spite of their very different fashions of shaving.

DON JUAN: Ah, here you are, my friend. Why don't you learn to sing the splendid music Mozart has written for you?

THE STATUE: Unluckily he has written it for a bass voice. Mine is a counter tenor. Well: have you repented yet?

DON JUAN: I have too much consideration for you to repent, Don Gonzalo. If I did, you would have no excuse for coming from Heaven to argue with me.

THE STATUE: True. Remain obdurate, my boy. I wish I had killed you, as I should have done but for an accident. Then I should have come here; and you would have had a statue and a reputation for piety to live up to. Any news?

DON JUAN: Yes: your daughter is dead.

THE STATUE [*puzzled*]: My daughter? [*Recollecting*] Oh! the one you were taken with. Let me see: what was her name?

DON JUAN: Ana.

THE STATUE: To be sure: Ana. A goodlooking girl, If I recollect aright. Have you warned Whatshisname—her husband?

DON JUAN: My friend Ottavio? No: I have not seen him since Ana arrived. *Ana comes indignantly to light.*

ANA: What does this mean? Ottavio here and your friend! And you, father, have forgotten my name. You are indeed turned to stone.

THE STATUE: My dear: I am so much more admired in marble than I ever was in my own person that I have retained the shape the sculptor gave me. He was one of the first men of his day: you must acknowledge that.

ANA: Father! Vanity! personal vanity! from you!

THE STATUE: Ah, you outlived that weakness, my daughter: you must be nearly 80 by this time. I was cut off (by an accident) in my 64th year, and am considerably your junior in consequence. Besides, my child, in this place, what our libertine friend here would call the farce of parental wisdom is dropped. Regard me, I beg, as a fellow creature, not as a father.

ANA: You speak as this villian speaks.

THE STATUE: Juan is a sound thinker, Ana. A bad fencer, but a sound thinker.

ANA [*horror creeping upon her*]: I begin to understand. These are devils, mocking me. I had better pray.

THE STATUE [*consoling her*]: No, no, no, my child: do not pray. If you do, you will throw away the main advantage of this place. Written over the gate here are the words "Leave every hope behind, ye who enter." Only think what a relief that is! For what is hope? A form of moral responsibility. Here there is no hope, and consequently no duty, no work, nothing to be gained by praying, nothing to be lost by doing what you like. Hell, in short, is a place where you have nothing to do but amuse yourself. [*Don Juan sighs deeply*]. You sigh, friend Juan; but if you dwelt in heaven, as I do, you would realize your advantages.

DON JUAN: You are in good spirits to-day, Commander. You are positively brilliant. What is the matter?

THE STATUE: I have come to a momentous decision, my boy. But first, where is our friend the Devil? I must consult him in the matter. And Ana would like to make his acquaintance, no doubt.

ANA: You are preparing some torment for me.

DON JUAN: All that is superstition, Ana. Reassure yourself. Remember: the devil is not so black as he is painted.

THE STATUE: Let us give him a call.

At the wave of the statue's hand the great chords roll out again; but this time Mozart's music gets grotesquely adulterated with Gounod's. A scarlet halo begins to glow; and into it the Devil rises, very Mephistophelean, and not at all unlike Mendoza, though not so interesting. He looks older; is getting prematurely bald; and, in spite of an effusion of good-nature and friendliness, is peevish and sensitive when his advances are not reciprocated. He does not inspire much confidence in his powers of hard work or endurance, and is, on the whole, a disagreeably self-indulgent looking person; but he is clever and plausible, though perceptibly less well bred than the two other men, and enormously less vital than the woman.

THE DEVIL [*heartily*]: Have I the pleasure of again receiving a visit from the illustrious Commander of Calatrava? [*Coldly*] Don Juan, your servant. [*Politely*] And a strange lady? My respects, Señora.

ANA: Are you—

THE DEVIL [*bowing*]: Lucifer, at your service.

ANA: I shall go mad.

THE DEVIL [*gallantly*]: Ah, Señora, do not be anxious. You come to us from earth, full of the prejudices and terrors of that priest-ridden place. You have heard me ill spoken of; and yet, believe me, I have hosts of friends there.

ANA: Yes: you reign in their hearts.

THE DEVIL [*shaking his head*]: You flatter me, Señora; but you are mistaken. It is true that the world cannot get on without me; but it never gives me credit for that: in its heart it mistrusts and hates me. Its sympathies are all with misery, with poverty, with starvation of the body and of the heart. I call on it to sympathize with joy, with love, and happiness, with beauty—

DON JUAN [*nauseated*]: Excuse me: I am going. You know I cannot stand this.

THE DEVIL [*angrily*]: Yes: I know that you are no friend of mine.

THE STATUE: What harm is he doing you, Juan? It seems to me that he was talking excellent sense when you interrupted him.

THE DEVIL [*warmly shaking the statue's hand*]: Thank you, my friend: thank you. You have always understood me: he has always disparaged and avoided me.

DON JUAN: I have treated you with perfect courtesy.

THE DEVIL: Courtesy! What is courtesy? I care nothing for mere courtesy. Give me warmth of heart, true sincerity, the bond of sympathy with love and joy—

DON JUAN: You are making me ill.

THE DEVIL: There! [*Appealing to the statue*] You hear, sir! Oh, by what irony of fate was this cold selfish egotist sent to my kingdom, and you taken to the icy mansions of the sky!

THE STATUE: I can't complain. I was a hypocrite; and it served me right to be sent to heaven.

THE DEVIL: Why, sir, do you not join us, and leave a sphere for which your temperament is too sympathetic, your heart too warm, your capacity for enjoyment too generous?

THE STATUE: I have this day resolved to do so. In future, excellent Son of the Morning, I am yours. I have left Heaven for ever.

THE DEVIL [*again grasping his hand*]: Ah, what an honor for me! What a triumph for our cause! Thank you, thank you. And now, my friend—

I may call you so at last—could you not persuade him to take the place you have left vacant above?

THE STATUE [*shaking his head*]: I cannot conscientiously recommend any-body with whom I am on friendly terms to deliberately make himself dull and uncomfortable.

THE DEVIL: Of course not; but are you sure he would be uncomfortable? Of course you know best: you brought him here originally; and we had the greatest hopes of him. His sentiments were in the best taste of our best people. You remember how he sang? [*He begins to sing in a nasal operatic baritone, tremulous from an eternity of misuse in the French manner*]

> Vivan le femmine!
> Viva il buon vino!

THE STATUE [*taking up the tune an octave higher in his counter tenor*]:

> Sostegno e gloria
> D'umanità.

THE DEVIL: Precisely. Well, he never sings for us now.

DON JUAN: Do you complain of that? Hell is full of musical amateurs: music is the brandy of the damned. May not one lost soul be per-mitted to abstain?

THE DEVIL: You dare blaspheme against the sublimest of the arts!

DON JUAN [*with cold disgust*]: You talk like a hysterical woman fawning on a fiddler.

THE DEVIL: I am not angry. I merely pity you. You have no soul; and you are unconscious of all that you lose. Now you, Señor Commander, are a born musician. How well you sing! Mozart would be delighted if he were still here; but he moped and went to heaven. Curious how these clever men, whom you would have supposed born to be popular here, have turned out social failures, like Don Juan!

DON JUAN: I am really very sorry to be a social failure.

THE DEVIL: Not that we don't admire your intellect, you know. We do. But I look at the matter from your own point of view. You don't get on with us. The place doesn't suit you. The truth is, you have—I won't say no heart; for we know that beneath all your affected cyni-cism you have a warm one—

DON JUAN [*shrinking*]: Don't, please don't.

THE DEVIL [*nettled*]: Well, you've no capacity for enjoyment. Will that satisfy you?

DON JUAN: It is a somewhat less insufferable form of cant than the other. But if you'll allow me, I'll take refuge, as usual, in solitude.

THE DEVIL: Why not take refuge in Heaven? That's the proper place for you. [*To Ana*] Come, Señora! could you not persuade him for his own good to try a change of air?

ANA: But can he go to Heaven if he wants to?

THE DEVIL: What's to prevent him?

ANA: Can anybody—can I go to Heaven if I want to?

THE DEVIL [*rather contemptuously*]: Certainly, if your taste lies that way.

ANA: But why doesn't everybody go to Heaven, then?

THE STATUE [*chuckling*]: I can tell you that, my dear. It's because heaven is the most angelically dull place in all creation: that's why.

THE DEVIL: His excellency the Commander puts it with military bluntness; but the strain of living in Heaven is intolerable. There is a notion that I was turned out of it; but as a matter of fact nothing could have induced me to stay there. I simply left it and organized this place.

THE STATUE: I don't wonder at it. Nobody could stand an eternity of heaven.

THE DEVIL: Oh, it suits some people. Let us be just, Commander: it is a question of temperament. I don't admire the heavenly temperament: I don't understand it: I don't know that I particularly want to understand it; but it takes all sorts to make a universe. There is no accounting for tastes: there are people who like it. I think Don Juan would like it.

DON JUAN: But—pardon my frankness—could you really go back there if you desired to; or are the grapes sour?

THE DEVIL: Back there! I often go back there. Have you never read the book of Job? Have you any canonical authority for assuming that there is any barrier between our circle and the other one?

ANA: But surely there is a great gulf fixed.

THE DEVIL: Dear lady: a parable must not be taken literally. The gulf is the difference between the angelic and the diabolic temperament. What more impassable gulf could you have? Think of what you have seen on earth. There is no physical gulf between the philosopher's class room and the bull ring; but the bull fighters do not come to the class room for all that. Have you ever been in the country where I have the largest following—England? There they have great racecourses, and also concert rooms where they play the classical compositions of his Excellency's friend Mozart. Those who go to the racecourses can stay away from them and go to the classical concerts instead if they like: there is no law against it; for Englishmen never will be slaves: they are free to do whatever the Government and public opinion allow them to do. And the classical concert is admitted to be a higher, more cultivated, poetic, intellectual, ennobling place than the racecourse. But do the lovers of racing desert their sport and flock to the concert room? Not they. They would suffer there all the weariness the Commander has suffered in heaven. There is the great gulf of the parable between the two places. A mere physical gulf they could bridge; or at least I could bridge it for them (the earth is full of Devil's Bridges); but the gulf of dislike is impassable and eternal. And that is the only gulf that separates my friends here from those who are invidiously called the blest.

ANA: I shall go to heaven at once.

THE STATUE: My child: one word of warning first. Let me complete my friend Lucifer's similitude of the classical concert. At every one of those concerts in England you will find rows of weary people who are there, not because they really like classical music, but because they think they ought to like it. Well, there is the same thing in heaven. A number of people sit there in glory, not because they are happy, but because they think they owe it to their position to be in heaven. They are almost all English.

THE DEVIL: Yes: the Southerners give it up and join me just as you have done. But the English really do not seem to know when they are thoroughly miserable. An Englishman thinks he is moral when he is only uncomfortable.

THE STATUE: In short, my daughter, if you go to Heaven without being naturally qualified for it, you will not enjoy yourself there.

ANA: And who dares say that I am not naturally qualified for it? The most distinguished princes of the Church have never questioned it. I owe it to myself to leave this place at once.

THE DEVIL [offended]: As you please, Señora. I should have expected better taste from you.

ANA: Father: I shall expect you to come with me. You cannot stay here. What will people say?

THE STATUE: People! Why, the best people are here—princes of the church and all. So few go to Heaven, and so many come here, that the blest, once called a heavenly host, are a continually dwindling minority. The saints, the fathers, the elect of long ago are the cranks, the faddists, the outsiders of to-day.

THE DEVIL: It is true. From the beginning of my career I knew that I should win in the long run by sheer weight of public opinion, in spite of the long campaign of misrepresentation and calumny against me. At bottom the universe is a constitutional one; and with such a majority as mine I cannot be kept permanently out of office.

DON JUAN: I think, Ana, you had better stay here.

ANA [jealously]: You do not want me to go with you.

DON JUAN: Surely you do not want to enter Heaven in the company of a reprobate like me.

ANA: All souls are equally precious. You repent, do you not?

DON JUAN: My dear Ana, you are silly. Do you suppose heaven is like earth, where people persuade themselves that what is done can be un- done by repentance; that what is spoken can be unspoken by with- drawing it; that what is true can be annihilated by a general agreement to give it the lie? No: heaven is the home of the masters of reality: that is why I am going thither.

ANA: Thank you: I am going to heaven for happiness. I have had quite enough of reality on earth.

DON JUAN: Then you must stay here; for hell is the home of the unreal and of the seekers for happiness. It is the only refuge from heaven, which is, as I tell you, the home of the masters of reality, and from earth, which is the home of the slaves of reality. The earth is a nursery in which men and women play at being heros and heroines, saints and sinners; but they are dragged down from their fool's paradise by their bodies: hunger and cold and thirst, age and decay and disease, death above all, make them slaves of reality: thrice a day meals must be eaten and digested: thrice a century a new generation must be engendered: ages of faith, of romance, and of science are all driven at last to have but one prayer "Make me a healthy animal." But here you escape this tyranny of the flesh; for here you are not an animal at all: you are a ghost, an appearance, an illusion, a convention, deathless, ageless: in a word, bodiless. There are no social questions here, no political questions, no religious questions, best of all, perhaps, no sanitary questions. Here you call your appearance beauty, your emotions love, your sentiments heroism, your aspirations virtue, just as you did on earth; but here there are no hard facts to contradict you, no ironic contrast of your needs with your pretensions, no human comedy, nothing but a perpetual romance, a universal melodrama. As our German friend put it in his poem, "the poetically nonsensical here is good sense; and the Eternal Feminine draws us ever upward and on"— without getting up a step farther. And yet you want to leave this paradise!

ANA: But if Hell be so beautiful as this, how glorious must heaven be!

The Devil, the Statue, and Don Juan all begin to speak at once in violent protest; then stop, abashed.

DON JUAN: I beg your pardon.

THE DEVIL: Not at all. I interrupted you.

THE STATUE: You were going to say something.

DON JUAN: After you, gentlemen.

THE DEVIL [*to Don Juan*]: You have been so eloquent on the advantages of my dominions that I leave you to do equal justice to the drawbacks of the alternative establishment.

DON JUAN: In Heaven, as I picture it, dear lady, you live and work instead of playing and pretending. You face things as they are; you escape nothing but glamor; and your steadfastness and your peril are your glory. If the play still goes on here and on earth, and all the world is a stage, Heaven is at least behind the scenes. But Heaven cannot be described by metaphor. Thither I shall go presently, because there I hope to escape at last from lies and from the tedious, vulgar pursuit of happiness, to spend my eons in contemplation—

THE STATUE: Ugh!

DON JUAN: Señor Commander: I do not blame your disgust: a picture gallery is a dull place for a blind man. But even as you enjoy the contemplation of such romantic mirages as beauty and pleasure; so would I enjoy the contemplation of that which interests me above all things: namely, Life: the force that ever strives to attain greater power of contemplating itself. What made this brain of mine, do you think? Not the need to move my limbs; for a rat with half my brains moves as well as I. Not merely the need to do, but the need to know what I do, lest in my blind efforts to live I should be slaying myself.

THE STATUE: You would have slain yourself in your blind efforts to fence but for my foot slipping, my friend.

DON JUAN: Audacious ribald: your laughter will finish in hideous boredom before morning.

THE STATUE: Ha ha! Do you remember how I frightened you when I said something like that to you from my pedestal in Seville? It sounds rather flat without my trombones.

DON JUAN: They tell me it generally sounds flat with them, Commander.

ANA: Oh, do not interrupt with these frivolities, father. Is there nothing in Heaven but contemplation, Juan?

DON JUAN: In the Heaven I seek, no other joy. But there is the work of helping Life in its struggle upward. Think of how it wastes and scatters itself, how it raises up obstacles to itself and destroys itself in its ignorance and blindness. It needs a brain, this irresistible force, lest in its ignorance it should resist itself. What a piece of work is man! says the poet. Yes: but what a blunderer! Here is the highest miracle of organization yet attained by life, the most intensely alive thing that exists, the most conscious of all the organisms; and yet, how wretched are his brains! Stupidity made sordid and cruel by the realities learnt from toil and poverty: Imagination resolved to starve sooner than face these realities, piling up illusions to hide them, and calling itself cleverness, genius! And each accusing the other of its own defect: Stupidity accusing Imagination of folly, and Imagination accusing Stupidity of ignorance: whereas, alas! Stupidity has all the knowledge, and Imagination all the intelligence.

THE DEVIL: And a pretty kettle of fish they make of it between them. Did I not say, when I was arranging that affair of Faust's, that all Man's reason has done for him is to make him beastlier than any beast. One splendid body is worth the brains of a hundred dyspeptic, flatulent philosophers.

DON JUAN: You forget that brainless magnificence of body has been tried. Things immeasurably greater than man in every respect but brain have existed and perished. The megatherium, the icthyosaurus have paced the earth with seven-league steps and hidden the day with cloud vast wings. Where are they now? Fossils in museums, and so few and imperfect at that, that a knuckle bone or a tooth of one of them is prized beyond the lives of a thousand soldiers. These things lived and wanted to live; but for lack of brains they did not know how to carry out their purpose, and so destroyed themselves.

THE DEVIL: And is Man any the less destroying himself for all this boasted brain of his? Have you walked up and down upon the earth lately? I have; and I have examined Man's wonderful inventions. And I tell you that in the arts of life man invents nothing; but in the arts of death he outdoes Nature herself, and produces by chemistry and machinery all the slaughter of plague, pestilence and famine. The peasant I tempt to-day eats and drinks what was eaten and drunk by the peasants of ten thousand years ago; and the house he lives in has not altered as much in a thousand centuries as the fashion of a lady's bonnet in a score of weeks. But when he goes out to slay, he carries a marvel of mechanism that lets loose at the touch of his finger all the hidden molecular energies, and leaves the javelin, the arrow, the blowpipe of his fathers far behind. In the arts of peace Man is a bungler. I have seen his cotton factories and the like, with machinery that a greedy dog could have invented if it had wanted money instead of food. I know his clumsy typewriters and bungling locomotives and tedious bicycles: they are toys compared to the machine gun, the submarine torpedo boat. There is nothing in Man's industrial machinery but his greed and sloth: his heart is in his weapons. This marvellous force of Life of which you boast is a force of Death: Man measures his strength by his destructiveness. What is his religion? An excuse for hating me. What is his law? An excuse for hanging you. What is his morality? Gentility! an excuse for consuming without producing. What is his art? An excuse for gloating over pictures of slaughter. What are his politics? Either the worship of a despot because a despot can kill, or parliamentary cockfighting. I spent an evening lately in a certain celebrated legislature, and heard the pot lecturing the kettle for its blackness, and ministers answering questions. When I left I chalked up on the door the old nursery saying "Ask no questions and you will be told no lies." I bought a sixpenny family magazine, and found it full of pictures of young men shooting and stabbing one another. I saw a man die: he was a London bricklayer's laborer with seven children. He left seventeen pounds club money; and his wife spent it all on his funeral and went into the workhouse with the children next day. She would not have spent sevenpence on her children's schooling: the law had to force her to let them be taught gratuitously; but on death she spent all she had. Their imagination glows, their energies rise up at the idea of death, these people: they love it; and the more horrible it is the more they enjoy it. Hell is a place far above their comprehension: they derive their notion of it from two of the greatest fools that ever lived, an Italian and an Englishman. The Italian described it as a place of mud, frost, filth, fire, and venomous serpents: all torture. This ass, when he was not lying about me, was maundering about some woman whom he saw once in the street. The Englishman described me as being expelled from Heaven by cannons and gunpowder; and to this day every Briton believes that the whole of his silly story is in the Bible. What else he says I do not know; for it is all in a long poem which neither I nor anyone else ever succeeded in wading through. It is the same in everything. The highest form of literature is the tragedy, a play in which everybody is murdered at the end. In the old chronicles you read of earthquakes and pestilences, and are told that these shewed the power and majesty of God and the littleness of Man. Nowadays the chronicles describe battles. In a battle two bodies of men shoot at one another with bullets and explosive shells until one body runs away, when the others chase the fugitives on horseback and cut them to pieces as they fly. And this, the chronicle concludes, shews the greatness and majesty of empires, and the littleness of the vanquished. Over such battles the people run about the streets yelling with delight, and egg their Governments on to spend hundreds of millions of money in the slaughter, whilst the strongest Ministers dare not spend an extra penny in the pound against the poverty and pestilence through which they themselves daily walk. I could give you a thousand instances; but they all come to the same thing: the power that governs the earth is not the power of Life but of Death; and the inner need that has nerved Life to the effort of organizing itself into the human being is not the need for higher life but for a more efficient engine of destruction. The plague, the famine, the earthquake, the tempest were too spasmodic in their action; the tiger and crocodile were too easily satiated and not cruel enough: something more constantly, more ruthlessly, more ingeniously destructive was needed; and that something was Man, the inventor of the rack, the stake, the gallows, and the electric chair; of the sword and gun; above all, of justice, duty, patriotism and all the other isms by which even those who are clever enough to be humanely disposed are persuaded to become the most destructive of all the destroyers.

DON JUAN: Pshaw! all this is old. Your weak side, my diabolic friend, is that you have always been a gull: you take Man at his own valuation. Nothing would flatter him more than your opinion of him. He loves to think of himself as bold and bad. He is neither one nor the other: he is only a coward. Call him tyrant, murderer, pirate, bully; and he will adore you, and swagger about with the consciousness of having the blood of the old sea kings in his veins. Call him liar and thief; and he will only take an action against you for libel. But call him coward; and he will go mad with rage: he will face death to outface that stinging truth. Man gives every reason for his conduct save one, every excuse for his crimes save one, every plea for his safety save one; and that one is his cowardice. Yet all his civilization is founded on his cowardice, on his abject tameness, which he calls his respectability. There are limits to what a mule or an ass will stand; but Man will suffer himself to be degraded until his vileness becomes so loathsome to his oppressors that they themselves are forced to reform it.

THE DEVIL: Precisely. And these are the creatures in whom you discover what you call a Life Force!

DON JUAN: Yes; for now comes the most surprising part of the whole business.

THE STATUE: What's that?

DON JUAN: Why, that you can make any of these cowards brave by simply putting an idea into his head.

THE STATUE: Stuff! As an old soldier I admit the cowardice: it's as universal as sea sickness, and matters just as little. But that about putting an idea into a man's head is stuff and nonsense. In a battle all you need to make you fight is a little hot blood and the knowledge that it's more dangerous to lose than to win.

DON JUAN: That is perhaps why battles are so useless. But men never really overcome fear until they imagine they are fighting to further a universal purpose—fighting for an idea, as they call it. Why was the Crusader braver than the pirate? Because he fought, not for himself, but for the Cross. What force was it that met him with a valor as reckless as his own? The force of men who fought, not for themselves, but for Islam. They took Spain from us, though we were fighting for our very hearths and homes; but when we, too, fought for that mighty idea, a Catholic Church, we swept them back to Africa.

THE DEVIL [*ironically*]: What! you a Catholic, Señor Don Juan! A devotee! My congratulations.

THE STATUE [*seriously*]: Come come! as a soldier, I can listen to nothing against the Church.

DON JUAN: Have no fear, Commander: this idea of a Catholic Church will survive Islam, will survive the Cross, will survive even that vulgar pageant of incompetent schoolboyish gladiators which you call the Army.

THE STATUE: Juan: you will force me to call you to account for this.

DON JUAN: Useless: I cannot fence. Every idea for which Man will die will be a Catholic idea. When the Spaniard learns at last that he is no better than the Saracen, and his prophet no better than Mahomet, he will arise, more Catholic than ever, and die on a barricade across the filthy slum he starves in, for universal liberty and equality.

THE STATUE: Bosh!

DON JUAN: What you call bosh is the only thing men dare die for. Later on, Liberty will not be Catholic enough: men will die for human perfection, to which they will sacrifice all their liberty gladly.

THE DEVIL: Ay: they will never be at a loss for an excuse for killing one another.

DON JUAN: What of that? It is not death that matters, but the fear of death. It is not killing and dying that degrades us, but base living, and accepting the wages and profits of degradation. Better ten dead men than one live slave or his master. Men shall yet rise up, father against son and brother against brother, and kill one another for the great Catholic idea of abolishing slavery.

THE DEVIL: Yes, when the Liberty and Equality of which you prate shall have made free white Christians cheaper in the labor market than black heathen slaves sold by auction at the block.

DON JUAN: Never fear! the white laborer shall have his turn too. But I am not now defending the illusory forms the great ideas take. I am giving you examples of the fact that this creature Man, who in his own selfish affairs is a coward to the backbone, will fight for an idea like a hero. He may be abject as a citizen; but he is dangerous as a fanatic. He can only be enslaved whilst he is spiritually weak enough to listen to reason. I tell you, gentlemen, if you can shew a man a piece of what he now calls God's work to do, and what he will later on call by many new names, you can make him entirely reckless of the consequences to himself personally.

. . .

. . . I tell you that as long as I can conceive something better than myself I cannot be easy unless I am striving to bring it into existence or clearing the way for it. That is the law of my life. That is the working within me of Life's incessant aspiration to higher organization, wider, deeper, intenser self-consciousness, and clearer self-understanding. It was the supremacy of this purpose that reduced love for me to the mere pleasure of a moment, art for me to the mere schooling of my faculties, religion for me to a mere excuse for laziness, since it had set up a God who looked at the world and saw that it was good, against the instinct in me that looked through my eyes at the world and saw that it could be improved. I tell you that in the pursuit of my own pleasure, my own health, my own fortune, I have never known happiness. It was not love for Woman that delivered me into her hands: it was fatigue, exhaustion. When I was a child, and bruised my head against a stone, I ran to the nearest woman and cried away my pain against her apron. When I grew up, and bruised my soul against the brutalities and stupidities with which I had to strive, I did again just what I had done as a child. I have enjoyed, too, my rests, my recuperations, my breathing times, my very prostrations after strife; but rather would I be dragged through all the circles of the foolish Italian's Inferno than through the pleasures of Europe. That is what has made this place of eternal pleasures so deadly to me. It is the absence of this instinct in you that makes you that strange monster called a Devil. It is the success with which you have diverted the attention of men from their real purpose, which in one degree or another is the same as mine, to yours, that has earned you the name of The Tempter. It is the fact that they are doing your will, or rather drifting with your want of will, instead of doing their own, that makes them the uncomfortable, false, restless, artificial, petulant, wretched creatures they are.

THE DEVIL [*mortified*]: Señor Don Juan: you are uncivil to my friends.

DON JUAN: Pooh! why should I be civil to them or to you? In this Palace of Lies a truth or two will not hurt you. Your friends are all the dullest dogs I know. They are not beautiful: they are only decorated.

They are not clean: they are only shaved and starched. They are not dignified: they are only fashionably dressed. They are not educated: they are only college passmen. They are not religious: they are only pewrenters. They are not moral: they are only conventional. They are not virtuous: they are only cowardly. They are not even vicious: they are only "frail." They are not artistic: they are only lascivious. They are not prosperous: they are only rich. They are not loyal, they are only servile; not dutiful, only sheepish; not public spirited, only patriotic; not courageous, only quarrelsome; not determined, only obstinate; not masterful, only domineering; not self-controlled, only obtuse; not self-respecting, only vain; not kind, only sentimental; not social, only gregarious; not considerate, only polite; not intelligent, only opinionated; not progressive, only factious; not imaginative, only superstitious; not just, only vindictive; not generous, only propitiatory; not disciplined, only cowed; and not truthful at all—liars every one of them, to the very backbone of their souls.

THE STATUE: Your flow of words is simply amazing, Juan. How I wish I could have talked like that to my soldiers.

THE DEVIL: It is mere talk, though. It has all been said before; but what change has it ever made? What notice has the world ever taken of it?

DON JUAN: Yes, it is mere talk. But why is it mere talk? Because, my friend, beauty, purity, respectability, religion, morality, art, patriotism, bravery and the rest are nothing but words which I or anyone else can turn inside out like a glove. Were they realities, you would have to plead guilty to my indictment; but fortunately for your self-respect, my diabolical friend, they are not realities. As you say, they are mere words, useful for duping barbarians into adopting civilization, or the civilized poor into submitting to be robbed and enslaved. That is the family secret of the governing caste; and if we who are of that caste aimed at more Life for the world instead of at more power and luxury for our miserable selves, that secret would make us great. Now, since I, being a nobleman, am in the secret too, think how tedious to me must be your unending cant about all these moralistic figments, and how squalidly disastrous your sacrifice of your lives to them! If you even believed in your moral game enough to play it fairly, it would be interesting to watch; but you don't: you cheat at every trick; and if your opponent outcheats you, you upset the table and try to murder him.

THE DEVIL: On earth there may be some truth in this, because the people are uneducated and cannot appreciate my religion of love and beauty; but here—

DON JUAN: Oh yes: I know. Here there is nothing but love and beauty. Ugh! it is like sitting for all eternity at the first act of a fashionable play, before the complications begin. Never in my worst moments of superstitious terror on earth did I dream that Hell was so horrible. I live, like a hairdresser, in the continual contemplation of beauty, toying with silken tresses. I breathe an atmosphere of sweetness, like a confectioner's shopboy. Commander: are there any beautiful women in Heaven?

THE STATUE: None. Absolutely none. All dowdies. Not two pennorth of jewellery among a dozen of them. They might be men of fifty.

DON JUAN: I am impatient to get there. Is the word beauty ever mentioned; and are there any artistic people?

THE STATUE: I give you my word they won't admire a fine statue even when it walks past them.

DON JUAN: I go.

THE DEVIL: Don Juan: shall I be frank with you?

DON JUAN: Were you not so before?

THE DEVIL: As far as I went, yes. But I will now go further, and confess to you that men get tired of everything, of heaven no less than of hell; and that all history is nothing but a record of the oscillations of the world between these two extremes. An epoch is but a swing of the pendulum; and each generation thinks the world is progressing because it is always moving. But when you are as old as I am; when you have a thousand times wearied of heaven, like myself and the Commander, and a thousand times wearied of hell, as you are wearied now, you will no longer imagine that every swing from heaven to hell is an emancipation, every swing from hell to heaven an evolution. Where you now see reform, progress, fulfilment of upward tendency, continual ascent by Man on the stepping stones of his dead selves to higher things, you will see nothing but an infinite comedy of illusion. You will discover the profound truth of the saying of my friend Koheleth, that there is nothing new under the sun. Vanitas vanitatum—

DON JUAN [out of all patience]: By Heaven, this is worse than your cant about love and beauty. Clever dolt that you are, is a man no better than a worm, or a dog than a wolf, because he gets tired of everything? Shall he give up eating because he destroys his appetite in the act of gratifying it? Is a field idle when it is fallow? Can the Commander expend his hellish energy here without accumulating heavenly energy for his next term of blessedness? Granted that the great Life Force has hit on the device of the clockmaker's pendulum, and uses the earth for its bob; that the history of each oscillation, which seems so novel to us the actors, is but the history of the last oscillation repeated; nay more, that in the unthinkable infinitude of time the sun throws off the earth and catches it again a thousand times as a circus rider throws up a ball, and that the total of all our epochs is but the moment between the toss and the catch, has the colossal mechanism no purpose?

THE DEVIL: None, my friend. You think, because you have a purpose, Nature must have one. You might as well expect it to have fingers and toes because you have them.

DON JUAN: But I should not have them if they served no purpose. And I, my friend, am as much a part of Nature as my own finger is a part of me. If my finger is the organ by which I grasp the sword and the mandolin, my brain is the organ by which Nature strives to understand itself. My dog's brain serves only my dog's purposes; but my brain labors at a knowledge which does nothing for me personally but make my body bitter to me and my decay and death a calamity. Were I not possessed with a purpose beyond my own I had better be a ploughman than a philosopher; for the ploughman lives as long as the philosopher, eats more, sleeps better, and rejoices in the wife of his bosom with less misgiving. This is because the philosopher is in the grip of the Life Force. This Life Force says to him "I have done a thousand wonderful things unconsciously by merely willing to live and following the line of least resistance: now I want to know myself and my destination, and choose my path; so I have made a special brain—a philosopher's brain—to grasp this knowledge for me as the husbandman's hand grasps the plough for me. And this" says the Life Force to the philosopher "must thou strive to do for me until thou diest, when I will make another brain and another philosopher to carry on the work."

THE DEVIL: What is the use of knowing?

DON JUAN: Why, to be able to choose the line of greatest advantage instead of yielding in the direction of the least resistance. Does a ship sail to its destination no better than a log drifts nowhither? The philosopher is Nature's pilot. And there you have our difference: to be in hell is to drift: to be in heaven is to steer.

THE DEVIL: On the rocks, most likely.

DON JUAN: Pooh! which ship goes oftenest on the rocks or to the bottom— the drifting ship or the ship with a pilot on board?

THE DEVIL: Well, well, go your way, Señor Don Juan. I prefer to be my own master and not the tool of any blundering universal force. I know that beauty is good to look at; that music is good to hear; that love is good to feel; and that they are all good to think about and talk about. I know that to be well exercised in these sensations, emotions, and studies is to be a refined and cultivated being. Whatever they may say of me in churches on earth, I know that it is universally admitted in good society that the Prince of Darkness is a gentleman; and that is enough for me. As to your Life Force, which you think irresistible, it is the most resistible thing in the world for a person of any character. But if you are naturally vulgar and credulous, as all reformers are, it will thrust you first into religion, where you will sprinkle water on babies to save their souls from me; then it will drive you from religion into science, where you will snatch the babies from the water sprinkling and inoculate them with disease to save them from catching it accidentally; then you will take to politics, where you will become the catspaw of corrupt functionaries and the henchman of ambitious

humbugs; and the end will be despair and decrepitude, broken nerve
and shattered hopes, vain regrets for that worst and silliest of wastes
and sacrifices, the waste and sacrifice of the power of enjoyment: in
a word, the punishment of the fool who pursues the better before he
has secured the good.

DON JUAN: But at least I shall not be bored. The service of the Life Force
has that advantage, at all events. So fare you well, Señor Satan.

THE DEVIL [*amiably*]: Fare you well, Don Juan. I shall often think of our
interesting chats about things in general. I wish you every happiness:
Heaven, as I said before, suits some people. But if you should change
your mind, do not forget that the gates are always open here to the
repentant prodigal. If you feel at any time that warmth of heart,
sincere unforced affection, innocent enjoyment, and warm, breathing,
palpitating reality—

DON JUAN: Why not say flesh and blood at once, though we have left
those two greasy commonplaces behind us?

THE DEVIL [*angrily*]: You throw my friendly farewell back in my teeth,
then, Don Juan?

DON JUAN: By no means. But though there is much to be learnt from a
cynical devil, I really cannot stand a sentimental one. Señor Commander: you know the way to the frontier of hell and heaven. Be good
enough to direct me.

THE STATUE: Oh, the frontier is only the difference between two ways of
looking at things. Any road will take you across it if you really want to
get there.

DON JUAN: Good. [*Saluting Doña Ana*] Señora: your servant.

THUS SPOKE ZARATHUSTRA
and
THE GAY SCIENCE
FRIEDRICH NIETZSCHE
(trans. by Walter Kaufmann)

Friedrich Nietzsche (1844–1900) was a German philosopher whose theory that every man seeks a richer, more powerful state of being greatly influenced literature, psychoanalysis, and existential philosophy. His ideas, often disjointed yet remarkably insightful, are contained in a variety of forceful works such as *The Birth of Tragedy, Thus Spoke Zarathustra, The Antichrist, Human, All-too-Human, The Joyful Wisdom (The Gay Science),* and *Beyond Good and Evil.*

Nietzsche greatly influenced G. B. Shaw and is directly responsible for Shaw's belief in eternal recurrence, the superman, and the virtue of power. However, Nietzsche goes further than Shaw and stresses such virtues as iconoclasm, avarice and cruelty, contempt for weakness, a warlike posture, and love of conquest. Almost everything that ordinary men call evil should be championed for the good of the species, and the overman (or superman) who creates new standards of excellence, is the ideal being with Zarathustra as his prophet. Only a small minority will be able to follow the image of the overman, for not only must a transvaluation of ordinary ethics be made, but the superior individual must also maintain his courage in the face of a universe in which all events recur and progress comes to nothing.

THUS SPOKE ZARATHUSTRA
3

When Zarathustra came into the next town, which lies on the edge of the forest, he found many people gathered together in the market place; for it had been promised that there would be a tightrope walker. And Zarathustra spoke thus to the people:

"*I teach you the overman.* Man is something that shall be overcome. What have you done to overcome him?

"All beings so far have created something beyond themselves; and do you want to be the ebb of this great flood and even go back to the beasts rather than overcome man? What is the ape to man? A laughingstock or a painful embarrassment. And man shall be just that for the overman: a laughingstock or a painful embarrassment. You have made your way from worm to man, and much in you is still worm. Once you were apes, and even now, too, man is more ape than any ape.

"Whoever is the wisest among you is also a mere conflict and cross between plant and ghost. But do I bid you become ghosts or plants?

"Behold, I teach you the overman. The overman is the meaning of the earth. Let your will say: the overman *shall be* the meaning of the earth! I beseech you, my brothers, *remain faithful to the earth,* and do not believe those who speak to you of otherworldly hopes! Poison-mixers are they, whether they know it or not. Despisers of life are they, decaying and poisoned ones themselves, of whom the earth is weary: so let them go.

"Once the sin against God was the greatest sin; but God died, and these sinners died with him. To sin against the earth is now the most dreadful thing, and to esteem the entrails of the unknowable higher than the meaning of the earth.

"Once the soul looked contemptuously upon the body, and then this contempt was the highest: she wanted the body meager, ghastly, and starved. Thus she hoped to escape it and the earth. Oh, this soul herself was still meager, ghastly, and starved: and cruelty was the lust of this soul. But you, too, my brothers, tell me: what does your body proclaim of your soul? Is not your soul poverty and filth and wretched contentment?

"Verily, a polluted stream is man. One must be a sea to be able to receive a polluted stream without becoming unclean. Behold, I teach you the overman: he is this sea; in him your great contempt can go under.

"What is the greatest experience you can have? It is the hour of the great contempt. The hour in which your happiness, too, arouses your disgust, and even your reason and your virtue.

"The hour when you say, 'What matters my happiness? It is poverty and filth and wretched contentment. But my happiness ought to justify existence itself.'

"The hour when you say, 'What matters my reason? Does it crave knowledge as the lion his food? It is poverty and filth and wretched contentment.'

"The hour when you say, 'What matters my virtue? As yet it has not made me rage. How weary I am of my good and my evil! All that is poverty and filth and wretched contentment.'

"The hour when you say, 'What matters my justice? I do not see that I am flames and fuel. But the just are flames and fuel.'

"The hour when you say, 'What matters my pity? Is not pity the cross on which he is nailed who loves man? But my pity is no crucifixion.'

"Have you yet spoken thus? Have you yet cried thus? Oh, that I might have heard you cry thus!

"Not your sin but your thrift cries to heaven; your meanness even in your sin cries to heaven.

"Where is the lightning to lick you with its tongue? Where is the frenzy with which you should be inoculated?

"Behold, I teach you the overman: he is this lightning, he is this frenzy."

When Zarathustra had spoken thus, one of the people cried: "Now we have heard enough about the tightrope walker; now let us see him too!" And all the people laughed at Zarathustra. But the tightrope walker, believing that the word concerned him, began his performance.

4

Zarathustra, however, beheld the people and was amazed. Then he spoke thus:

"Man is a rope, tied between beast and overman—a rope over an abyss. A dangerous across, a dangerous on-the-way, a dangerous looking-back, a dangerous shuddering and stopping.

"What is great in man is that he is a bridge and not an end: what can be loved in man is that he is an *overture* and a *going under*.

"I love those who do not know how to live, except by going under, for they are those who cross over.

"I love the great despisers because they are the great reverers and arrows of longing for the other shore.

"I love those who do not first seek behind the stars for a reason to go under and be a sacrifice, but who sacrifice themselves for the earth, that the earth may some day become the overman's.

"I love him who lives to know, and who wants to know so that the overman may live some day. And thus he wants to go under.

"I love him who works and invents to build a house for the overman and to prepare earth, animal, and plant for him: for thus he wants to go under.

"I love him who loves his virtue, for virtue is the will to go under and an arrow of longing.

"I love him who does not hold back one drop of spirit for himself, but wants to be entirely the spirit of his virtue: thus he strides over the bridge as spirit.

"I love him who makes his virtue his addiction and his catastrophe: for his virtue's sake he wants to live on and to live no longer.

"I love him who does not want to have too many virtues. One virtue is more virtue than two, because it is more of a noose on which his catastrophe may hang.

"I love him whose soul squanders itself, who wants no thanks and returns none: for he always gives away and does not want to preserve himself.

"I love him who is abashed when the dice fall to make his fortune, and asks, 'Am I then a crooked gambler?' For he wants to perish.

"I love him who casts golden words before his deeds and always does even more than he promises: for he wants to go under.

"I love him who justifies future and redeems past generations: for he wants to perish of the present.

"I love him who chastens his god because he loves his god: for he must perish of the wrath of his god.

"I love him whose soul is deep, even in being wounded, and who can perish of a small experience: thus he goes gladly over the bridge.

"I love him whose soul is overfull so that he forgets himself, and all things are in him: thus all things spell his going under.

"I love him who has a free spirit and a free heart: thus his head is only the entrails of his heart, but his heart drives him to go under.

"I love all those who are as heavy drops, falling one by one out of the dark cloud that hangs over men: they herald the advent of lightning, and, as heralds, they perish.

"Behold, I am a herald of the lightning and a heavy drop from the cloud; but this lightning is called *overman*."

5

When Zarathustra had spoken these words he beheld the people again and was silent. "There they stand," he said to his heart; "there they laugh. They do not understand me; I am not the mouth for these ears. Must one smash their ears before they learn to listen with their eyes? Must one clatter like kettledrums and preachers of repentance? Or do they believe only the stammerer?

"They have something of which they are proud. What do they call that which makes them proud? Education they call it; it distinguishes them from goatherds. That is why they do not like to hear the word 'contempt' applied to them. Let me then address their pride. Let me speak to them of what is most contemptible: but that is the *last man*."

And thus spoke Zarathustra to the people: "The time has come for man to set himself a goal. The time has come for man to plant the seed of his highest hope. His soil is still rich enough. But one day this soil will be poor and domesticated, and no tall tree will be able to grow in it. Alas, the time is coming when man will no longer shoot the arrow of his longing beyond man, and the string of his bow will have forgotten how to whir!

"I say unto you: one must still have chaos in oneself to be able to give birth to a dancing star. I say unto you: you still have chaos in yourselves.

"Alas, the time is coming when man will no longer give birth to a star. Alas, the time of the most despicable man is coming, he that is no longer able to despise himself. Behold, I show you the *last man*.

" 'What is love? What is creation? What is longing? What is a star?' thus asks the last man, and he blinks.

"The earth has become small, and on it hops the last man, who makes everything small. His race is as ineradicable as the flea-beetle; the last man lives longest.

" 'We have invented happiness,' say the last men, and they blink. They have left the regions where it was hard to live, for one needs warmth. One still loves one's neighbor and rubs against him, for one needs warmth.

"Becoming sick and harboring suspicion are sinful to them: one proceeds carefully. A fool, whoever still stumbles over stones or human beings! A little poison now and then: that makes for agreeable dreams. And much poison in the end, for an agreeable death.

"One still works, for work is a form of entertainment. But one is careful lest the entertainment be too harrowing. One no longer becomes poor or rich: both require too much exertion. Who still wants to rule? Who obey? Both require too much exertion.

"No shepherd and one herd! Everybody wants the same, everybody is the same: whoever feels different goes voluntarily into a madhouse.

" 'Formerly, all the world was mad,' say the most refined, and they blink.

"One is clever and knows everything that has ever happened: so there is no end of derision. One still quarrels, but one is soon reconciled—else it might spoil the digestion.

"One has one's little pleasure for the day and one's little pleasure for the night: but one has a regard for health.

" 'We have invented happiness,' say the last men, and they blink."

And here ended Zarathustra's first speech, which is also called "the Prologue"; for at this point he was interrupted by the clamor and delight of the crowd. "Give us this last man, O Zarathustra," they shouted. "Turn us into these last men! Then we shall make you a gift of the overman!" And all the people jubilated and clucked with their tongues.

But Zarathustra became sad and said to his heart: "They do not understand me: I am not the mouth for these ears. I seem to have lived too long in the mountains; I listened too much to brooks and trees: now I talk to them as to goatherds. My soul is unmoved and bright as the mountains in the morning. But they think I am cold and I jeer and make dreadful jests. And now they look at me and laugh: and as they laugh they even hate me. There is ice in their laughter."

from
THE GAY SCIENCE

EDITOR'S NOTE

Nietzsche's last really aphoristic work, first published in 1882. The title in the English collected edition, *Joyful Wisdom*, is a mistranslation. Aphorisms 285 and 341 are among the first statements of the "eternal recurrence." WALTER KAUFMANN

4

What preserves the species. The strongest and most evil spirits have so far advanced humanity the most: they have always rekindled the drowsing passions—all ordered society puts the passions to sleep; they have always reawakened the sense of comparison, of contradiction, of joy in the new, the daring, and the untried; they force men to meet opinion with opinion, model with model. For the most part by arms, by the overthrow of boundary stones, and by offense to the pieties, but also by new religions and moralities. The same "malice" is to be found in every teacher and preacher of the new. . . . The new is always *the evil*, as that which wants to conquer, to overthrow the old boundary stones and the old pieties; and only the old is the good. The good men of every age are those who dig the old ideas deep down and bear fruit with them, the husbandmen of the spirit. But all land is finally exhausted, and the plow of evil must always return.

There is a fundamentally erroneous doctrine in contemporary morality, celebrated particularly in England: according to this, the judgments "good" and "evil" are condensations of the experiences concerning "expedient" and "inexpedient"; what is called good preserves the species, while what is called evil is harmful to the species. In truth, however, the evil urges are expedient and indispensable and preserve the species to as high a degree as the good ones—only their function is different.

7

Something for the industrious. . . . So far, everything that has given color to existence still lacks a history: or, where could one find a history of love, of avarice, of envy, of conscience, of piety, or of cruelty? Even a comparative history of law, or merely of punishment, is completely lacking so far. Has anyone yet conducted research into the different ways of dividing the day and the consequences of a regular arrangement of work, holiday, and rest? Does one know the moral effects of food? Is there a philosophy of nourishment? (The ever-renewed clamor for and against vegetarianism is sufficient proof that there is no such philosophy as yet.) Have the experiences of living together been assembled; for example, the experiences in the monasteries? Has the dialectic of marriage and friendship been presented as yet? . . .

34

Historia abscondita. Every great human being has a retroactive force: all history is again placed in the scales for his sake, and a thousand secrets of the past crawl out of their hideouts—into *his* sun. There is no way of telling what may yet become history some day. Perhaps the past is still essentially undiscovered! So many retroactive forces are still required!

125

The Madman. Have you not heard of that madman who lit a lantern in the bright morning hours, ran to the market place, and cried incessantly, "I seek God! I seek God!" As many of those who do not believe in God were standing around just then, he provoked much laughter. Why, did he get lost? said one. Did he lose his way like a child? said another. Or is he hiding? Is he afraid of us? Has he gone on a voyage? or emigrated? Thus they yelled and laughed. The madman jumped into their midst and pierced them with his glances.

"Whither is God" he cried. "I shall tell you. *We have killed him—* you and I. All of us are his murderers. But how have we done this? How were we able to drink up the sea? Who gave us the sponge to wipe away the entire horizon? What did we do when we unchained this earth from its sun? Whither is it moving now? Whither are we moving now? Away from all suns? Are we not plunging continually? Backward, sideward, forward, in all directions? Is there any up or down left? Are we not straying as through an infinite nothing? Do we not feel the breath of empty space? Has it not become colder? Is not night and more night coming on all the while? Must not lanterns be lit in the morning? Do we not hear anything yet of the noise of the gravediggers who are burying God? Do we not smell anything yet of God's decomposition? Gods too decompose. God is dead. God remains dead. And we have killed him. How shall we, the murderers of all murderers, comfort ourselves? What was holiest and most powerful of all that the world has yet owned has bled to death under our knives. Who will wipe this blood off us? What water is there for us to clean ourselves? What festivals of atonement, what sacred games shall we have to invent? Is not the greatness of this deed too great for us? Must not we ourselves become gods simply to seem worthy of it? There has never been a greater deed; and whoever will be born after us—for the sake of this deed he will be part of a higher history than all history hitherto."

Here the madman fell silent and looked again at his listeners; and they too were silent and stared at him in astonishment. At last he threw his lantern on the ground, and it broke and went out. "I come too early," he said then; "my time has not come yet. This tremendous event is still on its way, still wandering—it has not yet reached the ears of man. Lightning and thunder require time, the light of the stars requires time, deeds require time even after they are done, before they can be seen and heard. This deed is still more distant from them than the most distant stars—*and yet they have done it themselves.*"

It has been related further that on that same day the madman entered divers churches and there sang his *requiem aeternam deo.* Led out and called to account, he is said to have replied each time, "What are these churches now if they are not the tombs and sepulchers of God?"

193

Kant's joke. Kant wanted to prove in a way that would dumfound the common man that the common man was right: that was the secret joke of this soul. He wrote against the scholars in favor of the popular prejudice, but for scholars and not popularly.

250

Guilt. Although the most acute judges of the witches, and even the witches themselves, were convinced of the guilt of witchery, the guilt nevertheless was nonexistent. It is thus with all guilt.

283

Preparatory men. I welcome all signs that a more manly, a warlike, age is almost to begin, an age which, above all, will give honor to valor once again. For this age shall prepare the way for one yet higher, and it shall gather the strength which this higher age will need one day—this age which is to carry heroism into the pursuit of knowledge and *wage wars* for the sake of thoughts and their consequences. To this end we now need many preparatory valorous men who cannot leap into being out of nothing—any more than out of the sand and slime of our present civilization and metropolitanism: men who are bent on seeking for that aspect in all things which must be *overcome*; men characterized by cheerfulness, patience, unpretentiousness, and contempt for all great vanities, as well as by magnanimity in victory and forbearance regarding the small vanities of the vanquished; men possessed of keen and free judgment concerning all victors and the share of chance in every victory and every fame; men who have their own festivals, their own weekdays, their own periods of mourning, who are accustomed to command with assurance and are no less ready to obey when necessary, in both cases equally proud and serving their own cause; men who are in greater danger, more fruitful, and happier! For, believe me, the secret of the greatest fruitfulness and the greatest enjoyment of existence is: to *live dangerously!* Build your cities under Vesuvius! Send your ships into uncharted seas! Live at war with your peers and yourselves! Be robbers and conquerors, as long as you cannot be rulers and owners, you lovers of knowledge! Soon the age will be past when you could be satisfied to live like shy deer, hidden in the woods! At long last the pursuit of knowledge will reach out for its due: it will want to *rule* and *own,* and you with it!

285

Excelsior! "You will never pray again, never adore again, never again rest in endless trust; you deny yourself any stopping before ultimate wisdom, ultimate goodness, ultimate power, while unharnessing your thoughts; you have no perpetual guardian and friend for your seven solitudes; you live without a view of mountains with snow on their peaks and fire in their hearts; there is no avenger for you, no eventual improver;

there is no reason any more in what happens, no love in what will happen to you; no resting place is any longer open to your heart, where it has only to find and no longer to seek; you resist any ultimate peace, you want the eternal recurrence of war and peace. Man of renunciation, do you want to renounce all this? Who will give you the necessary strength? Nobody yet has had this strength." There is a lake which one day refused to flow off and erected a dam where it had hitherto flowed off: ever since, this lake has been rising higher and higher. Perhaps that very renunciation will also lend us the strength to bear the renunciation itself; perhaps man will rise ever higher when he once ceases to *flow out* into a god.

290

One thing is needful. "Giving style" to one's character—a great and rare art! It is exercised by those who see all the strengths and weaknesses of their own natures and then comprehend them in an artistic plan until everything appears as art and reason and even weakness delights the eye. Here a large mass of second nature has been added; there a piece of original nature has been removed: both by long practice and daily labor. Here the ugly which could not be removed is hidden; there it has been reinterpreted and made sublime. . . . It will be the strong and domineering natures who enjoy their finest gaiety in such compulsion, in such constraint and perfection under a law of their own; the passion of their tremendous will relents when confronted with stylized, conquered, and serving nature; even when they have to build palaces and lay out gardens, they demur at giving nature a free hand. Conversely, it is the weak characters without power over themselves who *hate* the constraint of style. . . . They become slaves as soon as they serve; they hate to serve. Such spirits—and they may be of the first rank—are always out to interpret themselves and their environment as *free* nature—wild, arbitrary, fantastic, disorderly, astonishing; and they do well because only in this way do they please themselves. For one thing is needful: that a human being attain his satisfaction with himself—whether it be by this or by that poetry and art; only then is a human being at all tolerable to behold. Whoever is dissatisfied with himself is always ready to revenge himself therefor; we others will be his victims, if only by always having to stand his ugly sight. For the sight of the ugly makes men bad and gloomy. . . .

341

The greatest stress. How, if some day or night a demon were to sneak after you into your loneliest loneliness and say to you, "This life as you now live it and have lived it, you will have to live once more and innumerable times more; and there will be nothing new in it, but every pain and every joy and every thought and sigh and everything immeasurably small or great in your life must return to you—all in the same succession and sequence—even this spider and this moonlight between the trees, and even this moment and I myself. The eternal hourglass of existence is turned over and over, and you with it, a dust grain of dust." Would you not throw yourself down and gnash your teeth and curse the demon who spoke thus? Or did you once experience a tremendous moment when you would have answered him, "You are a god, and never have I heard anything more godly." If this thought were to gain possession of you, it would change you, as you are, or perhaps crush you. The question in each and every thing, "Do you want this once more and innumerable times more?" would weigh upon your actions as the greatest stress. Or how well disposed would you have to become to yourself and to life to *crave nothing more fervently* than this ultimate eternal confirmation and seal?

BIBLIOGRAPHY

A. PHILOSOPHIC WORKS

Aristotle. *The Nicomachean Ethics*. Translated by W. D. Ross. New York: Oxford University, 1963.

Baier, Kurt. *The Moral Point of View*. Ithaca, N.Y.: Cornell University, 1958.

Bentham, Jeremy. *Introduction to the Principles of Morals and Legislation*. London: Athlone Press, 1970.

Berdyaev, Nicolas. *The Fate of Man in the Modern World*. Translated by D. A. Lowrie. New York: Morehouse, 1935.

Bonhoeffer, Dietrich. *Ethics*. Edited by E. Bethge. New York: Macmillan, 1967.

Bradley, F. H. *Ethical Studies*. Oxford: Clarendon Press, 1927.

Brandt, Richard. *Ethical Theory*. Englewood Cliffs, N.J.: Prentice-Hall, 1959.

Broad, C. D. *Five Types of Ethical Theory*. London: Routledge and K. Paul, 1962.

Dewey, John. *Human Nature and Conduct*. New York: Henry Holt, 1922.

Epicurus. *Letter to Menoceus*. In *The Stoic and Epicurean Philosophers*, translated by C. Bailey, P. E. Matheson, H. Munro, and G. Long. New York: Random House, 1940.

Ewing, A. C. *The Definition of Good*. New York: Macmillan, 1947.

———. *Ethics*. London: English Universities Press, 1953.

Fletcher, Joseph. *Situation Ethics*. Philadelphia: Westminster Press, 1966.

Foot, Philippa, ed. *Theories of Ethics*. London: Oxford University, 1967.

Green, T. H. *Prolegomena to Ethics*. Edited by A. C. Bradley. Oxford: Clarendon Press, 1884.

Hare, R. M. *The Language of Morals*. New York: Oxford University, 1964.

Hartman, N. *Ethics*. Translated by S. Coit. London: Allen and Unwin, 1932.

Hegel, G. W. F. *Theory of Right, Duties, and Religion*. Translated by B. C. Burt. Ann Arbor: Inland Press, 1892.

Hocking, W. E. *Human Nature and Its Remaking*. New Haven: Yale University, 1918.

Hume, David. *An Inquiry Concerning the Principles of Morals*. Edited by C. W. Hendel. New York: Liberal Arts Press, 1957.

Lamont, Corliss. *The Philosophy of Humanism*. New York: Philosophical Library, 1957.

Mackinnon, D. M. *A Study in Ethical Theory*. London: A. and C. Black, 1957.

Martineau, James. *Types of Ethical Theory*. Oxford: Clarendon Press, 1901.

Moore, G. E. *Ethics*. New York: Henry Holt, 1912.

———. *Principia Ethica*. Cambridge: University Press, 1954.

Murray, Gilbert. *The Stoic Philosophy*. New York: G. P. Putnam's Sons, 1915.

Nietzsche, Friedrich. *Beyond Good and Evil, The Genealogy of Morals*, and *The Joyful Wisdom*. In *The Complete Works of Friedrich Nietzsche*, translated and edited by O. Levy. New York: Macmillan, 1896–1930.

Nowell-Smith, P. H. *Ethics*. New York: Philosophical Library, 1957.

Paley, William. *The Principles of Moral and Political Philosophy*. Boston: Richardson, 1825.

Perry, Ralph Barton. *Realms of Value*. Cambridge: Harvard University, 1954.

Plato. *Euthyphro, Gorgias, Meno, Protagoras*, and *Republic*. In *The Dialogues of Plato*, translated by B. Jovett. Oxford: Clarendon Press, 1871.

Rawls, John. *A Theory of Justice*. Cambridge: Harvard University, 1971.

Ross, W. D. *The Foundations of Ethics*. Oxford: Clarendon Press, 1939.

———. *The Right and the Good*. Oxford: Clarendon Press, 1930.

Sartre, Jean-Paul. *Existentialism*. Translated by B. Frechtman. New York: Philosophical Library, 1947.

Schlick, Moritz. *Problems of Ethics*. Translated by D. Rynin. New York: Dover, 1962.

Sidgwick, Henry. *Methods of Ethics*. Chicago: University Press, 1962.

———. *Outline of the History of Ethics*. Boston: Beacon Press, 1960.

Spencer, Herbert. *The Data of Ethics*. New York: Appleton, 1894.

Spinoza, Baruch. *Ethics*, esp. Parts 3–4. Translated by A. Boyle. New York: Dutton, 1950.

Stevenson, Charles. *Ethics and Language*. New Haven: Yale University, 1960.

Thomas Aquinas, St. *Summa Theologica*, Part II. Translated by the Dominican Fathers. New York: Benziger Brothers, 1947–48.

Toulmin, Stephen. *An Examination of the Place of Reason in Ethics*. Cambridge: University Press, 1960.

Urmson, J. O. *The Emotive Theory of Ethics*. London: Hutchinson, 1968.

Warnock, M. *Ethics Since 1900*. New York: Oxford University, 1963.

Wright, G. H. von. *The Varieties of Goodness*. London: Routledge and K. Paul, 1963.

B. LITERARY WORKS

Balzac, Honoré de. *The Quest of the Absolute*. Translated by E. Marriage. New York: Dutton, 1927.

Brecht, Bertolt. *Baal*. Translated by V. Sander. Waltham, Mass.: Blaisdell, 1969.

———. *The Good Woman of Setzuan*. In *Seven Plays*, edited by E. Bentley. New York: Grove Press, 1961.

Bunyan, John. *Pilgrim's Progress*. New York: Appleton, 1860.

Camus, Albert. *Caligula*. Translated by S. Gilbert. New York: Vintage Books, 1958.

———. *The Plague*. Translated by S. Gilbert. New York: Knopf, 1952.

Cather, Willa. *A Lost Lady*. New York: Knopf, 1923.

Clemens, Samuel L. *The Adventures of Huckleberry Finn*. Garden City, N.Y.: Doubleday, 1969.

Dostoevsky, Fedor. *Crime and Punishment*. Translated by C. Garnett. New York: Macmillan, 1937.

Dürrenmatt, Friedrich. *The Visit*. Translated by P. Bowles. New York: Grove Press, 1962.

Eliot, George. *Romola*. New York: Dutton, 1921.

———. *Silas Marner*. New York: Longmans, Green, 1895.

Eliot, T. S. *The Cocktail Party*. London: Faber and Faber, 1974.

Flaubert, Gustave. *Madame Bovary*. Translated by E. Marx-Aveling. New York: Knopf, 1924.

Fowles, John. *The Magus*. Boston: Little, Brown, 1965.

Galsworthy, John. *Justice*. London: Duckworth, 1910.

Gogol, Nikolai. *Dead Souls*. Translated by B. G. Guerney. New York: Limited Editions, 1944.

Hawthorne, Nathaniel. *The Scarlet Letter*. Boston: Ticknor and Fields, 1858.

Hesse, Hermann. *Steppenwolf*. Translated by B. Creighton. New York: Ungar, 1957.

Hofmannsthal, Hugo V. *Everyman*. Translated by G. Sterling and R. Ordynski. San Francisco: A. M. Robertson, 1917.

Hopkins, Gerard Manley. "The Wreck of the Deutschland." In *A Hopkins Reader*, edited by J. Pick. New York: Oxford University, 1953.

Melville, Herman. *Billy Budd*. Cambridge: Harvard University, 1948.

Molière, Jean Baptiste. *Le Misanthrope* and *Tartuffe*. Translated by R. Wilbur. New York: Harcourt Brace Jovanovich, Inc., 1965.

Montherlant, Henry de. *The Master of Santiago*. Translated by J. Griffin. New York: Knopf, 1951.

O'Conner, Flannery. "The Displaced Person." In *The Complete Stories*. New York: Farrar, Strauss and Giroux, 1972.

Pater, Walter. *Marius the Epicurean*. London: Macmillan, 1913.

Pushkin, Alexander. *Eugene Onegin*. In *The Works of Alexander Pushkin*. Translated by B. Deutsch. New York: Random House, 1936.

Rabelais, Francois. *Gargantua and Pantagruel*. In *The Complete Works of Rabelais*, translated by T. Urquhart and P. Motteux. New York: Boni and Liveright, 1927.

Sartre, Jean-Paul. *The Age of Reason*. Translated by E. Sutton. London: Hamilton, 1957.

Shakespeare, William. *Macbeth*. In *The Works of William Shakespeare*, edited by W. G. Clark and W. A. Wright. New York: St. Martin's Press, 1956.

Solzhenitsyn, Alexander. *Matryona's House.* In *We Never Make Mistakes,* translated by P. W. Blackstock. Columbia, S.C.: University of South Carolina, 1963.

Swift, Jonathan. *Gulliver's Travels.* New York: Dutton, 1909.

Thackeray, William M. *Vanity Fair.* Oxford: University Press, 1931.

Tolstoy, Leo. *Anna Karenina.* Translated by L. and A. Maude. London: Oxford University, 1939.

Wordsworth, William. "Ode to Duty." In *The Poetical Works,* edited by E. de Selincourt. New York: Oxford University, 1964.

FIVE

THE NATURE OF REALITY

In our more solemn and reflective moments, when we take a step backward to view ourselves in deeper perspective, we can experience a profound curiosity about the nature of the universe we inhabit. This is metaphysical wonder, a desire to understand and appreciate the overall scheme of which we are a part. We feel a need to comprehend not a fragment but the whole of things, and to realize through this understanding our position in the universe, the meaning of our individual lives and of human existence in general.

When we begin reflecting in a more deliberate way, we question whether we exist as an accident of biochemical forces in a world that is explicable wholly in terms of physical laws, or whether a purposive order prevails, informing every part of life with significance. This leads us to wonder whether the natural world is devoid of spiritual direction and is utterly meaningless, or whether a conscious intelligence is at work throughout the universe. We are also led to ask if the values we believe in, the central motives of our lives, have any objective foundation in universal principles, or if they are invented rather than discovered, merely reflecting our times, our society, and our personal tastes. If life is intrinsically meaningless, perhaps we can invest it with meaning through our choices and actions, and by our creative thrust bring purpose into being.

In less personal terms, we want to know whether space possesses an ultimate limit or is utterly limitless, whether the universe had a beginning and if it will end in time, with a bang or a whimper (that is, in a fiery, perhaps nuclear, apocalypse or in the gradual loss of all available energy). The concept of time can perplex us also, for the past and future resemble dreams and the present is a knife-edge instant, all of which causes us to doubt whether the passage of our lives through time is real. And as with space, we wonder whether time began and whether it will ever end. (If time is thought to have a beginning we would want to know what preceded it because time could not have begun at some point in time.)

In addition, we are curious to know the basic substance of the universe, that is, whether it is spiritual or material, and to discover its inherent structure and the process by which it operates. With regard to the last, we may regard the process as mechanical or organic, an evolution or devolution, a cyclical, spiral, linear, or stepwise pattern proceeding upward or downward. Or we may come to believe in the expansion and contraction of the entire universe in eternal cosmic pulsations that resemble the breathing of an enormous organism.

Metaphysicians theorize about the nature of reality in a rigorously logical and systematic way, using evidence from the sciences as the basis for their reasoned speculations but going beyond the bare facts to explore the implications of scientific discoveries. And though each person who engages in metaphysical thinking must find his answers afresh, the basic questions have been contemplated by philosophers since the time of ancient Greece.

The pre-Socratic Greek philosopher Thales in the sixth century B.C. was the first man known to history to speculate about the basic substance of the universe. In an imaginative leap of understanding, Thales reasoned that underlying the apparent diversity of things around us there might well be a single substance common to all matter, a substance that possesses a lawful arrangement and allows *explanation* to take place. Thales identified water as the essential constituent of all things and used numerous ingenious arguments to prove his contention,[1] but his particular choice and his "proofs" are philosophically and scientifically irrelevant. What matters is that Thales thought to reduce the multiplicity of objects to a unity, the seeming heterogeneity to a

---

[1] Thales argued that water transformed itself into air and earth through evaporation and into fire during lightning storms. Water underlies the earth as can be seen in wells and earthquakes, the latter due to storms at sea. Furthermore, water is essential to all life and actually creates life as can be seen by the organisms left wriggling in half-dried mud pools. With regard to the last, Thales is not far wrong, for life began as specks of protoplasmic jelly in the scum of tides.

homogeneity, which means that he saw beyond appearances to a universal essence, and accounted for why things exist as they do.

After Thales had broken the ground, a contemporary named Anaximander posited the Boundless or Indefinite as the primary source of matter, that "out of which all things arise and to which all return," but which does not itself possess determinate characteristics. And after Anaximander, Pythagoras declared numbers as basic, not just because everything could be expressed numerically but because numbers were thought to be fundamental entities with spatial magnitude. Following these philosophers were some fifth-century pre-Socratics who were impressed with the idea of constancy and change—Heraclitus, for whom change or *logos* (that is, process or measure) characterized everything, and Parmenides, who asserted that change is an illusion, for the universe rationally considered must be conceived as motionless, immutable, and wholly unified. Finally, Anaxagoras and Democritus spoke of particles that come into collision, mix, and combine to produce the physical world; Democritus, amazingly enough, offered a primitive theory of atomic interaction.

All these theories are little more than historical curiosities today, but they led to the more profound theories of Aristotle and Plato, St. Thomas Aquinas, Leibniz, Kant, Hegel, and Bertrand Russell, all of whom addressed themselves to similar problems using these early insights as stepping stones. And when we ourselves begin thinking in metaphysical categories we encounter the same problems and can profit enormously from what other thinkers have concluded. We too ask about the reality underlying appearances, the basis of things, and what remains constant throughout the perpetual flux of life. In short, metaphysical questions are the most perennial of all, for they are rooted in the human condition and obtrude themselves on every reflective mind.

In the reprinted works that follow three basic metaphysical views are described: *naturalism, spiritualism,* and *existentialism.* Each offers a characterization as to the basic nature of reality and indicates the response that is then appropriate for the conduct of our lives.

The *naturalist* maintains that the universe can be understood in wholly natural terms without any recourse to supernatural explanation. Human beings are a part of the natural order, and even though they have evolved to a position of supremacy among the other animals, they are not unique creations outside of nature.

In contrast to the naturalist, the *spiritualist* believes that soul or spirit constitutes the ultimate reality. Matter is thought to be dependent on some spiritual dimension for its existence or, perhaps, is merely an illusion rather than a reality in any form. Spiritualism and *idealism* are sometimes treated as synonymous, but idealism is a more comprehensive theory that reduces all of existence to ideas and mind.

Existentialism is a contemporary philosophy, embracing a metaphysical, epistemological, and ethical viewpoint. The existentialist maintains that man is a self-creating being who exists on earth with the consciousness to choose his own future, personally and collectively. The "essence" of a human being is not predetermined at birth but rather is formed by the decisions and commitments that are made during his lifetime. By crediting human beings with awareness and freedom of choice the existentialist regards man as having a spiritual part, but by stressing his physical position in a world without any discernible direction, the existentialist treats man as part of the natural not the spiritual universe.

1
Naturalism

THE OPEN BOAT
STEPHEN CRANE

Stephen Crane (1871–1900) was an American journalist, novelist, and short story writer who, together with Frank Norris, Jack London, Theodore Dreiser, and James T. Farrell, originated the movement of literary naturalism in this country. Although Crane is most celebrated for his Civil War novel *The Red Badge of Courage* and achieved recognition in literary circles for his realistic novel, *Maggie: A Girl of the Streets*, his major achievements lie in the genre of the short story. His Western tales, such as "The Blue Hotel," "One Dash-Horses," and "The Bride Comes to Yellow Sky," are classic in their tragic tone and symbolism, and his war stories rival or surpass *The Red Badge of Courage*, especially "Death and the Child," "The Price of the Harness," "An Episode of War," and "The Upturned Face."

"The Open Boat," here anthologized, exhibits many of Crane's literary themes including courage, isolation and companionship, chance, endurance, and death. In broader terms, however, the story shows the insignificance of man and the indifference of nature to his fate. The people in the boat do not deserve their suffering, and there is no reason why they should die (or live). Everything happens by accident, and life is pictured as rich in absurdity but devoid of justice or meaning. As Crane once wrote, there is only "this terrible and inscrutable wrath of nature."

It is interesting to note that the story is based on Crane's own experience when he was shipwrecked on his way to Cuba. He survived the ordeal but died a few years later of tuberculosis at the age of twenty-eight.

I

None of them knew the color of the sky. Their eyes glanced level, and were fastened upon the waves that swept toward them. These waves were of the hue of slate, save for the tops, which were of foaming white, and all of the men knew the colors of the sea. The horizon narrowed and widened, and dipped and rose, and at all times its edge was jagged with waves that seemed thrust up in points like rocks.

Many a man ought to have a bathtub larger than the boat which here rode upon the sea. These waves were most wrongfully and barbarously abrupt and tall, and each froth-top was a problem in small-boat navigation.

The cook squatted in the bottom, and looked with both eyes at the six inches of gunwale which separated him from the ocean. His sleeves were rolled over his fat forearms, and the two flaps of his unbuttoned vest dangled as he bent to bail out the boat. Often he said, "Gawd! that was a narrow clip." As he remarked it he invariably gazed eastward over the broken sea.

The oiler, steering with one of the two oars in the boat, sometimes raised himself suddenly to keep clear of water that swirled in over the stern. It was a thin little oar, and it seemed often ready to snap.

The correspondent, pulling at the other oar, watched the waves and wondered why he was there.

The injured captain, lying in the bow, was at this time buried in that profound dejection and indifference which comes, temporarily at least, to even the bravest and most enduring when, willy-nilly, the firm fails, the army loses, the ship goes down. The mind of the master of a vessel is rooted deep in the timbers of her, though he command for a day or a decade; and this captain had on him the stern impression of a scene in the grays of dawn of seven turned faces, and later a stump of a topmast with a white ball on it, that slashed to and fro at the waves, went low and lower, and down. Thereafter there was something strange in his voice. Although steady, it was deep with mourning, and of a quality beyond oration or tears.

"Keep'er a little more south, Billie," said he.

"A little more south, sir," said the oiler in the stern.

A seat in this boat was not unlike a seat upon a bucking broncho, and by the same token a broncho is not much smaller. The craft pranced and reared and plunged like an animal. As each wave came, and she rose for it, she seemed like a horse making at a fence outrageously high. The manner of her scramble over these walls of water is a mystic thing, and, moreover, at the top of them were ordinarily these problems in white water, the foam racing down from the summit of each wave requiring a new leap, and a leap from the air. Then, after scornfully bumping a crest, she would slide and race and splash down a long incline, and arrive bobbing and nodding in front of the next menace.

A singular disadvantage of the sea lies in the fact that after successfully surmounting one wave you discover that there is another behind it just as important and just as nervously anxious to do something effective in the way of swamping boats. In a ten-foot dinghy one can get an idea of the resources of the sea in the line of waves that is not probable to the average experience, which is never at sea in a dinghy. As each slaty wall of water approached, it shut all else from the view of the men in the boat, and it was not difficult to imagine that this particular wave was the final outburst of the ocean, the last effort of the grim water. There was a terrible grace in the move of the waves, and they came in silence, save for the snarling of the crests.

In the wan light the faces of the men must have been gray. Their eyes must have glinted in strange ways as they gazed steadily astern. Viewed from a balcony, the whole thing would doubtless have been weirdly picturesque. But the men in the boat had no time to see it, and if they had had leisure, there were other things to occupy their minds. The sun swung steadily up the sky, and they knew it was broad day because the color of the sea changed from slate to emerald-green streaked with amber lights, and the foam was like tumbling snow. The process of the breaking day was unknown to them. They were aware only of this effect upon the color of the waves that rolled toward them.

In disjointed sentences the cook and the correspondent argued as to the difference between a life-saving station and a house of refuge. The cook had said: "There's a house of refuge just north of the Mosquito Inlet Light, and as soon as they see us they'll come off in their boat and pick us up."

"As soon as who see us?" said the correspondent.

"The crew," said the cook.

"Houses of refuge don't have crews," said the correspondent. "As I understand them, they are only places where clothes and grub are stored for the benefit of shipwrecked people. They don't carry crews."

"Oh, yes, they do," said the cook.

"No, they don't," said the correspondent.

"Well, we're not there yet, anyhow," said the oiler, in the stern.

"Well," said the cook, "perhaps it's not a house of refuge that I'm thinking of as being near Mosquito Inlet Light; perhaps it's a lifesaving station."

"We're not there yet," said the oiler in the stern.

II

As the boat bounced from the top of each wave the wind tore through the hair of the hatless men, and as the craft plopped her stern down again the spray slashed past them. The crest of each of these waves was a hill, from the top of which the men surveyed for a moment a broad tumultuous expanse, shining and wind-riven. It was probably splendid, it was probably glorious, this play of the free sea, wild with lights of emerald and white and amber.

"Bully good thing it's an onshore wind," said the cook. "If not, where would we be? Wouldn't have a show."

"That's right," said the correspondent.

The busy oiler nodded his assent.

Then the captain, in the bow, chuckled in a way that expressed humor, contempt, tragedy, all in one. "Do you think we've got much of a show now, boys?" said he.

Whereupon the three were silent, save for a trifle of hemming and hawing. To express any particular optimism at this time they felt to be childish and stupid, but they all doubtless possessed this sense of the situation in their minds. A young man thinks doggedly at such times. On the other hand, the ethics of their condition was decidedly against any open suggestion of hopelessness. So they were silent.

"Oh, well," said the captain, soothing his children, "we'll get ashore all right."

But there was that in his tone which made them think; so the oiler quoth, "Yes! if this wind holds."

The cook was bailing. "Yes! if we don't catch hell in the surf."

Canton-flannel gulls flew near and far. Sometimes they sat down on the sea, near patches of brown seaweed that rolled over the waves with a movement like carpets on a line in a gale. The birds sat comfortably in groups, and they were envied by some in the dinghy, for the wrath of the sea was no more to them than it was to a covey of prairie chickens a thousand miles inland. Often they came very close and stared at the men with black bead-like eyes. At these times they were uncanny and sinister in their unblinking scrutiny, and the men hooted angrily at them, telling them to be gone. One came, and evidently decided to alight on the top of the captain's head. The bird flew parallel to the boat and did not circle, but made short sidelong jumps in the air in chicken fashion. His black eyes were wistfully fixed upon the captain's head. "Ugly brute," said the oiler to the bird. "You look as if you were made with a jackknife." The cook and the correspondent swore darkly at the creature. The captain naturally wished to knock it away with the end of the heavy painter, but he did not dare do it, because anything resembling an emphatic gesture would have capsized this freighted boat; and so, with his open hand, the captain gently and carefully waved the gull away. After it had been discouraged from the pursuit the captain breathed easier on account of his hair, and others breathed easier because the bird struck their minds at this time as being somehow gruesome and ominous.

In the meantime the oiler and the correspondent rowed. And also they rowed. They sat together in the same seat, and each rowed an oar. Then the oiler took both oars; then the correspondent took both oars; then the oiler; then the correspondent. They rowed and they rowed. The very ticklish part of the business was when the time came for the reclining one in the stern to take his turn at the oars. By the very last star of truth, it is easier to steal eggs from under a hen than it was to change seats in the dinghy. First the man in the stern slid his hand along the thwart and moved with care, as if he were of Sèvres. Then the man in the rowing-seat slid his hand along the other thwart. It was all done with the most extraordinary care. As the two sidled past each other, the whole party kept watchful eyes on the coming wave, and the captain cried: "Look out, now! Steady, there!"

The brown mats of seaweed that appeared from time to time were like islands, bits of earth. They were traveling, apparently, neither one way nor the other. They were, to all intents, stationary. They informed the men in the boat that it was making progress slowly toward the land.

The captain, rearing cautiously in the bow after the dinghy soared on a great swell, said that he had seen the lighthouse at Mosquito Inlet. Presently the cook remarked that he had seen it. The correspondent was at the oars then, and for some reason he too wished to look at the lighthouse; but his back was toward the far shore, and the waves were important, and for some time he could not seize an opportunity to turn his head. But at last there came a wave more gentle than the others, and when at the crest of it he swiftly scoured the western horizon.

"See it?" said the captain.

"No," said the correspondent, slowly; "I didn't see anything."

"Look again," said the captain. He pointed. "It's exactly in that direction."

At the top of another wave the correspondent did as he was bid, and this time his eyes chanced on a small, still thing on the edge of the swaying horizon. It was precisely like the point of a pin. It took an anxious eye to find a lighthouse so tiny.

"Think we'll make it, Captain?"

"If this wind holds and the boat don't swamp, we can't do much else," said the captain.

The little boat, lifted by each towering sea and splashed viciously by the crests, made progress that in the absence of seaweed was not apparent to those in her. She seemed just a wee thing wallowing, miraculously top up, at the mercy of five oceans. Occasionally a great spread of water, like white flames, swarmed into her.

"Bail her, cook," said the captain, serenely.

"All right, Captain," said the cheerful cook.

III

It would be difficult to describe the subtle brotherhood of men that was here established on the seas. No one said that it was so. No one mentioned it. But it dwelt in the boat, and each man felt it warm him. They were a captain, an oiler, a cook, and a correspondent, and they were friends— friends in a more curiously ironbound degree than may be common. The hurt captain, lying against the water jar in the bow, spoke always in a low voice and calmly; but he could never command a more ready and swiftly obedient crew than the motley three of the dinghy. It was more than a mere recognition of what was best for the common safety. There was surely in it a quality that was personal and heartfelt. And after this devotion to the commander of the boat, there was this comradeship, that the correspondent, for instance, who had been taught to be cynical of men, knew even at the time was the best experience of his life. But no one said that it was so. No one mentioned it.

"I wish we had a sail," remarked the captain. "We might try my overcoat on the end of an oar, and give you two boys a chance to rest." So the cook and the correspondent held the mast and spread wide the overcoat; the oiler steered; and the little boat made good way with her new rig. Sometimes the oiler had to scull sharply to keep a sea from breaking into the boat, but otherwise sailing was a success.

Meanwhile the lighthouse had been growing slowly larger. It had now almost assumed color, and appeared like a little gray shadow on the sky. The man at the oars could not be prevented from turning his head rather often to try for a glimpse of this little gray shadow.

At last, from the top of each wave, the men in the tossing boat could see land. Even as the lighthouse was an upright shadow on the sky, this land seemed but a long black shadow on the sea. It certainly was thinner than paper. "We must be about opposite New Smyrna," said the cook, who had coasted this shore often in schooners. "Captain, by the way, I believe they abandoned that lifesaving station there about a year ago."

"Did they?" said the captain.

The wind slowly died away. The cook and the correspondent were not now obliged to slave in order to hold high the oar. But the waves continued their old impetuous swooping at the dinghy, and the little craft, no longer under way, struggled woundily over them. The oiler or the correspondent took the oars again.

Shipwrecks are *apropos* of nothing. If men could only train for them and have them occur when the men had reached pink condition, there would be less drowning at sea. Of the four in the dinghy none had slept any time worth mentioning for two days and two nights previous to embarking in the dinghy, and in the excitement of clambering about the deck of a foundering ship they had also forgotten to eat heartily.

For these reasons, and for others, neither the oiler nor the correspondent was fond of rowing at this time. The correspondent wondered ingenuously how in the name of all that was sane could there be people who thought it amusing to row a boat. It was not an amusement; it was a diabolical punishment, and even a genius of mental aberrations could never conclude that it was anything but a horror to the muscles and a crime against the back. He mentioned to the boat in general how the amusement of rowing struck him, and the weary-faced oiler smiled in full sympathy. Previously to the foundering, by the way, the oiler had worked a double watch in the engine room of the ship.

"Take her easy now, boys," said the captain. "Don't spend yourselves. If we have to run a surf you'll need all your strength, because we'll sure have to swim for it. Take your time."

Slowly the land arose from the sea. From a black line it became a line of black and a line of white—trees and sand. Finally the captain said that he could make out a house on the shore. "That's the house of refuge, sure," said the cook. "They'll see us before long, and come out after us."

The distant lighthouse reared high. "The keeper ought to be able to make us out now, if he's looking through a glass," said the captain. "He'll notify the lifesaving people."

"None of those other boats could have got ashore to give word of this wreck," said the oiler, in a low voice, "else the lifeboat would be out hunting us."

Slowly and beautifully the land loomed out of the sea. The wind came again. It had veered from the northeast to the southeast. Finally a new sound struck the ears of the men in the boat. It was the low thunder of the surf on the shore. "We'll never be able to make the lighthouse now," said the captain. "Swing her head a little more north, Billie."

"A little more north, sir," said the oiler.

Whereupon the little boat turned her nose once more down the wind, and all but the oarsman watched the shore grow. Under the influence of this expansion doubt and direful apprehension were leaving the minds of the men. The management of the boat was still most absorbing, but it could not prevent a quiet cheerfulness. In an hour, perhaps, they would be ashore.

Their backbones had become thoroughly used to balancing in the boat, and they now rode this wild colt of a dinghy like circus men. The correspondent thought that he had been drenched to the skin, but happening to feel in the top pocket of his coat, he found therein eight cigars. Four of them were soaked with seawater; four were perfectly scatheless. After a search, somebody produced three dry matches; and thereupon the four waifs rode impudently in their little boat and, with an assurance of an impending rescue shining in their eyes, puffed at the big cigars, and judged well and ill of all men. Everybody took a drink of water.

IV

"Cook," remarked the captain, "there don't seem to be any signs of life about your house of refuge."

"No," replied the cook. "Funny they don't see us!"

A broad stretch of lowly coast lay before the eyes of the men. It was of low dunes topped with dark vegetation. The roar of the surf was plain, and sometimes they could see the white lip of a wave as it spun up the beach. A tiny house was blocked out black upon the sky. Southward, the slim lighthouse lifted its little gray length.

Tide, wind, and waves were swinging the dinghy northward. "Funny they don't see us," said the men.

The surf's roar was here dulled, but its tone was nevertheless thunderous and mighty. As the boat swam over the great rollers the men sat listening to this roar. "We'll swamp sure," said everybody.

It is fair to say here that there was not a lifesaving station within twenty miles in either direction; but the men did not know this fact, and in consequence they made dark and opprobrious remarks concerning the eyesight of the nation's lifesavers. Four scowling men sat in the dinghy and surpassed records in the invention of epithets.

"Funny they don't see us."

The light-heartedness of a former time had completely faded. To their sharpened minds it was easy to conjure pictures of all kinds of incompetency and blindness and, indeed, cowardice. There was the shore of the populous land, and it was bitter and bitter to them that from it came no sign.

"Well," said the captain, ultimately, "I suppose we'll have to make a try for ourselves. If we stay out here too long, we'll none of us have strength left to swim after the boat swamps."

And so the oiler, who was at the oars, turned the boat straight for the shore. There was a sudden tightening of muscles. There was some thinking.

"If we don't all get ashore," said the captain—"if we don't all get ashore, I suppose you fellows know where to send news of my finish?"

They then briefly exchanged some addresses and admonitions. As for the reflections of the men, there was a great deal of rage in them. Perchance they might be formulated thus: "If I am going to be drowned—if I am going to be drowned—if I am going to be drowned, why, in the name of the seven mad gods who rule the sea, was I allowed to come thus far and contemplate sand and trees? Was I brought here merely to have my nose dragged away as I was about to nibble the sacred cheese of life? It is preposterous. If this old ninny-woman, Fate, cannot do better than this, she should be deprived of the management of men's fortunes. She is an old hen who knows not her intention. If she has decided to drown me, why did she not do it in the beginning and save me all this trouble? The whole affair is absurd. . . . But no; she cannot mean to drown me. She dare not drown me. She cannot drown me. Not after all this work." Afterward the man might have had an impulse to shake his fist at the clouds. "Just you drown me, now, and then hear what I call you!"

The billows that came at this time were more formidable. They seemed always just about to break and roll over the little boat in a turmoil of foam. There was a preparatory and long growl in the speech of them. No mind unused to the sea would have concluded that the dinghy could ascend these sheer heights in time. The shore was still afar. The oiler was a wily surfman. "Boys," he said swiftly, "she won't live three minutes more, and we're too far out to swim. Shall I take her to sea again, Captain?"

"Yes; go ahead!" said the captain.

This oiler, by a series of quick miracles and fast and steady oarsmanship, turned the boat in the middle of the surf and took her safely to sea again.

There was a considerable silence as the boat bumped over the furrowed sea to deeper water. Then somebody in gloom spoke: "Well, anyhow, they must have seen us from the shore by now."

The gulls went in slanting flight up the wind toward the gray, desolate east. A squall, marked by dingy clouds and clouds brick-red, like smoke from a burning building, appeared from the southeast.

"What do you think of those lifesaving people? Ain't they peaches?"

"Funny they haven't seen us."

"Maybe they think we're out here for sport! Maybe they think we're fishin'. Maybe they think we're damned fools."

It was a long afternoon. A changed tide tried to force them southward, but wind and wave said northward. Far ahead, where coastline, sea, and sky formed their mighty angle, there were little dots which seemed to indicate a city on the shore.

"St. Augustine?"

The captain shook his head. "Too near Mosquito Inlet."

And the oiler rowed, and then the correspondent rowed; then the oiler rowed. It was a weary business. The human back can become the seat of more aches and pains than are registered in books for the composite anatomy of a regiment. It is a limited area, but it can become the theater of innumerable muscular conflicts, tangles, wrenches, knots, and other comforts.

"Did you ever like to row, Billie?" asked the correspondent.

"No," said the oiler; "hang it!"

When one exchanged the rowing-seat for a place in the bottom of the boat, he suffered a bodily depression that caused him to be careless of everything save an obligation to wiggle one finger. There was cold seawater swashing to and fro in the boat, and he lay in it. His head, pillowed on a thwart, was within an inch of the swirl of a wave-crest, and sometimes a particularly obstreperous sea came inboard and drenched him once more. But these matters did not annoy him. It is almost certain that if the boat had capsized he would have tumbled comfortably out upon the ocean as if he felt sure that it was a great soft mattress.

"Look! There's a man on the shore!"

"Where?"

"There! See 'im? See 'im?"

"Yes, sure! He's walking along."

"Now he's stopped. Look! He's facing us!"

"He's waving at us!"

"So he is! By thunder!"

"Ah, now we're all right! Now we're all right! There'll be a boat out here for us in half an hour."

"He's going on. He's running. He's going up to that house there."

The remote beach seemed lower than the sea, and it required a searching glance to discern the little black figure. The captain saw a floating stick, and they rowed to it. A bath towel was by some weird chance in the boat, and, tying this on the stick, the captain waved it. The oarsman did not dare turn his head, so he was obliged to ask questions.

"What's he doing now?"

"He's standing still again. He's looking, I think. . . . There he goes again—toward the house. . . . Now he's stopped again."

"Is he waving at us?"

"No, not now; he was, though."

"Look! There comes another man!"

"He's running."

"Look at him go, would you!"

"Why, he's on a bicycle. Now he's met the other man. They're both waving at us. Look!"

"There comes something up the beach."

"What the devil is that thing?"

"Why, it looks like a boat."

"Why, certainly, it's a boat."

"No; it's on wheels."

"Yes, so it is. Well, that must be the lifeboat. They drag them along shore on a wagon."

"That's the lifeboat, sure."

"No, by God, it's—it's an omnibus."

"I tell you it's a lifeboat."

"It is not! It's an omnibus. I can see it plain. See? One of these big hotel omnibuses."

"By thunder, you're right. It's an omnibus, sure as fate. What do you suppose they are doing with an omnibus? Maybe they are going around collecting the life-crew, hey?"

"That's it, likely. Look! There's a fellow waving a little black flag. He's standing on the steps of the omnibus. There come those other two fellows. Now they're all talking together. Look at the fellow with the flag. Maybe he ain't waving it!"

"That ain't a flag, is it? That's his coat. Why, certainly, that's his coat."

"So it is; it's his coat. He's taken it off and is waving it around his head. But would you look at him swing it!"

"Oh, say, there isn't any lifesaving station there. That's just a winter-resort hotel omnibus that has brought over some of the boarders to see us drown."

"What's that idiot with the coat mean? What's he signaling, anyhow?"

"It looks as if he were trying to tell us to go north. There must be a lifesaving station up there."

"No; he thinks we're fishing. Just giving us a merry hand. See? Ah, there, Willie!"

"Well, I wish I could make something out of those signals. What do you suppose he means?"

"He don't mean anything; he's just playing."

"Well, if he'd just signal us to try the surf again, or to go to sea and wait, or go north, or go south, or go to hell, there would be some reason in it. But look at him! He just stands there and keeps his coat revolving like a wheel. The ass!"

"There come more people."

"Now there's quite a mob. Look! Isn't that a boat?"

"Where? Oh, I see where you mean. No, that's no boat."

"That fellow is still waving his coat."

"He must think we like to see him do that. Why don't he quit it? It don't mean anything."

"I don't know. I think he is trying to make us go north. It must be that there's a lifesaving station there somewhere."

"Say, he ain't tired yet. Look at 'im wave!"

"Wonder how long he can keep that up. He's been revolving his coat ever since he caught sight of us. He's an idiot. Why aren't they getting men to bring a boat out? A fishing boat—one of those big yawls—could come out here all right. Why don't he do something?"

"Oh, it's all right now."

"They'll have a boat out here for us in less than no time, now that they've seen us."

A faint yellow tone came into the sky over the low land. The shadows on the sea slowly deepened. The wind bore coldness with it, and the men began to shiver.

"Holy smoke!" said one, allowing his voice to express his impious mood, "if we keep on monkeying out here! If we've got to flounder out here all night!"

"Oh, we'll never have to stay here all night! Don't you worry. They've seen us now, and it won't be long before they'll come chasing out after us."

The shore grew dusky. The man waving a coat blended gradually into this gloom, and it swallowed in the same manner the omnibus and the group of people. The spray, when it dashed uproariously over the side, made the voyagers shrink and swear like men who were being branded.

"I'd like to catch the chump who waved the coat. I feel like socking him one, just for luck."

"Why? What did he do?"

"Oh, nothing, but then he seemed so damned cheerful."

In the meantime the oiler rowed, and then the correspondent rowed, and then the oiler rowed. Gray-faced and bowed forward, they mechanically, turn by turn, plied the leaden oars. The form of the lighthouse had vanished from the southern horizon, but finally a pale star appeared, just lifting from the sea. The streaked saffron in the west passed before the all-merging darkness, and the sea to the east was black. The land had vanished, and was expressed only by the low and drear thunder of the surf.

"If I am going to be drowned—if I am going to be drowned—if I am going to be drowned, why, in the name of the seven mad gods who rule the sea, was I allowed to come thus far and contemplate sand and trees? Was I brought here merely to have my nose dragged away as I was about to nibble the sacred cheese of life?"

The patient captain, drooped over the water jar, was sometimes obliged to speak to the oarsman.

"Keep her head up! Keep her head up!"

"Keep her head up, sir." The voices were weary and low.

This was surely a quiet evening. All save the oarsman lay heavily and listlessly in the boat's bottom. As for him, his eyes were just capable of noting the tall black waves that swept forward in a most sinister silence, save for an occasional subdued growl of a crest.

The cook's head was on a thwart, and he looked without interest at the water under his nose. He was deep in other scenes. Finally he spoke. "Billie," he murmured, dreamfully, "what kind of pie do you like best?"

V

"Pie!" said the oiler and the correspondent, agitatedly. "Don't talk about those things, blast you!"

"Well," said the cook, "I was just thinking about ham sandwiches, and—"

A night on the sea in an open boat is a long night. As darkness settled finally, the shine of the light, lifting from the sea in the south, changed to full gold. On the northern horizon a new light appeared, a small bluish gleam on the edge of the waters. These two lights were the furniture of the world. Otherwise there was nothing but waves.

Two men huddled in the stern, and distances were so magnificent in the dinghy that the rower was enabled to keep his feet partly warm by thrusting them under his companions. Their legs indeed extended far under the rowing-seat until they touched the feet of the captain forward. Sometimes, despite the efforts of the tired oarsman, a wave came piling into the boat, an icy wave of the night, and the chilling water soaked them anew. They would twist their bodies for a moment and groan, and sleep the dead sleep once more, while the water in the boat gurgled about them as the craft rocked.

The plan of the oiler and the correspondent was for one to row until he lost the ability, and then arouse the other from his sea-water couch in the bottom of the boat.

The oiler plied the oars until his head drooped forward and the overpowering sleep blinded him; and he rowed yet afterward. Then he touched a man in the bottom of the boat, and called his name. "Will you spell me for a little while?" he said meekly.

"Sure, Billie," said the correspondent, awaking and dragging himself to a sitting position. They exchanged places carefully, and the oiler, cuddling down in the seawater at the cook's side, seemed to go to sleep instantly.

The particular violence of the sea had ceased. The waves came without snarling. The obligation of the man at the oars was to keep the boat headed so that the tilt of the rollers would not capsize her, and to preserve her from filling when the crests rushed past. The black waves were silent and hard to be seen in the darkness. Often one was almost upon the boat before the oarsman was aware.

In a low voice the correspondent addressed the captain. He was not sure that the captain was awake, although this iron man seemed to be always awake. "Captain, shall I keep her making for that light north, sir?"

The same steady voice answered him. "Yes. Keep it about two points off the port bow."

The cook had tied a lifebelt around himself in order to get even the warmth which this clumsy cork contrivance could donate, and he seemed almost stove-like when a rower, whose teeth invariably chattered wildly as soon as he ceased his labor, dropped down to sleep.

The correspondent, as he rowed, looked down at the two men sleeping underfoot. The cook's arm was around the oiler's shoulders, and, with their fragmentary clothing and haggard faces, they were the babes of the sea—a grotesque rendering of the old babes in the wood.

Later he must have grown stupid at his work, for suddenly there was a growling of water, and a crest came with a roar and a swash into the boat, and it was a wonder that it did not set the cook afloat in his lifebelt. The cook continued to sleep, but the oiler sat up, blinking his eyes and shaking with the new cold.

"Oh, I'm awful sorry, Billie," said the correspondent, contritely.

"That's all right, old boy," said the oiler, and lay down again and was asleep.

Presently it seemed that even the captain dozed, and the correspondent thought that he was the one man afloat on all the oceans. The wind had a voice as it came over the waves, and it was sadder than the end.

There was a long, loud swishing astern of the boat, and a gleaming trail of phosphorescence, like blue flame, was furrowed on the black waters. It might have been made by a monstrous knife.

Then there came a stillness, while the correspondent breathed with open mouth and looked at the sea.

Suddenly there was another swish and another long flash of bluish light, and this time it was alongside the boat, and might almost have been reached with an oar. The correspondent saw an enormous fin speed like a shadow through the water, hurling the crystalline spray and leaving the long glowing trail.

The correspondent looked over his shoulder at the captain. His face was hidden, and he seemed to be asleep. He looked at the babes of the sea. They certainly were asleep. So, being bereft of sympathy, he leaned a little way to one side and swore softly into the sea.

But the thing did not then leave the vicinity of the boat. Ahead or astern, on one side or the other, at intervals long or short, fled the long sparkling streak, and there was to be heard the *whirroo* of the dark fin. The speed and power of the thing was greatly to be admired. It cut the water like a gigantic and keen projectile.

The presence of this biding thing did not affect the man with the same horror that it would if he had been a picnicker. He simply looked at the sea dully and swore in an undertone.

Nevertheless, it is true that he did not wish to be alone with the thing. He wished one of his companions to awake by chance and keep him company with it. But the captain hung motionless over the water jar, and the oiler and the cook in the bottom of the boat were plunged in slumber.

VI

"If I am going to be drowned—if I am going to be drowned—if I am going to be drowned, why, in the name of the seven mad gods who rule the sea, was I allowed to come thus far and contemplate sand and trees?"

During this dismal night, it may be remarked that a man would conclude that it was really the intention of the seven mad gods to drown him, despite the abominable injustice of it. For it was certainly an abominable injustice to drown a man who had worked so hard, so hard. The man felt it would be a crime most unnatural. Other people had drowned at sea since galleys swarmed with painted sails, but still—

When it occurs to a man that nature does not regard him as important, and that she feels she would not maim the universe by disposing of him, he at first wishes to throw bricks at the temple, and he hates deeply the fact that there are no bricks and no temples. Any visible expression of nature would surely be pelleted with his jeers.

Then, if there be no tangible thing to hoot, he feels, perhaps, the desire to confront a personification and indulge in pleas, bowed to one knee, and with hands supplicant, saying, "Yes, but I love myself."

A high cold star on a winter's night is the word he feels that she says to him. Thereafter he knows the pathos of his situation.

The men in the dinghy had not discussed these matters, but each had, no doubt, reflected upon them in silence and according to his mind. There was seldom any expression upon their faces save the general one of complete weariness. Speech was devoted to the business of the boat.

To chime the notes of his emotion, a verse mysteriously entered the correspondent's head. He had even forgotten that he had forgotten this verse, but it suddenly was in his mind.

A soldier of the Legion lay dying in Algiers;
There was lack of woman's nursing, there was dearth of woman's tears;

But a comrade stood beside him, and he took that comrade's hand,
And he said, "I never more shall see my own, my native land."

In his childhood the correspondent had been made acquainted with the
fact that a soldier of the Legion lay dying in Algiers, but he had never
regarded the fact as important. Myriads of his schoolfellows had informed
him of the soldier's plight, but the dinning had naturally ended by making
him perfectly indifferent. He had never considered it his affair that a
soldier of the Legion lay dying in Algiers, nor had it appeared to him as a
matter for sorrow. It was less to him than the breaking of a pencil's point.

Now, however, it quaintly came to him as a human, living thing. It was
no longer merely a picture of a few throes in the breast of a poet, meanwhile drinking tea and warming his feet at the grate; it was an actuality
—stern, mournful, and fine.

The correspondent plainly saw the soldier. He lay on the sand with his
feet out straight and still. While his pale left hand was upon his chest in
an attempt to thwart the going of his life, the blood came between his
fingers. In the far Algerian distance, a city of low square forms was set
against a sky that was faint with the last sunset hues. The correspondent,
plying the oars and dreaming of the slow and slower movements of the
lips of the soldier, was moved by a profound and perfectly impersonal comprehension. He was sorry for the soldier of the Legion who lay dying in
Algiers.

The thing which had followed the boat and waited had evidently grown
bored at the delay. There was no longer to be heard the slash of the cut-
water, and there was no longer the flame of the long trail. The light in
the north still glimmered, but it was apparently no nearer to the boat.
Sometimes the boom of the surf rang in the correspondent's ears, and he
turned the craft seaward then and rowed harder. Southward, some one
had evidently built a watch fire on the beach. It was too low and too far
to be seen, but it made a shimmering, roseate reflection upon the bluff in
back of it, and this could be discerned from the boat. The wind came
stronger, and sometimes a wave suddenly raged out like a mountain cat,
and there was to be seen the sheen and sparkle of a broken crest.

The captain, in the bow, moved on his water jar and sat erect. "Pretty
long night," he observed to the correspondent. He looked at the shore.
"Those lifesaving people take their time."

"Did you see that shark playing around?"

"Yes, I saw him. He was a big fellow, all right."

"Wish I had known you were awake."

Later the correspondent spoke into the bottom of the boat. "Billie!"
There was a slow and gradual disentanglement. "Billie, will you spell me?"

"Sure," said the oiler.

As soon as the correspondent touched the cold, comfortable seawater in
the bottom of the boat and had huddled close to the cook's lifebelt he was

deep in sleep, despite the fact that his teeth played all the popular airs. This sleep was so good to him that it was but a moment before he heard a voice call his name in a tone that demonstrated the last stages of exhaustion. "Will you spell me?"

"Sure, Billie."

The light in the north had mysteriously vanished, but the correspondent took his course from the wide-awake captain.

Later in the night they took the boat farther out to sea, and the captain directed the cook to take one oar at the stern and keep the boat facing the seas. He was to call out if he should hear the thunder of the surf. This plan enabled the oiler and the correspondent to get respite together. "We'll give those boys a chance to get into shape again," said the captain. They curled down and, after a few preliminary chatterings and trembles, slept once more the dead sleep. Neither knew they had bequeathed to the cook the company of another shark, or perhaps the same shark.

As the boat caroused on the waves, spray occasionally bumped over the side and gave them a fresh soaking, but this had no power to break their repose. The ominous slash of the wind and the water affected them as it would have affected mummies.

"Boys," said the cook, with the notes of every reluctance in his voice, "she's drifted in pretty close. I guess one of you had better take her to sea again." The correspondent, aroused, heard the crash of the toppled crests.

As he was rowing, the captain gave him some whiskey-and-water, and this steadied the chills out of him. "If I ever get ashore and anybody shows me even a photograph of an oar—"

At last there was a short conversation.

"Billie! . . . Billie, will you spell me?"

"Sure," said the oiler.

VII

When the correspondent again opened his eyes, the sea and the sky were each of the gray hue of the dawning. Later, carmine and gold was painted upon the waters. The morning appeared finally, in its splendor, with a sky of pure blue, and the sunlight flamed on the tips of the waves.

On the distant dunes were set many little black cottages, and a tall white windmill reared above them. No man, nor dog, nor bicycle appeared on the beach. The cottages might have formed a deserted village.

The voyagers scanned the shore. A conference was held in the boat. "Well," said the captain, "if no help is coming, we might better try a run through the surf right away. If we stay out here much longer we will be too weak to do anything for ourselves at all." The others silently acquiesced in this reasoning. The boat was headed for the beach. The correspondent wondered if none ever ascended the tall wind-tower, and if then they never looked seaward. This tower was a giant, standing with its back to the plight of the ants. It represented in a degree, to the correspondent, the serenity of nature amid the struggles of the individual—nature in the wind, and nature in the vision of men. She did not seem cruel to him then, nor beneficent, nor treacherous, nor wise. But she was indifferent, flatly indifferent. It is, perhaps, plausible that a man in this situation, impressed with the unconcern of the universe, should see the innumerable flaws of his life, and have them taste wickedly in his mind, and wish for another chance. A distinction between right and wrong seems absurdly clear to him, then, in this new ignorance of the grave-edge, and he understands that if he were given another opportunity he would mend his conduct and his words, and be better and brighter during an introduction or at a tea.

"Now, boys," said the captain, "she is going to swamp sure. All we can do is to work her in as far as possible, and then when she swamps, pile out and scramble for the beach. Keep cool now, and don't jump until she swamps sure."

The oiler took the oars. Over his shoulders he scanned the surf. "Captain," he said, "I think I'd better bring her about and keep her head-on to the seas and back her in."

"All right, Billie," said the captain. "Back her in." The oiler swung the boat then, and, seated in the stern, the cook and the correspondent were obliged to look over their shoulders to contemplate the lonely and indifferent shore.

The monstrous inshore rollers heaved the boat high until the men were again enabled to see the white sheets of water scudding up the slanted beach. "We won't get in very close," said the captain. Each time a man could wrest his attention from the rollers, he turned his glance toward the shore, and in the expression of the eyes during this contemplation there was a singular quality. The correspondent, observing the others, knew that they were not afraid, but the full meaning of their glances was shrouded.

As for himself, he was too tired to grapple fundamentally with the fact. He tried to coerce his mind into thinking of it, but the mind was dominated at this time by the muscles, and the muscles said they did not care. It merely occurred to him that if he should drown it would be a shame.

There were no hurried words, no pallor, no plain agitation. The men simply looked at the shore. "Now, remember to get well clear of the boat when you jump," said the captain.

Seaward the crest of a roller suddenly fell with a thunderous crash, and the long white comber came roaring down upon the boat.

"Steady now," said the captain. The men were silent. They turned their eyes from the shore to the comber and waited. The boat slid up the incline, leaped at the furious top, bounced over it, and swung down the long back of the wave. Some water had been shipped, and the cook bailed it out.

But the next crest crashed also. The tumbling, boiling flood of white water caught the boat and whirled it almost perpendicular. Water swarmed in from all sides. The correspondent had his hands on the gunwale at this time, and when the water entered at that place he swiftly withdrew his fingers, as if he objected to wetting them.

The little boat, drunken with this weight of water, reeled and snuggled deeper into the sea.

"Bail her out, cook! Bail her out!" said the captain.

"All right, Captain," said the cook.

"Now, boys, the next one will do for us sure," said the oiler. "Mind to jump clear of the boat."

The third wave moved forward, huge, furious, implacable. It fairly swallowed the dinghy, and almost simultaneously the men tumbled into the sea. A piece of lifebelt had lain in the bottom of the boat, and as the correspondent went overboard he held this to his chest with his left hand.

The January water was icy, and he reflected immediately that it was colder than he had expected to find it off the coast of Florida. This appeared to his dazed mind as a fact important enough to be noted at the time. The coldness of the water was sad; it was tragic. This fact was somehow mixed and confused with his opinion of his own situation, so that it seemed almost a proper reason for tears. The water was cold.

When he came to the surface he was conscious of little but the noisy water. Afterward he saw his companions in the sea. The oiler was ahead in the race. He was swimming strongly and rapidly. Off to the correspondent's left, the cook's great white and corked back bulged out of the water; and in the rear the captain was hanging with his one good hand to the keel of the overturned dinghy.

There is a certain immovable quality to a shore, and the correspondent wondered at it amid the confusion of the sea.

It seemed also very attractive; but the correspondent knew that it was a long journey, and he paddled leisurely. The piece of life preserver lay under him, and sometimes he whirled down the incline of a wave as if he were on a hand-sled.

But finally he arrived at a place in the sea where travel was beset with difficulty. He did not pause swimming to inquire what manner of current had caught him, but there his progress ceased. The shore was set before him like a bit of scenery on a stage, and he looked at it and understood with his eyes each detail of it.

As the cook passed, much farther to the left, the captain was calling to him, "Turn over on your back, cook! Turn over on your back and use the oar."

"All right, sir." The cook turned on his back, and, paddling with an oar, went ahead as if he were a canoe.

Presently the boat also passed to the left of the correspondent, with the captain clinging with one hand to the keel. He would have appeared like a man raising himself to look over a board fence if it were not for the extraordinary gymnastics of the boat. The correspondent marveled that the captain could still hold to it.

They passed on nearer to shore—the oiler, the cook, the captain—and following them went the water jar, bouncing gaily over the seas.

The correspondent remained in the grip of this strange new enemy—a current. The shore, with its white slope of sand and its green bluff topped with little silent cottages, was spread like a picture before him. It was very near to him then, but he was impressed as one who, in a gallery, looks at a scene from Brittany or Algiers.

He thought: "I am going to drown? Can it be possible? Can it be possible? Can it be possible?" Perhaps an individual must consider his own death to be the final phenomenon of nature.

But later a wave perhaps whirled him out of this small deadly current, for he found suddenly that he could again make progress toward the shore. Later still he was aware that the captain, clinging with one hand to the keel of the dinghy, had his face turned away from the shore and toward him, and was calling his name. "Come to the boat! Come to the boat!"

In his struggle to reach the captain and the boat, he reflected that when one gets properly wearied drowning must really be a comfortable arrangement—a cessation of hostilities accompanied by a large degree of relief; and he was glad of it, for the main thing in his mind for some moments had been horror of the temporary agony. He did not wish to be hurt.

Presently he saw a man running along the shore. He was undressing with most remarkable speed. Coat, trousers, shirt, everything flew magically off him.

"Come to the boat!" called the captain.

"All right, Captain." As the correspondent paddled, he saw the captain let himself down to bottom and leave the boat. Then the correspondent performed his one little marvel of the voyage. A large wave caught him and flung him with ease and supreme speed completely over the boat and far beyond it. It struck him even then as an event in gymnastics and a true miracle of the sea. An overturned boat in the surf is not a plaything to a swimming man.

The correspondent arrived in water that reached only to his waist, but his condition did not enable him to stand for more than a moment. Each wave knocked him into a heap, and the undertow pulled at him.

Then he saw the man who had been running and undressing, and undressing and running, come bounding into the water. He dragged ashore the cook, and then waded toward the captain; but the captain waved him away and sent him to the correspondent. He was naked—naked as a tree in winter; but a halo was about his head, and he shone like a saint. He gave a strong pull, and a long drag, and a bully heave at the correspondent's hand. The correspondent, schooled in the minor formulae, said,

"Thanks, old man." But suddenly the man cried, "What's that?" He pointed a swift finger. The correspondent said, "Go."

In the shallows, face downward, lay the oiler. His forehead touched sand that was periodically, between each wave, clear of the sea.

The correspondent did not know all that transpired afterward. When he achieved safe ground he fell, striking the sand with each particular part of his body. It was as if he had dropped from a roof, but the thud was grateful to him.

It seems that instantly the beach was populated with men with blankets, clothes, and flasks, and women with coffeepots and all the remedies sacred to their minds. The welcome of the land to the men from the sea was warm and generous; but a still and dripping shape was carried slowly up the beach, and the land's welcome for it could only be the different and sinister hospitality of the grave.

When it came night, the white waves paced to and fro in the moonlight, and the wind brought the sound of the great sea's voice to the men on the shore, and they felt that they could then be interpreters.

A FREE MAN'S WORSHIP

BERTRAND RUSSELL

Bertrand Russell (1872–1970) was a British philosopher usually included among the outstanding minds of the twentieth century. His principal contribution to philosophy lies in the field of logic, especially the theory of descriptions and the theory of types, and in his attempt to introduce scientific method into philosophic inquiry. Russell's major works include *Principia Mathematica* (with A. N. Whitehead), *The Problems of Philosophy, Our Knowledge of the External World, The Analysis of Mind,* and *An Enquiry into Meaning and Truth.* Books such as *Marriage and Morals* and *Why I am not a Christian* were written for a more general audience.

Russell followed the tradition of British empiricism, relying upon sense-perception for determining genuine knowledge (although this was modified somewhat by a bent toward rationalism). In the following essay, Russell presents a thoroughgoing naturalistic view of life as contrasted with a more comforting but illusory religious belief. He offers a lyrical and heroic defense of honesty in the conduct of our lives—an acceptance and affirmation of our position as fragile, unsupported beings in a wholly natural world.

To Dr. Faustus in his study Mephistopheles told the history of the Creation, saying:

"The endless praises of the choirs of angels had begun to grow wearisome; for, after all, did he not deserve their praise? Had he not given them endless joy? Would it not be more amusing to obtain undeserved praise, to be worshipped by beings whom he tortured? He smiled inwardly, and resolved that the great drama should be performed.

"For countless ages the hot nebula whirled aimlessly through space. At length it began to take shape, the central mass threw off planets, the planets cooled, boiling seas and burning mountains heaved and tossed, from black masses of cloud hot sheets of rain deluged the barely solid crust. And now the first germ of life grew in the depths of the ocean, and developed rapidly in the fructifying warmth into vast forest trees, huge ferns springing from the damp mould, sea monsters breeding, fighting, devouring, and passing away. And from the monsters, as the play unfolded itself, Man was born, with the power of thought, the knowledge of good and evil, and the cruel thirst for worship. And Man saw that all is passing in this mad, monstrous world, that all is struggling to snatch, at any cost, a few brief moments of life before Death's inexorable decree. And Man said: 'There is a hidden purpose, could we but fathom it, and the purpose is good; for we must reverence something, and in the visible world there is nothing worthy of reverence.' And Man stood aside from the struggle, resolving that God intended harmony to come out of chaos by human efforts. And when he followed the instincts which God had transmitted to him from his ancestry of beasts of prey, he called it Sin, and asked God to forgive him. But he doubted whether he could be justly forgiven, until he invented a divine Plan by which God's wrath was to have been appeased. And seeing the present was bad, he made it yet worse, that thereby the future might be better. And he gave God thanks for the strength that enabled him to forgo even the joys that were possible. And God smiled; and when he saw that Man had become perfect in renunciation and worship, he sent another sun through the sky, which crashed into Man's sun; and all returned again to nebula.

"'Yes,' he murmured, 'it was a good play; I will have it performed again.'"

Such, in outline, but even more purposeless, more void of meaning, is the world which Science presents for our belief. Amid such a world, if anywhere, our ideals henceforward must find a home. That Man is the product of causes which had no prevision of the end they were achieving; that his origin, his growth, his hopes and fears, his loves and his beliefs, are but the outcome of accidental collocations of atoms; that no fire, no heroism, no intensity of thought and feeling, can preserve an individual life beyond the grave; that all the labours of the ages, all the devotion, all the inspiration, all the noonday brightness of human genius, are destined to extinction in the vast death of the solar system, and that the whole temple of Man's achievement must inevitably be buried beneath the débris of a universe in ruins—all these things, if not quite beyond dispute, are yet so nearly certain, that no philosophy which rejects them can hope to stand. Only within the scaffolding of these truths, only on the firm foundation of unyielding despair, can the soul's habitation henceforth be safely built.

How, in such an alien and inhuman world, can so powerless a creature as Man preserve his aspirations untarnished? A strange mystery it is that Nature, omnipotent but blind, in the revolutions of her secular hurryings through the abysses of space, has brought forth at last a child, subject still to her power, but gifted with sight, with knowledge of good and evil, with the capacity of judging all the works of his unthinking Mother. In spite of Death, the mark and seal of the parental control, Man is yet free, during his brief years, to examine, to criticise, to know, and in imagination to create. To him alone, in the world with which he is acquainted, this freedom belongs; and in this lies his superiority to the resistless forces that control his outward life.

The savage, like ourselves, feels the oppression of his impotence before the powers of Nature; but having in himself nothing that he respects more than Power, he is willing to prostrate himself before his gods, without inquiring whether they are worthy of his worship. Pathetic and very terrible is the long history of cruelty and torture, of degradation and human sacrifice, endured in the hope of placating the jealous gods: surely, the trembling believer thinks, when what is most precious has been freely given, their lust for blood must be appeased, and more will not be required. The religion of Moloch—as such creeds may be generically called

—is in essence the cringing submission of the slave, who dare not, even in his heart, allow the thought that his master deserves no adulation. Since the independence of ideals is not yet acknowledged, Power may be freely worshipped, and receive an unlimited respect, despite its wanton infliction of pain.

But gradually, as morality grows bolder, the claim of the ideal world begins to be felt; and worship, if it is not to cease, must be given to gods of another kind than those created by the savage. Some, though they feel the demands of the ideal, will still consciously reject them, still urging that naked Power is worthy of worship. Such is the attitude inculcated in God's answer to Job out of the whirlwind: the divine power and knowledge are paraded, but of the divine goodness there is no hint. Such also is the attitude of those who, in our own day, base their morality upon the struggle for survival, maintaining that the survivors are necessarily the fittest. But others, not content with an answer so repugnant to the moral sense, will adopt the position which we have become accustomed to regard as specially religious, maintaining that, in some hidden manner, the world of fact is really harmonious with the world of ideals. Thus Man creates God, all-powerful and all-good, the mystic unity of what is and what should be.

But the world of fact, after all, is not good; and, in submitting our judgment to it, there is an element of slavishness from which our thoughts must be purged. For in all things it is well to exalt the dignity of Man, by freeing him as far as possible from the tyranny of non-human Power. When we have realised that Power is largely bad, that man, with his knowledge of good and evil, is but a hopeless atom in a world which has no such knowledge, the choice is again presented to us: Shall we worship Force, or shall we worship Goodness? Shall our God exist and be evil, or shall he be recognised as the creation of our own conscience?

The answer to this question is very momentous, and affects profoundly our whole morality. The worship of Force, to which Carlyle and Nietzsche and the creed of Militarism have accustomed us, is the result of failure to maintain our own ideals against a hostile universe: it is itself a prostrate submission to evil, a sacrifice of our best to Moloch. If strength indeed is to be respected, let us respect rather the strength of those who refuse that false "recognition of facts" which fails to recognise that facts are often bad. Let us admit that, in the world we know, there are many things that would be better otherwise, and that the ideals to which we do and must adhere are not realised in the realm of matter. Let us preserve our respect for truth, for beauty, for the ideal of perfection which life does not permit us to attain, though none of these things meet with the approval of the unconscious universe. If Power is bad, as it seems to be, let us reject it from our hearts. In this lies Man's true freedom: in determination to worship only the God created by our own love of the good, to respect only the heaven which inspires the insight of our best moments. In action, in desire, we must submit perpetually to the tyranny of outside forces; but in thought, in aspiration, we are free, free from our fellowmen, free from the petty planet on which our bodies impotently crawl, free even, while we live, from the tyranny of death. Let us learn, then, that energy of faith which enables us to live constantly in the vision of the good; and let us descend, in action, into the world of fact, with that vision always before us.

When first the opposition of fact and ideal grows fully visible, a spirit of fiery revolt, of fierce hatred of the gods, seems necessary to the assertion of freedom. To defy with Promethean constancy a hostile universe, to keep its evil always in view, always actively hated, to refuse no pain that the malice of Power can invent, appears to be the duty of all who will not bow before the inevitable. But indignation is still a bondage, for it compels our thoughts to be occupied with an evil world; and in the fierceness of desire from which rebellion springs there is a kind of self-assertion which it is necessary for the wise to overcome. Indignation is a submission of our thoughts, but not of our desires; the Stoic freedom in which wisdom consists is found in the submission of our desires, but not of our thoughts. From the submission of our desires springs the virtue of resignation; from the freedom of our thoughts springs the whole world of art and philosophy, and the vision of beauty by which, at last, we half reconquer the reluctant world. But the vision of beauty is possible only to unfettered contemplation, to thoughts not weighted by the load of eager wishes; and thus Freedom comes only to those who no longer ask of life that it shall yield them any of those personal goods that are subject to the mutations of Time.

Although the necessity of renunciation is evidence of the existence of evil, yet Christianity, in preaching it, has shown a wisdom exceeding that of the Promethean philosophy of rebellion. It must be admitted that, of the things we desire, some, though they prove impossible, are yet real goods; others, however, as ardently longed for, do not form part of a fully purified ideal. The belief that what must be renounced is bad, though sometimes false, is far less often false than untamed passion supposes; and the creed of religion, by providing a reason for proving that it is never false, has been the means of purifying our hopes by the discovery of many austere truths.

But there is in resignation a further good element: even real goods, when they are unattainable, ought not to be fretfully desired. To every man comes, sooner or later, the great renunciation. For the young, there is nothing unattainable; a good thing desired with the whole force of a passionate will, and yet impossible, is to them not credible. Yet, by death, by illness, by poverty, or by the voice of duty, we must learn, each one of us, that the world was not made for us, and that, however beautiful may be the things we crave, Fate may nevertheless forbid them. It is the part of courage, when misfortune comes, to bear without repining the ruin of our hopes, to turn away our thoughts from vain regrets. This degree of submission to Power is not only just and right: it is the very gate of wisdom.

But passive renunciation is not the whole of wisdom; for not by renunciation alone can we build a temple for the worship of our own ideals. Haunting foreshadowings of the temple appear in the realm of imagination, in music, in architecture, in the untroubled kingdom of reason, and in the golden sunset magic of lyrics, where beauty shines and glows, remote from the touch of sorrow, remote from the fear of change, remote from the failures and disenchantments of the world of fact. In the contemplation of these things the vision of heaven will shape itself in our hearts, giving at once a touchstone to judge the world about us, and an inspiration by which to fashion to our needs whatever is not incapable of serving as a stone in the sacred temple.

Except for those rare spirits that are born without sin, there is a cavern of darkness to be traversed before that temple can be entered. The gate of the cavern is despair, and its floor is paved with the gravestones of abandoned hopes. There Self must die; there the eagerness, the greed of untamed desire must be slain, for only so can the soul be freed from the empire of Fate. But out of the cavern the Gate of Renunciation leads again to the daylight of wisdom, by whose radiance a new insight, a new joy, a new tenderness, shine forth to gladden the pilgrim's heart.

When, without the bitterness of impotent rebellion, we have learnt both to resign ourselves to the outward rule of Fate and to recognise that the non-human world is unworthy of our worship, it becomes possible at last so to transform and refashion the unconscious universe, so to transmute it in the crucible of imagination, that a new image of shining gold replaces the old idol of clay. In all the multiform facts of the world—in the visual shapes of trees and mountains and clouds, in the events of the life of man, even in the very omnipotence of Death—the insight of creative idealism can find the reflection of a beauty which its own thoughts first made. In this way mind asserts its subtle mastery over the thoughtless forces of Nature. The more evil the material with which it deals, the more thwarting to untrained desire, the greater is its achievement in inducing the reluctant rock to yield up its hidden treasures, the prouder its victory in compelling the opposing forces to swell the pageant of its triumph. Of all the arts, Tragedy is the proudest, the most triumphant; for it builds its shining citadel in the very centre of the enemy's country, on the very summit of his highest mountain; from its impregnable watch-towers, his camps and arsenals, his columns and forts, are all revealed; within its walls the free life continues, while the legions of Death and Pain and Despair, and all the servile captains of tyrant Fate, afford the burghers of that dauntless city new spectacles of beauty. Happy those sacred ramparts, thrice happy the dwellers on that all-seeing eminence. Honour to those brave warriors who, through countless ages of warfare, have preserved for us the priceless heritage of liberty, and have kept undefiled by sacrilegious invaders the home of the unsubdued.

But the beauty of Tragedy does but make visible a quality which, in more or less obvious shapes, is present always and everywhere in life. In the spectacle of Death, in the endurance of intolerable pain, and in the irrevocableness of a vanished past, there is a sacredness, an overpowering awe, a feeling of the vastness, the depth, the inexhaustible mystery of existence, in which, as by some strange marriage of pain, the sufferer is bound to the world by bonds of sorrow. In these moments of insight, we lose all eagerness of temporary desire, all struggling and striving for petty ends, all care for the little trivial things that, to a superficial view, make up the common life of day by day; we see, surrounding the narrow raft illumined by the flickering light of human comradeship, the dark ocean on whose rolling waves we toss for a brief hour; from the great night without, a chill blast breaks in upon our refuge; all the loneliness of humanity amid hostile forces is concentrated upon the individual soul, which must struggle alone, with what of courage it can command, against the whole weight of a universe that cares nothing for its hopes and fears. Victory, in this struggle with the powers of darkness, is the true baptism into the glorious company of heroes, the true initiation into the overmastering beauty of human existence. From that awful encounter of the soul with the outer world, enunciation, wisdom, and charity are born; and with their birth a new life begins. To take into the inmost shrine of the soul the irresistible forces whose puppets we seem to be—Death and change, the irrevocableness of the past, and the powerlessness of man before the blind hurry of the universe from vanity to vanity—to feel these things and know them is to conquer them.

This is the reason why the Past has such magical power. The beauty of its motionless and silent pictures is like the enchanted purity of late autumn, when the leaves, though one breath would make them fall, still glow against the sky in golden glory. The Past does not change or strive; like Duncan,[1] after life's fitful fever it sleeps well; what was eager and grasping, what was petty and transitory, has faded away, the things that were beautiful and eternal shine out of it like stars in the night. Its beauty, to a soul not worthy of it, is unendurable; but to a soul which has conquered Fate it is the key of religion.

The life of Man, viewed outwardly, is but a small thing in comparison with the forces of Nature. The slave is doomed to worship Time and Fate and Death, because they are greater than anything he finds in himself, and because all his thoughts are of things which they devour. But, great as they are, to think of them greatly, to feel their passionless splendour, is greater still. And such thought makes us free men; we no longer bow before the inevitable in Oriental subjection, but we absorb it, and make it a

---

[1] From Shakespeare's *Macbeth*.

part of ourselves. To abandon the struggle for private happiness, to expel all eagerness of temporary desire, to burn with passion for eternal things—this is emancipation, and this is the free man's worship. And this liberation is effected by a contemplation of Fate; for Fate itself is subdued by the mind which leaves nothing to be purged by the purifying fire of Time.

United with his fellow-men by the strongest of all ties, the tie of a common doom, the free man finds that a new vision is with him always, shedding over every daily task the light of love. The life of Man is a long march through the night, surrounded by invisible foes, tortured by weariness and pain, towards a goal that few can hope to reach, and where none may tarry long. One by one, as they march, our comrades vanish from our sight, seized by the silent orders of omnipotent Death. Very brief is the time in which we can help them, in which their happiness or misery is decided. Be it ours to shed sunshine on their path, to lighten their sorrows by the balm of sympathy, to give them the pure joy of a never-tiring affection, to strengthen failing courage, to instil faith in hours of despair. Let us not weigh in grudging scales their merits and demerits, but let us think only of their need—of the sorrows, the difficulties, perhaps the blindnesses, that make the misery of their lives; let us remember that they are fellow-sufferers in the same darkness, actors in the same tragedy with ourselves. And so, when their day is over, when their good and their evil have become eternal by the immortality of the past, be it ours to feel that, where they suffered, where they failed, no deed of ours was the cause; but wherever a spark of the divine fire kindled in their hearts, we were ready with encouragement, with sympathy, with brave words in which high courage glowed.

Brief and powerless is Man's life; on him and all his race the slow, sure doom falls pitiless and dark. Blind to good and evil, reckless of destruction, omnipotent matter rolls on its relentless way; for Man, condemned to-day to lose his dearest, to-morrow himself to pass through the gate of darkness, it remains only to cherish, ere yet the blow falls, the lofty thoughts that ennoble his little day; disdaining the coward terrors of the slave of Fate, to worship at the shrine that his own hands have built; undismayed by the empire of chance, to preserve a mind free from the wanton tyranny that rules his outward life; proudly defiant of the irresistible forces that tolerate, for a moment, his knowledge and his condemnation, to sustain alone, a weary but unyielding Atlas, the world that his own ideals have fashioned despite the trampling march of unconscious power.

2

Spiritualism

SIDDHARTHA
HERMANN HESSE
(trans. by Hilda Rosner)

Hermann Hesse (1877–1962) was a German poet and novelist who is best known for *Steppenwolf* and *Siddhartha*. Several of his other novels also attained considerable popular success, including *Magister Ludi (The Glass-Bead Game)*, *Narcissus and Goldmund*, and *Demian*. In all of Hesse's works he is persistently concerned not with social issues but with problems of how the individual in his striving can build a harmonious personality and an adequate relationship to the world.

In his novel *Siddhartha*, excerpted below, Hesse presents an interpretation of the world view of Indian religion, and he does so in a serene and musical style suggestive of the eternal flow of life itself. Siddhartha advances in his spiritual development from the stage of self-denial in which home, family, and caste are ascetically abandoned, to the life of sensual love, wealth, and power, to the simple existence of a ferryman absorbing the lessons of eternity taught by the river itself. In this last stage of final enlightenment, Siddhartha reaches an awareness of the interconnectedness of all things, their simultaneity and oneness, and through the medium of mystical experience is able to impart his vision to others.

Siddhartha's vision is essentially that of Indian scripture which comprehends the universe as an immense, all-encompassing, unified whole, with the individual soul (Atman) actually one with the Absolute or world spirit (Brahman). Any separation then, between self and world, subject and object is artificial; there is only the All. This is the essential view of Guatama, the Buddha, founder of Buddhism, whose given name was Siddhartha.

In the following passage, Siddhartha (as an old man), tells his boyhood friend, Govinda, of the truth he has found.

GOVINDA

Govinda once spent a rest period with some other monks in the pleasure grove which Kamala, the courtesan, had once presented to the followers of Gotama. He heard talk of an old ferryman who lived by the river, a day's journey away, and whom many considered to be a sage. When Govinda moved on, he chose the path to the ferry, eager to see this ferryman, for although he had lived his life according to the rule and was also regarded with respect by the younger monks for his age and modesty, there was still restlessness in his heart and his seeking was unsatisfied.

He arrived at the river and asked the old man to take him across. When they climbed out of the boat on the other side, he said to the old man: "You show much kindness to the monks and pilgrims; you have taken many of us across. Are you not also a seeker of the right path?"

There was a smile in Siddhartha's old eyes as he said: "Do you call yourself a seeker, O venerable one, you who are already advanced in years and wear the role of Gotama's monks?"

"I am indeed old," said Govinda, "but I have never ceased seeking. I will never cease seeking. That seems to be my destiny. It seems to me that you also have sought. Will you talk to me a little about it, my friend?"

Siddhartha said: "What could I say to you that would be of value, except that perhaps you seek too much, that as a result of your seeking you cannot find."

"How is that?" asked Govinda.

"When someone is seeking," said Siddhartha, "it happens quite easily that he only sees the thing that he is seeking; that he is unable to find anything, unable to absorb anything, because he is only thinking of the thing he is seeking, because he has a goal, because he is obsessed with his goal. Seeking means: to have a goal; but finding means: to be free, to be receptive, to have no goal. You, O worthy one, are perhaps indeed a seeker, for in striving towards your goal, you do not see many things that are under your nose."

"I do not yet quite understand," said Govinda. "How do you mean?"

Siddhartha said: "Once, O worthy one, many years ago, you came to this river and found a man sleeping there. You sat beside him to guard him while he slept, but you did not recognize the sleeping man, Govinda."

Astonished and like one bewitched the monk gazed at the ferryman.

"Are you Siddhartha?" he asked in a timid voice. "I did not recognize you this time, too. I am very pleased to see you again, Siddhartha, very pleased. You have changed very much, my friend. And have you become a ferryman now?"

Siddhartha laughed warmly. "Yes, I have become a ferryman. Many people have to change a great deal and wear all sorts of clothes. I am one of those, my friend. You are very welcome, Govinda, and I invite you to stay the night in my hut."

Govinda stayed the night in the hut and slept in the bed that had once been Vasudeva's. He asked the friend of his youth many questions and Siddhartha had a great deal to tell him about his life.

When it was time for Govinda to depart the following morning, he said with some hesitation: "Before I go on my way, Siddhartha, I should like to ask you one more question. Have you a doctrine, belief or knowledge which you uphold, which helps you to live and do right?"

Siddhartha said: "You know, my friend, that even as a young man, when we lived with the ascetics in the forest, I came to distrust doctrines and teachers and to turn my back on them. I am still of the same turn of mind, although I have, since that time, had many teachers. A beautiful courtesan was my teacher for a long time, and a rich merchant and a dice player. On one occasion, one of the Buddha's wandering monks was my teacher. He halted in his pilgrimage to sit beside me when I fell asleep in the forest. I also learned something from him and I am grateful to him, very grateful. But most of all, I have learned from this river and from my predecessor, Vasudeva. He was a simple man; he was not a thinker, but he realized the essential as well as Gotama. He was a holy man, a saint."

Govinda said: "It seems to me, Siddhartha, that you still like to jest a little. I believe you and know that you have not followed any teacher, but have you not yourself, if not a doctrine, certain thoughts? Have you not discovered certain knowledge yourself that has helped you to live? It would give me great pleasure if you would tell me something about this."

Siddhartha said: "Yes, I have had thoughts and knowledge here and there. Sometimes, for an hour or for a day, I have become aware of knowledge, just as one feels life in one's heart. I have had many thoughts, but it would be difficult for me to tell you about them. But this is one thought that has impressed me, Govinda. Wisdom is not communicable. The wisdom which a wise man tries to communicate always sounds foolish."

"Are you jesting?" asked Govinda.

"No, I am telling you what I have discovered. Knowledge can be communicated, but not wisdom. One can find it, live it, be fortified by it, do wonders through it, but one cannot communicate and teach it. I suspected this when I was still a youth and it was this that drove me away from teachers. There is one thought I have had, Govinda, which you will again think is a jest or folly: that is, in every truth the opposite is equally true. For example, a truth can only be expressed and enveloped in words if it is one-sided. Everything that is thought and expressed in words is one-sided, only half the truth; it all lacks totality, completeness, unity. When the Illustrious Buddha taught about the world, he had to divide it into Sansara and Nirvana, into illusion and truth, into suffering and salvation. One cannot do otherwise, there is no other method for those who teach. But the world itself, being in and around us, is never one-sided. Never is a man or a deed wholly Sansara or wholly Nirvana; never is a man wholly a saint or a sinner. This only seems so because we suffer the illusion that time is something real. Time is not real, Govinda. I have realized this repeatedly. And if time is not real, then the dividing line that seems to lie between this world and eternity, between suffering and bliss, between good and evil, is also an illusion."

"How is that?" asked Govinda, puzzled.

"Listen, my friend! I am a sinner and you are a sinner, but someday the sinner will be Brahma again, will someday attain Nirvana, will someday become a Buddha. Now this 'someday' is illusion; it is only a comparison.

The sinner is not on the way to a Buddha-like state; he is not evolving, although our thinking cannot conceive things otherwise. No, the potential Buddha already exists in the sinner; his future is already there. The potential hidden Buddha must be recognized in him, in you, in everybody. The world, Govinda, is not imperfect or slowly evolving along a long path to perfection. No, it is perfect at every moment; every sin already carries grace within it, all small children are potential old men, all sucklings have death within them, all dying people—eternal life. It is not possible for one person to see how far another is on the way; the Buddha exists in the robber and dice player; the robber exists in the Brahmin. During deep meditation it is possible to dispel time, to see simultaneously all the past, present and future, and then everything is good, everything is perfect, everything is Brahman. Therefore, it seems to me that everything that exists is good—death as well as life, sin as well as holiness, wisdom as well as folly. Everything is necessary, everything needs only my agreement, my assent, my loving understanding; then all is well with me and nothing can harm me. I learned through my body and soul that it was necessary for me to sin, that I needed lust, that I had to strive for property and experience nausea and the depths of despair in order to learn not to resist them, in order to learn to love the world, and no longer compare it with some kind of desired imaginary world, some imaginary vision of perfection, but to leave it as it is, to love it and be glad to belong to it. These, Govinda, are some of the thoughts that are in my mind."

Siddhartha bent down, lifted a stone from the ground and held it in his hand.

"This," he said, handling it, "is a stone, and within a certain length of time it will perhaps be soil and from the soil it will become plant, animal or man. Previously I should have said: This stone is just a stone; it has no value, it belongs to the world of Maya, but perhaps because within the cycle of change it can also become man and spirit, it is also of importance. That is what I should have thought. But now I think: This stone is stone; it is also animal, God and Buddha. I do not respect and love it because it was one thing and will become something else, but because it has already long been everything and always is everything. I love it just because it is a stone, because today and now it appears to me a stone. I see value and meaning in each one of its fine markings and cavities, in the yellow, in the grey, in the hardness and the sound of it when I knock it, in the dryness or dampness of its surface. There are stones that feel like oil or soap, that look like leaves or sand, and each one is different and worships Om in its own way; each one is Brahman. At the same time it is very much stone, oily or soapy, and that is just what pleases me and seems wonderful and worthy of worship. But I will say no more about it. Words do not express thoughts very well. They always become a little different immediately they are expressed, a little distorted, a little foolish. And yet it also pleases me and seems right that what is of value and wisdom to one man seems nonsense to another."

Govinda had listened in silence.

"Why did you tell me about the stone?" he asked hesitatingly after a pause.

"I did so unintentionally. But perhaps it illustrates that I just love the stone and the river and all these things that we see and from which we can learn. I can love a stone, Govinda, and a tree or a piece of bark. These are things and one can love things. But one cannot love words. Therefore teachings are of no use to me; they have no hardness, no softness, no colors, no corners, no smell, no taste—they have nothing but words. Perhaps that is what prevents you from finding peace, perhaps there are too many words, for even salvation and virtue. Sansara and Nirvana are only words, Govinda. Nirvana is not a thing; there is only the word Nirvana."

Govinda said: "Nirvana is not only a word, my friend; it is a thought."

Siddhartha continued: "It may be a thought, but I must confess, my friend, that I do not differentiate very much between thoughts and words. Quite frankly, I do not attach great importance to thoughts either. I attach more importance to things. For example, there was a man at this ferry who was my predecessor and teacher. He was a holy man who for many years believed only in the river and nothing else. He noticed that the river's voice spoke to him. He learned from it; it educated and taught him. The river seemed like a god to him and for many years he did not know that every wind, every cloud, every bird, every beetle is equally divine and knows and can teach just as well as the esteemed river. But when this holy man went off into the woods, he knew everything; he knew more than you and I, without teachers, without books, just because he believed in the river."

Govinda said: "But what you call thing, is it something real, something intrinsic? Is it not only the illusion of Maya, only image and appearance? Your stone, your tree, are they real?"

"This also does not trouble me much," said Siddhartha. "If they are illusion, then I also am illusion, and so they are always of the same nature as myself. It is that which makes them so lovable and venerable. That is why I can love them. And here is a doctrine at which you will laugh. It seems to me, Govinda, that love is the most important thing in the world. It may be important to great thinkers to examine the world, to explain and despise it. But I think it is only important to love the world, not to despise it, not for us to hate each other, but to be able to regard the world and ourselves and all beings with love, admiration and respect."

"I understand that," said Govinda, "but that is just what the Illustrious One called illusion. He preached benevolence, forbearance, sympathy, patience—but not love. He forbade us to bind ourselves to earthly love."

"I know that," said Siddhartha smiling radiantly, "I know that, Govinda, and here we find ourselves within the maze of meanings, within the conflict of words, for I will not deny that my words about love are in apparent contradiction to the teachings of Gotama. That is just why I distrust words so much, for I know that this contradiction is an illusion. I know that I am at one with Gotama. How, indeed, could he not know love, he who has recognized all humanity's vanity and transitoriness, yet loves humanity so much that he has devoted a long life solely to help and teach people? Also with this great teacher, the thing to me is of greater importance than the words; his deeds and life are more important to me than his talk, the gesture of his hand is more important to me than his opinions. Not in speech or thought do I regard him as a great man, but in his deeds and life."

The two old men were silent for a long time. Then as Govinda was preparing to go, he said: "I thank you, Siddhartha, for telling me something of your thoughts. Some of them are strange thoughts. I cannot grasp them all immediately. However, I thank you, and I wish you many peaceful days."

Inwardly, however, he thought: Siddhartha is a strange man and he expresses strange thoughts. His ideas seem crazy. How different do the Illustrious One's doctrines sound! They are clear, straightforward, comprehensible; they contain nothing strange, wild or laughable. But Siddhartha's hands and feet, his eyes, his brow, his breathing, his smile, his greeting, his gait affect me differently from his thoughts. Never, since the time our Illustrious Gotama passed into Nirvana, have I ever met a man with the exception of Siddhartha about whom I felt: This is a holy man! His ideas may be strange, his words may sound foolish, but his glance and his hand, his skin and his hair, all radiate a purity, peace, serenity, gentleness and saintliness which I have never seen in any man since the recent death of our illustrious teacher.

While Govinda was thinking these thoughts and there was conflict in his heart, he again bowed to Siddhartha, full of affection towards him. He bowed low before the quietly seated man.

"Siddhartha," he said, "we are now old men. We may never see each other again in this life. I can see, my dear friend, that you have found peace. I realize that I have not found it. Tell me one more word, my esteemed friend, tell me something that I can conceive, something I can understand! Give me something to help me on my way, Siddhartha. My path is often hard and dark."

Siddhartha was silent and looked at him with his calm, peaceful smile. Govinda looked steadily in his face, with anxiety, with longing. Suffering, continual seeking and continual failure were written in his look.

Siddhartha saw it and smiled.

"Bend near to me!" he whispered in Govinda's ear. "Come, still nearer, quite close! Kiss me on the forehead, Govinda."

Although surprised, Govinda was compelled by a great love and presentiment to obey him; he leaned close to him and touched his forehead with his lips. As he did this, something wonderful happened to him. While he was still dwelling on Siddhartha's strange words, while he strove in vain to dispel the conception of time, to imagine Nirvana and Sansara as one, while even a certain contempt for his friend's words conflicted with a tremendous love and esteem for him, this happened to him.

He no longer saw the face of his friend Siddhartha. Instead he saw

other faces, many faces, a long series, a continuous stream of faces—
hundreds, thousands, which all came and disappeared and yet all seemed
to be there at the same time, which all continually changed and renewed
themselves and which were yet all Siddhartha. He saw the face of a fish,
of a carp, with tremendous painfully opened mouth, a dying fish with
dimmed eyes. He saw the face of a newly born child, red and full of
wrinkles, ready to cry. He saw the face of a murderer, saw him plunge a
knife into the body of a man; at the same moment he saw this criminal
kneeling down, bound, and his head cut off by an executioner. He saw the
naked bodies of men and women in the postures and transports of
passionate love. He saw corpses stretched out, still, cold, empty. He saw
the heads of animals, boars, crocodiles, elephants, oxen, birds. He saw
Krishna and Agni. He saw all these forms and faces in a thousand relationships to each other, all helping each other, loving, hating and destroying each other and become newly born. Each one was mortal, a
passionate, painful example of all that is transitory. Yet none of them
died, they only changed, were always reborn, continually had a new face:
only time stood between one face and another. And all these forms and
faces rested, flowed, reproduced, swam past and merged into each other,
and over them all there was continually something thin, unreal and yet
existing, stretched across like thin glass or ice, like a transparent skin,
shell, form or mask of water—and this mask was Siddhartha's smiling face
which Govinda touched with his lips at that moment. And Govinda saw
that this mask-like smile, this smile of unity over the flowing forms, this
smile of simultaneousness over the thousands of births and deaths—this
smile of Siddhartha—was exactly the same as the calm, delicate, impenetrable, perhaps gracious, perhaps mocking, wise, thousand-fold smile
of Gotama, the Buddha, as he had perceived it with awe a hundred times.
It was in such a manner, Govinda knew, that the Perfect One smiled.

No longer knowing whether time existed, whether this display had
lasted a second or a hundred years, whether there was a Siddhartha, or a
Gotama, a Self and others, wounded deeply by a divine arrow which gave
him pleasure, deeply enchanted and exalted, Govinda stood yet a while
bending over Siddhartha's peaceful face which he had just kissed, which
had just been the stage of all present and future forms. His countenance
was unchanged after the mirror of the thousand-fold forms had disappeared
from the surface. He smiled peacefully and gently, perhaps very graciously,
perhaps very mockingly, exactly as the Illustrious One had smiled.

Govinda bowed low. Uncontrollable tears trickled down his old face. He
was overwhelmed by a feeling of great love, of the most humble venera-
tion. He bowed low, right down to the ground, in front of the man sitting
there motionless, whose smile reminded him of everything that he had
ever loved in his life, of everything that had ever been of value and holy
in his life.

THE VARIETIES OF RELIGIOUS EXPERIENCE

(Lectures XVI and XVII)

WILLIAM JAMES

William James (1842–1910) was an American philosopher and psychologist chiefly associated with the early beginnings of behaviorism in psychology and the philosophic movement of Pragmatism. His two-volume work *The Principles of Psychology* contributed to establishing psychology as a science, and *The Varieties of Religious Experience* still stands as a definitive study of the philosophy and psychology of religion. James's distinctively philosophic works include *The Will to Believe* and *Pragmatism*.

In the following chapter "Mysticism" from James's *Varieties of Religious Experience*, four characteristics of the mystical state are described,[1] all of which agree with the transcendental experiences reported by Indian mystics as well as Christian ones. After presenting various accounts of the mystical experience, James logically assesses the validity of the claims, questioning the more extravagant conclusions but sympathizing with the mystic's contention that we cannot dismiss what may be a genuine means of knowing profound and hidden realities.

It is instructive to compare the mystical concept of the universe, which affirms the spiritual nature of reality, with that of materialism, which maintains that everything, including the mind and conscious events, can be explained in terms of matter and motion.

MYSTICISM

Over and over again in these lectures I have raised points and left them open and unfinished until we should have come to the subject of Mysticism. Some of you, I fear, may have smiled as you noted my reiterated postponements. But now the hour has come when mysticism must be faced in good earnest, and those broken threads wound up together. One may say truly, I think, that personal religious experience has its root and centre in mystical states of consciousness; so for us, who in these lectures are treating personal experience as the exclusive subject of our study, such states of consciousness ought to form the vital chapter from which the other chapters get their light. Whether my treatment of mystical states will shed more light or darkness, I do not know, for my own constitution shuts me out from their enjoyment almost entirely, and I can speak of them only at second hand. But though forced to look upon the subject so externally, I will be as objective and receptive as I can; and I think I shall at least succeed in convincing you of the reality of the states in question, and of the paramount importance of their function.

First of all, then, I ask, What does the expression 'mystical states of consciousness' mean? How do we part off mystical states from other states?

[1] Cf. Underhill, E. *Mysticism* (London: Methuen and Co., 1911) p. 96ff.

The words 'mysticism' and 'mystical' are often used as terms of mere reproach, to throw at any opinion which we regard as vague and vast and sentimental, and without a base in either facts or logic. For some writers a 'mystic' is any person who believes in thought-transference, or spirit-return. Employed in this way the word has little value: there are too many less ambiguous synonyms. So, to keep it useful by restricting it, I will do what I did in the case of the word 'religion,' and simply propose to you four marks which, when an experience has them, may justify us in calling it mystical for the purpose of the present lectures. In this way we shall save verbal disputation, and the recriminations that generally go therewith.

1. *Ineffability.*—The handiest of the marks by which I classify a state of mind as mystical is negative. The subject of it immediately says that it defies expression, that no adequate report of its contents can be given in words. It follows from this that its quality must be directly experienced; it cannot be imparted or transferred to others. In this peculiarity mystical states are more like states of feeling than like states of intellect. No one can make clear to another who has never had a certain feeling, in what the quality or worth of it consists. One must have musical ears to know the value of a symphony; one must have been in love one's self to understand a lover's state of mind. Lacking the heart or ear, we cannot interpret the musician or the lover justly, and are even likely to consider him weak-minded or absurd. The mystic finds that most of us accord to his experiences an equally incompetent treatment.

2. *Noetic quality.*— Although so similar to states of feeling, mystical states seem to those who experience them to be also states of knowledge. They are states of insight into depths of truth unplumbed by the discursive intellect. They are illuminations, revelations, full of significance and importance, all inarticulate though they remain; and as a rule they carry with them a curious sense of authority for after-time.

These two characters will entitle any state to be called mystical, in the sense in which I use the word. Two other qualities are less sharply marked, but are usually found. These are:—

3. *Transiency.*—Mystical states cannot be sustained for long. Except in rare instances, half an hour, or at most an hour or two, seems to be the limit beyond which they fade into the light of common day. Often, when faded, their quality can but imperfectly be reproduced in memory; but when they recur it is recognized; and from one recurrence to another it is susceptible of continuous development in what is felt as inner richness and importance.

4. *Passivity.*—Although the oncoming of mystical states may be facilitated by preliminary voluntary operations, as by fixing the attention, or going through certain bodily performances, or in other ways which manuals of mysticism prescribe; yet when the characteristic sort of consciousness once has set in, the mystic feels as if his own will were in abeyance, and indeed sometimes as if he were grasped and held by a

superior power. This latter peculiarity connects mystical states with certain definite phenomena of secondary or alternative personality, such as prophetic speech, automatic writing, or the mediumistic trance. When these latter conditions are well pronounced, however, there may be no recollection whatever of the phenomenon, and it may have no significance for the subject's usual inner life, to which, as it were, it makes a mere interruption. Mystical states, strictly so called, are never merely interruptive. Some memory of their content always remains, and a profound sense of their importance. They modify the inner life of the subject between the times of their recurrence. Sharp divisions in this region are, however, difficult to make, and we find all sorts of gradations and mixtures.

These four characteristics are sufficient to mark out a group of states of consciousness peculiar enough to deserve a special name and to call for careful study. Let it then be called the mystical group.

Our next step should be to gain acquaintance with some typical examples. Professional mystics at the height of their development have often elaborately organized experiences and a philosophy based thereupon. But you remember what I said in my first lecture: phenomena are best understood when placed within their series, studied in their germ and in their over-ripe decay, and compared with their exaggerated and degenerated kindred. The range of mystical experience is very wide, much too wide for us to cover in the time at our disposal. Yet the method of serial study is so essential for interpretation that if we really wish to reach conclusions we must use it. I will begin, therefore, with phenomena which claim no special religious significance, and end with those of which the religious pretensions are extreme.

The simplest rudiment of mystical experience would seem to be that deepened sense of the significance of a maxim or formula which occasionally sweeps over one. "I've heard that said all my life," we exclaim, "but I never realized its full meaning until now." "When a fellow-monk," said Luther, "one day repeated the words of the Creed: 'I believe in the forgiveness of sins,' I saw the Scripture in an entirely new light; and straightway I felt as if I were born anew. It was as if I had found the door of paradise thrown wide open."[2] This sense of deeper significance is not confined to rational propositions. Single words,[3] and conjunctions of words, effects of light on land and sea, odors and musical sounds, all bring it when the mind is tuned aright. Most of us can remember the

---

2 Newman's *Securus pudicat orbis terrarum* is another instance. [William James.]

3 'Mesopotamia' is the stock comic instance.—An excellent old German lady, who had done some traveling in her day, used to describe to me her *Sehnsucht* that she might yet visit 'Phīladelphiā,' whose wondrous name had always haunted her imagination. Of John Foster it is said that "single words (as *chalcedony*), or the names of ancient heroes, had a mighty fascination over him. 'At any time the word *hermit* was enough to transport him.' The words *woods* and *forests* would produce the most powerful emotion." Foster's Life, by RYLAND, New York, 1846, p. 3. [William James.]

strangely moving power of passages in certain poems read when we were young, irrational doorways as they were through which the mystery of fact, the wildness and the pang of life, stole into our hearts and thrilled them. The words have now perhaps become mere polished surfaces for us; but lyric poetry and music are alive and significant only in proportion as they fetch these vague vistas of a life continuous with our own, beckoning and inviting, yet ever eluding our pursuit. We are alive or dead to the eternal inner message of the arts according as we have kept or lost this mystical susceptibility.

A more pronounced step forward on the mystical ladder is found in an extremely frequent phenomenon, that sudden feeling, namely, which sometimes sweeps over us, of having 'been here before,' as if at some indefinite past time, in just this place, with just these people, we were already saying just these things. As Tennyson writes:

> "Moreover, something is or seems,
> That touches me with mystic gleams,
> Like glimpses of forgotten dreams—
>
> "Of something felt, like something here;
> Of something done, I know not where;
> Such as no language may declare."[4]

Sir James Crichton-Browne has given the technical name of 'dreamy states' to these sudden invasions of vaguely reminiscent consciousness.[5] They bring a sense of mystery and of the metaphysical duality of things, and the feeling of an enlargement of perception which seems imminent but which never completes itself. In Dr. Crichton-Browne's opinion they connect themselves with the perplexed and scared disturbances of self-consciousness which occasionally precede epileptic attacks. I think that this learned alienist takes a rather absurdly alarmist view of an intrinsically insignificant phenomenon. He follows it along the downward ladder,

---

[4] The Two Voices. In a letter to Mr. B. P. Blood, Tennyson reports of himself as follows:—

"I have never had any revelations through anaesthetics, but a kind of waking trance—this for lack of a better word—I have frequently had, quite up from boyhood, when I have been all alone. This has come upon me through repeating my own name to myself silently, till all at once, as it were out of the intensity of the consciousness of individuality, individuality itself seemed to dissolve and fade away into boundless being, and this not a confused state but the clearest, the surest of the surest, utterly beyond words—where death was an almost laughable impossibility—the loss of personality (if so it were) seeming no extinction, but the only true life. I am ashamed of my feeble description. Have I not said the state is utterly beyond words?"

Professor Tyndall, in a letter, recalls Tennyson saying of this condition: "By God Almighty! there is no delusion in the matter! It is no nebulous ecstasy, but a state of transcendent wonder, associated with absolute clearness of mind." Memoirs of Alfred Tennyson, ii. 473. [William James.]

[5] The Lancet, July 6 and 13, 1895, reprinted as the Cavendish Lecture, on Dreamy Mental States, London, Baillière, 1895. They have been a good deal discussed of late by psychologists. See, for example, BERNARD-LEROY: L'Illusion de Fausse Reconnaissance, Paris, 1898. [William James.]

to insanity; our path pursues the upward ladder chiefly. The divergence shows how important it is to neglect no part of a phenomenon's connections, for we make it appear admirable or dreadful according to the context by which we set it off.

Somewhat deeper plunges into mystical consciousness are met with in yet other dreamy states. Such feelings as these which Charles Kingsley describes are surely far from being uncommon, especially in youth:—

> "When I walk the fields, I am oppressed now and then with an innate feeling that everything I see has a meaning, if I could but understand it. And this feeling of being surrounded with truths which I cannot grasp amounts to indescribable awe sometimes. . . . Have you not felt that your real soul was imperceptible to your mental vision, except in a few hallowed moments?" [6]

A much more extreme state of mystical consciousness is described by J. A. Symonds; and probably more persons than we suspect could give parallels to it from their own experience.

> "Suddenly," writes Symonds, "at church, or in company, or when I was reading, and always, I think, when my muscles were at rest, I felt the approach of the mood. Irresistibly it took possession of my mind and will, lasted what seemed an eternity, and disappeared in a series of rapid sensations which resembled the awakening from anæsthetic influence. One reason why I disliked this kind of trance was that I could not describe it to myself. I cannot even now find words to render it intelligible. It consisted in a gradual but swiftly progressive obliteration of space, time, sensation, and the multitudinous factors of experience which seem to qualify what we are pleased to call our Self. In proportion as these conditions of ordinary consciousness were subtracted, the sense of an underlying or essential consciousness acquired intensity. At last nothing remained but a pure, absolute, abstract Self. The universe became without form and void of content. But Self persisted, formidable in its vivid keenness, feeling the most poignant doubt about reality, ready, as it seemed, to find existence break as breaks a bubble round about it. And what then? The apprehension of a coming dissolution, the grim conviction that this state was the last state of the conscious Self, the sense that I had followed the last thread of being to the verge of the abyss, and had arrived at demonstration of eternal Maya or illusion, stirred or seemed to stir me up again. The return to ordinary conditions of sentient existence began by my first recovering the power of touch, and then by the gradual though rapid influx of familiar impressions and diurnal interests. At last I felt myself once more a human being; and though the riddle of what is meant by life remained unsolved, I was thankful for this return from the abyss—this deliverance from so awful an initiation into the mysteries of skepticism.

[6] Charles Kingsley's Life, i. 55, quoted by INGE: Christian Mysticism, London, 1899, p. 341. [William James.]

"This trance recurred with diminishing frequency until I reached the age of twenty-eight. It served to impress upon my growing nature the phantasmal unreality of all the circumstances which contribute to a merely phenomenal consciousness. Often have I asked myself with anguish, on waking from that formless state of denuded, keenly sentient being, Which is the unreality?—the trance of fiery, vacant, apprehensive, skeptical Self from which I issue, or these surrounding phenomena and habits which veil that inner Self and build a self of flesh-and-blood conventionality? Again, are men the factors of some dream, the dream-like unsubstantiality of which they comprehend at such eventful moments? What would happen if the final stage of the trance were reached?" [7]

In a recital like this there is certainly something suggestive of pathology.[8] The next step into mystical states carries us into a realm that public opinion and ethical philosophy have long since branded as pathological, though private practice and certain lyric strains of poetry seem still to bear witness to its ideality. I refer to the consciousness produced by intoxicants and anæsthetics, especially by alcohol. The sway of alcohol over mankind is unquestionably due to its power to stimulate the mystical faculties of human nature, usually crushed to earth by the cold facts and dry criticisms of the sober hour. Sobriety diminishes, discriminates, and says no; drunkenness expands, unites, and says yes. It is in fact the great exciter of the *Yes* function in man. It brings its votary from the chill periphery of things to the radiant core. It makes him for the moment one with truth. Not through mere perversity do men run after it. To the poor and the unlettered it stands in the place of symphony concerts and of literature; and it is part of the deeper mystery and tragedy of life that whiffs and gleams of something that we immediately recognize as excellent should be vouchsafed to so many of us only in the fleeting earlier phases of what in its totality is so degrading a poisoning. The drunken consciousness is one bit of the mystic consciousness, and our total opinion of it must find its place in our opinion of that larger whole.

Nitrous oxide and ether, especially nitrous oxide, when sufficiently diluted with air, stimulate the mystical consciousness in an extraordinary degree. Depth beyond depth of truth seems revealed to the inhaler. This truth fades out, however, or escapes, at the moment of coming to; and if any words remain over in which it seemed to clothe itself, they prove to be the veriest nonsense. Nevertheless, the sense of a profound meaning having been there persists; and I know more than one person who is persuaded that in the nitrous oxide trance we have a genuine metaphysical revelation.

---

[7] H. F. Brown: J. A. Symonds, a Biography, London, 1895, pp. 29–31, abridged. [William James.]

[8] Crichton-Browne expressly says that Symonds's "highest nerve centres were in some degree enfeebled or damaged by these dreamy mental states which afflicted him so grievously." Symonds was, however, a perfect monster of many-sided cerebral efficiency, and his critic gives no objective grounds whatever for his strange opinion, save that Symonds complained occasionally, as all susceptible and ambitious men complain, of lassitude and uncertainty as to his life's mission. [William James.]

Some years ago I myself made some observations on this aspect of nitrous oxide intoxication, and reported them in print. One conclusion was forced upon my mind at that time, and my impression of its truth has ever since remained unshaken. It is that our normal waking consciousness, rational consciousness as we call it, is but one special type of consciousness, whilst all about it, parted from it by the filmiest of screens, there lie potential forms of consciousness entirely different. We may go through life without suspecting their existence; but apply the requisite stimulus, and at a touch they are there in all their completeness, definite types of mentality which probably somewhere have their field of application and adaptation. No account of the universe in its totality can be final which leaves these other forms of consciousness quite disregarded. How to regard them is the question,—for they are so discontinuous with ordinary consciousness. Yet they may determine attitudes though they cannot furnish formulas, and open a region though they fail to give a map. At any rate, they forbid a premature closing of our accounts with reality. Looking back on my own experiences, they all converge towards a kind of insight to which I cannot help ascribing some metaphysical significance. The keynote of it is invariably a reconciliation. It is as if the opposites of the world, whose contradictoriness and conflict make all our difficulties and troubles, were melted into unity. Not only do they, as contrasted species, belong to one and the same genus, but *one of the species*, the nobler and better one, *is itself the genus, and so soaks up and absorbs its opposite into itself*. This is a dark saying, I know, when thus expressed in terms of common logic, but I cannot wholly escape from its authority.

. . .

We have now seen enough of this cosmic or mystic consciousness, as it comes sporadically. We must next pass to its methodical cultivation as an element of the religious life. Hindus, Buddhists, Mohammedans, and Christians all have cultivated it methodically.

In India, training in mystical insight has been known from time immemorial under the name of yoga. Yoga means the experimental union of the individual with the divine. It is based on persevering exercise; and the diet, posture, breathing, intellectual concentration, and moral discipline vary slightly in the different systems which teach it. The yogi, or disciple, who has by these means overcome the obscurations of his lower nature sufficiently, enters into the condition termed *samâdhi*, "comes face to face with facts which no instinct or reason can ever know." He learns—

"That the mind itself has a higher state of existence, beyond reason, a superconscious state, and that when the mind gets to that higher state, then this knowledge beyond reasoning comes. . . . All the different steps in yoga are intended to bring us scientifically to the superconscious state or samâdhi. . . . Just as unconscious work is beneath consciousness, so there is another work which is above consciousness, and which, also, is not accompanied with the feeling of egoism. . . . There is no feeling of *I*, and yet the mind works, desireless, free from restlessness, objectless, bodiless. Then the Truth shines in its full effulgence, and we know ourselves—for Samâdhi lies potential in us all—for what we truly are, free, immortal, omnipotent, loosed from the finite, and its contrasts of good and evil altogether, and identical with the Atman or Universal Soul." [9]

The Vedantists say that one may stumble into superconsciousness sporadically, without the previous discipline, but it is then impure. Their test of its purity, like our test of religion's value, is empirical: its fruits must be good for life. When a man comes out of Samâdhi, they assure us that he remains "enlightened, a sage, a prophet, a saint, his whole character changed, his life changed, illumined."[10]

The Buddhists use the word 'samâdhi' as well as the Hindus; but 'dhyâna' is their special word for higher states of contemplation. There seem to be four stages recognized in dhyâna. The first stage comes through concentration of the mind upon one point. It excludes desire, but not discernment or judgment: it is still intellectual. In the second stage the intellectual functions drop off, and the satisfied sense of unity remains. In the third stage the satisfaction departs, and indifference begins, along with memory and self-consciousness. In the fourth stage the indifference, memory, and self-consciousness are perfected. [Just what 'memory' and 'self-consciousness' mean in this connection is doubtful. They cannot be the faculties familiar to us in the lower life.] Higher stages still of contemplation are mentioned—a region where there exists nothing, and where the meditator says: "There exists absolutely nothing," and stops. Then he reaches another region where he says: "There are neither ideas nor absence of ideas," and stops again. Then another region where, "having reached the end of both idea and perception, he stops finally." This would seem to be, not yet Nirvâna, but as close an approach to it as this life affords.[11]

In the Mohammedan world the Sufi sect and various dervish bodies are the possessors of the mystical tradition. The Sufis have existed in Persia from the earliest times, and as their pantheism is so at variance with the hot and rigid monotheism of the Arab mind, it has been suggested that

9 My quotations are from VIVEKANANDA, Raja Yoga, London, 1896. The completest source of information on Yoga is the work translated by VIHARI LALA MITRA: Yoga Vasishta Maha Ramayana, 4 vols., Calcutta, 1891–99. [William James.]

10A European witness, after carefully comparing the results of Yoga with those of the hypnotic or dreamy states artificially producible by us, says: "It makes of its true disciples good, healthy, and happy men. . . . Through the mastery which the yogi attains over his thoughts and his body, he grows into a 'character.' By the subjection of his impulses and propensities to his will, and the fixing of the latter upon the ideal of goodness, he becomes a 'personality' hard to influence by others, and thus almost the opposite of what we usually imagine a 'medium' so-called, or 'psychic subject' to be." KARL KELLNER: Yoga: Eine Skizze, München, 1896, p. 21. [William James.]

11 I follow the account in C. F. KOEPPEN: Die Religion des Buddha, Berlin, 1857, i. 585 ff. [William James.]

Sufism must have been inoculated into Islam by Hindu influences. We Christians know little of Sufism, for its secrets are disclosed only to those initiated. To give its existence a certain liveliness in your minds, I will quote a Moslem document, and pass away from the subject.

Al-Ghazzali, a Persian philosopher and theologian, who flourished in the eleventh century, and ranks as one of the greatest doctors of the Moslem church, has left us one of the few autobiographies to be found outside of Christian literature. Strange that a species of book so abundant among ourselves should be so little represented elsewhere—the absence of strictly personal confessions is the chief difficulty to the purely literary student who would like to become acquainted with the inwardness of religions other than the Christian.

M. Schmölders has translated a part of Al-Ghazzali's autobiography into French:[12]—

"The Science of the Sufis," says the Moslem author, "aims at detaching the heart from all that is not God, and at giving to it for sole occupation the meditation of the divine being. Theory being more easy for me than practice, I read [certain books] until I understood all that can be learned by study and hearsay. Then I recognized that what pertains most exclusively to their method is just what no study can grasp, but only transport, ecstasy, and the transformation of the soul. How great, for example, is the difference between knowing the definitions of health, of satiety, with their causes and conditions, and being really healthy or filled. How different to know in what drunkenness consists,—as being a state occasioned by a vapor that rises from the stomach,—and *being* drunk effectively. Without doubt, the drunken man knows neither the definition of drunkenness nor what makes it interesting for science. Being drunk, he knows nothing; whilst the physician, although not drunk, knows well in what drunkenness consists, and what are its predisposing conditions. Similarly there is a difference between knowing the nature of abstinence, and *being* abstinent or having one's soul detached from the world.—Thus I had learned what words could teach of Sufism, but what was left could be learned neither by study nor through the ears, but solely by giving one's self up to ecstasy and leading a pious life.

"Reflecting on my situation, I found myself tied down by a multitude of bonds—temptations on every side. Considering my teaching, I found it was impure before God. I saw myself struggling with all my might to achieve glory and to spread my name. [Here follows an account of his six months' hesitation to break away from the conditions of his life at Bagdad, at the end of which he fell ill with a paralysis of the tongue.] Then, feeling my own weakness, and having entirely given up my own will, I repaired to God like a man in distress who has no more resources. He answered, as he answers the wretch who invokes him. My heart no longer felt any difficulty in renouncing glory, wealth, and my children.

12 For a full account of him, see D. B. MACDONALD: The Life of Al-Ghazzali, in the Journal of the American Oriental Society, 1899, vol. xx. p. 71. [William James.]

So I quitted Bagdad, and reserving from my fortune only what was indispensable for my subsistence, I distributed the rest. I went to Syria, where I remained about two years, with no other occupation than living in retreat and solitude, conquering my desires, combating my passions, training myself to purify my soul, to make my character perfect, to prepare my heart for meditating on God—all according to the methods of the Sufis, as I had read of them.

"This retreat only increased my desire to live in solitude, and to complete the purification of my heart and fit it for meditation. But the vicissitudes of the times, the affairs of the family, the need of subsistence, changed in some respects my primitive resolve, and interfered with my plans for a purely solitary life. I had never yet found myself completely in ecstasy, save in a few single hours; nevertheless, I kept the hope of attaining this state. Every time that the accidents led me astray, I sought to return; and in this situation I spent ten years. During this solitary state things were revealed to me which it is impossible either to describe or to point out. I recognized for certain that the Sufis are assuredly walking in the path of God. Both in their acts and in their inaction, whether internal or external, they are illumined by the light which proceeds from the prophetic source. The first condition for a Sufi is to purge his heart entirely of all that is not God. The next key of the contemplative life consists in the humble prayers which escape from the fervent soul, and in the meditations on God in which the heart is swallowed up entirely. But in reality this is only the beginning of the Sufi life, the end of Sufism being total absorption in God. The intuitions and all that precede are, so to speak, only the threshold for those who enter. From the beginning, revelations take place in so flagrant a shape that the Sufis see before them, whilst wide awake, the angels and the souls of the prophets. They hear their voices and obtain their favors. Then the transport rises from the perception of forms and figures to a degree which escapes all expression, and which no man may seek to give an account of without his words involving sin.

"Whoever has had no experience of the transport knows of the true nature of prophetism nothing but the name. He may meanwhile be sure of its existence, both by experience and by what he hears the Sufis say. As there are men endowed only with the sensitive faculty who reject what is offered them in the way of objects of the pure understanding, so there are intellectual men who reject and avoid the things perceived by the prophetic faculty. A blind man can understand nothing of colors save what he has learned by narration and hearsay. Yet God has brought prophetism near to men in giving them all a state analogous to it in its principal characters. This state is sleep. If you were to tell a man who was himself without experience of such a phenomenon that there are people who at times swoon away so as to resemble dead men, and who [in dreams] yet perceive things that are hidden, he would deny it [and give his reasons]. Nevertheless, his arguments would be refuted by actual experience. Wherefore, just as the understanding is a stage of human life in which an eye opens to discern various intellectual objects uncomprehended by sensation; just so in the prophetic the sight is illumined by a light which uncovers hidden things and objects which the intellect fails to reach. The chief properties of prophetism are perceptible only during the transport, by those who embrace the Sufi life. The prophet is endowed with qualities to which you possess nothing analogous, and which consequently you cannot possibly understand. How should you know their true nature, since one knows only what one can comprehend? But the transport which one attains by the method of the Sufis is like an immediate perception, as if one touched the objects with one's hand." [13]

This incommunicableness of the transport is the keynote of all mysticism. Mystical truth exists for the individual who has the transport, but for no one else. In this, as I have said, it resembles the knowledge given to us in sensations more than that given by conceptual thought. Thought, with its remoteness and abstractness, has often enough in the history of philosophy been contrasted unfavorably with sensation. It is a commonplace of metaphysics that God's knowledge cannot be discursive but must be intuitive, that is, must be constructed more after the pattern of what in ourselves is called immediate feeling, than after that of proposition and judgment. But *our* immediate feelings have no content but what the five senses supply; and we have seen and shall see again that mystics may emphatically deny that the senses play any part in the very highest type of knowledge which their transports yield.

In the Christian church there have always been mystics. Although many of them have been viewed with suspicion, some have gained favor in the eyes of the authorities. The experiences of these have been treated as precedents, and a codified system of mystical theology has been based upon them, in which everything legitimate finds its place.[14] The basis of the system is 'orison' or meditation, the methodical elevation of the soul towards God. Through the practice of orison the higher levels of mystical experience may be attained. It is odd that Protestantism, especially evangelical Protestantism, should seemingly have abandoned everything methodical in this line. Apart from what prayer may lead to, Protestant mystical experience appears to have been almost exclusively sporadic. It has been left to our mind-curers to reintroduce methodical meditation into our religious life.

The first thing to be aimed at in orison is the mind's detachment from outer sensations, for these interfere with its concentration upon ideal things. Such manuals as Saint Ignatius's Spiritual Exercises recommend the disciple to expel sensation by a graduated series of efforts to imagine holy scenes. The acme of this kind of discipline would be a semi-hallucinatory mono-ideism—an imaginary figure of Christ, for example, coming

[13] A. SCHMÖLDERS: Essai sur les écoles philosophiques chez les Arabes, Paris, 1842, pp. 54–68, abridged. [William James.]

[14] GÖRRES's Christliche Mystik gives a full account of the facts. So does RIBET's Mystique Divine, 2 vols., Paris, 1890. A still more methodical modern work is the Mystica Theologia of VALLGORNERA, 2 vols., Turin, 1890. [William James.]

fully to occupy the mind. Sensorial images of this sort, whether literal or symbolic, play an enormous part in mysticism.[15] But in certain cases imagery may fall away entirely, and in the very highest raptures it tends to do so. The state of consciousness becomes then insusceptible of any verbal description. Mystical teachers are unanimous as to this. Saint John of the Cross, for instance, one of the best of them, thus describes the condition called the 'union of love,' which, he says, is reached by 'dark contemplation.' In this the Deity compenetrates the soul, but in such a hidden way that the soul—

"finds no terms, no means, no comparison whereby to render the sublimity of the wisdom and the delicacy of the spiritual feeling with which she is filled. . . . We receive this mystical knowledge of God clothed in none of the kinds of images, in none of the sensible representations, which our mind makes use of in other circumstances. Accordingly in this knowledge, since the senses and the imagination are not employed, we get neither form nor impression, nor can we give any account or furnish any likeness, although the mysterious and sweet-tasting wisdom comes home so clearly to the inmost parts of our soul. Fancy a man seeing a certain kind of thing for the first time in his life. He can understand it, use and enjoy it, but he cannot apply a name to it, nor communicate any idea of it, even though all the while it be a mere thing of sense. How much greater will be his powerlessness when it goes beyond the senses! This is the peculiarity of the divine language. The more infused, intimate, spiritual, and supersensible it is, the more does it exceed the senses, both inner and outer, and impose silence upon them. . . . The soul then feels as if placed in a vast and profound solitude, to which no created thing has access, in an immense and boundless desert, desert the more delicious the more solitary it is. There, in this abyss of wisdom, the soul grows by what it drinks in from the well-springs of the comprehension of love, . . . and recognizes, however sublime and learned may be the terms we employ, how utterly vile, insignificant, and improper they are, when we seek to discourse of divine things by their means."[16]

I cannot pretend to detail to you the sundry stages of the Christian mystical life.[17] Our time would not suffice, for one thing; and moreover,

---

15 M. RÉCÉJAC, in a recent volume, makes them essential. Mysticism he defines as "the tendency to draw near to the Absolute morally, *and by the aid of Symbols.*" See his Fondements de la Connaissance mystique, Paris, 1897, p. 66. But there are unquestionably mystical conditions in which sensible symbols play no part. [William James.]

16 Saint John of the Cross: The Dark Night of the Soul, book ii. ch. xvii., in Vie et Œuvres, 3me édition, Paris, 1893, iii. 428–432. Chapter xi. of book ii. of Saint John's Ascent of Carmel is devoted to showing the harmfulness for the mystical life of the use of sensible imagery. [William James.]

17 In particular I omit mention of visual and auditory hallucinations, verbal and graphic automatisms, and such marvels as 'levitation,' stigmatization, and the healing of disease. These phenomena, which mystics have often presented (or are believed to have presented), have no essential mystical significance, for they occur with no consciousness of illumination whatever, when they occur, as they often do, in persons of non-mystical mind. Consciousness of illumination is for us the essential mark of 'mystical' states. [William James.]

I confess that the subdivisions and names which we find in the Catholic books seem to me to represent nothing objectively distinct. So many men, so many minds: I imagine that these experiences can be as infinitely varied as are the idiosyncrasies of individuals.

The cognitive aspects of them, their value in the way of revelation, is what we are directly concerned with, and it is easy to show by citation how strong an impression they leave of being revelations of new depths of truth. Saint Teresa is the expert of experts in describing such conditions, so I will turn immediately to what she says of one of the highest of them, the 'orison of union.'

> "In the orison of union," says Saint Teresa, "the soul is fully awake as regards God, but wholly asleep as regards things of this world and in respect of herself. During the short time the union lasts, she is as it were deprived of every feeling, and even if she would, she could not think of any single thing. Thus she needs to employ no artifice in order to arrest the use of her understanding: it remains so stricken with inactivity that she neither knows what she loves, nor in what manner she loves, nor what she wills. In short, she is utterly dead to the things of the world and lives solely in God. . . . I do not even know whether in this state she has enough life left to breathe. It seems to me she has not; or at least that if she does breathe, she is unaware of it. Her intellect would fain understand something of what is going on within her, but it has so little force now that it can act in no way whatsoever. So a person who falls into a deep faint appears as if dead. . . .
>
> "Thus does God, when he raises a soul to union with himself, suspend the natural action of all her faculties. She neither sees, hears, nor understands, so long as she is united with God. But this time is always short, and it seems even shorter than it is. God establishes himself in the interior of this soul in such a way, that when she returns to herself, it is wholly impossible for her to doubt that she has been in God, and God in her. This truth remains so strongly impressed on her that, even though many years should pass without the condition returning, she can neither forget the favor she received, nor doubt of its reality. If you, nevertheless, ask how it is possible that the soul can see and understand that she has been in God, since during the union she has neither sight nor understanding, I reply that she does not see it then, but that she sees it clearly later, after she has returned to herself, not by any vision, but by a certitude which abides with her and which God alone can give her. I knew a person who was ignorant of the truth that God's mode of being in everything must be either by presence, by power, or by essence, but who, after having received the grace of which I am speaking, believed this truth in the most unshakable manner. So much so that, having consulted a half-learned man who was as ignorant on this point as she had been before she was enlightened, when he replied that God is in us only by 'grace,' she disbelieved his reply, so sure she was of the true answer; and when she came to ask wiser doctors, they confirmed her in her belief, which much consoled her. . . .
>
> "But how, you will repeat, *can* one have such certainty in respect to

what one does not see? This question, I am powerless to answer. These are secrets of God's omnipotence which it does not appertain to me to penetrate. All that I know is that I tell the truth; and I shall never believe that any soul who does not possess this certainty has ever been really united to God." [18]

The kinds of truth communicable in mystical ways, whether these be sensible or supersensible, are various. Some of them relate to this world,— visions of the future, the reading of hearts, the sudden understanding of texts, the knowledge of distant events, for example; but the most important revelations are theological or metaphysical.

"Saint Ignatius confessed one day to Father Laynez that a single hour of meditation at Manresa had taught him more truths about heavenly things than all the teachings of all the doctors put together could have taught him. . . . One day in orison, on the steps of the choir of the Dominican church, he saw in a distinct manner the plan of divine wisdom in the creation of the world. On another occasion, during a procession, his spirit was ravished in God, and it was given him to contemplate, in a form and images fitted to the weak understanding of a dweller on the earth, the deep mystery of the holy Trinity. This last vision flooded his heart with such sweetness, that the mere memory of it in after times made him shed abundant tears." [19]

[18] The Interior Castle, Fifth Abode, ch. i., in Œuvres, translated by BOUIX, iii. 421–424. [William James.]

[19] BARTOLI-MICHEL: Vie de Saint Ignace de Loyola, i. 34–36. Others have had illuminations about the created world, Jacob Boehme, for instance. At the age of twenty-five he was "surrounded by the divine light, and replenished with the heavenly knowledge: insomuch as going abroad into the fields to a green, at Görlitz, he there sat down, and viewing the herbs and grass of the field, in his inward light he saw into their essences, use, and properties, which was discovered to him by their lineaments, figures, and signatures." Of a later period of experience he writes: "In one quarter of an hour I saw and knew more than if I had been many years together at an university. For I saw and knew the being of all things, the Byss and the Abyss, and the eternal generation of the holy Trinity, the descent and origin of the world and of all creatures through the divine wisdom. I knew and saw in myself all the three worlds, the external and visible world being of a procreation or extern birth from both the internal and spiritual worlds; and I saw and knew the whole working essence, in the evil and in the good, and the mutual origin and existence; and likewise how the fruitful bearing womb of eternity brought forth. So that I did not only greatly wonder at it, but did also exceedingly rejoice, albeit I could very hardly apprehend the same in my external man and set it down with the pen. For I had a thorough view of the universe as in a chaos, wherein all things are couched and wrapt up, but it was impossible for me to explicate the same." Jacob Behmen's Theosophic Philosophy, etc., by EDWARD TAYLOR, London, 1691, pp. 425, 427, abridged. So George Fox: "I was come up to the state of Adam in which he was before he fell. The creation was opened to me; and it was showed me, how all things had their names given to them, according to their nature and virtue. I was at a stand in my mind, whether I should practice physic for the good of mankind, seeing the nature and virtues of the creatures were so opened to me by the Lord." Journal, Philadelphia, no date, p. 69. Contemporary 'Clairvoyance' abounds in similar revelations. Andrew Jackson Davis's cosmogonies, for example, or certain experiences related in the delectable 'Reminiscences and Memories of Henry Thomas Butterworth,' Lebanon, Ohio, 1886. [William James.]

Similarly with Saint Teresa. "One day, being in orison," she writes, "it was granted me to perceive in one instant how all things are seen and contained in God. I did not perceive them in their proper form, and nevertheless the view I had of them was of a sovereign clearness, and has remained vividly impressed upon my soul. It is one of the most signal of all the graces which the Lord has granted me. . . . The view was so subtile and delicate that the understanding cannot grasp it." [20]

.   .   .

I have now sketched with extreme brevity and insufficiency, but as fairly as I am able in the time allowed, the general traits of the mystic range of consciousness. *It is on the whole pantheistic and optimistic, or at least the opposite of pessimistic. It is anti-naturalistic, and harmonizes best with twice-bornness and so-called other-worldly states of mind.*

My next task is to inquire whether we can invoke it as authoritative. Does it furnish any *warrant for the truth* of the twice-bornness and super-naturality and pantheism which it favors? I must give my answer to this question as concisely as I can.

In brief my answer is this,—and I will divide it into three parts:—

(1) Mystical states, when well developed, usually are, and have the right to be, absolutely authoritative over the individuals to whom they come.

(2) No authority emanates from them which should make it a duty for those who stand outside of them to accept their revelations uncritically.

(3) They break down the authority of the non-mystical or rationalistic consciousness, based upon the understanding and the senses alone. They show it to be only one kind of consciousness. They open out the possibility of other orders of truth, in which, so far as anything in us vitally responds to them, we may freely continue to have faith.

I will take up these points one by one.

1.

As a matter of psychological fact, mystical states of a well-pronounced and emphatic sort *are* usually authoritative over those who have them. [21] They have been 'there', and know. It is vain for rationalism to grumble about this. If the mystical truth that comes to a man proves to be a force that he can live by, what mandate have we of the majority to order him to live in another way? We can throw him into prison or a madhouse, but we cannot change his mind—we commonly attach it only the more stub-

20 Vie, pp. 581, 582. [William James.]
21 I abstract from weaker states, and from those cases of which the books are full, where the director (but usually not the subject) remains in doubt whether the experience may not have proceeded from the demon. [William James.]

bornly to its beliefs.[22] It mocks our utmost efforts, as a matter of fact, and in point of logic it absolutely escapes our jurisdiction. Our own more 'rational' beliefs are based on evidence exactly similar in nature to that which mystics quote for theirs. Our senses, namely, have assured us of certain states of fact; but mystical experiences are as direct perceptions of fact for those who have them as any sensations ever were for us. The records show that even though the five senses be in abeyance in them, they are absolutely sensational in their epistemological quality, if I may be pardoned the barbarous expression,—that is, they are face to face presentations of what seems immediately to exist.

The mystic is, in short, *invulnerable*, and must be left, whether we relish it or not, in undisturbed enjoyment of his creed. Faith, says Tolstoy, is that by which men live. And faith-state and mystic state are practically convertible terms.

2.

But I now proceed to add that mystics have no right to claim that we ought to accept the deliverance of their peculiar experiences, if we are ourselves outsiders and feel no private call thereto. The utmost they can ever ask of us in this life is to admit that they establish a presumption. They form a consensus and have an unequivocal outcome; and it would be odd, mystics might say, if such a unanimous type of experience should prove to be altogether wrong. At bottom, however, this would only be an appeal to numbers, like the appeal of rationalism the other way; and the appeal to numbers has no logical force. If we acknowledge it, it is for 'suggestive,' not for logical reasons: we follow the majority because to do so suits our life.

But even this presumption from the unanimity of mystics is far from being strong. In characterizing mystic states as pantheistic, optimistic, etc., I am afraid I over-simplified the truth. I did so for expository reasons, and to keep the closer to the classic mystical tradition. The classic religious mysticism, it now must be confessed, is only a 'privileged case.' It is an *extract*, kept true to type by the selection of the fittest specimens and their preservation in 'schools.' It is carved out from a much larger mass; and if we take the larger mass as seriously as religious mysticism has historically taken itself, we find that the supposed unanimity largely disappears. To begin with, even religious mysticism itself, the kind that accumulates traditions and makes schools, is much less unanimous than I have allowed. It has been both ascetic and antinomianly self-indulgent

---

[22] Example: Mr. John Nelson writes of his imprisonment for preaching Methodism: "My soul was as a watered garden, and I could sing praises to God all day long; for he turned my captivity into joy, and gave me to rest as well on the boards, as if I had been on a bed of down. Now could I say, 'God's service is perfect freedom,' and I was carried out much in prayer that my enemies might drink of the same river of peace which my God gave so largely to me." Journal, London, no date, p. 172. [William James.]

within the Christian church.[23] It is dualistic in Sankhya, and monistic in Vedanta philosophy. I called it pantheistic; but the great Spanish mystics are anything but pantheists. They are with few exceptions non-metaphysical minds, for whom 'the category of personality' is absolute. The 'union' of man with God is for them much more like an occasional miracle than like an original identity.[24] How different again, apart from the happiness common to all, is the mysticism of Walt Whitman, Edward Carpenter, Richard Jefferies, and other naturalistic pantheists, from the more distinctively Christian sort.[25] The fact is that the mystical feeling of enlargement, union, and emancipation has no specific intellectual content whatever of its own. It is capable of forming matrimonial alliances with material furnished by the most diverse philosophies and theologies, provided only they can find a place in their framework for its peculiar emotional mood. We have no right, therefore, to invoke its prestige as distinctively in favor of any special belief, such as that in absolute idealism, or in the absolute monistic identity, or in the absolute goodness, of the world. It is only relatively in favor of all these things—it passes out of common human consciousness in the direction in which they lie.

So much for religious mysticism proper. But more remains to be told, for religious mysticism is only one half of mysticism. The other half has no accumulated traditions except those which the text-books on insanity supply. Open any one of these, and you will find abundant cases in which 'mystical ideas' are cited as characteristic symptoms of enfeebled or deluded states of mind. In delusional insanity, paranoia, as they sometimes call it, we may have a *diabolical* mysticism, a sort of religious mysticism turned upside down. The same sense of ineffable importance in the smallest events, the same texts and words coming with new meanings, the same voices and visions and leadings and missions, the same controlling by extraneous powers; only this time the emotion is pessimistic: instead of consolations we have desolations; the meanings are dreadful; and the powers are enemies to life. It is evident that from the point of view of their psychological mechanism, the classic mysticism and these lower mysticisms spring from the same mental level, from that great subliminal or transmarginal region of which science is beginning to admit the existence, but of which so little is really known. That region contains every kind of matter: 'seraph and snake' abide there side by side. To come from thence is no infallible credential. What comes must be sifted and tested, and run the gauntlet of confrontation with the total context of experience, just like what comes from the outer world of sense. Its value

---

[23] RUYSBROECK, in the work which Maeterlinck has translated, has a chapter against the antinomianism of disciples. H. DELACROIX's book (Essai sur le mysticisme spéculatif en Allemagne au XIVme Siècle, Paris, 1900) is full of antinomian material. Compare also A. JUNDT: Les Amis de Dieu au XIVme Siècle, Thèse de Strasbourg, 1879. [William James.]

[24] Compare PAUL ROUSSELOT: Les Mystiques Espagnois, Paris, 1869, ch. xii. [William James.]

[25] See CARPENTER's Towards Democracy, especially the latter parts, and JEFFERIES's wonderful and splendid mystic rhapsody, The Story of my Heart. [William James.]

must be ascertained by empirical methods, so long as we are not mystics ourselves.

Once more, then, I repeat that non-mystics are under no obligation to acknowledge in mystical states a superior authority conferred on them by their intrinsic nature.[26]

3.

Yet, I repeat once more, the existence of mystical states absolutely overthrows the pretension of non-mystical states to be the sole and ulti-mate dictators of what we may believe. As a rule, mystical states merely add a supersensuous meaning to the ordinary outward data of conscious-ness. They are excitements like the emotions of love or ambition, gifts to our spirit by means of which facts already objectively before us fall into a new expressiveness and make a new connection with our active life. They do not contradict these facts as such, or deny anything that our senses have immediately seized.[27] It is the rationalistic critic rather who plays the part of denier in the controversy, and his denials have no strength, for there never can be a state of facts to which new meaning may not truthfully be added, provided the mind ascend to a more en-veloping point. It must always remain an open question whether mystical states may not possibly be such superior points of view, windows through which the mind looks out upon a more extensive and inclusive world. The difference of the views seen from the different mystical windows need not prevent us from entertaining this supposition. The wider world would in that case prove to have a mixed constitution like that of this world, that is all. It would have its celestial and its infernal regions, its tempting and its saving moments, its valid experiences and its counterfeit ones, just as our world has them; but it would be a wider world all the same. We should have to use its experiences by selecting and subordinating and substituting just as is our custom in this ordinary naturalistic world; we should be liable to error just as we are now; yet the counting in of that wider world of meanings, and the serious dealing with it, might, in spite of all the perplexity, be indispensable stages in our approach to the final fullness of the truth. . . .

26 In chapter i. of book ii. of his work Degeneration, 'MAX NORDAU' seeks to undermine all mysticism by exposing the weakness of the lower kinds. Mysticism for him means any sudden perception of hidden significance in things. He explains such perception by the abundant uncompleted associations which experiences may arouse in a degenerate brain. These give to him who has the experience a vague and vast sense of its leading further, yet they awaken no definite or useful consequent in his thought. The explanation is a plausible one for certain sorts of feeling of significance; and other alienists (WERNICKE, for example, in his Grundriss der Psychiatrie, Theil ii., Leipzig, 1896) have explained 'paranoiac' conditions by a laming of the association-organ. But the higher mystical flights, with their positiveness and abruptness, are surely products of no such merely negative condition. It seems far more reasonable to ascribe them to inroads from the subconscious life, of the cerebral activity correlative to which we as yet know nothing. [William James.]

27 They sometimes add subjective audita et visa to the facts, but as these are usually in-terpreted as transmundane, they oblige no alteration in the facts of sense. [William James.]

3

Existentialism

THE PLAGUE

ALBERT CAMUS

(trans. by Stuart Gilbert)

Albert Camus (1913–1960) was a French essayist, novelist, and dramatist closely associated with Jean-Paul Sartre as one of the leaders of the existentialist movement. In works such as *The Myth of Sisyphus, The Fall, The Rebel, Caligula, The Stranger*, and *The Plague,* Camus sounds some of the principal themes of existentialism, including absurdity, meaninglessness, anguish, freedom, despair, and commitment.

In his celebrated essay, *The Myth of Sisyphus,* Camus offers an answer to the metaphysical despair portrayed by Hemingway. Instead of a response of suicide, either spiritual or physical, we can revolt against the absurdity of a universe that does not contain the meaning we require. While maintaining our consciousness that life has no meaning, we can refuse the resignation and despondency that often follow this realization, and affirm the value of life even in the face of its ultimate pointlessness. Although we all resemble Sisyphus who ceaselessly rolled his rock up a mountain only to have it fall back again each time, and seem condemned to repetitive, meaningless labor, we can transcend our fate by finding joy in the very experience of living itself.

In the selection from *The Plague* included below, Camus presents a humanistic rather than just an individualistic type of existentialism. Even in the absence of God, Camus finds reason for human beings to commit themselves to the alleviation of suffering and to refuse to join the oppressors of the human race. He seems to be saying that out of a natural sense of compassion we should strive to mitigate the pain inherent in man's condition on earth. Although we all live meaningless lives in a metaphysical sense, devoid of any ultimate cosmic purpose, we can try to help rather than harm one another. In this way, Camus believes, we will fully exist as human beings.

The following excerpts consist of conversations between a man named Tarrou and a Dr. Rieux, both of whom have joined an organized medical effort to combat a mysterious plague that is ravaging the city. In the first section the two men are talking after having heard a sermon by Father Paneloux in which he justified the plague as God's way of purifying man through suffering. The second section takes place much later when Rieux and Tarrou take a brief respite from their exhausting labor of tending to the sick.

"Do you believe in God, doctor?"

Again the question was put in an ordinary tone. But this time Rieux took longer to find his answer.

"No—but what does that really mean? I'm fumbling in the dark, struggling to make something out. But I've long ceased finding that original."

"Isn't that it—the gulf between Paneloux and you?"

"I doubt it. Paneloux is a man of learning, a scholar. He hasn't come in contact with death; that's why he can speak with such assurance of the truth—with a capital T. But every country priest who visits his parishioners and has heard a man gasping for breath on his deathbed thinks as I do. He'd try to relieve human suffering before trying to point out its excellence." Rieux stood up; his face was now in shadow. "Let's drop the subject," he said, "as you won't answer."

Tarrou remained seated in his chair; he was smiling again.

"Suppose I answer with a question."

The doctor now smiled, too.

"You like being mysterious, don't you? Yes, fire away."

"My question's this," said Tarrou. "Why do you yourself show such devotion, considering you don't believe in God? I suspect your answer may help me to mine."

His face still in shadow, Rieux said that he'd already answered: that if he believed in an all-powerful God he would cease curing the sick and leave that to Him. But no one in the world believed in a God of that sort; no, not even Paneloux, who believed that he believed in such a God. And this was proved by the fact that no one ever threw himself on Providence completely. Anyhow, in this respect Rieux believed himself to be on the right road—in fighting against creation as he found it.

"Ah," Tarrou remarked. "So that's the idea you have of your profession?"

"More or less." The doctor came back into the light.

Tarrou made a faint whistling noise with his lips, and the doctor gazed at him.

"Yes, you're thinking it calls for pride to feel that way. But I assure you I've no more than the pride that's needed to keep me going. I have no idea what's awaiting me, or what will happen when all this ends. For the moment I know this; there are sick people and they need curing. Later on, perhaps, they'll think things over; and so shall I. But what's wanted now is to make them well. I defend them as best I can, that's all."

"Against whom?"

Rieux turned to the window. A shadow-line on the horizon told of the presence of the sea. He was conscious only of his exhaustion, and at the same time was struggling against a sudden, irrational impulse to unburden himself a little more to his companion; an eccentric, perhaps, but who, he guessed, was one of his own kind.

"I haven't a notion, Tarrou; I assure you I haven't a notion. When I entered this profession, I did it 'abstractedly,' so to speak; because I had a desire for it, because it meant a career like another, one that young men often aspire to. Perhaps, too, because it was particularly difficult for a workman's son, like myself. And then I had to see people die. Do you know that there are some who *refuse* to die? Have you ever heard a woman scream 'Never!' with her last gasp? Well, I have. And then I saw that I could never get hardened to it. I was young then, and I was outraged by the whole scheme of things, or so I thought. Subsequently I grew more modest. Only, I've never managed to get used to seeing people die. That's all I know. Yet after all—"

Rieux fell silent and sat down. He felt his mouth dry.

"After all—?" Tarrou prompted softly.

"After all," the doctor repeated, then hesitated again, fixing his eyes on Tarrou, "it's something that a man of your sort can understand most likely, but, since the order of the world is shaped by death, mightn't it be better for God if we refuse to believe in Him and struggle with all our might against death, without raising our eyes toward the heaven where He sits in silence."

Tarrou nodded.

"Yes. But your victories will never be lasting; that's all."

Rieux's face darkened.

"Yes, I know that. But it's no reason for giving up the struggle."

"No reason, I agree. Only, I now can picture what this plague must mean for you."

"Yes. A never ending defeat."

Tarrou stared at the doctor for a moment, then turned and tramped heavily toward the door. Rieux followed him and was almost at his side when Tarrou, who was staring at the floor, suddenly said:

"Who taught you all this, doctor?"

The reply came promptly:

"Suffering."

. . .

"Rieux," Tarrou said in a quite ordinary tone, "do you realize that you've never tried to find out anything about me—the man I am? Can I regard you as a friend?"

"Yes, of course, we're friends; only so far we haven't had much time to show it."

"Good. That gives me confidence. Suppose we now take an hour off— for friendship?"

Rieux smiled by way of answer.

"Well, here goes!"

There was a long faint hiss some streets off, the sound of a car speeding

on the wet pavement. It died away; then some vague shouts a long way
off broke the stillness again. Then, like a dense veil slowly falling from the
starry sky on the two men, silence returned. Tarrou had moved and now
was sitting on the parapet, facing Rieux, who was slumped back in his
chair. All that could be seen of him was a dark, bulky form outlined
against the glimmering sky. He had much to tell; what follows gives it
more or less in his own words.

"To make things simpler, Rieux, let me begin by saying I had plague
already, long before I came to this town and encountered it here. Which
is tantamount to saying I'm like everybody else. Only there are some
people who don't know it, or feel at ease in that condition; others know
and want to get out of it. Personally, I've always wanted to get out of it.

"When I was young I lived with the idea of my innocence; that is to
say, with no idea at all. I'm not the self-tormenting kind of person, and I
made a suitable start in life. I brought off everything I set my hand to, I
moved at ease in the field of the intellect, I got on excellently with women,
and if I had occasional qualms, they passed as lightly as they came. Then
one day I started thinking. And now—

"I should tell you I wasn't poor in my young days, as you were. My
father had an important post—he was prosecuting attorney; but to look at
him, you'd never have guessed it; he appeared, and was, a kindly, good-
natured man. My mother was a simple, rather shy woman, and I've always
loved her greatly; but I'd rather not talk about her. My father was always
very kind to me, and I even think he tried to understand me. He wasn't
a model husband. I know that now, but I can't say it shocks me particularly. Even in his infidelities he behaved as one could count on his behaving and never gave rise to scandal. In short, he wasn't at all original
and, now he's dead, I realize that, while no plaster saint, he was a very
decent man as men go. He kept the middle way, that's all; he was the
type of man for whom one has an affection of the mild but steady order
—which is the kind that wears best.

"My father had one peculiarity; the big railway directory was his bed-
side book. Not that he often took a train; almost his only journeys were to
Brittany, where he had a small country house to which we went every
summer. But he was a walking timetable; he could tell you the exact times
of departure and arrival of the Paris-Berlin expresses; how to get from
Lyon to Warsaw, which trains to take and at what hours; the precise
distance between any two capital cities you might mention. Could you
tell me offhand how to get from Briançon to Chamonix? Even a station-
master would scratch his head, I should say. Well, my father had the
answer pat. Almost every evening he enlarged his knowledge of the subject,
and he prided himself on it. This hobby of his much amused me; I would
put complicated travel problems to him and check his answers afterwards
by the railway directory. They were invariably correct. My father and I got
on together excellently, thanks largely to these railway games we played in

the evenings; I was exactly the audience he needed, attentive and appreciative. Personally I regarded this accomplishment of his as quite as admirable in its ways as most accomplishments.

"But I'm letting my tongue run away with me and attributing too much importance to that worthy man. Actually he played only an indirect role in the great change of heart about which I want to tell you. The most he did to me was to touch off a train of thoughts. When I was seventeen my father asked me to come to hear him speak in court. There was a big case on at the assizes, and probably he thought I'd see him to his best advantage. Also I suspect he hoped I'd be duly impressed by the pomp and ceremony of the law and encouraged to take up his profession. I could tell he was keen on my going, and the prospect of seeing a side of my father's character so different from that we saw at home appealed to me. Those were absolutely the only reasons I had for going to the trial. What happened in a court had always seemed to me as natural, as much in the order of things, as a military parade on the Fourteenth of July or a school speech day. My notions on the subject were purely abstract, and I'd never given it serious thought.

"The only picture I carried away with me of that day's proceedings was a picture of the criminal. I have little doubt he was guilty—of what crime is no great matter. That little man of about thirty, with sparse, sandy hair, seemed so eager to confess everything, so genuinely horrified at what he'd done and what was going to be done with him, that after a few minutes I had eyes for nothing and nobody else. He looked like a yellow owl scared blind by too much light. His tie was slightly awry, he kept biting his nails, those of one hand only, his right. . . . I needn't go on, need I? You've understood—he was a living human being.

"As for me, it came on me suddenly, in a flash of understanding; until then I'd thought of him only under his commonplace official designation, as 'the defendant.' And though I can't say I quite forgot my father, something seemed to grip my vitals at that moment and riveted all my attention on the little man in the dock. I hardly heard what was being said; I only knew that they were set on killing that living man, and an uprush of some elemental instinct, like a wave, had swept me to his side. And I did not really wake up until my father rose to address the court.

"In his red gown he was another man, no longer genial or good-natured; his mouth spewed out long, turgid phrases like an endless stream of snakes. I realized he was clamoring for the prisoner's death, telling the jury that they owed it to society to find him guilty; he went so far as to demand that the man should have his head cut off. Not exactly in those words, I admit. 'He must pay the supreme penalty,' was the formula. But the difference, really, was slight, and the result the same. He had the head he asked for. Only of course it wasn't he who did the actual job. I, who saw the whole business through to its conclusion, felt a far closer, far more terrifying intimacy with that wretched man than my father can ever have felt. Nevertheless, it fell to him, in the course of his duties, to be present at what's politely termed the prisoner's last moments, but what would be better called murder in its most despicable form.

"From that day on I couldn't even see the railway directory without a shudder of disgust. I took a horrified interest in legal proceedings, death sentences, executions, and I realized with dismay that my father must have often witnessed those brutal murders—on the days when, as I'd noticed without guessing what it meant, he rose very early in the morning. I remembered he used to wind his alarm-clock on those occasions, to make sure. I didn't dare to broach the subject with my mother, but I watched her now more closely and saw that their life in common had ceased to mean anything, she had abandoned hope. That helped me to 'forgive her,' as I put it to myself at the time. Later on, I learned that there'd been nothing to forgive; she'd been quite poor until her marriage, and poverty had taught her resignation.

"Probably you're expecting me to tell you that I left home at once. No, I stayed on many months, nearly a year, in fact. Then one evening my father asked for the alarm-clock as he had to get up early. I couldn't sleep that night. Next day, when he came home, I'd gone.

"To cut a long story short, I had a letter from my father, who had set inquiries on foot to find me, I went to see him, and, without explaining my reasons, told him quite calmly that I'd kill myself if he forced me to return. He wound up by letting me have my way—he was, as I've said, a kindly man at bottom—gave me a lecture on the silliness of wanting to 'live my life' (that was how he accounted for my conduct and I didn't undeceive him), and plenty of good advice. I could see he really felt it deeply and it was an effort for him to keep back his tears. Subsequently—but quite a long time after that—I formed a habit of visiting my mother periodically, and I always saw him on these occasions. I imagine these infrequent meetings satisfied my father. Personally, I hadn't the least antipathy to him, only a little sadness of heart. When he died I had my mother come to live with me, and she'd still be with me if she were alive.

"I've had to dwell on my start in life, since for me it really was the start of everything. I'll get on more quickly now. I came to grips with poverty when I was eighteen, after an easy life till then. I tried all sorts of jobs, and I didn't do too badly. But my real interest in life was the death penalty; I wanted to square accounts with that poor blind owl in the dock. So I became an agitator, as they say. I didn't want to be pestiferous, that's all. To my mind the social order around me was based on the death sentence, and by fighting the established order I'd be fighting against murder. That was my view, others had told me so, and I still think that this belief of mine was substantially true. I joined forces with a group of people I then liked, and indeed have never ceased to like. I spent many years in close co-operation with them, and there's not a country in Europe in whose struggles I haven't played a part. But that's another story.

"Needless to say, I knew that we, too, on occasion, passed sentences of death. But I was told that these few deaths were inevitable for the building up of a new world in which murder would cease to be. That also was true up to a point—and maybe I'm not capable of standing fast where that order of truths is concerned. Whatever the explanation, I hesitated. But then I remembered that miserable owl in the dock and it enabled me to keep on. Until the day when I was present at an execution—it was in Hungary—and exactly the same dazed horror that I'd experienced as a youngster made everything reel before my eyes.

"Have you ever seen a man shot by a firing-squad? No, of course not; the spectators are hand-picked and it's like a private party, you need an invitation. The result is that you've gleaned your ideas about it from books and pictures. A post, a blindfolded man, some soldiers in the offing. But the real thing isn't a bit like that. Do you know that the firing-squad stands only a yard and a half from the condemned man? Do you know that if the victim took two steps forward his chest would touch the rifles? Do you know that, at this short range, the soldiers concentrate their fire on the region of the heart and their big bullets make a hole into which you could thrust your fist? No, you didn't know all that; those are things that are never spoken of. For the plague-stricken their peace of mind is more important than a human life. Decent folks must be allowed to sleep easy o' nights, mustn't they? Really it would be shockingly bad taste to linger on such details, that's common knowledge. But personally I've never been able to sleep well since then. The bad taste remained in my mouth and I've kept lingering on the details, brooding over them.

"And thus I came to understand that I, anyhow, had had plague through all those long years in which, paradoxically enough, I'd believed with all my soul that I was fighting it. I learned that I had had an indirect hand in the deaths of thousands of people; that I'd even brought about their deaths by approving of acts and principles which could only end that way. Others did not seem embarrassed by such thoughts, or anyhow never voiced them of their own accord. But I was different; what I'd come to know stuck in my gorge. I was with them and yet I was alone. When I spoke of these matters they told me not to be so squeamish; I should remember what great issues were at stake. And they advanced arguments, often quite impressive ones, to make me swallow what none the less I couldn't bring myself to stomach. I replied that the most eminent of the plague-stricken, the men who wear red robes, also have excellent arguments to justify what they do, and once I admitted the arguments of necessity and *force majeure* put forward by the less eminent, I couldn't reject those of the eminent. To which they retorted that the surest way of playing the game of the red robes was to leave to them the monopoly of the death penalty. My reply to this was that if you gave in once, there was no reason for not continuing to give in. It seems to me that history has borne me out; today there's a sort of competition who will kill the most.

They're all mad over murder and they couldn't stop killing men even if
they wanted to.

"In any case, my concern was not with arguments. It was with the poor
owl; with that foul procedure whereby dirty mouths stinking of plague told
a fettered man that he was going to die, and scientifically arranged things
so that he should die, after nights and nights of mental torture while he
waited to be murdered in cold blood. My concern was with that hole in
a man's chest. And I told myself that meanwhile, so far anyhow as I was
concerned, nothing in the world would induce me to accept any argument
that justified such butcheries. Yes, I chose to be blindly obstinate, pending
the day when I could see my way more clearly.

"I'm still of the same mind. For many years I've been ashamed,
mortally ashamed, of having been, even with the best intentions, even at
many removes, a murderer in my turn. As time went on I merely learned
that even those who were better than the rest could not keep themselves
nowadays from killing or letting others kill, because such is the logic by
which they live; and that we can't stir a finger in this world without the
risk of bringing death to somebody. Yes, I've been ashamed ever since; I
have realized that we all have plague, and I have lost my peace. And today
I am still trying to find it; still trying to understand all those others and
not to be the mortal enemy of anyone. I only know that one must do what
one can to cease being plague-stricken, and that's the only way in which
we can hope for some peace or, failing that, a decent death. This, and only
this, can bring relief to men and, if not save them, at least do them the
least harm possible and even, sometimes, a little good. So that is why I
resolved to have no truck with anything which, directly or indirectly, for
good reasons or for bad, brings death to anyone or justifies others' putting
him to death.

"That, too, is why this epidemic has taught me nothing new, except
that I must fight it at your side. I know positively—yes, Rieux, I can say I
know the world inside out, as you may see—that each of us has the plague
within him; no one, no one on earth is free from it. And I know, too, that
we must keep endless watch on ourselves lest in a careless moment we
breathe in somebody's face and fasten the infection on him. What's
natural is the microbe. All the rest—health, integrity, purity (if you like)—
is a product of the human will, of a vigilance that must never falter. The
good man, the man who infects hardly anyone, is the man who has the
fewest lapses of attention. And it needs tremendous will-power, a never
ending tension of the mind, to avoid such lapses. Yes, Rieux, it's a wearying business, being plague-stricken. But it's still more wearying to refuse
to be it. That's why everybody in the world today looks so tired; everyone
is more or less sick of plague. But that is also why some of us, those who
want to get the plague out of their systems, feel such desperate weariness,
a weariness from which nothing remains to set us free except death.

"Pending that release, I know I have no place in the world of today;

once I'd definitely refused to kill, I doomed myself to an exile that can never end. I leave it to others to make history. I know, too, that I'm not qualified to pass judgment on those others. There's something lacking in my mental make-up, and its lack prevents me from being a rational murderer. So it's a deficiency, not a superiority. But as things are, I'm willing to be as I am; I've learned modesty. All I maintain is that on this earth there are pestilences and there are victims, and it's up to us, so far as possible, not to join forces with the pestilences. That may sound simple to the point of childishness; I can't judge if it's simple, but I know it's true. You see, I'd heard such quantities of arguments, which very nearly turned my head, and turned other people's heads enough to make them approve of murder; and I'd come to realize that all our troubles spring from our failure to use plain, clean-cut language. So I resolved always to speak—and to act—quite clearly, as this was the only way of setting myself on the right track. That's why I say there are pestilences and there are victims; no more than that. If, by making that statement, I, too, become a carrier of the plague-germ, at least I don't do it willfully. I try, in short, to be an innocent murderer. You see, I've no great ambitions.

"I grant we should add a third category: that of the true healers. But it's a fact one doesn't come across many of them, and anyhow it must be a hard vocation. That's why I decided to take, in every predicament, the victims' side, so as to reduce the damage done. Among them I can at least try to discover how one attains to the third category; in other words, to peace."

Tarrou was swinging his leg, tapping the terrace lightly with his heel, as he concluded. After a short silence the doctor raised himself a little in his chair and asked if Tarrou had an idea of the path to follow for attaining peace.

"Yes," he replied. "The path of sympathy."

Two ambulances were clanging in the distance. The dispersed shouts they had been hearing off and on drew together on the outskirts of the town, near the stony hill, and presently there was a sound like a gunshot. Then silence fell again. Rieux counted two flashes of the revolving light. The breeze freshened and a gust coming from the sea filled the air for a moment with the smell of brine. And at the same time they clearly heard the low sound of waves lapping the foot of the cliffs.

"It comes to this," Tarrou said almost casually; "what interests me is learning how to become a saint."

"But you don't believe in God."

"Exactly! Can one be a saint without God?—that's the problem, in fact the only problem, I'm up against today."

A sudden blaze sprang up above the place the shouts had come from and, stemming the wind-stream, a rumor of many voices came to their ears. The blaze died down almost at once, leaving behind it only a dull red glow. Then in a break of the wind they distinctly heard some strident yells and the discharge of a gun, followed by the roar of an angry crowd. Tarrou stood up and listened, but nothing more could be heard.

"Another skirmish at the gates, I suppose."

"Well, it's over now," Rieux said.

Tarrou said in a low voice that it was never over, and there would be more victims, because that was in the order of things.

"Perhaps," the doctor answered. "But, you know, I feel more fellowship with the defeated than with saints. Heroism and sanctity don't really appeal to me, I imagine. What interests me is being a man." . . .

THE HUMANISM OF EXISTENTIALISM

JEAN-PAUL SARTRE
(trans. by Bernard Frechtman)

Jean-Paul Sartre (1905–   ) is a French philosopher, novelist, and playwright who is generally considered the dean of contemporary existentialism. His massive *Being and Nothingness* presents a definitive account of his metaphysics, while his literary works, such as *No Exit, Nausea, The Age of Reason,* and *The Wall,* dramatize various aspects of the existentialist ethic.

In explicating the basic philosophy of existentialism in the following essay, Sartre asserts that individuals define their essence by freely chosen actions, and are responsible to themselves and mankind for the person they have elected to become. Despite the anguish of responsibility and the forlornness of decision without the guidance of God, we must nevertheless make a commitment; otherwise we are nothing. Once our choice is made, integrity demands that we accept the consequences, standing by the self that we have created.

What can be said from the very beginning is that by existentialism we mean a doctrine which makes human life possible and, in addition, declares that every truth and every action implies a human setting and a human subjectivity.

As is generally known, the basic charge against us is that we put the emphasis on the dark side of human life. Someone recently told me of a lady who, when she let slip a vulgar word in a moment of irritation, excused herself by saying, "I guess I'm becoming an existentialist." Consequently, existentialism is regarded as something ugly; that is why we are said to be naturalists; and if we are, it is rather surprising that in this day and age we cause so much more alarm and scandal than does naturalism, properly so called. The kind of person who can take in his stride such a novel as Zola's *The Earth* is disgusted as soon as he starts reading an existentialist novel; the kind of person who is resigned to the wisdom of the ages—which is pretty sad—finds us even sadder. Yet, what can be more disillusioning than saying "true charity begins at home" or "a scoundrel will always return evil for good"?

We know the commonplace remarks made when this subject comes up, remarks which always add up to the same thing: we shouldn't struggle against the powers-that-be; we shouldn't resist authority; we shouldn't try to rise above our station; any action which doesn't conform to authority is romantic; any effort not based on past experience is doomed to failure; experience shows that man's bent is always toward trouble, that there must be a strong hand to hold him in check, if not, there will be anarchy. There are still people who go on mumbling these melancholy old saws, the people who say, "It's only human!" whenever a more or less repugnant act is pointed out to them, the people who glut themselves on *chansons réalistes*; these are the people who accuse existentialism of being too gloomy, and to such an extent that I wonder whether they are complaining about it, not for its pessimism, but much rather its optimism. Can it be that what really scares them in the doctrine I shall try to present here is that it leaves to man a possibility of choice? To answer this question, we must re-examine it on a strictly philosophical plane. What is meant by the term *existentialism?*

Most people who use the word would be rather embarrassed if they had to explain it, since, now that the word is all the rage, even the work of a musician or painter is being called existentialist. A gossip columnist in *Clartés* signs himself *The Existentialist*, so that by this time the word has been so stretched and has taken on so broad a meaning, that it no longer means anything at all. It seems that for want of an advanced-guard doctrine analogous to surrealism, the kind of people who are eager for scandal and flurry turn to this philosophy which in other respects does not at all serve their purposes in this sphere.

Actually, it is the least scandalous, the most austere of doctrines. It is intended strictly for specialists and philosophers. Yet it can be defined easily. What complicates matters is that there are two kinds of existentialists; first, those who are Christian, among whom I would include Jaspers and Gabriel Marcel, both Catholic; and on the other hand the atheistic existentialists among whom I class Heidegger, and then the French existentialists and myself. What they have in common is that they think that existence precedes essence, or, if you prefer, that subjectivity must be the starting point.

Just what does that mean? Let us consider some object that is manufactured, for example, a book or a paper-cutter: here is an object which has been made by an artisan whose inspiration came from a concept. He referred to the concept of what a paper-cutter is and likewise to a known method of production, which is part of the concept, something which is, by and large, a routine. Thus, the paper-cutter is at once an object produced in a certain way and, on the other hand, one having a specific use; and one cannot postulate a man who produces a paper-cutter but does not know what it is used for. Therefore, let us say that, for the paper-cutter, essence—that is, the ensemble of both the production routines and the properties which enable it to be both produced and defined—precedes existence. Thus, the presence of the paper-cutter or book in front of me is determined. Therefore, we have here a technical view of the world whereby it can be said that production precedes existence.

When we conceive God as the Creator, He is generally thought of as a superior sort of artisan. Whatever doctrine we may be considering, whether one like that of Descartes or that of Leibniz, we always grant that will more or less follows understanding or, at the very least, accompanies it, and that when God creates He knows exactly what He is creating. Thus, the concept of man in the mind of God is comparable to the concept of a paper-cutter in the mind of the manufacturer, and, following certain techniques and a conception, God produces man, just as the artisan, following a definition and a technique, makes a paper-cutter. Thus, the individual man is the realization of a certain concept in the divine intelligence.

In the eighteenth century, the atheism of the *philosophers* discarded the idea of God, but not so much for the notion that essence precedes existence. To a certain extent, this idea is found everywhere; we find it in Diderot, in Voltaire, and even in Kant. Man has a human nature; this human nature, which is the concept of the human, is found in all men, which means that each man is a particular example of a universal concept, man. In Kant, the result of this universality is that the wild-man, the natural man, as well as the bourgeois, are circumscribed by the same definition and have the same basic qualities. Thus, here too the essence of man precedes the historical existence that we find in nature.

Atheistic existentialism, which I represent, is more coherent. It states that if God does not exist, there is at least one being in whom existence precedes essence, a being who exists before he can be defined by any concept, and that this being is man, or, as Heidegger says, human reality. What is meant here by saying that existence precedes essence? It means that, first of all, man exists, turns up, appears on the scene, and, only afterwards, defines himself. If man, as the existentialist conceives him, is indefinable, it is because at first he is nothing. Only afterward will he be something, and he himself will have made what he will be. Thus, there is no human nature, since there is no God to conceive it. Not only is man what he conceives himself to be, but he is also only what he wills himself to be after this thrust toward existence.

Man is nothing else but what he makes of himself. Such is the first principle of existentialism. It is also what is called subjectivity, the name we are labeled with when charges are brought against us. But what do we mean by this, if not that man has a greater dignity than a stone or table? For we mean that man first exists, that is, that man first of all is the being who hurls himself toward a future and who is conscious of imagining himself as being in the future. Man is at the start a plan which is aware of itself, rather than a patch of moss, a piece of garbage, or a cauliflower; nothing exists prior to this plan; there is nothing in heaven; man will be what he will have planned to be. Not what he will want to be. Because by the word "will" we generally mean a conscious decision, which is subsequent to what we have already made of ourselves. I may want to belong to a political party, write a book, get married; but all that is only a manifestation of an earlier, more spontaneous choice that is called "will." But if existence really does precede essence, man is responsible for what he is. Thus, existentialism's first move is to make every man aware of what he is and to make the full responsibility of his existence rest on him. And when we say that a man is responsible for himself, we do not only mean that he is responsible for his own individuality, but that he is responsible for all men.

The word subjectivism has two meanings, and our opponents play on the two. Subjectivism means, on the one hand, that an individual chooses and makes himself; and, on the other, that it is impossible for man to transcend human subjectivity. The second of these is the essential meaning of existentialism. When we say that man chooses his own self, we mean that every one of us does likewise; but we also mean by that that in making this choice he also chooses all men. In fact, in creating the man that we want to be, there is not a single one of our acts which does not at the same time create an image of man as we think he ought to be. To choose to be this or that is to affirm at the same time the value of what we choose, because we can never choose evil. We always choose the good, and nothing can be good for us without being good for all.

If, on the other hand, existence precedes essence, and if we grant that we exist and fashion our image at one and the same time, the image is valid for everybody and for our whole age. Thus, our responsibility is much greater than we might have supposed, because it involves all mankind. If I am a workingman and choose to join a Christian trade-union rather than be a communist, and if by being a member I want to show that the best thing for man is resignation, that the kingdom of man is not of this world, I am not only involving my own case—I want to be resigned for everyone. As a result, my action has involved all humanity. To take a more individual matter, if I want to marry, to have children; even if this marriage depends solely on my own circumstances or passion or wish, I am involving all humanity in monogamy and not merely myself. Therefore, I am responsible for myself and for everyone else. I am creating a certain image of man of my own choosing. In choosing myself, I choose man.

This helps us understand what the actual content is of such rather grandiloquent words as anguish, forlornness, despair. As you will see, it's all quite simple.

First, what is meant by anguish? The existentialists say at once that man is anguish. What that means is this: the man who involves himself and who realizes that he is not only the person he chooses to be, but also a lawmaker who is, at the same time, choosing all mankind as well as himself, cannot help escape the feeling of his total and deep responsibility. Of course, there are many people who are not anxious; but we claim that they are hiding their anxiety, that they are fleeing from it. Certainly, many people believe that when they do something, they themselves are the only ones involved, and when someone says to them, "What if everyone acted that way?" they shrug their shoulders and answer, "Everyone doesn't act that way." But really, one should always ask himself, "What would happen if everybody looked at things that way?" There is no escaping this disturbing thought except by a kind of double-dealing. A man who lies and makes excuses for himself by saying "Not everybody does that," is someone with an uneasy conscience, because the act of lying implies that a universal value is conferred upon the lie.

Anguish is evident even when it conceals itself. This is the anguish that Kierkegaard called the anguish of Abraham. You know the story:

an angel has ordered Abraham to sacrifice his son; if it really were an angel who has come and said, "You are Abraham, you shall sacrifice your son," everything would be all right. But everyone might first wonder, "Is it really an angel, and am I really Abraham? What proof do I have?"

There was a madwoman who had hallucinations; someone used to speak to her on the telephone and give her orders. Her doctor asked her, "Who is it who talks to you?" She answered, "He says it's God." What proof did she really have that it was God? If an angel comes to me, what proof is there that it's an angel? And if I hear voices, what proof is there that they come from heaven and not from hell, or from the subconscious, or a pathological condition? What proves that they are addressed to me? What proof is there that I have been appointed to impose my choice and my conception of man on humanity? I'll never find any proof or sign to convince me of that. If a voice addresses me, it is always for me to decide that this is the angel's voice; if I consider that such an act is a good one, it is I who will choose to say that it is good rather than bad.

Now, I'm not being singled out as an Abraham, and yet at every moment I'm obliged to perform exemplary acts. For every man, everything happens as if all mankind had its eyes fixed on him and were guiding itself by what he does. And every man ought to say to himself, "Am I really the kind of man who has the right to act in such a way that humanity might guide itself by my actions?" And if he does not say that to himself, he is masking his anguish.

There is no question here of the kind of anguish which would lead to quietism, to inaction. It is a matter of a simple sort of anguish that anybody who has had responsibilities is familiar with. For example, when a military officer takes the responsibility for an attack and sends a certain number of men to death, he chooses to do so, and in the main he alone makes the choice. Doubtless, orders come from above, but they are too broad; he interprets them, and on this interpretation depend the lives of ten or fourteen or twenty men. In making a decision he cannot help having a certain anguish. All leaders know this anguish. That doesn't keep them from acting; on the contrary, it is the very condition of their action. For it implies that they envisage a number of possibilities, and when they choose one, they realize that it has value only because it is chosen. We shall see that this kind of anguish, which is the kind that existentialism describes, is explained, in addition, by a direct responsibility to the other men whom it involves. It is not a curtain separating us from action, but is part of action itself.

When we speak of forlornness, a term Heidegger was fond of, we mean only that God does not exist and that we have to face all the consequences of this. The existentialist is strongly opposed to a certain kind of secular ethics which would like to abolish God with the least possible expense. About 1880, some French teachers tried to set up a secular ethics which went something like this: God is a useless and costly hypothesis; we are discarding it; but, meanwhile, in order for there to be an ethics, a society, a civilization, it is essential that certain values be taken seriously and that they be considered as having an *a priori* existence. It must be obligatory, *a priori*, to be honest, not to lie, not to beat your wife, to have children, etc., etc. So we're going to try a little device which will make it possible to show that values exist all the same, inscribed in a heaven of ideas, though otherwise God does not exist. In other words—and this, I believe, is the tendency of everything called reformism in France— nothing will be changed if God does not exist. We shall find ourselves with the same norms of honesty, progress, and humanism, and we shall have made of God an outdated hypothesis which will peacefully die off by itself.

The existentialist, on the contrary, thinks it very distressing that God does not exist, because all possibility of finding values in a heaven of ideas disappears along with Him; there can no longer be an *a priori* Good, since there is no infinite and perfect consciousness to think it. No- where is it written that the Good exists, that we must be honest, that we must not lie; because the fact is we are on a plane where there are only men. Dostoievsky said, "If God didn't exist, everything would be possible." That is the very starting point of existentialism. Indeed, everything is per- missible if God does not exist, and as a result man is forlorn, because neither within him nor without does he find anything to cling to. He can't start making excuses for himself.

If existence really does precede essence, there is no explaining things away by reference to a fixed and given human nature. In other words, there is no determinism, man is free, man is freedom. On the other hand, if God does not exist, we find no values or commands to turn to which legitimize our conduct. So, in the bright realm of values, we have no excuse behind us, nor justification before us. We are alone, with no ex- cuses.

That is the idea I shall try to convey when I say that man is con- demned to be free. Condemned, because he did not create himself, yet, in other respects is free; because, once thrown into the world, he is responsi- ble for everything he does. The existentialist does not believe in the power of passion. He will never agree that a sweeping passion is a ravaging torrent which fatally leads a man to certain acts and is therefore an ex- cuse. He thinks that man is responsible for his passion.

The existentialist does not think that man is going to help himself by finding in the world some omen by which to orient himself. Because he thinks that man will interpret the omen to suit himself. Therefore, he thinks that man, with no support and no aid, is condemned every moment to invent man. Ponge, in a very fine article, has said, "Man is the future of man." That's exactly it. But if it is taken to mean that this future is recorded in heaven, that God sees it, then it is false, because it would really no longer be a future. If it is taken to mean that, whatever a man may be, there is a future to be forged, a virgin future before him, then this remark is sound. But then we are forlorn.

To give you an example which will enable you to understand forlorn-ness better, I shall cite the case of one of my students who came to see me under the following circumstances: his father was on bad terms with his mother, and, moreover, was inclined to be a collaborationist; his older brother had been killed in the German offensive of 1940, and the young man, with somewhat immature but generous feelings, wanted to avenge him. His mother lived alone with him, very much upset by the half-treason of her husband and the death of her older son; the boy was her only consolation.

The boy was faced with the choice of leaving for England and joining the Free French Forces—that is, leaving his mother behind—or remaining with his mother and helping her to carry on. He was fully aware that the woman lived only for him and that his going-off—and perhaps his death—would plunge her into despair. He was also aware that every act that he did for his mother's sake was a sure thing, in the sense that it was helping her to carry on, whereas every effort he made toward going off and fighting was an uncertain move which might run aground and prove completely useless; for example, on his way to England he might, while passing through Spain, be detained indefinitely in a Spanish camp; he might reach England or Algiers and be stuck in an office at a desk job. As a re-sult, he was faced with two very different kinds of action: one, concrete, immediate, but concerning only one individual; the other concerned an incomparably vaster group, a national collectivity, but for that very reason was dubious, and might be interrupted en route. And, at the same time, he was wavering between two kinds of ethics. On the one hand, an ethics of sympathy, of personal devotion; on the other, a broader ethics, but one whose efficacy was more dubious. He had to choose between the two.

Who could help him choose? Christian doctrine? No. Christian doctrine says, "Be charitable, love your neighbor, take the more rugged path, etc., etc." But which is the more rugged path? Whom should he love as a brother? The fighting man or his mother? Which does the greater good, the vague act of fighting in a group, or the concrete one of helping a particular human being to go on living? Who can decide *a priori*? Nobody. No book of ethics can tell him. The Kantian ethics says, "Never treat any person as a means, but as an end." Very well, if I stay with mother, I'll treat her as an end and not as a means; but by virtue of this very fact, I'm running the risk of treating the people around me who are fighting, as means; and, conversely, if I go to join those who are fighting, I'll be treating them as an end, and, by doing that, I run the risk of treating my mother as a means.

If values are vague, and if they are always too broad for the concrete and specific case that we are considering, the only thing left for us is to trust our instincts. That's what this young man tried to do; and when I saw him, he said, "In the end, feeling is what counts. I ought to choose whichever pushes me in one direction. If I feel that I love my mother enough to sacrifice everything else for her—my desire for vengeance, for action, for adventure—then I'll stay with her. If, on the contrary, I feel that my love for my mother isn't enough, I'll leave."

But how is the value of a feeling determined? What gives his feeling for his mother value? Precisely the fact that he remained with her. I may say that I like so-and-so well enough to sacrifice a certain amount of money for him, but I may say so only if I've done it. I may say "I love my mother well enough to remain with her" if I have remained with her. The only way to determine the value of this affection is, precisely, to perform an act which confirms and defines it. But, since I require this affection to justify my act, I find myself caught in a vicious circle.

On the other hand, Gide has well said that a mock feeling and a true feeling are almost indistinguishable; to decide that I love my mother and will remain with her, or to remain with her by putting on an act, amount somewhat to the same thing. In other words, the feeling is formed by the acts one performs; so, I can not refer to it in order to act upon it. Which means that I can neither seek within myself the true condition which will impel me to act, nor apply to a system of ethics for concepts which will permit me to act. You will say, "At least, he did go to a teacher for advice." But if you seek advice from a priest, for example, you have chosen this priest; you already knew, more or less, just about what advice he was going to give you. In other words, choosing your adviser is involving yourself. The proof of this is that if you are a Christian, you will say, "Consult a priest." But some priests are collaborating, some are just marking time, some are resisting. Which to choose? If the young man chooses a priest who is resisting or collaborating, he has already decided on the kind of advice he's going to get. Therefore, in coming to see me he knew the answer I was going to give him, and I had only one answer to give: "You're free, choose, that is, invent." No general ethics can show you what is to be done; there are no omens in the world. The Catholics will reply, "But there are." Granted—but, in any case, I myself choose the meaning they have.

When I was a prisoner, I knew a rather remarkable young man who was a Jesuit. He had entered the Jesuit order in the following way: he had had a number of very bad breaks; in childhood, his father died, leaving him in poverty, and he was a scholarship student at a religious institution where he was constantly made to feel that he was being kept out of charity; then, he failed to get any of the honors and distinctions that children like; later on, at about eighteen, he bungled a love affair; finally, at twenty-two, he failed in military training, a childish enough matter, but it was the last straw.

This young fellow might well have felt that he had botched everything. It was a sign of something, but of what? He might have taken refuge in bitterness or despair. But he very wisely looked upon all this as a sign that he was not made for secular triumphs, and that only the triumphs of religion, holiness, and faith were open to him. He saw the hand of God in all this, and so he entered the order. Who can help seeing that he alone decided what the sign meant?

Some other interpretation might have been drawn from this series of setbacks; for example, that he might have done better to turn carpenter or revolutionist. Therefore, he is fully responsible for the interpretation. Forlornness implies that we ourselves choose our being. Forlornness and anguish go together.

As for despair, the term has a very simple meaning. It means that we shall confine ourselves to reckoning only with what depends upon our will, or on the ensemble of probabilities which make our action possible. When we want something, we always have to reckon with probabilities. I may be counting on the arrival of a friend. The friend is coming by rail or street-car; this supposes that the train will arrive on schedule, or that the street-car will not jump the track. I am left in the realm of possibility; but possibilities are to be reckoned with only to the point where my action comports with the ensemble of these possibilities, and no further. The moment the possibilities I am considering are not rigorously involved by my action, I ought to disengage myself from them, because no God, no scheme, can adapt the world and its possibilities to my will. When Descartes said, "Conquer yourself rather than the world," he meant essentially the same thing.

The Marxists to whom I have spoken reply, "You can rely on the support of others in your action, which obviously has certain limits because you're not going to live forever. That means: rely on both what others are doing elsewhere to help you, in China, in Russia, and what they will do later on, after your death, to carry on the action and lead it to its fulfillment, which will be the revolution. You even *have* to rely upon that, otherwise you're immoral." I reply at once that I will always rely on fellow-fighters insofar as these comrades are involved with me in a common struggle, in the unity of a party or a group in which I can more or less make my weight felt; that is, one whose ranks I am in as a fighter and whose movements I am aware of at every moment. In such a situation, relying on the unity and will of the party is exactly like counting on the fact that the train will arrive on time or that the car won't jump the track. But, given that man is free and that there is no human nature for me to depend on, I can not count on men whom I do not know by relying on human goodness or man's concern for the good of society. I don't know what will become of the Russian revolution; I may make an example of it to the extent that at the present time it is apparent that the proletariat plays a part in Russia that it plays in no other nation. But I can't swear that this will inevitably lead to a triumph of the proletariat. I've got to limit myself to what I see.

Given that men are free and that tomorrow they will freely decide what man will be, I cannot be sure that, after my death, fellow-fighters will carry on my work to bring it to its maximum perfection. Tomorrow, after my death, some men may decide to set up Fascism, and the others may be cowardly and muddled enough to let them do it. Fascism will then be the human reality, so much the worse for us.

Actually, things will be as man will have decided they are to be. Does that mean that I should abandon myself to quietism? No. First, I should involve myself; then, act on the old saw, "Nothing ventured, nothing gained." Nor does it mean that I shouldn't belong to a party, but rather that I shall have no illusions and shall do what I can. For example, suppose I ask myself, "Will socialization, as such, ever come about?" I know nothing about it. All I know is that I'm going to do everything in my power to bring it about. Beyond that, I can't count on anything. Quietism is the attitude of people who say, "Let others do what I can't do." The doctrine I am presenting is the very opposite of quietism, since it declares, "There is no reality except in action." Moreover, it goes further, since it adds, "Man is nothing else than his plan; he exists only to the extent that he fulfills himself; he is therefore nothing else than the ensemble of his acts, nothing else than his life."

According to this, we can understand why our doctrine horrifies certain people. Because often the only way they can bear their wretchedness is to think, "Circumstances have been against me. What I've been and done doesn't show my true worth. To be sure, I've had no great love, no great friendship, but that's because I haven't met a man or woman who was worthy. The books I've written haven't been very good because I haven't had the proper leisure. I haven't had children to devote myself to because I didn't find a man with whom I could have spent my life. So there remains within me, unused and quite viable, a host of propensities, inclinations, possibilities, that one wouldn't guess from the mere series of things I've done."

Now, for the existentialist there is really no love other than one which manifests itself in a person's being in love. There is no genius other than one which is expressed in works of art; the genius of Proust is the sum of Proust's works; the genius of Racine is his series of tragedies. Outside of that, there is nothing. Why say that Racine could have written another tragedy, when he didn't write it? A man is involved in life, leaves his impress on it, and outside of that there is nothing. To be sure, this may seem a harsh thought to someone whose life hasn't been a success. But, on the other hand, it prompts people to understand that reality alone is what counts, that dreams, expectations, and hopes warrant no more than to define a man as a disappointed dream, as miscarried hopes, as vain expectations. In other words, to define him negatively and not positively. However, when we say, "You are nothing else than your life," that does not imply that the artist will be judged solely on the basis of his works of art; a thousand other things will contribute toward summing him up. What we mean is that a man is nothing else than a series of undertakings, that he is the sum, the organization, the ensemble of the relationships which make up these undertakings.

When all is said and done, what we are accused of, at bottom, is not our pessimism, but an optimistic toughness. If people throw up to us our works of fiction in which we write about people who are soft, weak, cowardly, and sometimes even downright bad, it's not because these people are soft, weak, cowardly, or bad; because if we were to say, as Zola did, that they are that way because of heredity, the workings of environment, society, because of biological or psychological determinism, people would be reassured. They would say, "Well, that's what we're like, no one can do anything about it." But when the existentialist writes about a coward, he says that this coward is responsible for his cowardice. He's not like that because he has a cowardly heart or lung or brain; he's not like that on account of his physiological make-up; but he's like that because he has made himself a coward by his acts. There's no such thing as a cowardly constitution; there are nervous constitutions; there is poor blood, as the common people say, or there are strong constitutions. But the man whose blood is poor is not a coward on that account, for what makes cowardice is the act of renouncing or yielding. A constitution is not an act; the coward is defined on the basis of the acts he performs. People feel, in a vague sort of way, that this coward we're talking about is guilty of being a coward, and the thought frightens them. What people would like is that a coward or a hero be born that way.

One of the complaints most frequently made about *The Ways of Freedom*[1] can be summed up as follows: "After all, these people are so spineless, how are you going to make heroes out of them?" This objection almost makes me laugh, for it assumes that people are born heroes. That's what people really want to think. If you're born cowardly, you may set your mind perfectly at rest; there's nothing you can do about it; you'll be cowardly all your life, whatever you may do. If you're born a hero, you may set your mind just as much at rest; you'll be a hero all your life; you'll drink like a hero and eat like a hero. What the existentialist says is that the coward makes himself cowardly, that the hero makes himself heroic. There's always a possibility for the coward not to be cowardly any more and for the hero to stop being heroic. What counts is total involvement; some one particular action or set of circumstances is not total involvement.

Thus, I think we have answered a number of the charges concerning existentialism. You see that it can not be taken for a philosophy of quietism, since it defines man in terms of action; nor for a pessimistic description of man—there is no doctrine more optimistic, since man's destiny is within himself; nor for an attempt to discourage man from acting, since it tells him that the only hope is in his acting and that action is the only thing that enables a man to live. Consequently, we are dealing here with an ethics of action and involvement.

---

[1] *Les Chemins de la Liberté,* Sartre's trilogy of novels. [Bernard Frechtman.]

BIBLIOGRAPHY

A. PHILOSOPHIC WORKS

Aristotle. *Categories* and *Physics*. Translated by W. D. Ross. In *The Works*. Oxford: Clarendon Press, 1908–31.

Ayer, A. J. *Language, Truth and Logic*. New York: Dover, 1936.

Bergson, Henri. *The Creative Mind*. Translated by M. L. Andison. New York: Philosophical Library, 1946.

Bradley, F. H. *Appearance and Reality*. Oxford: Clarendon Press, 1930.

Collingwood, R. G. *An Essay on Metaphysics*. Oxford: Clarendon Press, 1940.

Copleston, F. C. *A History of Philosophy*, 7 vols. Westminster, Md.: Newman Bookshops, 1946–66.

Coreth, Emerich. *Metaphysics*. Translated by J. Donceel. New York: Herder and Herder, 1968.

De George, Richard T., ed. *Classical and Contemporary Metaphysics*. New York: Krieger, 1962.

Descartes, René. *Meditations on First Philosophy*. Translated by L. J. Lafleur. Indianapolis: Liberal Arts Press, 1960.

Emmet, Dorothy M. *The Nature of Metaphysical Thinking*. London: Macmillan, 1946.

Farrer, Austin. *Finite and Infinite*. London: Westminster Press, 1959.

Hamlyn, D. W. *Sensations and Perception*. New York: Humanities Press, 1961.

Hegel, G. W. F. *Phenomenology of Mind*. Edited and translated by W. Kaufmann. Garden City, N.Y.: Anchor Books, 1966.

———. Philosophy of History. Translated by J. Sibree. London: George Bell and Sons, 1894.

Heidegger, Martin. *Being and Time* and *An Introduction to Metaphysics*. In *Basic Writings*. Edited and translated by D. F. Krell. New York: Harper and Row, 1977.

Hoernle, R. F. Alfred. *Studies in Contemporary Metaphysics*. New York: Harcourt Brave Jovanovich, Inc., 1920.

Hook, Sidney. *The Quest for Being*. New York: St. Martin's Press, 1961.

Hume, David. *Enquiry Concerning Human Understanding*. Edited by L. A. Selby-Bigge. Oxford: Clarendon Press, 1962.

———. A Treatise of Human Nature. Edited by L. A. Selby-Bigge. Oxford: Clarendon Press, 1928.

James, William. *Varieties of Religious Experience*. New York: Longmans, Green, 1935.

Kant, Immanuel. *Critique of Practical Reason*. Translated by L. W. Beck. Chicago: University of Chicago, 1949.

———. Critique of Pure Reason. Translated by N. Kemp-Smith. New York: St. Martin's Press, 1965.

———. Prolegomena to Every Future Metaphysics. Translated by P. Carus. Chicago: Open Court, 1902.

Klubertanz, George P., and Holloway, M. R. *Being and God*. New York: Appleton-Century-Crofts, 1963.

Lazerowitz, Morris. *The Structure of Metaphysics*. London: Routledge and K. Paul, 1955.

Leibniz, G. W. *The Monadology and Other Philosophical Writings*. Edited by R. Latta. New York: Oxford University, 1898.

Leighton, J. A. *Man and the Cosmos—An Introduction to Metaphysics*. New York: D. Appleton, 1922.

Lovejoy, Arthur. *The Great Chain of Being*. Cambridge: Harvard University, 1936.

Lucretius. *De Rerum Natura*. Translated by W. H. D. Rouse. New York: G. Putnam's Sons, 1924.

MacIntyre, Alasdair, ed. *Metaphysical Beliefs*. London: S. C. M. Press, 1957.

Mackinnon, D. M. *The Problems of Metaphysics*. New York: Cambridge University, 1974.

Marcel, Gabriel. *The Mystery of Being*. Translated by R. Hague. Chicago: Regnery, 1950–51.

Maritain, Jacques. *A Preface to Metaphysics*. London: Sheed and Ward, 1939.

Mascall, E. L. *Existence and Analogy*. New York: Longmans, Green, 1949.

Moore, G. E. *Philosophical Papers*. New York: Macmillan, 1959.

———. *Some Main Problems of Philosophy*. New York: Humanities Press, 1953.

Passmore, John. *A Hundred Years of Philosophy*. London: Duckworth, 1957.

Pears, D. F., ed. *The Nature of Metaphysics*. New York: St. Martin's Press, 1957.

Plato. *Parmenides, Republic* (esp. VI–VII), *Sophist*, and *Timaeus*. In *The Dialogues of Plato*, translated by B. Jowett. Oxford: Clarendon Press, 1871.

Ross, W. D. *Aristotle*. London: Methuen, 1923.

Russell, Bertrand. *Human Knowledge: Its Scope and Limitations*. New York: Simon and Schuster, 1948.

———. *The Problems of Philosophy*. London: Oxford University, 1950.

Santayana, George. *Realms of Being*, 4 vols. New York: C. Scribner's Sons, 1940.

Schopenhauer, Arthur. *The World as Will and Idea*. Translated by R. B. Haldane and J. Kemp. London: K. Paul, Trench, Trubner, 1896.

Slote, Michael. *Metaphysics and Essence*. New York: New York University, 1975.

Taylor, Richard. *Metaphysics*. Englewood Cliffs, N.J.: Prentice-Hall, 1963.

Underhill, Evelyn. *Mysticism*. New York: E. P. Dutton, 1911.

Vaske, Martin O. *An Introduction to Metaphysics*. New York: McGraw-Hill, 1963.

Walsh, W. H. *Metaphysics*. London: Hutchinson University Library, 1963.

Warnock, G. J., ed. *The Philosophy of Perception*. London: Oxford University, 1967.

Weiss, Paul. *Reality*. Princeton: Princeton University, 1938.

Whitehead, A. N. *Process and Reality*. New York: Macmillan, 1929.

———. *Science and the Modern World*. New York: Macmillan, 1925.

Wittgenstein, Ludwig. *Philosophical Investigations*. Translated by G. E. M. Anscombe. New York: Macmillan, 1953.

———. *Tractatus Logico-Philosophicus*. Translated by D. F. Pears and B. F. McGuinness. New York: Humanities Press, 1963.

B. LITERARY WORKS

Aiken, Conrad. "Time in the Rock." *Collected Poems*. New York: Oxford University, 1970.

Anderson, Sherwood. *Key Largo*. Washington, D.C.: Anderson House, 1939.

Arnold, Matthew. "The Buried Life," "Self-Deception," and "To an Independent Preacher." In *The Works of Matthew Arnold*. London, Macmillan, 1903–04.

Baudelaire, Charles Pierre. "L'Horloge." In *The Flowers of Evil*. Translated by G. Dillon. New York: Harper and Brothers, 1936.

Beckett, Samuel. *Endgame*. New York: Grove Press, 1958.

———. *Malloy, Malone Dies and The Unnamable*. New York: Grove Press, 1958.

———. *Waiting for Godot*. New York: Grove Press, 1954.

Borges, Jorge Luis. *The Aleph and Other Stories*. Translated by N. T. di Giovanni. New York: E. P. Dutton, 1970.

———. *Labyrinths*. New York: New Directions, 1964.

Camus, Albert. *Caligula and Three Other Plays*. Translated by J. O'Brien. New York: Knopf, 1958.

———. *The Stranger*. Translated by S. Gilbert. New York: Knopf, 1946.

Conrad, Joseph. *The Heart of Darkness*. Edited by R. Kimbrough. New York: Norton, 1963.

Dante Alighieri. *The Divine Comedy*. Translated by C. E. Norton. New York: Houghton Mifflin, 1941.

Edman, Irwin. *Poems*, esp. "Eternity." New York: Simon and Schuster, 1925.

Emerson, Ralph Waldo. "Xenophanes." In *The Collected Works*. Cambridge: Harvard University, 1971.

Frost, Robert. "The Bear" and "Design." In *Collected Poems*. New York: Henry Holt, 1930.

Genet, Jean. *The Balcony*. Translated by B. Frechtman. New York: Grove Press, 1958.

Goethe, Johann Wolfgang von. *Faust*. Translated by G. M. Priest. New York: Knopf, 1950.

Hardy, Thomas. "Nature's Questioning" and "Convergence of the Twain." In *Collected Poems*. London: Macmillan, 1930.

Ibsen, H. *Brand*. Translated by F. E. Garrett. London: Dent, 1961.

Ionesco, E. *Exit the King*. In *Plays*. Translated by D. Watson. London: J. Calder, 1958.

——. *Fragments of a Journal*. Translated by J. Stewart. New York: Grove Press, 1968.

Joyce, James. *Finnegan's Wake*. New York: Viking Press, 1947.

——. *Ulysses*. New York: Random House, 1961.

Kafka, Franz. *The Castle*. Translated by W. and E. Muir. New York: Knopf, 1954.

——. *The Trial*. Translated by W. and E. Muir. New York: Knopf, 1957.

Mann, Thomas. *Doctor Faustus*. Translated by H. T. Lowe-Porter. New York: Knopf, 1948.

——. *Magic Mountain*. Translated by H. T. Lowe-Porter. New York: Knopf, 1953.

Maugham, W. Somerset. *Of Human Bondage*. Garden City, N.Y.: Doubleday, Doran, 1936.

Melville, Herman. *Moby Dick*. New York: Dutton, 1907.

Milton, John. "Paradise Lost." In *The Works*. New York: Columbia University, 1931–38.

Pater, Walter. *Marius the Epicurean*. New York: Macmillan, 1900.

Pirandello, Luigi. *It Is So (If You Think So)*. In *Naked Masks*. Edited by E. Bentley. New York: Dutton, 1952.

Proust, Marcel. *Remembrance of Things Past*. Translated by C. K. Scott-Moncrieff. London: Chatto and Windus, 1957.

Santayana, George. *The Last Puritan*. New York: C. Scribner's Sons, 1936.

Sartre, Jean-Paul. *Nausea*. Translated by L. Alexander. New York: New Directions, 1964.

——. *No Exit* and *The Flies*. Translated by S. Gilbert. New York: Knopf, 1947.

Shakespeare, William. *King Lear*. In *The Works of William Shakespeare*, edited by W. G. Clark and W. A. Wright. New York: St. Martin's Press, 1956.

Tennyson, Alfred. "The Ancient Sage," "The Flower in the Crannied Wall," "In Memoriam," and "Ulysses." In *Complete Poetical Works*. Boston: Houghton Mifflin, 1963.

Thompson, Francis. "The Hound of Heaven." In *Complete Poetical Works*. New York: Boni and Liveright, 1918.

Tolstoy, Leo. *War and Peace*. Translated by L. and A. Maude. New York: Simon and Schuster, 1942.

Unamuno, Miguel de. *The Song of the Eternal Waters*. In *Perplexities and Paradoxes*. Translated by S. Gross. New York: Philosophical Library, 1945.

Wordsworth, William. "Lines Composed a Few Miles Above Tintern Abbey," and "My Heart Leaps Up When I Behold." In *The Poetical Works*. Edited by E. de Selincourt. Oxford: Clarendon Press, 1952–59.

COPYRIGHTS AND ACKNOWLEDGMENTS

For permission to use the selections reprinted in this book, the author is grateful to the following publishers and copyright holders:

BARNES & NOBLE BOOKS For "A Free Man's Worship" from *Mysticism and Logic and Other Essays* by Bertrand Russell. Reprinted by permission of Barnes & Noble Books.

THE BOBBS-MERRILL COMPANY, INC. For the excerpt from *Dialogues Concerning Natural Religion* by David Hume, edited by Norman Kemp Smith, copyright © 1947, by Thomas Nelson & Sons Ltd., reprinted by permission of the Bobbs-Merrill Company, Inc.

THE CATHOLIC UNIVERSITY OF AMERICA PRESS For the excerpts from *City of God* by Saint Augustine from the series *Fathers of the Church*, edited by Bernard M. Peebles. Reprinted by permission of The Catholic University of America Press.

DOVER PUBLICATIONS, INC. For the excerpt from *The Tragic Sense of Life* by Miguel de Unamuno. Dover Publications, Inc., New York, 1954. Reprinted through the permission of the publisher.

E. P. DUTTON & CO., INC. For the excerpt from *Notes from Underground* by Fyodor Dostoevsky. From the book *Notes from Underground* and *The Grand Inquisitor* by Fyodor Dostoevsky. Trans. by Ralph Matlaw. Copyright © 1960 by E. P. Dutton & Co., Inc., publishers, and used with their permission.

HARCOURT BRACE JOVANOVICH, INC. For the excerpt from *Murder in the Cathedral* by T. S. Eliot, copyright, 1935, by Harcourt Brace Jovanovich, Inc.; copyright 1963, by T. S. Eliot. Reprinted by permission of the publishers.

HARPER & ROW, PUBLISHERS For the excerpt from *Brave New World* by Aldous Huxley. Copyright 1932, 1960 by Aldous Huxley. By permission of Harper & Row, Publishers. For the excerpt from *Groundwork of the Metaphysic of Morals* by Immanuel Kant, translated and analysed by H. J. Paton (New York: Harper & Row, 1964), pp. 61-73. Reprinted by permission of the publisher.

HOUGHTON MIFFLIN COMPANY For the excerpt from *J. B.* by Archibald Mac-Leish. Copyright © 1956, 1957, 1958 by Archibald MacLeish. Reprinted by permission of Houghton Mifflin Company.

ALFRED A. KNOPF, INC. For the excerpt from *The Plague* by Albert Camus, translated by Stuart Gilbert. Copyright 1948 by Stuart Gilbert. Reprinted by permission of Alfred A. Knopf, Inc.

MACMILLAN PUBLISHING CO., INC. For the excerpts from *Science and Human Behavior* by B. F. Skinner. Reprinted with permission of Macmillan Publishing Co., Inc. from *Science and Human Behavior* by B. F. Skinner. Copyright 1953 by Macmillan Publishing Co., Inc.

NEW DIRECTIONS PUBLISHING CORP. For the excerpt from *Siddhartha* by Herman Hesse, translated by Hilda Rosner. Copyright 1951 by New Directions Publishing Corporation.

W. W. NORTON & COMPANY, INC. For the selections reprinted from *The Notebooks of Malte Laurids Brigge* by Rainer Maria Rilke, translated by M. D. Herter Norton. By permission of W. W. Norton & Company, Inc. Copyright 1949 by W. W. Norton & Company, Inc. Copyright renewed 1977 by M. D. Herter Norton.

PENGUIN BOOKS LTD. For the excerpt from *Germinal* by Emile Zola, translated by L. W. Tancock (Penguin Classics, 1954). Copyright © L. W. Tancock, 1954.

PHILOSOPHICAL LIBRARY, PUBLISHERS For the excerpt from "The Humanism of Existentialism" from *Existentialism and Humanism* by Jean-Paul Sartre, translated by Bernard Frechtman. Reprinted by permission of Philosophical Library, Publishers.

RANDOM HOUSE, INC.   For the excerpt from *Antigone* by Jean Anouilh, adapted and translated by Lewis Galantiere. Copyright 1946 by Random House and renewed 1974 by Lewis Galantiere. Reprinted by permission of Random House, Inc.

SCHOCKEN BOOKS INC.   For the excerpt from "The Metamorphosis" by Franz Kafka. Reprinted by permission of Schocken Books Inc. from *The Penal Colony* by Franz Kafka. Copyright © 1948 by Schocken Books Inc. Copyright renewed © 1975 by Schocken Books Inc.

THE VIKING PRESS, INC.   For the excerpts from *Thus Spoke Zarathustra* and *The Gay Science* by Friedrich Nietzsche. From *The Portable Nietzsche*, selected and translated by Walter Kaufmann. Copyright 1954 by The Viking Press, Inc. Reprinted by permission of The Viking Press, Inc.

YALE UNIVERSITY PRESS   For the excerpt from *The Self: Its Body and Freedom* by William Ernest Hocking. Copyright © 1928, 1956 by Yale University Press. Reprinted by permission of the publisher.

A 0
B 1
C 2
D 3
E 4
F 5
G 6
H 7
I 8
J 9